早稲田大学学術叢書 35
Waseda University Academic Series

An Automodular View of English Grammar

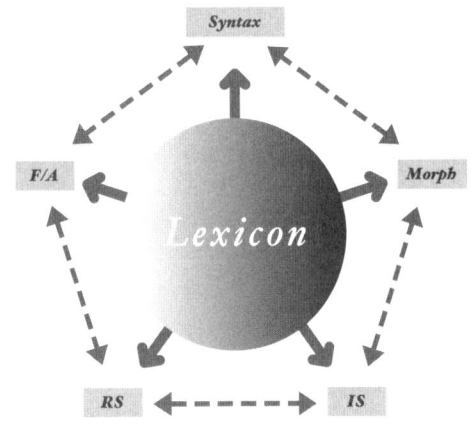

Yoshio Ueno

早稲田大学出版部
Waseda University Press

An Automodular View of English Grammar

Yoshio Ueno is professor of linguistics at the Center for English Language Education in Science and Engineering, Waseda University and was visiting scholar at the Department of Linguistics, the University of Chicago in the academic year of 2012/13.

First published in 2014 by
Waseda University Press Co., Ltd.
1-1-7 Nishiwaseda
Shinjuku-ku, Tokyo 169-0051
www.waseda-up.co.jp

© 2014 by Yoshio Ueno

All rights reserved. Except for short extracts used for academic purposes or book reviews, no part of this publication may be reproduced, stored in a retrieval system or transmitted in any form whatsoever—electronic, mechanical, photocopying or otherwise—without the prior and written permission of the publisher.

ISBN 978-4-657-14705-9

Printed in Japan

Contents

Foreword by Jerrold M. Sadock
Preface

Introduction 1
    About this book   1

1 Modules 3
    1.1 Morphology and Morphophonology Overview   3
        1.1.1 Morphology   3
        1.1.2 Morphophonology   10
    1.2 Syntax Overview   14
    1.3 Semantics 1: Function-Argument Structure Overview   23
    1.4 Semantics 2: Role Structure Overview   34
    1.5 Information Structure Overview   42
    1.6 Lexical Items and Lexical Entries   43

2 Clause Structures 47
    2.1 Inversion   47
    2.2 Propositional Negation by *not*   59
    2.3 Negative Inversion   66
    2.4 Dummy *there*   74
    2.5 Clausal Subject   81
    2.6 Locative Inversion   87
    2.7 Extraposition   91

3 Passive 95
    3.1 Agentless Passives of Transitive Verbs   95
        3.1.1 The syntax, F/A, and RS of agentless passives   95
        3.1.2 Passive Lexical Rule   98
        3.1.3 Middle Lexical Rule   101
    3.2 Exploration of Unassociable Roles   102

3.3	Passive *by*-Phrase	104
	3.3.1 The syntax, F/A, and RS of passive *by*-phrase	104
	3.3.2 Propositional agentive phrase	108
3.4	Prepositional Passives	108
	3.4.1 Prepositional Passive Lexical Rule	108
	3.4.2 Extending the coverage of Prepositional Passive Lexical Rule	111
	3.4.3 On the notions of agent and patient	114
3.5	Verb Classes and Their Passives	117
	3.5.1 The verb class of *express*	117
	3.5.2 The verb class of *suppose*	118
	3.5.3 The verb class of *depend*	119
	3.5.4 The verb class of *hope*	120
	3.5.5 The verb class of *wonder*	121
	3.5.6 The verb class of *rain*	123
3.6	VP Idioms and Their Passives	126
3.7	Double Passives	130
3.8	Locative Inversion in the Passive	133
3.9	Imperatives in the Passive	135
3.10	The Acceptability of Passive Sentences	137
3.11	The Family of Passive Lexical Rules	139

4 Raising and Control 141

4.1	Subject Raising	141
	4.1.1 Subject raising as innocuous mismatch	142
	4.1.2 The distribution of the dummy *it*	147
	4.1.3 Subject raising and EQNP	149
	4.1.4 Subject raising in the inversion constructions	150
	4.1.5 Subject raising and idiom chunks	154
	4.1.6 The subject raising verb *strike*	156
	4.1.7 Subject raising in the imperative	158
	4.1.8 Subject raising in coordination	159
4.2	Object Raising	160
	4.2.1 Traditional analyses of object raising	160
	4.2.2 AMG analysis of object raising	161
	4.2.3 Passivization of object raising verbs	164

		4.2.4 Dummy NPs and idiom chunks in object raising	166
		4.2.5 Characterizing raising predicates	167
		4.2.6 Evidence for the ternary branching VP	168
	4.3	Event Hierarchy and Control	182
		4.3.1 Event Hierarchy	182
		4.3.2 The control construction	184
	4.4	Unique Control	185
		4.4.1 Unique control verbs of *order* and *promise*	185
		4.4.2 Notes on determining the controller	188
	4.5	On the Controlled Argument RHO	190
	4.6	Passivization of Unique Control Verbs	195
		4.6.1 Passivization of object-control verbs	195
		4.6.2 Passivization of subject control verbs	196
		4.6.3 Impersonal passive with VP[*to*]	199
	4.7	Causative Coercion	201
		4.7.1 Need for causative coercion	201
		4.7.2 More examples of causative coercion	203
	4.8	Controller Shift	208
		4.8.1 Controller shift and its triggering factors	208
		4.8.2 Passivization of *promise*: revisited	211
		4.8.3 Other pragmatic and semantic factors	213
	4.9	Partial Control	217
5	Quantification		221
	5.1	Internal Structure of Proposition	221
	5.2	NP with Multiple Quantifiers	226
	5.3	Quantifiers and Bound Variables	229
	5.4	Set Arguments and Set Variables	234
	5.5	Domain Expressions and Split Antecedents	240
	5.6	Quantifier-Float	243
6	Unbounded Dependency		253
	6.1	*Wh*-Questions	253
		6.1.1 Direct *wh*-questions	256
		6.1.2 ATB "*wh*-movement"	261
		6.1.3 Unbounded dependency and islands	262

		6.1.4	F/A dominance path condition and role sharing	275
		6.1.5	WH[Q] and preposition stranding	280
		6.1.6	Multiple *wh*-questions	284
		6.1.7	Lexical entries	286
		6.1.8	Crossover phenomena and presuppositions	291
		6.1.9	Quiz questions	296
		6.1.10	Nonbridge verbs	299
		6.1.11	The Coordinate Structure Constraint revisited	303
	6.2	Relative Clauses		311
		6.2.1	The WH[R] feature and its percolation	311
		6.2.2	Relative pronouns	313
		6.2.3	Restrictive *wh*-relative clauses	317
		6.2.4	Nonrestrictive relative clauses	324
		6.2.5	*That*-relatives and bare relatives	330
		6.2.6	Infinitival *wh*-questions and relative clauses	339
		6.2.7	Reduced relative clauses	346
		6.2.8	Restrictive relative clause constructions in inheritance hierarchy	349
7	Speech Acts			353
	7.1	Speech Act Superstructure		353
	7.2	Indirect Speech Acts		361
	7.3	Embedded Performative Verbs		364
	7.4	Antecedents in "Performative Clauses"		367
	7.5	Referring to "Performative Clauses"		368
	7.6	"Performative Clause" Modifiers		370
		7.6.1 Style disjuncts		370
		7.6.2 Performative adverb *hereby*		375
		7.6.3 "Performative clause" modifying PPs		376

Appendix: List of Definitions, Features, and Rules 381
References 397
Index 403

Foreword

Mainstream grammatical thinking assumes that a single, very intricate, and fragile computational system connects the conceptual dimension of language with the physical dimension. Studies that adhere to such a program tend to concentrate on a rather small range of phenomena, many of which were introduced into the literature in the early days of modern linguistic theory. The descriptions of grammatical fact within the newest versions are generally very approximate, making numerous poorly supported assumptions and referring vaguely to "some version" of a huge array of highly abstract notions. This allows for a seemingly endless variety of speculative avenues of escape from the constraints imposed by linguistic fact.

By contrast, Yoshio Ueno's *Automodular View of English Grammar* employs a multimodular framework of grammatical description consisting of a number of separate generative components, each of which is quite simple, easily formalized, and much closer to observable fact than what we find in the Minimalist Program. As Ueno shows, the individual grammars of the independent dimensions of representation can be made quite explicit and therefore falsifiable. In his hands, Automodular Grammar comes close to being a *theory* of grammar, rather than just a program for speculating about language.

The independent generative components that are invoked in Ueno's *Automodular View* are connected largely by the lexicon, which, because of the explicitness of the components, can once again be sharply defined. The properties of lexical items can therefore be made explicit and subject to disconfirmation, a property not much in evidence in mainstream descriptions. Ueno also demonstrates that a grammar built from autonomous components can provide a description of a very wide range of grammatical phenomena in a single language, something approaching, in fact, a full grammar of a language, in which the account of any given set of facts meshes well with the accounts of the others. While accepting much of the mechanics and analyses in my recent *Modular Architecture of Grammar*, Ueno goes far beyond that work, modeling many of the insights and much of the coverage of McCawley's magisterial *Syntactic Phenomena of*

English. He both deepens and broadens the range of phenomena dealt with in my work, greatly deepening, for example, the treatment of unbounded dependencies and syntactic islands found in earlier work. Its breadth of coverage is expanded to include, among other things, a remarkably effective account of speech acts, which are handled by adding an illocutionary superstructure—reminiscent of the performative hypothesis—to event structure representations, where it is far more comfortable than in the left periphery of syntactic trees.

An Automodular View of English Grammar is an impressively careful, far-ranging, and original contribution to the study of modular grammar. It contains lessons that would be valuable to any linguistic researcher and it deserves a wide audience.

Jerrold M. Sadock
The Glen A. Lloyd Distinguished Service
Professor Emeritus in the Department of Linguistics
at the University of Chicago

Preface

This book concerns major "syntactic phenomena of English" (including inversion, clausal subjects, extraposition, passivization, raising, control, controller shift, quantification, unbounded dependency, island phenomena, speech acts, and "performative" clauses) from a multi-modular perspective, namely, Automodular Grammar (AMG), the latest version of which is presented in Jerrold M. Sadock's (2012) *The Modular Architecture of Grammar*, Cambridge University Press.

An Automodular View of English Grammar grew out of my lecture notes on English syntax from my graduate syntax class in 2009 at Waseda University. In the spring semester of that year, I used the late James D. McCawley's (1998) *The Syntactic Phenomena of English*, Second edition, University of Chicago Press. In this book, Jim adopted his long-held "highly revisionist version of transformational grammar," in which the deep structure of a sentence is its semantic representation and the surface structure is its surface syntactic structure, and a series of transformations connects the two representations guided by his "strict cyclic principle" in such a way that the transformations resolve the mismatches between the two and the derivation converges to the surface structure that meets his "surface combinatoric rules." At the end of the spring semester, I was planning to teach a nonderivational approach to English syntax in the fall semester and looking for introductory materials to Lexical Functional Grammar (LFG), Head-driven Phrase Structure Grammar (HPSG), and Autolexical Syntax, when Jerry kindly sent me his book manuscript, which was then titled *An Introduction to Automodular Grammar* and which came out in 2012. In the fall semester, I used the manuscript together with his earlier book *Autolexical Syntax*.

While I was writing this book on the basis of my lecture notes, I had in mind two pieces of advice that Jim gave me when I was a student at Chicago. The first was to learn not just one but several approaches to syntax and try to see the advantages and disadvantages of each approach, and the second was that once you have decided which framework to use for your linguistic analysis, you must apply it thoroughly and consistently to as large a set of data as possible. Following his first advice, this book is greatly influenced in various ways by LFG,

Generalized Phrase Structure Grammar (GPSG), HPSG, and Ray Jackendoff's Parallel Architecture. As for his second piece of advice, I tried to explore the full potential of Jerry's latest formulation of AMG. One example is my adoption of two-tiered participant roles for his Role Structure. Another is my extension of his Role Structure to speech acts and "performative" clauses.

I am well aware that the AMG view presented in this book is only one of the many possible alternative multi-modular views of English grammar. As an anonymous reviewer pointed out to me, there may be a better way of looking at the syntactic phenomena discussed in the book, and the worth of publishing this work lies in promoting research on similar approaches to linguistic analysis and on comparison between competing analyses.

The first draft of this book was completed in 2012 while I was at the University of Chicago as a visiting researcher. I cannot thank Jerry enough for reading the entire first draft and giving me advice and detailed comments on every chapter as well as for writing a foreword to this book. Without his support, it would have been impossible to finish this work. I would also like to express my gratitude to my LFG teacher Amy Dahlstrom, who was kind enough to be my sponsor at Chicago. For numerous encouragements and/or comments at various stages of this book project, I would like to thank first and foremost my family members, and my friends, Syugo Hotta, Hisano Nakamoto, Saeko Reynolds, Yoko Sugioka, Etsuyo Yuasa, and especially Ichiro Yuhara, whose comments on most of the chapters were very useful. Finally, I would like to thank Atsushi Kanamaru, Waseda University Press, for his painstaking editorial work. The publication of this book was made possible by a publishing grant from Waseda University, for which I am most grateful.

Yoshio Ueno

Introduction

About this book

The aim of this book is to present a multi-modular view of English grammar, in which English, or for that matter, any natural language, is described and explained as a result of interactions between several autonomous modules. There is no derivation, transformation (movement), insertion, or deletion. The view of English grammar from a multi-modular perspective presented in this book is based on and, in some cases, is an extension of Jerrold Sadock's *Modular Architecture of Grammar* (2012). Over the past three decades, he has been developing in a series of books and papers, especially his 1985, 1991, and 2012, a multi-modular grammar called Automodular Grammar (AMG) or Autolexical Syntax, according to which the grammar of a natural language consists of several autonomous modules, including morphology, syntax, and semantics, each of them being generative in its own way and formulated in context-free phrase structure grammar (PSG). Each module only does its own work with its own primitives and grammar rules. All the modules are connected by an interface including default correspondences. Because of this architecture, lexical entries and lexical rules are expressed module by module, which forms the basis of the interface.

This book is organized as follows. Chapter 1 Modules gives a brief sketch of each module, namely, Morphology, Morphophonology, Syntax, Function Argument Structure, Role Structure, and Information Structure, which are illustrated with plenty of examples. These modules are applied and extended in the subsequent chapters. In Chapter 2 Clause Structures, inversion (including negative inversion and locative inversion), negation, dummy *there*, clausal subject, and extraposition are discussed and analyzed in a multi-modular fashion. In Chapter 3 Passive, we apply Sadock's (2012) analysis of passivization in terms of module-by-module lexical rules to a much wider range of data, including the passivization of verbs that do not take an NP complement. Chapter 4 Raising and

Control concerns subject-to-subject raising, subject-to-object raising, and control. These are analyzed and formalized from a multi-modular perspective. The discussion on obligatory control and controller shift shows that semantic and pragmatic factors play an important role. In Chapter 5 Quantification, we discuss the internal structure of a proposition, quantifier scope ambiguities, and quantifier float. Chapter 6 Unbounded Dependency deals with wh-questions, relative clauses, islands, and crossover phenomena, which are analyzed from a multi-modular perspective. In Chapter 7 Speech Acts, we extend the notion of Role Structure to speech acts and their illocutionary forces, and explain various phenomena that were dealt with under the Performative Hypothesis.

Much of the data in the subsequent chapters is taken from the late Jim McCawley's monumental works, his logic book (McCawley 1993) and syntax book (McCawley 1998). As readers go through these chapters, it will become evident that the view presented in this book is greatly influenced by Generalized Phrase Structure Grammar (GPSG), Head-driven Phrase Structure Grammar (HPSG), Lexical Functional Grammar (LFG), and the parallel architecture by Ray Jackendoff.

The aim of this book is best summarized in the following quote from Sadock (2012: 7): "I will try to convince readers of the virtues of the automodular arrangement by providing a wide-ranging and detailed analysis of grammatical phenomena."

Chapter 1
Modules

In this chapter, a sketch of each module, namely, Morphology, Morphophonology, Syntax, Function Argument Structure, Role Structure, and Information Structure, is given with plenty of examples.

1.1 Morphology and Morphophonology Overview

1.1.1 Morphology

Morphology is the grammar of word structure and deals with productive morphological facts. It is one of the autonomous modules with its own categories and its own rules of combination, and is formalized in terms of a context-free phrase structure grammar (Sadock 2012:147–148). The three basic morphological categories we need are a morphological word (technically, a morphological entity with the BAR feature whose value is 1, represented as <BAR, 1>), a sub-word category that we call stem (<BAR, 0>), and the other sub-word category that we call affix (AF). In derivational morphology, a derivational affix is added to a stem (<BAR, 0>) and produces a larger stem (<BAR, 0>), keeping the BAR value unchanged. On the other hand, in inflectional morphology, an inflectional affix is added to a stem (<BAR, 0>) and produces a morphological word (<BAR, 1>), changing the BAR value from 0 to 1 (Sadock 1991: 28–29, Sadock 2012: 148). An affix that comes before the stem is called prefix, whereas an affix that comes after the stem is called suffix.

We will be looking at four morphological structures: derivation, inflection, cliticization, and compounding. As described above, derivation is a morphological structure in which a larger stem (<BAR, 0>) consists of a smaller stem (<BAR, 0>) and a derivational affix (1a), whereas inflection is a morphological structure in which a morphological word (<BAR, 1>) consists of a stem (<BAR, 0>) and an inflectional affix (1b). Cliticization is a morphological structure in which a larger morphological word (<BAR, 1>) consists of a smaller morphological word

(<BAR, 1>) and a clitic (CL) (1c). Compounding is a morphological structure that consists of two stems, two words, or a stem and a word (1d).

(1) a. derivation   [$_{X[0]}$ Y[0], AF]   (Sadock 2012: 148 (1), Sadock 1991: 28 MF2)

```
      X[0]           or        X[0]
     /    \                   /    \
   Y[0]    AF               AF    Y[0]
```

b. inflection   [$_{X[1]}$ X[0], AF]   (Sadock 2012: 148 (2), Sadock 1991: 28 MF1)

```
      X[1]           or        X[1]
     /    \                   /    \
   X[0]    AF               AF    X[0]
```

c. cliticization   [$_{Y[1]}$ X[1], CL]   (Sadock 2012: 148 (3), Sadock 1991: 29 MF3)

d. compounding   [$_{Z[0]}$ X[m], Y[n]], where m, n = 0 or 1
(Sadock 1991: 29 MF4)

In (1), the comma (,) between two categories in the bracket notations indicates that the linear order between them is not specified. (Without a comma, the order between two categories is specified.) Moreover, the numbers 0 and 1 within the square brackets indicate the BAR value of the morphological category in question. In derivation (1a), the notation [$_{X[0]}$ Y[0], AF] is equivalent to the two local trees (i.e., two-story tree structures), one with the AF as a suffix and the other with the AF as a prefix. A derivational affix takes a stem of a specific morphological category and derives a larger stem of a specific morphological category. In inflection (1b), an inflectional affix attaches to a stem of a specific category (X[0]) and creates a morphological word (X[1]) of the same morphological category. Note that derivation keeps its BAR value at 0 and hence can be applied recursively, but inflection changes its BAR value from 0 to 1, which captures the fact that there can be only one inflectional affix added to a stem.

As an example of derivation (1a), the derivational suffix *-ness* attaches to an adjective stem (A[0]) and derives a noun stem (N[0]). Therefore, the noun *kindness* (as morphological word) has the morphological structure: [$_{N[1]}$ [$_{N[0]}$ [$_{A[0]}$ kind] [$_{AF}$ -ness]]]. This morphological structure shows that the noun (N[1]) consists of its own noun stem (N[0]) with no inflectional affix. Inflection with no overt inflectional affix is called zero inflection (Sadock 2012: 150). The noun stem in turn consists of the adjective stem (A[0]) *kind* and the derivational affix (AF) *-ness*.

Consider another example, *unkind*, whose morphological structure is shown in (2a).

(2) examples of derivation
 a. [_A[1] [_A[0] [_AF un-] [_A[0] kind]]] b. [_ADV[1] [_ADV[0] [_A[0] [_AF un-] [_A[0] kind]] [_AF -ly]]]

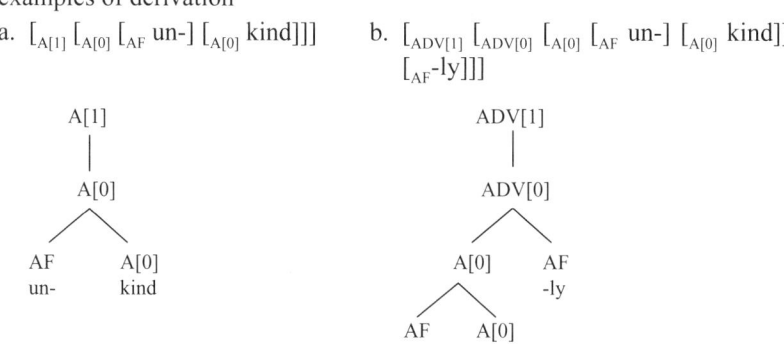

In (2a), the prefix (AF) *un-* and the adjective stem (A[0]) *kind* form a larger adjective stem (A[0]), which in turn constitutes an adjective as a morphological word (A[1]) with no inflectional affix, another example of zero inflection. The three-story tree structure in (2a) is equivalent to the bracket notation in (2a).

When we need to clearly indicate the order between two categories, the symbol (<) is used to mean "precedes." For example, [_A[1] A[0] < AF], which is the same as [_A[1] A[0] AF], means that the adjective (as a morphological word) consists of two parts, an adjective stem (A[0]) and an affix (AF) and the former precedes the latter, which is an inflectional suffix, as in (3b).

(2b) shows the morphological structure of *unkindly*, which is an adverb (morphological word) ADV[1]. It consists of the adverb stem (ADV[0]) with no overt inflectional affix (zero inflection). The adverb stem in turn consists of the adjective stem (A[0]) *unkind* and the derivational suffix *-ly*. Again, this four-story morphological structure is equivalent to the bracket notation in (2b). To save space, we will be using these bracket notations with category labels instead of tree structures.

Inflection (1b) is illustrated by the regular past tense inflectional suffix *-ed* (cf. 1.1.2 (2) and (5)) that attaches to a verb stem (V[0]) and produces a morphological word of the same category (V[1]), which is shown in (3a) below. (3b) shows that the comparative adjective (as morphological word A[1]) *kinder* consists of the adjective stem (A[0]) *kind* and the comparative inflectional suffix *-er*.

(3) examples of inflection
a. [$_{V[1]}$ [$_{V[0]}$ kick] [$_{AF}$ -ed]]   b. [$_{A[1]}$ [$_{A[0]}$ kind] [$_{AF}$ -er]]

English possessive 's, as in [$_{NP}$ [$_{NP[POS]}$ *the king of England's*] *daughters*] is an example of cliticization (1c). The possessive clitic is morphologically attached to the last word ([$_{N[1, POS]}$ [$_{N[1]}$ England] [$_{CL}$'s]]) of an NP and turns the NP into a possessive NP (NP[POS]).

Compounding (1d) is illustrated with the compound noun *communications director jobs*, which is formed by compounding two noun stems [$_{N[0]}$ communications director] and [$_{N[0]}$ job] into [$_{N[0]}$ N[0] N[0]] and this larger noun stem is inflected for plural ([$_{N[1]}$ [$_{N[0]}$ N[0] N[0]] [$_{AF}$ -s]]). Within the compound noun *communications director jobs*, the first part *communications director* is also a compound noun stem, which consists of an inflected noun *communications* and a noun stem *director* ([$_{N[0]}$ N[1] N[0]]). The entire morphological structure is shown in (4).

(4) the morphological structure of compound noun *communications director jobs*

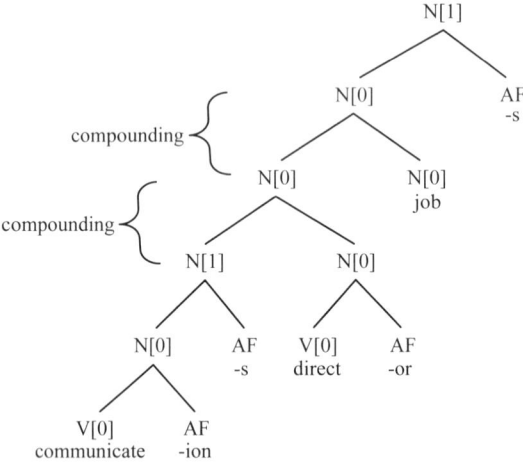

Morphological categories are in principle distinct from syntactic categories. However, in the majority of cases, there is no mismatch in category between the morphological and syntactic modules. In these default cases, a verb in morphology is a verb in syntax, and a morphological noun is a syntactic noun. For example, the word *observe* is a verb in morphology, because it inflects as a morphological verb: it takes the regular past tense suffix -*ed* and the third person singular present tense suffix -*s*. It is also a verb in syntax, because it functions as a verb in syntax: it takes an NP object and forms a verb phrase (VP). The word *student* is morphologically a noun because it inflects as a morphological noun: it takes the plural suffix -*s*. Syntactically, it is also a noun because it functions as a syntactic noun: it takes a prepositional phrase headed by *of* (PP[*of*]) and forms a phrase N', as in [$_{NP}$ *a* [$_{N'}$ *student* [$_{PP[of]}$ *of linguistics*]]]. These informal observations can be made precise as (5) and (6) (Sadock 2012: 150).

(5) *observe*
    syntax: V in [$_{VP}$ __, NP]
    morph: V[0]

(6) *student*
    syntax: N in [$_{N'}$ __, PP[*of*]]
    morph: N[0]

Under default correspondences, a syntactic verb (V in syntax) corresponds to a verb as a morphological word (V[1] in morphology), whereas a syntactic noun (N in syntax) corresponds to a noun as a morphological word (N[1] in morphology). In (5), the morphological category of *observe* is specified as V[0], which indicates that it is capable of inflection. In (6), the morphological category of *student* is specified as N[0], which again indicates that it is capable of inflection.

Where there is no mismatch between syntactic category and morphological category (i.e., in default cases), either one can be omitted from the lexical entry. In (7) and (8), the syntactic category is specified and the morphological category is to be predicted from it. Conversely, in (9) and (10), the morphological category is specified and the syntactic category is to be predicted from it.

(7) *observe*
    syntax: H in [$_{VP}$ __, NP]
    morph: {<BAR, 0>}

(8) *student*
    syntax: H in [$_{N'}$ __, (PP[*of*])]
    morph: {<BAR, 0>}

(9) *observe*
    syntax: H in [$_{HP}$ __, NP]
    morph: V[0]

(10) *student*
    syntax: H in [$_{H'}$ __, (PP[*of*])]
    morph: N[0]

The symbol H stands for the head of a phrase in syntax, and its category is predicted by its mother node (phrasal category) in syntax, as in (7) and (8), or by the morphological category, as in (9) and (10): in (9), a verb in morphology is a verb in syntax and in (10), a noun in morphology is a noun in syntax.

(11) is the lexical entry for *fun* (cf. Sadock 2012: 150). The syntactic field specifies that this is [+N], that is, N (whose feature specification is [+N, −V]) or A (whose feature specification is [+N, +V]), and the morphological field specifies that this is a morphological word; that is, it is incapable of inflection (**funs*, **funner*) or derivation (**funly*, **funness*, **unfun*).

(11) *fun*
 syntax: [+N]
 morph: Word (i.e., {<BAR, 1>})

In morphology, we find conversion (zero derivation) of morphological categories, in which a morphological category is changed with no overt derivational affix. For example, the word *surprising* is morphologically ambiguous. On the one hand, it is the present participle form of the transitive verb *surprise*, as in *You're always surprising me*. On the other hand, it is also an adjective, as in *The news was very surprising to me*. (12) is the lexical entry for the adjective *surprising*, whose syntactic category is adjective and whose morphological field says that it is an adjective stem (A[0]) consisting of a present participle (V[1, PRP]), an example of conversion.

(12) adjective *surprising*
 (as in *very surprising to me*)
 syntax: A
 morph: [_A[0]_ V[1, PRP]]

(13)
```
              ADV(in syntax)
              ⋮
              ADV[1] (in morphology)
              |  ⎫ zero inflection
              ADV[0]
              ╱╲  ⎫ derivation
             A[0]  AF
                   -ly
   derivation ⎰
             AF   A[0]
             un-  |   ⎫ V-to-A conversion
                  V[1, PRP]
                  ╱╲  ⎫ inflection
                 V[0] AF
                 surprise -ing
```

The reason why *surprising* is an adjective stem in morphology in (12) is that it can undergo regular derivations as an adjective stem, such as *un-surprising* and *surprising-ly*. The word *unsurprising* is morphologically an adjective stem derived from the prefix *un-* and the adjective stem *surprising* (cf. (2a)). The adjective stem *surprising* can take the derivational suffix *-ly* and forms an adverb stem (ADV[0]) (cf. (2b)). The morphological structure of the adverb *unsurprisingly* is shown in (13).

Note that English has two *un-* prefixes: the prefix that attaches to an adjective stem and derives an adjective stem with negative meaning (2a) and the prefix that attaches to a verb stem and derives a verb stem that means the reversal of an action, such as *undo* or *uncover*. Because there is no such verb as **unsurprise*, the *unsurprising* we have been talking about is not a verb in the present participle form (V [1, PRP]) but morphologically an adjective stem (A[0]).

The word *killing* is morphologically ambiguous. On the one hand, it is a verb, namely, the present participle form (V [1, PRP]) of the transitive verb *kill*, as in *this economic downturn is killing jobs*. On the other hand, it is also a noun, as in *the brutal killings of innocent civilians*, in which *killing* takes the plural suffix *-s*, a hallmark of a morphological noun, and this is modified by the adjective *brutal* and takes the definite article and a complement PP headed by *of* (PP [*of*]), hallmarks of a syntactic noun. This is another example of conversion (V-to-N conversion).

(14) *killing*
(as in *a killing of a person*)
syntax: N in [$_{N'}$ __, (PP [*of*])]
morph: [$_{N[0]}$ V [1, PRP]]

(15) *breaking down*
(as in *a breaking down of barriers*)
syntax: N in [$_{N'}$ __, (PP [*of*])]
morph: [$_{N[0]}$ [$_{N[0]}$ V [1, PRP]] PRT [1]]

(14) shows that *killing* is an N in syntax and its morphological field says that it is a noun stem (N[0]) consisting of a present participle (V [1, PRP]). Historically, *-ing* was a derivational suffix that was added to a verb and derived a derivational noun, just as the German *-ung*, as in *Wohnung* from the verb *wohnen*.

(15) is an example of compounding. In this example, *breaking down* is syntactically a noun and in its morphological structure, the verb in the present participle form (V[1, PRP]) *breaking* first undergoes the same V-to-N conversion, resulting in a noun stem (N[0]), which in turn combines with the particle (PRT) *down* (a morphological word) by compounding, producing a larger noun stem (N[0]). This is the same morphological structure as the noun *looker-on*, which is a compound of a noun stem (*looker*) and a particle (*on*). This morphological

structure of *breaking down* is justified by looking at its plural form. There are two plural forms found on the Internet, *the breaking downs of* ..., in which the plural inflectional suffix *-s* is added to the larger noun stem *breaking down*, and *the breakings down of* ..., in which it is added to the smaller noun stem *breaking*, just as *lookers-on*.

A local morphological structure (i.e., a two-story morphological tree structure, such as [$_X$ Y, AF]), is well formed if and only if it is an instantiation of one of the local morphological rules (e.g., local morphological rules in (1)) permitted by the language in question and satisfies the morphological properties of the morphemes involved. A morphological structure is well formed iff all the local morphological structures contained in it are well formed.

1.1.2 Morphophonology

Morphophonology concerns "the phonological realization of productive morphological alternations and must be kept clearly separate from pure morphology" (Sadock 2012: 150). For example, in the lexical entries for English regular verbs, the morphophonological (mphon) field only lists the phonological realization of its stem (1), and all the other regular inflectional forms are specified by productive morphophonological rules (2).

(1) lexical entry for *kick*
 syntax: V in [$_{VP}$ __, NP]
 morph: V [0]
 mphon: [$_{V[0]}$ /kɪk/]

(2) morphophonological rules for regular verbs
 a. [$_{V[1, BSE]}$ V[0]]
 b. [$_{V[1, PRP]}$ V[0] [$_{AF}$ /ɪŋ/]]
 c. [$_{V[1, PRES]}$ V[0]]
 d. [$_{V[1, PRES, 3SG]}$ V[0] [$_{AF}$ {Z}]]
 e. [$_{V[1, PAST]}$ V[0] [$_{AF}$ {D}]]
 f. [$_{V[1, PSP]}$ V[0] [$_{AF}$ {D}]]

(2a) says that the phonological form of a verb (as a morphological word) in the base form (the form that is not inflected for tense, for example, the form *be* of the verb *be*, which is represented morphologically as V[1, BSE]) is phonologically the same as its verb stem (V[0]). (2b) says that the phonological form of a verb in the present participle form (V[1, PRP]) consists of its verb stem (V[0]) and the suffix /ɪŋ/. (2c) says that the phonological form of a verb in the present tense (V[1, PRES]) is the same as that of its verb stem (V[0]). (2d) says that the phonological form of a verb in the present tense third person singular form (V[1, PRES, 3SG]) consists of its verb stem (V[0]) and the suffix {Z}. The latter is the regular third person singular present tense morpheme and consists of three allomorphs /s/, /z/, and /ɪz/. {Z} is understood as an abbreviation for {/s/ | /z/ | /ɪz/}, that is, one of the three alternative phonological realizations /s/, /z/, and /ɪz/. The notation {A | B | C} denotes alternatives. The three allomorphs are phonologically conditioned and in complementary distribution. The affix {D} in (2e, f) is the regular past and past participle morpheme and consists of three allomorphs /t/, /d/, and /ɪd/. {D} is understood as an abbreviation for {/t/ | /d/ | /ɪd/}. V[1, PAST] in (2e) refers to a verb in the past tense form (as a morphological word). V[1, PSP] in (2f) refers to a verb in the past participle form (as a morphological word).

The relationship between (2c) and (2d) is such that the latter, whose mother node is V[1, PRES, 3SG], is a special case of the former, whose mother node is V[1, PRES]. Therefore, the choice of the more specific (2d) preempts that of the more general (2c), due to the Elsewhere Principle (3), which was due originally to a Sanskrit grammarian Panini (ca. 500 B.C.) and was reintroduced into modern linguistics in 1969 by Stephen R. Anderson in his dissertation on the ordering of phonological rules.

(3) Elsewhere Principle (McCawley 1998: 163)
When the conditions of application for one rule are a special case of those for another rule, the more general rule is inapplicable in those cases in which the conditions for the more specific rule are met; that is, specific rules preempt the application of general rules.

When the mother node of a verb is the more specific V[1, PRES, 3SG], (2c) with the more general mother node V[1, PRES] becomes inapplicable, thus excluding the ungrammatical *[$_{V[1, PRES, 3SG]}$ V[0]].

Here is another example of the Elsewhere Principle. The rules in (4) determine which phonological realization of {D} is chosen under which environment. The notation A ≤ B in (4) denotes A immediately precedes B.

(4) a. {D} → /t/ in [–voice] ≤ __   b. {D} → /ɪd/ in /t/ ≤ __
    c. {D} → /d/ in [+voice] ≤ __   d. {D} → /ɪd/ in /d/ ≤ __

(4a) says that the morpheme {D} in (2e, f) is realized as /t/ when it is immediately preceded by a voiceless segment, as in *capped*. (4b) says that {D} is realized as /ɪd/ when it is immediately preceded by /t/, as in *patted*. (4c) says that {D} is realized as /d/ when it is immediately preceded by a voiced segment, as in *cabbed*.

(4d) says that {D} is realized as /ɪd/ when it is preceded by /d/, as in *padded*. The condition of application of (4b) is a special case of that of (4a) and therefore, (4b) preempts (4a), by the Elsewhere Principle. The same is true of (4c) and (4d).

We are now ready to give the lexical entry for the morpheme {D} based on (4). (5) and (6) are lexical entries for the regular past tense suffix {D} and the regular past participle suffix {D}, respectively. We ignore their semantic information (F/A and RS), which will be discussed later.

(5) lexical entry for the regular past tense suffix {D}
syntax: nil
morph: [$_{AF}$ {D}] in [$_{V[1, PAST]}$ V[0] __]
mphon: /t/ in [−voice] ⩽ __
/ɪd/ in /t/ ⩽ __
/d/ in [+voice] ⩽ __
/ɪd/ in /d/ ⩽ __

(6) lexical entry for the regular past participle suffix {D}
syntax: nil
morph: [$_{AF}$ {D}] in [$_{V[1, PSP]}$ V[0] __]
mphon: /t/ in [−voice] ⩽ __
/ɪd/ in /t/ ⩽ __
/d/ in [+voice] ⩽ __
/ɪd/ in /d/ ⩽ __

In (5) and (6), the suffix {D} is not represented in syntax. This is an example of a defective lexical item, which lacks representation in one or more modules in its lexical entry (Sadock 1991: 29, 2012: 183, Jackendoff 2002: 131). The tense PAST in (5) does not appear as a syntactic node, which is indicated by the syntactic field of (5) as "syntax: nil." It only appears in syntax as a value of the VFORM feature borne by a verb in syntax, as in V[PAST], which, by default, the morphological category V[1, PAST] corresponds to.

There is a lot of information common to (5) and (6). We can separate common lexical information from a family of lexical entries and organize the member lexical entries in an inheritance hierarchy, as in (8). An inheritance hierarchy places more general, more common, lexical information at a higher node in the hierarchy and more specific, less common, lexical information at a lower node, and each node in the hierarchy inherits by default all the information listed on the nodes that dominate it (Pollard and Sag 1987: 193ff., Pollard and Sag 1994: 36–37, Jackendoff 2002: 184, Sag, Wasow and Bender 2003: 229ff. and 470ff.). Some pieces of lexical information are very common, some are very limited, and others come in between. Under these circumstances, we can simplify all the lexical entries of a family by organizing them in an inheritance hierarchy (7), in which the common information is extracted from each lexical entry and is placed at the top node of the hierarchy, and the most restricted lexical information is placed at the bottom node of the hierarchy. The lexical information on a higher node trickles down the hierarchy to lower nodes; that is, the information at each node of the hierarchy by default inherits the information placed at all the higher nodes.

(7) inheritance hierarchy

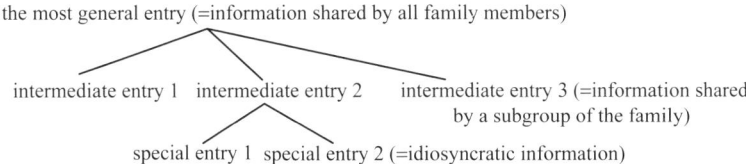

(8) inheritance hierarchy for the lexical entries for the suffix {D}

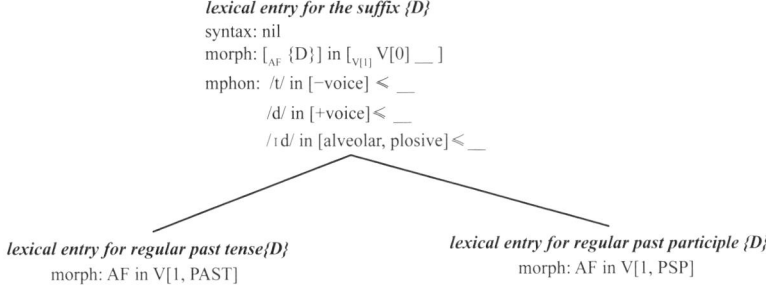

In the case of irregular verbs, their stem forms and all the irregular forms must be listed in the morphophonological field of their lexical entry. For example, (9) is the lexical entry for the irregular verb *sing*.

(9) lexical entry for *sing*
 syntax: V in [$_{VP}$ __, (NP)]
 morph: V[0]
 mphon: [$_{V[0]}$ /sɪŋ/], [$_{V[1, PAST]}$ /sæŋ/], [$_{V[1, PSP]}$ /sʌŋ/]

When a morphophonological value is registered in the lexical entry of a lexeme, the productive morphophonological rule of the same morphological category, such as one of (2), becomes inapplicable. This phenomenon is called blocking. For example, because /sæŋ/ is registered in the lexical entry for the verb *sing* (9) as the value of V[1, PAST], the productive rule (2e) becomes inapplicable. We can attribute this effect to the Elsewhere Principle (3), if we understand that the condition of application of [$_{V[1, PAST]}$ /sæŋ/] is a special case of that of (2e) in the sense that the specification of a phonological realization is the most specific in all the morphophonological rules.

Some irregular verbs have two V[1, PAST] (and V[1, PSP]) forms: one is an irregular form and the other is a regular form (10). For such verbs, not only irregular forms but also regular forms must be listed so that irregular forms do not block regular forms (cf. Jackendoff 1997: 230 note 4).

(10)

V[0]	regular V[1, PAST]	irregular V[1, PAST]
dream	dreamed	dreamt
learn	learned	learnt
burn	burned	burnt
bust	busted	bust
awake	awaked	awoke
dive	dived	dove

1.2 Syntax Overview

For the syntax module of English, we use phrase structure (PS) grammar (1). Recall that the comma between categories in PS rules means that the linear order is not included. That is, all the PS rules in (1) only show constituent structures without specifying the linear order between the sisters. The underlying assumption here is that the linear order between sisters can be specified separately from the specification of constituent structures along the lines of GPSG's ID/LP format (Gazdar et al. 1985: 46ff.).

The PS rules, such as [$_{VP}$ V, NP], [$_{PP}$ P, NP], or [$_{CP}$ C, S], that introduce the lexical head of a phrase (indicated by the symbol H[0], a head with <BAR, 0>) and its complements (i.e., GPSG's lexical ID rules (Gazdar et al. 1985: 54)) are not listed in (1), because they are lexical information (the subcategorization frame of each word) and are included in the syntactic field of each lexical entry. Therefore, except (1a, b), the PS rules in (1) are all adjunction rules for modification (i.e., GPSG's nonlexical ID rules). The notation {A | B} in (1) means alternatives. For example, (1b) is the same as [$_{NP}$ DET, N'] or [$_{NP}$ NP[POS], N'].

(1) English PS rules
   a. [$_S$ NP, VP]   b. [$_{NP}$ {DET | NP[POS]}, N']   c. [$_{N'}$ {A | RRC}, N']
   d. [$_{AP}$ {PP | ADVP}, AP] e. [$_{VP}$ {PP | ADVP}, VP]   f. [$_S$ {PP | ADVP}, S]

In (1c), RRC stands for restrictive relative clause, which includes what McCawley (1998: 393) called reduced relative clauses, such as *any person proud of himself*, *the little house on the prairie*, *a child taking a nap*. See 6.2.7 for details.

We will use the term subject (in syntax) only for descriptive purposes and not as a theoretical primitive, to refer to the NP in (1a), that is, the NP that is directly dominated by an S and is a sister of its VP.

All syntactic categories are sets of feature-value pairs. For the part-of-speech categories (N, A, V, P), we assume the standard feature specifications: N = {<N, +>, <V, –>} (or alternatively, {[+N], [–V]}), A = {<N, +>, <V, +>}, V = {<N, –>, <V, +>}, P = {<N, –>, <V, –>}. For the feature BAR, following McCawley (1998), we use <BAR, 0> for word level and <BAR, 1> for phrase level. Clauses (S), whose syntactic head is V (Gazdar et al. 1985: 23), are {<N, –>, <V, +>, <BAR, 2>}, namely, V[2] or alternatively V" (V double prime). As for noun (N), again following McCawley (1998), N' (or alternatively N[1]) is {<N, +>, <V, +>, <BAR, 1>} and NP (alternatively N" or N[2]) is {<N, +>, <V, +>, <BAR, 2>}. That is, NP = N", S = V" and otherwise, XP = X'. Although BAR is used both in morphology and in syntax, the definitions are different: in morphology, <BAR, 0> refers to a stem and <BAR, 1> refers to a morphological word.

(2) BAR values in syntax

category	N	V	A	P	ADV	C
<BAR, 0>	N	V	A	P	ADV	C
<BAR, 1>	N'	VP	AP	PP	ADVP	CP
<BAR, 2>	NP	S				

We can rewrite the PS rules in (1) by using the BAR value of each category and the head (H) symbol.

(1') English PS rules:
a. [$_{V[2]}$ N[2], H[1]]
b. [$_{N[2]}$ {DET | N[2, POS]}, H[1]]
c. [$_{N[1]}$ {A | RRC}, H[1]]
d. [$_{A[1]}$ ADV[1], H[1]]
e. [$_{V[n]}$ {P[1] | ADV[1]}, H[n]] (n=1, 2)

One of the advantages of feature-based syntactic categories is that we can capture similarities between different categories. For example, nouns and adjectives (i.e., [+N] categories) cannot take an NP complement, whereas verbs and prepositions (i.e., [−N] categories) can take an NP complement.

We assume a very loose version of the Head Feature Convention (HFC) for default cases, which can be overridden by specific requirements (cf. Gazdar et al. 1985: 94ff.).

(3) Head Feature Convention (HFC)
In each headed local tree, the mother and its head daughter must meet the conditions (i) and (ii), unless specified otherwise.
(i) The set of head features on the mother is identical to that on its head daughter.
(ii) For each head feature in (i), its value on the mother must be identical to that on the daughter.

(4) list of head features
BAR, form features (NFORM, PFORM, VFORM, and CFORM), part-of-speech features (<N, ±>, <V, ±>), AUX, INV, AGREEMENT (AGR), which subsumes PERSON (PER), NUMBER (NUM), and GENDER (GEN),

The head features INV (inversion) and AGR will be discussed in 2.1 and 1.3, respectively.

Here are examples of how the Head Feature Convention (HFC) works in syntax. First, because part-of-speech features are head features, they and their values must be shared between a phrase (<BAR, 1>) and its head daughter (<BAR, 0>). This excludes such ill-formed phrases as [$_{VP}$ N ...], where the head of a verb phrase (VP) is a noun (N). Therefore, the fact that the head of XP is X, where X ∈ {N, A, V, P}, is due to the HFC.

Second, as shown in (5), one of the values of VFORM feature is PAST, and because this feature is a head feature, this feature-value pair <VFORM, PAST> must be shared between a verb in the past tense (V[PAST], whose feature composition is {<N, −>, <V, +>, <BAR, 0>, <VFORM, PAST>}), its verb phrase

(VP[PAST]), and its clause (S[PAST]). Therefore, the fact that a finite clause in the past tense is headed by a finite verb in the past tense is due to the HFC.

Third, PFORM is another head feature and one of its values is *of*. Therefore, the prepositional phrase headed by the preposition *of* (PP[*of*], whose feature composition is {<N, –>, <V, –>, <BAR, 1>, <PFORM, *of*>}) has the syntactic structure [$_{PP[of]}$ P[*of*], NP], in which the head of PP[*of*] is P[*of*].

Fourth, the HFC is overridden when specific requirements are stated in rules. For example, the syntactic structure of a phrase is [$_{X[1]}$ X[0] ...], where the phrasal node is <BAR, 1> and its head is <BAR, 0>. The value of the head feature BAR on the mother and that on the head daughter are specified in the PS rules (1a, b) and in the syntactic field of lexical entries, such as 1.1.1 (5) and (6). Therefore, the HFC is overridden in these cases. Otherwise, the value of the BAR feature is maintained by the HFC. This means that adjunction structures ([$_{XP}$ YP, XP]), which keep the head's category and BAR value unchanged, are always licensed by the HFC, unless specified otherwise.

Fifth, when there is no head daughter in a phrase (i.e., an exocentric phrase), the HFC is not violated, because it only applies to headed local trees. Examples of exocentric phrases are *wh*-questions and *wh*-relative clauses, which will be discussed in Chapter 6. The syntactic category of *wh*-questions is CP[WH[Q]], which consists of an interrogative *wh*-phrase (XP[WH[Q]]) and an S, namely, [$_{CP[WH[Q]]}$ XP[WH[Q]], S]. The syntactic category of *wh*-relative clauses is CP[WH[R]], which consists of a relative *wh*-phrase (XP[WH[R]]) and an S, namely, [$_{CP[WH[R]]}$ XP[WH[R]], S]. These are exocentric phrase structures and are not excluded by the HFC.

The VFORM feature takes the following values.

(5) VFORM values
BSE (base form), PRP (present participle form), PSP (past participle form), PAS (passive participle form), *to*, FIN (finite, covering PRES (present tense) and PAST (past tense))

Here are examples of the internal structures of clauses. In (6), the verb *want* takes an S[*to*] complement, which is a clause headed by a V[*to*], whose lexical entry is given in (12c). The V[*to*] takes a VP[BSE] complement.

(6) a. John wants Mary to stay home.
b. [$_{S[PRES]}$ [$_{NP}$ John] [$_{VP[PRES]}$ wants [$_{S[to]}$ Mary [$_{VP[to]}$ [$_{V[to]}$ to] [$_{VP[BSE]}$ stay home]]]]].

In (7), the verb *arrange* takes a CP[*for*] complement, a complementizer phrase (CP) headed by the complementizer (C) *for*, which takes an S[*to*] complement.

(7) a. John arranged for Mary to stay home.
 b. [$_{S[PAST]}$ [$_{NP}$ John] [$_{VP[PAST]}$ arranged [$_{CP[for]}$ [$_{C[for]}$ for] [$_{S[to]}$ Mary [$_{VP[to]}$ to stay home]]]]].

In (8), the verb *count* takes a PP[*on*] complement, a prepositional phrase headed by the preposition *on*. The preposition *on*, in turn, takes an S[PRP] complement, a clause headed by a verb in the present participle form (V[PRP]).

(8) a. John counted on Mary staying home.
 b. [$_{S[PAST]}$ [$_{NP}$ John] [$_{VP[PAST]}$ counted [$_{PP[on]}$ [$_{P[on]}$ on] [$_{S[PRP]}$ Mary [$_{VP[PRP]}$ staying home]]]]].

In (9), the verb *seem* takes a VP[*to*] complement. This is an example of subject raising.

(9) a. John seems to like Mary.
 b. [$_{S[PRES]}$ [$_{NP}$ John] [$_{VP[PRES]}$ seems [$_{VP[to]}$ to [$_{VP[BSE]}$ like Mary]]]].

In (10), the verb *persuade* takes two complements, NP and VP[*to*]. This is an example of object control. Raising and control will be discussed in Chapter 4.

(10) a. John persuaded Mary to stay home.
 b. [$_{S[PAST]}$ [$_{NP}$ John] [$_{VP[PAST]}$ persuaded [$_{NP}$ Mary] [$_{VP[to]}$ to [$_{VP[BSE]}$ stay home]]]].

The subject-verb agreement is achieved in syntax through the PS rule (11a).

(11) a. subject-verb agreement
 [$_{S[FIN, AGR[<PER, 3>, <NUM, SG>, <GEN, N>]]}$ NP[AGR[<PER, α>, <NUM, β>]], VP[FIN, AGR[<PER, α>, <NUM, β>]], where α ∈ {1, 2, 3} and β ∈ {SG, PL}
 b. [$_{VP[FIN, AGR[<PER, α>, <NUM, β>]]}$ V[FIN, AGR[<PER, α>, <NUM, β>]], ...]

The AGR feature is one of the head features listed in (4) and consists of three features: PERSON (PER) with its values 1, 2, and 3, NUMBER (NUM) with its values SG and PL, and GENER (GEN) with its values M, F, and N. In English subject-verb agreement, only PER and NUM are relevant. (In French, GEN and NUM are relevant in subject-past participle agreement, as in *Vous êtes allées*, and in object-past participle agreement, as in *Je les ai vues*.) (11a) says that the AGR values are shared in a finite clause between its subject NP and finite VP. The AGR value on the mother node S[FIN] is specified as third person singular neuter (<PER, 3>, <NUM, SG>, <GEN, N>). Because AGR is a head feature, (11b), in which the AGR on VP and that on its head V are shared, is forced by the HFC (3). However, because the AGR value is already specified on the mother S (=V[2]) node in (11a), the HFC (3) does not force the VP's AGR value onto the mother S[FIN].

For ease of future reference, we will give sample lexical entries in (12), including lexical information about the semantic modules F/A and RS, which will be discussed in 1.3 and 1.4. Some lexical items are defective in that they lack representation in one or more modules, which is indicated as *nil* in (12c, d, e). As for the syntactic field of a lexical entry, we adopt the convention that we omit the phrasal category of the subcategorization frame in question: for example, V in [__, NP] in place of V in [$_{VP}$ __, NP], because the category information of a phrasal node is predictable from that of the head node by the HFC.

(12) sample lexical entries with annotations

a. *sneeze*
syntax: V (syntactic category: verb) in [__] (subcategorization frame)
F/A: Fa (a functor that takes one argument and returns a proposition: [$_{PROP}$ Fa, ARG])
RS: [$_{TYPE}$ "sneeze"] in [$_{EV}$ __ AG] (a verb that denotes an event (EV) that takes one participant role, namely, agent (AG))
morph: V[0] (morphological category: verb stem)
mphon: [$_{V[0]}$ /sni:z/] (a regular verb; the other forms are supplied by 1.1.2 (2))

b. *take*
syntax: V in [__, NP]
F/A: Faa (a functor that takes one argument and returns an Fa: [$_{Fa}$ Faa, ARG])
RS: [$_{TYPE}$ "take"] in [$_{EV}$ __ AG PT] (a verb that denotes an event (EV) that takes two participant roles, namely, agent (AG) and patient (PT))
morph: V[0]
mphon: [$_{V[0]}$ /teɪk/], [$_{V[1, PAST]}$ /tʊk/], [$_{V[1, PSP]}$ /teɪkən/]

c. *to*
   syntax: V[AUX, *to*] in [__, VP[BSE]] (a nonfinite auxiliary verb (AUX) with <VFORM, *to*> that takes a VP[BSE] complement, which is a VP headed by a verb in the base form (V[BSE]))
   F/A: nil (no representation in F/A)
   RS: nil (no representation in RS)
   morph: Word (<BAR, 1> morphological category. This means no inflection or derivation.)
   mphon: /tə/

d. complementizer *that*
   syntax: C[*that*] in [__, {S[FIN] | S[BSE]}] (C with <CFORM, *that*>, which takes as its complement an S[FIN] or S[BSE])
   F/A: nil
   RS: nil
   morph: Word
   mphon: /ðæt/

e. complementizer *for*
   syntax: C[*for*] in [__, S[*to*]] (C with <CFORM, *for*>, which takes S[*to*] as its complement)
   F/A: nil
   RS: nil
   morph: Word
   mphon: /fɚ/

In (12c), the infinitival *to* is treated as a semantically null nonfinite auxiliary verb V[AUX, *to*] (a verb with the feature AUX and the VFORM value *to*), which is supported by the similarities between *to* and auxiliary verbs: (i) VP ellipsis (... *but I don't think I can.* vs. ... *but I don't want to.*), (ii) VP preposing (... *and buy a new car I really should.* vs. ... *and buy a new car I really want to.*), (iii) *to* occupies the Modal position in the sequence: Modal + Have(-en) + Be(-ing) (*John may have been at home last night* vs. *John seems to have been at home last night.*), (iv) no inflection for modal auxiliaries and *to*, and (v) modal auxiliaries and *to* take a VP[BSE] complement. Note that *to* cannot undergo inversion because it is not a finite auxiliary verb (cf. 2.1 (3)).

In (12d), the complementizer C[*that*] takes two kinds of complement, S[FIN] or S[BSE]. Verbs such as *think* and *say* take a CP[*that*] complement with an S[FIN] (*John said [that Mary stayed home]*), whereas verbs such as *propose* and *demand* take a CP[*that*] complement with an S[BSE] (*John demanded* [*that Mary stay home*] and *I demand* [*that John not be here*]). The selection of complement type between S[FIN] and S[BSE] is not syntactic but semantic and pragmatic, which is illustrated by *John demanded something. It was that Mary stay home* and *What is the Case Filter? It is that an NP be assigned Case*. See 6.2.6 (7) for some discussion on this.

In the remainder of this section, we will give the definitions of dominate, c-command, S-mates, and well-formedness of syntactic trees, which we need in the subsequent chapters.

(13) definition of directly dominate
For two nodes X and Y in a given tree, X <u>directly dominates</u> Y iff there is a branch in the tree that connects X and Y with X immediately above Y.

(14) definition of dominate
For two nodes X and Y in a given tree, X <u>dominates</u> Y iff there is a series of nodes in the tree X = X_1, ..., X_n = Y, such that for each pair of X_i and X_{i+1}, X_i directly dominates X_{i+1}.

The notion of c-command is a member of the command family. Each family member x-command shares the same basic definition and is parameterized by the set of bounding nodes $\phi(x)$ (McCawley 1984, 1998: 352–353).

(15) definition of x-command
For two nodes X and Y in a given tree, X <u>x-commands</u> Y iff (i) the first (lowest) non-adjoined node that dominates X and is a member of $\phi(x)$, the set of bounding nodes for x, also dominates Y, and (ii) X does not dominate Y.

(16) definition of non-adjoined node
The <u>non-adjoined node</u> in an adjunction structure is the node that dominates all the adjoined nodes.

For example, in a syntactic structure [$_S$ NP [$_{VP}$ [$_{VP}$ [$_{VP}$ VP PP] PP] PP]], where three PPs are adjoined to the VP, the highest VP node (underlined) is the non-adjoined node.

(17) definition of c-command
For two nodes X and Y in a given syntactic structure, X <u>c-commands</u> Y iff X x-commands Y, where $\phi(x)$ = {all nodes in the syntactic structure}.

(18) definition of asymmetric c-command
For two nodes X and Y in a given syntactic structure, X asymmetrically c-commands Y iff X c-commands Y and Y does not c-command X.

(19) definition of S-command
For two nodes X and Y in a given syntactic structure, X S-commands Y iff X x-commands Y, where $\phi(x) = \{S\}$.

(20) definition of S-mates
For two nodes X and Y in a given syntactic structure, X and Y are S-mates iff X and Y S-command each other.

Here are the definitions of well-formedness for a local tree (21) and a tree (22).

(21) definition of a well-formed syntactic local tree
A syntactic local tree (a two-story tree structure in syntax, for example, [$_S$ NP, VP]), is well formed iff it is either (ia) an instantiation of one of the syntactic PS rules admitted by the language in question (i.e., (1) for English) or (ib) an instantiation of the syntactic field (i.e., subcategorization frame) of one of the lexical entries of the language in question, and (ii) it also meets all the relevant syntactic constraints on syntactic structures (e.g., the HFC).

For example, a local tree is an instantiation of [$_S$ NP VP] iff the mother node of the local tree is labeled S and directly dominates two daughter nodes, one labeled NP and the other labeled VP, and the former precedes the latter. In other words, PS rules are interpreted as "node admissibility conditions" (McCawley 1973: 39–40, cf. Carnie 2008: 88–89).

(22) definition of a well-formed syntactic structure
A syntactic structure is well formed iff all the local trees that it contains are well formed.

For example, the syntactic structure [$_{S[PAST]}$ [$_{NP[3SGM]}$ he] [$_{VP[PAST, 3SG]}$ [$_{V[PAST, 3SG]}$ ran]]] is well formed, because this contains two local syntactic structures, [$_{VP[PAST, 3SG]}$ [$_{V[PAST, 3SG]}$ ran]] and [$_{S[PAST]}$ NP[3SGM] VP[PAST, 3SG]] and both are well formed. The former is an instantiation of the syntactic field of the lexical entry for the verb *run* (V in [$_{VP}$ __]), and the latter is an instantiation of the phrase structure rule (1a) ([$_S$ NP VP]). Furthermore, the Head Feature Convention (3) and the subject-verb agreement (11) are satisfied.

1.3 Semantics 1: Function-Argument Structure Overview

Function-Argument (F/A) structures are representations of logical structures (semantic forms) of sentences and consist of such semantic categories as proposition (PROP), argument (ARG), and various functors (Fφ). They are order-free phrase structures that are binary-branching except for cases of coordination. An infinite set of such F/A structures is generated by the phrase structure (PS) grammar (1). In (1a), *a* and *p* refer to ARG and PROP, respectively.

(1) PS rules for F/A
  a. [$_{Fφ}$ Fxφ, x], where x is either *a* or *p*, and φ is a finite string of *a*'s and *p*'s, and Fe = PROP for the empty string e. (Sadock 2012: 16 (4))
  b. [$_α$ Mα, α], where Mα is a modifier of an F/A category α. (Sadock 2012: 17–18)

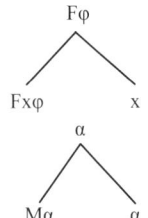

Here are examples of F/A structures generated by (1a).

(2) a. [$_{PROP}$ Fa, ARG], where Fa is an intransitive functor, such as *dance*.
  b. [$_{Fa}$ Faa, ARG], where Faa is a transitive functor, such as *kick*.
  c. [$_{Faa}$ Faaa, ARG], where Faaa is a ditransitive functor, such as *give*.
  d. [$_{PROP}$ Fp, PROP], where Fp is a SEEM-type functor, which includes TENSE (PRES and PAST) and NOT.
  e. [$_{Fa}$ Fpa, PROP], where Fpa is a functor, such as *know*, that takes an internal PROP and the subject ARG.
  f. [$_{Faa}$ Fpaa, PROP], where Fpaa is a functor, such as *tell*, that takes internal PROP and ARG and the subject ARG.

We will use the term subject ARG (in F/A) for descriptive purposes, and not as a theoretical primitive, to refer to the ARG in (2a), that is, the ARG that is directly dominated by a PROP and is a sister of its Fa.

In (1b), a modifier of the F/A category Mα is adjoined to the F/A category α and returns a more complex member of the same category α. The following are examples of F/A structures generated by (1b).

24 1 MODULES

(3) common types of F/A modifier (Sadock 2012: 17–18 (8))
   a. [PROP Mp, PROP], where Mp is a propositional modifier, such as *probably*
   b. [Fa M_Fa, Fa], where M_Fa is a predicate modifier, such as *intentionally*
   c. [ARG Ma, ARG], where Ma is an argument modifier, for example, an attributive adjective or a restrictive or reduced relative clause.

Here is the definition of a well-formed F/A structure.

(4) definition of a well-formed F/A structure
   a. A local F/A structure (a local F/A tree) is well formed iff it is an instantiation of (i.e., generated by) (1a) or (1b), and its terminal nodes, if any, are instantiations of the F/A field of one of the lexical entries of the language in question.
   b. An F/A structure is well formed iff all the local F/A structures that it contains are well formed.

(5) is an example of a well-formed F/A structure of a sentence.
   a. John knows that Mary met a tall boy yesterday.
   b. the F/A structure of (5a).

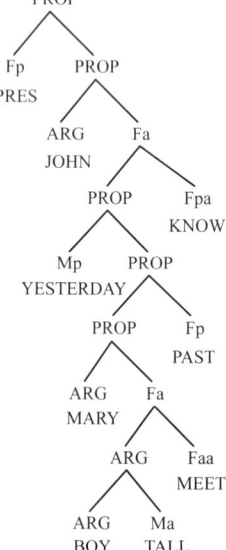

Note that each local F/A structure in (5b) is well formed by (4a) and therefore the whole F/A structure is well formed by (4b). We capitalize each word in (5b) to indicate the F/A aspects of its meaning (i.e., the F/A field of its lexical entry).

Coreference relations between two NPs are primarily a semantic notion and are represented in F/A. However, this information is accessible from the other modules (e.g., syntax, RS, and Information Structure) through an extended interpretation of Feature Osmosis (Sadock 2012: 154 (19)), which roughly says that in the unmarked situations, there will be a correspondence of features between modules. To indicate coreference between ARGs, we use the INDEX (IND) feature, which consists of the referential index (ref) and the AGREEMENT (AGR) feature with PERSON (PER), NUMBER (NUM), and GENDER (GEN) (cf. Pollard and Sag 1994: 24–25).

(6) the feature structure of INDEX (IND)

$$\text{IND} \begin{pmatrix} \text{ref} & i \\ \text{AGR} & \begin{pmatrix} \text{PER} & \{1|2|3\} \\ \text{NUM} & \{\text{SG}|\text{PL}\} \\ \text{GEN} & \{\text{M}|\text{F}|\text{N}\} \end{pmatrix} \end{pmatrix}$$

For example, if in *John loves her*, *John*'s referential index is i and that of *her* is j, their respective ARGs in F/A are [$_{\text{ARG[IND[i, 3SGM]]}}$ JOHN] and ARG[IND[j, 3SGF]]. That is, each ARG has its own IND value. In fact, the AGR value (i.e., PER, NUM, and GEN values) is a function of the referential index (IND[j, AGR(j)]) in the sense that once the referential index is determined (i.e., the referent is determined), its AGR value is determined as a result. For example, in *Vous êtes gentilles*, the adjective *gentilles* is in the feminine plural form only if the referent of *vous*, the set of people referred to by the second person pronoun, is feminine plural. We will treat nonreflexive pronouns as consisting only of the INDEX feature (i.e., their referential index and AGR value) (cf. McCawley 1998: 480 note 2). We define coreference as follows. Two ARGs are coreferential iff they share the same referential index. From this definition, it follows that when two ARGs are coreferent, they have the same AGR value, because AGR is a function of the referential index.

Not only TENSE (PRES and PAST) but also auxiliary verbs (V[AUX]) are treated as an Fp. For example, the perfect auxiliary *have* is [$_{Fp}$ PAST] in F/A (McCawley 1998: 221, Sadock 2012: 161–162). In (7), mismatches (crossings of association lines) arise between syntax and F/A, which are all innocuous mismatches of subject-raising type, which will be discussed in 4.1. These mismatches are unavoidable, because the TENSE and other Fp functors, although taking scope over their sister PROP, are all realized within the VP in syntax. Therefore, Fp functors c-command the subject ARG in F/A, whereas this c-command relation is reversed in syntax. See (25) for the definition of c-command in F/A.

(7) innocuous mismatches between syntax and F/A

a. [$_{S[PAST]}$ John [$_{VP[PAST]}$ [$_{V[PAST]}$ kicked] the dog]].

[$_{Fp}$ PAST]([$_{ARG}$ JOHN]([$_{Faa}$ KICK]([$_{ARG}$ DOG])))

b. [$_{S[PRES]}$ John [$_{VP[PRES]}$[$_{V[PRES]}$ has] [$_{VP[PSP]}$ kicked the dog]]].

PRES(PAST(JOHN(KICK(DOG))))

c. [$_{S[PRES]}$ John [$_{VP[PRES]}$ has [$_{VP[PSP]}$ been [$_{VP[PRP]}$ kicking the dog]]]].

PRES(PAST(PROG(JOHN(KICK(DOG)))))

d. [$_{S[PRES]}$ John [$_{VP[PRES]}$ may [$_{VP[BSE]}$ have [$_{VP[PSP]}$ been [$_{VP[PRP]}$ kicking the dog]]]]].

PRES(MAY(PAST(PROG(JOHN(KICK(DOG))))))

Note that in (7b, c), the perfect auxiliary verb in the present tense *has* corresponds to PRES and PAST, the latter being within the scope of the former.

(8a) is an example in which a common noun is used as a predicate and its F/A and RS are given in (8b). (RS, the module that represents events and their participant roles, will be discussed in the next section.) In (8b), the predicative BABY, which is the second argument of the Faa functor =, carries the INDEX value IND[3SG] without a referential index, because it is not referentially used. See (22) for the lexical entry for the Faa functor =.

(8) a. John is a baby.
b. the F/A and RS of (8a)

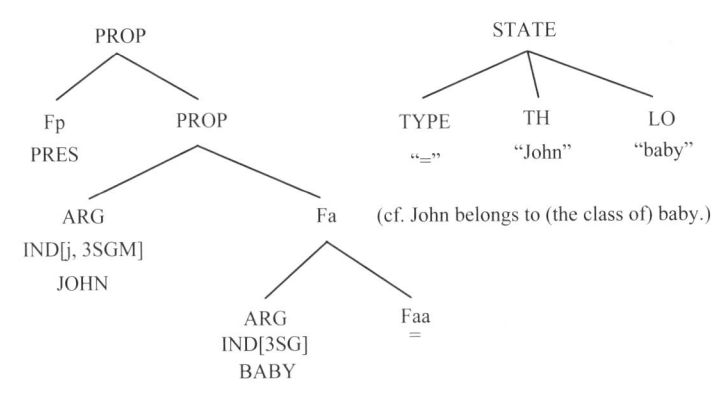

```
        PROP                              STATE
       /    \                            /  |   \
     Fp     PROP                      TYPE  TH   LO
     PRES  /    \                      "="  "John" "baby"
         ARG     Fa          (cf. John belongs to (the class of) baby.)
     IND[j, 3SGM]
       JOHN    /    \
             ARG    Faa
          IND[3SG]   =
            BABY
```

The common noun *baby* has the following lexical entry, in which the referential index (ref) is optional. Note that a common noun, whether used predicatively or as an argument, is treated as ARG in F/A. (The other way of treating a predicative noun is to treat it as an Fa, as in Sadock 2012: 28 (10), 62 (96). But we will explore the first way.)

(9) lexical entry for the common noun *baby*
syntax: N in [_N'_ __]
F/A: ARG[IND[(ref), 3SGN]]
RS: ROLE

When a common noun is used as a predicate, as in (8a), it serves as the lower ARG of the Faa type-identity functor = and forms an Fa, as in (8b). (See (22) for the lexical entry for the type-identity Faa =.) "α = β" means that α is equal to β in type or α is an instance of type β. (See Jackendoff 1983: 78ff. and Lyons 1977: 13ff. for type-token distinction.) We assume that a predicate NP, when representing a type as the second argument of the type-identity functor =, lacks its referential index, as in (8b). The verb *is* and the indefinite article *a* in (8a) are meaningless and lack their F/A representation (except, of course, the tense PRES and agreement information carried by *is*) (Sadock 2012: 29). In *Mary considers John a baby*, the meaning of type-identity functor = is evident, although there is no *be* verb. Therefore, we claim that the source of the meaning "=" in (8a) is not the verb *be* and that *be* in (8a) is meaningless.

An NP in syntax corresponds to an ARG in F/A in default cases (1.4 (7a), Sadock 2012: 26 (6)). When a noun is modified in syntax by an adjective, as in (*a*) [$_{N'}$ *cute baby*], BABY in F/A is an ARG and CUTE is an Ma (modifier of an argument). Therefore, the F/A of the N' is [$_{ARG}$ [$_{Ma}$ CUTE], [$_{ARG}$ BABY]] and when the NP is used predicatively, its F/A is [$_{Fa}$ [$_{Faa}$ =][$_{ARG}$ [$_{Ma}$ CUTE], [$_{ARG}$ BABY]]]. When a noun takes a complement CP[*that*], the F/A category of the noun is ARGp, which shows that it takes a PROP and returns ARG (i.e., [$_{ARG}$ ARGp, PROP]). An example of ARGp is the noun *fact* (as in *the fact that John passed the exam*). When a noun takes a PP complement, its F/A category is ARGa, which shows that it takes an ARG and returns an ARG (i.e., [$_{ARG}$ ARGa, ARG]). The head of the PP complement of a noun is either a semantically empty *of*, as in (10a) (Sadock 2012: 34 (22)) or a preposition lexically selected by the head noun, as in (11a), where the head noun *attack* selects the head (*on*) of its complement PP. In both cases, we treat the prepositions as semantically empty in F/A, because the head of the complement PP cannot be substituted by some other preposition P in such a way that the P gives a different meaning to the NP *the attack* P *the government*, and the meaning difference between *the attack on the government* and *the attack* P *the government* is reducible to the meaning difference between the prepositions that head the complement PPs. (See Cruse 2011: 84–85 on how to identify semantic constituents.)

(10) a. the king of England
 b. the [$_{N'}$ [$_N$ king] [$_{PP[of]}$ of [$_{NP}$ England]]]
 c. [$_{ARG}$ [$_{ARGa}$ KING] [$_{ARG}$ ENGLAND]]

(11) a. the attack on the government
 b. the [$_{N'}$ [$_N$ attack] [$_{PP[on]}$ on [$_{NP}$ the government]]]
 c. [$_{ARG}$ [$_{ARGa}$ ATTACK] [$_{ARG}$ GOVERNMENT]]

Sometimes, the meaning of the complement PP of a noun is expressed by a prenominal adjective, as in (12). (Note that (12a, b) are in fact ambiguous. For example, (12a) means either 'the king of England,' as in *the English king from France* or 'the king who is English,' as in *the English king of France*.) In such a case, there is a mismatch between syntax and F/A in that a prenominal adjective does not correspond to an Ma (modifier of ARG) but to an ARG, as in (13). This mismatched correspondence between adjective in syntax and ARG in F/A is needed later to treat such control structures as *an American attempt to dominate the Middle East* (Culicover and Jackendoff 2005: 418). (See 4.4 (1d) and (2d) for adjective controllers.)

(12) a. the English king (in the sense of 'the king of England')
 b. the Russian president (in the sense of 'the president of Russia')

(13) a. [$_{ARG}$ [$_{ARGa}$ KING] [$_{ARG}$ ENGLAND]]   b. [$_{ARG}$ [$_{ARGa}$ PRESIDENT] [$_{ARG}$ RUSSIA]]

The lexical entry for the adjective *English*, for example, must include in its F/A field Ma (attributive use), Fa (predicative use), and ARG (complement use).

When a noun is preceded by both a complement adjective (ARG in F/A) and a modifier adjective (Ma in F/A), the complement adjective must be placed closer to the head noun (14a). The same is true of a complement PP and a modifier PP (14b). This is because the F/A category of the head noun is ARGa, which must be combined with ARG, and because the F/A category of a modifier adjective or PP is Ma, which must be combined with ARG and not with ARGa. Therefore, (14c) is the only F/A structure that meets these requirements. In (14a, b), the notation A < B means A precedes B.

(14) a. [$_{N'}$ modifier adjective < complement adjective < N]
 [$_{N'}$ modifier adjective [$_{N'}$ complement adjective N]]
 *the English bald king, cf. the bald English king
 *the Russian young president   cf. the young Russian president
 b. [$_{N'}$ N < complement PP < modifier PP]
 [$_{N'}$ [$_{N'}$ N complement PP] modifier PP]
 *the king from France of England   cf. the king of England from France
 c. [$_{ARG}$ Ma, [$_{ARG}$ ARG, ARGa]]

The F/A constituent structure (14c) is isomorphic to the syntactic structures (14a) and (14b). That is, (14c) entails the linear orders of modifier before complement in (14a) and complement before modifier in (14b).

The F/A module is the place where quantifiers and their scopes are represented. (15) is a set of conditions that well-formed quantifier phrases (QPs) must satisfy and is largely based on McCawley's (1993: 34) coherence conditions on variables. In (15), a QP that quantifies a variable x is denoted by QP_x with the subscript x.

(15) the well-formed conditions on QPs (cf. Sadock 2012: 61)
   a. [$_{PROP}$ QP_x, PROP], where the matrix PROP must contain x.
   b. [$_{QPx}$ Q, PROP], where the domain expression PROP must contain x.
   c. All the instances of a variable x must be either dominated or c-commanded by a single QP_x.

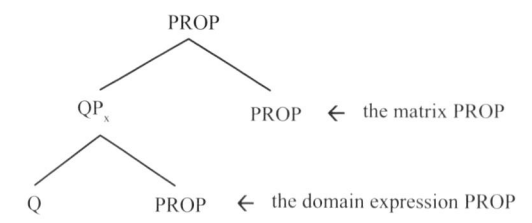

```
            PROP
           /    \
         QP_x    PROP    ← the matrix PROP
         /  \
        Q    PROP        ← the domain expression PROP
```

Sadock (2012: 61) formulated his well-formedness conditions on quantification based on his assumption that a variable is a foot feature. We will try a different approach by eliminating a foot feature from our syntax and F/A and develop our theory of quantification along the lines of more traditional conditions, such as (15). (15c) entails that the set {x, y, z, ...} of all the distinct variables contained in the topmost PROP and the set {QP_x, QP_y, QP_z, ...} of all the distinct QPs contained in that PROP must correspond one to one. That is, the correspondence from x to QP_x defines a bijective mapping from the set of all the distinct variables to the set of all the QPs in the sense that (i) for each variable x, there is only one QP_x, (ii) QP_x and QP_y are distinct QPs if x and y are distinct variables, and (iii) for each QP contained in the topmost PROP, there is a variable x contained in that PROP such that QP = QP_x. The three examples in (16) are ill-formed F/A structures. (16a, b, c) violate (15a, b, c), respectively.

(16) a. [[$_{QPx}$ [$_Q$ ALL] [$_{PROP}$ x = BOY]] [$_{PROP}$ JOHN ADMIRE MARY]]
   b. [[$_{QPx}$ [$_Q$ ALL] [$_{PROP}$ JOHN ADMIRE MARY]] [$_{PROP}$ x LAUGH]]
   c. [[$_{QPy}$ [$_Q$ ALL] [$_{PROP}$ x FRIEND y]] [$_{QPx}$ [$_Q$ ALL] [$_{PROP}$ x = BOY]] [$_{PROP}$ x ADMIRE y]]

(17a) below has a quantified NP (QNP) *every baby* as its subject. The lexical entry for *every* is given in (18). The syntax of (17a) is (17c) and its F/A structure that meets the well-formedness conditions (15) is (17b).

(17) a. Every baby sleeps.

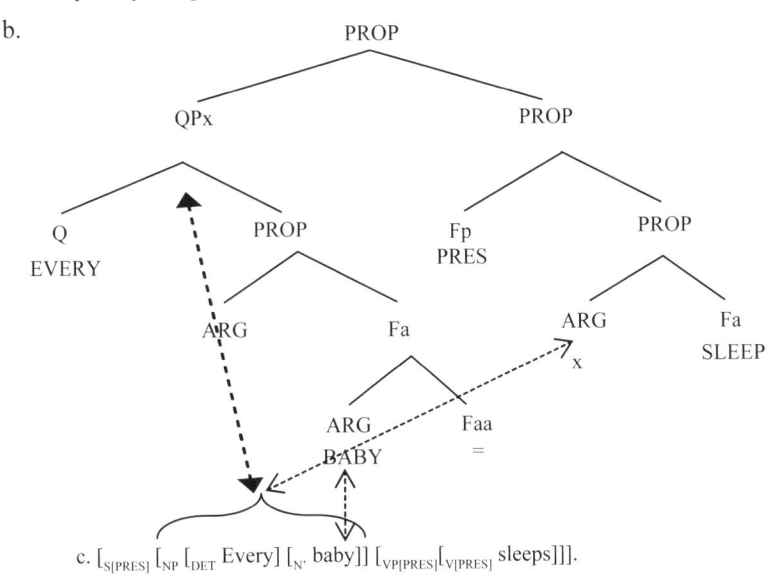

b.
```
                    PROP
                   /    \
                 QPx     PROP
                /  \    /    \
               Q   PROP Fp    PROP
             EVERY /  \ PRES  /   \
                ARG   Fa    ARG    Fa
                              x   SLEEP
                       ARG   Faa
                       BABY   =
```

c. [_{S[PRES]} [_{NP} [_{DET} Every] [_{N'} baby]] [_{VP[PRES]} [_{V[PRES]} sleeps]]].

(18) lexical entry for *every* (Sadock 2012: 61 (95a))
syntax: DET in [_{NP} __, N'[3SG]]
F/A: [_{Q} EVERY]
RS: nil

In (17b, c) above, the QNP *every baby* in syntax corresponds to the QP_x and one of the variables [_{ARG} x] in the matrix PROP. (In (17b), there happens to be only one variable in the matrix PROP.) This is because a QP in F/A is required to be outside the matrix PROP by (15a), whereas in syntax, a QNP is required to occupy an ordinary syntactic argument position, since it is an NP. Also, the N' of the QNP corresponds to the second ARG of the type-identity Faa functor = in the domain expression PROP. The type-identity Faa functor = in (17b) shows that 'x is equal to BABY in type' (i.e., 'x is an instance of type BABY'). (19a) is an example with two QNPs. As is well known, it has two interpretations: (i) *every student* has wide scope or (ii) *a professor* has wide scope. Interpretations (i) and (ii) can be roughly expressed as (19b) and (19c), respectively.

(19) a. Every student admires a professor. (cf. Sadock 2012: 62)
b. [[$_{QPx}$ EVERY x = STUDENT] [[$_{QPy}$ A y = PROFESSOR] [x ADMIRE y]]]
c. [[$_{QPy}$ A y = PROFESSOR] [[$_{QPx}$ EVERY x = STUDENT] [x ADMIRE y]]]

The detailed F/A structure of (19a) with interpretation (i) is given in (20). Note that in (20), QP$_x$ asymmetrically c-commands QP$_y$, which represents the fact that QP$_x$ has scope over QP$_y$.

(20) the F/A of *Every student admires a professor* with interpretation (i)

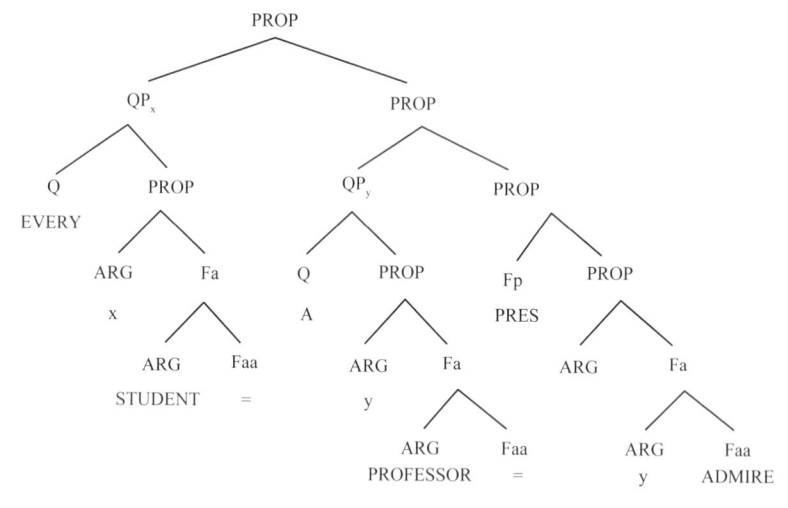

```
                        PROP
                   /          \
               QP_x            PROP
              /    \          /    \
             Q     PROP      QP_y   PROP
          EVERY   /   \     /   \   /   \
               ARG    Fa   Q   PROP Fp  PROP
                x    / \   A   / \ PRES /  \
                   ARG Faa  ARG Fa    ARG   Fa
                STUDENT  =   y      /   \
                                  ARG   Faa   ARG    Faa
                               PROFESSOR  =    y    ADMIRE
```

In (20), the indefinite article is treated as a kind of existential quantifier. The lexical entry for this use of the indefinite article is given in (21). (22) is the lexical entry for the type-identity Faa functor =.

(21) lexical entry for the indefinite article *a* (as an existential quantifier)
syntax: DET in [$_{NP}$ __, N'[3SG]]
F/A: [$_Q$ A]
RS: nil

(22) lexical entry for the type-identity Faa functor = (cf. (8b))
syntax: nil
F/A: [$_{Faa}$ =]
RS: [$_{TYPE}$ "="] in [$_{STATE}$ __ [$_{TH}$ *token*] [$_{LO}$ *type*]]
mphon: nil

In the RS of (22), which will be discussed in the next section, the functor takes a theme role (TH) representing a token, and a locative role (LO) representing a type. Note that TH outranks LO by the Role Hierarchy (1.4 (6a)) and therefore

TH corresponds to the subject ARG in F/A and LO to the lower ARG under the default geometric correspondences (1.4 (7b)). Note also that in the RS of (22), the label STATE is used instead of EVENT (EV). The former is a subcategory of the latter. See the Event Hierarchy (4.3 (5)). Later we will also need another Faa functor ∈ in (23), to deal with set membership. This functor takes an individual as the theme role (TH) and a set as the locative role (LO) in the sense that an individual belongs to a set. Along with the indefinite article in (21), we will be treating the definite article *the* (24) as a kind of existential quantifier (McCawley 1993: 205).

(23) lexical entry for the set-
 membership Faa functor ∈
 syntax: nil
 F/A: [$_{Faa}$∈]
 RS: [$_{TYPE}$ "∈"] in [$_{STATE}$ ___
  [$_{TH}$ *individual*] [$_{LO}$ *set*]]
 mphon: nil

(24) lexical entry for the definite
 article *the* (as an existential
 quantifier)
 syntax: DET in [$_{NP}$ ___, N'[3]]
 F/A: [$_Q$ THE]
 RS: nil

The quantifier-like property of *the* is evident in *Every man admires the woman who raised him* (McCawley 1993: 205), where the definite noun phrase *the woman who raised him* is in the scope of *every man*. Also in *Each teacher heard the rumor that the best student in his class had cheated* (ibid.), the definite noun phrase *the best student in his class* is in the scope of *each teacher*.

In the discussion on the F/A structure (20), we used the notion of c-command. This notion can be defined easily on F/A structures, in exactly the same way we defined it on syntactic structures. The definitions of directly dominate, dominate, x-command, and non-adjoined node are the same as 1.2 (13), (14), (15), and (16).

(25) definition of c-command in F/A
 For two nodes X and Y in a given F/A structure, X c-commands Y iff X x-commands Y,
 where ϕ(x) = {all nodes in an F/A structure}.

Going back to the F/A structure (20), we claimed that QP$_x$ asymmetrically c-commands QP$_y$. Note that QP$_y$ does not c-command QP$_x$ in (20), because the two QPs are not adjoined to the matrix PROP. For one thing, their F/A category is not Mp (i.e., a modifier of PROP, as in [$_{PROP}$ Mp, PROP]), and for another, QP is obligatory in the sense that if we omitted QP$_x$ or QP$_y$ from the well-formed F/A in (20), it would violate (15c) and would be ill formed.

1.4 Semantics 2: Role Structure Overview

The Role Structure (RS) module is the one in which the cognitive content of events and the cognitive status of the participants in them are represented. The grammar of RS is another autonomous order-free phrase structure grammar (PSG) (Sadock 2012: 73–75).

(1) PS rules for RS (cf. Sadock 2012: 77 (1))
    a. [$_{EV}$ TYPE, ROLE^n]   b. [$_{ROLE}$ EV]

This grammar specifies in an iterative way an event type and the list of roles that the participants play in it (Sadock 2012: 76). (1a) says that each event (EV) consists of its event type (TYPE) and a certain number of roles (ROLE^n) that the event type requires. Later in Chapter 4 (4.3 (5)), we will propose the Event Hierarchy and introduce various kinds of events, including state, action, and volitional action. Therefore, the term event is used as a cover term for these kinds of events. (1b) says that any role (ROLE) can directly dominate an event (EV). (1b) captures such semantic relations as we observe between [$_{agent}$ *John*] *explained* [$_{theme}$ *the fact*] *to* [$_{goal}$ *Mary*] and [$_{agent}$ *John*] *explained to* [$_{goal}$ *Mary*] [$_{theme}$ *that Sam died*], in which the NP *the fact* in the former example and the CP[*that*] *that Sam died* in the latter carry the same role, namely, theme. (2) gives two sample RSs. (2a) is the RS of [$_{agent}$ *John*] *explained* [$_{theme}$ *the fact*] *to* [$_{goal}$ *Mary*] and (2b) is the RS of [$_{agent}$ *John*] *explained to* [$_{goal}$ *Mary*] [$_{theme}$ *that Sam died*].

(2) sample RSs

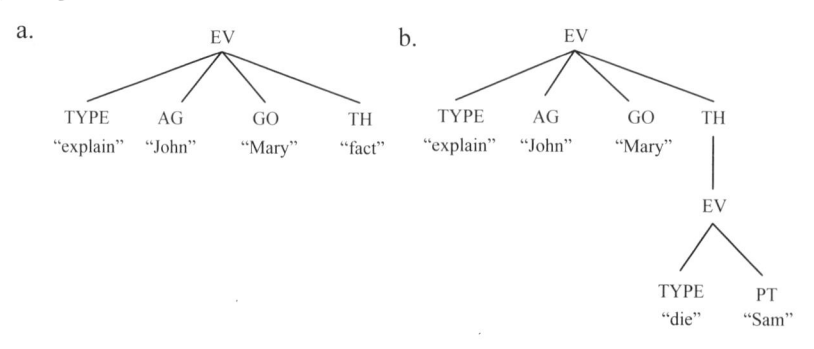

a.
```
              EV
    ┌────┬────┬────┐
   TYPE  AG   GO   TH
"explain" "John" "Mary" "fact"
```

b.
```
              EV
    ┌────┬────┬────┐
   TYPE  AG   GO   TH
"explain" "John" "Mary"  │
                         EV
                        ╱ ╲
                      TYPE  PT
                     "die" "Sam"
```

In (2a, b), the participant roles that the verb requires are represented as sisters: agent (AG), goal (GO), theme (TH). In (2b), the theme role directly dominates another event, which is licensed by (1b). The following is the definition of a well-formed RS.

(3) definition of a well-formed RS
   a. A local RS tree is well formed iff it is an instantiation of (i.e., generated by) (1a) or (1b), and it is matched by the RS field of one of the lexical entries of the language in question.
   b. An RS tree is well formed iff all the local RS trees that it contains are well formed.

As for the participant roles, we employ the two-tiered roles first proposed in Jackendoff (1990: 126–127), according to which, a participant role is a combination of two roles: one from the action tier and the other from the thematic tier. The action tier consists of agent (AG) and patient (PT), and the thematic tier consists of source (SO), goal (GO), theme (TH), and locative (LO). (See (6a) below.) For example, in (2a) [$_{agent}$ *John*] *explained* [$_{theme}$ *the fact*] to [$_{goal}$ *Mary*], *John* is not only an agent who did the explaining, but also a source (SO), because *the fact* was conveyed from *John* to *Mary*. We notate the role carried by *John* as [AG, SO], which combines AG from the action tier and SO from the thematic tier. The object NP *the fact* is not only a theme (TH) that was conveyed but also a patient (PT) of the event, because *the fact* changed its possessor from *John* to *Mary* by being explained to *Mary*, and in this sense, *the fact* was affected by the explaining: *the fact* known to John became known to Mary. We notate the role carried by *the fact* as [PT, TH], which is a combination of PT from the action tier and TH from the thematic tier. Sometimes, a role may lack its action tier specification (i.e., specification of AG or PT) or thematic tier specification (i.e., specification of SO, GO, TH, or LO). For example, the role carried by *Mary* in *John explained the fact to Mary* is GO on the thematic tier but lacks its action tier specification.

Let us consider another set of examples, two uses of the verb *give*. In *John gave a book to Mary*, *John* carries the role of [AG, SO], which is AG on the action tier and at the same time SO on the thematic tier, *a book* carries the role of [PT, TH], which is PT on the action tier and TH on the thematic tier, and *Mary* carries GO, which is GO on the thematic tier with no specification for the action tier. By contrast, in the ditransitive use of *give*, as in *John gave Mary a book*,

Mary assumes the role of [PT, GO] (i.e., recipient) and *a book* carries the role TH without an action tier specification. Therefore, these two uses of *give* differ in which role the speaker conceptualizes as the patient (PT) of the *giving* event, theme (TH) or goal (GO). In other words, there are two ways the speaker can conceptualize a *giving* event. Here are the lexical entries for the two kinds of *give* (cf. Sadock 2012: 213 (11), 244 note 6).

(4) lexical entry for *give*
(ditransitive)
syntax: V in [__, NP, NP]
F/A: Faaa
RS: [$_{TYPE}$ "give"] in [$_{EV}$ __ [AG, SO] [PT, GO] TH]
morph: V[0]
mphon: [$_{V[0]}$ /gɪv/], [$_{V[1, PAST]}$ /geɪv/], [$_{V[1, PSP]}$ /gɪvṇ/]

(5) lexical entry for *give*
(transitive with *to*)
syntax: V in [__, NP, PP[*to*]]
F/A: Faaa
RS: [$_{TYPE}$ "give"] in [$_{EV}$ __ [AG, SO] [PT, TH] GO]
morph: V[0]
mphon: [$_{V[0]}$ /gɪv/], [$_{V[1, PAST]}$ /geɪv/], [$_{V[1, PSP]}$ /gɪvṇ/]

The difference in RS between (4) and (5) is clearly perceived if we look at the verb *send*, another verb that has lexical entries similar to (4) and (5). Observe the contrast between *John sent a package to Chicago* and **John sent Chicago a package* (pointed out in Goldsmith 1980 and McCawley 1993: 602 note 18). When the goal NP is a person, as in *John sent Mary a package*, it can be easily interpreted as the [PT, GO] in (4), that is, the recipient of the *sending* event that resulted in Mary having the package. However, when the goal NP is a place, such interpretation is hard to come by, because a place is not perceived as being affected by the *sending* event and therefore does not qualify as the patient of the event. In contrast, in *John sent the White House a package* (pointed out by Ichiro Yuhara (p.c.)), *the White House* is perceived not as a pure place name but as the place where the President and his staff stay (an instance of place-for-institution metonymy in Cruse 2011: 258), which facilities its interpretation as patient. By the same token, *John sent Chicago a package* sounds much better if we can recognize a metonymic extension by which *Chicago* refers to an institution, such as *the Chicago office* or *the University of Chicago* (McCawley 1993: 602 note 18). Another advantage of separating the two tiers is that in Japanese, the postpositions that mark the agent role can be transparent to their concomitant role on the thematic tier. For example, the [AG, SO] can be marked by *kara* ('from'), as in *Taro kara Hanako ni tegami wo okut-ta* (Taro from Hanako DAT letter ACC send-PAST) (due to Ichiro Yuhara (p.c.)).

In syntax and F/A, the structural relation c-command was defined naturally (1.2 (17) for syntax and 1.3 (25) for F/A) as a useful way of measuring the prominence of each NP or ARG, but since RS trees in (1a) are flat, the c-command relation cannot be defined in RS in a similar fashion. Instead, we define the relation outrank to compare the prominence of two roles based on the Role Hierarchy (cf. Sadock 2012: 81, Bresnan 2001: 213).

(6) a. Role Hierarchy
 (action tier) AG > PT > ø (Sadock 2012: 81 (13))
 (thematic tier) SO > GO > TH > LO (cf. Bresnan 2001: 307 (14), Dalrymple 2001: 206)

 b. definition of outrank
  i. Outrank (">") is determined on the action tier. Otherwise, it is determined on the thematic tier.
  ii. If A outranks B and B dominates C in RS, then A outranks C.
  iii. If A outranks B and B outranks C, then A outranks C.

The Role Hierarchy (6a) says that on the action tier, AG outranks PT, which in turn outranks a role that has no specification for the action tier (i.e., a role that has a specification for the thematic tier alone), whereas on the thematic tier, the outrank relations are indicated in (6a). We define the general notion of outrank as (6bi) based on the tier-specific notion of outrank in (6a) (cf. LFG's definition of outrank in Bresnan 1995: 247, HPSG's definition of o-command in Pollard and Sag 1994: 253 and outrank in Sag et al. 2003: 222, and McCawley's definition of outrank in 1998: 362). (6bi) says, for example, that any role with AG outranks any role with PT, which in turn outranks any role that is not specified for the action tier. If roles are not specified for the action tier, SO outranks GO, GO outranks TH, TH outranks LO. For example, the roles are listed in the outrank order in the lexical entries (4) and (5). (6biii) says that outrank (">") is a transitive relation: if A > B and B > C, then A > C.

The default correspondences between syntax, F/A, and RS are given in (7).

(7) default correspondences
 a. default categorial correspondences (Sadock 2012: 78 (8))
syntax	F/A	RS
S	<-------> PROP <------->	EV
NP	<-------> ARG <------->	ROLE
VP	<-------> Fa	

b. default geometrical correspondences (Sadock 2012: 35 (24))
  i. Dominance relations should be preserved between corresponding nodes in each module.
  ii. C-command relations in syntax and F/A should be preserved in RS as corresponding outrank relations.

Because of (7), we have the following default correspondences between the syntax, F/A, and RS of a transitive sentence. In (8), NP_1 corresponds to ARG_1 and $ROLE_1$ and NP_2 corresponds to ARG_2 and $ROLE_2$ (Sadock 2012: 81 (14)).

(8) default correspondences of a transitive sentence

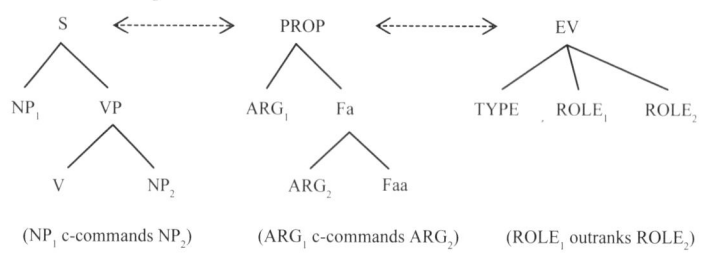

```
      S  <------->   PROP  <------->   EV
     / \             / \             / | \
   NP₁  VP        ARG₁  Fa       TYPE ROLE₁ ROLE₂
        / \            / \
       V  NP₂        ARG₂  Faa

  (NP₁ c-commands NP₂)   (ARG₁ c-commands ARG₂)   (ROLE₁ outranks ROLE₂)
```

Here is another set of examples, the lexical entries for ditransitive *buy* and transitive *buy*. [PT, GO_{+aff}] in the RS field of (9) is intended as beneficiary recipient, as opposed to neutral recipient ([PT, GO]) and adversative goal (GO_{-aff}), as in *My car broke down on me* (cf. Jackendoff 1990: 186–187). The feature [+affected] means positively affected and [−affected] negatively affected (Jackendoff 1990: 134).

(9) lexical entry for *buy* (ditransitive)
   (*I bought her a book (from him)*)
   syntax: V in [__, NP, NP]
   F/A: Faaa
   RS: [$_{TYPE}$ "buy"] in [$_{EV}$ __ AG
   [PT, GO_{+aff}] TH]
   morph: V[0]
   mphon: [$_{V[0]}$ /baɪ/], [$_{V[1, PAST]}$ /bɔːt/],
   [$_{V[1, PSP]}$ /bɔːt/]

(10) lexical entry for *buy* (transitive)
   (*I bought a book (for her) (from him)*)
   syntax: V in [__, NP]
   F/A: Faa
   RS: [$_{TYPE}$ "buy"] in [$_{EV}$ __ AG
   [PT, TH]]
   morph: V[0]
   mphon: [$_{V[0]}$ /baɪ/], [$_{V[1, PAST]}$ /bɔːt/],
   [$_{V[1, PSP]}$ /bɔːt/]

In (10), the PP[*for*] that denotes beneficiary goal is a VP-adjunct (cf. McCawley 1998: 70).

In the remainder of this section, we would like to consider the default linear orders between sisters in general, and those between VP complements in particular. The default linear orders in syntax between sisters are determined by the factor of complexity of linguistic entities. In terms of syntactic complexity, semantic/informational complexity, and phonological complexity (or heaviness), a word in syntax (N, A, V, P, ADV, DET, PRT) is less complex than a phrase (NP, AP, VP, PP, ADVP), which in turn is less complex than a clause (S, CP). If we assume that a less complex sister precedes a more complex sister by default, we arrive at the default linear order rules in (11).

(11) the default linear order between sisters based on complexity
A less complex sister precedes a more complex sister by default.
a. pronoun < word < phrase < clause
b. NP < PP
c. syntactic correspondent of ARG < syntactic correspondent of Fa or PROP

In (11), the notation A < B means A precedes B. Because a pronoun (PN) is less complex than a full word in terms of syntactic, semantic/informational, and phonological complexity, pronoun < word in (11a) is predicted. In (11b), we claim, following Sadock (2012: 115), that a PP is more complex syntactically than an NP, because PP consists of NP and the head P: [$_{PP}$ P, NP]. (11c) is a syntactic reflection of semantic (F/A) complexity. PROP is more complex than ARG because PROP consists of ARG and Fa: [$_{PROP}$ ARG, Fa]. Moreover, Fa is more complex than ARG because Fa consists of ARG and Faa: [$_{Fa}$ ARG, Faa]. (These are the same kind of argument we used to motivate (11b).) Note that the syntactic correspondent of ARG is usually NP or PP, whereas the syntactic correspondent of Fa or PROP is usually VP, AP, S, or CP. Because {NP | PP} < {S | CP} is already covered by (11a), the net effect of (11c) is {NP | PP} < {AP | VP | PP}, where the latter PP corresponds to an Fa in F/A.

(11) is a natural consequence of the Principle of Linguistic Gravity (Sadock 2012: 211 (4)), which states that "Heavy constituents tend to occur later than light constituents," which is a restatement of Behagel's (1909) celebrated *das Gesetz der wachsenden Glieder*, which says "Von zwei Satzgliedern geht, wenn möglich, das kürzere dem längeren voraus."

Because (11) only talks about the default orders between sisters in general, we need a separate, more specific, statement (12) about where the head comes in head-complement structures (i.e., the head parameter).

(12) English is a head-initial language. That is, in head-complement structures, where a lexical head (H[0]) takes one or more complements within its phrase (H[1]), the head must precede all the complements.

(12) is more specific than (11) in that the former only applies to head-complement structures. Therefore, the application of (12) preempts that of (11) by the Elsewhere Principle in 1.1.2 (3). Although (12) only concerns itself with head-initial languages, much of (11) holds for head-final languages, as well.

Let us look at examples of (11) and (12). First of all, because of (12), we have [$_{PP}$ P < {NP | S}], [$_{AP}$ A < {PP | CP}], [$_{ADVP}$ ADV < PP] (as in *fortunately for John* or *independently of this conclusion*), [$_{N'}$ N <{PP | CP}], and [$_{VP}$ V < complement(s)]. Second, pronoun < word in (11a) predicts the following orders. Particles (PRT) such as *up* and *down* are words and we observe the contrast between **John picked* [$_{PRT}$ *up*] [$_{PN}$ *it*] vs. *John picked* [$_{PN}$ *it*] [$_{PRT}$ *up*]. Note that the VP node of this example dominates three words: [$_{VP}$ [$_{V}$ *picked*], [$_{PN}$ *it*], [$_{PRT}$ *up*]]. Because this is a head-complement structure, (12) applies preemptively over (11) by the Elsewhere Principle, and the head V is placed at the initial position. The remaining two complements *it* and *up* are ordered by (11a). As another example of (11a), the quantifiers (Q) *all* and *both* are words and we find the following contrast between the sister Q and PN: *John liked* [[$_{Q}$ *all*] [$_{NP}$ *the books*]] vs. **John liked* [[$_{Q}$ *all*] [$_{PN}$ *them*]] vs. *John liked* [[$_{PN}$ *them*] [$_{Q}$ *all*]]. As for ditransitive verbs, such as *give* (4) or *buy* (9), we have been assuming that they form a ternary branching VP, in which the two NP objects are sisters. We observe the contrast between *John gave* [$_{PN}$ *her*] [$_{NP}$ *Fido*] and **John gave* [$_{NP}$ *Mary*] [$_{PN}$ *it*]. French is a head-initial language but it has gone to extremes along with other Romance languages to allow pronoun objects to appear to the left of the finite head V: *Tu vois souvent <u>tes parents</u>?—No, je ne <u>les</u> vois pas souvent.* (In fact, the direct object pronoun *les* is cliticized to the finite verb *vois*, as in [$_{V[FIN]}$ PN V[FIN]] (cf. 1.1.1 (1c)), and forms a word *les vois*. This is why the complex *les vois* appears between the negative *ne ... pas*.) Third, let us look at examples of word < phrase in (11a). This order is seen in VPs consisting of V, PRT, and PP, such as *look forward* PP[*to*] and *give up* PP[*on*], in such PRT + PP combinations as *away* PP[*from*] and *back* PP[*to*], and in coordinating conjunctions [*both* XP] [*and* YP] and [*either* XP] [*or* YP]. (For the last set of examples, the interpretation that *both, and, either, or* are heads is also possible. If so, the order is due not to (11a) but to (12).) Fourth, by combining (11b) and (12), we get

[$_{VP}$ V NP PP]. Finally, let us consider (11c). First and foremost, this predicts [$_S$ NP VP]. Although VP (=V[1]) is the head of S (=V[2]), (12) has nothing to say about this structure, because it is not a head (H[0])-complement structure within its phrase (H[1]). In addition, (11c) together with (12) predicts various cases including (i) [$_{VP}$ [$_V$ *think*] PP[*of*] PP[*as*]], [$_{VP}$ [$_V$ *look*] PP[*on*] PP[*as*]], [$_{VP}$ [$_V$ *regard*] NP PP[*as*]], where PP[*as*] corresponds to Fa in F/A; (ii) [$_{VP}$ [$_V$ *make*] NP AP] and [$_{VP}$ [$_V$ *hammered*] [$_{NP}$ *the metal*] [$_{AP}$ *flat*]] (change-of-state transitive verbs and the resultative construction); (iii) [$_{VP}$ [$_V$ *consider*] NP XP] (small clause), [$_{PP}$ [$_P$ *with*] NP XP] (small clause), [$_{VP}$ [$_V$ *believe*] NP VP[*to*]] (object raising), where XP and VP[*to*] correspond to Fa (cf. 4.2.1 (2)); (iv) [$_{VP}$ [$_V$ *promise*] NP VP[*to*]] (subject control), [$_{VP}$ [$_V$ *order*] NP VP[*to*]] (object control), [$_{VP}$ [$_V$ *appeal*] PP[*to*] VP[*to*]] (object control), [$_{VP}$ [$_V$ *plead*] PP[*with*] VP[*to*]] (object control), and [$_{VP}$ [$_V$ *depend*] PP[*on*] VP[*to*]] (object control), where VP[*to*] corresponds to PROP in F/A (cf. 4.4 (4) and (5)).

Before closing this section, we would like to go back to the English PS rules in 1.2 (1), repeated below as (13), and see how much of the linear orders in them both (11) and (12) can predict and how much must be specified as marked orders. We exclude (1d, e, f) in 1.2 from our consideration, because on the one hand, the distribution of ADVP and adjunct PP is very free, and on the other hand, their exact distribution depends on their semantic types. This leaves only three PS rules to consider.

(13) English PS rules:
 a. [$_S$ NP, VP]   b. [$_{NP}$ {DET | NP[POS]}, N']   c. [$_{N'}$ {A | RRC}, N']

As stated already, the order [$_S$ NP < VP] in (13a) follows from (11c). The order [$_{NP}$ DET < N'] in (13b) follows from (11a). In (13c), the order [$_{N'}$ A < N'] also follows from (11a). We claim that the stacked modifiers *occasionally very offensive* in such NPs as *his occasionally very offensive behaviour* (Huddleston and Pullum 2002: 547) have the adjunction structure: [$_A$ *occasionally* [$_A$ *very* [$_A$ *offensive*]]]. To license this structure, we need a new PS rule with a marked order [$_A$ ADV < A]. An order is marked if it is not predictable from (11) or (12). The order [$_{N'}$ N' < RRC] in (13c) is predictable. If the RRC in question is a relative clause (CP), the order follows from (11a). However, if the RRC is a reduced relative clause (AP, PP, or nonfinite VP), we claim that the RRC in syntax corresponds to [$_{PROP}$ ARG, Fa] in F/A, where the ARG is coreferent with the head N' (6.2.7 (5)). Therefore, the order follows from (11c). This much consideration of (13) leaves (13b) [$_{NP}$ NP[POS] < N'] as another PS rule with a marked order. In German, an NP[GEN] (an NP in the genitive case) comes after the head noun, as in *das Buch des Lehrers* except when the NP[GEN] consists of a proper noun without a determiner, in which case the NP[GEN] comes before the head noun, as in *Peters Buch* or *Deutschlands Grenzen*.

1.5 Information Structure Overview

In this section, we will give a very brief description of what Information Structure (IS) does in the subsequent chapters. A full-scale investigation of IS in AMG awaits future research, in which we will need to take into consideration such important works as Birner and Ward 1998, Dik 1997, Erteschik-Shir 1997, Erteschik-Shir 2007, Firbas 1992, and Lambrecht 1994.

First, IS represents familiarity status (old vs. new) of information with respect to discourse or addressee (Huddleston and Pullum 2002: 1368ff.). Old information tends to precede new information. For example, the topic of a clause, which expresses what the clause is about and is discourse-old, precedes the rest of the clause (comment). The subject of a clause comes first and tends to be a default topic (1.6 (1) and (2)). On the other hand, the focus of a clause bears the strongest stress and carries addressee-new information, whereas the rest of the clause is addressee-old information. Therefore, the focus tends to occur at the clause-final position (1.6 (1) and (2)). For example, in the Heavy Constituent Shift (4.2.2 (4)), a phonologically heavy sister of the verb in a VP occurs as focus at the clause-final position. In the locative inversion construction (2.6 (4)), the locative PP comes first as the topic of the clause and the theme NP comes last as (presentational) focus. In the predicate inversion construction (4.1 (26)), the discourse-old predicate phrase comes first and the subject NP or CP comes last as focus.

Second, IS also represents a more general distinction between foreground information (FI) and background information (BI). FI is the part of an utterance that the speaker intends to convey to the addressee. This includes new information, focus, and assertion. The rest of the utterance represents BI, the information the speaker takes for granted. This includes old information, topic, and presupposition. For example, a factive verb takes a CP[*that*] that carries

BI (6.1.10 (7)). In the case of manner-of-speaking verbs, such as *mumble*, the meaning component of the manner of speaking 'mumblingly' is FI (6.1.10 (10)). The PP that modifies a performative clause in *In case you haven't heard, Bob and Frieda have decided to get married* (7.6.3 (1a)) carries BI and the main clause FI (7.6.3 (5)).

Finally, order requirements in IS are stronger than and override those in syntax. See, for example, the locative inversion construction (2.6 (4)) and the predicate inversion construction (4.1 (26)).

1.6 Lexical Items and Lexical Entries

In the chapters that follow, we will be giving module-by-module lexical entries for lexical items, as we have done so far in this chapter. Lexical items are things that are stored in the mental lexicon, the long-term memory repository of lexical items in the brain. They are not only words (lexemes) but also morphemes, idioms (including clichés and fixed expressions), collocations, constructions, and even the entire text of *Hamlet*, if it is memorized and stored in the long-term memory of the brain (Jackendoff 2002: 152ff). Note that the adjective *lexical*, as in *lexical entry* and *lexical item* does not mean 'of lexemes (<BAR, 0> syntactic entities)' but 'of or in the lexicon.' From this perspective, phrase structure rules themselves are viewed as lexical items stored in the lexicon (Sadock 1996, Jackendoff 2002: 154, Jackendoff 2010: 17–20).

Lexical entries for lexical items, whether they are entries for morphemes, words, idioms, constructions, or phrase structure rules, are all constraints on linguistic forms in which they are instantiated in the sense that lexical entries (as well as other constraints, such as the Head Feature Convention) impose constraints on linguistic forms and guarantee their well-formedness (Pollard and Sag 1987: 44, Jackendoff 2002: 48). Because lexical entries are given module by module, they provide the basis of the interface that connects various autonomous modules (Sadock 1991: 36, 2012: 25, Jackendoff 2002: 131, 425, Marantz 1984: 53).

For example, the default transitive and ditransitive clauses are registered in the lexicon as (1) and (2) without any phonological information. The Information Structure (IS) field in (1) and (2) says that the topic (TOP) and focus (FOC) appear utterance-initially and utterance-finally, respectively.

(1) lexical entry for the default transitive construction

syntax: [$_S$ NP [$_{VP}$ V NP]]

F/A: [$_{PROP}$ ARG [$_{Fa}$ Faa, ARG]]

RS: [$_{EV}$ TYPE [AG PT]

IS: [$_U$ TOP < rest < FOC]

(2) lexical entry for the default ditransitive construction

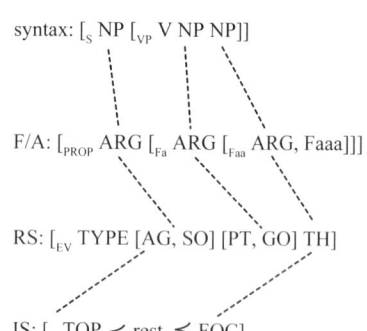

syntax: [$_S$ NP [$_{VP}$ V NP NP]]

F/A: [$_{PROP}$ ARG [$_{Fa}$ ARG [$_{Faa}$ ARG, Faaa]]]

RS: [$_{EV}$ TYPE [AG, SO] [PT, GO] TH]

IS: [$_U$ TOP < rest < FOC]

Because the intermodular correspondences in (1) and (2) are default, much of the information in them is predictable and hence redundant. However, the advantage of registering redundant information in (1) and (2) is to help facilitate the process of language acquisition in such a way that when a baby hears a transitive or ditransitive clause with an unknown verb, they can still guess the basic semantic and discourse information, which would help them learn the unknown verb. Or when a baby wants to express a message that has a transitive or ditransitive semantics, they can guess its syntactic form from (1) and (2).

Wide-scale redundancy of function exists between the modules (Sadock 1983). In addition, lexical items are often redundantly specified for various properties (Sadock 1984). Redundancy in the lexicon and the grammatical modules is important and useful in the processes of language acquisition and verbal communication (Sadock 1991: 14). It not only helps language acquisition, as stated above, but it also allows for language to work under less than ideal circumstances (Sadock 2012: 227). Therefore, redundancy is NOT something that is pernicious and should be purged from the lexicon and grammar. Rather, it is a fundamental feature of the design of language that helps facilitate language acquisition and verbal communication (Sadock 2012: 225, Sadock 1991: 14–15). We take this view very seriously.

There is no reason to think that the brain stores information nonredundantly (Jackendoff 2002: 153). McCawley (1998: 8–9) wrote:

"The popular idea that grammars must be nonredundant is quite implausible when viewed from the perspective of a scenario for language acquisition in which children extend the coverage of their internalized grammars by making minimal alternations in them. Under such a conception of language acquisition, a child might learn several highly specific rules before hitting on an insight that enabled it to learn a general rule that rendered them superfluous; but learning the general rule would not cause the child to purge the now-redundant special rules from its mental grammar."

Redundancy that arises between different modules and between different fields of a lexical entry or a lexical rule is strictly speaking "degeneracy" (Sadock 2012: 225–226). Degeneracy is the mechanism in which the same function, goal, or output is achieved by structurally different elements, whereas redundancy is the mechanism in which the same function, goal, or output is achieved by structurally identical or isomorphic elements. The biologists Gerald M. Edelman and Joseph A. Gally, who first introduced this distinction, claimed that "degeneracy is a ubiquitous biological property" and that "it is a feature of complexity at genetic and cellular levels" (Edelman and Gally 2001). Sadock (2012: 226) states that "degeneracy is exactly the kind of functional duplication that automodular analysis imputes to the system of natural languages."

Chapter 2
Clause Structures

> In this chapter, we consider how we can analyze in a multi-modular fashion such important issues on clause structures as inversion (including negative inversion and locative inversion), negation, dummy *there*, clausal subject, and extraposition.

2.1 Inversion

In Automodular Grammar (AMG), an inverted clause (i.e., a clause with subject-auxiliary inversion), such as (1a), can be treated in two ways: (i) by formulating a linear order rule that places the finite auxiliary verb in the clause initial position without changing the constituent structure (Sadock 2012: 124 (33)), as in (1b), or (ii) by introducing an inversion phrase structure (PS), as in (1c).

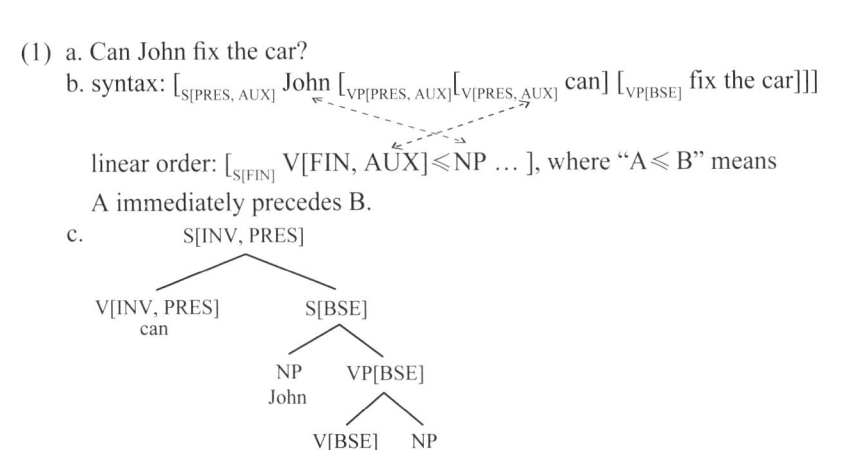

(1) a. Can John fix the car?
  b. syntax: [$_{S[PRES, AUX]}$ John [$_{VP[PRES, AUX]}$[$_{V[PRES, AUX]}$ can] [$_{VP[BSE]}$ fix the car]]]

  linear order: [$_{S[FIN]}$ V[FIN, AUX]⩽NP ...], where "A ⩽ B" means A immediately precedes B.
  c.   S[INV, PRES]
         /   \
    V[INV, PRES]   S[BSE]
       can   /   \
                  NP   VP[BSE]
                 John   /   \
                      V[BSE]   NP
                       fix   /\
                            the car

Recall that PRES and BSE in (1b, c) are values of the VFORM feature (1.2 (5)). For example, V[BSE] is a verb in the base form (BSE) and VP[BSE] is a VP whose head is V[BSE]. Recall also that VFORM is a head feature (1.2 (4)) and thus obeys the Head Feature Convention (HFC) (1.2 (3)), which explains why the head of VP[BSE] is V[BSE]. Recall furthermore that the head of S is V; that is, S = V[2] (1.2 (2)). S[BSE] is an S whose head is V[BSE]. In (1b), V[PRES, AUX] is an auxiliary verb (AUX) in the present tense (PRES).

We choose the second way, the inversion PS (1c), so that we can deal with such an inverted clause as (2a) that has coordinated nonfinite clauses as its complement. The PS of (2a) is (2b), where the inverted finite auxiliary verb *did* is the head of the whole clause and takes coordinated S[BSE] clauses as its complement.

(2) a. Did John fix the car and Mary mow the lawn? (McCawley 1998: 490)
  b. [$_{S[PAST, INV]}$ [$_{V[PAST, INV]}$ Did] [$_{S[BSE]}$ [$_{S[BSE]}$ John fix the car] and [$_{S[BSE]}$ Mary mow the lawn]]]?

(3a) is the PS rule that licenses the inversion PS in (1c) and (2b).

(3) a. inversion PS rule
   [$_{S[INV]}$ V[INV] S[α]], where [$_{S[INV]}$ V[INV] ⋖ NP…]
  b. Inversion Lexical Rule
   input lexical entry   output lexical entry
   syntax: V[AUX, FIN] in → V[INV] in [$_{S[INV]}$ __, S[α]],
   [$_{VP}$ __, VP[α]]   where [$_{S[INV]}$ V[INV] ⋖ NP…]
  c. INV Feature Co-occurrence Restriction (FCR)
   INV → {AUX, <VFORM, FIN>, <V, +>, <N, −>}

An inverted clause (S[INV]) in (3a) consists of its head V[INV] and its complement clause S[α], where α is the VFORM value of the head verb of the S[α] and is determined by the Inversion Lexical Rule (3b). (Note again that VFORM is a head feature and the head of an S is the verb from which the S is projected.) The linear order in (3a) between the head V[INV] and its complement S[α] is predicted by the English rule that a head precedes its complement(s) (1.4 (12)). However, the connection between V[INV] and the subject NP of S[α] is so tight that nothing can intervene (*ptu*Did sometimes John fix the car?* cf. *Did John sometimes fix the car?*). Therefore, the symbol ⋖ (immediately precedes) is specified in (3a). Note that a simpler specification, such as [$_{S[INV]}$ V[INV] ⋖ S[α]], is not enough, because it would wrongly allow a modifier (an adverb or an adverbial phrase) to be adjoined to the S[α] and would result in *[$_{\text{S[INV]}}$ V[INV] ⩽ [$_{\text{S[α]}}$ ADV S[α]]]. Note also that technically speaking, (3a) need not be listed as one of the English PS rules in 1.2 (1), because this PS rule has a lexical head (V[INV]) (i.e., lexical ID rule in GPSG) and as such should be included in the syntactic field of the lexical entry of each V[INV] (as the subcategorization frame for V[INV]). This means that every lexical entry for V[INV] contains the same information (i.e., (3a)). However, this redundancy can be captured by means of inheritance hierarchy along the lines of 1.1.2 (8).

We formulate the relationship between an inverted auxiliary verb and its corresponding noninverted auxiliary verb in terms of the lexical rule (3b). A lexical rule is a rule that captures relationships between two sets of lexical entries in the lexicon. More specifically, a lexical rule says that if there is a lexical entry in the lexicon that meets the input conditions of the lexical rule, there is another lexical entry in the lexicon that meets the output conditions. The input to the Inversion Lexical Rule (3b) is a lexical entry of a finite auxiliary verb (V[FIN, AUX]) and the lexical rule guarantees the existence of another lexical entry in the lexicon for the same auxiliary verb but with the INV feature. The inverted auxiliary verb (V[INV]) in the output takes as its complement an S[α] that has the same VFORM value as that of the input auxiliary's complement VP[α]. For example, the auxiliary *can* (V[AUX, PRES]) takes a VP[BSE] complement and therefore its output of (3b) (V[INV, PRES]) takes an S[BSE] complement with the same VFORM value BSE.

We adopt the feature co-occurrence restriction (FCR) (3c) (Gazdar et al. 1985: 28, 63), which guarantees that whenever the INV feature is present, {AUX, <VFORM, FIN>, <V, +>, <N, –>} must also be present. Therefore, the INV feature can only appear on finite auxiliary verbs. This prevents an unwanted inversion of finite main verbs (V[FIN]), such as *Speak you Japanese?*. Languages that allow the inversion of finite main verbs (as well as finite auxiliary verbs), such as German (*Sprechen Sie Japanisch?*) or French (*Parlez-vous japonais?*), have a simpler verb feature system that lacks the AUX feature, which implies that all finite verbs can be input to the Inversion Lexical Rule (3b).

Our inversion PS (1c) is a binary branching structure assumed in the Mainstream Generative Grammar (MGG), McCawley (1998: 233), LFG (Dalrymple 2001: 63), and Huddleston and Pullum (2002: 50, 97), and not a ternary branching structure ([$_{\text{S}}$ V[AUX] NP VP]) assumed in GPSG (Gazdar et al. 1985: 62), HPSG (Pollard and Sag 1994: 42 and Sag et al. 2003: 410), Culicover and Jackendoff (2005: 309), and Culicover (2009: 330). Our choice of binary branching structure for an inverted clause is primarily because only the binary branching structure

50   2 CLAUSE STRUCTURES

allows coordination of the complement of the inverted auxiliary verb, as in (2b) and secondarily because this binary branching structure is needed to account for a gapping construction, such as *Will* [$_{S[BSE]}$ [*John watch the Red Sox game*] *and* [*Lucy the quiz show*]]? (McCawley 1998: 306).

Furthermore, in (1c), (3a), and the output lexical entry of (3b), the INV feature is shared between the mother S and the head daughter V, because INV is a head feature (1.2 (4)). However, this is different from regular PS rules in that the mother S[INV] has <BAR, 2>, namely, it is a clause, but its head daughter V[INV] has <BAR, 0>; that is, it is a word. (4) gives the feature compositions of the three nodes in (3a). Recall that all syntactic categories are sets of features or feature-value pairs (1.2). Although BAR is a head feature (1.2 (4)) and its values on the mother S[INV] and the head daughter V[INV] are different, this is not a violation of the HFC (1.2 (3)), because the HFC says, "unless specified otherwise" and the relevant BAR values are already specified in the PS rule (3a).

(4) feature compositions of the three nodes in (3a)
   S[INV] = {<V, +>, <N, –>, <BAR, 2>, INV, AUX, <VFORM, FIN>}
   V[INV] = {<V, +>, <N, –>, <BAR, 0>, INV, AUX, <VFORM, FIN>}
   S[α] = {<V, +>, <N, –>, <BAR, 2>, <VFORM, α>}

(5) is an example of how the Inversion Lexical Rule (3b) works when the input is the auxiliary verb *can*. The lexical rule only affects the syntactic field of the input lexical entry. The INV feature is added to the input finite auxiliary verb and at the same time, the subcategorization frame is changed from [$_{VP}$ __, VP[BSE]] to [$_{S}$ __, S[BSE]].

(5) example of the Inversion Lexical Rule (3b)
   input   output
   lexical entry for *can*   lexical entry for inverted *can*
   syntax: V[AUX, PRES] in [$_{VP}$ __, VP[BSE]]   V[INV, PRES] in [$_{S}$ __, S[BSE]]

As for the INV feature, there are two ways we can treat it: as a binary feature <INV, ±> or as a unary feature INV. If we treat it as a binary feature, all the inverted finite auxiliary verbs and all the clauses that they head bear <INV, +>, whereas noninverted finite auxiliary verbs and noninverted finite clauses are all <INV, –>. In (4), the INV feature is treated as a unary feature. For one thing, S[INV] has the lexical head V[INV] and, as such, the INV feature is encoded in the lexical entry of the V[INV] in question: V[INV] in [$_{S[INV]}$ __, S[α]]. For another, those verbs that have the INV feature also have the features FIN and AUX by the inversion FCR (3c). Therefore, if we compare the two PS rules, [$_{S[FIN]}$ NP, VP[FIN]] and [$_{S[INV]}$ V[INV], S[α]], we can claim that the latter is more specific than the former in terms of both the status of the PS rules (nonlexical information (i.e., nonlexical ID rule) in the former and lexical information (i.e., lexical ID rule) in the latter) and their feature compositions (the feature composition of S[FIN] is a proper subset of that of S[INV]). Consequently, whenever the INV feature is present on an S node, the more specific S[INV] PS rule overrides the less specific S[FIN] PS rule, due to the Elsewhere Principle (1.1.2 (3)). This means that there is no need for such specification as <INV, –>, because S[FIN] is interpreted as a noninverted finite clause. The AUX feature is also encoded in the lexical entries for auxiliary verbs and we treat it as a unary feature, as we have done so far. Therefore, the notations V and V[AUX] refer to a nonauxiliary main verb and an auxiliary verb, respectively. V[(AUX)] refers to either a main verb or an auxiliary verb.

The dummy *do* in *I do not smoke* and *Do you smoke?* has its own lexical entries (6) and (7), which each consist of the three subentries for *do*, *does*, and *did*. (7a, b, c) are the outputs of (6a, b, c), respectively, by the Inversion Lexical Rule (3b). Because there is no insertion rule in AMG (Sadock 2012: 30), there is no "*do*-support" rule (Sadock 2012: 169), either. In (6) and (7), FIN (a VFORM value) in syntax and TENSE in F/A have two subcategories PRES and PAST. The dummy *do* has only finite forms and lacks nonfinite forms (*[$_{V[BSE]}$ do], *[$_{V[PSP]}$ done], *[$_{V[PRP]}$ doing]). In (7), everything except the syntactic field is inherited from (6), because the Inversion Lexical Rule (3b) only affects the syntactic field of the input lexical entry.

(6) lexical entry for dummy *do*
   a. syntax: V[AUX, PRES]
      in [__, VP[BSE]]
      F/A: [$_{Fp}$ PRES]
      RS: nil
      morph: V[1, PRES]
      mphon: /duː/
   c. syntax: V[AUX, PAST]
      in [__, VP[BSE]]
      F/A: [$_{Fp}$ PAST]
      RS: nil
      morph: V[1, PAST]
      mphon: /dɪd/

   b. syntax: V[AUX, PRES, 3SG] in [__, VP[BSE]]
      F/A: [$_{Fp}$ PRES]
      RS: nil
      morph: V[1, PRES, 3SG]
      mphon: /dʌz/
   d. syntax: V[AUX, FIN]
      in [__, VP[BSE]]
      F/A: [$_{Fp}$ TENSE]
      RS: nil
      morph: V[1, FIN]
      mphon: [$_{V[1, PRES]}$/duː/], [$_{V[1, PRES, 3SG]}$/dʌz/], [$_{V[1, PAST]}$/dɪd/]

There is a lot of information in common between (6a), (6b), and (6c). The shared information can be factored out by organizing the three lexical entries in an inheritance hierarchy (1.1.2 (7) and (8)), or we can conflate them into a single lexical entry (6d) under the assumption that the subcategory of FIN is identical to the value of TENSE (i.e., PRES or PAST) and is determined by the morphological category specified in each of the three mphon representations.

(7) lexical entry for inverted dummy *do* (output of the Inversion Lexical Rule (3b))
    a. syntax: V[INV, PRES]
       in $[_{S[INV]}\_\_, S[BSE]]$
      F/A: $[_{F_p} PRES]$
      RS: nil
      morph: V[1, PRES]
      mphon: /du:/
    b. syntax: V[INV, PRES, 3SG] in $[_{S[INV]}\_\_, S[BSE]]$
      F/A: $[_{F_p} PRES]$
      RS: nil
      morph: V[1, PRES, 3SG]
      mphon: /dʌz/
    c. syntax: V[INV, PAST]
      in $[_{S[INV]}\_\_, S[BSE]]$
      F/A: $[_{F_p} PAST]$
      RS: nil
      morph: V[1, PAST]
      mphon: /dɪd/
    d. syntax: V[INV, FIN]
      in $[_{S[INV]}\_\_, S[BSE]]$
      F/A: $[_{F_p} TENSE]$
      RS: nil
      morph: V[1, FIN]
      mphon: $[_{V[1, PRES]}$ /du:/], $[_{V[1, PRES, 3SG]}$ /dʌz/], $[_{V[1, PAST]}$ /dɪd/]

Some inverted auxiliary verbs lack their corresponding noninverted auxiliary verbs. In these cases, the lexical entry for such an inverted auxiliary verb should be specified separately in the lexicon. The existence of such cases shows the need for the lexical entry for an inverted auxiliary verb separately from the lexical entry for the corresponding noninverted auxiliary verb, although in most cases, inverted and noninverted auxiliary verbs are related by the Inversion Lexical Rule (3b). Here are two such examples: inverted *aren't* and *mightn't*. As shown in (8), *aren't* can be used as the first person singular only in inverted clauses.

(8) first person singular inverted *aren't* (Gazdar et al. 1985: 64)
    *I aren't going.   Aren't I going?

(9) lexical entry for first person singular inverted *aren't*
    syntax: V[INV, PRES, 1SG] in $[_{S[INV, PRES]}\_\_, S[\alpha]]$

F/A: [$_{Fp}$ PRES] ∘ [$_{Fp}$ NOT]
RS: nil
morph: V[1, PRES, PL ∨ 2SG]
mphon: /ɑɚnt/

The lexical entry (9) says that *aren't* is used as an inverted auxiliary for the first person singular in syntax, although it is morphologically a verb in the plural or second person singular, just as regular *are* and *aren't*. (9) does not block the output of the Inversion Lexical Rule (3b) when it is applied to *aren't* for 2SG, 2PL, 1PL, and 3PL, because *aren't* in (9) is specified as 1SG in syntax. In (9), the F/A is a composite Fp functor [$_{Fp}$ PRES]∘[$_{Fp}$ NOT], which is defined as the composition of the two Fp functors: ([$_{Fp}$ PRES]∘[$_{Fp}$ NOT]) PROP = [$_{Fp}$ PRES] ([$_{Fp}$ NOT] PROP). (The symbol ∘ is a standard notation for composite mappings in mathematics.) In general, Fp^n is a composite Fp functor defined as Fp^n (PROP) = Fp^{n-1} (Fp (PROP)).

Mightn't in (10) is another example. It has negation within the scope of *might* when used in the declarative, as shown in the paraphrase in (10a), whereas the inverted *mightn't* in (10b) has the reverse scope, that is, *might* being within the scope of negation (Gazdar et al. 1985: 64; cf. Huddleston and Pullum 2002: 205 (b)). Therefore, we need to posit the lexical entry for inverted *mightn't* (12) separately from the lexical entry for noninverted *mightn't* (11). The output of the Inversion Lexical Rule (3b) is blocked when it is applied to the lexical entry (11), because of the existence of (12) in the lexicon.

(10) a. Kim mightn't go. ('Possibly Kim will not go.' MIGHT > NOT)
 b. Mightn't Kim go? ('Is it not the case that possibly Kim will go?' NOT > MIGHT)

(11) lexical entry for noninverted
 mightn't
 syntax: V[AUX, PRES]
 in [__, VP[BSE]]
 F/A: [$_{Fp}$ PRES]∘[$_{Fp}$ MIGHT]∘
 [$_{Fp}$ NOT]
 RS: nil
 morph: V[1, PRES]
 mphon: /maɪtn̩t/

(12) lexical entry for inverted
 mightn't
 syntax: V[PRES, INV]
 in [$_{S[PRES, INV]}$ __, S[BSE]]
 F/A: [$_{Fp}$ PRES]∘[$_{Fp}$ NOT]∘
 [$_{Fp}$ MIGHT]
 RS: nil
 morph: V[1, PRES]
 mphon: /maɪtn̩t/

54   2 CLAUSE STRUCTURES

Of all the auxiliary verbs, the verb *be* is special, because it takes not only a VP complement (such cases as passive *be* and progressive *be*) but also a non-VP complement, when used as an empty verb (13e), as in *Sally is a carpenter* (Sadock 2012: 28–29). When *be* is used as such, its inverted form has as its complement not a full-fledged nonfinite S but a small clause (SC), as in (13a–d), a clause that lacks its head verb.

(13) a. Is [$_{SC}$ [$_{NP}$ Sally] [$_{NP}$ a carpenter]]?
 b. Is [$_{SC}$ [$_{NP}$ Sally] [$_{AP}$ very kind to you]]?
 c. Is [$_{SC}$ [$_{NP}$ Sally] [$_{PP}$ in the room]]? (locative PP)
 d. Is [$_{SC}$ [$_{NP}$ Sally] [$_{PP}$ in good shape]]? (predicative PP)
 e. partial lexical entry for empty *be* (cf. Sadock 2012: 29 (11))
  syntax: V[AUX, FIN] in [$_{VP}$ __ XP], where XP ∈ {NP, AP, PP, VP[PAS]}
  F/A: [$_{Fp}$ TENSE]
  RS: nil
  morph: V[1]
  mphon: [$_{V[1, PRES]}$ /aɚ/], [$_{V[1, PRES, 1SG]}$ /æm/], [$_{V[1, PRES, 3SG]}$ /ɪz/],
   [$_{V[1, PAST]}$ /wɚː/], [$_{V[1, PAST, 1SGv3SG]}$ /wəz/]

So far, we have been assuming that VP is a phrase (<BAR, 1>) headed by a verb and that S is a clause (<BAR, 2>) headed by a verb. Therefore, strictly speaking, S should be represented as VS, a clause headed by a verb (14a), just as a phrase headed by a verb is represented as VP. If we extend this notation to other head categories, as in (14) and (15), what we have just labeled SC in (13a) is nothing but a clause headed by a noun, namely, NS (14b).

(14) a. [$_{VS}$ [$_{NP}$ Sally] [$_{VP}$ likes music]].   b. [$_{NS}$ [$_{NP}$ Sally] [$_{NP}$ a carpenter]]

(15) extended clause structures

head category	predicate phrase XP (<BAR, 1> except NP)	clause [$_{XS}$ NP, XP] (<BAR, 2> except NS)	
V	[$_{VP}$ likes music]	[$_{VS}$ Sally [$_{VP}$ likes music]]	VS (abbreviated as S)
N	[$_{NP}$ a carpenter]	[$_{NS}$ Sally [$_{NP}$ a carpenter]]	⎫
A	[$_{AP}$ very kind to you]	[$_{AS}$ Sally [$_{AP}$ very kind to you]]	⎬ SC (cover term)
P	[$_{PP}$ in the room]	[$_{PS}$ Sally [$_{PP}$ in the room]]	⎭

Note that the predicate phrase XP corresponds to Fa in F/A. Note also that NP is <BAR, 2> and all the other predicate XPs are <BAR, 1>. Furthermore, when an NP forms a predicate phrase in *Sally is a carpenter*, the NP corresponds to the lower ARG in F/A of the type-identity Faa functor = (1.3 (22)). Therefore, the F/A structure of *Sally is a carpenter* is [$_{PROP}$ [$_{Fp}$ PRES] ([$_{PROP}$ [$_{ARG}$ SALLY] [$_{Fa}$ [$_{ARG}$ CARPENTER] [$_{Faa}$ =]]])]. The tense PRES in the F/A structure comes from *is*, which carries the tense and agreement information but no other semantic information, hence an empty verb.

The relationship between the noninverted *be* that takes an XP complement and the inverted *be* that takes a small clause complement is captured by the following lexical rule that only affects the syntactic field of the lexical entry for *be*.

(16) lexical rule for *be*, when it takes a non-VP complement
 input lexical entry   output lexical entry
 syntax: V[AUX, FIN] in [__, XP] → syntax: V[INV] in [$_S$ __, XS]
 where X∈{N, A, P}

There are two cases when the verb *be* takes two complements, thereby giving rise to a ternary branching VP structure: the *there* construction (17a) (McCawley 1998: 95, 635; Sadock 2012: 65; Pollard and Sag 1994: 147 and Sag et al. 2003: 337) and the *it*-cleft construction (17b) (Gazdar et al. 1985: 159; Pollard and Sag 1994: 261; pace McCawley 1998: 465). When (17a, b) are inverted, the resultant constituent structure is (17a', b'), where the verb, the subject (*there* in a' and *it* in b'), the NP, and the PP or RRC form a quaternary branching clause, as in (18).

(17) a. There [$_{VP}$ is [$_{NP}$ a book] [$_{PP}$ on the table]].
 a'. [Is there [$_{NP}$ a book] [$_{PP}$ on the table]]?
  cf. How many books are there on the table?/*How many books on the table are there?
  cf. Although he said there was only him in that department, I could hear call center busy voices in the background. (from the web)
 b. It [$_{VP}$ is [$_{NP}$ John] [$_{RRC}$ that Mary was talking about]]. (RRC = restrictive relative clause)
 b'. [Is it [$_{NP}$ John] [$_{RRC}$ that Mary was talking about]]?
  cf. Who is it that Mary was talking about?

(18) a. [$_{S[INV]}$ Is [$_{NP[there]}$ there] [$_{NP}$ a book] [$_{PP}$ on the table]]?
 b. [$_{S[INV]}$ Is [$_{NP[it]}$ it] [$_{NP}$ John] [$_{RRC}$ that Mary was talking about]]?

Following GPSG (Gazdar et al. 1985: 115) and HPSG (Sag et al. 2003: 336), we introduce the NFORM feature whose value is the dummy *it* or *there*. We stipulate the PS rules (19a, b) (by brute force) to deal with the inverted clause structures in (18a, b). A small piece of evidence for this flat structure is that the NP in (19a) can undergo the Heavy Constituent Shift (HCS), which is discussed in 4.2.5 (4), as in *Are there on the desk all the books John has read?*, which shows that the NP is a sister of the verb before the application of HCS.

(19) a. PS rule for inverted *be* and NP[*there*]
 [$_{S[INV]}$ V[INV] < NP[*there*] < NP < PP]
 b. PS rule for inverted *be* and NP[*it*]
 [$_{S[INV]}$ V[INV] < NP[*it*] < XP < RRC]

The linear order in (19a, b) follows from the general linear order rules we discussed at the end of 1.4. The finite *be* verb comes first, because it is the head of the clause. *There* and *it* come next because they are pronouns.

The subject-verb agreement in an inverted clause is achieved in syntax, which is shown in (20). The inverted auxiliary verb (V[INV]) agrees with the NP[NOM] that is the subject of its nonfinite complement clause S[γ], where γ is a VFORM value. Because the embedded VP[γ] in (20) is nonfinite and cannot carry its own AGR value, the subject-verb agreement 1.2 (11a) is not applicable to S[γ]. AGRα is an abbreviation for {<PER, $α_1$>, <NUM, $α_2$>}, where $α_1 \in \{1, 2, 3\}$ and $α_2 \in$ {SG, PL}.

(20) [$_{S[INV]}$ V[INV, AGRα], [$_{S[γ]}$ NP[NOM, AGRα], VP[γ]]

Recall how agreement in a finite noninverted clause is achieved (1.2 (11a, b), repeated here as (21a, b)).

(21) a. subject-verb agreement
 [$_{S[FIN, AGR[3SGN]]}$ NP[AGRα] VP[FIN, AGRα]]
 b. [$_{VP[FIN, AGRα]}$ V[FIN, AGRα], ...]
 c. [$_{PROP}$ [$_{Fp}$ TENSE](∘Fp), [$_{PROP}$ ARG[IND[AGRα]], Fa]]

(21a) says in part that the subject NP and the finite VP in a finite clause must share the same AGR value. Because AGR is a head feature (1.2 (4)), the AGR on the VP[FIN] node is shared with its head V[FIN], as in (21b) by the Head Feature Convention (1.2 (3)). At the same time, in the F/A structure (21c) that corresponds to (21a), the subject NP corresponds to the subject ARG that is c-commanded by the TENSE that is realized on the finite verb. An ARG carries the INDEX (IND) feature that takes as its value the referential index j and AGR value α: IND[j, AGRα] (1.3 (6)). Note that the F/A of the noninverted clause (21a) and that of the inverted clause (20) are almost identical. The only difference between them is that when (20) is used as an interrogative sentence, it has an interrogative operator Q, as in (22). (The co-occurrence of an inverted clause in syntax and the Q in F/A is guaranteed by (24).)

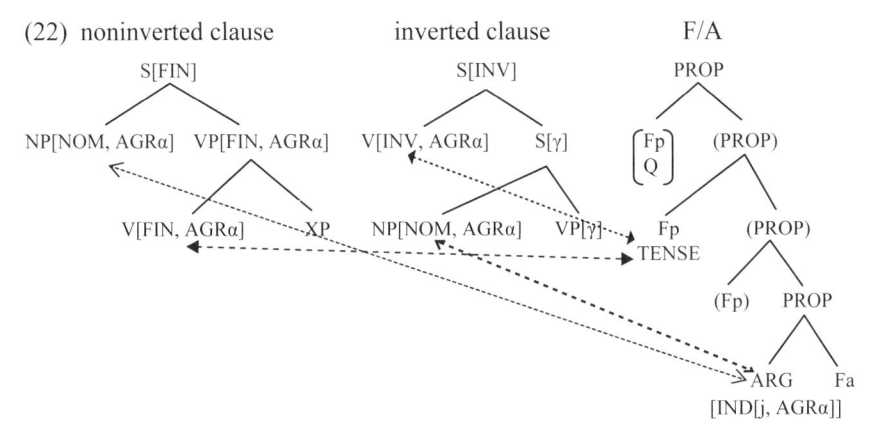

(22) noninverted clause   inverted clause   F/A

```
         S[FIN]                S[INV]                PROP
        /      \              /      \              /    \
NP[NOM, AGRα] VP[FIN, AGRα] V[INV, AGRα] S[γ]    ⎡Fp⎤  (PROP)
                                                 ⎣Q ⎦
                                                         \
       V[FIN, AGRα]   XP   NP[NOM, AGRα] VP[γ]    Fp      (PROP)
                                                 TENSE   /    \
                                                       (Fp)   PROP
                                                              /    \
                                                            ARG    Fa
                                                          [IND[j, AGRα]]
```

We would like to unify the two agreement patterns, the agreement in a noninverted clause (21a, b) and the agreement in an inverted clause (20), through the common F/A structure in (22) by redefining the subject-verb agreement in more general terms.

(23) subject-verb agreement (generalized)
   a. definition of agreement controller
      The agreement controller of a finite (auxiliary) verb is the NP that the finite (auxiliary) verb agrees with.
      (cf. Gazdar et al. 1985: 84–85)

   b. generalized agreement
      The agreement controller of a finite (auxiliary) verb is the NP whose F/A correspondent is the subject ARG that is c-commanded by the TENSE that is realized on the finite (auxiliary) verb in question.

Recall the definition of subject ARG in F/A: the subject ARG is the ARG that is directly dominated by a PROP and is the sister of its Fa. For the definition of c-command in F/A, see 1.3 (25). With these definitions at hand, we can now claim that the NPs with AGRα in the noninverted and inverted clauses in (22) are the agreement controllers of the finite (auxiliary) verb, because in their F/A structure, the TENSE c-commands the subject ARG with AGRα.

When a finite clause (inverted and noninverted) has the dummy subject NP[*it*], which is not represented in F/A (2.4 (9)), the same agreement patterns as in (22) are maintained in syntax; that is, the agreement controller is NP[*it*], although (23b) is not applicable. We claim that in the case of the dummy subject *it*, agreement is achieved purely syntactically by means of (20) for an inverted clause and (21a) for a noninverted clause. On the other hand, when the subject of a finite clause is the dummy (existential) *there* (NP[*there*]) (2.4 (8)), (23b) correctly predicts that the agreement controller is the theme NP, which will be discussed in 2.4 (14).

A yes/no question (polar question), such as (1a), has the modular representations (24) as a construction (cf. 7.1 (6b)).

(24) lexical entry for direct
  yes/no question
  (as a construction)
  syntax: S[INV]
  F/A: [$_{PROP}$ [$_{Fp}$ Q], PROP]
  RS: [$_{SA}$ [$_{IF}$ #inquire#] [$_{[AG, SO]}$ SP]
  [$_{[PT, GO]}$ AD]
  [$_{TH}$ EV]]
  phonology: rising intonation

(25) lexical entry for exclamative
  inversion
  (as a construction)
  syntax: S[INV]
  F/A: PROP
  RS: [$_{SA}$ [$_{IF}$ #exclaim#]
  [$_{[AG, SO]}$ SP] [$_{[PT, GO]}$ AD]
  [$_{TH}$ EV]]
  phonology: falling intonation

The F/A of a yes/no question consists of the interrogative operator Q and the matrix PROP whose truth or falsity the speaker is requesting the addressee to determine. The Q has the sister PROP within its scope. In the RS module, a direct question represents a speech act (SA) with the illocutionary force (IF) #inquire#, in which the speaker (SP) asks the addressee (AD) about the truth of the event (EV), which corresponds to the matrix PROP in F/A that is the sister of Q. See Chapter 7 for the details of speech acts. Inversion is not limited to yes/no questions. It is also used in exclamative sentences, such as *God, was I hungry!* and

Have things ever been happening! (McCawley 1998: 554). We need a separate entry (25) for this exclamative use of inversion.

2.2 Propositional Negation by *not*

The distribution of *not* is different from apparently similar VP-adverbs, such as *never* and *hardly*. In a nonfinite clause, such as (1c, d), *not* precedes the verb phrase just as any other VP-adverb. However, in a finite clause, such as (1a, b), *not* cannot precede a finite (auxiliary) verb. (1e, e') show that a single clause can contain multiple occurrences of *not*. Syntactically, *not* takes its sister constituent in its scope. For example, in (1g), the negative polarity item (NPI) *any* is dominated by the sister constituent of *not*, namely, VP[BSE], whereas *any* in (1g') is not. (1f) is ambiguous and its ambiguity arises from whether or not the PP[*because*] is within the scope of *not*. In fact, (1f) is syntactically ambiguous in three ways, as is shown in (1f', f", f'"). Only in (1f') is the PP[*because*] in the scope of *not*. Considering these facts, we give the lexical entry for *not* in (2) (cf. Sadock 2012: 174 (65)).

(1) McCawley 1998: 572–573
    a. Sam is not/*not is a Catholic.
    b. Sam does not like/*not likes Reagan.
    c. Sam is believed not to/to not be a Catholic.
    d. I'm surprised at Sam not being a Catholic/not liking Reagan.
    e. Sam hasn't been not paying taxes recently.
    e'. When I received first-hand credible evidence of more than one woman being sexually harassed, I could not not act. (*The Rachel Maddow Show* on MSNBC, July 31, 2013)
    f. John does not beat his wife [because he loves her]. (ambiguous)
    f'. John does not [$_{VP[BSE]}$ beat his wife PP[*because*]]. (PP[*because*] adjoined to VP[BSE])
    f". John [$_{VP[AUX, PRES]}$ [does not beat his wife] PP[*because*]]. (PP[*because*] adjoined to VP[AUX, PRES])
    f'". [$_{S[AUX, PRES]}$ [John does not beat his wife] PP[*because*]]. (PP[*because*] adjoined to S[AUX, PRES])
    g. John did not give me any help.
    g'. *Any help was not given to me.

(2) lexical entry for proposition-negating *not*
syntax: Word in [$_{XP}$ __, XP], where XP ≠ VP[FIN] and either XP corresponds to Fa or the head X corresponds to Fp.
F/A: [$_{Fp}$ NOT]
RS: nil
morph: Word (= {<BAR, 1>})
mphon: /nɑt/

The syntactic and morphological fields of (2) say that *not* is a word without category specification. This means that it is a word that is not capable of inflection, just as particles. In addition, the syntactic field requires that it be adjoined to a nonfinite VP or a non-VP phrase (e.g., *John is not* [$_{NP}$ *a student*]/[$_{PP}$ *from Chicago*]/ [$_{AP}$ *fond of Chicago*]). In (1b), the sister of *not* is [$_{VP[BSE]}$ *like Reagan*], which corresponds to Fa. In *John has not been smoking*, the sister of *not* is [$_{VP[PSP]}$ *been smoking*], whose head *been* corresponds to [$_{Fp}$ PROG]. We will use a short-hand notation VP[−FIN] to refer to a nonfinite VP. This syntax allows multiple occurrences of *not* in a clause, which is illustrated in (1e, e'). The linear order between *not* and the following phrase is determined by the default order rule between sisters: word < phrase (1.4 (11a)). In F/A, *not* is an Fp functor ([$_{PROP}$ [$_{Fp}$ NOT], PROP]).

When there is a finite auxiliary verb (V[FIN, AUX]) and a proposition-negating *not* in the VP, because of the lexical entry (2), the finite auxiliary verb must precede *not*, as in (3a), resulting in the VP structure [$_{VP[FIN, AUX]}$ V[FIN, AUX] [$_{XP}$ *not* XP]]. In (3a), *not* is adjoined to a nonfinite VP and meets the lexical requirement in (2). On the other hand, (3b) is ungrammatical, because *not* is adjoined to a finite VP and violates the syntactic requirement in (2).

(3) a. John does [not [$_{VP[BSE]}$ smoke]].   VP[PRES, AUX]
    b. *John [not [$_{VP[PRES]}$ smokes]].

```
        VP[PRES, AUX]
         /      \
   V[PRES, AUX]  VP[BSE]
       does      /    \
                not   VP[BSE]
                        |
                      V[BSE]
                      smoke
```

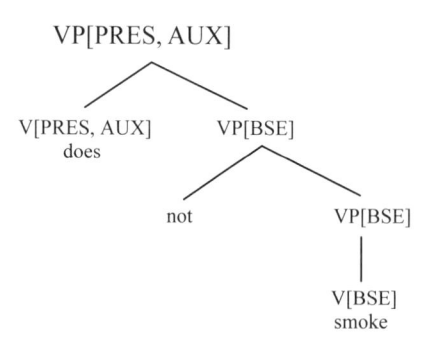

As for the dummy *do*, whose lexical entry is given in 2.1 (6), we regard a finite VP headed by it (e.g., [$_{VP[AUX, PRES]}$ *does* [$_{VP[BSE]}$ *smoke*]]) as always available along with a finite VP without it (e.g., [$_{VP[PRES]}$ *smokes*]). Both express exactly the same semantic information. Because the latter is simpler than the former in terms of the syntactic structure involved and the number of words used, the simpler form [$_{VP[PRES]}$ *smokes*] is chosen over the more complex [$_{VP[AUX, PRES]}$ *does* [$_{VP[BSE]}$ *smoke*]] whenever possible, due to the economy of language use. The more complex form is ONLY pressed into service when the presence of V[FIN, AUX] is required: for allowing *not* to appear in a VP, for emphasizing the polarity of a sentence (e.g., *John DOES smoke*), or for introducing a VP ellipsis (e.g., *John smokes and Mary does too*).

As for the scope relations in F/A between the two Fp functors, NOT and TENSE, it has often been claimed that TENSE is within the scope of NOT, that is, NOT(TENSE(PROP)) in F/A (Sadock 2012: 175 (67), McCawley 1998: 571). However, when the sentence in the past tense *John smoked* is negated by *not*, as in *John did not smoke*, what is semantically negated by *not* seems to be the proposition SMOKE(JOHN) and not the proposition PAST(SMOKE(JOHN)); that is, the tense PAST is not within the negative scope. In other words, we usually interpret the sentence *John did not smoke* as PAST(NOT(SMOKE(JOHN))), that is, about something in the past, namely, about a nonoccurrence in the past of the event of John's smoking. For example, in *John did not smoke but he smokes now*, what is contrasted is the nonoccurrence of John's smoking in the past, that is, PAST(NOT(SMOKE(JOHN))), and the occurrence of John's smoking at present, that is, PRES(SMOKE(JOHN)). Therefore, we assume that in default cases, NOT is in the scope of TENSE, that is, TENSE(NOT(PROP)). Here are two examples of F/A structure of a past-tense sentence. (4b) shows John's lack of ability in the past to swim.

(4) a. the F/A of *John did not smoke*   b. the F/A of *John could not swim (ten years ago)*
    PAST(NOT(SMOKE (JOHN)))   PAST(NOT(CAN(SWIM (JOHN))))

The advantages of this analysis are not only that it is semantically more plausible but also that it reduces the amount of mismatch between syntax and F/A. In (5), the c-command relations of the functors between syntax and F/A are preserved.

(5) syntax and F/A of (4a) *John did not smoke*

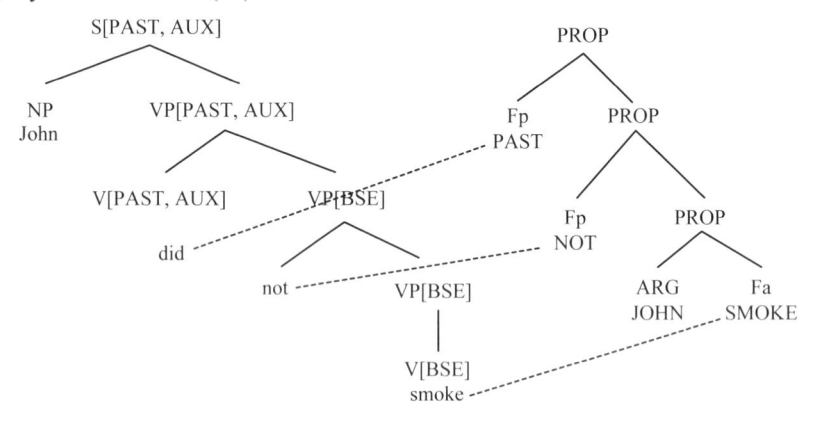

As for (4b), a certain amount of mismatch is forced between syntax and F/A. In (6), the syntactic field of the lexical entry for *not* (2) requires that it be adjoined to a nonfinite VP. With this F/A structure, there is no way of avoiding the mismatch, namely, that *not* is c-commanded by *could* in syntax, whereas NOT is not c-commanded by both PAST and CAN.

(6) syntax and F/A of (4b) *John could not swim*

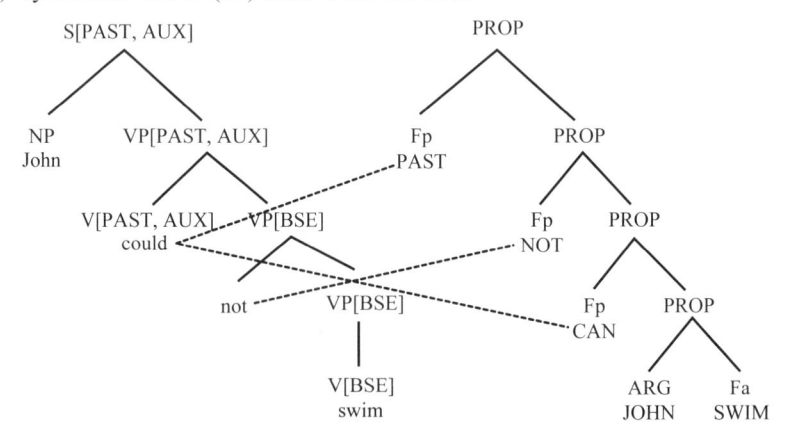

When there are a string of auxiliary verbs and *not* in a finite VP and *not* purports to negate the whole proposition, *not* must be placed immediately after the finite auxiliary verb (i.e., the first auxiliary verb), because this is the position where there is the least amount of mismatch between syntax and F/A. In (7a), for example, *not* can be adjoined to one of the four nonfinite VPs. But the option of adjoining it to the VP[BSE], the highest nonfinite VP node, exhibits the least amount of mismatch between (7a) and (7b), which is shown in (7c) and is the same mismatch as we saw in (6).

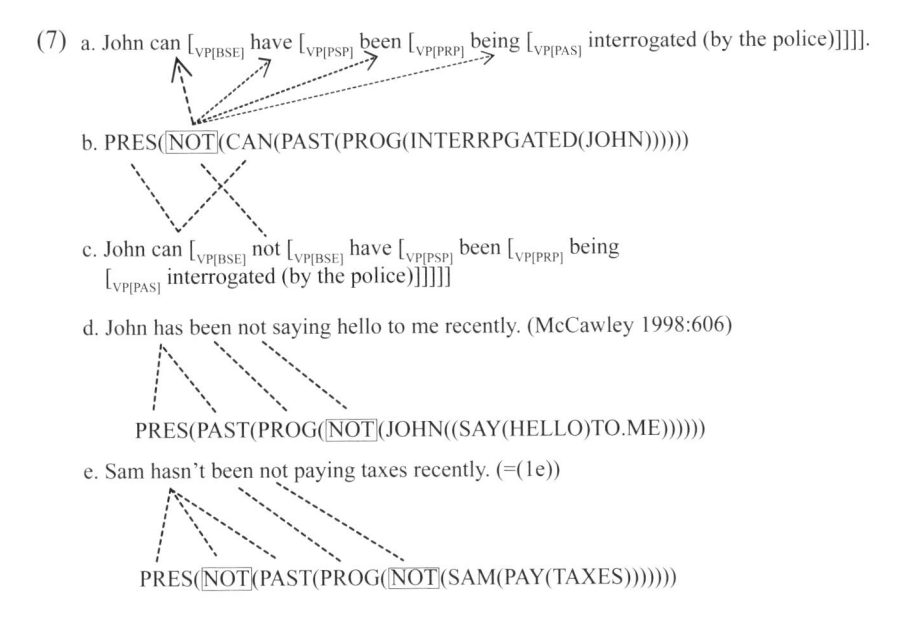

(7) a. John can [$_{VP[BSE]}$ have [$_{VP[PSP]}$ been [$_{VP[PRP]}$ being [$_{VP[PAS]}$ interrogated (by the police)]]]].

b. PRES(NOT(CAN(PAST(PROG(INTERRPGATED(JOHN))))))

c. John can [$_{VP[BSE]}$ not [$_{VP[BSE]}$ have [$_{VP[PSP]}$ been [$_{VP[PRP]}$ being [$_{VP[PAS]}$ interrogated (by the police)]]]]]

d. John has been not saying hello to me recently. (McCawley 1998:606)

PRES(PAST(PROG(NOT(JOHN((SAY(HELLO)TO.ME))))))

e. Sam hasn't been not paying taxes recently. (=(1e))

PRES(NOT(PAST(PROG(NOT(SAM(PAY(TAXES)))))))

Of course, when *not* takes a different scope and purports to negate an embedded proposition, an option different from (7c) becomes available, as in (7d, e).

(8a) is ambiguous (Sadock 2012: 176) because it corresponds to two F/A structures. One reading is that permission to participate is denied (8b) and the other is that permission to refrain from participation is granted (8c). (8a) with the reading (8c) exhibits no mismatch between syntax and F/A (except, of course, for the innocuous mismatch caused by subject raising, which will be discussed in 4.1). On the other hand, (8a) with the reading (8b) (i.e., denied permission reading) shows the same mismatch that we saw in (6) and (7b, c). Evidently, this mismatch is innocuous in English.

(8) a. Students may not participate in the convocation. (ambiguous) (Sadock 2012: 176)
b. PRES(NOT(MAY([(PARTICIPATE(CONVOCATION)STUDENTS)])))
c. PRES(MAY(NOT([(PARTICIPATE(CONVOCATION)STUDENTS)])))

(9b) is ungrammatical because *not* does not satisfy the lexical requirement (2) that it be adjoined to a nonfinite VP. In contrast, (9c) is grammatical and the contracted form *don't*, whose syntactic category is V[INV, PRES], is permitted in the inverted auxiliary verb position.

(9) a. What problem do the students not [$_{VP[BSE]}$ have to do]? (Sadock 2012: 177)
b. *What problem do not [$_{S[BSE]}$ the students have to do]?
c. What problem [$_{S[INV, PRES]}$ [$_{V[INV, PRES]}$ don't] [$_{S[BSE]}$ the students have to do]]?

We need to list all the contracted forms of finite auxiliary verbs and *not* in the lexicon, in order to record their phonological idiosyncrasies, such as those in *don't* and *won't*, and semantic idiosyncrasies, such as those in *mightn't*, in 2.1 (11) and (12) (Sadock 2012: 177–178). This is also necessary partly because some finite auxiliary verbs lack their contracted form (**amn't*, **mayn't*) and partly because some only exist as contracted forms, for example, first person singular inverted *aren't* in 2.1 (9) and *ain't*, as in *I/You/She ain't going nowhere/been there*. The syntactic category of these contracted forms is V[AUX, FIN], which undergoes the Inversion Lexical Rule (2.1 (3b)), which turns them into V[INV]. Therefore, *don't* in (9c) is a regular V[INV] and takes an S[BSE] complement, as specified in the lexical entry for the inverted *don't*.

(10a) means 'Mendel is forbidden to refrain from singing *Home on the Range*' with its F/A (10b), which is logically equivalent to 'Mendel must sing *Home on the Range*.' However, it cannot mean that 'Mendel is permitted to sing *Home on the Range*,' whose F/A would be (10c) (Sadock 2012: 180–181).

(10) a. Mendel mustn't not sing Home on the Range. (Sadock 2012: 180)
b. PRES(MUST(NOT(NOT([$_{PROP}$ (SING(H.R.)MENDEL)]))))
c. *PRES(NOT(MUST(NOT([$_{PROP}$ (SING(H.R.)MENDEL)]))))

The narrow negative scope of *mustn't*, that is, MUST(NOT(PROP)), is fixed lexically (Sadock 2012: 178) and registered in its lexical entry. Because the tense PRES comes at the top, the Fp sequence PRES(MUST(NOT ...)), which means 'it is forbidden to,' is lexically fixed for *mustn't*. In the F/A structures (10b, c), the lexically fixed parts are underlined. The unavailability of (10c) shows that although the mismatch in (6) and (7b, c) is innocuous, the mismatch between (10a) and (10c) is too great to tolerate (Sadock 2012: 181 (82)). This is shown in (11). First, there are two association line crossings in (11b). Second, NOT intervenes in the lexically fixed part, the underlined part in (11b). Third, the two instances of *not* in syntax and the two instances of NOT in F/A reverse their c-command relations in (11b); that is, the lower *not* in syntax tries to take the higher *not* within its scope.

(11) a. (10a) with the interpretation (10b)   b. (10a) with the interpretation (10c)

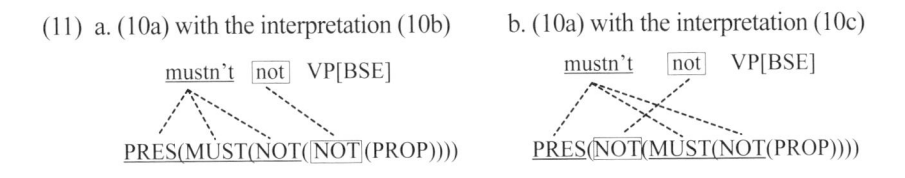

   mustn't [not] VP[BSE]   mustn't [not] VP[BSE]

   PRES(MUST(NOT([NOT](PROP))))   PRES(NOT(MUST(NOT(PROP))))

Jerry Sadock (p.c.) pointed out to me that (12a) only means 'Mendel must sing' and cannot mean 'Mendel can sing'; that is, the interpretation PRES(NOT (NOT(CAN(SING(MENDEL)))))) is not available. The contracted auxiliary *can't*, when used as an expression of prohibition ('not be allowed to do'), has a lexically fixed scope PRES(NOT(CAN(PROP))). The non-mismatched correspondence between the syntax and F/A of *Mendel can't not sing* is shown in (12). Note that NOT(CAN(NOT(PROP))) means 'prohibition against refraining from doing something,' that is, 'not allowed not to do something,' which is semantically equivalent to 'must' (cf. McCawley 1993: 378–379: "for any proposition A, □A if ~◊~A," where □ is necessity and ◊ is possibility).

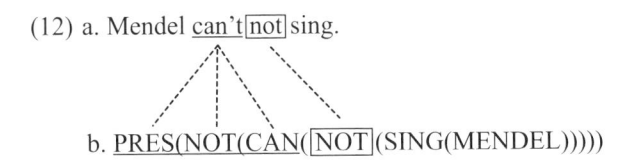

(12) a. Mendel can't [not] sing.

   b. PRES(NOT(CAN([NOT](SING(MENDEL))))))

When we try to interpret (12a) as 'Mendel can sing' with its F/A (13a') or (13b'), this interpretation is not available. On the one hand, (13a, a') show two association line crossings, which is too great a mismatch to tolerate, as in (11b). On the other hand, in (13b, b'), the lower *not* intervenes in the lexically fixed PRES∘NOT∘CAN.

(13) a. Mendel can't not sing.

a'. PRES(NOT (NOT(CAN(SING(MENDEL))))

b. Mendel can't not sing. (=(13a))

b'. PRES(NOT(NOT (CAN(SING(MENDEL)))))

Considering (11), (12), and (13), we conclude that NOT cannot intervene in lexically specified Fp sequences such as PRES∘MUST∘NOT and PRES∘NOT∘CAN.

2.3 Negative Inversion

Negative inversion is a type of inversion in which a negative phrase (XP[NG]), a phrase with the unary NG feature, occurs clause-initially (i.e., is "preposed") and is followed by an inverted clause (1a, b).

(1) a. At no time did anything unusual happen. (McCawley 1998: 582)
 b. Nothing did I know about cats. (from the web)

The most frequent type of negative inversion is the one in which the negative phrase is a sentential modifier (Mp in F/A), as in (1a). The inversion with a negative nonsubject argument (1b) is much less common. A clause-initial negative VP-adjunct (MFa in F/A) is very rare. Such apparent manner adverbials as *by no means*, *in no way*, or *in no manner* do occur with negative inversion but their meaning is almost the same as such propositional modifiers (Mp) as 'not at all' or 'never.' The lexical entry for negative inversion is given in (2).

(2) lexical entry for negative inversion (as a construction)
 IS: [_U FOC ≺ rest]

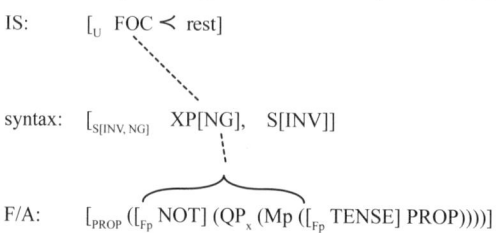

 syntax: [_S[INV, NG] XP[NG], S[INV]]

 F/A: [_PROP ([_Fp NOT) (QP_x (Mp ([_Fp TENSE] PROP))))]

2.3 NEGATIVE INVERSION

In syntax, a negative phrase XP[NG] is adjoined to an inverted clause S[INV] that lacks a negative phrase, creating a larger clause S[INV, NG]. Because this PS rule is not recursive, it correctly predicts the ungrammaticality of negative inversion with two or more negative phrases: *[XP[NG], [$_{S[INV, NG]}$ YP[NG], S[INV]]]. The negative phrase XP[NG] in (2) corresponds to the F/A complex [$_{Fp}$ NOT] QP$_x$ Mp, on the one hand, and to the focus (FOC) in Information Structure (IS), on the other. Negative inversion is a focus-initial construction along with a *wh*-question, in which the *wh*-phrase is the focus, although some authors treat the preposed negative phrase as a topic ("stage topic"). See Erteschik-Shir (1997: 221, 234) and Erteschik-Shir (2007: 172) for the latter view.

The inverted auxiliary verb in (1a) is essential in extending to the whole clause the negative scope triggered by a negative element in the negative phrase XP[NG]. For example, compare (1a) with *In no time, something unusual happened*. In the latter, which lacks negative inversion, the negative scope does not extend to the whole proposition. The same contrast is found in (14c, d). Therefore, negative inversion is required in syntax to extend the negative scope of the negation contained in the negative phrase to the entire proposition. Note that the subject NP of the negative inversion construction is in the scope of its negation, as shown by the NPI *anything* in (1a). In contrast, *not* adjoined to a VP cannot have its subject within its scope (2.2 (1 g)).

In the syntax of (2), neither < nor ⩽ is indicated to order the two constituents. Their order follows from the default order phrase < clause (1.4 (11a)) and also from the order specified in IS. Note that a parenthetical phrase can intervene between XP[NG] and S[INV], as in (3a). By contrast, (3b) shows that nothing can intervene between V[INV] and its complement nonfinite S, as we discussed in 2.1 (3a).

(3) a. Under no circumstances, <u>I think/in my opinion</u>, should John be arrested.
    b. *Under no circumstances should, <u>I think/in my opinion</u>, John be arrested.

The negation in negative inversion negates the whole clause, as shown in (1a). (4b, c) cannot be understood as the negative inversion counterpart of (4a).

(4) a. I said that he had <u>never</u> lied to me.   b. *<u>Never</u> did I say that he had lied to me.
    c. *<u>Never</u> had I said that he lied to me.   d. I said that <u>never</u> had he lied to me.

This is explained by the F/A requirement in (2) that NOT contained in XP[NG] must be the topmost Fp having scope over the entire clause.

Because the negative inversion PS, namely, the syntactic field of (2), specifically mentions S[INV] and the presence of the INV feature requires the presence of <VFORM, FIN> by the FCR in 2.1 (3c), repeated here as (5a), negative inversion is impossible in a nonfinite clause, such as S[BSE], which is illustrated by (6), whereas it is possible with a CP[*that*] taking an S[FIN] complement, as in (7). Note that because the VFORM feature on the head verb cannot have two values BSE and FIN at the same time, S[BSE, INV] in (5b) is an ill-formed syntactic category.

(5) a. INV Feature Co-occurrence Restriction
INV → {AUX, <VFORM, FIN>, <V, +>, <N, –>}
b. the feature composition of the ill-formed category S[BSE, INV]
{<u><VFORM, BSE></u>, INV, AUX, <u><VFORM, FIN></u>, <V, +>, <N, –>, <BAR, 2>}

(6) *I demand that [under no circumstances [$_{S[BSE, INV]}$ [$_{V[BSE, INV]}$ be] [$_{S[PAS]}$ he arrested]. (Rizzi 1990: 117 note 19)
cf. I demand that [$_{S[INV, NG]}$ under no circumstances should he be arrested].

(7) I think that [never before have the media played such a major role in a kidnapping]. (McCawley 1998: 598)

The negative phrase XP[NG] of the negative inversion construction must be either an adjunct or a nonsubject argument, which was shown in (1). (8a, b) show that a subject with negation does not trigger negative inversion. (8c) is the syntactic structure we would have if negative inversion appeared with the subject *nobody*. Note that we would need to posit a phonologically null NP gap (NP[G]) in the subject position of the S[BSE].

(8) a. Nobody loves me.
b. *Nobody does love me. (no stress on *does*)
c. [$_{S[INV, PRES, NG]}$ [$_{NP[NG]}$ Nobody] [$_{S[INV, PRES]}$ [$_{V[INV, PRES]}$ does] [$_{S[BSE]}$ NP[G] [$_{VP[BSE]}$ love me]]]]
d. ... or maybe, nobody DOES love me anymore. (stress on DOES) (from the web)

The unacceptability of (8b) with unstressed *does* can be explained in two ways, in pragmatic and syntactic terms. First, the syntactic structure (8c) of the unacceptable (8b) is much more complex than that of the acceptable (8a), though both express the same information. In the simpler (8a), the hallmark of negative inversion that a negative phrase comes first and a finite verb comes second is already achieved by the default linear order [$_{S[FIN]}$ NP < VP[FIN]] (1.4 (11c)) without negative inversion. We claim that when there are two or more competing options available, the simplest one, and in this case (8a), must be chosen for the sake of the economy of language use. Second, the syntactic structure (8c) with "extraction" from the subject position is not syntactically possible. It has been observed since Bresnan's Fixed Subject Condition (McCawley 1998: 544) that the "extraction" of a subject NP is possible only if it is the subject of an embedded clause that is immediately preceded by and is a sister of the (nonauxiliary) main verb. This is shown in (9).

(9) a. *Which applicant would you like [$_{CP[for]}$ for [$_{S[to]}$ __ to get the job]]? (McCawley 1998: 528)
  b. *Who did you say [$_{CP[that]}$ that [$_{S[PAST]}$ __ called me]]?
  c. *John is the one who I'm counting [$_{PP[on]}$ on [$_{S[PRP]}$ __ marrying her]]. (Kayne 1984: 29)
  d. Who do you [$_{VP}$ think [$_{S[PRES]}$ __ loves Mary]]?
  e. Who do you [$_{VP}$ want [$_{S[to]}$ __ to call you]]?

In (9a), the clause in question (S[*to*]) is the complement of the C[*for*]. In (9b), the clause (S[PAST]) is the complement of the C[*that*]. In (9c), the clause (S[PRP]) is the complement of the P[*on*]. (9d) is fine, because the clause (S[PRES]) is the complement of the verb *think*. (9e) is fine too, because the clause (S[*to*]) is the complement of the verb *want*. Going back to (8c), the extraction site (NP[G]) is the subject of the clause (S[BSE]) that is the complement of the inverted auxiliary verb (V[INV, PRES]), not a complement of a main verb, as in (9d, e).

Note that (8d) with a stressed dummy *do* (emphatic *do*) is acceptable. Our view about the dummy *do* is that a VP[AUX, FIN] headed by the dummy *do* ([$_{VP[AUX, FIN]}$ [$_{V[AUX, FIN]}$ *do*(*es*)/*did*] VP[BSE]]) is always available along with VP[FIN] (VP headed by a nonauxiliary V[FIN]) and that the former is chosen only when there is a reason for such a choice. That is, when there is no such reason, the simpler, shorter form (VP[FIN]) must be chosen, again, for the sake of the economy of language use. If we take (8b) as an instance of a finite VP headed by an unstressed dummy *do*, the simpler (8a) and the more complex (8b) express the same information, and therefore, there is no reason to choose (8b) over (8a). However, when the dummy *do* serves a purpose, for example, the purpose of emphasizing the polarity of the clause with stress, its use becomes possible, as in (8d).

When a nonsubject argument NP[NG] is "preposed," as in (1b), we need to posit a phonologically null NP gap (NP[G]) in its original position to meet the subcategorization requirement of the verb that the gap is a complement of. (10) gives the syntax and F/A of (1b).

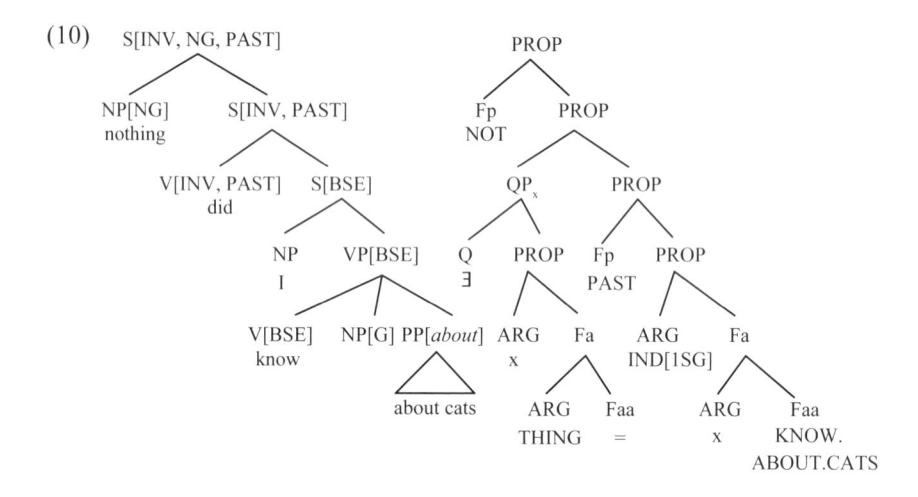

(10)

```
        S[INV, NG, PAST]                    PROP
        /        \                         /    \
    NP[NG]     S[INV, PAST]              Fp     PROP
    nothing    /        \                NOT    /    \
          V[INV, PAST]  S[BSE]                QP_x   PROP
              did      /      \               / \    /  \
                     NP      VP[BSE]          Q  PROP Fp  PROP
                     I      /      \          ∃  / \  PAST /  \
                       V[BSE] NP[G] PP[about] ARG Fa  ARG  Fa
                       know              x   / \      IND[1SG] / \
                            about cats      ARG Faa    ARG    Faa
                                           THING  =     x    KNOW.
                                                              ABOUT.CATS
```

Note that *nothing* is treated as the combination of NOT and SOMETHING, the latter being an existential quantifier in F/A (cf. 1.3 (15) and (16)). The F/A structure is determined in such a way that there is the least amount of mismatch between it and its syntax in terms of geometrical correspondences (1.4 (7b)). The NP[G] in syntax corresponds to the variable [$_{ARG}$ x]. This gap licenses a parasitic gap, which is shown in (11).

(11) a. Nothing can you learn __ without trying __.
     cf. *Nothing can you learn it without trying __.
     b. Nothing did he ever file __ without reading __.
     cf. *Nothing did he ever file it without reading __.

The VP[BSE] and S[BSE] nodes in (10) can be the locus of coordination of gapped VP and gapped S, respectively.

(12) a. Nothing at all did I [say __ to Mary or hear __ from her]. (coordination of gapped VP[BSE])
b. Nothing at all did [I tell you __ or you tell me __]. (coordination of gapped S[BSE])

When an XP[NG] happens to be a locative PP, it looks as if both negative inversion (2) and locative inversion 2.6 (4) were possible. However, recall that in the negative inversion construction (2), the presence of an inverted auxiliary was essential to extending the negative scope to the whole clause. Furthermore, the PP[NG] in negative inversion is FOC in IS, whereas the locative PP in locative inversion is TOP. Therefore, the two types of PP are different information-wise. For these reasons, only negative inversion is possible with a negative locative PP, such as (13a, b). In (13c), *there*-insertion appears with negative inversion.

(13) a. *[Nowhere in the world] exists anything simple. (locative inversion)
b. [Nowhere in the world] does anything simple exist. (negative inversion)
c. Nowhere in the world does there exist anything simple. (from the web)

A PP[NG] is sometimes used in two ways, with or without negative inversion, accompanied by corresponding semantic differences.

(14) a. At no time did they reveal what they wanted. (McCawley 1998: 582)
b. In no time, we were approaching Toledo. (McCawley 1998: 582)
c. In no clothes does Mary look attractive. (Jackendoff 1972: 364)
= 'There are no clothes in which Mary looks attractive.'
d. In no clothes, Mary looks attractive. (Jackendoff 1972: 365)
= 'Mary looks attractive when wearing no clothes.'

(14a, c) have negative inversion and their F/A is along the lines of (2). As might be expected from the usual paraphrase of *no* as *not any*, we analyze the determiner *no* as the combination of negative Fp functor NOT and existential quantifier $\exists$, as in (15) and (16) (cf. negative incorporation in McCawley 1998: 579). *In no clothes* in (14c) is assumed to be Mp. For instance, (15) shows how the syntax and F/A of (14c) correspond to each other. In its F/A, NOT immediately c-commands the QP_x ($[_{QPx} \exists x = CLOTHES]$), which in turn immediately c-commands the Mp ($[_{Mp} IN [_{ARG} x]]$), thus satisfying (2).

(15) [$_{PP[NG]}$ In [$_{NP[NG]}$ [$_{DET[NG]}$ no] clothes]] [$_{S[PRES, INV]}$ does [$_{S[BSE]}$ Mary look attractive]]

[$_{Fp}$ NOT] ([$_{QPx}$ ∃x = CLOTHES] ([$_{PROP}$ [$_{Mp}$ IN, [$_{ARG}$ x]] ([$_{Fp}$ PRES]
([$_{PROP}$ LOOK.ATTRACTIVE(MARY)])))])

(16) lexical entry of negative determiner *no*
    syntax: DET[NG]
    F/A: [$_{Fp}$ NOT] [$_{QPx}$ ∃ x = [$_{ARG}$ ...]], where the value of [$_{ARG}$ ...] comes from the sister N' in syntax.
    RS: nil

The fact that NOT is at the top of the whole proposition and has the rest of the proposition within its scope, as required by (2), is clearly seen in (17), where the NPIs *anything* and *anyone* show that they are in the scope of negation.

(17) At no time was anything shown to anyone. (McCawley 1998: 578)
    cf. *Anything was shown to anyone at no time.

(14b, d) lack negative inversion, showing that the negation in the sentence-initial PPs does not take the whole proposition within its scope and that its negative scope stays within the PP. *In no time* in (14b) roughly means 'very soon' and *in no clothes* in (14d) 'when not wearing any clothes.' Here are two more examples of apparent negative PP.

(18) a. For no reason, he suddenly punched someone. (McCawley 1998: 582)
    b. Out of nowhere appeared a little mouse. (locative inversion, from the web)

The distribution of negative adverb *never* is quite different from that of *not*. Although *not* alone does not trigger negative inversion, *never* does, as in (19c). This means that *never* (but not *not*) counts as XP[NG] in the negative inversion construction (2). (Compare the lexical entries for *never* in (21) below and *not* in 2.2 (2).) *Never* is semantically equivalent to 'not ever, not at any time.' Therefore, in (20) and (21), we treat *never* as a combination of NOT and existential quantifier.

(19) a. He never/*not smokes.
    b. He does not/*never smoke.
    c. Never/*Not did he smoke.

2.3 NEGATIVE INVERSION

(20) [$_{\text{ADVP[NG]}}$ [$_{\text{ADV[NG]}}$ never]] [$_{\text{S[PAST, INV]}}$ did [$_{\text{S[BSE]}}$ he smoke]]

[$_{\text{Fp}}$ NOT] ([$_{\text{QPx}}$ ∃ x = TIME] ([$_{\text{PROP}}$ [$_{\text{Mp}}$ AT, [$_{\text{ARG}}$ x]] ([$_{\text{Fp}}$ PAST] ([$_{\text{PROP}}$ SMOKE(ARG[IND[j, 3SGM])])))

(21) lexical entry for *never*
syntax: ADV[NG]
F/A: [$_{\text{Fp}}$ NOT] [$_{\text{QPx}}$ ∃ x = TIME] [$_{\text{Mp}}$ AT, [$_{\text{ARG}}$ x]]
RS: nil

The remaining issue is how the NG feature percolates in syntax. For this purpose, we propose four local PS rules (22a-d).

(22) percolation of the feature NG in syntax
    a. [$_{\text{NP[NG]}}$ DET[NG] N']   b. [$_{\text{PP[NG]}}$ P NP[NG]]
    c. [$_{\text{PP[NG]}}$ ADV[NG] PP]   d. [$_{\text{PP[NG]}}$ *not* PP]
    e. [$_{\text{S[INV, NG]}}$ XP[NG], S[INV]] (from (2))   f. [$_{\text{XP[NG]}}$ ... X[NG] ...]

(22a, b) are needed to account for examples like [$_{\text{PP[at, NG]}}$ at [$_{\text{DET[NG]}}$ no] time] in (14a). (22c) is needed for (23a) and (13b, c), in which a negative word *never* or *nowhere* is adjoined to a PP. (22d) is needed for (23b, c). What is interesting about (22d) is that although *not* alone cannot trigger negative inversion (19c), when it is adjoined to a PP, it can. (22f) says that NG is a head feature. This is needed to account for such trivial cases as [$_{\text{ADVP[NG]}}$ [$_{\text{ADV[NG]}}$ never]] in (19c) and (1b). In the latter, we treat *nothing* as N[NG] in syntax, which accounts for such examples as *Nothing about it did I hate* (from the web). The syntax of the preposed NP *nothing about it* is [$_{\text{NP[NG]}}$ [$_{\text{N'[NG]}}$ [$_{\text{N'[NG]}}$ [$_{\text{N[NG]}}$ nothing]] [$_{\text{PP[about]}}$ about it]]], in which the PP[*about*] is adjoined to the N'[NG] consisting of the N[NG] *nothing*.

(23) a. Never in my life have I seen such a mess! (from the web)
    b. ... but please tell Melissa that not under any circumstances did I think we should have to pay 150 dollars ... (from the web)
    c. Not at any time did the United States occupy nor rule Mexico. (from the web)

Note that (22a) and (22c) might be subsumed under (22f). As for (22a), if we employ the DP analysis, according to which the head of NP with a determiner is not N but DET, then this will be a special case of (22f). The same is true of (22c). If we assume that the head of the constituent [ADV[NG] PP] in (22c) is not PP but ADV[NG], that is, that the adverbs *never* and *nowhere* take a PP complement, just like *independently* PP[*of*], *fortunately* PP[*for*], or *separately* PP[*from*], (22c) will be a special case of (22f), too. Note also that the percolation of the feature NG is very similar to the percolation of the WH[Q] feature in a *wh*-phrase (6.1.5 (3)).

2.4 Dummy *there*

In such uses of the verb *be* as *Sally is a carpenter*, it is an empty verb whose F/A and RS are nil (2.1 (13e); cf. Sadock 2012:29 (11)). There is another use of the verb *be* as a verb of existence (1a, b). Although the empty *be* is optional in some environments (1c), the verb-of-existence *be* is not optional in those environments (1d). This use of *be* belongs to the same group of verbs of existence and appearance that includes *exist*, *remain*, and *appear*, which typically take two roles: theme (TH) and locative (LO).

(1) a. a way of life that has long since ceased to be (from the web)
  b. I think, therefore I am. (from "Cogito, ergo sum")
  c. I consider John (to be) in good shape. (empty *be*) cf. John is considered (to be) in good shape.
  d. I consider John *(to be) in Chicago. (verb of existence) cf. John is considered *(to be) in Chicago.

When *be* is used in the *there* construction, we find two subtypes. One is when *be* is a verb of existence (2a). The locative PP is optional and can be temporal, as in the second example in (2a). The other is when *be* is empty and takes two complements, NP and XP, the latter being either AP, predicative PP, or nonfinite VP, as in (2b). In the examples of (2b), the XP corresponds to an Fa in F/A and the NP and the XP form a PROP (cf. (6)).

(2) a. the *there* construction with verb-of-existence *be*
    There is [$_{NP}$ a mistake] ([$_{PP}$ in the book]). There is [$_{NP}$ a concert] ([$_{PP}$ on Sunday]).

b. the *there* construction with empty *be*
There is [$_{NP}$ a copy of the book] [$_{XP}$ available/in good shape/bought by our library/lying on the floor].

The lexical entries for these two types of the *there* construction are given in (3) and (6).

(3) lexical entry for the *there* construction with verb-of-existence *be*

syntax: [$_{V[AUX]}$ be] in [__, EQNP, (PP)]
F/A: [$_{F(a)a}$ BE]
RS: [$_{TYPE}$ "be"] in [__, TH, {LO | <LO>}]

IS: [$_U$ … new …]

The verb-of-existence *be* takes as its complements an existentially quantified NP (EQNP) and an optional PP in syntax, and two roles, TH and LO, in RS. EQNP, which is shown in (10), is an NP that is interpreted as existentially quantified. The LO can be an unassociable role (<LO>), which counts as a role in RS and is interpreted as such but does not correspond to anything in syntax or in F/A (3.2 (2); cf. Sadock 2012:82). The TH role that corresponds to the EQNP in syntax is specified as new in Information Structure (IS), because it introduces "addressee-new entities into the discourse" (Huddleston and Pullum 2002: 1396). Therefore, the EQNP is quite often an indefinite NP. Because TH outranks LO by the Role Hierarchy (1.4 (6)) and LO corresponds to a PP in syntax, we have the following default correspondences (shown by numbers) between syntax, F/A, and RS (cf. 1.4 (7)). The word order in the VP follows from the default order rules 1.4 (11b) and (12).

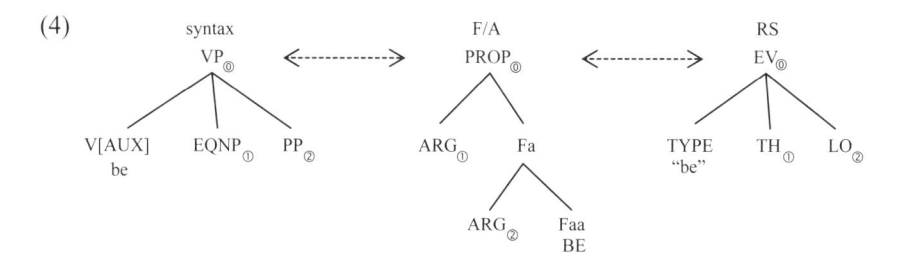

(4)

syntax: VP$_{⓪}$ — V[AUX] be, EQNP$_①$, PP$_②$

F/A: PROP$_⓪$ — ARG$_①$, Fa — ARG$_②$, Faa BE

RS: EV$_⓪$ — TYPE "be", TH$_①$, LO$_②$

Note that the VP in (4) is a ternary-branching structure and not a binary-branching [be [$_{SC}$ NP PP]], which is confirmed by the Heavy Constituent Shift (HCS) (a.k.a. Heavy NP Shift). In descriptive terms, HCS "moves" a "heavy" constituent that is a sister of a verb to the S-final focus position crossing other complements and adjuncts. (This test will be examined in 4.2.2 (4).)

(5) HCS applied to the theme EQNP
   a. There were __ in his in-tray [no fewer than thirty unpaid bills]. (Huddleston and Pullum 2002: 1392)
   b. There will be __ in the syntax of sentences [an illocutionary force indicating device and a representation of the propositional content]. (Searle 1989: 540)

Note also that the VP in (4) is semantically saturated and therefore, its subject position must be filled by a dummy element, namely, the existential *there*, whose lexical entry will be given later in (8).

Here is the lexical entry for the other type of the *there* construction.

(6) lexical entry for the *there* construction with empty *be* (cf. Sadock 2012: 64 (98))
   syntax: [$_{VP}$ [$_{V[AUX]}$ be], EQNP, XP], where XP is AP, PP, VP[–FIN].
   F/A: [$_{PROP}$ ARG, Fa]
   RS: [$_{EV}$ TYPE TH]
   IS: [$_U$ ... new ...]

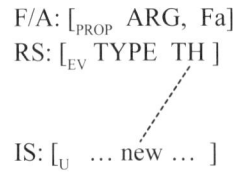

In a very few cases, an NP is possible as the XP in (6), such as *There were few persons still his friends* (McCawley 1998: 113 note 8) and *Is there anything the matter?* (Huddleston and Pullum 2002: 1394). The EQNP and XP in syntax correspond respectively to ARG and Fa in F/A, which form a PROP. Also, the EQNP corresponds to TH in RS and carries new information in IS. The word order in the VP follows from the default order rules 1.4 (11c) and (12). The intermodular correspondences are shown in (7).

(7)

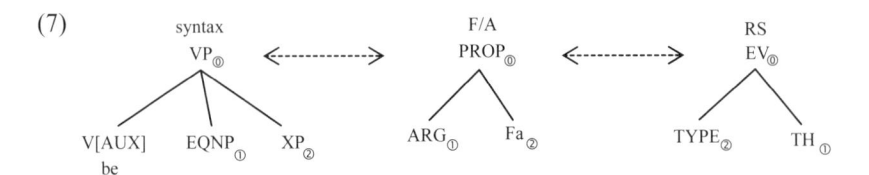

```
       syntax                    F/A                    RS
       VP₀       <------->      PROP₀     <------->    EV₀
      /  |  \                   /   \                  /   \
  V[AUX] EQNP  XP₂            ARG₁  Fa₂             TYPE₂  TH₁
    be    ₁
```

Note that here again, the VP is semantically saturated, and therefore, the subject position must be filled by a dummy element.

In English, there are two kinds of dummy NP, NP[*there*] and NP[*it*]. They are NPs with their NFORM value *there* and *it* (2.1 (18)). Their lexical entries are given below. As for the definition of S-mates, see 1.2 (20).

(8) lexical entry for dummy *there* (cf. Sadock 2012: 65 (99))
   syntax: NP[*there*, 3]
   ➢ NP[*there*] and an existentially quantified NP (EQNP) must be S-mates.
   ➢ NP[*there*] and its licensing verb must be S-mates.
   F/A: nil
   RS: nil
   morph: Word
   mphon: /ðɛɚ/

Although the number (NUM) of *there* is not specified in (8), the person (PER) is specified as third person in syntax (Pollard and Sag 1994: 147 (141), Sag et al. 2003: 338 (13)), which is illustrated with *There is only you in my heart* (from the web). NP[*there*] needs an S-mate licensing verb, which includes the verb *be*. This means that in the *there* constructions (3) and (6), the presence of *be* is obligatory. Observe the contrast between *I consider there to be a solution* and **I consider there a solution* (Chomsky 1995: 158). The licensing verbs for NP[*there*] also include verbs of existence and appearance, such as *remain*, *appear*, and *seem*, as in *There seems no reason for it* (from the web).

(9) lexical entry for dummy *it* (cf. Sadock 2012: 33 (20))
   syntax: NP[*it*, 3SGN]
   F/A: nil
   RS: nil
   morph: Word
   mphon: /ɪt/

Although (8) and (9) are the same in their F/A, RS, and morphology, the syntactic field of (8) is more specific than that of (9), because the former has two additional conditions. Therefore, wherever NP[*there*] can occur, NP[*it*] is prevented from appearing in the same environment by the Elsewhere Principle (1.1.2 (3)).

Remarkable characteristics of the *there* construction are not only that the theme NP in (3) and (6) must carry new information, but also that it must be interpretable as existentially quantified (EQ) (McCawley 1993: 225, 1998: 635, 1999: 42):

the EQNP appears in most cases in the form of a syntactically indefinite NP but in some cases in the form of a syntactically definite NP, as in *There were the usual people at the party* (i.e., people whom one might expect to find) or *There's this funny-looking guy at the door* (i.e., some funny looking guy to whom I now shift the topic) (Sadock 2012: 65). Huddleston and Pullum (2002: 1398–1401) list five distinct cases where a definite NP is interpreted as new information.

Our claim about (8) is that the existential quantifier that is found in the F/A of the *there* construction in (12) is not introduced by the dummy ("existential") *there* (Sadock 2012: 65 (99)), but by the existentially quantified theme NP (EQNP) (McCawley 1993: 225–226, McCawley 1998: 635, McCawley 1999: 42), whose modular correspondences are given in (10).

(10) modular correspondences for an EQNP
 syntax: [$_{NP}$ (DET) N']
 F/A: [$_{QPx}$ [$_Q$ ∃] [$_{PROP}$ [$_{ARG}$ x], [$_{Fa}$ ARG, [$_{Faa}$ =]]]]
 ➢ The value of the ARG comes from the N'.

Note that the existential quantifier (∃) in (10) comes from existential quantifier uses of the indefinite article (1.3 (20)) and the definite article (1.3 (23)), or from EQNP uses of a singular mass noun (*There is time left*) and a plural count noun (11b) (cf. 5.4 (10)). Our approach avoids the problem pointed out by Sadock (2012: 235 note 33) that there would be two existential quantifiers in the *there* construction, one coming from the "existential" *there* and the other from the theme EQNP.

There is reason to believe that in the number agreement pattern of the *there* construction in Standard English, the dummy *there* carries the same NUMBER (NUM) value as the theme EQNP.

(11) a. There seems/*seem to be [$_{EQNP[3SG]}$ a solution] {in the book | available}.
 b. There *seems/seem to be [$_{EQNP[3PL]}$ solutions] {in the book | available}.
 c. There is [$_{EQNP[3SG]}$ a solution] {in the book | available}, isn't/*aren't there?
 d. There are [$_{EQNP[3PL]}$ solutions] {in the book | available}, *isn't/aren't there?
 e. You said there is [$_{EQNP[3SG]}$ a solution] {in the book | available}, but I think there isn't/*aren't.
 f. You said there are [$_{EQNP[3PL]}$ solutions] {in the book | available}, but I think there *isn't/aren't.

The verb *seem* in (11a, b) agrees in number with the theme EQNP. If we take the view that in tag questions, the auxiliary verb and the pronoun subject agree in person and number, as in *isn't he?* and *aren't they?*, then the dummy *there* in the tag questions in (11c, d) must have its own AGR value. (11e, f) are VP ellipsis examples with the *there* construction. Here again, we need to assume that the dummy *there* must have its own AGR value.

Let us look at two examples of the *there* construction, the modular representations of *there is a solution in the book* (an instance of (3)) and *there is a solution available* (an instance of (6)) and consider how agreement is achieved between the dummy *there* and the verb *be*.

(12) a. F/A of *There is a solution in the book*   b. F/A of *There is a solution available*

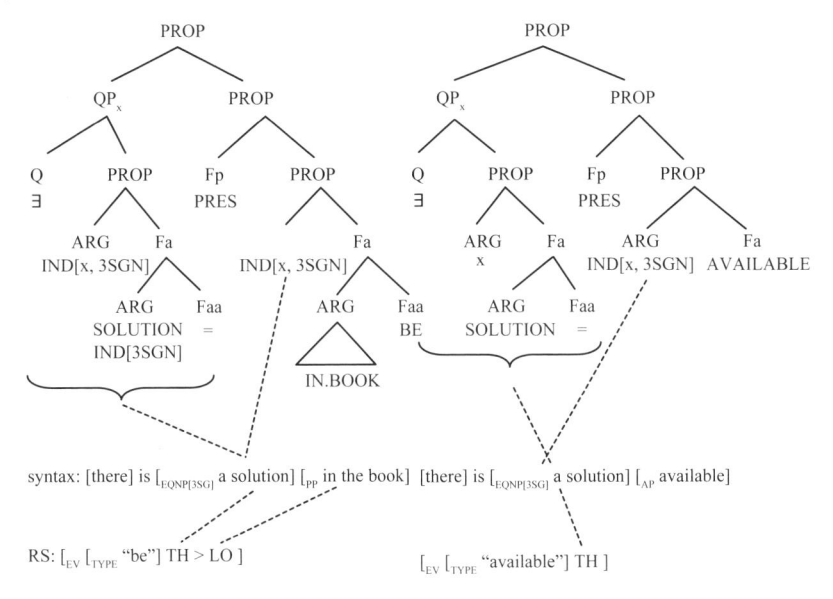

[tree diagrams]

syntax: [there] is [$_{EQNP[3SG]}$ a solution] [$_{PP}$ in the book]   [there] is [$_{EQNP[3SG]}$ a solution] [$_{AP}$ available]

RS: [$_{EV}$ [$_{TYPE}$ "be"] TH > LO]   [$_{EV}$ [$_{TYPE}$ "available"] TH]

In (12), the agreement controller of the *there* construction is the theme EQNP, according to the generalized agreement (2.1 (23)), repeated here as (13).

(13) agreement (generalized)
   a. definition of agreement controller
      The agreement controller of a finite (auxiliary) verb is the NP that the finite (auxiliary) verb agrees with.

b. generalized agreement
The agreement controller of a finite (auxiliary) verb is the NP whose F/A correspondent is the subject ARG that is c-commanded by the TENSE that is realized on the finite (auxiliary) verb in question.

In (12a, b), the agreement controller of the finite verb *is* is the theme EQNP. Note that the quantifier phrase QP_x and the variable ARG[IND[x, 3SGN]] in the matrix PROP correspond to the theme EQNP *a solution*. Therefore, one of the F/A correspondents of the theme EQNP is the variable ARG[IND[x, 3SGN]], which is the subject ARG that is c-commanded by the PRES tense that is realized on the finite verb *is*. The agreement between *there* and the verb *is* is achieved through (i) agreement between the EQNP and the finite verb by the generalized agreement (13b), (ii) the finite verb and its mother VP node sharing the agreement value by the Head Feature Convention (HFC) (1.2 (3)), and (iii) agreement between the VP and the subject NP *there* by the regular agreement in syntax (2.1 (21a)). The whole picture of agreement in the *there* construction is given in (14).

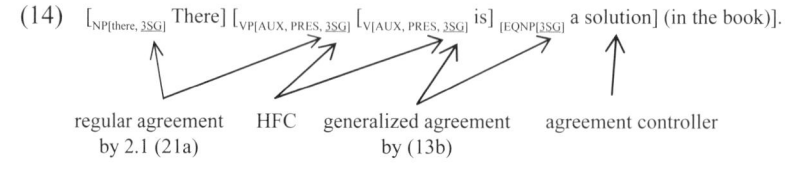

(14) [_NP[there, 3SG] There] [_VP[AUX, PRES, 3SG] [_V[AUX, PRES, 3SG] is] _[EQNP[3SG] a solution] (in the book)].

regular agreement   HFC   generalized agreement   agreement controller
by 2.1 (21a)   by (13b)

Some remarks on the F/A structures in (12) are in order. First, the Faa functor = is a type-identity functor that takes two arguments and denotes that the first (higher) ARG is equal to the second (lower) ARG in type; that is, 'x is equal to SOLUTION in type' or 'x is an instance of SOLUTION' (1.3 (8b) and (21)). Second, a predicate noun lacks a referential index (1.3 (8)). Third, the INDEX (IND) feature consists of the referential index (ref) and the AGREEMENT (AGR) feature, which in turn consists of PER, NUM, and GEN (IND[ref, AGR]) (1.3 (6)). Fourth, a variable is technically the INDEX feature whose referential index is the variable (IND[x, AGR]). Finally, the ARG SOLUTION has IND[3SGN] (third person, singular, neuter) without its referential index. The subject ARG in the QP_x is a variable IND[x, 3SGN], whose AGR value 3SGN comes from that of SOLUTION through the type-identity Faa functor =. The variable in the matrix PROP must have the same IND value IND[x, 3SGN].

The agreement pattern when the dummy *there* undergoes subject raising (4.1) is explained in the same way. In this example, just as in the previous example, the agreement controller of the finite verb *seems* is the theme EQNP *a mistake*, because the F/A correspondent of the theme EQNP is the subject variable ARG[IND[x, 3SGN]] that is c-commanded by the PRES tense that is realized on the finite verb in question.

(15) the *there* construction in subject raising: *There seems to have been a mistake in the proof*
RS: [$_{EV}$ [$_{TYPE}$ "seem"] [$_{TH}$ [$_{EV}$ [$_{TYPE}$ "be"] TH > LO]]]

F/A:

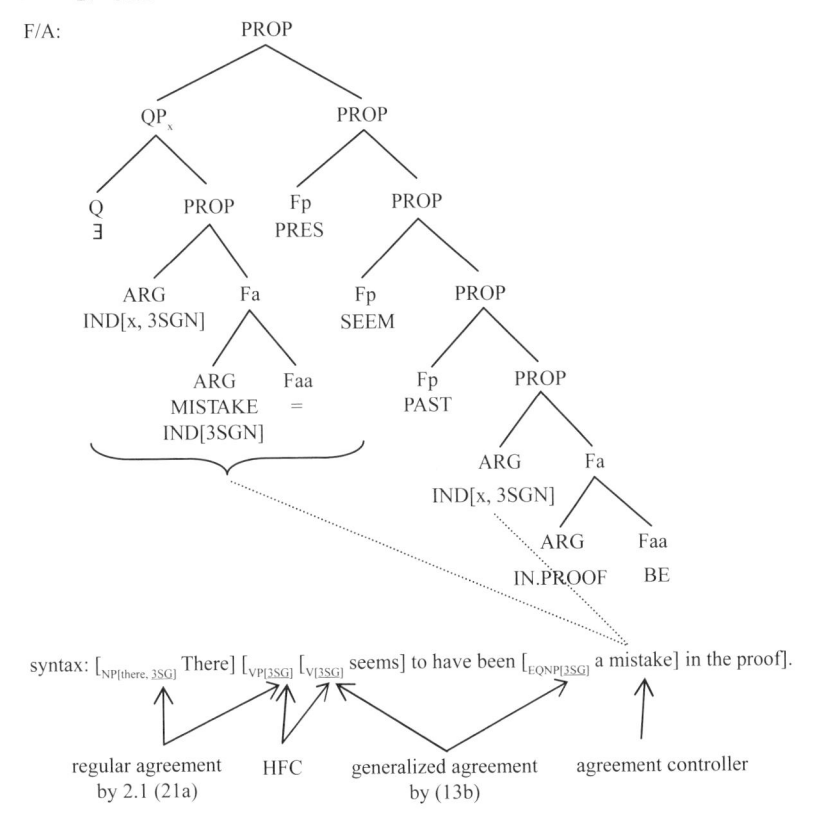

```
                           PROP
                    ┌────────┴────────┐
                   QP_x              PROP
                 ┌──┴──┐          ┌───┴───┐
                 Q    PROP        Fp     PROP
                 ∃   ┌─┴─┐       PRES   ┌──┴──┐
                   ARG   Fa            Fp    PROP
                 IND[x, 3SGN] ┌─┴─┐   SEEM  ┌──┴──┐
                            ARG  Faa        Fp   PROP
                          MISTAKE  =        PAST ┌──┴──┐
                          IND[3SGN]             ARG    Fa
                                             IND[x, 3SGN] ┌─┴─┐
                                                        ARG   Faa
                                                     IN.PROOF  BE
```

syntax: [$_{NP[there, 3SG]}$ There] [$_{VP[3SG]}$ [$_{V[3SG]}$ seems] to have been [$_{EQNP[3SG]}$ a mistake] in the proof].

regular agreement   HFC   generalized agreement   agreement controller
by 2.1 (21a)   by (13b)

2.5 Clausal Subject

An NP subject and a clausal subject are different in that the former (1a) but not the latter (1b) can appear as the subject of an inverted clause (S[INV]).

82   2 CLAUSE STRUCTURES

(1) a. [$_{S[INV, PRES]}$ Has [$_{S[PSP]}$ [$_{NP}$ the fact] surprised John]]?
    b. *[$_{S[INV, PRES]}$ Has [$_{S[PSP]}$ [$_{CP[that]}$ that Mary passed the exam] surprised John]]?
    c. [$_{S[PRES]}$ [$_{CP[that]}$ That Mary passed the exam] has surprised John].
    d. A: John said that Mary passed the exam.
       B: That's/It's not true.

We explain this fact by claiming that the syntactic category of a clausal subject in (1b) is CP[*that*] and introducing the PS rule (2a), in which CP[*that*] is the subject of a noninverted FINITE clause. We already have the default PS rule (2b) and these two PS rules exclude a clausal subject from a nonfinite clause: for example, in (1b), where CP[*that*] is directly dominated by the nonfinite S[PSP] node, thus violating (2a). In (2a, b), the VFORM value on VP and that on its mother S are identical due to the Head Feature Convention (1.2 (3)). The syntax, F/A, and RS of a clausal subject sentence are given in (2c) as an example.

(2) a. [$_{S[FIN]}$ CP[*that*], VP[FIN]]
    b. [$_{S[\alpha]}$ NP, VP[α]] (α = VFORM value)
    c. the syntax, F/A, and RS of *That Mary passed the exam shocked John*

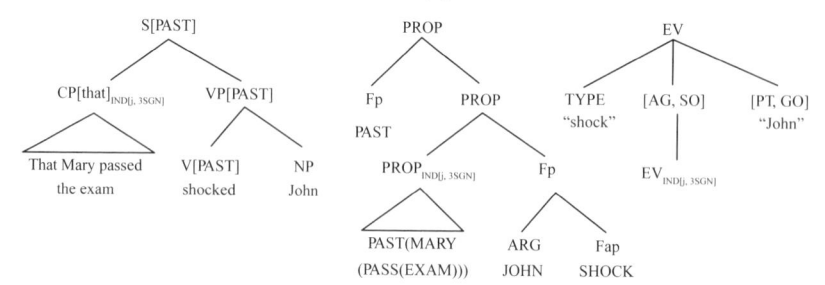

```
              S[PAST]                        PROP                              EV
             /       \                      /     \                         /      \
    CP[that]$_{IND[j, 3SGN]}$  VP[PAST]   Fp      PROP                  TYPE   [AG, SO]   [PT, GO]
       /    \              / \           |                            "shock"
                                        PAST
  That Mary passed    V[PAST]   NP    PROP$_{IND[j, 3SGN]}$     Fp            EV$_{IND[j, 3SGN]}$
    the exam         shocked   John         /    \             / \
                                      PAST(MARY     ARG     Fap
                                     (PASS(EXAM)))  JOHN   SHOCK
```

In (1c), the clausal subject (CP[*that*]) and the finite auxiliary verb (*has*) agree in PERSON and NUMBER (third person singular), which is a semantically controlled agreement (Jerry Sadock (p.c.)). In general, a PROP in F/A, when referred to by an anaphoric device, is third person singular neuter (3SGN). For example, in (1d), either the whole proposition 'John said that Mary passed the exam' or the internal proposition 'Mary passed the exam' is referred to by the 3SGN form *it* or *that*. Therefore, we assume that a PROP in F/A carries the INDEX feature IND[j, 3SGN] with 3SGN as its AGR value (cf. the AGR value 3SGN on the S node in 2.1 (21a)) and with the referential index j. We assume further that CP[*that*] in syntax and EVENT in RS that this PROP corresponds to also share the same INDEX value by Feature Osmosis (cf. the paragraph before 1.3 (6)).

When the subject is coordinated clauses, as in (3), the NUMBER value on the finite verb has a semantic effect: whether distributive reading is available or not. (3a) with singular agreement means that the conjunction of the two propositions 'the price of gas went up' and 'the price of gold went down' is not surprising. The distributive reading, in which each of the two propositions isn't surprising, is not available, because there is only one CP[*that*] in the subject position and thus singular agreement is required. See (3a', a"). In contrast, in (3b), the subject is coordinated CP[*that*] clauses, and both singular and plural agreements are possible. When the agreement is in the singular, nondistributive reading (namely, the conjunction of the two propositions is not surprising) obtains. On the other hand, when the agreement is in the plural, distributive reading obtains. See (3b', b").

(3) McCawley 1998: 117
    a. [That the price of gas went up and the price of gold went down] isn't/*aren't surprising.
    a'. [$_{CP[that,\ IND[j,\ 3\underline{SG}N]]}$ S[FIN] and S[FIN]] isn't surprising. (nondistributive reading)
    a". PRES(NOT([$_{PROP[IND[j,\ 3\underline{SG}N]]}$ PROP AND PROP] [$_{Fp}$ SURPRISING])) (nondistributive reading)
    b. [That the price of gas went up] and [that the price of gold went down] isn't/aren't surprising.
    b'. [$_{CP[that,\ IND[\{j,\ k\},\ 3\underline{PL}N]]}$ CP[*that*, IND[j, 3$\underline{SG}$N]] and CP[*that*, IND[k, 3$\underline{SG}$N]]] aren't surprising. (distributive reading)
    b". PRES(NOT([$_{PROP[IND[\{j,\ k\},\ 3\underline{PL}N]]}$ PROP[IND[j, 3$\underline{SG}$N]] AND PROP[IND[k, 3$\underline{SG}$N]]] [$_{Fp}$ SURPRISING])) (distributive reading)

The mechanism of distributive reading involved (3b) is the same mechanism by which an ordinary NP-subject clause, such as *The books are interesting*, is interpreted (cf. See related discussion on individual predicate and de-aggregation in 5.4 (8)).

Some verbs, such as *capture*, *express*, *describe*, and *support*, take an NP complement but do not take a CP[*that*] complement (4a, b), (namely, V in [$_{VP}$ __ {NP | *CP[*that*]}]), although they can semantically take a propositional complement, as in (4a). When verbs of this class are passivized, a clausal subject becomes possible (4b') in a finite clause. The same situation arises with object-raising verbs, such as *believe*. The object position of this class of verbs can be occupied by an NP and not by a CP[*that*] (4c, d), although semantically a propositional complement is acceptable (4c). When these verbs are passivized, a clausal subject becomes possible (4d') in a finite clause. The details will be discussed in 3.5 (1c) and 4.2.1 (8d).

(4) a. This theory captures [$_{NP}$ the fact that any language is learnable].
 b. *This theory captures [$_{CP[that]}$ that any language is learnable].
 b'. [$_{CP[that]}$ That any language is learnable] is captured by this theory.
 c. I believe [$_{NP}$ the report that the country is hiding nuclear facilities] to be true.
 d. *I believe [$_{CP[that]}$ that the country is hiding nuclear facilities] to be true.
 d'. [$_{CP[that]}$ That the country is hiding nuclear facilities] is believed to be true.

Some speakers accept inverted clauses with a clausal subject, such as (1b). For example, in Gazdar et al. (1982: 613), *Does that she is here surprise you?* is judged acceptable. On the other hand, Grosu and Thompson (1977: 163) reported that some speakers do not even accept noninverted finite clauses with a clausal subject. According to Traugott (1972: 102) and Stockwell (1977: 310), clausal subjects became established in the history of the English language as recently as in the 19th century. We can interpret the idiolectal/dialectal fluctuations of the acceptability of clausal subjects as due to two factors: (i) that the clausal subject first became established in the most stable and least marked subject position, that is, the matrix subject position of a noninverted finite clause, and (ii) that its distribution is in the process of being extended to the subject position in an inverted clause. If we understand the clausal subject this way, the two PS rules in (2a, b) look quite natural as a reflection of this ongoing process. Those speakers who accept a clausal subject only in a noninverted finite clause have (2a) as well as (2b). Those who do not accept a clausal subject anywhere have only (2b). Those who accept a clausal subject in an inverted clause have generalized (2a) to [$_{S[\alpha]}$ CP[*that*], VP[α]] by eliminating the restriction of finiteness.

It has often been claimed (Safir 1985: 85–86, Koster 1978: 59–60, Koster 1987: 262–263, Bresnan 2001: 20 among others) that a clausal subject is a topic and occupies the topic position that is higher than the subject position. The motivation for this claim is that it explains why a clausal subject cannot undergo subject-auxiliary inversion. However, this claim is fraught with problems and we reject it categorically. First, this claim predicts that the distribution of a clausal subject is the same as that of a topic NP. However, there are syntactic environments where a clausal subject can occur but a topic NP cannot.

(5) PP[*because*] (Grosu and Thompson 1977: 123)
   a. Sam is eating at home, not because <u>for him to dine out</u> would be against social conventions, but because he enjoys his wife's cooking.
   b. *Sam is eating at home, not because <u>pheasant</u> he dislikes, but because <u>beans</u> he prefers.

Second, Kuno (1972: 297ff.) showed that an NP subject can be interpreted in four ways: noncontrastive topic, contrastive topic, exhaustive listing, and part of a neutral description, whereas a topicalized NP allows only contrastive topic interpretation. According to Grosu and Thompson (1977: 123–124), a clausal subject allows all the four interpretations. Third, according to Grosu and Thompson (1977: 124), comma intonation is possible at the end of a topicalized NP, whereas it is impossible at the end of an NP subject and a clausal subject. Fourth, a clausal subject allows a clausal subject within itself (6a, b), which would amount to topicalization within a topic. However, a topicalized CP[*that*] does not allow a topicalized NP within itself (6c, d).

(6) a. That <u>for Bill to resign</u> would cause a commotion has never been in the slightest doubt. (Grosu and Thompson 1977: 109)
    b. That <u>for Americans to visit Cuba</u> is illegal is unthinkable. (McCawley 1988: 312)
    c. *That <u>Bill</u>, Mary loves, I simply can't believe. (Grosu and Thompson 1977: 109)
    d. *That <u>Bill</u>, Mary loves, everyone thinks is not true. (Grosu and Thompson 1977: 109)

Fifth, "*wh*-movement" is possible out of a clausal subject, as in (7), under certain restricted conditions. However, "*wh*-movement" out of a topicalized NP is always pretty bad (8).

(7) a. This is something which for you to try to understand would be futile. (Kuno and Takami 1993: 51)
b. This is something which I think for you to try to understand would be futile.

(8) a. ??Who do you think that pictures of, John wanted? (Lasnik and Saito 1992: 101)
a'. *This is someone who I think that pictures of, John wanted.
b. ??Vowel harmony, I think that articles about, you should read carefully. (Lasnik and Saito 1992: 101)
b'. *This is the topic (that) I think that articles about, you should read carefully.

Sixth, if a clausal subject was always a topic, it would predict that it could not appear at the sentence-final position and bear a focus/new information status. However, a clausal subject can occur in the subject-predicate inversion construction (4.1 (26)), just as a regular NP subject.

(9) a. Even more important is for the outside guarantors to pre-empt divisions among themselves by making sure the parties fulfill their commitments to arrest and extradite suspects, supply requested evidence and permit unhindered access to crime scenes. (*The Washington Post*, January 23, 1996 editorial)
b. Underlying our view of elliptical structure is that in order for it to count as projected structure, it must be reconstructed, that is, satisfy structural identity conditions. (Fiengo and May. 1994. *Indices and Identity*. MIT Press. p. 258)
c. Of particular interest is that if a factive is embedded to a proposition with past tense, then the factive complement can be past or nonpast. (Elizabeth Closs Traugott. 1972. *A History of English Syntax*. p. 61)
d. The criterion I have given for distinguishing factives from nonfactives is primarily a semantic one; there are, however, many syntactic reasons for distinguishing factives from nonfactives. Among them is that in 2. 198 it can be replaced by the fact .... (E. C. Traugott. 1972. *A History of English Syntax*. p.60)

2.6 Locative Inversion

The locative inversion construction, which is illustrated in (1), begins with a locative PP and ends with a theme NP. It has a special discourse property that the theme NP is presentationally focused. This is as if a scene (the sentence-initial PP and the finite verb) is set and a referent (the sentence-final theme NP) is introduced or reintroduced on the scene to become a new focus of attention (Bresnan 1994: 90, 92).

(1) Bresnan 1994: 75
 a. In the corner was a lamp.
 b. Among the guests was sitting my friend Rose.
 c. Back to the village came the tax collector.
 d. Crashing through the woods came a wild boar.
 e. Coiled on the floor lay a one-hundred-fifty-foot length of brailed nylon climbing rope three-eighths of an inch thick.

The sentence-initial PP is locative in a broad sense, covering goal (1c) and path (1d). Also, the sentence-initial scene can be a VP[PRP] (i.e., present participle VP) or VP[PAS] (i.e., passive participle VP) that contains a locative PP (1d, e). It is well known that a transitive verb cannot occur in the construction; that is, the verb must be intransitive including a passivized transitive. (See 3.8 for passive locative inversion.) This is because transitive verbs take two NPs (subject and object) but the locative inversion construction requires only one NP (the presentationally focused theme NP). The theme NP is in the accusative, which is clear when it is a pronoun.

(2) Among the guests of honor was sitting HER. [*her* stressed with a pointing gesture] (Bresnan 1994: 86)

Although the construction must have a theme (TH) and a locative (LO), the theme NP can be agentive, which is shown in (3). (Jerry Sadock (p.c.) pointed out to me that (3) sounds "very odd" to some speakers including himself.) This is because, according to Bresnan, the scene of shooting through the window serves to locate the sniper. Therefore, the construction must impose the theme interpretation of the agent (shooter) in (3). Since we have been using the two-tiered participant roles (1.4), we claim that the TH-LO requirement of the locative construction (4) refers only to the thematic tier of the roles involved in the construction.

(3) Through the window on the second story was shooting a sniper. (Bresnan 1994: 84)
     _____/   _____/
                        LO   [AG, TH]

The role of the NP *a sniper* in (3) is [AG, TH], that is, agent (AG) on the action tier and theme (TH) on the thematic tier. Note that the RS field of the lexical entry for the verb *shoot* is [$_{EV}$ [$_{TYPE}$ "shoot"] [AG, SO] [PT, TH] GO], as in *shoot* [$_{[PT, TH]}$ *a bullet*] [$_{GO}$ *at the target*] or [$_{EV}$ [$_{TYPE}$ "shoot"] [AG, SO] [PT, GO]], as in *shoot* [$_{[PT, GO]}$ *a rabbit*]. In either RS field, a locative that shows the location of the AG (shooter) is not a required role in a shooting event. Also, the shooter role in both RSs is [AG, SO], not [AG, TH]. Therefore, we claim that the TH-LO requirement of locative inversion does not come from the lexical information of the verb that appears in the construction, but rather must come from the construction itself. For this reason, locative inversion can be better formalized as a construction than as a lexical rule. The lexical entry for the locative inversion construction is given in (4).

(4) lexical entry for the locative inversion construction

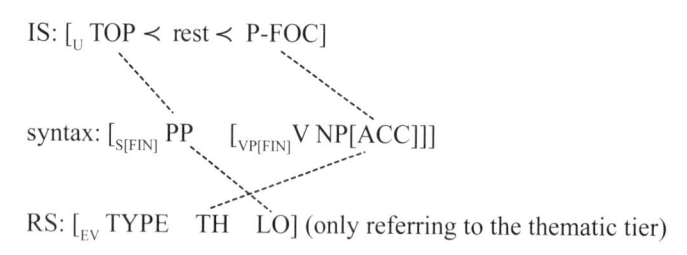

   IS: [$_U$ TOP ≺ rest ≺ P-FOC]

   syntax: [$_{S[FIN]}$ PP   [$_{VP[FIN]}$ V NP[ACC]]]

   RS: [$_{EV}$ TYPE   TH   LO] (only referring to the thematic tier)

The locative PP and the theme NP correspond respectively to the topic (TOP) ("stage topic" in Erteschik-Shir 2007: 68) and the presentational focus (P-FOC) in IS, where the order is specified: the topic is utterance-initial and the presentational focus utterance-final. There is a mismatch between syntax and RS, which is due to the ordering requirement in IS. In syntax, the PP asymmetrically c-commands the NP, whereas in RS, TH outranks LO on the thematic tier (1.4 (6)).

2.6 LOCATIVE INVERSION

The F/A of the locative inversion construction is not included in (4), because it is predictable from the RS specification. The F/A is [$_{PROP}$ ARG [$_{Fa}$ ARG Faa]], in which the subject ARG and the lower ARG correspond harmoniously to TH and LO in RS, respectively.

In the syntax of (4), the locative PP and the VP are directly dominated by an S[FIN]. However, locative inversion cannot occur in an inverted clause (5), because the locative PP in an inverted clause would be directly dominated by a nonfinite S. This violates 2.5 (2b), which only licenses an NP subject for a non-finite S.

(5) Bresnan 1994: 108
   a. Do you remember? *Did [$_{S[BSE]}$ [on the wall] hang a Mexican serape]?
   b. *Was [$_{S[PAS]}$ [among the ruins] found a skeleton]?

We claim that the locative PP occupies the same syntactic position as the run-of-the-mill NP subject, that is, the NP position that is a sister of VP and is directly dominated by the mother S. First, in a tag question, the subject of the tag must be the pronoun corresponding to the matrix subject and in the case of locative inversion, *there* is used as the subject of the tag (6a). This shows that *there* is the pro-form of the locative PP and the PP occupies the subject position in syntax. Second, the locative PP, when "moved," shows the "*that*-trace effect," showing that a phonologically null PP gap (PP[G]) must occupy the position right after the complementizer *that* (6b). Third, an interrogative *wh*-phrase appears before the locative PP (6c). As will be discussed in 6.1.1 (1a), the internal syntax of a *wh*-question is [$_{CP[WH[Q]]}$ XP[WH[Q]] S]. Therefore, the only place the locative PP can occupy is the subject position of the matrix S. Fourth, when the locative PP contains a *wh*-word, a *wh*-question is possible without subject-auxiliary inversion (6d, e), exactly like a subject *wh*-question. (6h) is an example of locative inversion in a nonrestrictive relative clause. Fifth, the locative PP, just like an NP subject, undergoes subject-to-subject raising (6f, g), which will be discussed in 4.1 (21) and (22).

(6) a. In the garden is a beautiful statue, isn't there? (Bresnan 1994: 97)
   b. It's in these villages that we all believe (*that) [$_S$ __ can be found the best examples of this cuisine]. (Bresnan 1994: 97)
   c. We all witnessed how [$_S$ [down the hill] came rolling a huge baby carriage]. (Bresnan 1994: 102)

d. On which wall hung a portrait of the artist? (Bresnan 1994: 102)
e. *On which wall did hang a portrait of the artist? (*did* unstressed)
f. [Over my window sill] seems to have crawled an entire army of ants. (Bresnan 1994: 96)
g. [In these villages] are likely to be found the best examples of this cuisine. (Bresnan 1994: 96)
h. He (*referring to John L. Austin*) produces a tentative five-fold classification that he implies emerges naturally, as genera might if you were collecting butterflies, into which may be sorted the many thousands of performative verbs that he estimates to be in the language. (Levinson 1983: 234)

The agreement on the finite verb of the locative inversion construction is not determined by the locative PP. Although it occupies the same syntactic position as the ordinary NP subject ([$_S$ NP VP]), the PP lacks an AGREEMENT feature (AGR). The agreement is determined by the theme NP in the VP (7), because the agreement controller (2.1 (23a)) is the theme NP.

(7) a. In the swamp was/*were found [a child]. (Bresnan 1994: 95)
   b. In the swamp were/*was found [two children].
   c. the F/A and RS of (7a)

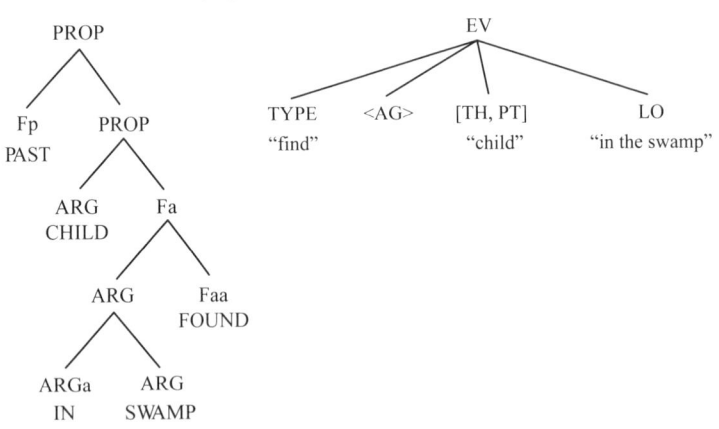

```
        PROP                                EV
       /    \                          /     |    \
     Fp    PROP           TYPE    <AG>  [TH, PT]    LO
     PAST  /    \         "find"        "child"   "in the swamp"
         ARG    Fa
         CHILD  /  \
              ARG   Faa
              /  \  FOUND
           ARGa  ARG
           IN    SWAMP
```

This agreement pattern is predicted by the generalized agreement (2.1 (23b)): the agreement controller of a finite (auxiliary) verb is the NP whose F/A correspondent is the subject ARG that is c-commanded by the TENSE that is realized on the finite verb in question. In the case of (7a, b), the subject ARG in F/A is the theme ARG, because TH outranks LO, according to the Role Hierarchy (1.4 (6)). This theme ARG is c-commanded by the PAST that is realized on the finite verbs *was* and *were*. Therefore, the theme NP is the agreement controller. Note that the other ARG (i.e., the locative ARG, which corresponds to the PP in syntax) lacks its AGR feature and hence cannot be the agreement controller, anyway.

2.7 Extraposition

There are three types of extraposition: extraposition from subject (1a), extraposition from object (1b, c, d), and extraposition from prepositional object (1e). Extraposition of CP[*that*] arises when a speaker wants to express a proposition (PROP) as one of the arguments of a verb, but its syntactic correspondent (CP[*that*]) is not allowed by the syntactic field of the lexical entry for that verb, or when a speaker wants to postpone the clausal subject or object (PROP in F/A) to the clause-final position for processing or informational purposes. Under these circumstances, the speaker can fill the NP position with the dummy *it* (NP[*it*]), whose lexical entry is given in 2.4 (9), and express the PROP as a clause-final CP[*that*] in syntax. Note that the verbs in (1b, c, d, e) cannot take a CP[*that*] complement directly.

(1) a. It surprised me [that John quit his job]. (McCawley 1998: 103)
 b. I took it for granted [that George would help us]. (McCawley 1998: 105)
  cf. *I took [that George would help us] for granted.
 c. He never gave it a thought [that Bolshies are human beings]. (McCawley 1998: 105)
  cf. *He never gave [that Bolshies are human beings] a thought.
 d. I can't help it [that I'm madly in love with Edith]. (McCawley 1998: 105)
  cf. *I can't help [that I'm madly in love with Edith].
 e. You can depend on it [that he'll try to make trouble]. (McCawley 1998: 105)
  cf. *You can depend on [that he'll try to make trouble].

The constituent structure of extraposition is such that the extraposed CP[*that*] is adjoined to the VP.

(2) [$_{VP}$ [$_{VP}$ V ...] CP[*that*]] (McCawley 1998: 106)

This constituent structure is confirmed by (i) VP-preposing (3), (ii) coordination of the inner VP (4), and (iii) *too* placement (4). As discussed in McCawley (1998: 70), the test of placing the focus bearing element *too* is to determine where a constituent ends.

(3) I warned you that it would upset Rosa that you smoke, and [upset her that you smoked] it certainly did. (Reinhart 1983: 51, cited in McCawley 1998: 107)

(4) a. It [shocked me] and [angered me] too that Mary dumped me without telling me anything.
   b. I [gave it a thought] and [took it for granted] too that Mary and I would get married some day.
   c. I [gave it a thought] and [counted on it] too that John would help me whenever I needed him.

We can capture the relationships between the two sets of lexical entries (non-extraposed entries and extraposed entries) by the Extraposition Lexical Rule (cf. Gazdar et al. 1985: 118, Sag et al. 2003: 346, cf. Sadock 2012: 37 (29)).

(5) Extraposition Lexical Rule
   input   output
   syntax: V in [$_{VP}$ _, Σ]   →   V in [[$_{VP}$ _, Σ], CP[*that*]]
   F/A: Fφαχ   →   Fφpχ

What this lexical rule says is that when there is a verb that takes an argument (ARG) in F/A that is semantically compatible with a proposition, there is another lexical entry for this verb in which (i) CP[*that*] is adjoined to the VP headed by the verb in syntax, and (ii) in F/A, a PROP appears in place of the ARG. With this much specification, we can deduce the following: (i) the CP[*that*] in the syntax output of the lexical rule corresponds to the newly introduced PROP in the F/A output, (ii) in the RS output of the lexical rule, the participant role that corresponds to the ARG mentioned in the input comes to dominate an EV that corresponds to the introduced PROP, namely, [$_{ROLE}$ EV] (cf. (6)-(8) below), but this relation between the input ROLE and the output [$_{ROLE}$ EV] is predictable from the introduction of a new PROP in F/A and as such is not specified in the RS input and output of the lexical rule, and (iii) the NP that corresponds to the ARG mentioned in the input must be filled with the dummy *it* (NP[*it*]); otherwise, the output would be ill-formed, on the one hand, because (a) if the ARG mentioned in the input F/A is the subject, there would be no subject NP in the output syntax, or (b) if the ARG is the object, there would be no object NP in the output syntax, hence the output would violate the subcategorization of the verb, and on the other hand, because if an ordinary NP was used instead of the dummy *it*, there would be no role available to this NP in the RS of the verb's output lexical entry.

The lexical rule (5) correctly predicts that extraposition is only possible out of an argument. No extraposition is possible out of a modifier. For example, extraposition out of a passive *by*-phrase is impossible: **by it* CP[*that*]. (See 3.3 (5) for the passive *by*-phrase.)

(6) is an example, in which the lexical rule (5) is applied to the lexical entry for *shock*. The output lexical entry is needed for such an extraposition example as *It shocked me that Mary and John got married so soon*. Note that the subject NP of the output must be the dummy *it*, because there is no role available that corresponds to this NP. For ease of understanding, we have added the predictable, automatic changes in syntax and RS.

(6) input
    lexical entry for *shock*
    syntax: V in [__, NP]
    F/A: Faa
    RS: [$_{TYPE}$ "shock"] in
        [$_{EV}$ __ [AG, SO] [PT, GO]]

output
    lexical entry for *shock* with extraposition
    → V in [[__, NP], CP[*that*]]
    → Fap
    → [$_{TYPE}$ "shock"] in [$_{EV}$ __ [$_{[AG, SO]}$ EV]
        [PT, GO]]

(7) is an example, in which the lexical rule (5) is applied to the lexical entry for *regret*. The output lexical entry is needed for such an extraposition example as *I regretted it that Mary and I got married so soon*. Note that the object NP of the output must be the dummy *it*, again for the same reason that there is no role available that corresponds to this NP.

(7) input
    lexical entry for *regret*
    syntax: V in [__, NP]
    F/A: Faa

output
    lexical entry for *regret* with extraposition
    → V in [[__, NP[*it*]], CP[*that*]]
    → Fpa

94   2 CLAUSE STRUCTURES

RS: [$_{\text{TYPE}}$ "regret"] in   → [$_{\text{TYPE}}$ "regret"] in [$_{\text{EV}}$ __ [AG, LO]
[$_{\text{EV}}$ __ [AG, LO] [PT, TH]]   [$_{\text{[PT, TH]}}$ EV]]

(8) is an example, in which the lexical rule (5) is applied to the lexical entry for *depend*. The output lexical entry is needed for such an extraposition example as (1e). Note that the prepositional object NP of the output must be the dummy *it* for the same reason.

(8) input   output
     lexical entry for *depend*   lexical entry for *depend* with extraposition
     syntax: V in [__, PP[*on*]]   → V in [[__, [$_{\text{PP[}on\text{]}}$ P[*on*] NP[*it*]]], CP[*that*]]
     F/A: Faa   → Fpa
     RS: [$_{\text{TYPE}}$ "depend"] in   → [$_{\text{TYPE}}$ "depend"] in [$_{\text{EV}}$ __ [AG, TH]
     [$_{\text{EV}}$ __ [AG, TH] [PT, LO]]   [$_{\text{[PT, LO]}}$ EV]]

Chapter 3
Passive

> In this chapter, we review Sadock's (2012) analysis of passivization in terms of module-by-module lexical rule and extend it to a much wider range of data, including prepositional passives, and passivization of VP idioms and verbs that do not take an NP complement.

3.1 Agentless Passives of Transitive Verbs

3.1.1 The syntax, F/A, and RS of agentless passives

The syntax, F/A, and RS of an active sentence (1a) and its agentless passive counterpart (1b) are given below.

(1) a. The boy kicked the dog.

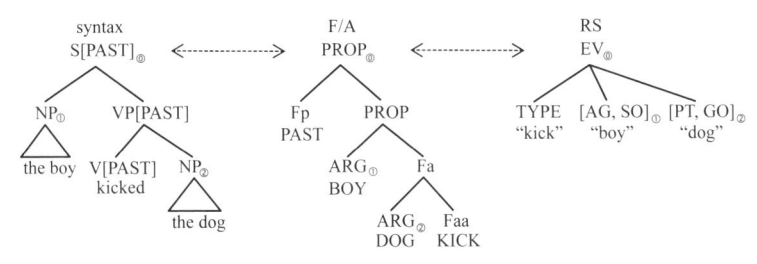

```
      syntax                    F/A                      RS
      S[PAST]_①    <------>    PROP_①    <------>     EV_①
       /    \                   /   \                  / | \
     NP_①   VP[PAST]          Fp    PROP          TYPE  [AG, SO]_①  [PT, GO]_②
     /\     /    \            PAST  /  \          "kick"   "boy"      "dog"
  the boy V[PAST] NP_②             ARG_①  Fa
          kicked  /\                BOY
                 /  \                   /  \
                the dog              ARG_②  Faa
                                     DOG    KICK
```

  b. The dog was kicked.

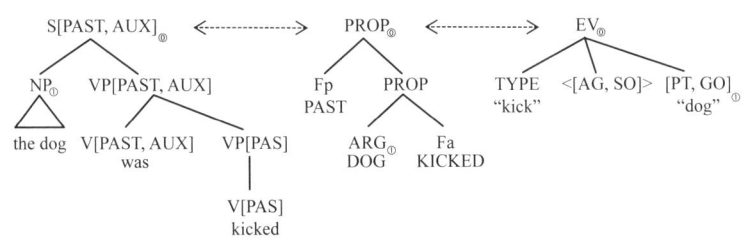

```
      S[PAST, AUX]_①  <------>  PROP_①  <------>  EV_①
       /       \                 /  \              / | \
     NP_①   VP[PAST, AUX]       Fp   PROP      TYPE  <[AG, SO]>  [PT, GO]_①
     /\      /        \         PAST  /  \     "kick"              "dog"
  the dog V[PAST, AUX]  VP[PAS]      ARG_①  Fa
           was            |          DOG    KICKED
                       V[PAS]
                       kicked
```

The intermodular correspondences between syntax, F/A, and RS in (1a) and those in (1b), which are indicated by circled numbers, are established by the default correspondence rules in 1.4 (7), repeated below as (2i).

(2i) a. default categorial correspondences
syntax   F/A   RS
S   <--->   PROP   <--->   EV
NP   <--->   ARG   <--->   ROLE
VP   <--->   Fa

b. default geometrical correspondences
  i. Dominance relations should be preserved between corresponding nodes in each module.
  ii. C-command relations in syntax and F/A should be preserved in RS as corresponding outrank relations.

(1a) is an active transitive sentence, which was discussed in 1.4 (8) and 1.6 (1). The subject $NP_①$ in syntax corresponds to the subject $ARG_①$ in F/A and the agent $[AG, SO]_①$ in RS, whereas the object $NP_②$ in syntax corresponds to the object $ARG_②$ in F/A and the patient $[PT, GO]_②$ in RS. Recall that subject NP in syntax and subject ARG in F/A refer to the NP in $[_S$ NP VP] (1.2 (1a)) and the ARG in $[_{PROP}$ ARG, Fa] (1.3 (2a)), respectively. Similarly, object NP in syntax and object ARG in F/A refer to the NP in $[_{VP}$ V NP] and the ARG in $[_{Fa}$ ARG, Faa], respectively. The intermodular correspondences in (1a) are established by (2ia, b). Note that $NP_①$ c-commands $NP_②$ in syntax, $ARG_①$ c-commands $ARG_②$ in F/A, and $[AG, SO]_①$ outranks $[PT, GO]_②$ in RS. The definitions of c-command in syntax, c-command in F/A, and outrank in RS are given in 1.2 (17), 1.3 (24), and 1.4 (6) (repeated here as (2ii)), respectively.

(1b) is a passive sentence. The subject $NP_①$ in syntax corresponds to the subject $ARG_①$ in F/A and the patient $[PT, GO]_①$ in RS. The empty verb *be* (2.1 (13e), Sadock 2012:29 (11)) is used (i) to carry the tense, because the passive participle (V[PAS] in syntax) is morphologically a full-fledged word (V[1, PSP] in morphology) and hence cannot inflect for tense, or (ii) to satisfy the subcategorization requirement of a lexical item that takes a VP complement. For example, in *The dog seemed* $[_{VP[to]}$ to $[_{VP[BSE]}$ *(be) kicked*]], *to* takes as its complement VP[BSE] (1.2 (12c)), but cannot take a VP[PAS] complement. The empty *be* is pressed into service to satisfy this requirement. The dummy verb *do* (2.1 (6d)) is impossible here (*_The dog did kicked_), because it takes a VP[BSE] (a VP headed by a V[BSE]) as its complement. Except for the presence of the empty verb _be_, (1b) is an intransitive sentence, which is evident in its F/A, in which an Fa takes an ARG to form a PROP. The <AG> in the RS is an unassociable agent role (a.k.a. suppressed agent role) that counts as an agent in RS and is interpreted as such but corresponds to nothing in syntax and F/A (Sadock 2012: 82 (15)).

The relation c-command is defined in syntax (1.2 (17)) and in F/A (1.3 (24)). In RS, in place of c-command, the relation outrank is defined based on the Role Hierarchy (1.4 (6)), repeated here as (2ii).

(2ii) a. Role Hierarchy
 (action tier) AG > PT > ø
 (thematic tier) SO > GO > TH > LO
 b. definition of outrank
  i. Outrank (" > ") is determined by the action tier. Otherwise, it is determined by the thematic tier.
  ii. If A outranks B and B dominates C in RS, then A outranks C.
  iii. If A outranks B and B outranks C, then A outranks C.

As for participant roles in RS, we have been assuming two-tiered roles (cf. the paragraph after 1.4 (3); Jackendoff 1990: 126–127); that is, a role is a combination of two roles: one from the action tier consisting of agent (AG) and patient (PT), and the other from the thematic tier consisting of source (SO), goal (GO), theme (TH), and locative (LO). For example, in _John gave a book to Mary_, _John_ carries the role of [AG, SO], which is AG on the action tier and at the same time SO on the thematic tier, _a book_ carries the role of [PT, TH], and _Mary_ carries GO, which is GO on the thematic tier but no specification on the action tier. The definition of outrank (2iib) says that any role with AG (i.e., AG with or without a thematic tier specification) outranks any role with PT (i.e., PT with or without a thematic tier specification) (i.e., AG > PT), which in turn outranks any role that is not specified for the action tier. If roles are not specified for the action tier, SO outranks GO, GO outranks TH, and TH outranks LO (i.e., SO > GO > TH > LO). For example, in the above example of _give_, [AG, SO] > [PT, TH] > GO. Also, in _The book lay on the desk_, _the book_ is TH and _the desk_ is LO. Because both lack their specification for the action tier, TH outranks LO and the former corresponds to the subject NP in syntax.

3.1.2 Passive Lexical Rule

The relationships between active transitive clauses, such as (1a), and their agentless passive counterparts, such as (1b), can be stated in the lexicon by the Passive Lexical Rule (3) as regular relationships between lexical entries of transitive verbs and those of their passive participles. As we discussed in 2.1 (3b), a lexical rule is a rule that captures relationships between two sets of lexical entries in the lexicon. More specifically, a lexical rule says that if there is a lexical entry in the lexicon that meets its input conditions, there is another lexical entry in the lexicon that meets its output conditions. The Passive Lexical Rule captures the regular relationships between the set of lexical entries for active transitive verbs and the set of lexical entries for passive participles (V[PAS]).

(3) Passive Lexical Rule for transitive verbs (Sadock 2012: 83 (17), 152 (14))
input (active) output (passive)
syntax: V in [__, NP, ψ]   →   V[PAS] in [__, ψ]
F/A: Fφaa   →   Fφa
RS: TYPE in [$_{EV}$ __ AG PT χ]   →   TYPE in [$_{EV}$ __ <AG> PT χ]
morph: V[0]   →   V[1, PSP]

The specification of each module in this lexical rule is not independent of each other but closely related: in the output lexical entry, an NP is lost in syntax, an ARG is lost in F/A, and AG is made unassociable (suppressed) in RS. This output lexical entry, together with the default correspondences in (2i), predicts that the subject NP in syntax must correspond to the subject ARG in F/A, which in turn must correspond to the highest associable role PT in RS.

The defining property of the Passive Lexical Rule is its specification <AG> in the RS of the output lexical entry, which forces the passive participle in syntax and the corresponding functor in F/A to reduce its valance by one. The net result is that if we compare an active transitive clause and its passive counterpart side by side, a transitive verb corresponds to an intransitive verb (i.e., passive participle) in syntax, and the object ARG of the input transitive functor corresponds to the subject ARG of the output intransitive functor in F/A. This creates an illusion of the object NP moving to the subject NP position in syntax ("NP-movement") under passivization. Note that the V[PAS] in the syntax of the output lexical entry is passive participle, which is past participle (V[1, PSP]) in morphology. Below is an example of how the Passive Lexical Rule applies to the transitive verb *kick*.

(4) active
lexical entry for *kick*
syntax: V in [__, NP]   →   V[PAS] in [__]
F/A: Faa   →   Fa
RS: [_TYPE_ "kick"] in   →   [_TYPE_ "kick"] in [_EV_ __ <[AG, SO]>
   [_EV_ __ [AG, SO]   [PT, GO]]
    [PT, GO]]
morph: V[0]   →   V[1, PSP]

passive
lexical entry for the passive participle *kicked*

the F/A of the active *kick*   the F/A of the passive *kicked*

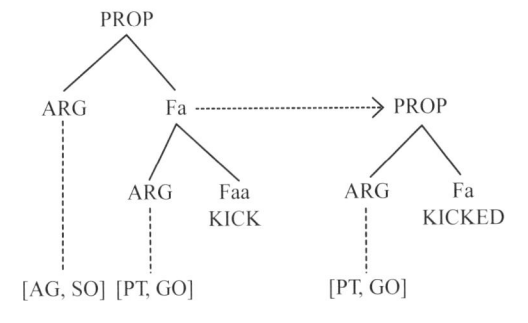

```
        PROP
       /    \
     ARG     Fa --------------→ PROP
            /   \              /    \
          ARG    Faa         ARG     Fa
                 KICK                KICKED

     [AG, SO] [PT, GO]             [PT, GO]
```

Lexical entries for passive participles (V[PAS]) are needed independently of whether the corresponding active lexical entries exist or not. There are a handful of verbs that are used only in the passive voice (Huddleston and Pullum 2002: 1435 and Quirk et al. 1985: 162). *Rumor* is such an example: *It is rumored that John failed the test* and *John is rumored to have failed the test* but **They rumored that John failed the test*. *Say* has a subject-raising use in the passive (*John is said to have failed the test*) without its corresponding object-raising use in the active (**People say John to have failed the test*). Furthermore, there are VP idioms that only exist in the passive: *be taken aback*, *be caught short*, and *be written/carved/ engraved/set in stone*.

Passive participles have an unassociable agent (<AG>) in the RS field of their lexical entry. Therefore, they can support intentional modifiers, such as *purposely* or *in order to* … (Sadock 2012: 81). On the other hand, the RS of the intransitive (unaccusative) verb *fall* is [_EV_ "fall" [PT, TH]], which lacks an agent, and it cannot support intentional modifiers. This is illustrated in (5).

(5) a. The tree was purposely felled. (Sadock 2012: 81)
   a'. The windows were broken in order to enter the house.
   b. *The tree purposely fell. (Sadock 2012: 80)
   b'. *The windows broke in order to enter the house.

The Passive Lexical Rule (3) requires that there be agent and patient in the RS field of an input lexical entry. (See 3.4 (14) and (15) on the notions of agent and patient.) If a verb lacks one or the other, it cannot passivize. For example, the transitive verb *compose* does not form a regular passive (6a). This is because it does not take agent or patient in its RS field and hence cannot be an input to the Passive Lexical Rule. The event described by this verb (6a') is stative, because it cannot be used in the progressive.

(6) a. *Water is composed by hydrogen and oxygen. (Bolinger 1975: 57)
   cf. Water is [$_A$ composed] *(of hydrogen and oxygen).
   a'. Hydrogen and oxygen compose/*are composing water.
   RS: [$_{TYPE}$ "compose"] in [$_{STATE}$ __ SO TH]
   b. *The University of Hawaii was entered by John in 1960. (Kuno 1983: 201)
   b'. The nuclear reactor was entered by a team of scientists for the first time yesterday. (Kuno 1983: 202)
   RS: [$_{TYPE}$ "enter"] in [$_{VA}$ __ <[AG, TH]> [PT, LO]]
   b''. The nuclear reactor was entered for the first time after the accident.

(6b) is unacceptable because *the University of Hawaii* does not qualify as a patient, an entity that has been affected by the event in question. We can only perceive *the University of Hawaii* as LO and not as [PT, LO]; that is, we cannot perceive it as having been affected by the event of John's entering it. However, *the nuclear reactor* in (6b') is easy to perceive as [PT, LO] because we understand easily that it was inspected by *a team of scientists*. This pair (6b, b') shows that the acceptability of a passive sentence depends on how easily the addressee/audience can perceive the referent of the patient role as having been affected by the event described. This cannot be determined grammatically on the basis of the syntactic structure of a passive sentence, but rather determined semantically and pragmatically in linguistic and nonlinguistic context.

Although the passive lexical rule in English requires the presence of both agent and patient in its input lexical entries, German passive is quite different in this respect: it does not require the presence of PT in RS or the presence of NP[ACC] in syntax. German allows intransitive verbs to be passivized, as in *Hier wurde gestorben und geliebt, gefeiert und geweint, demonstriert und getrunken ...* (Sadock 2012: 109), in which not only unergatives (*feiern, weinen, demonstrieren*) but also unaccusatives (*sterben*) are passivized. German also allows verbs with a dative object to be passivized and the dative NP stays in the dative under passivization, as in *Wir helfen dem Nachbarn* vs. *Dem Nachbarn wird* (*von uns*) *geholfen*.

Bolinger (1977: 10) observed that whether a passive sentence is acceptable or not cannot be determined by its transitive verb alone and claimed that for its acceptability, it is essential for us to be able to perceive the passive subject as having been "affected" by the event in question ("an effect is produced"), a hallmark of a patient role. This was illustrated in (6). Bolinger illustrated the same point with (7). In (7a), *the pages* are perceived as affected in the sense that they were moved and their positions were changed. In (7b), *the corner* is not perceived as affected, because it was "only where George was at the time." In (7c), *that corner* is perceived as affected by whether or not it has been turned already. (7c) allows the interpretation that whether *that corner* has been turned already or not is a salient, characterizing property of *that corner*. (A plausible situation is that a group of runners is running a course along which there are many corners they must turn.) Note that the demonstrative *that* is used, which helps distinguish *that corner* from all the other corners by the characterizing property. Note also that the present perfect is used to make the affectedness more prominent (cf. 3.4 (17)). The RS for each of (7a–c) shows that the role of the object NP can be different depending on how we conceptualize the turning event in question.

(7) Bolinger 1977: 10
 a. The pages were turned by George.
  RS: [$_{TYPE}$ "turn"] in [$_{EV}$ __ <AG> [PT, TH]]
 b. *The corner was turned by George.
 c. That corner hasn't been turned yet.
  RS: [$_{TYPE}$ "turn"] in [$_{EV}$ __ <[AG, TH]> [PT, LO]]

3.1.3 Middle Lexical Rule

A lexical rule is a useful mechanism to capture regular relationships in the lexicon between two sets of lexical entries. The middle construction (8b, d) can be stated easily as a lexical rule (9), which removes an agent role and adds a manner adverb complement.

(8) a. The books were sold in large numbers in order to raise money for charity.
  b. The books sold in large numbers (??in order to raise money for charity). (Sadock 2012: 81)
  b'. *The books sold briskly by the store. (Jerry Sadock (p.c.))
  c. The students drove cars.
  d. These cars drive easily. (Sag et al. 2003: 262)

(9) Middle Lexical Rule
    input (transitive verb)   output (middle)
    syntax: V in [__, NP]   →   V in [__, {ADVP | PP}]
    F/A: Faa   →   Faa
    RS: TYPE in [$_{VA}$ __ AG [PT, TH]] → TYPE in [$_{STATE}$ __ TH, MANNER]
    morph: V[0]   →   V[0]

The event type in the input RS of (9) is a volitional action (VA) but it is a state (STATE) in the output RS. (See the Event Hierarchy in 4.3 (5).) Furthermore, the output RS lacks an agent role, which explains why the intentional modifier *in order to* in (8b) and the *by*-phrase in (8b') cannot modify the middle construction. In the output of (9), the ADVP or PP complement in syntax corresponds to the lower ARG in F/A and MANNER in RS. The middle construction is an expression of a property of the theme argument: in (8b), the property of selling in large numbers is true of *the books* and in (8d), the property of driving easily is true of *these cars*.

3.2 Exploration of Unassociable Roles

Suppression of a ROLE takes place in the RS field of a lexical entry by turning the ROLE into the corresponding unassociable role <ROLE>, a role that exists in RS but does not correspond to anything in syntax or in F/A (Sadock 2012: 82, cf. Bresnan 2001: 310; Dalrymple 2001: 208). Role suppression in RS must be accompanied by the reduction of valence by one in syntax and F/A. Otherwise, there would be more NPs in syntax and more ARGs in F/A than the number of associable roles available in RS. Under normal circumstances, a ROLE in the RS field of a lexical entry must correspond to an NP in syntax and an ARG in F/A by the default correspondence 3.1 (2ia). On the other hand, an unassociable <ROLE> is exempted from this default correspondence. In other words, an unassociable role <ROLE> in RS is not visible to or accessible from the other modules.

3.2 EXPLORATION OF UNASSOCIABLE ROLES

The unassociable agent (<AG>) in the agentless passive provides a perfect example of an unassociable role. The interpretation of <AG> can be singular or plural (1a), specific (1d) or nonspecific (1b), and in some cases almost nonexistent (1c). (1e) can be interpreted as 'I want someone or some people to leave me alone,' where the referent of 'someone or some people' is determined pragmatically in discourse, or can be interpreted as a universally quantified proposition 'I want everyone to leave me alone.' These examples show that the semantic range of <AG> goes far beyond simply assuming *someone* (human and singular) as the hidden/underlying agent for agentless passives (McCawley 1998: 91).

(1) McCawley 1998: 91
   a. We have been outvoted.
   b. The Earth was formed 4 billion years ago.
   c. My brother was drowned in a boating accident.
   d. Chomsky's *Syntactic Structures* was written in 1956.
   e. I want to be left alone.

We generalize the unassociable agent <AG> to any other role <ROLE>. (2c) is an example where two roles are suppressed. In (2d), a new selectional restriction is added to the unassociable role.

(2) a. Beat with a wire whisk. (recipe) (Sadock 2012: 232 note 9)
   a'. Add sugar and beat till fluffy.   RS: [$_{EV}$ [$_{TYPE}$ "beat"] AG <PT>]
   b. She sent the letter by airmail.
      RS: [$_{EV}$ [$_{TYPE}$ "send"] [AG, SO] [PT, TH] <GO>]
   c. Some people steal.
      RS: [$_{EV}$ [$_{TYPE}$ "steal"] [AG, GO] <[PT, TH]> <SO>]
   d. John drinks every night.
      RS: [$_{EV}$ [$_{TYPE}$ "drink"] AG <[$_{PT}$ ALCOHOL]>]

Some verbs allow multiple suppressions ((2c) and (3d)).

(3) a. People donate money to the institution whenever they can.
      RS: [$_{EV}$ [$_{TYPE}$ "donate"] [AG, SO] [PT, TH] GO]
   b. People donate money whenever they can.
      RS: [$_{EV}$ [$_{TYPE}$ "donate"] [AG, SO] [PT, TH] <GO>]

c. People donate to the institution whenever they can.
RS: [$_{EV}$ [$_{TYPE}$ "donate"] [AG, SO] <[PT, TH]> GO]
d. People donate whenever they can.
RS: [$_{EV}$ [$_{TYPE}$ "donate"] [AG, SO] <[PT, TH]> <GO>]

Because an unassociable role only exists in RS and does not correspond to anything in F/A, it does not give rise to scope ambiguities, although it is often interpreted existentially (Sadock 2012: 96). Observe that *Every problem was solved* is not ambiguous in the way that *Every problem was solved by some student* is ambiguous (Sadock 2012: 96, Bresnan 1982: 38–39). The situation is exactly the same between *Everyone is reading* and *Everyone is reading something* (Bresnan 1982: 38). The former is not ambiguous but the latter is. Recall that quantifier scopes are represented in F/A (1.3 (15), (16)).

3.3 Passive *by*-Phrase

3.3.1 The syntax, F/A, and RS of passive *by*-phrase

The passive *by*-phrase PP[*by*] of an agentive passive is part of VP[PAS], a VP headed by a passive participle. This is confirmed by VP ellipsis (1a) and VP coordination (1b). We take it as a VP-adjunct in syntax (Sadock 2012: 95 (49), McCawley 1998: 87 (5)). In (1c), in which two VP[PAS]s are coordinated, the PP[*by*] is adjoined to the entire VP[PAS]. By contrast, Gazdar et al. (1985: 59–60), Pollard and Sag (1994: 153), Sag et al. (2003: 314–315), Culicover and Jackendoff (2005: 203), and Huddleston and Pullum (2002: 1428) treated the passive *by*-phrase as a complement of V[PAS]. One piece of evidence for the adjuncthood of the agentive PP[*by*] is that in (1d), the focus-bearing element *too* is placed before the PP[*by*] and the sentence is interpreted in such a way that *too* takes the verb *sent* as its focus. This shows that the constituent whose first word is *sent* ends with *book*. See McCawley 1998: 70 for the details of the *too*-placement test.

(1) a. John was [$_{VP[PAS]}$ kicked by Mary] and Tom was too/but Tom wasn't.
b. John was [$_{VP[PAS]}$ kicked by Mary] and [$_{VP[PAS]}$ slapped by Jane].
c. John was [[[sentenced to five years' hard labor] and [ordered to leave the courtroom]] by Judge Hoffman].
d. He was [sent the book] too by its author.

The preposition *by* of the agentive PP[*by*] in the passive construction is grammatically specified, just as the preposition *into* of *look into* 'investigate' is lexically specified (Sadock 2012: 33 (21)). These prepositions cannot be changed to another preposition, thereby expressing a slightly different meaning in such a way that the resultant meaning difference can be attributed to the meaning difference between the prepositions. (See Cruse 2011: 84 on how to identify a semantic constituent.) In the lexical entry for *look into* (2a), the preposition *into* is not represented in F/A or in RS. The PT in RS corresponds to the lower ARG (i.e., object ARG) in F/A, which in turn corresponds to the object NP of the PP[*into*] in syntax. This is in striking contrast to the lexical entry for the verb *lie* (2b), in which the LO in RS corresponds to the lower ARG in F/A, which corresponds to the PP in syntax. If the preposition is changed, for example, from *on* to *under*, the sentence meaning changes accordingly. Therefore, the head of the PP is represented as ARGa in F/A. For example, the F/A of *The book lies on the desk* is [$_{PROP}$ [$_{ARG}$ BOOK], [$_{Fa}$ [$_{Faa}$ LIE], [$_{ARG}$ [$_{ARGa}$ ON], [$_{ARG}$ DESK]]]].

(2) a. lexical entry for *look into*
   syntax: V, P[*into*] in [$_{VP}$ __, [$_{PP}$ __, NP]]
   F/A: Faa
   RS: [$_{TYPE}$ "investigate"] in [$_{EV}$__AGPT]
   mphon: [$_{V[0]}$ /lʊk/], [$_{P[1]}$ /ɪntʊ/]

b. lexical entry for *lie* (as in *The book lies on the desk*)
   syntax: V in [__, PP]
   F/A: Faa
   RS: [$_{TYPE}$ "lie"] in [$_{EV}$ __ TH LO]

Because the preposition *by* of the agentive passive is grammatically specified, we give the passive *by* the same treatment as that of the preposition *into* of *look into* in (2a), namely, no F/A exponent of the preposition. See the lexical entry for the passive *by*-phrase in (5) and the intermodular representations of an agentive passive sentence in (6). Note that because the passive *by*-phrase (PP[*by*]) is a VP-adjunct in syntax and a VP[PAS] corresponds to an Fa, the passive *by*-phrase corresponds to M$_{Fa}$, a modifier of Fa.

In the RS of an agentive passive, such as (6), the passive *by*-phrase adds the meaning of who or what caused the situation described by the agentless passive. For example, the agentive passive sentence *The cathedral was built by Wren* (Sadock 2012: 95 (48)) is paraphrased as 'Wren brought about/caused the situation that the cathedral was built.' To account for this semantic effect of the passive *by*-phrase, we resort to causative coercion and role sharing, which will be discussed in 4.7 and 6.1.4 (8), (9), respectively. (3) is the lexical entry for causative coercion.

(3) lexical entry for causative coercion (=4.7 (3))
 syntax: nil
 F/A: nil
 RS: [$_{TYPE}$ "cause$_2$"] in [$_{VA}$ __ AG [$_{PT}$ SITU]]
 mphon: nil

(4) RS after causative coercion and role sharing

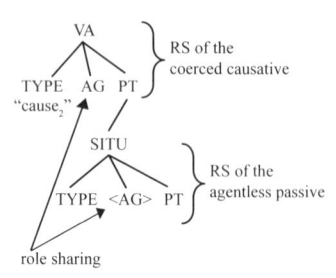

```
         VA
        /  \                } RS of the
    TYPE  AG  PT             } coerced causative
   "cause₂"    \
                \
               SITU
              /    \         } RS of the
          TYPE  <AG>  PT     } agentless passive

         role sharing
```

(3) is another defective lexical item, whose RS field specifies that the two-place "cause$_2$" constitutes a volitional action (VA) and takes two roles AG and PT, the latter dominating a situation (SITU). (See the Event Hierarchy in 4.3 (5).) Causative coercion needs a trigger, without which its appearance in RS cannot be sanctioned. In the case of agentive passives, it is triggered by (i) the presence of PP[*by*] in a passive VP (VP[PAS]) in syntax and (ii) the presence of an unassociable agent (<AG>) in RS. Once causative coercion is triggered, it will add its own RS to the RS of the original passive sentence, which is shown in (4). Furthermore, role sharing takes place in (4) between the AG of the "cause$_2$" and the unassociable AG of the SITU, and the two agents are shared (identified or unified). (Recall that an unassociable role is a full-fledged role in RS and interpreted as such, but it is not accessible from the other modules.) Role sharing in RS will be needed in 6.1.4 to account for the light verb construction and the cognate object construction. On the basis of these observations, we propose (5) as our lexical entry for the passive *by*-phrase, whose RS results from causative coercion and role sharing. (6) is an example of an agentive passive sentence.

(5) lexical entry for passive *by*-phrase (cf. Sadock 2012: 94 (47))
 syntax: PP[*by*] in [$_{VP[PAS]}$ VP[PAS], __]
 F/A: [$_{MFa}$ ARG]
 RS: AG in [$_{VA}$ [$_{TYPE}$ "cause$_2$"] __ [$_{PT}$ [$_{SITU}$ <AG>]]] (due to causative coercion and role sharing)

(6) syntax, F/A, and RS of *The cathedral was built by Wren* (cf. Sadock 2012: 95 (48))

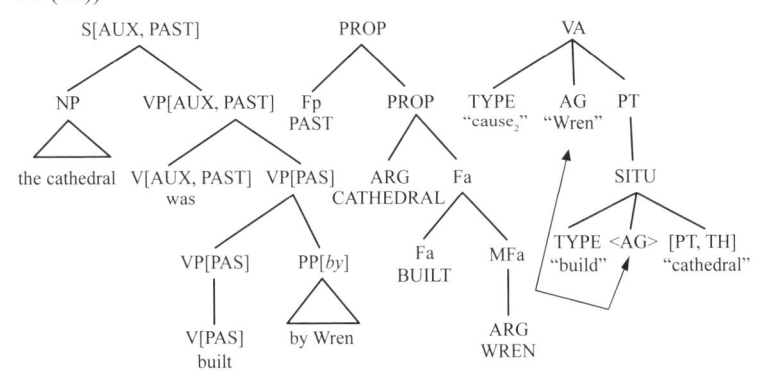

```
S[AUX, PAST]                    PROP                        VA
   /\                            /\                         /\
  NP   VP[AUX, PAST]           Fp   PROP              TYPE   AG    PT
  /\        /\                PAST   /\              "cause₂" "Wren"
the cathedral V[AUX, PAST] VP[PAS]  ARG   Fa                   |
              was          /\      CATHEDRAL                  SITU
                         VP[PAS] PP[by]   Fa    MFa      TYPE <AG> [PT, TH]
                           |      /\    BUILT   |        "build"    "cathedral"
                         V[PAS]  by Wren               ARG
                          built                        WREN
```

The passive *by*-phrase in (5) and (6) is a modifier in syntax and F/A, and therefore is not required to appear in passive sentences ((1b) and (3) in 3.1, and (7a) below). However, in some cases, such as (7b), a passive *by*-phrase is obligatory.

(7) a. We were met (by our friends). (Bolinger 1975: 57)
    b. We were joined *(by our friends). (ibid.)
       RS: [_VA [_TYPE "cause₂"] [_AG X] [_PT [_SITU [_TYPE "join"] <[AG, TH]> [_[PT, GO] Y]]]] &

       [_EV [_TYPE "become one group"] [_PT X and Y]]
    c. We were joined together in holy matrimony (by a priest).
       RS: [_EV [_TYPE "join"] <AG> [_PT "we"; PAIR]]

What is peculiar about (7b) is that when *we were joined by our friends*, we were affected by the joining event in the sense that *we* became a part of a newly formed larger group consisting of *we* and *our friends*, but at the same time, *our friends* were also affected by the same event in exactly the same way. (Some dictionaries define the verb as "to come into the company of" or "if one group joins another, they come together to form one group.") In this respect, *our friends* in (7b) is not a pure external causer we saw in the RS of (6) that causes the subordinate event from outside. In other words, *our friends* is a causer of the joining event, but at the same time, it is part of the patient of the same event. This semantic factor prevents the omission of the PP[*by*] in (7b). If we drop the PP[*by*] in (7b), the only interpretation available is that the suppressed agent (the causer) is an external causer, just as in (6). Under this interpretation, *we*, for example, the speaker and someone else, came to form a pair or a group. This is the interpretation of (7c), in which the PP[*by*] is omissible, as expected.

3.3.2 Propositional agentive phrase

When an active sentence headed by a transitive verb has a clausal subject CP[*that*] (2.5) and the transitive verb is passivizable, the agentive phrase of the agentive passive counterpart cannot be a PP[*by*], because prepositions cannot take a CP[*that*] complement. In such cases, the passive agentive phrase appears in the form of CP[*that*] without the agentive preposition *by*, which is illustrated in (8). This is the same kind of phenomenon that we see in complement alternations between PP and CP[*that*], such as *hope* ([$_{VP}$ V, PP[*for*]] ~ [$_{VP}$ V, CP[*that*]]), *insist* ([$_{VP}$ V, PP[*on*]] ~ [$_{VP}$ V, CP[*that*]]), and *content* ([$_{AP}$ A, PP[*with*]] ~ [$_{AP}$ A, CP[*that*]]) (McCawley 1998: 121). In these alternations, when a PP complement expresses a propositional content, it appears as CP[*that*]. In (8), the adverb *very much* is added to exclude the possibility of the past participle being an adjective.

(8) a. [$_{CP[that]}$ That John passed the test] surprised/shocked/disappointed/impressed us very much.
 b. We were/got surprised/shocked/disappointed/impressed very much (*by) [$_{CP[that]}$ that John passed the test].

(9) is the lexical entry for a propositional agentive phrase, in which the RS field is the result of causative coercion and role sharing, just as in (5).

(9) lexical entry for propositional agentive phrase (cf. 3.3.1 (5))
 syntax: CP[*that*] in [$_{VP[PAS]}$ VP[PAS], __]
 F/A: [$_{MFa}$ PROP]
 RS: [$_{AG}$ EV] in [$_{VA}$ "cause$_2$" __ [$_{PT}$ [$_{SITU}$ <AG>]]] (due to causative coercion and role sharing)

3.4 Prepositional Passives

3.4.1 Prepositional Passive Lexical Rule

When a verb takes not an NP complement but a PP complement (V in [$_{VP}$ __, PP]), the object NP of the PP can often appear as the subject of the passive counterpart, as in (1). This phenomenon is generally known as prepositional passive or pseudo-passive.

(1) a. This lock has been tinkered with (by an amateur). (Sadock 2012: 96)
b. The police were spat on (by the crowd). (ibid.)
c. Robin was being stared at. (Culicover and Jackendoff 2005: 207)
d. Sandy can be relied on. (ibid.)
e. Max is being talked about. (ibid.)
f. The subject was gone into thoroughly. (Bolinger 1975: 58)
g. *The room was gone into at once. (ibid.)

The V+P combinations that appear in prepositional passives often have synonymous transitive verbs: *set upon* ~ *beset*, *engage in* ~ *practice*, *look into* ~ *investigate* (Bolinger 1975: 58, Takami 1992: 95, Sadock 2012: 99). This suggests that the meaning of the preposition in these V+P combinations is not a semantic unit separate from the verb meaning, but rather each of these V+P combinations constitutes a single semantic unit and there is no semantic contribution of the preposition to the meaning of the V+P combination. These V+P combinations are Faa in F/A (cf. 3.3 (2a)), and have often been called natural predicates (Riemsdijk and Williams 1986: 118). To deal with prepositional passives, we need to revise the Passive Lexical Rule for transitive verbs (3.1 (3)) as follows.

(2) Prepositional Passive Lexical Rule (Sadock 2012: 100 (74))
Active input   Passive output
syntax: V, P in [$_{VP}$ __, [$_{PP}$ __, NP], ψ]   →   V[PAS], P in [$_{VP}$ __, [$_{PP}$ __], ψ]
F/A: Fφaa   →   Fφa
RS: TYPE in [$_{EV}$ __ AG PT χ]   →   TYPE in [$_{EV}$ __ <AG> PT χ]
morph: V[0]   →   V[1, PSP]

In the input of (2), the NP object of the PP in syntax corresponds to the second highest ARG (i.e., object ARG) in F/A and PT in RS. For example, in (1f), *go into* means 'investigate' and its F/A and RS are Faa and [$_{EV}$ TYPE AG PT], respectively. Therefore, it can be an input to the Prepositional Passive Lexical Rule (2) and is passivizable. On the other hand, the RS of *go into* in (1g) is [$_{EV}$ TYPE [AG, TH] LO], in which LO corresponds to PP[*into*] in syntax and the object NP of PP[*into*] is not perceived as being affected by the event of going into a place (i.e., it is not a patient). Furthermore, the latter *go into* is not a single semantic unit Faa in F/A but semantically complex, because *go into* contrasts with, for example, *go out of*, which shows the preposition *into* has its own semantic contribution to the combination *go into* in (1g). Therefore, the F/A of this *go into* is [$_{Fa}$ [$_{Faa}$ GO] [$_{ARG}$ [$_{ARGa}$ INTO] ARG]]. In addition, the ARG of INTO does not correspond to PT in RS (cf. 3.3

(2b)). Hence prepositional passivization is impossible with this *go into*. Here is an example of (2) applying to the lexical entry of *go into* ('investigate') in (1f).

(3) example of (2) applying to the lexical entry for *go into* 'investigate'
Active input   Passive output
lexical entry for *go into*   lexical entry for passive *gone into*
syntax: V, P[*into*] in [$_{VP}$ __, [$_{PP}$ __, NP]]   → V[PAS], P[*into*] in [$_{VP}$ __, [$_{PP}$ __]]
F/A: Faa   → Fa
RS: [$_{TYPE}$ "investigate"] in [$_{EV}$ __ AG PT] → TYPE in [$_{EV}$ __ <AG> PT]
morph: V[0]   → V[1, PSP]

In the syntactic output above, PP[*into*] consists only of P[*into*] without an NP complement. On the other hand, we have a lexical entry for the preposition *into*, whose syntactic field specifies P[*into*] in [$_{PP}$ __, NP]. These two kinds of PP[*into*] nodes compete with each other. However, if we compare the PP[*into*] node in the syntactic output of (3) ([$_{VP[PAS]}$ V[PAS], [$_{PP[into]}$ P[*into*]]) and the PP[into] node in the lexical entry for *into* ([$_{PP[into]}$ P[*into*], NP]), the former is more specific than the latter in the sense that the external syntax of PP[*into*] is specified in the former but not in the latter. Therefore, the former preempts the latter by the Elsewhere Principle (1.1.2 (3)) and every time the former PP[*into*] is applicable, the latter PP[*into*] is not. In other words, there is no violation of subcategorization requirement for prepositions in the syntactic output [$_{PP}$ P] in (2) and (3) (cf. McCawley's (1998: 173) discussion on tense in relation to the Elsewhere Principle).

The stranded preposition in prepositional passives is syntactically a separate word, as specified in the output syntactic field in (2) and (3). Although Bresnan (1982: 51) and others claimed that the preposition is incorporated into the passive participle in prepositional passives, it is not, because an adverb can be inserted in (4a-d) between the passive participle and the stranded preposition.

(4) a. Sandy was relied very heavily on. (Culicover and Jackendoff 2005: 208)
  b. Jill was being looked intently at by Ann. (Culicover and Jackendoff 2005: 208)
  c. John was spoken critically/severely to. (Takami 1992: 99)
  d. John's lecture was listened carefully/attentively to by his students. (Takami 1992: 99)
  e. This linguistic phenomenon has been continually [talked and argued] about. (Takami 1992: 99)
  f. This desk should not be [written or typed] on. (Takami 1992: 99)

Examples such as (4a-d) are often felt degraded in acceptability, because they have better sounding competitors in which the adverbs are placed before or after the V+P combination (Jerry Sadock (p.c.)), such as *Sandy was very heavily relied on* and *Sandy was relied on very heavily*, which exhibit a smaller amount of mismatch between syntax and F/A. In (4e, f), the two passive participles are coordinated and the stranded preposition follows the coordinate structure. If the V[PAS]+P combination was a syntactic word, this coordination would have been impossible.

In languages that do not allow preposition stranding, such as German, the prepositional object is retained as such under passivation, as in [$_{PP[auf]}$ *Auf* [$_{NP[ACC]}$ *die Frage*]] *wird nicht geantwortet* and [$_{PP[für]}$ *Für* [$_{NP[ACC]}$ *die Kinder*]] *wird gesorgt*.

3.4.2 Extending the coverage of Prepositional Passive Lexical Rule

In (5), the object NP of a locative PP that is a VP-adjunct appears as the subject of the corresponding prepositional passive. We assume that the locative adjunct PPs in (5) are listed in the RS field of each verb as a result of PP incorporation (10) and that the referent of the NP object of each locative PP is conceptualized as being affected by the action in question; that is, the NP bears a patient role ([PT, LO]).

(5) a. This rock used to be slid down when we were kids. (Davison 1980: 45)
    [$_{EV}$ "slide-down" <AG> [PT, LO]]
  b. Being tiptoed behind makes me nervous. (Davison 1980: 45)
    [$_{EV}$ "tiptoe-behind" <AG> [PT, LO]]
  c. The bridge has been walked under by generations of lovers. (Bolinger 1977: 9)
    cf. *The bridge was walked under by the dog.
    [$_{EV}$ "walk-under" <AG> [PT, LO]]
  d. This lake is not to be camped beside by anybody! (Bolinger 1977: 10)
    cf. *The lake was camped beside by my sister.
    [$_{EV}$ "camp-beside" <AG> [PT, LO]]
  e. This river should not be swum in. (Takami 1992: 101)
    cf. This river should not be swum in by {*John | children}.
    [$_{EV}$ "swim-in" <AG> [PT, LO]]

Jerry Sadock (p.c.) pointed out that these examples tend to be more degraded than the examples in (1) and that the prepositional passives with a complement PP (1) and those with an adjunct PP (5), (6), (7) vary in their acceptability.

(6) is an example of prepositional passive with a goal adjunct PP[*for*]. Here again, we assume that the goal adjunct PP in (6) is listed on the RS of the verb as

a result of PP incorporation (10) and that the referent of the NP is conceptualized as being affected by the action in question.

(6) These rights were fought for in these very halls. (Bresnan 1994: 79)
 [$_{EV}$ "fight-for" <AG> [PT, GO]]

It is also well known that the object NP of an instrumental adjunct PP[*with*] often appears as the subject of the prepositional passive counterpart, as in (7). Again, we assume that the instrumental adjuncts (PP[*with*]) in (7) are listed in the RS field of each verb as a result of PP incorporation (10) and that the referents of the NPs are conceptualized as a new patient ([PT, INSTR]), and at the same time, the original patient role of each verb is made unassociable (<PT>), which prevents two patient NPs and ARGs from appearing in syntax and F/A.

(7) a. I won't use a razor that has been shaved with by anyone. (McCawley 1998: 90)
 [$_{EV}$ "shave-with" <AG> <[PT, TH]> [PT, INSTR]]   cf. [$_{EV}$ "shave" AG [PT, TH]]
 b. That knife has been cut with too often without being sharpened. (Davison 1980: 45)
 [$_{EV}$ "cut-with" <AG> <[PT, TH]> [PT, INSTR]]   cf. [$_{EV}$ "cut" AG [PT, TH]]
 c. This spoon has been eaten with. (Davison 1980: 45)
 [$_{EV}$ "eat-with" <AG> <[PT, TH]> [PT, INSTR]]   cf. [$_{EV}$ "eat" AG [PT, TH]]
 d. This brand-new fountain pen has never be written with. (Takami 1992: 101)
 [$_{EV}$ "write-with" <AG> <[PT, TH]> [PT, INSTR]]   cf. [$_{EV}$ "write" AG [PT, TH]]

The following (8a) is a prepositional passive in which a source adjunct is involved. Again, we assume that the source (SO) role is listed in the RS field of the verb *drink* as a result of PP incorporation (10). The referent of the source NP *that glass* is being conceptualized as a new patient role and at the same time, the original patient role is made unassociable.

(8) a. That glass has been drunk out of (by someone). (Davison 1980: 53)
 [$_{EV}$ "drink-out-of" <AG> <[PT, TH]> [PT, SO]]   cf. [$_{EV}$ "drink" AG [PT, TH]]

b. (intransitive *drink*) John drinks every night.
[$_{EV}$ "drink" AG <[$_{[PT, TH]}$ ALCOHOL]>] (=3.2 (2d))

The meaning of (8a) with respect to 'what was drunk out of that glass' is not restricted to alcoholic drinks, which is part of the meaning of intransitive *drink* (8b). This shows that the passive (8a) is based on the transitive *drink*.

When a verb takes both NP and PP complements (V in [$_{VP}$ __, NP, PP]), the patient role that corresponds to the NP object must be made unassociable, as in (9), for the verb to occur in a prepositional passive. This is again for the same reason: to prevent two patient NPs and ARGs from appearing in syntax and F/A.

(9) a. Bob Hope is often stolen from.   cf. *Bob Hope is often stolen jokes from. (McCawley 1998: 168)
[$_{EV}$ "steal" <[AG, GO]> <[PT, TH]> [PT, SO]]   cf. [$_{EV}$ "steal" [AG, GO] [PT, TH] SO].
  b. This spoon has been eaten with. (Davison 1980: 45)   cf. *This fork has been eaten spaghetti with. (Davison 1980: 49)
[$_{EV}$ "eat" <AG> <[PT, TH]> [PT, INSTR]]   cf. [$_{EV}$ "eat" AG [PT, TH]]
  c. Aikhenvald's book on classifiers is always being quoted from. (from the web)   cf. *The book is always being quoted passages from.
[$_{EV}$ "quote" <[AG, GO]> <[PT, TH]> [PT, SO]]   cf. [$_{EV}$ "quote" [AG, GO] [PT, TH] SO]
  d. I've never been written to by Maria. (Dixon 2005: 374)   cf. *I've never been written letters to by Maria.
[$_{EV}$ "write" <[AG, SO]> <[PT, TH]> [PT, GO]]   cf. [$_{EV}$ "write" [AG, SO] [PT, TH] GO]
  e. Mayor Schaefer indicated neither organization has been donated to in the past. (from the web)   cf. *Neither organization has been donated money to in the past.
[$_{EV}$ "donate" <[AG, SO]> <[PT, TH]> [PT, GO]]   cf. [$_{EV}$ "donate" [AG, SO] [PT, TH] GO]

If the patient role that corresponds to the NP object is made unassociable in RS, the syntax of the verb is V in [$_{VP}$ __, PP] and qualifies as an input to the Prepositional Passive Lexical Rule (2). Otherwise, the verb's syntax is V in [$_{VP}$ __, NP, PP] and can only be an input to the regular Passive Lexical Rule (3.1 (3)).

In order for the Prepositional Passive Lexical Rule (2) to apply to the cases (5)–(8), where a new patient NP is introduced as the NP object of a VP-adjunct

PP, we propose the following lexical rule, which turns a locative, source, goal, or instrumental PP adjunct into a PP complement under certain conditions, when the object NP of the PP is perceived as being affected by the action in question.

(10) PP Incorporation Lexical Rule
    a. input   output
        syntax: V in [$_{VP}$ __]   → V in [$_{VP}$ __, [$_{PP}$ P, NP]]
        RS: [$_{TYPE}$ χ] in [$_{EV}$ __] → [$_{TYPE}$ χ-P] in [$_{EV}$ __, [PT, ROLE]],
                                                 where ROLE is either LO, GO, SO,
                                                 or INSTR.

    b. input   output
        syntax: V in [$_{VP}$ __]   → V in [$_{VP}$ __, [$_{PP}$ P, NP]]
        RS: [$_{TYPE}$ χ] in [$_{EV}$ __ <PT>] → [$_{TYPE}$ χ-P] in [$_{EV}$ __ <PT> [PT, ROLE]],
                                                 where ROLE is either LO, GO, SO,
                                                 or INSTR.

In the output syntax in (10), a new PP complement is added and its NP object corresponds to the PT role on the action tier and one of the roles on the thematic tier. (10a) applies to the cases in (5) and (6). (10b) applies to the cases in (7), (8), and (9). Note that in the input of (10b), the PT is already made unassociable, which predicts that only the verbs that can make their patient role unassociable can appear in a prepositional passive. One piece of evidence for this prediction is the contrast between *This spoon has been eaten with* (=(5c)) and **This spoon has been devoured with*. As is often pointed out, the transitive verb *devour* must express its patient role, as in *He devoured *(food)*.

3.4.3 On the notions of agent and patient
Sadock (2012: 99) observed graded acceptability in prepositional passives in (11) and stated a general tendency that the more patient-like the referent of the subject NP (i.e., the object of the preposition in the corresponding active) is perceived to be by the speaker/addressee (cf. (13)) and the more agent-like the referent of the object NP of the agentive PP[*by*] (i.e., the subject in the corresponding active), if there is one, is perceived to be (cf. (12)), the more acceptable the prepositional passive is.

(11) a. The safe has been tampered with. >
    b. The table has been sat on. >
    c. The closet has been slid into.

We adopt Dowty's (1991) notions of proto-agent and proto-patient and regard the agent and the patient as cluster concepts with several contributing properties (Sadock 2012: 76). Dowty gave five contributing properties for his proto-agent and proto-patient. The more contributing properties for agenthood the referent of an NP has and the more fully it has these contributing properties, the more agent-like it is. The same is true of a patient.

(12) contributing properties for agenthood (Dowty 1991 (27), (29))
    a. volition
       John is being polite to Bill.
    b. sentience
       John knows the statement. John sees Mary.
    c. causing an event or change of state in another participant
       His loneliness causes his happiness.
    d. movement (relative to the position of another participant)
       The bullet overtook the arrow.
    e. existing independently of the event named by the verb
       John needs a new car.

(13) contributing properties for patienthood (Dowty 1991 (28), (30))
    a. undergoes change of state or location
       John made a mistake. John erased the error. John moved the rock.
    b. incremental theme
       John crossed the driveway. John filled the glass with water.
    c. causally affected by another participant
       Smoking causes cancer.
    d. stationary (relative to movement of another participant)
       The bullet overtook the arrow.
    e. does not exist independently of the event
       John built a house. This situation constitutes a major dilemma.

These contributing properties (in terms of to what degree an NP has a contributing property and how many of the five contributing properties it has) are not determined by the main verb alone; other factors, such as modifiers (14) and (17) and auxiliary verbs (15), also influence them.

(14) a. <u>John</u> broke the window. <u>John</u> intentionally/inadvertently broke the window.
 b. <u>John</u> broke his finger. <u>John</u> intentionally/inadvertently broke his finger.
 c. <u>That careless boy</u> broke the PC again. <u>That naughty boy</u> broke the PC again.

In (15b) below and in (5c), (7b, c, d), (8a), and (9b, d, e), the use of present perfect makes more readily available the interpretation of the referent of the subject NP being "causally affected" (13c).

(15) McCawley 1998: 90
 a. *A straight razor is shaved with by John.
 b. I won't use a razor that has been shaved with by anyone. (=(7a))

The affectedness in (13c) "causally affected" can be either physical or psychological. The prepositional passive *be stepped on* in (16) can be interpreted either physically or psychologically, as in *I don't want to be stepped on or pushed around. I don't want to be the person who people think they need to lead, because I have my own compass and can find my own direction* (from the web).

(16) a. I don't want to be stepped on. (Davison 1980: 53)
 b. I feel as though I'm being snuck up on.

When the agent of an action that acts on another participant is a famous person, the acted-on participant (i.e., patient) increases its patienthood because "acted on by a famous person" is a salient property that characterizes the patient.

(17) a. This porch was [$_{VP[PAS]}$ walked on by Teddy Roosevelt]. (Davison 1980: 54)
 b. This chair was [$_{VP[PAS]}$ sat on by Adolf Hitler]. (ibid.)
 c. That cup was [$_{VP[PAS]}$ drunk out of by Napoleon]. (ibid.)
 d. This building was [$_{VP[PAS]}$ walked in front of by the Japanese Emperor] last month. (Takami 1992: 108)

3.5 Verb Classes and Their Passives

3.5.1 The verb class of *express*

Jacobson (1992: 284–5) pointed out that verbs such as *express*, *capture*, *support*, and *describe* take an NP object but not a CP[*that*] complement (1a, b), namely, V in [__, {NP | *CP[*that*]}], although the complement NP of this verb class (with a patient role) is semantically compatible with a proposition. However, when they are passivized, they allow a clausal subject. These points are illustrated in (1a, b, c).

(1) a. This principle expresses/captures [$_{NP}$ the fact that languages are learnable]. (Jacobson 1992: 284)
   b. *This principle expresses/captures [$_{CP[that]}$ that languages are learnable]. (ibid.)
   c. [$_{CP[that]}$ That languages are learnable] is expressed/captured by this principle. (Jacobson 1992: 285) (=2.6 (4b'))
   d. It is expressed/captured by this principle [$_{CP[that]}$ that languages are learnable].
   e. lexical entry for passive participle
      syntax: V[PAS] in [__]
      F/A: Fa
      RS: TYPE in [__ <AG> PT]
   f. lexical entry for passive participle with a clausal subject
      syntax: V[PAS] in [__]
      F/A: Fp
      RS: TYPE in [__ <AG> [$_{PT}$ EV]]
   g. lexical entry for passive participle with extraposition
      syntax: V[PAS] in [[__] CP[*that*]]
      F/A: Fp
      RS: TYPE in [__ <AG> [$_{PT}$ EV]]

As predicted by the Passive Lexical Rule (3.1 (3)), the lexical entry for the passive participle of these verbs is (1e). Because the patient role of this verb class is semantically compatible with a proposition, the RS of the passive participle can be [$_{PT}$ EV], and concomitantly, the F/A can be Fp, instead of Fa. Therefore, we have another lexical entry (1f) for these passive participles. This lexical entry licenses the clausal subject in (1c) (cf. 2.5 (2)). This option of turning PT and ARG into [$_{PT}$ EV] and PROP, respectively, is not possible with the active lexical entry, because PT is required in the active to correspond to an NP object. Once the verb is passivized, there ceases to be a requirement for an NP object in the lexical entry and this option becomes available. In addition, the Extraposition Lexical Rule (2.7 (5)) predicts (by being applied to (1e)) that there is still another lexical entry (1g) for this passive participle. This lexical entry licenses (1d). (1g) is an example of composition of two lexical rules: the Passive Lexical Rule feeding the Extraposition Lexical Rule. See (4d).

3.5.2 The verb class of *suppose*

When a verb only takes a CP[*that*] complement but no NP object or PP complement, namely, V in [$_{VP}$ __, {CP[*that*] | *NP | *PP}]), it is still passivizable if it has a right semantics for passivization. *Suppose* is such a verb. (The object-raising use of *suppose*, as in *I suppose John's answer to be correct* is irrelevant here.)

(2) a. *I suppose the correctness of John's answer.   cf. *What I suppose is the correctness of John's answer.
 b. I suppose that John's answer is correct.   cf. What I suppose is correct is John's answer.
 c. It is supposed that John's answer is correct.
 d. *That John's answer is correct is supposed.

When we try to apply the Passive Lexical Rule (3.1 (3)) to *suppose*, although the input condition is not quite met (because (i) no NP complement is in the input syntax and (ii) no Faa is in the input F/A), its effects should look like (3), in which the complement CP[*that*] must stay in situ in the output syntax in view of (2c, d), the subject argument is lost in the output F/A, and AG is turned into an unassociable role (<AG>) in the output RS. The output lexical entry in (3) licenses (2c).

(3) Passive Lexical Rule for verbs taking a clausal complement
  input   output
  syntax: V in [__, CP[*that*]]   →   V[PAS] in [__, CP[*that*]]
  F/A: Fpa   →   Fp
  RS: TYPE in [$_{EV}$ __ AG [$_{PT}$ EV]] →   TYPE in [$_{EV}$ __ <AG> [$_{PT}$ EV]]
  morph: V[0]   →   V[1, PSP]

Because the CP[*that*] complement in the output lexical entry corresponds to the sole associable role [$_{PT}$ EV] in RS, there is no associable role left that can correspond to the subject NP. Therefore, the subject NP must be filled with the dummy *it* (2.4 (9)), as in (2c). (2d) is ungrammatical because it violates the syntactic field of the output lexical entry in (3), where the CP[*that*] must be a complement, not a subject. As far as syntax and F/A are concerned, the output lexical entry in (3) is of the *seem*-class, which does not allow a CP[*that*] subject, and is not of the *stink*-class, which allows a CP[*that*] subject.

3.5.3 The verb class of *depend*

Verbs such as *depend* only take a PP complement but no NP object or CP[*that*] complement, namely, V in [$_{VP}$ __, {*CP[*that*] | *NP | PP}]. They undergo the Prepositional Passive Lexical Rule (3.4 (2)), whose output passive participle licenses (4a). (4b) is licensed in exactly the same way as (1c), because the patient role of *depend on* is semantically compatible with a proposition, which is shown in such examples as *You can depend on my assistant and that he will be on time* (Sag et al. 1985: 165).

(4) a. This route is depended on by many commuters. (from the web)
 b. [$_{CP[that]}$ That Channel 5 will cover it] can be depended on. (from the web)
 c. Every year it can be depended on [$_{CP[that]}$ [that Channel 5 will cover it] and [that Natalie Jacobson will be there]]. (from the web)
 d. the composition of two lexical rules

lexical entry for *depend*	Prepositional Passive Lexical Rule
syntax: V in [$_{VP}$ __, [$_{PP[on]}$ P, NP]	⟶ V[PAS] in [$_{VP}$ __, [$_{PP[on]}$ P]]
F/A: Faa	Fa
RS: [$_{TYPE}$ "depend-on"] in [$_{EV}$ __ [AG, TH] [PT, LO]]	[$_{TYPE}$ "depend-on"] in [$_{EV}$ __ <[AG, TH]> [PT, LO]]

Extraposition Lexical Rule

V[PAS] in [$_{VP}$ [$_{VP}$ __, [$_{PP[on]}$ P]], CP[*that*]]

Fp

[$_{TYPE}$ "depend-on"] in
 [$_{EV}$ __ <[AG, TH]> [$_{[PT, LO]}$ EV]]

The syntactic structure of (4c) is the one in which the subject of the prepositional passive is the dummy *it* and a CP[*that*] is adjoined to the VP[PAS]. This structure is licensed by the lexical entry for the passive participle *depended* whose presence in the lexicon is predicted, as in (4d) by the Prepositional Passive Lexical Rule (3.4 (2)) feeding the Extraposition Lexical Rule (2.8 (5)). Here, "one lexical rule feeds another" means that when the output lexical entries of the first lexical rule meet the input conditions for the second lexical rule, the two lexical rules can be applied in succession. Recall that a lexical rule is a mapping in the lexicon from a set of lexical entries to another set of lexical entries. Therefore, the composition of two lexical rules is possible, as long as the range of the first mapping (i.e., the output of the first lexical rule) is within the domain of the second mapping (i.e., satisfies the input conditions of the second lexical rule). This is shown in (4d).

3.5.4 The verb class of *hope*

Verbs such as *hope, insist, agree* take a PP complement or a CP[*that*] complement but not an NP object, namely, V in [$_{VP}$ __, {CP[*that*] | *NP | PP}]. The (b) examples of these verbs in (5), (6), and (7) without a stranded preposition show again that verbs that do not take an NP object can passivize, just as *suppose* in (2). The unacceptable (c) examples of prepositional passive show that the source of the (b) examples is the subcategorization frame [$_{VP}$ V, CP[*that*]], exactly as in (3). Furthermore, prepositional passives with clausal subjects (the (e) examples) are acceptable, whereas their extraposed counterparts (the (c) examples) are bad. Note that we cannot formulate the Extraposition Lexical Rule in such a way that it cannot apply to the prepositional passive lexical entries, because we have cases such as *depend on* in (4c).

(5) a. syntax of *hope*: V in [__, CP[*that*]], [__, PP[*for*]], *[__, NP]
 b. It is hoped [that a solution will be found]. (Dixon 2005: 18)
 c. *It is hoped for [that a solution will be found].
 d. *[That a solution will be found] is hoped. (Dixon 2005: 18)
 e. [That a better solution would be found] was earnestly hoped for. (Dixon 2005: 18)

(6) a. syntax of *insist*: V in [__, CP[*that*]], [__, PP[*on*]], *[__, NP]
 b. It was insisted that the President could not constitutionally exercise the power. (from the web)

c. *It was insisted on that the President could not constitutionally exercise the power.
d. *[That the President could not constitutionally exercise the power] was insisted.
e. [That the President could not constitutionally exercise the power] was insisted on.

(7) a. syntax of *agree*: V in [__, CP[*that*]], [__, PP[*on*]], *[__, NP]
b. It is agreed that we should eat less fat. (from the web)
c. *It is agreed on that we should eat less fat.
d. *[That we should eat less fat] is agreed.
e. [That we should eat less fat] is agreed on.

We claim that although both the (b) sentences without a stranded preposition and the (c) sentences with a stranded preposition express the same meaning and are grammatically possible (and hence are competing with each other), only the (b) sentences are chosen as acceptable. Note that the (b) sentences result from the lexical rule (3) whereas the (c) sentences result from the Prepositional Passive Lexical Rule feeding the Extraposition Lexical Rule. Note also that the (b) sentences are structurally shorter and simpler than the (c) sentences, because the former lack the prepositions that the latter have. In other words, although they express the same information, the (c) sentences are more complex than the (b) sentences in terms of the number of lexical rules involved, the number of words used, and the complexity of constituent structure. Therefore, the less complex (b) sentences are chosen over the more complex (c) sentences, thanks to the economy of language use. This situation, in which there are two or more competing grammatical forms with the same meaning and the simplest one overrides the occurrence of the other more complex forms, is of the same nature as the situation we found with the distribution of dummy *do* discussed in 2.2 (3) and 2.3 (8b).

3.5.5 The verb class of *wonder*

The verb *wonder* also belongs to the previous class of *hope*, namely, V in [$_{VP}$ __, {CP[WH[Q]] | *NP | PP}]. It takes as its complement an indirect question (CP[WH[Q]]) (8) or a PP[*about*] (9), but it does not take an NP object. However, it can be turned into passive (10) and prepositional passive (11).

(8) lexical entry for *wonder*
syntax: V in [__, CP[WH[Q]]]
F/A: Fpa
RS: [_TYPE "wonder"] in
[_EV __ [AG, LO] [_[PT, TH] EV]]

(9) lexical entry for *wonder*
syntax: V in [__, PP[*about*]]
F/A: Faa
RS: [_TYPE "wonder"] in
[_EV __ [AG, LO] [_[PT, TH] EV]]

In the RS of (9), the [PT, TH] role is interpreted as an event (EV) (Jerry Sadock (p.c.)), which explains the fact that *John wondered about the time*, for example, is interpreted as *John wondered what time it was* with a concealed question interpretation (Grimshaw 1979: 297ff.).

(10) (from the web)
   a. Likewise, it was wondered whether the reverse is also possible.
   b. When the place "caught on fire," it was wondered what would happen to all of the residents. Of course, it was revealed that only half of the hotel burned down and miraculously everyone still had a place to live.
   c. As a result, it was wondered what purpose another meeting would serve other than to possibly challenge the city manager's efforts.
   d. The campaign had been temporarily suspended and it was wondered what effect the death of the Princess of Wales would have on the election.
   e. Every holiday it was wondered what we would celebrate and how. Even when my father passed away, it was asked how and when he would be honored.

(11) a. It's time to ask a question that has been wondered about for a long time. (from the web)
   b. The relationship between reason and the emotions is one that has been wondered about for a very long time. (from the web)

Chomsky (1995: 33) observed that "In English, generally only objective Case-assigning verbs can occur in the passive" and claimed on the basis of the following two sets of data, (12) and (13), that the verb *ask* can assign Case to the NP object (12a) and therefore it can passivize when it takes a CP complement (12c), whereas the verb *wonder* cannot assign Case to the NP object (13a) and therefore it cannot passivize when it takes a CP complement (13c).

(12) a. Mary asked the time.
  b. Mary asked [$_{CP}$ what time it was].
  c. It was asked what time it was.

(13) a. *Mary wondered the time.
  b. Mary wondered what time it was.
  c. *It was wondered what time it was.

What we have shown abundantly so far is that a verb that does not take an NP object and hence does not have the capacity of Case assignment still passivizes as long as its semantics is right, which means that passivizability of a verb has nothing to do with its capacity of Case assignment.

3.5.6 The verb class of *rain*

The last verb class we would like to consider is weather verbs, such as *rain* and *snow*. English weather verbs are passivizable when they take an adversative PP[*on*] adjunct. This is shown in (14b). The passive subject expresses the adversely affected patient role that is expressed in the active as the NP object of the preposition *on*. In (14b), the agentive phrase *by it* is unacceptable, because the passive *by* requires its object to be an agent (3.3 (5), (6)), for which the dummy *it* does not qualify. Recall the lexical entry of the dummy *it* in 2.4 (9), in which the RS field is nil, meaning that the dummy *it* cannot assume any role.

(14) a. It rained/snowed on John.
  b. John was rained/snowed on (*by it). (Sadock 2012: 236 note 9)

If weather verbs, such as *rain* and *snow*, did not have an agent role when used with the impersonal subject *it*, then these passives would be examples of the promotion of patient role to the syntactic subject without a concomitant agent suppression or demotion, which would look as if unaccusative verbs were passivized. Three lexical entries for *rain* are given in (15). (15b) is illustrated by (16a), in which *rain* takes a PP complement in syntax and the two roles TH and GO in RS. (15c) is its transitive counterpart and illustrated in (16b). On the other hand, in (15a), the lexical entry for the impersonal weather verb *rain*, the F/A is a PROP, that is, semantically saturated, which means that the dummy *it* (2.4 (9)) is required to fill the subject NP position to form a clause (S). We claim that there is an unassociable agent (<AG>) in the RS field of (15a). This is supported by (16c-f).

124   3 PASSIVE

(15) lexical entries for *rain*
  a. intransitive (weather)
     syntax: V in [__]
     F/A: PROP
     RS: [$_{\text{TYPE}}$ "rain"] in [$_{\text{EV}}$ __ <AG>]
  b. intransitive (unaccusative)
     syntax: V in [__, PP]
     F/A: Fa
     RS: [$_{\text{TYPE}}$ "fall"] in [$_{\text{EV}}$ __ TH GO]
  c. transitive
     syntax: V in [__, NP, PP]
     F/A: Faa
     RS: [$_{\text{TYPE}}$ "make-fall"] in [$_{\text{EV}}$ __ [AG, SO] [PT, TH] GO]

In (16c, c'), the passive *by*-phrase is present, which requires the presence of an unassociable AG role in the subordinate event (3.3 (6)). Note that the PP Incorporation Lexical Rule (3.4 (10)) applies to the lexical entry (15a), and the Prepositional Passive Lexical Rule (3.4 (2)) applies to its output. In (16d, d'), *raining* (underlined) is used without *it*, as if (speaking in GB terms) it were structurally *without* [PRO *raining*], where PRO is assigned the external θ-role by the verb. In (16e), *rain* is used in the imperative, which requires the presence of an agent role in RS (3.9 (2)). In (16f), *rain* is used as the complement of the verb *try*, which requires the presence of AG in its complement clause (4.7 (6)).

(16) a. The volcano erupted and hot ash rained over a wide area.
  b. The volcano erupted and rained hot ash over a wide area.
     cf. Hot ash was rained over a wide area.
  c. Most of the 2005 festival was rained on by remnants of tropical storm Arlene. (from the web)
     RS: [$_{\text{TYPE}}$ "rain-on"] in [$_{\text{EV}}$ __ <AG> [PT, GO$_{-\text{aff}}$]]
  c'. Mitt Romney was rained on by the loss of the election and walked away humiliated as President Barack Obama celebrated his reelection. (from the web)
  d. It can be cloudy without <u>raining</u>. (from the web)
  d'. A tornado watch is going on where I live…. What worries me is that it's not raining or anything, it's storming without <u>raining</u>. (from the web)
  e. Please don't rain today. (McCawley 1998: 566, originally due to Susan Schmerling)
  f. It's been trying to rain all day, but it just can't make it. (Chomsky 1981: 141 note 40)

The PP[*on*] in (14a) is a VP-adjunct that expresses an entity (typically a person) that is adversely affected by the event, whose role is GO$_{-aff}$, which is a negatively affected goal (cf. 1.4 (9)). This PP[*on*] can be added as a VP-adjunct to a transitive VP (e.g., *She shut the door on me* or *Every year he raised the rent on me*) or to an intransitive VP (e.g., *My hair drier broke on me*, *My wife died on me*, *My husband cheated on me*, *She hung up on me*). When a transitive verb is used together with this PP[*on*], its prepositional passive is impossible, because there is an intervening NP object (3.4 (9)). When an intransitive verb is used together with the PP[*on*], if the intransitive verb is unaccusative (i.e., an intransitive verb that takes a patient subject), its prepositional passive is impossible (e.g., **I was broken on* (*by my hair drier*), **I was died on* (*by my wife*)), because the Prepositional Passive Lexical Rule (3.4 (2)) is not applicable to unaccusative verbs due to the absence of an AG role. However, if the intransitive verb is unergative (i.e., an intransitive verb that takes an agent subject), its prepositional passive is possible (e.g., *I was cheated on* (*by my husband*), *I was hung up on* (*by the boss*)). Because *rain on* allows prepositional passive (14b), the intransitive verb *rain* resembles not an unaccusative but an unergative, such as the lexical entry (15a), whose agent role happens to be unassociable (<AG>).

(17) is the lexical entry for *rain on*. This is the result of the PP incorporation (3.4 (10)) being applied to the lexical entry (15a).

(17) lexical entry for *rain on* (output of the PP Incorporation Lexical Rule (3.4 (10))
 syntax: V, P[*on*] in [$_{VP}$ _ , [$_{PP}$ _ , NP]]
 F/A: Fa
 RS: TYPE "rain-on" [$_{EVENT}$ _ <AG> [PT, GO$_{-aff}$]]

Note that in (17), the sole ARG in F/A must correspond to the object NP of the PP[*on*] in syntax and the [PT, GO$_{-aff}$] role in RS. (Recall that (17) is an output of the PP Incorporation Lexical Rule (3.4 (10)); that is, the PP[*on*] was originally a VP-adjunct with its NP object carrying a GO$_{-aff}$ role.) This means that the subject NP position must be filled by the dummy *it*.

Technically, the Prepositional Passive Lexical Rule (3.4 (2)) is not applicable to (17). Although <AG> counts as a genuine AG within the domain of RS (the only difference between <AG> and AG is that the former is unassociable, that is, an AG that does not correspond to anything in syntax or in F/A (3.2 (1))), the input F/A of the Prepositional Passive Lexical Rule is specified as Fφaa, which is not satisfied by (17). To avoid this problem, we would like to propose that we drop the F/A specification in the Prepositional Passive Lexical Rule, because this part is predictable, anyway, from the specifications both in syntax, where the object of the preposition is lost in the output, and in RS, where the AG is made unassociable in the output. Here is the revised Prepositional Passive Lexical Rule.

(18) Prepositional Passive Lexical Rule (revised)
Active input   Passive output
syntax: V in [__, [$_{PP}$ P, NP], ψ]   →   V[PAS] in [__, [$_{PP}$ P], ψ]
RS: TYPE in [$_{EV}$ __ AG PT χ]   →   TYPE in [$_{EV}$ __ <AG> PT χ]
morph: V[0]   →   V[1, PSP]

3.6 VP Idioms and Their Passives

Those VP idioms with transitive verbs (i.e., [$_{VP}$ V, NP] in syntax) but with intransitive semantics (i.e., Fa in F/A and TYPE with one ROLE in RS, therefore, their syntactic object NP is nonreferential) cannot passivize, because they do not meet the input conditions of the Passive Lexical Rule (3.1 (3)) (Sadock 2012: 98). For example, the VP idioms that mean 'die,' such as *kick the bucket*, *pop one's clogs*, and *snuff it*, do not passivize with their idiomatic meaning: **The bucket was kicked (by John)*, **His clogs were popped (by John)*, and **It was snuffed (by John)*.

On the other hand, those VP idioms with meanings that are construed as having transitive semantics (i.e., Faa in F/A and TYPE with AG and PT in RS) can passivize (Sadock 2012: 98). Their meaning is distributed over their parts in a harmonious way. For example, the VP idiom [$_{VP}$ [$_V$ *pull*] [$_{NP}$ *strings*]] means 'exploit personal connections' and this meaning is distributed over the two parts of the idiom in such a way that the verb *pull* carries the meaning 'exploit' when it takes *strings* as its object and the NP *strings* carries the meaning 'personal connections' when it occurs as the object of the verb *pull*. Idioms of this type are called idiomatically combining expression (ICE) (Nunberg et al. 1994: 496). We propose the following bi-partite lexical entry for the VP idiom *pull strings* (1a) (cf. Sadock 2012: 59–60 (90) and (91)). In (1a), the first part gives the entry for the idiom as a whole and serves as record keeping. The second part gives the entry for the verb in the idiom. Note that the default correspondence rules (3.1 (2i)) establish from the first part the intermodular correspondences in the idiom: [$_{NP[3PL]}$ strings] ↔ [$_{ARG}$ PERSONAL.CONNECTIONS] ↔ [$_{PT}$ "personal connections"] and [$_V$ pull] ↔ [$_{Faa}$ EXPLOIT] ↔ [$_{TYPE}$ "exploit"].

(1) a. bi-partite lexical entry for *pull strings* (as ICE)
syntax: [$_{VP}$ [$_V$ pull] [$_{NP[3PL]}$ strings]]
F/A: [$_{Fa}$ [$_{Faa}$ EXPLOIT], [$_{ARG}$ PERSONAL.CONNECTIONS]]
RS: [$_{EV}$ [$_{TYPE}$ "exploit"] AG [$_{PT}$ "personal connections"]]

syntax: V in [__, NP]
F/A: Faa
RS: TYPE in [EV __ AG PT]
morph: V[0]

b. passive lexical entry for *pull strings* (as ICE)
syntax: [$_{VP}$ [$_V$ pull] [$_{NP[3PL]}$ strings]]
F/A: [$_{Fa}$ [$_{Faa}$ EXPLOIT], [$_{ARG}$ PERSONAL.CONNECTIONS]]
RS: [$_{EV}$[$_{TYPE}$ "exploit"] AG [$_{PT}$ "personal connections"]]

syntax: V[PAS] in [__]
F/A: Fa
RS: TYPE in [$_{EV}$ __ <AG> PT]
morph: V[1, PSP]

The Passive Lexical Rule (3.1 (3)) is applicable to the second part of (1a) and its output, the passive lexical entry for the idiom, is (1b), in which the first part is kept intact. In fact, this idiom is passivizable, just as a regular transitive verb (2a, g). In the passive lexical entry (1b), we can tell from the second part, the patient (PT) corresponds to the sole ARG in F/A and the subject NP in syntax. From the first part of the passive lexical entry, we can tell further that this patient corresponds to the NP [$_{NP[3PL]}$ strings] in syntax.

Because the NP object of this idiom carries a specific meaning ('connections') as part of the idiom, its syntactic behavior is expected to be just like a regular NP. This expectation is borne out. The object NP can be modified (2b, g), can be quantified (2a, e, f, g), can be topicalized (2d), can be raised (2 g), can be referred to by anaphoric devices (pronouns) (2e, f), can appear in the *tough* construction (2f), and can be relativized (2c).

(2) a. What strings were pulled to give the heretofore heartless Cheney a new heart? (from the web)
b. Pat pulled the strings that got Chris the job. (Nunberg et al. 1994: 510)
c. The strings that Pat pulled got Chris the job. (Nunberg et al. 1994: 510)

d. Those strings, he wouldn't pull for you. (Nunberg et al. 1994: 501)
e. Kim's family pulled some strings on her behalf, but they weren't enough to get her the job. (Nunberg et al. 1994: 502)
f. Some strings are harder to pull than others. (Nunberg et al. 1994: 517)
g. All the right strings seem to have been pulled in securing the proper state-of-the-art support staff. (from the web)

Here are two more examples of ICE (3) and (5). Again, we use bi-partite lexical entries.

(3) a. lexical entry for *spill the beans* (as ICE)
syntax: [$_{VP}$ [$_V$ spill] [$_{NP[3PLN]}$ the beans]]
F/A: [$_{Fa}$ [$_{Faa}$ REVEAL], [$_{ARG}$ THE.SECRET]]
RS: [$_{EV}$ [$_{TYPE}$ "reveal"] [AG, SO] [$_{[PT, TH]}$ "secret"]]

syntax: V in [__, NP]
F/A: Faa
RS: TYPE in [$_{EV}$ __ [AG, SO] [PT, TH]]
morph: V[0]

b. passive lexical entry for *spill the beans* (as ICE)
syntax: [$_{VP}$ [$_V$ spill] [$_{NP[3PLN]}$ the beans]]
F/A: [$_{Fa}$ [$_{Faa}$ REVEAL], [$_{ARG}$ THE.SECRET]]
RS: [$_{EV}$ [$_{TYPE}$ "reveal"] [AG, SO] [$_{[PT, TH]}$ "secret"]]

syntax: V[PAS] in [__]
F/A: Fa
RS: TYPE in [$_{EV}$ __ <[AG, SO]> [PT, TH]]
morph: V[1, PSP]

This idiom is passivizable, as in (4a), which is licensed by the passive entry (3b). The noun *beans*, which carries the meaning of 'secret,' can be modified by an adjective that can modify *secret* (4b). Sadock (1974: 100) observed that idioms have co-occurrence properties that reflect their meaning rather than their form. In fact, this idiom allows a PP[*to*] complement, as in (4c), that denotes the recipient of the secret, though the verb *spill* per se in its literal use does not take a PP[*to*] complement. Furthermore, the VP idiom can be modified by a PP[*about*], as in (4c), and the noun *beans* allows a CP[*that*] complement, as in (4d), because it means 'secret.'

(4) (from the web)
   a. Ironically, the beans were spilled by an analyst during an HP conference call!
   b. Within a few short moments, a former White House aide named Alexander Butterfield had spilled the political beans.
   c. Just one day before his birthday, my little brother spilled the beans to my dad about the party.
   d. Asus spilled the beans that Google's first Android tablet is coming this month.

The idiom *pull X's leg* is another example of ICE, whose bi-partite lexical entry is in (5). The transitive meaning 'tease' is borne by *pull __ 's leg*. That is, the NP within the NP[POS] corresponds to the ARG in F/A and the PT in RS. The CL[POS] in (5) is a possessive clitic.

(5) a. lexical entry for *pull X's leg* (as ICE)
   syntax: [$_{VP}$ [$_V$ pull] [$_{NP[3SG]}$ [$_{NP[POS]}$ NP, CL[POS]], [$_{N'[3SG]}$ leg]]]
   F/A: [$_{Fa}$ [$_{Faa}$ TEASE], ARG]
   RS: [$_{EV}$ [$_{TYPE}$ "tease"] AG PT]

   syntax: V in [__, NP]
   F/A: Faa
   RS: [$_{EV}$ TYPE AG PT]
   morph: V[0]

   b. passive lexical entry for *pull X's leg* (as ICE)
   syntax: [$_{VP}$ [$_V$ pull] [$_{NP[3SG]}$ [$_{NP[POS]}$ NP, CL[POS]], [$_{N'[3SG]}$ leg]]]
   F/A: [$_{Fa}$ [$_{Faa}$ TEASE], ARG]
   RS: [$_{EV}$ [$_{TYPE}$ "tease"] AG PT]

   syntax: V[PAS] in [__]
   F/A: Fa
   RS: [$_{EV}$ TYPE <AG> PT]

When the idiom is passivized (5b), the noun *leg* is pied-piped with the patient argument, as in (6a), because the Passive Lexical Rule changes the syntax from V in [__, NP] to V[PAS] in [__]. Note that because the noun *leg* is specified as singular in (5), we get a singular agreement in the passive (6a). The patient argument can be quantified (6b, c) and it can be used in the *tough* construction (6d). The idiom chunk *leg* is referred to in (6b, c) by the possessive NP (*John's* in (6b) and *the audience's* in (6c)) and by the pronoun *it* in (6c).

(6) a. My/Our leg was pulled. (from the web)
 b. We are still wondering <u>whose leg</u> was pulled, and beginning to suspect that <u>it</u> was not <u>John's</u>. (from the web)
 c. So, <u>someone's leg</u> was pulled? Are you sure <u>it</u> wasn't <u>the audience's</u>? (from the web)
 d. Your leg is easy to pull. (McCawley 1998: 75)

3.7 Double Passives

Some VP idioms in the form of V+N+PP allow two kinds of passive structure, which is shown in (1).

(1) *take advantage of* (Nunberg et al. 1994: 520)
 a. Advantage was [$_{V[PAS]}$ taken] (of the students). (inner passive)
 b. The students were [$_{V[PAS]}$ taken advantage of]. (outer passive)

Following Bresnan (1982: 61) and Nunberg et al. (1994: 520), we will explain (1a, b) by giving two lexical entries to the VP idiom *take advantage of*: (2a) as a morphologically complex verb and (3a) as an idiomatically combining expression (ICE).

(2) a. lexical entry for *take-advantage-of*
   syntax: V in [__, NP]
   F/A: Faa
   RS: TYPE in [$_{EV}$ [$_{TYPE}$ "exploit"] AG PT]
   morph: [$_{V[0]}$ [$_{V[0]}$ take] ≼ [$_{N[0]}$ advantage] ≼ [$_P$ of]]
 b. passive lexical entry
   syntax: V[PAS] in [__]
   F/A: Fa
   RS: TYPE in [$_{EV}$ [$_{TYPE}$ "exploit"] <AG> PT]
   morph: [$_{V[1, PSP]}$ [$_{V[1, PSP]}$ taken] ≼ [$_{N[0]}$ advantage] ≼ [$_P$ of]]
 c. It was more likely that they were simply taking advantage of, exploiting, if you will, mistakes that had been made by others and that had gone undetected. (from the web)

(2c) is an example in which a parenthetical (*exploiting, if you will*) is inserted right after *taking advantage of* and is semantically coordinated with it and shows that *take advantage of* is a semantic unit equivalent to the transitive verb *exploit* (Faa in F/A), thus supporting the lexical entry (2a).

The lexical entry (2a) undergoes the Passive Lexical Rule (3.1 (3)) and its output lexical entry (2b) licenses the outer passive (1b). Because the noun *advantage* in (2b) is not present as an ARG in F/A, nor is its corresponding role present in RS, it cannot be referred to by a pronoun (e.g., *They claimed John was taken advantage of but nobody was taken it of*), and it cannot be quantified (e.g., *How much advantage were the students taken of?*) (Nunberg et al. 1994: 521–523).

As for modification of the noun *advantage* by an adjective, although it is not impossible (e.g., *These students were taken unfair advantage of*, which means 'These students were unfairly taken advantage of,' just as *make considerable progress* means 'considerably make progress'; more examples in Takami 1992: 104), it is decidedly much less common than adjective modification in (3) below (e.g., *Unfair advantage was taken of the students*) (Nunberg et al. 1994: 521).

The morphological field of the passive output (2b) is specified as V[1, PSP] and the VFORM value PSP is realized on the head of the complex [$_{V[0]}$ [$_{V[0]}$ take] ≼ [$_{N[0]}$ advantage] ≼ [$_P$ of]], because VFORM is a head feature both in syntax and in morphology. In this entry, the complex *take advantage of* is treated as a single verb stem (V[0]), which is very plausible if we look at web examples, such as *I'm going through a taken advantage of moment myself* and *I'm feeling a little taken advantage of* and *This is not an opportunity that should go un-taken-advantage-of.* The first two examples show that the *taken advantage of* is used as an adjective in syntax, which is only possible if the complex undergoes the V[1, PSP]-to-A[0] conversion in morphology (cf. 1.1.1 (12)). This shows that the complex must be a single word (V[1, PSP]) in morphology. The third example shows that the converted *taken-advantage-of* is in fact an adjective stem (A[0]) in morphology, because the prefix *un-* is added to it (1.1.1 (2a), (13)). Again, the complex must have undergone the V[1, PSP]-to-A[0] conversion in morphology. The complex passive participle *taken-unfair-advantage-of* in *These students were taken unfair advantage of* has the morphological structure [$_{V[1, PSP]}$ V[1, PSP], ≼ A[0] ≼ N[0] ≼ P[1]], which seems to be very rare, as opposed to the more frequent morphological structure [$_{V[1, PSP]}$ V[1, PSP] ≼ N[0] ≼ P[1]]. For example, a simple Google search shows that the word strings *was well taken care of* and *was effectively made use of* are far more frequent than *was taken good care of* and *was made effective use of*, respectively.

Here is the second entry for *take advantage of*, which is treated as an ICE.

(3) a. bi-partite lexical entry for *take advantage of* (as ICE)
     syntax: [$_{VP}$ [$_V$ take], [$_{NP}$ advantage], (PP[*of*])]

132   3 PASSIVE

   F/A: [_Fa_ [_ARG_ BENEFIT], [[_F(a)aa_ GAIN], ([_ARG_ FROM ARG])]]
   RS: TYPE in [_EV_ [_TYPE_ "gain"] [AG, GO] [_[PT, TH]_ "benefit"] {SO | <SO>}]

   syntax: V in [__, NP, (PP[*of*])]
   F/A: F(a)aa
   RS: TYPE in [_EV_ __ [AG, GO] [PT, TH] {SO | <SO>}]
   morph: V[0]

   b. passive bi-partite lexical entry for *take advantage of* (as ICE)
   syntax: [_VP_ [_V_ take], [_NP_ advantage], (PP[*of*])]
   F/A: [_Fa_ [_ARG_ BENEFIT], [[_F(a)aa_ GAIN], ([_ARG_ FROM ARG])]]
   RS: TYPE in [_EV_ [_TYPE_ "gain"] [AG, GO] [_[PT, TH]_ "benefit"] {SO | <SO>}]

   syntax: V[PAS] in [__,(PP[*of*])]
   F/A: F(a)a
   RS: TYPE in [_EV_ __ <[AG, GO]> [PT, TH] {SO | <SO>}]
   morph: V[1, PSP]

The second part of the lexical entry (3a) undergoes the Passive Lexical Rule and its output lexical entry (3b) licenses the inner passive (1a) (cf. 3.6 (1a, b)). Because *advantage* in (3) is an ARG in F/A and carries PT in RS, it behaves as a regular referential NP: *advantage* can be quantified (4b, b'), referred to by a pronoun (4c), and modified by an adjective (4d). As pointed out by Nunberg et al. (1994: 520 note 34), *take advantage of* can be used without a PP[*of*], as in (4a). For this reason, the PP[*of*] in the syntactic field of (3) is optional, which corresponds to the RS field specification {SO | <SO>}; that is, when the PP[*of*] is present in syntax, it corresponds to the lowest ARG of the Faaa in F/A and corresponds to SO in RS, whereas when the PP[*of*] does not appear in syntax, the verb corresponds to an Faa in F/A and the unassociable <SO> appears in RS.

(4) a. The way in which the deregulation was done was faulty; it allowed interest seeking traders to take advantage to their own profit.
   b. How much advantage do you think we can take of his failure?
   b'. That some advantage could be taken of Shoal Creek was proved by Morgan. (Nunberg at al. 1994: 523)
   c. They claimed that advantage was taken of Pat, but it wasn't taken of anyone. (Nunberg at al. 1994: 522)
   d. Maximum advantage is taken of the natural beauties of the place. (Nunberg et al. 1994: 521)

3.8 Locative Inversion in the Passive

Although a transitive verb cannot appear in the locative inversion construction (2.6), its passive counterpart can occur if it fits the locative inversion construction lexical entry (2.6 (4)), repeated here as (1). Two examples of passive locative inversion are given in (2).

(1) lexical entry for the locative inversion construction
IS: [$_U$ TOP < *rest* < P-FOC]

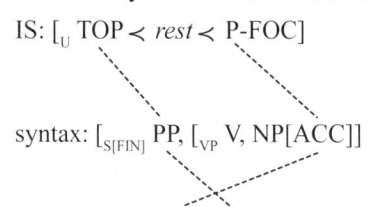

syntax: [$_{S[FIN]}$ PP, [$_{VP}$ V, NP[ACC]]]

RS: [$_{EV}$ TYPE TH LO] (only referring to the thematic tier)

(2) Bresnan 1994: 78–79
a. [Among the guests of honor] was seated [my mother] (??by my friend Rose).
b. [On the table] has been placed [a tarte Tatin] (??by Susan).
c. By a "ball" is meant an open ball or a closed ball.
(Maxwell Rosenlicht 1968 *Introduction to Analysis*, p.37)

If we apply the Passive Lexical Rule (3.1 (3)) to the lexical entry for the transitive verb *seat*, the output is (3).

(3) input: lexical entry for *seat*   passive output
syntax: V in [__, NP, PP]   →   V[PAS] in [__, PP]
F/A: Faaa   →   Faa
RS: [$_{TYPE}$ "seat"] in [$_{EV}$ __ AG   →   [$_{TYPE}$ "seat"] in [$_{EV}$ __ <AG>
[PT, TH] LO]   [PT, TH] LO]

In the output syntax, V[PAS] takes a subject NP and a PP complement. Under the default correspondence rules (1.4 (7)), the subject NP in syntax corresponds to the subject ARG in F/A and the [PT, TH] role in RS, whereas the PP complement in syntax corresponds to the lower ARG in F/A and the LO role in RS. Note that the AG in RS is an unassociable role. So, if we only look at the thematic tier of the output RS in (3), it consists of TH and LO, which meets the RS of the locative inversion construction (1), in which the locative PP and the theme NP correspond to the utterance-initial topic (TOP) and the utterance-final presentational focus (P-FOC), respectively. Although the passive participle *seated* can appear in the two syntactic environments, satisfying the lexical entry for the locative inversion construction (1) takes precedence over satisfying the passive lexical entry in (3), due to the Elsewhere Principle.

Examples (2a, b) show that adding a passive *by*-phrase reduces the acceptability. This is because the presence of the agentive PP[*by*] at the utterance-final position violates the requirement in (1) that the theme NP be placed utterance-finally.

(4) the syntax of (2a) with the passive *by*-phrase

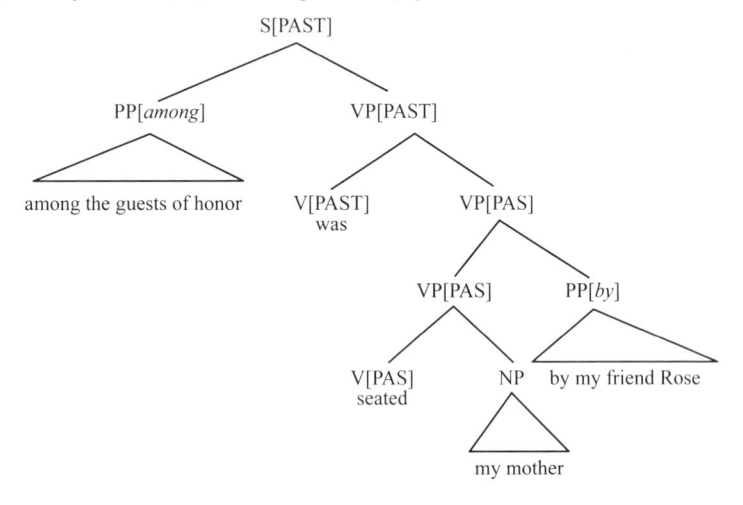

```
                    S[PAST]
                   /       \
           PP[among]        VP[PAST]
           /      \         /      \
  among the guests of honor V[PAST]  VP[PAS]
                            was     /      \
                                 VP[PAS]   PP[by]
                                /     \
                            V[PAS]    NP   by my friend Rose
                            seated    |
                                   my mother
```

(5) the RS of (2a) with causative coercion and role sharing

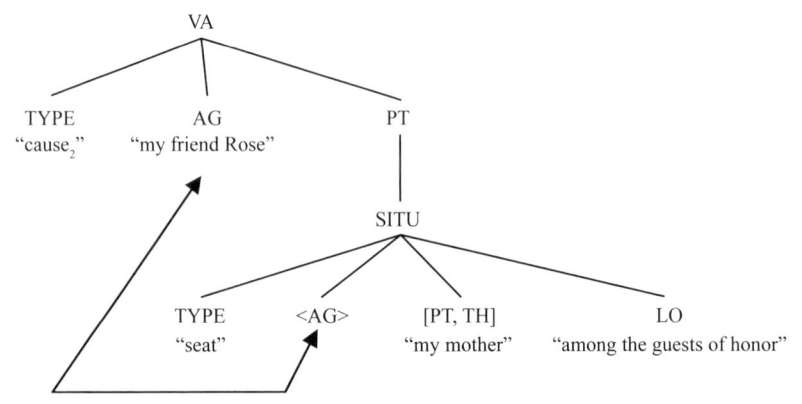

```
                        VA
                      / |  \
                TYPE   AG    PT
              "cause₂" "my friend Rose" |
                                      SITU
                                    / |  \  \
                              TYPE <AG> [PT, TH]   LO
                              "seat"    "my mother" "among the guests of honor"
```

In fact, Jerry Sadock (p.c.) pointed out that when the agentive PP[*by*] and the presentationally focused theme NP reverse their order and the latter comes sentence-finally, as in ?*Among the guests of honor was seated* [*by my friend Rose*] [*my mother*], the acceptability improves. Acceptability improves even more, if the theme NP is heavy (and undergoes the Heavy Constituent Shift (cf. 2.4 (5))), as in (?)*Among the guests of honor were seated* [*by my friend Rose*] [*my parents and relatives who came all the way from Japan*].

3.9 Imperatives in the Passive

The examples in (1) show that passive VPs can occur as imperative sentences. McCawley (1998: 548) observed that imperatives sound normal only when the surface VP "denotes something whose occurrence is under the control of the person denoted by the understood subject," that is, the addressee. The low acceptability of (1b) is due to a violation of this condition. Being admired by everyone is not something you have control over.

(1) a. Be examined by a doctor! (Culicover and Jackendoff 2005: 428).
　　b. ?Be admired by everyone. (McCawley 1998: 548)
　　c. Don't be intimidated by those bullies. (McCawley 1998: 548)

We will propose in 7.1 the lexical entry for the imperative construction (2).

(2) the default lexical entry for imperatives (as a construction) (=7.1 (6c))

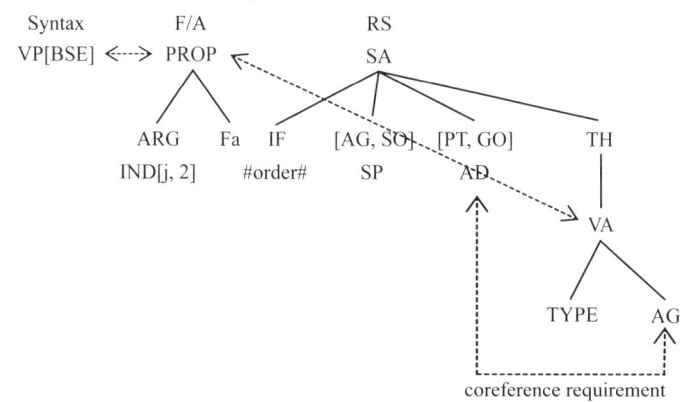

```
    Syntax      F/A              RS
   VP[BSE]  <---> PROP           SA
           /\          ⤺     /  |    \
         /    \             /    |      \
       ARG    Fa   IF   [AG, SO] [PT, GO]  TH
      IND[j, 2]  #order#  SP        AD
                                   ↑  ⤵
                                   :    VA
                                   :   /  \
                                   : TYPE   AG
                                   :        ↑
                                   :........:
                                   coreference requirement
```

phonology: falling intonation

In the RS of (2), the speech act (SA) with its illocutionary force (IF) #order# takes three roles, [AG, SO], [PT, GO], and TH, the last dominating a volitional action (VA). The [AG, SO] role is the speaker (SP) and the [PT, GO] role is the addressee (AD) and there is a requirement in the imperative construction that the AD and the AG role of the embedded volitional action (VA) be coreferent. This coreference requirement comes from the definition of what an act of order is, which is part of pragmatic knowledge: a (speech) act is an order if it counts as an attempt by the speaker to get the addressee to do something (Searle 1969: 69). Note that the subject ARG in the F/A structure carries IND[j, 2] (cf. 1.3 (6)) with the referential index j and the AGR value second person.

When the VP[BSE] of the imperative construction is in the passive, as in (1), two factors trigger causative coercion (3.3 (3) and 4.7 (3)). First, the subject ARG in F/A of the passive VP corresponds to the patient (PT), not the agent (AG) in RS. Therefore, the coreference requirement in (2) is not met. Second, the passive VP does not qualify as a volitional action (VA). For example, although the active sentence *The doctor examined the patient* qualifies as one, its passive counterpart *John was examined by the doctor* does not. Observe the contrast in (3).

(3) a. A: What did the doctor do?
B: He examined the patient.

A: What did the patient do?
B: ??He was examined by the doctor.
b. *John was examined by the doctor and Mary did so too.

Volitional action VPs can be asked by *What did/does X do?* or can be replaced by *do so* (cf. Culicover and Jackendoff 2005: 284). These two factors trigger causative coercion, which produces a new RS of (1a), namely, (4), where there are two instances of "cause$_2$." The lower one is triggered by the presence of the agentive PP[*by*] in the VP[PAS] and the presence of <AG> in RS, exactly as in 3.3 (6). The higher one is triggered by the two factors just mentioned.

(4) the RS after the causative coercion

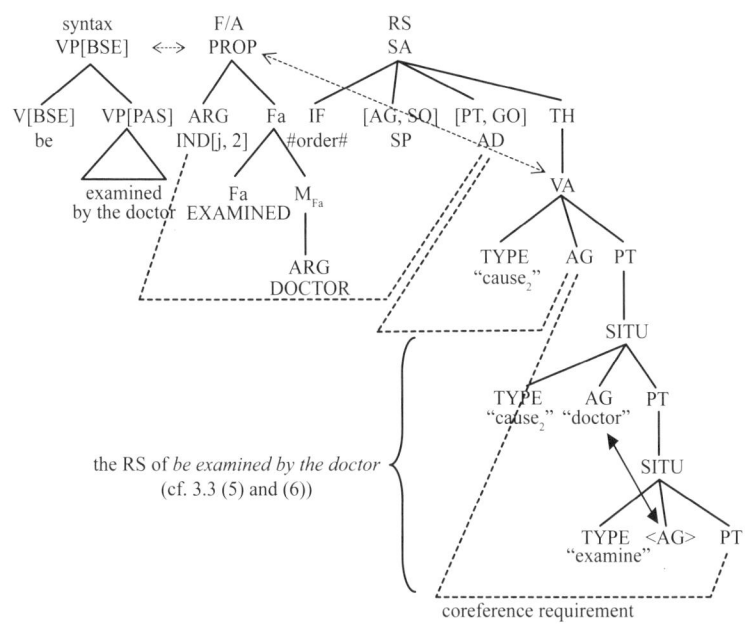

In (4), the coreference requirement in (2) between the AD and the AG of the volitional action (VA) is met. The coreference between the AG of the VA and the PT of "examine" is due to the fact that the addressee is the one who will be examined. In other words, the coreference relation between the AD of the ordering speech act and the PT of "examine" is divided into two coreference relations: the coreference relation between the AD and the AG of "cause$_2$," and the one between the AG and the PT of "examine." The intended interpretation of (1a) is paraphrased as 'I order you that you bring it about that you be examined by a doctor,' which is directly reflected in the RS in (4).

3.10 The Acceptability of Passive Sentences

Kuno and Takami claimed in their books (Kuno 1983, Takami 1992, 1997, 2011, Takami and Kuno 2002) that the acceptability of passive sentences is not determined lexically or syntactically, but is determined semantically and pragmatically based on the meaning of the passive sentence and its relation to the context in which it is uttered. (See related discussion in 3.1.2 (6).) They proposed three functional constraints on English passive sentences.

(1) Kuno and Takami's functional constraints on passive sentences (Takami and Kuno 2002: 218)
English passive sentences are acceptable if
   (i) the passive *by*-phrase, whether it is overtly expressed or not, represents an agent or something close to it (i.e., experiencer or external causer),
   (ii) the referent of the passive subject is involved in the verb's action or state (i.e., something is done to the referent by the verb's action or state), and
   (iii) the referent of the passive subject is characterized and distinguished from others by a salient property expressed by the passive VP.

(i) and (ii) roughly correspond to Bolinger's "affectedness" and seem to be equivalent to Sadock's observation in 3.4.3 about prepositional passives that the more patient-like the referent of the subject NP (i.e., the object of the preposition in the corresponding active) is perceived to be by the speaker/addressee and the more agent-like the referent of the object NP of the agentive PP[*by*] (i.e., the subject in the corresponding active), if there is one, is perceived to be, the more acceptable the passive is. However, the contrast in the passive pairs (2) and (3) is difficult to explain with (1i, ii). The contrast can be better explained by their third constraint (1iii) on characterizability. The referent of the subject NP of b-sentences is clearly characterized by the salient property expressed by the passive VP.

(2) a. *London was visited by John yesterday. (Takami and Kuno 2002: 215)
    b. London is visited by millions of tourists every year.

(3) a. *The mountain was flown over by the plane. (Takami and Kuno 2002: 208)
    b. The mountain was flown over by the Air Force.

Their third constraint also better explains the examples we have considered so far.

(4) a. That corner hasn't been turned yet. (=3.1.2 (7c))
cf. *The corner was turned by George. (=3.1.2 (7b))
b. The bridge has been walked under by generations of lovers. (=3.4.2 (5c))
cf. *The bridge was walked under by the dog.
c. This lake is not to be camped beside by anybody! (=3.4.2 (5d))
*The lake was camped beside by my sister.
d. This porch was walked on by Teddy Roosevelt. (=3.4.3 (17a))
e. This chair was sat on by Adolf Hitler. (=3.4.3 (17b))
f. That cup was drunk out of by Napoleon. (=3.4.3 (17c))

To better characterize the referent of the subject NP of a passive sentence, not only the subject NP and the *by*-phrase but also modifiers of various sorts play an important role. This is shown in (5)-(7), where the relevant modifiers are underlined.

(5) a. *The couple next door is known by John. (Takami and Kuno 2002: 215)
b. The couple next door is only known by John.

(6) a. ??*Shogun* was read by John. (Takami and Kuno 2002: 204)
b. *Shogun* was read even by John.

(7) a. *The room was walked through by the boy.
b. This room was walked through by the boy before he killed his mother.
(Takami 1992: 119)

We conclude that the acceptability of passive sentences is determined by some constraints along the lines of Kuno and Takami's functional constraints (1), which are applied not to passive participle lexical entries or to passive subjects or to passive *by*-phrases, but to passive sentences and the context in which they were uttered. All we can say at this moment is that their constraints, especially (1iii), can best be stated in our Information Structure module. However, we need further research to determine exactly how we can implement their insight.

3.11 The Family of Passive Lexical Rules

So far, we have proposed three passive lexical rules: for transitive verbs (3.1.2 (3)), for prepositional passives (3.4.1 (2), 3.5 (18)), and for verbs taking clausal complement (3.5.2 (3)). In addition, the passive lexical rule for transitive verbs will be generalized to 4.2.3 (9) to cover the passivization of object raising verbs. This family of passive lexical rules have much in common and we can organize the family of passive lexical rules in an inheritance hierarchy, in the same way as a family of similar lexical entries is organized in an inheritance hierarchy (1.1.2 (7), (8)).

(1) the family of passive lexical rules

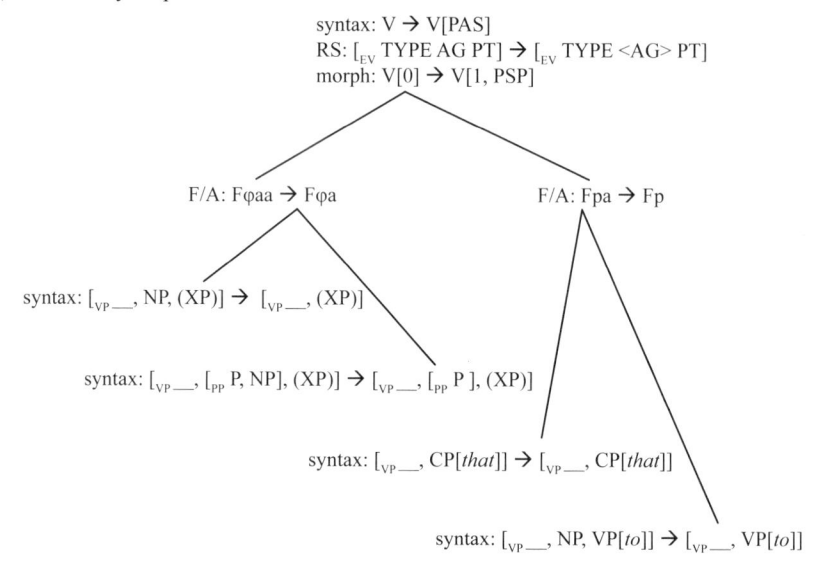

syntax: V → V[PAS]
RS: [$_{EV}$ TYPE AG PT] → [$_{EV}$ TYPE <AG> PT]
morph: V[0] → V[1, PSP]

F/A: Fφaa → Fφa

F/A: Fpa → Fp

syntax: [$_{VP}$__, NP, (XP)] → [$_{VP}$__, (XP)]

syntax: [$_{VP}$__, [$_{PP}$ P, NP], (XP)] → [$_{VP}$__, [$_{PP}$ P], (XP)]

syntax: [$_{VP}$__, CP[*that*]] → [$_{VP}$__, CP[*that*]]

syntax: [$_{VP}$__, NP, VP[*to*]] → [$_{VP}$__, VP[*to*]]

Chapter 4
Raising and Control

> In this chapter, raising and control phenomena are discussed from a multi-modular perspective. In the discussion on subject-to-object raising, the ternary-branching VP structure is defended. The discussion on obligatory control includes passivization of unique control verbs, impersonal passives, and the semantic and pragmatic factors involved in controller shift.

4.1 Subject Raising

Subject-to-subject raising (henceforth, subject raising), which is illustrated in (1b), is said to occur with verbs such as *seem, appear,* and *happen* and adjectives such as *likely, sure,* and *certain*. Semantically, these subject raising predicates take only one role (i.e., theme) that corresponds to a proposition, which is expressed in syntax as a CP[*that*] or S[FIN]. This is shown in (1a). The matrix subject NP position is filled by the dummy *it* (2.4 (9)), because the VP *seems that John likes Mary* is semantically saturated, and hence, there is no role left that the subject NP can bear.

(1) a. It seems [$_{CP[that]}$ that John likes Mary].
 b. John seems [$_{VP[to]}$ to like Mary].
 c. [$_{NP}$] seems [$_{S[to]}$ [$_{NP}$ John] [$_{VP[to]}$ to like Mary]].

The other way of expressing the same meaning is (1b), in which the subject raising predicate *seem* takes a VP[*to*] complement and the subject *John* of the embedded clause appears as the matrix subject. We call this sentence pattern the subject raising construction, which has been explained in transformational grammars by means of a rule (NP-movement or, more generally, Move α) that "moves" the NP subject of the embedded clause to the matrix subject position, as in (1c). Although we do not, and in fact cannot, adopt the "movement" analysis of the subject raising construction, because there is no such thing as a "movement" rule in AMG, we will continue using the term subject raising for descriptive purposes.

4.1.1 Subject raising as innocuous mismatch

Subject raising occurs, first and foremost, when an Fp in F/A (a functor that takes a proposition and returns a proposition: [$_{PROP}$ Fp, PROP]) is realized on a verb in the case of TENSE, or its syntactic correspondent takes a VP complement in the case of auxiliary verbs (cf. Sadock 2012: 161, 167). In fact, tenses and auxiliary verbs have been treated as subject raising predicates in some versions of transformational grammar (e.g., McCawley 1973: 259, 1998: 217–224, 1999: 45). For example, in (2), the tense [$_{Fp}$ PRES] and the functor [$_{Faa}$ LOVE] in F/A correspond to the finite verb [$_{V[PRES]}$ loves] in syntax. This correspondence involves a mismatch between syntax and F/A in that *John* c-commands the verb *loves* in the present-tense in syntax, whereas JOHN is c-commanded by PRES in F/A.

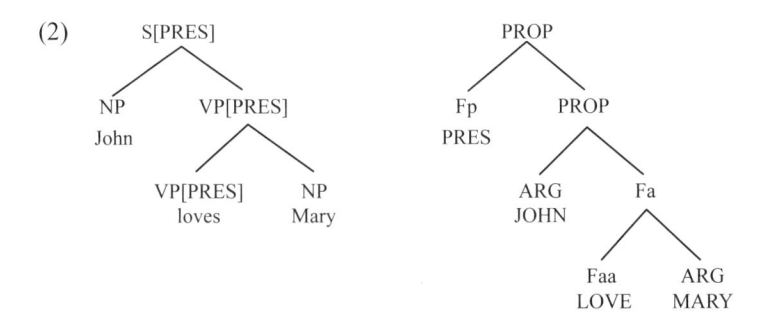

(2)   S[PRES]   PROP

      NP   VP[PRES]   Fp   PROP
     John   PRES
           VP[PRES]   NP   ARG   Fa
            loves   Mary   JOHN
                                                Faa   ARG
                                                LOVE   MARY

This mismatch can be displayed either in (3), in which the F/A structure is shown upside down, or in (4), in which the bracket notation is used to represent the syntactic and F/A structures. In (4), the mismatch shows up as a crossing of association lines. To save space, we will use the bracket notation to indicate mismatches between syntax and F/A. (5) is the lexical entry for the present tense.

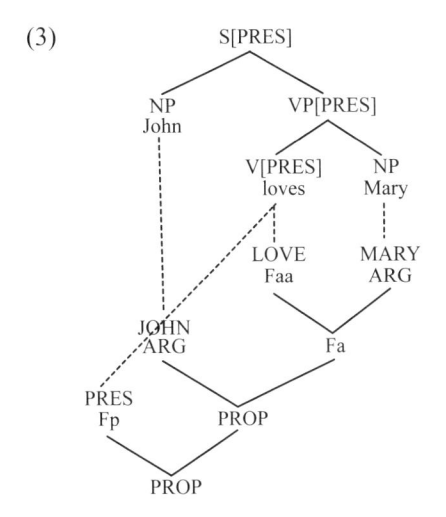

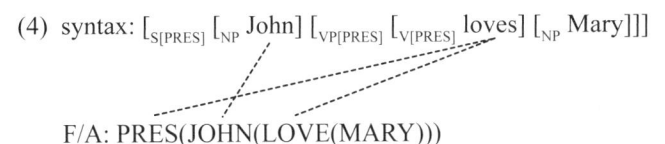

(3)
```
                S[PRES]
              /        \
           NP            VP[PRES]
          John          /        \
                   V[PRES]        NP
                    loves        Mary
                      |            |
                    LOVE         MARY
                    Faa          ARG
           JOHN
           ARG            Fa
        PRES
         Fp      PROP

              PROP
```

(4) syntax: [$_{S[PRES]}$ [$_{NP}$ John] [$_{VP[PRES]}$ [$_{V[PRES]}$ loves] [$_{NP}$ Mary]]]

F/A: PRES(JOHN(LOVE(MARY)))

(5) lexical entry for the present tense (cf. Sadock 2012: 163 (37))
syntax: PRES in V[__] (VFORM value)
F/A: [$_{Fp}$ PRES]
RS: nil
morph: PRES in V[1, __] (VFORM value)
mphon: PRES in [$_{V[1, \_]}$ V[0]] (=1.2.2 (2c)) and [$_{V[1, \_, 3SG]}$ V[0] [$_{AF}$ {Z}]] (=1.1.2 (2d))

This type of mismatch is unavoidable in English, and for that matter, in any language in which the tense is realized on the verb, because TENSE in F/A is an Fp that asymmetrically c-commands the subject ARG, as in [$_{PROP}$ [$_{Fp}$ TENSE], [$_{PROP}$ ARG, Fa]], whereas the syntactic correspondent of TENSE is morphologically realized on a finite V. This is an innocuous mismatch between syntax and F/A and as such can occur in a clause more than once without any loss of acceptability. (6a) is an example of a sentence with the finite auxiliary verb *may*, which corresponds to [$_{Fp}$ PRES]∘[$_{Fp}$ MAY] in F/A, the composition of two Fp functors. As discussed in 2.1 (9), the composition of two Fp functors $Fp_1 \circ Fp_2$ is defined as $Fp_1 \circ Fp_2(PROP) = Fp_1(Fp_2(PROP))$. The composition of Fp functors is, again, an Fp functor.

144 4 RAISING AND CONTROL

(6) a. John may like Mary.
  b. syntax: [$_{S[PRES]}$ John [$_{VP[PRES]}$ may [$_{VP[BSE]}$ like Mary]]]

  F/A: PRES(MAY(JOHN(LIKE(MARY))))
  ⎵⎵⎵⎵⎵⎵
  composite Fp

  c. John may have been seeing Mary.
  d. syntax: [$_{S[PRES]}$ John [$_{VP[PRES]}$ may [$_{VP[BSE]}$ have [$_{VP[PSP]}$ been [$_{VP[PRP]}$ seeing Mary]]]]]

  F/A: PRES(MAY(PAST(PROG(JOHN(SEE(MARY))))))
  ⎵⎵⎵⎵⎵⎵⎵⎵⎵⎵⎵⎵
  composite Fp

In (6b), the syntactic correspondent of the F/A subject [$_{ARG}$ JOHN], namely, [$_{NP}$ John], and that of its associate predicate [$_{Fa}$ LIKE(MARY)], namely, [$_{VP[BSE]}$ like Mary], are separated by *may*, the syntactic correspondent of the composite Fp, namely, [$_{Fp}$ PRES]∘[$_{Fp}$ MAY]. (6c) is an example of a sentence with a series of auxiliary verbs. Again, the correspondence between its syntax and F/A is the same. That is, the syntactic correspondent of the F/A subject [$_{ARG}$ JOHN] and that of its associate predicate [$_{Fa}$ SEE(MARY)] are separated by the string *may have been*, which is the syntactic correspondent of the composite Fp, namely, [$_{Fp}$ PRES]∘[$_{Fp}$ MAY]∘[$_{Fp}$ PAST]∘[$_{Fp}$ PROG]. There are two association line crossings in (6b) and four in (6d), each due to the innocuous subject raising mismatch. This type of innocuous mismatch between syntax and F/A must be allowed in any language in which the subject NP appears outside the VP headed by a finite auxiliary verb (V[FIN, AUX]), as in (7). Otherwise, a sentence with a finite auxiliary verb would be ungrammatical.

(7) [$_S$ NP, [$_{VP[FIN, AUX]}$ V[FIN, AUX], VP]] cf. [$_S$ NP [$_{VP[PAST]}$ [$_{V[PAST]}$ seemed] VP]]
  He <u>has</u> bought a car. She <u>seemed</u> to be sleeping.
  Er <u>hat</u> einen Wagen gekauft. Sie <u>schien</u> zu schlafen.
  Il <u>a</u> acheté une voiture. Elle <u>semblait</u> dormir.

The innocuous mismatches that involve subject raising that we have been considering so far are characterized as (8), in which (i) the outermost subject NP and the innermost VP in syntax correspond respectively to the ARG and Fa of the innermost PROP in F/A and (ii) the two are separated in syntax by a string of (auxiliary) verbs that corresponds in F/A to a string of Fp functors, namely, the composite Fp.

(8) innocuous mismatches in subject raising

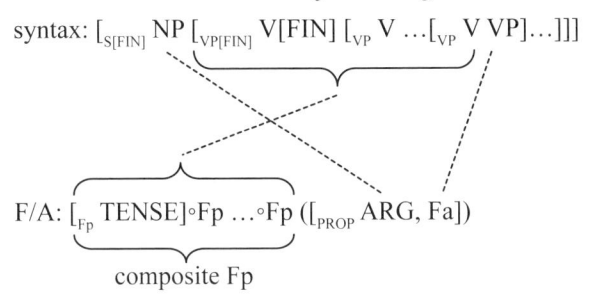

syntax: [$_{S[FIN]}$ NP [$_{VP[FIN]}$ V[FIN] [$_{VP}$ V ...[$_{VP}$ V VP]...]]]

F/A: [$_{Fp}$ TENSE]∘Fp ...∘Fp ([$_{PROP}$ ARG, Fa])

composite Fp

In (6d), the functor [$_{Fp}$ PAST] that occurs in a nonfinite environment corresponds to the perfect auxiliary verb *have* in syntax (McCawley 1973: 259–260, 1998: 221–223, 1999: 45, Sadock 2012: 161–162). The lexical entry for the perfect auxiliary verb *have* is given in (9).

(9) lexical entry for the perfect auxiliary *have*
syntax: V[AUX] in [__, VP[PSP]]
F/A: [$_{Fp}$ PAST]
RS: nil
morph: V[0]
mphon: [$_{V[0]}$ /hæv/]
        [$_{V[1, BSE]}$ /hæv/] (from 1.1.2 (2a))
        [$_{V[1, PRP]}$ /hæv ɪŋ/] (from 1.1.2 (2b))
        %[$_{V[1, PSP]}$ /hæd/]
        [$_{V[1, PRES]}$ /hæv/] (with F/A [$_{Fp}$ PRES]∘[$_{Fp}$ PAST]) (from 1.1.2 (2c))
        [$_{V[1, PRES, 3SG]}$ /hæz/] (with F/A [$_{Fp}$ PRES]∘[$_{Fp}$ PAST])
        [$_{V[1, PAST]}$ /hæd/] (with F/A [$_{Fp}$ PAST]∘[$_{Fp}$ PAST])

The symbol % in front of the past participle form (V[1, PSP]) indicates that there is individual variation about this form (McCawley 1998: 226–227): some speakers have it and others don't. For those who have NOT learned this form, such sentences as *Nancy is believed to have already mailed the letter when I talked to her* (McCawley 1998: 221) sound acceptable, though the embedded proposition must have two PAST tenses semantically: PAST(PAST(NANCY (MAIL(LETTER)))). They reject *Nancy is believed to have had already mailed the letter when I talked to her* (McCawley 1998: 221; Sadock 2012: 174). For those who have learned this form, the latter sentence sounds more acceptable than the former sentence (McCawley 1998: 227).

Here are examples of the subject raising verb *seem*, whose F/A category is Fp, and which works in exactly the same way as tense and auxiliary verbs. The lexical entry for subject raising *seem* is given in (11).

(10) a. John seems to like Mary.

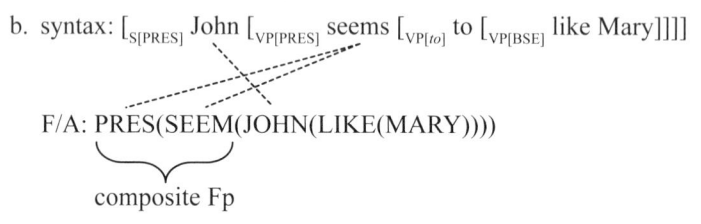

  b. syntax: [_{S[PRES]} John [_{VP[PRES]} seems [_{VP[to]} to [_{VP[BSE]} like Mary]]]]

  F/A: PRES(SEEM(JOHN(LIKE(MARY))))

  composite Fp

  c. John seems to have been seeing Mary.

  d. syntax: [_{S[PRES]} John [_{VP[PRES]} seems [_{VP[to]} to have [_{VP[PSP]} been [_{VP[PRP]} seeing Mary]]]]]

  F/A: PRES(SEEM(PAST(PROG(JOHN(SEE(MARY))))))

  composite Fp

  e. John may seem to have been seeing Mary.

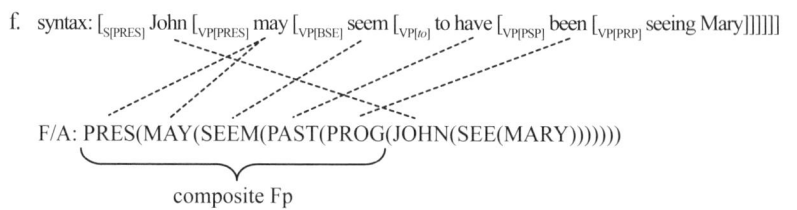

  f. syntax: [_{S[PRES]} John [_{VP[PRES]} may [_{VP[BSE]} seem [_{VP[to]} to have [_{VP[PSP]} been [_{VP[PRP]} seeing Mary]]]]]]

  F/A: PRES(MAY(SEEM(PAST(PROG(JOHN(SEE(MARY)))))))

  composite Fp

(11) lexical entry for subject raising *seem* (cf. Sadock 2012: 40(38))
  Syntax: V in [__, VP[*to*]]
  F/A: [_{Fp} SEEM]
  RS: [_{TYPE} "seem"] in [_{EV}__[_{TH} EV]]

The mismatches represented by the association line crossings between the syntax and F/A in (10b, d, f) are all innocuous subject raising mismatches characterized by (8).

4.1.2 The distribution of the dummy *it*

The subject raising verb *seem*, whose F/A category is Fp, can be expressed in syntax in two ways. One way is to take a VP[*to*] complement as a subject raising predicate (11). The other is to take a CP[*that*] complement as an expression that lacks subject raising, which is illustrated in (1a) and (12). The lexical entry for this use of *seem* is given in (13), where there is no ARG in F/A or role in RS that corresponds to the subject NP of *seem* in syntax, or in other words, the VP [$_{\text{VP}}$ *seem* CP[*that*]] is semantically saturated and there is no more role left that the matrix subject NP can carry. In such circumstances, the dummy *it* (2.5 (9)) is pressed into service to fill the subject NP position in syntax. Epistemic modal auxiliaries function in exactly the same way in this respect, which is shown in (14).

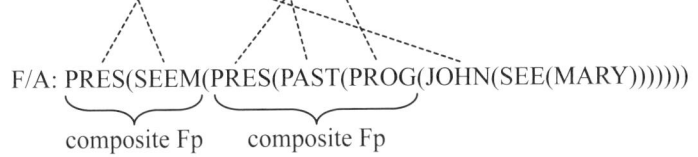

(12) syntax: It seems that John has been seeing Mary.

F/A: PRES(SEEM(PRES(PAST(PROG(JOHN(SEE(MARY)))))))

  composite Fp   composite Fp

(13) lexical entry for *seem*
 syntax: V in [__ , CP[*that*]]
 F/A: [$_{\text{Fp}}$ SEEM]
 RS: [$_{\text{TYPE}}$ "seem"] in [$_{\text{EV}}$ __ [$_{\text{TH}}$ EV]]

(14) syntax: It may be that John has been seeing Mary. cf. (6c)

F/A: PRES(MAY(PRES(PAST(PROG(JOHN(SEE(MARY)))))))

In (14), *may* takes a VP[BSE] complement and cannot take a CP[*that*] complement directly (**It may that John has been seeing Mary*). For this reason, the empty *be*, whose F/A and RS are nil (2.1 (13e); Sadock 2012: 29 (11)), is used to project a VP[BSE] node and *be* in turn takes a CP[*that*] complement. Note that the dummy *do* cannot be used here (**It may do that John has been seeing Mary*), because, on the one hand, it only has finite forms (V[PRES] and V[PAST]) and lacks a V[BSE] form, and on the other, it only takes a VP[BSE] complement and cannot take a CP[*that*] complement (2.1 (6)).

As for the lexical entry for *seem* in (13), this use of subject raising verbs does not allow a clausal subject (**That John has been seeing Mary seems*), which is evident from the syntactic field in (13). Note that clausal subjects are interpreted as factive by default (Sadock 2012: 37 (28)), which contradicts with this use of subject raising verbs, because they are nonfactive predicates (Sadock 2012: 36 (26)). Note further that the grammatical sentence *That John has been seeing Mary seems to be true* comes from not (13) but (11) and the CP[*that*] subject is an argument of not *seem* but *true*.

The dummy *it* also appears as the subject of weather verbs, such as *rain* (15a), and as the subject of extraposition (2.7 (5)) of such verbs as *shock* (16a). In these cases, too, the VP is already saturated semantically, and there is no role left that the subject NP can carry. This is why the dummy *it* is pressed into service.

(15) a. syntax: [$_{S[PRES]}$ [$_{NP[it]}$ It] [$_{VP[PRES]}$ rains]].
F/A: PRES([$_{PROP}$ RAIN])
b. syntax: [$_{S[PRES]}$ [$_{NP[it]}$ It] [$_{VP[PRES]}$ seems to have been raining]].
F/A: PRES(SEEM(PAST(PROG([$_{PROP}$ RAIN]))))
$\underbrace{\qquad\qquad\qquad\qquad}_{\text{composite Fp}}$

(16) a. syntax: [$_{S[PAST]}$ [$_{NP[it]}$ It] [$_{VP[PAST]}$ shocked John that Mary danced]].
F/A: PAST([PROP([$_{Fap}$ SHOCK](JOHN))]), where PROP = [$_{PROP}$ PAST (DANCE(MARY))]
b. syntax: [$_{S[PRES]}$ [$_{NP[it]}$ It] [$_{VP[PRES]}$ may seem to have shocked John that Mary danced]].
F/A: PRES(MAY(SEEM(PAST([PROP([$_{Fap}$ SHOCK](JOHN))]))))
$\underbrace{\qquad\qquad\qquad\qquad}_{\text{composite Fp}}$ where PROP = [$_{PROP}$ PAST(DANCE(MARY))]

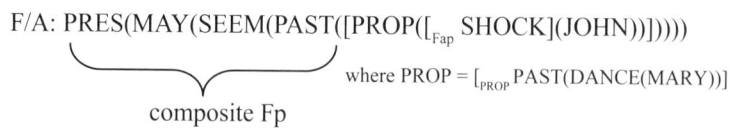

In (15b), the innermost VP *raining* is semantically saturated, and hence the largest VP *seems to have been raining* is also semantically saturated. In (16b), the innermost VP *shocked John that Mary danced* is semantically saturated, and hence the largest VP *may seem to have shocked John that Mary danced* is too. In both cases, the dummy subject is used to fill the matrix subject position, as expected. The lexical entries for *rain* and *shock* are given in (17) and (18) below.

(17) lexical entry for *rain* (=3.5 (15))
syntax: V in [$_{VP}$ __]

F/A: PROP
RS: [$_{TYPE}$ "rain"] in [$_{EV}$ __ <AG>]

(18) lexical entry for *shock* (output of the Extraposition Lexical Rule (2.7 (5)))
syntax: V in [$_{VP}$ [$_{VP}$ __, NP], CP[*that*]]
F/A: Fap
RS: TYPE "shock" in [$_{EV}$ __ [$_{[AG, SO]}$ EV] [PT, GO]]

4.1.3 Subject raising and EQNP

When an existentially quantified NP (EQNP), an NP that is interpreted as existentially quantified (2.4 (10)), is used as the subject of a raising predicate (19a), there are two interpretations available: wide scope interpretation of the EQNP (19b), in which the existential quantifier phrase (QP$_x$) that corresponds to the EQNP has scope over the composite Fp PRES∘LIKELY, and narrow scope interpretation of the EQNP (19c), in which the scope relations between the QP and the composite Fp are reversed (Sadock 2012: 58–59, McCawley 1998: 132, 652). (See 1.3 (15) for quantifier phrases.)

(19) a. [$_{EQNP}$ 500 Americans] are likely to die in accidents this weekend. (McCawley 1998: 132)

  b. [$_{QPX}$ ∃ X = 500 AMERICANS][∀x∈X](PRES(LIKELY(DIE(x)))) (wide scope)
      _____
      composite Fp

  'There are 500 Americans each of whom is likely to die in an accident this weekend.'

  c. (PRES(LIKELY([$_{QPX}$ ∃ X = 500 AMERICANS][∀x∈X] DIE(x)))) (narrow scope)
      _____
      composite Fp

  'It is likely that there will be 500 American accident victims this weekend.'

  d. innocuous mismatches between (19a) and (19b)

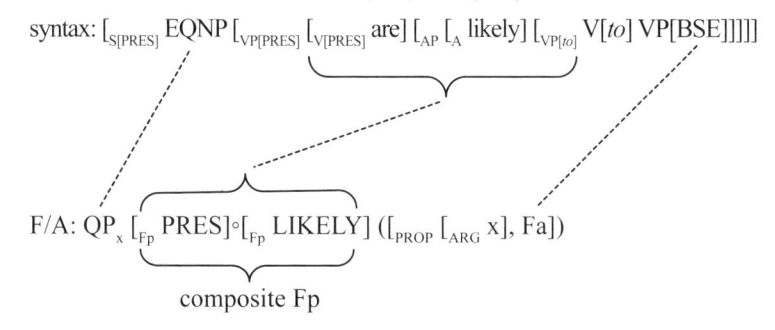

  syntax: [$_{S[PRES]}$ EQNP [$_{VP[PRES]}$ [$_{V[PRES]}$ are] [$_{AP}$ [$_A$ likely] [$_{VP[to]}$ V[*to*] VP[BSE]]]]]

  F/A: QP$_x$ [$_{Fp}$ PRES]∘[$_{Fp}$ LIKELY] ([$_{PROP}$ [$_{ARG}$ x], Fa])
           _____
              composite Fp

e. innocuous mismatches between (19a) and (19c)

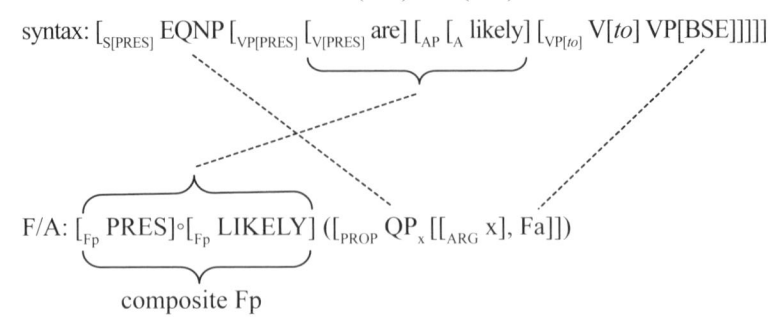

syntax: [$_{S[PRES]}$ EQNP [$_{VP[PRES]}$ [$_{V[PRES]}$ are] [$_{AP}$ [$_A$ likely] [$_{VP[to]}$ V[*to*] VP[BSE]]]]]

F/A: [$_{Fp}$ PRES]∘[$_{Fp}$ LIKELY] ([$_{PROP}$ QP$_x$ [[$_{ARG}$ x], Fa]])

composite Fp

In (19d, e), QPx represents the complex in (19b, c) [$_{QPX}$ ∃ X = 500 AMERICANS] [∀x∈ X]. Note that there is no mismatch in correspondence between the syntax (19a) and the F/A (19b), as is shown in (19d), whereas there is one between the syntax (19a) and the F/A (19c), which is shown in (19e). However, the mismatch found in the latter is of the same type as the innocuous mismatches found in (8).

The existential quantifier ∃ in (19b, c) comes from the EQNP *500 Americans* in (19a). Here are the intermodular representations of an EQNP, repeated from 2.4 (10).

(20) intermodular representations of an EQNP
syntax: [$_{NP}$ (DET) N']
F/A: [$_{QPx}$ [$_Q$ ∃] [$_{PROP}$ [$_{ARG}$ x], [$_{Fa}$ ARG, [$_{Faa}$ =]]]]
 • The value of the ARG comes from the N'

4.1.4 Subject raising in the inversion constructions

In this section, we would like to consider how subject raising interacts with the locative inversion construction (21) and the predicate inversion construction (24). The locative PP of the locative inversion construction (2.6 (4), repeated here as (21c)) occurs in the subject raising construction (21a, b). Because the Information Structure (IS) of (21c) requires that the locative PP be the utterance-initial topic (TOP) and the theme NP be the utterance-final presentational focus (P-FOC), the locative PP must appear before the subject raising predicate in (21a, b), creating innocuous mismatches between syntax and F/A, as in (22). Because the agreement controller is the theme NP in syntax (2.1 (23) and 2.6 (7)), the finite verbs (*seems* in (21a) and *are* in (21b)) agree with the S-final theme NP. Recall that TH outranks LO in RS (1.4 (6)) and therefore, TH corresponds to the subject ARG in F/A, which in turn corresponds to the S-final NP in syntax.

(21) a. [Over my window sill] seems to have crawled [an entire army of ants]. (Bresnan 1994: 96)
   b. [In these villages] are likely to be found [the best examples of this cuisine]. (Bresnan 1994: 96)
   c. lexical entry for the locative inversion construction (=2.6 (4))

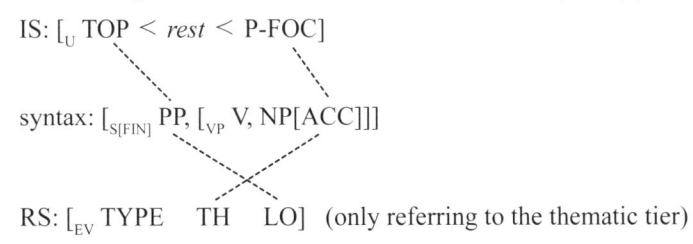

   IS: [$_U$ TOP < *rest* < P-FOC]

   syntax: [$_{S[FIN]}$ PP, [$_{VP}$ V, NP[ACC]]]

   RS: [$_{EV}$ TYPE   TH   LO]   (only referring to the thematic tier)

The intermodular correspondences of (21a) are shown below.

(22) a. intermodular correspondences of (21a)

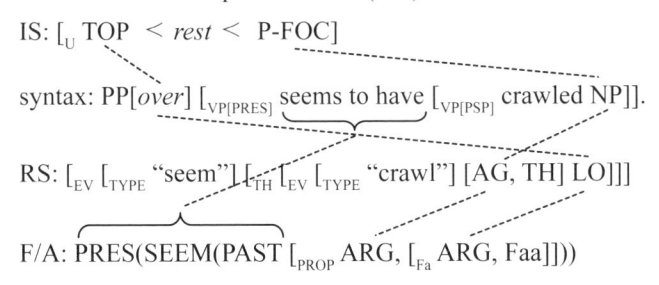

   IS: [$_U$ TOP < *rest* < P-FOC]

   syntax: PP[*over*] [$_{VP[PRES]}$ seems to have [$_{VP[PSP]}$ crawled NP]].

   RS: [$_{EV}$ [$_{TYPE}$ "seem"] [$_{TH}$ [$_{EV}$ [$_{TYPE}$ "crawl"] [AG, TH] LO]]]

   F/A: PRES(SEEM(PAST [$_{PROP}$ ARG, [$_{Fa}$ ARG, Faa]]))

   b. PP [$_{VP[PAST]}$ V[PAST] NP]

   PAST(ARG [$_{Fa}$ ARG, Faa])

   Out of the house came a tiny old lady and three or four enormous people ... (Levin and Rappaport Hovav 1995: 221)

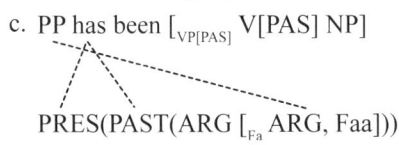

   c. PP has been [$_{VP[PAS]}$ V[PAS] NP]

   PRES(PAST(ARG [$_{Fa}$ ARG, Faa]))

On the house roof has been mounted a copper lightning rod oxidized green and ...
(Levin and Rappaport Hovav 1995: 222)

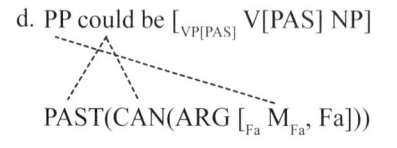

d. PP could be [$_{VP[PAS]}$ V[PAS] NP]

PAST(CAN(ARG [$_{Fa}$ M$_{Fa}$, Fa]))

... the benches under the elm from which could be seen an endless avenue of dark pink May trees ...
(Levin and Rappaport Hovav 1995: 222)

It is a matter of course that the locative PP of the locative inversion construction, or for that matter the predicate phrase of the predicate inversion construction (24) and subject idiom chunks (30), is allowed to raise, because on the one hand, the locative PP appears in a finite locative inversion clause (22b), which involves raising due to the tense PAST on the finite verb, and on the other hand, it appears in a finite locative inversion clause with a finite auxiliary verb (22c, d), which also involves raising.

The innocuous mismatches between syntax and F/A characterized by (8) do not cover (22a), because the S-initial phrase in (8) is an NP that corresponds to the subject ARG in F/A. This is not true in (22a). We need to generalize (8) to (23), so that it covers both (8) and (22a).

(23) innocuous mismatches in subject raising (generalized)

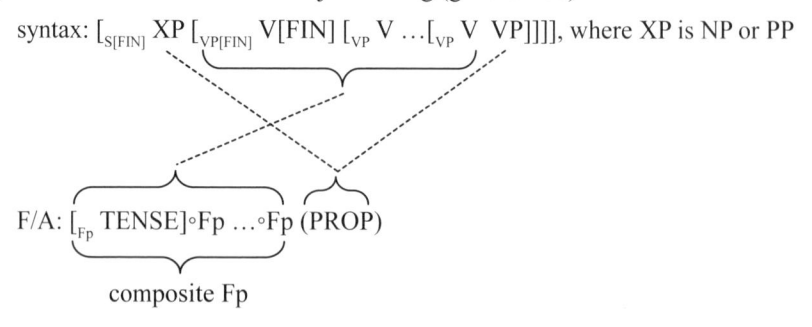

syntax: [$_{S[FIN]}$ XP [$_{VP[FIN]}$ V[FIN] [$_{VP}$ V ...[$_{VP}$ V VP]]]], where XP is NP or PP

F/A: [$_{Fp}$ TENSE]∘Fp ...∘Fp (PROP)

composite Fp

The predicate inversion construction is illustrated in (24a, a', a"). The preposed predicate phrases are shown by brackets. Three characteristics have been observed of this construction: (i) the empty verb *be* is required; (ii) the preposed predicate (AP, VP[PAS], or VP[PRP]) is linked to the immediately preceding discourse context (D-linked) (for example, the preposed APs in (24a, a') are in the comparative and the preposed VP[PAS] in (24a") is modified by the adverb *equally*), and (iii) the S-final NP or CP is the focus of the sentence. The preposed predicate phrase of this construction also occurs in the subject raising construction (24b, b').

(24) a. [Even more likely] is that you'll be able to easily acquire new clients from the wider web. (from the web)
 a'. [More damaging] is the auditor's report. (Huddleston and Pullum 2002: 97)
 a". [Equally flawed] had been the financial arguments. (Huddleston and Pullum 2002: 243)
 b. The versions of the outcome vary from source to source, but [the most likely] seems to have been that the Roman killed the Numidian, and then with the help of a slave ran himself through. (from the web)
 b'. But [even more damaging] seems to have been their regard for food staples. (from the web)

The syntax-F/A correspondences in (24b, b') are shown below.

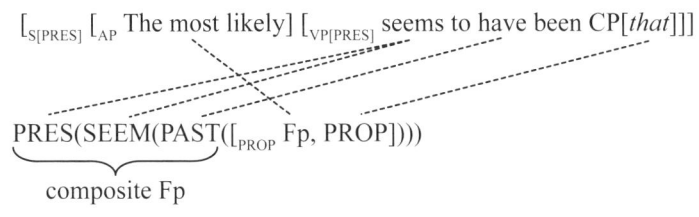

(25) a. the syntax and F/A of (24b)

[$_{S[PRES]}$ [$_{AP}$ The most likely] [$_{VP[PRES]}$ seems to have been CP[*that*]]]

PRES(SEEM(PAST([$_{PROP}$ Fp, PROP])))

composite Fp

 b. the syntax and F/A of (24b')

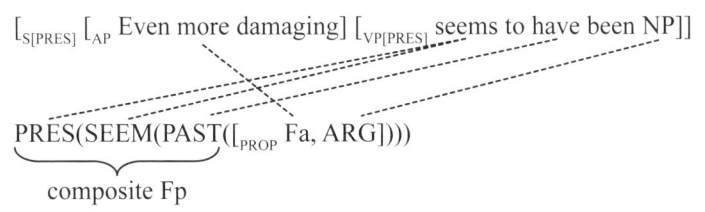

[$_{S[PRES]}$ [$_{AP}$ Even more damaging] [$_{VP[PRES]}$ seems to have been NP]]

PRES(SEEM(PAST([$_{PROP}$ Fa, ARG])))

composite Fp

(26) is the lexical entry for the predicate inversion construction, in which syntax requires the presence of the empty verb *be* and Information Structure (IS) requires that old/accessible information be utterance-initial and focused/new information be utterance-final.

(26) lexical entry for the predicate inversion construction
IS: [$_U$ OLD/ACCESSIBLE < rest < NEW/FOC]

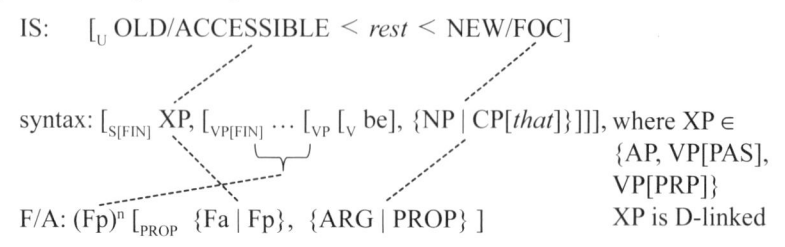

syntax: [$_{S[FIN]}$ XP, [$_{VP[FIN]}$ ... [$_{VP}$ [$_V$ be], {NP | CP[*that*]}]]], where XP ∈
{AP, VP[PAS],
VP[PRP]}
F/A: (Fp)^n [$_{PROP}$ {Fa | Fp}, {ARG | PROP}]   XP is D-linked

Note that because of the IS requirements, the predicate phrase (XP) must come sentence-initially and the NP or CP[*that*] must come sentence-finally. Here again, the characterization of innocuous mismatches in its pristine form (8) does not cover (25a, b). We need to generalize (23) still further.

(27) innocuous mismatches in subject raising (final version)
syntax: [$_{S[FIN]}$ XP [$_{VP[FIN]}$ V[FIN] [$_{VP}$ V ...[$_{VP}$ V VP]]]], where XP is NP, PP,
or predicate phrase,
such as AP, VP[PRP],
VP[PAS]

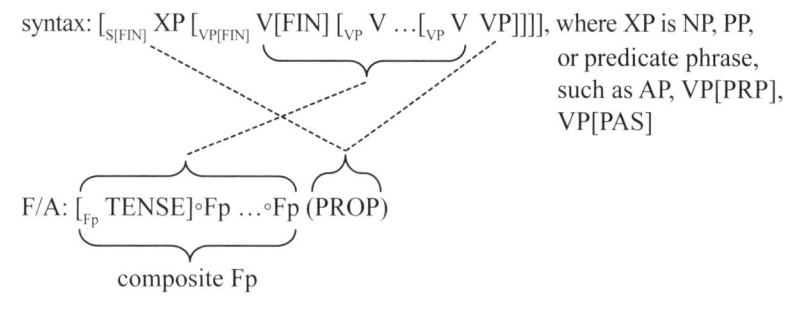

F/A: [$_{Fp}$ TENSE]∘Fp ...∘Fp (PROP)

composite Fp

4.1.5 Subject raising and idiom chunks

An idiom chunk, such as *all hell*, when used with the VP *break loose* (28a), occurs with subject raising (28b) (cf. Nunberg et al. 1994: 510 (32)).

(28) a. All hell broke loose.
b. All hell seems to have broken loose. (Sadock 2012: 59 (89))

The sentence idiom *all hell breaks loose* is an idiomatically combining expression (ICE) (3.6 (1)) in that *all hell* carries the meaning of 'pandemonium' and *breaks loose* "arises suddenly." We follow our treatment of VP idioms in (3.6) and propose a bi-partite lexical entry (29), which consists of two parts, the entry for the subject NP and that for the VP.

(29) bi-partite lexical entry for the sentence idiom *all hell break loose*
(cf. 3.6 (1a), Sadock 2012: 59–60 (90) and (91))
syntax: [$_{NP[3SGN]}$ all hell] in [$_S$ __, [$_{VP}$ break loose]]
F/A: [$_{ARG}$ PANDEMONIUM] in [$_{PROP}$ __, [$_{Fa}$ ARISE.SUDDENLY]]
RS: [$_{TH}$ "pandemonium"] in [$_{EV}$ [$_{TYPE}$ "arise suddenly"] __]

syntax: [$_{VP}$ break loose] in [$_S$ [$_{NP[3SGN]}$ all hell], __]
F/A: [$_{Fa}$ ARISE.SUDDENLY] in [$_{PROP}$ [$_{ARG}$ PANDEMONIUM], __]
RS: [$_{TYPE}$ "arise suddenly"] in [$_{EV}$ __ [$_{TH}$ "pandemonium"]]

The unacceptability of *All hell arose suddenly and *Pandemonium broke loose is due to the facts that the NP *all hell* is required to co-occur with the VP *break loose* in the syntax of the first part of (29) and that the VP *break loose* is required to co-occur with the NP *all hell* in the syntax of the second part of (29).

As expected, all kinds of innocuous mismatches are allowed in (30) just as ordinary sentences and, of course, subject raising with *seem* is one of them (30e, f). In (30), PROP is an abbreviation for [$_{PROP}$ [$_{ARG}$ PANDEMONIUM], [$_{Fa}$ ARISE.SUDDENLY]]. The syntax-F/A correspondences in (30e) are given in (31).

(30) a. All hell broke loose. (=(28a)) (PAST(PROP))
b. All hell has broken loose. (PRES(PAST(PROP)))
c. All hell may have broken loose. (PRES(MAY(PAST(PROP))))
d. All hell may have been breaking loose. (PRES(MAY(PAST(PROG(PROP)))))
e. All hell seems to have broken loose. (=(28b)) (PRES(SEEM(PAST(PROP))))
f. All hell may seem to have broken loose. (from the web) (PRES(MAY(SEEM(PAST(PROP)))))

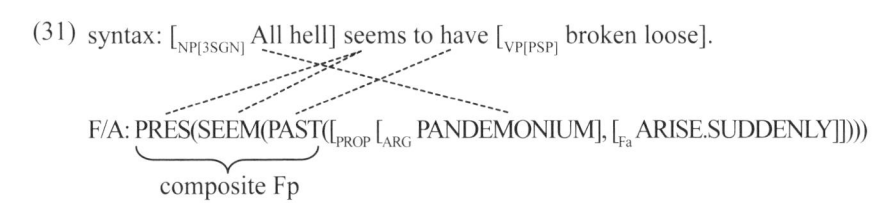

(31) syntax: [$_{NP[3SGN]}$ All hell] seems to have [$_{VP[PSP]}$ broken loose].

F/A: PRES(SEEM(PAST([$_{PROP}$ [$_{ARG}$ PANDEMONIUM], [$_{Fa}$ ARISE.SUDDENLY]])))
⏟
composite Fp

The syntax-F/A mismatches in (30) and (31) are all innocuous and captured by (8), or its generalization (27).

Because each of the NP and the VP of this sentential ICE carries its own meaning when they occur together; that is, when they are S-mates (1.2 (20)), it is possible for the NP to be the subject of a subject control verb (32a, b, c) (cf. Nunberg et al. 1994: 517 (50)). (Subject control verbs will be discussed in 4.4.) It is also possible for the NP to be referred to by a pronoun and at the same time for the VP to be referred to by a VP ellipsis (32d) (cf. Nunberg et al. 1994: 501 (7), 502 (10)). In (32e), *all hell* is the head of the relative clause *that broke loose*.

(32) examples from the web
  a. All hell threatened to break loose if the matter was put to parliamentary debate. An election was imminent.
  b. Then Matt Capps came in for the top of the ninth, and all hell attempted to break loose. Capps' first pitch was deposited into the left field seats ....
  c. I had to put a barrier wall of covers up so the kittens couldn't see each other.... They finally must have caught a glimpse of each other in the middle of the night and all hell tried to break loose.
  d. ... especially around the time my next son was born, I was worried about reverting so much I had a secret dummy stashed in case all hell broke loose but it did not and I worried for nothing!
  e. In light of the "All Hell" that "Broke Loose" the other day, it seems that life and business will soon return to normal.

Jerry Sadock (p.c.) observed that when the idiom appears in the pseudo-cleft and cleft constructions, it is degraded in acceptability (**What broke loose was all hell. ?It was all hell that broke loose*). A reason for the degraded acceptability seems to be that both sentences share the ill-formed presupposition 'Something broke loose,' in which *broke loose* violates the second part of (29), which requires that the VP *break loose* co-occur with the NP *all hell* in order to be interpreted as part of the idiom *all hell break loose*.

4.1.6 The subject raising verb *strike*

The transitive verb *strike*, when it takes an NP and a PP[*as*] as its complements, as in (33a), is a subject raising verb (33b). The lexical entry for this use of the verb is given in (34). Although *strike* is a passivizable transitive verb, the passivization of this use is ungrammatical (33c).

(33) a. You've always struck me as (being) an angry person.
b. There struck me as being too few women in positions of power. (Bresnan 1982: 358)
c. *Mary was struck (by Tom) as smart. (Bresnan 1982: 367)

(34) lexical entry for subject raising *strike*
syntax: V in [__, NP, PP[*as*]]
F/A: Fap
RS: [$_{TYPE}$ "strike"] in [__ [$_{[AG, TH]}$ EV] [PT, GO]]

Considering that the verb *strike* in (33a) has a closely related use that takes a CP[*that*] complement, as in *It struck me that you are (being) an angry person* and that the F/A of the verb in this use is Fap, we take the F/A category of the verb in (33a, b) as the same category, namely, Fap. In the lexical entry (34), the subject NP and the PP[*as*] complement in syntax correspond respectively to the ARG and Fa of the PROP of Fap in F/A, which in turn corresponds to the role [$_{[AG, TH]}$ EV] in RS. The intermodular correspondences of this lexical entry are shown in (35).

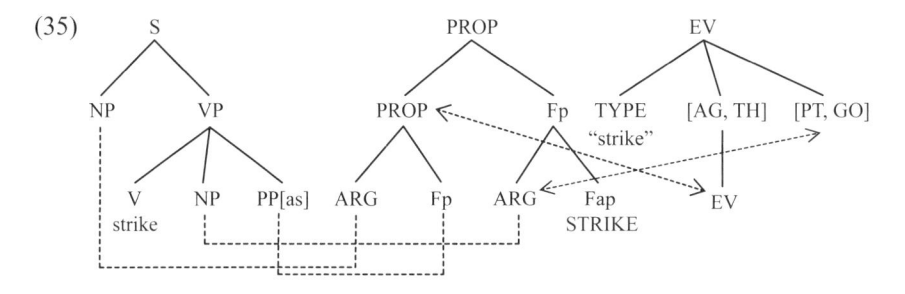

(35)

If the Passive Lexical Rule (3.1 (3)) were applicable to this entry, the output would be as follows.

(36) input: subject raising *strike*　　　　　　　　*output
syntax: V in [__, NP, PP[*as*]]　　→　V[PAS] in [__, PP[*as*]]
F/A: Fap　　　　　　　　　　　　　→　Fa
RS: [$_{TYPE}$ "strike"] in [__ [$_{[AG, TH]}$ EV]　→　[__ <[$_{[AG, TH]}$ EV]> [PT, GO]]
　　[PT, GO]]
morph: V[0]　　　　　　　　　　　→　V[1, PSP]

This output is ill formed, as (33c) illustrates. Note first that, as a general rule, a verb complement PP[*as*] canonically corresponds to an Fa in F/A. For example, in

[_VP_ *regard* NP PP[*as*]] and [_VP_ *think* PP[*of*] PP[*as*]], the PP[*as*] is an Fa, and it and the other complement form a complement PROP of the Fpa functors REGARD and THINK. In the output lexical entry above, the output V[PAS] takes one ARG in F/A that corresponds to the [PT, GO] in RS, which in turn must correspond to the subject NP in syntax. This means that there is no ARG available that can combine with the Fa of the PP[*as*] to form a PROP. In other words, there is no F/A subject for the Fa that corresponds to the PP[*as*]. For this reason, the output entry in (36) is ill formed. Note that when the PROP of Fap is expressed as a clausal subject (i.e., as a CP[*that*]), as in *That Mary was smart struck me*, its passive is well formed (*I was struck that Mary was smart*), as expected, which was explained in 3.3.2 (8) and (9). Strictly speaking, however, the subject raising *strike* (34) cannot be input to the Passive Lexical Rule (3.1 (3)), because the F/A of the verb is Fap, but the lexical rule requires Faa as its F/A input. This already explains the ill-formedness of the output of (36). Note also that a passive *by*-phrase (3.3.1 (5), (6)) does not help improve the acceptability of (33c). This is because the NP object *Tom* of the passive *by*-phrase in (33c), due to role sharing (3.3.1 (5)), must be interpreted as coreferent with the unassociable <[_[AG, TH]_ EV]> in the output of (36), which is impossible. In other words, an event-like interpretation of *Tom* is unavailable.

4.1.7 Subject raising in the imperative

Subject raising verbs can be used in the imperative (37). We can account for these sentences by means of causative coercion (3.3 (3), 4.7 (3)) in the same way as passive imperative sentences (3.9 (1), (4)).

(37) a. ?Appear to be working hard. (McCawley 1998:548)
  b. Don't appear to be wasting time. (ibid.)
  c. [_SA_ #order# SP AD_j_ [_VA_ "cause_2_," AG_j_ [_PT_ [_EV_ "appear" [_TH_ [_EV_ "waste" AG_j_ [_PT_ "time"]]]]]].

The RS of the imperative construction (3.9 (2)) requires that the addressee (AD) be coreferent with the agent (AG) of the volitional action (VA) that corresponds to the PROP in F/A, which is NOT(APPEAR(PROG(YOU(WASTE(TIME))))) in (37b). However, this is not a volitional action, and hence, there is no AG that the AD corefers with. This triggers causative coercion, resulting in the RS given in (37c), where the AD is coreferent with the AG of the "cause_2_," which in turn corefers with the AG of "waste." The paraphrase of (37b) that reflects the RS of (37c) is 'I order you$_j$ that you$_j$ bring it about that it does not appear that you$_j$ are wasting time.'

4.1.8 Subject raising in coordination

In this section, we would like to consider how subject raising interacts with coordinate structures. (38a-c) are examples of coordinated VPs. (38a) illustrates a coordination of subject raising predicates, and (38b), a coordination of finite VPs with different tenses.

(38) a. The girl seems tired and is likely to leave earlier.

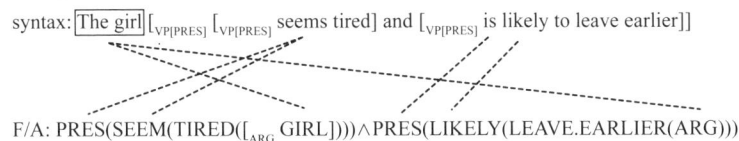

syntax: The girl [$_{VP[PRES]}$ [$_{VP[PRES]}$ seems tired] and [$_{VP[PRES]}$ is likely to leave earlier]]

F/A: PRES(SEEM(TIRED([$_{ARG}$ GIRL])))∧PRES(LIKELY(LEAVE.EARLIER(ARG)))

b. The girl liked John a year ago but hates him now.

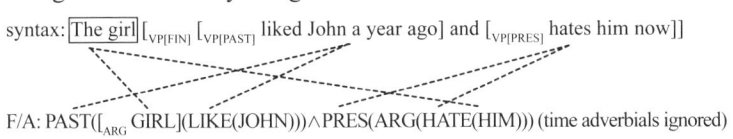

syntax: The girl [$_{VP[FIN]}$ [$_{VP[PAST]}$ liked John a year ago] and [$_{VP[PRES]}$ hates him now]]

F/A: PAST([$_{ARG}$ GIRL](LIKE(JOHN)))∧PRES(ARG(HATE(HIM))) (time adverbials ignored)

c. The girl went and bought beer.

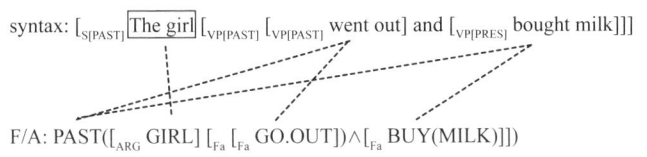

syntax: [$_{S[PAST]}$ The girl [$_{VP[PAST]}$ [$_{VP[PAST]}$ went out] and [$_{VP[PRES]}$ bought milk]]]

F/A: PAST([$_{ARG}$ GIRL] [$_{Fa}$ [$_{Fa}$ GO.OUT])∧[$_{Fa}$ BUY(MILK)]])

In each conjunct in (38a) and (38b), we find the same innocuous mismatches between syntax and F/A as we saw in (4), (6), and (10), which are all captured by (8). However, there is an important difference in (38a, b): VP coordination. We need to allow the association of the single subject NP of the coordinated VPs in syntax and the subject ARG of each conjunct PROP in F/A. Note that in (38a, b), the VP coordination in syntax corresponds not to an Fa coordination but to a PROP coordination. The mismatched association between a single subject NP in syntax and multiple subject ARGs in F/A must be countenanced when a finite VP coordination with different tenses in syntax corresponds to a PROP coordination in F/A. Such an innocuously mismatched association is in effect what the Conjunction Reduction transformation (McCawley 1998: 272–280) does in transformational approaches.

The ARG in the second conjunct in (38a, b), which corresponds to the subject NP in syntax, is required to be present for the sake of the well-formedness of the F/A, a result of the autonomy of the F/A module in the AMG architecture. This ARG contains the same IND value (referential index and agreement values) as the subject NP in syntax and the ARG in the first conjunct, but it does not correspond to anything in syntax, morphology, or (morpho-)phonology.

As for (38c), where VPs with the same tense are coordinated, its F/A structure is ambiguous. On the one hand, it can be a PROP coordination with each PROP headed by its own tense (PAST in this case), namely, [$_{PROP}$ [$_{Fp}$ PAST], PROP], and the innocuously mismatched association is allowed between syntax and F/A, exactly as in (38a, b). On the other hand, the F/A structure of (38c) can be an Fa coordination with a single TENSE, as in the F/A given in (38c). In the syntax of (38c), the entire clause is S[PAST] and since PAST is a VFORM value, it is shared with its VP, each VP conjunct, and each V, all due to the HFC (1.2 (3)). Note that if one of the verbs in (38c) had a different VFORM value, the HFC would be violated. It seems that when a VP coordination with the same tense is interpreted as representing a "scenario" of a "natural course of events" (Lakoff 1986), as in *Here's the whisky which I went to the store and bought* (Ross 1986: 103), Fa coordination is preferred. We will explore this possibility in 6.1.11, where we will deal with well-known counterexamples to the Coordinate Structure Constraint.

4.2 Object Raising

4.2.1 Traditional analyses of object raising

Subject-to-object raising (henceforth, object raising) occurs with verbs such as *believe* and *think*. These verbs take two arguments, as in (1a): a person who holds a belief or thought that is expressed as the subject NP and the content of the belief or thought as a CP[*that*] complement. Verbs of this class allow the meaning of (1a) to be expressed in another way, as in (1b), in which the verb takes an object NP and a complement VP[*to*] that are understood semantically as forming an embedded proposition. This sentence pattern is called the object raising construction. In transformational grammars, the object raising construction was explained either (i) by a rule that "moves" the subject NP of the complement clause to the matrix object NP position, as in (1c), or (ii) by "Exceptional Case Marking" (ECM), an "exceptional" way of assigning accusative Case to the subject NP of the embedded nonfinite clause, as in (1d). The ECM analysis of object raising (1d) assumes the binary-branching VP structure [$_{VP}$ V S[*to*]], which will be argued against in 4.2.6.

(1) a. John believes that Mary likes music.
 b. John believes Mary to like music.
 c. John believes [$_{NP}$] [$_{S[to]}$[$_{NP}$ Mary] to like music]

 d. John believes [$_{S[to]}$[$_{NP}$ Mary] to like music]
  accusative Case

Although we do not adopt these analyses, we will continue using the term object raising for descriptive purposes.

The French and German verbs of the same semantic class lack this construction (i.e., [$_{VP}$ V NP[ACC] VP[–FIN]]), although both languages allow the small clause construction for this class of verbs, just like English, as in *Je te trouve amusant* (from the web) and *Ich finde dich witzig* (from the web), both of which mean 'I find you funny.' However, they allow the subject control use (4.3 (7a) and (8a)) of these verbs. For example, the French verb *croire* and the German verb *glauben* both mean 'believe' and they take not only a CP[*that*] complement (CP[*dass*] in German and CP[*que*] in French) but also a nonfinite VP complement: *Je crois* [$_{VP[BSE]}$ *pouvoir l'aider*] (from the web) and *Ich glaube* [$_{VP[zu]}$ *ihm helfen zu können*] (from the web), both of which mean 'I believe myself to be able to help him.'

4.2.2 AMG analysis of object raising

In AMG terms, object raising verbs, such as *assume, believe, consider, expect, find, suppose, think,* and *understand,* take two complements in syntax, an NP object and a VP[*to*] complement, and their F/A category is Fpa. The default correspondence rules (1.4 (7)) establish the correspondences between the three modules shown in (2): NP$_①$ ↔ ARG$_①$ ↔ [AG, LO]$_①$ and NP$_②$ ↔ ARG$_②$ ↔ ROLE$_②$. Note that there is no constituent in syntax that corresponds to the PROP and EV enclosed in a rectangle.

162   4 RAISING AND CONTROL

(2)   S[PRES]   ⟵--------⟶   PROP   ⟵--------⟶   EV
       ╱   ╲   ╱   ╲   ╱   ╲
     NP①   VP[PRES]   Fp   PROP   TYPE   [AG, LO]① [PT, TH]
      I   ╱   ╲   PRES   ╱   ╲   "believe"   "I"
        VP[PRES] NP② VP[to]   ARG①   Fa   EV
        believe John ╱   ╲   IND[1SG] ╱   ╲   ╱   ╲
              to be fond of Mary   PROP   Fpa   TYPE   ROLE② ROLE
                                         BELIEVE "fond"   "John" "Mary"
                                         ╱   ╲
                                       ARG②   Fa
                                       JOHN FOND(MARY)

syntax: [S[PRES] I [VP[PRES] believe [NP John] [VP[to] to be fond of Mary]]]

F/A: PRES(I(BELIEVE(JOHN(FOND(MARY)))))

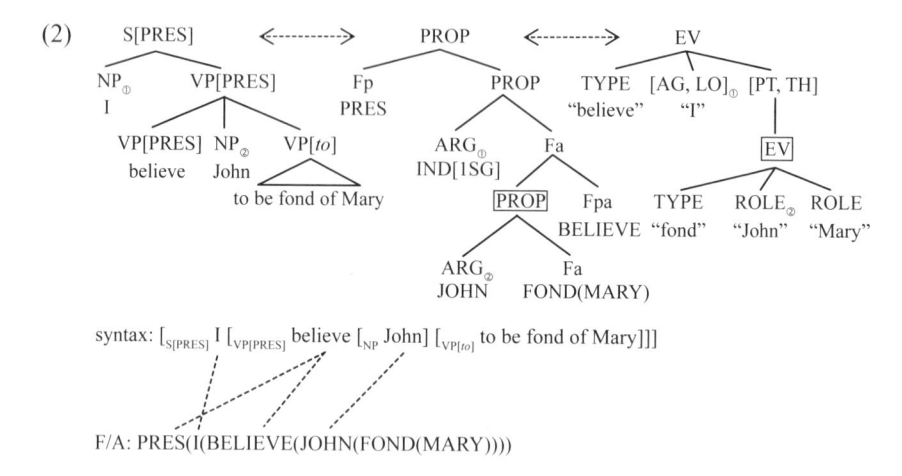

There is a mismatch between syntax and semantics (F/A and RS) in (2) in that the object NP of the matrix clause in syntax corresponds to the subject of the complement clause in semantics (Sadock 2012: 52–53). This mismatch must be innocuous in English, though it is not in French and German, which lack this construction. (3) is the lexical entry for object raising verbs.

(3) lexical entry for object raising verbs in English
    syntax: V in [__ NP[ACC] VP[to]]
    F/A: Fpa
    RS: TYPE in [EV __ [AG, LO] [[PT, TH] EV]]

Note that the linear order within the VP in (3) is due to the default order rules (1.4 (11c), (12)). (4) is another set of examples of the object raising construction in which the complement PROP has its own Fp (TENSE and ASPECT) functors. (4a) is interpreted as a nonfinite counterpart of *I believe that John has been seeing Mary (for a year now)*, in which the present perfect progressive ([Fp PRES]∘[Fp PAST]∘[Fp PROG] in F/A) corresponds to the string of *to have been*. Even the sentence *I believe John to be fond of Mary* in (2) is interpreted as a nonfinite counterpart of *I believe that John is fond of Mary* (4b). Note that the PRES in the embedded PROP in (4a, b) is another defective lexical item that has only the F/A value PRES and nil in all the other modules (5). (See McCawley's (1998: 221–222) arguments to motivate his Tense-replacement transformation (Pres → ø in nonfinite S) based on co-occurrence restrictions between tenses and time adverbials.)

(4) a. I believe John to have been seeing Mary (for a year now).

syntax: [$_{S[PRES]}$ I [$_{VP[PRES]}$ believe [$_{NP}$ John] [$_{VP[to]}$ to have been seeing Mary]]]

F/A: PRES(I(BELIEVE([$_{PROP}$ PRES(PAST(PROG(JOHN(SEE(MARY)))))])))

composite Fp

b. I believe John to be fond of Mary. (=(2))

syntax: [$_{S[PRES]}$ I [$_{VP[PRES]}$ believe [$_{NP}$ John] [$_{VP[to]}$ to be fond of Mary]]]

F/A: PRES(I(BELIEVE([$_{PROP}$ PRES(JOHN(FOND(MARY)))])))

Fp

(5) lexical entry for nonfinite PRES
syntax: nil
F/A: [$_{Fp}$ PRES] with the mother PROP corresponding to a nonfinite S or VP in syntax
RS: nil
morph: nil
mphon: nil

The presence of (5) in a nonfinite PROP in F/A can account for the contrast in *I believe John to be sick in bed {today | *yesterday}* and *John seems to be sick in bed {today | *yesterday}*.

The hallmark of the object raising construction is that there is no syntactic constituent S or CP that corresponds to the complement PROP (the PROP enclosed in a rectangle in (2) above) of the Fpa functor of an object raising verb. This is in exact parallel with the subject raising construction, in which there is no syntactic constituent S or CP that corresponds to the complement PROP of the Fp functor of a subject raising verb, such as *seem*. Therefore, the subject ARG of these complement PROPs must find its expression somewhere in syntax, and it corresponds to the matrix object NP in the case of an object raising verb and the matrix subject NP in the case of a subject raising verb. Note that these NPs do not carry any role of the matrix raising verb. (The existence of an object NP position that does not carry any participant role is abundantly demonstrated in Postal and Pullum 1988.)

As noted above, the matrix object NP of an object raising verb does not carry any of the verb's participant roles, since the theme role (in fact, [$_{[PT, TH]}$ EV]) is borne by the embedded PROP in F/A that corresponds to two nonconstituent phrases in syntax, the matrix object NP and the following VP[*to*]. (See (2) and (3).) This is again in exact parallel with the subject raising construction, in which the matrix subject NP of a subject raising verb does not carry any of the verb's participant roles. The theme role (in fact, [$_{[PT, TH]}$ EV]) of a subject raising verb is borne by the embedded PROP in F/A that corresponds to two nonconstituent phrases in syntax, the matrix subject NP and the complement VP[*to*].

Based on these exact parallels between object raising verbs and subject raising verbs and the characterization of innocuous mismatches in subject raising (4.1.1 (8)), we propose the following characterization of innocuous mismatches in object raising.

(6) characterization of innocuous mismatches in object raising
   (i) The subject ARG of the complement PROP of an object raising verb (V_{OR}) is allowed to correspond to the matrix object NP in syntax.
   (ii) syntax: [$_{VP}$ V_{OR} NP [$_{VP[to]}$ V ...[$_{VP}$ V VP]...]]]

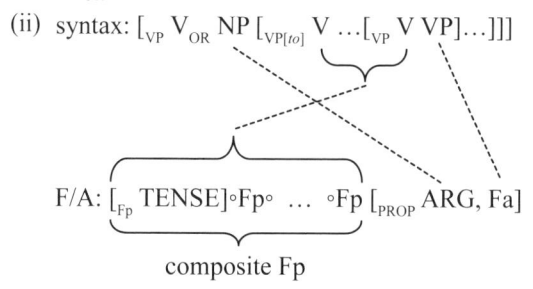

F/A: [$_{Fp}$ TENSE]∘Fp∘ ... ∘Fp [$_{PROP}$ ARG, Fa]

composite Fp

(6i) is a language particular property, and captures the correspondence in (2) between the matrix object NP and the subject ARG of the complement PROP of an object raising verb. For example, French and German lack (6i). On the other hand, (6ii) captures the type of innocuous mismatches countenanced by object raising verbs, which are exactly the same as the type of innocuous mismatches permitted by subject raising verbs (4.1.1 (8)).

4.2.3 Passivization of object raising verbs

When the Passive Lexical Rule for transitive verbs (3.1 (3)) applies to the lexical entry for object raising verbs (3), its output in (7) is the same as the lexical entry for subject raising verbs (cf. 4.1.1 (11)). For example, (8a) is an instance of the object raising construction, and its passive counterpart (8b) is an instance of the subject raising construction.

(7) applying the generalized Passive Lexical Rule (9) to object raising verbs
input: lexical entry for object raising verbs   output
syntax: V in [_, NP, VP[*to*]]   → V[PAS] in [_, VP[*to*]]
F/A: Fpa   → Fp
RS: TYPE in [$_{EV}$ __ [AG, LO] [$_{[PT, TH]}$ EV]]   → TYPE in [$_{EV}$ __ <[AG, LO]>
        [$_{[PT, TH]}$ EV]]
morph: V[0]   → V[1, PSP]

The output lexical entry in (7) shows that passivization of an object raising verb is a subject raising verb. The effect of passivization on the F/A structure of object raising verbs is shown in (8c). The passive participle *believed* is a subject raising verb (i.e., Fp in F/A) and permits a clausal subject (CP[*that*]) when it takes a VP[*to*] complement (8d), just as other subject raising verbs do.

(8) a. People believe those politicians to be trustworthy.
  b. Those politicians are believed to be trustworthy.
  c.   PROP   passivization of object raising verbs

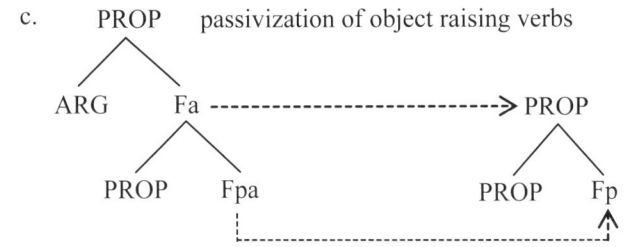

```
        PROP
       /    \
     ARG     Fa ---------------------> PROP
            /  \                      /    \
         PROP   Fpa                 PROP    Fp
                 └─────────────────────────↑
```

  d. [$_{CP[that]}$ That the country is hiding nuclear facilities] is believed to be true. (=2.5 (4d'))
  cf. *We believe [$_{CP[that]}$ that the country is hiding nuclear facilities] to be true.
  cf. [$_{CP[that]}$ That the country is hiding nuclear facilities] seems to be true.

Strictly speaking, for the Passive Lexical Rule to apply to object raising verbs (3), we need to generalize the Passive Lexical Rule for transitive verbs (3.1 (3)) to (9), because the pristine Passive Lexical Rule for transitive verbs only applies to verbs of the F/A category Fφaa, which excludes the F/A category of object raising verbs Fpa.

(9) Passive Lexical Rule for transitive verbs (generalized)
  Active input   Passive output
  syntax: V in [__, NP, ψ]   → V[PAS] in [__, ψ]

F/A: Fφa   → Fφ
RS: TYPE in [$_{EV}$ __ AG PT χ]   → TYPE in [$_{EV}$ __ <AG> PT χ]
morph: V[0]   → V[1, PSP]

Not all subject raising verbs in the passive are the result of the generalized Passive Lexical Rule (9) applying to the lexical entry for an object raising verb. Some passive verbs (V[PAS] in syntax) are listed in the lexicon as subject raising verbs with no corresponding object raising verbs. Verbs such as *say*, *rumor*, *allege*, *repute*, *state* have a subject raising passive use (e.g., *John is said/rumored to be at home*), but they lack an object raising use (**Mary says/rumors John to be at home*). The existence of such passive verbs confirms that the lexical entry of a passive verb is needed independently of whether or not it is "derived" from its corresponding active verb.

4.2.4 Dummy NPs and idiom chunks in object raising

When the VP[*to*] complement of an object raising verb is semantically saturated, the dummy *it* (2.4 (9)) is used to fill the matrix object NP position of the object raising verb. (This is exactly the same as the circumstances under which the dummy *it* is used to fill the matrix subject NP position of a subject raising verb, as in *It seems to be raining*, when its VP[*to*] complement is semantically saturated.) This is illustrated in (10a).

When the VP[*to*] complement of an object raising verb consists of an existentially quantified theme NP (EQNP), an optional locative PP, and a verb that licenses the dummy *there* (2.4 (8)), and hence is semantically saturated, the matrix object position of the object raising verb must be filled with the dummy *there* (10b). Recall that because the environment in which the dummy *there* occurs is more specific than the environment in which the dummy *it* occurs, the appearance of the former preempts that of the latter, due to the Elsewhere Principle (1.1.2 (3)).

(10) a. People believe [$_{NP[it]}$ it] [$_{VP[to]}$ to be raining].
   PRES(PEOPLE(BELIEVE([$_{PROP}$ PROG([$_{PROP}$ RAIN])])))
b. People believe [$_{NP[there]}$ there] to be [$_{EQNP}$ mistakes] in the proof.
   cf. *People believe [$_{NP[it]}$ it] to be [$_{EQNP}$ mistakes] in the proof.
   PRES(PEOPLE(BELIEVE([$_{QPX}$ ∃ X$_{+Set}$ = MISTAKES] PRES [(X)(BE (IN.THE.PROOF))])))

Some object raising verbs take a PP[*as*] complement instead of VP[*to*]. *Regard* is such a verb with its subcategorization frame [__, NP, PP[*as*]]: *We regard there as being no solution to this problem* (Pollard and Sag 1994: 108) and *There is regarded as being no issue that needs further investigation* (from the web). They are passivizable, just as the other object raising verbs, and the result is a subject raising verb with a PP[*as*] complement.

We observed in 4.1 (28b) that an idiom chunk NP subject of an idiomatically combining expression (ICE) occurs as the matrix subject of the subject raising construction. It is also true that such an NP occurs as the matrix object of the object raising construction, as in (11). See the bi-partite lexical entry for *all hell break loose* (4.1 (29)).

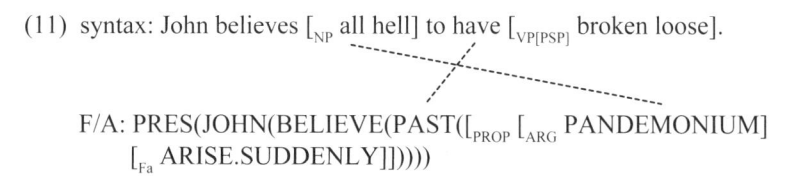

(11) syntax: John believes [$_{NP}$ all hell] to have [$_{VP[PSP]}$ broken loose].

F/A: PRES(JOHN(BELIEVE(PAST([$_{PROP}$ [$_{ARG}$ PANDEMONIUM] [$_{Fa}$ ARISE.SUDDENLY]]))))

The mismatch in (11) between syntax and F/A is captured by (6ii).

4.2.5 Characterizing raising predicates

Some of the semantic characteristics of raising verbs are (i) that they express how the speaker conceives the content of the complement proposition (the speaker's epistemic attitude toward the content of the proposition), for example, how plausible he takes it to be, or how he comes to know it, and (ii) that they assert the content of the proposition; that is, it is not a presupposed background part but an asserted foreground part of the sentence meaning. (The subject raising verb *happen* is an implicative verb, but (i) and (ii) still hold.) Because factive verbs express that the speaker takes the content of the complement proposition for granted, the complement proposition is not an asserted part. Therefore, subject and object raising verbs are not factive verbs (Kiparsky and Kiparsky 1971: 346, 348). Factivity also explains why subject raising verbs cannot have a clausal subject (*CP[*that*] *seems/ appears/happens*). A clausal subject is interpreted as factive, that is, presupposed (background) information (Sadock 2012: 36, Kiparsky and Kiparsky 1971: 366), which contradicts with the nonfactive characteristic of subject raising verbs.

We would like to conflate 4.1.1 (8) and 4.2.2 (6), which describe innocuous mismatches in English between syntax and F/A, into a single condition on raising predicates that guarantees innocuous mismatches between syntax and F/A.

(12) Raising Principle
 (i) The subject ARG of the complement PROP of a raising predicate X_R ($X = V$ or A) is allowed to correspond to a matrix NP position in syntax.
 (ii) syntax: NP, X_R, $[_{VP[-FIN]}$ V ...$[_{VP}$ V VP[−FIN]]...]

 F/A: $[_{Fp}$ TENSE]∘Fp∘...∘Fp $[_{PROP}$ ARG, Fa]

 IS: foreground information

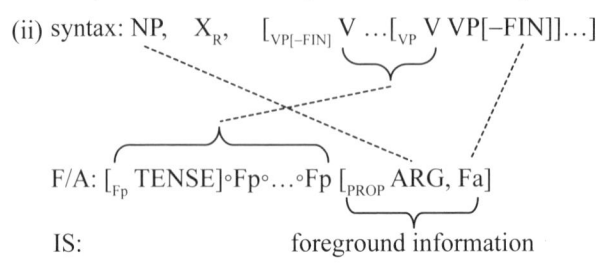

In (12i), the matrix NP that the subject ARG corresponds to cannot carry a role of the raising predicate X_R, which is entailed by the default correspondence 1.4 (7a), which says in part that NP ◄--► ROLE (one to one correspondence between NPs and ROLEs). (12ii) says that the matrix NP and its nonfinite associate VP can be separated in syntax by a string of verbs if the string corresponds to a composite Fp.

4.2.6 Evidence for the ternary branching VP

In this section, we would like to critically review the syntactic evidence that has been claimed to support the ternary branching VP structure ($[_{VP}$ V NP[ACC] VP[*to*]]) of object raising verbs and contrast it with the Exceptional Case Marking (ECM) analysis (4.2.1 (1d)), according to which the syntactic structure of the VP headed by an object raising verb is binary branching, namely, $[_{VP}$ V $[_{S[to]}$ NP[ACC] VP[*to*]]].

The first evidence for the ternary branching VP structure of the object raising construction is about backward control. When a VP[PRP]—a VP headed by a verb in the present participle form (V[PRP])—is used as the subject of a clause, the semantic subject (RHO) of the VP[PRP] can take as its antecedent the object NP in the matrix clause (1a, 2a), but not the subject of the complement clause (1b, 2b). (See 4.5 for the details on RHO, the semantic subject of a nonfinite VP.) In the object raising construction, the post-verbal NP can be the antecedent of the semantic subject of the VP[PRP] in the matrix subject position (1c, 2c). Therefore, in terms of backward control, the post-verbal NP of the object raising construction behaves in the same way as the matrix object NP of a transitive verb and not as the subject NP of a complement clause.

(1) a. Contradicting himself will discredit [Mr. Jones]. (Bresnan 1982: 380)
   b. *Contradicting himself will prove that [Mr. Jones] is a liar. (Bresnan 1982: 380)
   c. Contradicting himself will prove [Mr. Jones] to be a liar. (Bresnan 1982: 380)

(2) a. Shooting himself amused [Tony]. (Postal 1974: 124)
   b. *Criticizing himself proved/showed (that) [Bob] was humble. (Postal 1974: 125)
   c. ?Criticizing himself proved/showed [Bob] to be humble. (Postal 1974: 125)

The same contrast between (b) and (c) examples is observed with the *picture* noun reflexive.

(3) a. This picture of herself shocked [Mary].
   b. *This picture of herself shows that [Mary] was an excellent dancer. (Imanishi and Asano 1990: 104)
   c. This picture of herself shows [Mary] to be an excellent dancer. (Imanishi and Asano 1990: 104)

This argument for the ternary branching VP structure is weak in at least two respects. First, there is still a possibility left that the difference between (1b) and (2b) on the one hand and (1c) and (2c) on the other is either due to the presence in the former and the absence in the latter of a CP boundary, or due to the finiteness of the former and the nonfiniteness of the latter. If so, one can both maintain the ECM analysis and account for the difference between them by claiming, for example, that the controlled NP (PRO in GB terms) and the controller NP must be CP-mates (although this condition has a counterexample, such as *It was making a display of his emotions that resulted in Muskie's losing the primary* (Bresnan 1976: 493)). Second and more importantly, the data is about coreference relations, and various theories formulate (non)coreference conditions in various ways that are not always purely syntactic, because coreference is primarily a semantic and pragmatic phenomenon (Sadock 2012: 190). Therefore, this evidence is only convincing to the extent that (non)coreference between NPs (or ARGs) depends on syntactic structures and (non)coreference conditions are formulated in purely syntactic terms.

The second evidence concerns Heavy Constituent Shift (HCS) (a.k.a. Heavy NP Shift). HCS (McCawley 1998: 93, 529, 540, Sadock 2012: 212) "moves" a heavy constituent that is a sister of a verb to the S-final focus position crossing over other complements and VP-adjuncts (Bresnan 1982: 380, Rochemont and Culicover 1990: 24). This is illustrated in (4). In AMG terms, HCS is not "shifting things from one order to another" but simply a phenomenon in which the two conditions on Information Structure (IS), namely, that a heavy constituent tends to occur later than light constituents (Sadock 2012: 211 (4)) and that the new/focused information appears at the utterance-final position (Sadock 2012: 217 (30)), override the default word order in syntax, as in (4d).

(4) a. I insisted on [the fact that I was neutral] throughout the discussion. (Postal 1971)
   b. *I insisted on __ throughout the discussion [the fact that I was neutral].
   c. I insisted __ throughout the discussion [on the fact that I was neutral].
   d. syntax: [$_{VP}$ [$_{VP}$ V PP[*on*]] PP[*throughout*]]

   IS: [$_U$ *rest* < heavy/focus]

When a verb takes a clausal complement, HCS can "move" the entire complement to the S-final position, which is shown in (5b), but not the subject of the clausal complement, which is shown in (5c), (6).

(5) Bresnan 1982: 380
   a. I discussed [$_{S[PRP]}$ all those women riding motorcycles nowadays] with my sister.
   b. I discussed __ with my sister [$_{S[PRP]}$ all those women riding motorcycles nowadays].
   c. *I discussed [$_{S[PRP]}$ __ riding motorcycles nowadays] with my sister [all those women].

(6) Postal 1974: 105
   a. *I resent [$_{S[PRP]}$ __ happening to me] [all sorts of bad accidents and other unpleasant occurrences].
   b. *I favor [$_{S[PRP]}$ __ being fired] [everyone who disagrees with that policy].

In (7), HCS "moves" the NP after an object raising verb to the S-final position, which shows that the NP in question is a sister of the object raising verb.

(7) a. I will consider __ to be fools in the weeks ahead [all those who drop this course]. (Bresnan 1982: 381)
   b. I believe __ to have been tortured by Brazilians [the priests who are going to speak today]. (Postal 1974: 84)
   c. I believe __ very strongly to be a Turkish spy [the doctor who you met yesterday in Ankara]. (Postal 1974: 278)

However, the sequence NP[ACC] VP[*to*] after an object raising verb cannot be "moved" by HCS, whereas the sequence NP[ACC] VP[PRP] after a transitive verb can. This contrast is shown in (8). This confirms that the former does not form a constituent (*[$_{VP}$ believe [$_{S[to]}$ NP[ACC] VP[*to*]]]) but the latter does ([$_{VP}$ support [$_{S[PRP]}$ NP[ACC] VP[PRP]]]).

(8) a. *I believe __ in the strongest terms possible [(for) the man to have been spying on us for a long time].
   b. I support __ in the strongest terms possible [the student getting all the financial help he needs].

The above conclusions about (7) and (8a) are consistent with the ternary branching VP structure but inconsistent with the binary branching ECM analysis.

A caveat about HCS is that it is not true that any constituent that is a sister of a verb can undergo HCS, as shown in (9). What we can conclude from HCS data is that if a constituent in a VP successfully undergoes HCS, the constituent, before its application, was a sister of the verb that heads the VP. That is, a successful HCS of a constituent in a VP is a sufficient (but not necessary) condition for a pre-HCS syntactic structure in which the constituent was a sister of the verb that heads the VP.

(9) Bresnan 1976: 487
   a. *I forced to leave [all the rowdy boys].
   b. *I convinced to disqualify themselves [all of the antifeminist candidates].

Incidentally, the HCS test in (10a) shows that the theme NP of the locative inversion construction is a sister of the verb, which supports the syntactic structure of the construction given in 2.6 (4), namely, [$_S$ PP, [$_{VP}$ V, NP[ACC]]]. The contrast between (10b) and (10b') confirms that HCS is at work.

(10) a. Over my windowsill climbed __ every day [an entire army of ants]. (Bresnan 1976: 486)
   b. Near the factory sat __ on Tuesday [an old rusting wreck covered with spider webs]. (Postal 1977: 145)
   b'. ??Near the factory sat __ on Tuesday [a wreck]. (Jerry Sadock (p.c.))

The HCS test also shows that the existentially quantified theme NP in the *there* construction is a sister of the verb *be* (2.4 (5)).

The third piece of evidence comes from coordination. The sequence NP VP[*to*] after an object raising verb in (11a) apparently allows coordination. However, we cannot conclude from this fact that the sequence comprises a single constituent, because English permits nonconstituent coordination, such as (11b, c). It has been observed (e.g., Postal 1974: 419–420) that inserting *both* or *either* before the first conjunct in (12) lowers the acceptability of a nonconstituent coordination.

(11) a. I believe Bob to know French and Sally to know Spanish. (Postal 1974: 417)
   b. I promised Bob to leave and Sally to stay. (Postal 1974: 132)
   c. Kim gave a dollar to Bobbie and a dime to Jean. (Sag et al. 1985: 159)

(12) McCawley 1998: 63–64
   a. John donated (??both) $50 to the Anti-Vivisection Society and $75 to the Red Cross.
   b. I didn't put (??either) potatoes in the pantry or the milk in the refrigerator.

When *both* or *either* is inserted between an object raising verb and the first conjunct of a coordination of the sequence NP VP[*to*] (cf. (11a)), the result is unacceptable, as in (13). This shows that (13a-c) are instances of nonconstituent coordination and that the sequence NP VP[*to*] does not form a syntactic constituent.

(13) a. *He believes either Melvin to be insane or Joan to have been giving him drugs. (Postal 1974: 420)
cf. He believes either Melvin is insane or Joan has been giving him drugs.
b. *He believes both Bob to be immoral and Joan to be promiscuous. (Postal 1974: 420)
c. *Mary believes both George to be the culprit and greed to be the motive. (McCawley 1998: 137)

Note, however, that the sequence NP[ACC] VP[PRP] after a transitive verb allows a coordination of this type, showing yet again that the sequence forms a syntactic constituent.

(14) Mary favors both Greenland being admitted to the U.N. and Congress repealing the Hatch Act. (McCawley 1998: 137)

Lasnik and Uriagereka (1988: 10–11) treated [$_{CP[for]}$ *for* [$_{S[to]}$ NP VP[*to*]]] as another instance of the ECM construction. They were correct about the constituent structure of CP[*for*]. In fact, the NP VP[*to*] sequence in a CP[*for*] in (15) can be coordinated and introduced by *either* or *both*, and therefore forms a constituent. (But they were wrong about object raising verbs and claimed the binary branching VP structure [$_{VP}$ V [$_{S[to]}$ NP VP[*to*]]]. As was shown in (13), the NP VP[*to*] sequence after an object raising verb does not allow this type of coordination and hence does not form a syntactic constituent.)

(15) a. For either John to tell Bill such a lie or Bill to believe it is outrageous. (McCawley 1998: 118)
b. It would be disastrous for either John to open the letter or Mary to find the money. (McCawley 1984: 171)

The fourth piece of evidence for the ternary branching VP structure of the object raising construction is concerned with adverbial insertion. Some sentence-modifying adverbials (ad-S) cannot modify the matrix clause when they occur in an embedded clause.

(16) Pollard and Sag 1994: 117
   a. [To this very day], I have been hoping for Kim to be proven innocent.
   b. *I have been hoping for Kim [to this very day] to be proven innocent.
   c. [In spite of myself], I have been hoping for Kim to get the job.
   d. *I have been hoping for Kim [in spite of myself] to get the job.

These adverbials in (16) can be placed between the NP and the VP[*to*] of an object raising verb, and the interpretation is still available in which they modify the matrix clause.

(17) Pollard and Sag 1994: 117
   a. I believe George Washington [to this very day] to have been a great statesman.
   b. I believe Kim [in spite of myself] to be the most qualified.

By contrast, the sequence NP VP[PRP] after a transitive verb does not allow a matrix-clause-modifying adverbial to be inserted between the two phrases.

(18) *I favor Greenland, [to this very day], being admitted to the U.N.
   cf. I favor [to this very day] Greenland being admitted to the U.N.

The contrast between (17) and (18) shows that the adverbials in (17) are not dominated by an embedded clausal node S[*to*], (hence, it is possible for the adverbial to modify the matrix clause) but that the adverbial in (18) is dominated by a clausal node, namely, S[PRP]. However, this argument is weak in two respects. First, there is still a possibility left that one can maintain the ECM analysis and claim that the difference between (16b, d) and (17) is due to the presence in (16b, d) and the absence in (17) of a complement CP node that dominates the adverbial, if the constituent NP VP[PRP] in (18) can also be analyzed as a CP. Second, the data is about modification, which is first and foremost a semantic phenomenon. Therefore, this argument is only valid to the extent that the possibility of modification depends on syntactic structures.

The fifth piece of evidence concerns gapping. When gapping is applied to a coordinated clause and leaves behind three or more constituents in the affected clause (19b, d), the sentence is unacceptable.

(19) McCawley 1998: 280
   a. Fred sent the President a nasty letter, and [Bernice] [a bomb].
   b. *Fred sent the President a nasty letter, and [Bernice] [the governor] [a bomb].

c. Bob intends to travel to Hong Kong in August, and [Ann] [in July].
d. *Bob intends to travel to Hong Kong in August, and [Ann] [to Djakarta] [in July].

When gapping is applied to the object raising construction (20a) and to the construction in which a transitive verb is followed by a sequence NP[ACC] VP[PRP] (21a), the sequence NP[ACC] VP[*to*] after an object raising verb cannot be retained (20b), whereas the post-verbal sequence NP[ACC] VP[PRP] can be retained (21b).

(20) Postal 1974: 130
  a. I believe Tom to be weird, and Joan believes Sally to be paranoiac.
  b. *I believe Tom to be weird, and [Joan] [Sally] [to be paranoiac].

(21) Postal 1974: 131
  a. Bob resents this happening to him, and I resent that happening to me.
  b. Bob resents this happening to him, and [I] [that happening to me].

This contrast shows again, on the one hand, that the sequence NP[ACC] VP[*to*] after an object raising verb does not form a single constituent, and hence, an unacceptable sequence of three constituents (NP[NOM] NP[ACC] VP[*to*]) is left behind in (20b), and, on the other hand, that the sequence NP[ACC] VP[PRP] after a transitive verb does form a single constituent, namely, S[PRP], and hence, two constituents (NP[NOM] S[PRP]) are retained in (21b).

What is interesting about gapping is that it interacts with "*wh*-movement" (6.1) or Right Node Raising (RNR) in such a way that unacceptable gapped sentences with two constituents left in the affected VP (19b, d) can be improved by extracting one of them out of the coordinate structure by across-the-board (ATB) "*wh*-movement" or RNR. This is shown in (22). The same is true of object raising verbs (23).

(22) a. *Fred sent the President a nasty letter, and [Bernice] [the governor] [a bomb]. (=(19b))
  b. Tell me who Fred sent a nasty letter, and [Bernice] [a bomb]. (ATB "*wh*-movement")
  c. Fred sent the President, and [Bernice] [the governor], a homemade bomb with a timing device. (RNR)

(23) a. Tell me which book John believes to be interesting and [Mary] [to be boring]. (ATB "*wh*-movement" cf. (20b))
b. John believes this book, and [Mary] [that book], to be very interesting and informative. (RNR)
c. John believes to be interesting, and [Mary] [to be boring], this book about generative phonology. (HCS + RNR)

This improvement in acceptability in (23) shows that the reason why (20b) is unacceptable is that two constituents are left in the affected VP after gapping, thus proving the ternary branching VP structure [$_{VP}$ V NP[ACC] VP[*to*]]).

The sixth piece of evidence is about passivization. The Passive Lexical Rule (3.1 (3)), or its generalized version (4.2.3 (9)), picks out the NP that is a sister of a transitive verb as the NP that is turned into a passive subject. This means that the NP embedded in a larger constituent that is a complement of a transitive verb ([$_{VP}$ V [$_{XP}$ NP ...] ...]) cannot be passivized. In particular, the NP[ACC] in the constituent [$_{S[PRP]}$ NP[ACC] VP[PRP]] after a transitive verb cannot be turned into a passive subject (24a, c), while the whole constituent [$_{S[PRP]}$ NP[ACC] VP[PRP]] can (24b, d).

(24) a. *Greenland is favored (by many people) being admitted to the U.N. (McCawley 1998: 137)
cf. Many people favor Greenland being admitted to the U.N.
b. Greenland being admitted to the U.N. is favored by many people. (McCawley 1998: 137)
c. *Mary is regretted having sold the car by John. (McCawley 1998: 139)
cf. John regrets Mary having sold the car.
d. Mary having sold the car is regretted by John. (McCawley 1998: 139)

Such transitive verbs as *hate*, *like*, and *prefer* take an S[*to*] complement (25a). This is confirmed in two ways. First, the complementizer *for* is permitted after each transitive verb (25b). Second, the NP after the transitive verbs cannot be postposed by HCS (25c). (As for coordination, there seems to be idiolectal variation in acceptability (25f, g).) Because these verbs take an S[*to*] complement, the matrix VP is a binary branching structure [$_{VP}$ V [$_{S[to]}$ NP[ACC] VP[*to*]]], where the NP[ACC] is not a sister of the matrix verb. This predicts that passivization is not possible (25e), although these verbs are passivizable when used as a transitive verb (25d).

(25) a. I would hate/like/prefer [$_{S[to]}$ you [$_{VP[to]}$ to say things like that]].
b. I would hate/like/prefer [$_{CP[for]}$ for [$_{S[to]}$ you [$_{VP[to]}$ to say things like this]]].
c. *I would hate/like/prefer__ to say things like that [anyone who is interested in linguistics]. (cf. Postal 1974: 181, 407)
d. That was generally hated/liked/preferred. (Postal 1974:179)
e. *You are hated/liked/preferred to say things like that. (cf. Postal 1974: 18)
f. ?Everyone wants both John to resign and Alice to be named his successor. (McCawley 1998: 140)
g. *He wishes both Larry to be discrete and Tom to be cautious. (Postal 1974: 420)

On the other hand, the post-verbal NP of object raising verbs can be made a passive subject, as we saw in 4.2.1 (8b). Therefore, the passivization test shows [$_{VP}$ V [$_{NP}$ S[PRP]]] for *favor* and *regret* in (24), [$_{VP}$ V [$_{S[to]}$ NP[ACC] VP[*to*]]] for *like* and *hate* in (25), and, most importantly, [$_{VP}$ V NP[ACC] VP[*to*]] for object raising verbs.

The seventh piece of evidence is concerned with the focus-bearing element *only*. This focus-bearing element assigns its focus on the basis of (surface) syntactic structure, according to the following rule (McCawley 1998: 68–69, Jackendoff 1972: 247ff.).

(26) the focus of *only*
X is interpreted as the focus of *only* iff
(i) X is a single constituent in syntax, and
(ii) *only* is adjoined to the left of a constituent Y that dominates or is equal to X: [$_Y$ *only* [$_Y$ ...X...]]

For example, when *only* is adjoined to a VP, as in (27a), the PP can be interpreted as its focus, because the PP is dominated by the VP to which *only* is adjoined. However, both the NP and PP at once cannot be the focus (27b), because they do not form a constituent. When *only* is adjoined to the NP in (27c), the PP cannot be interpreted as its focus, because it is not dominated by a node to which *only* is adjoined.

(27) McCawley 1998: 68 (intended focus underlined)
    a. John only [_VP_ put [_NP_ flowers] [_PP_ in the vase]].
    b. *John only [_VP_ put [_NP_ flowers] [_PP_ in the vase]]
    c. *John [_VP_ put only [_NP_ flowers] [_PP_ in the vase]].

McCawley observed in a lecture titled "Discontinuous and other 'nonstandard' kinds of constituent structure" given at Keio University, Tokyo in 1997 that the underlined sequence NP VP[*to*] in (28b) cannot be interpreted as the focus of *only*, whereas the S[FIN] in (28a) can. If the sequence NP VP[*to*] after the object raising verb *believe* does not form a single constituent, the unacceptability of (28b) can be accounted for as a violation of (26i).

(28) a. Sam only believes (that) [_S[FIN]_ Bush is incompetent]. (intended focus underlined)
    b. *Sam only believes Bush to be incompetent. (intended focus underlined)
    c. *Sam believes only Bush to be incompetent. (intended focus underlined)

Note that although *Bush to be incompetent* cannot be the focus of *only* in (28b), *Bush* can be interpreted as the focus by being contrasted with other people or *to be incompetent* by being contrasted with other properties. This is consistent with (26), because the NP and the VP[*to*] are dominated by the VP to which *only* is adjoined: [_VP_ only [_VP_ believes [_NP_ Bush] [_VP[to]_ to be incompetent]].

Furthermore, when *only* is placed in front of the post-verbal NP (28c), the VP[*to*] cannot be interpreted as its focus. If the VP structure were binary branching, as the ECM analysis claims, we would expect wrongly that the VP[*to*] can be interpreted as the focus, because *only* was adjoined to the S[*to*] that dominates the VP[*to*] in question.

When we apply the *only* test to the *want*-class (that includes *want, hate, like,* and *prefer*), which is characterized by their property of taking a CP[*for*] complement and their impossibility of the post-verbal NP to be turned into a passive subject, the post-verbal sequence NP VP[*to*] can be interpreted as the focus of *only*, which shows again that the VP structure of verbs of this class is [_VP_ V [_S[to]_ NP[ACC] VP[*to*]]], that is, an "ECM" structure.

(29) Sam only wants Bush to be competent. (intended focus underlined)

The eighth and last piece of evidence is about *make out, prevent from,* and other object raising verbs whose subcategorization frame is not [$_{VP}$ V, NP[ACC], VP[*to*]]. Admittedly, this evidence is weak in that there might be a possible way of reducing the VP structures in (30) and (31) to a binary branching structure but is still important because it shows the variety of object raising verbs. Two classes of such verbs have been pointed out so far. The first class (30) is object raising verbs such as *keep, prevent,* and *stop* that take NP[ACC] and PP[*from*] as their complements.

(30) [$_{VP}$ V, NP[ACC], [$_{PP[from]}$ P[*from*], VP[PRP]]]
   a. He kept there from being a riot. (Postal 1974: 159)
   b. Harry kept tabs from being kept on Joan's movements (Postal 1974: 159)
   c. Mary prevented John's leg from being pulled. (McCawley 1998: 135)
   d. We prevented it from becoming obvious that things were out of control. (Postal and Pullum 1988: 637)
   e. The Lord stopped it from raining. (Postal and Pullum 1988: 637)

The other class (31) is such object raising verbs as *make, figure,* and *reason* that take NP[ACC], the particle *out*, and VP[*to*].

(31) [$_{VP}$ V, NP[ACC], [$_{PRT}$ *out*], VP[*to*]]
   a. I figured it out to be impossible to do that. (Culicover 1997: 50)
   b. I figured it out to be more than 300 miles from here to Tulsa. (Postal and Pullum 1988: 646)
   c. She made it out to be only 49% probable that we would get there on time. (Postal and Pullum 1988: 646)
   d. Helen made there out to be seven gorillas in the clearing. (Postal 2004: 110)
   e. He reasoned it out to be incorrect to make that assumption. (Postal and Pullum 1988: 646)

Before closing this section, a few remarks are in order about RNR and pseudo-cleft. In the past, RNR data, such as (32), was used to show that the sequence NP VP[*to*] after an object raising verb does not comprise a single constituent, in view of the fact that RNR can "extract" only a single constituent.

(32) a. *Mary believes, but Catherine doesn't believe, Peter to be fat. (Bresnan 1982: 382)
  b. *I find it easy to believe—but Joan finds it hard to believe—Tom to be dishonest. (Postal 1974: 128)

However, if there is a restriction on the syntactic category of a constituent that can be "extracted" by RNR, and if the sentences in (32) violate that restriction, then we cannot determine why (32a, b) are ungrammatical: are they ungrammatical because the NP VP[*to*] sequence does not form a constituent? Or are they ungrammatical because they simply violate the categorical restriction on RNR-ed phrases? We have taken the view, following McCawley (1998: 141), that the verb class that includes *want, like, prefer*, and *hate* takes two types of clausal complement: CP[*for*] and S[*to*] (cf. (25a, b) above). This class allows the RNR of CP[*for*] but not that of S[*to*] (33). Therefore, we must admit that there is indeed a restriction on RNR about which syntactic category can undergo RNR and that S[*to*] is not such a syntactic category. To the extent that this restriction is real, we cannot use RNR data to falsify the ECM analysis of the object raising construction.

(33) I didn't expect to prefer—but I did like— *(for) that to happen. (cf. Postal 1974: 185)

The same restriction is at work in the pseudo-cleft construction. Although S[PRP] in (34a), CP[*that*] in (34b), and CP[*for*] in (34c, d) can occupy the post-copula focus position of pseudo-cleft, S[FIN] and S[*to*] in (34e, f) cannot. Note that (34b, c) show that an NP gap is needed in the subject of pseudo-cleft (as a "trace" of *what*). The syntactic field of the lexical entry for *ashamed* is A in [__, PP[*of*]] and [__, CP[*that*]] and that for *eager* is A in [__, PP[*for*]] and [__, CP[*for*]]. As for (34f), if comma intonation is used at the end of *What I believe is*, it becomes acceptable, as in *What I believe is, I have no intention to do that at this time* (Bill Clinton). By contrast, comma intonation does not improve (34e).

(34) a. What Mary favors is [Greenland being admitted to the U.N.] (McCawley 1998: 137)
  b. What I'm ashamed *(of) is [that I neglected you]. (McCawley 1998: 121)
  c. What I'm most eager *(for) is [for you to visit us]. (McCawley 1998: 121)
  d. What I hate is [for people to play radios on buses]. (McCawley 1998: 67)
  e. *What everyone wants is [John to resign]. (McCawley 1998: 140)
  f. What I believe is [*(that) Bill is intelligent]. (Postal 1974: 133)

In the past, such data as (35) below was used to show that the sequence NP VP[*to*] after an object raising verb does not form a constituent. However, this conclusion is not warranted in view of (34e), where the matrix verb is *want*, whose subcategorization frames are V in [__, NP], [__, S[*to*]] (when the V and the S[*to*] are adjacent), and [__, CP[*for*]]. Because S[*to*] cannot be the focus of pseudo-cleft in (34e), we cannot tell why (35a, b) are unacceptable: are they unacceptable because of the syntactic category restriction on the focus position of the pseudo-cleft construction? Or are they unacceptable because the NP VP[*to*] sequence does not form a constituent?

(35) a. *What I believe is [Bill to be intelligent]. (Postal 1974: 137)
 b. *What John believes is [(for) George to be the culprit]. (McCawley 1998: 140)

So far, we have argued for and confirmed the conclusion that the verb class of *believe* has the (surface) syntax of [$_{VP}$ V NP VP[*to*]], the verb class of *want* [$_{VP}$ V S[*to*]], and the verb class of *favor* [$_{VP}$ V [$_{NP}$ S[PRP]]]. To the extent that this conclusion is correct, the Mainstream Generative Grammar (MGG)'s terminology "Exceptional Case Marking (ECM)," which has been applied to the *believe*-class, is a misnomer and should have been applied to the *want*-class. Also, through the examination of various sorts of data, it seems to have become clear that the syntactic category S[*to*] (i.e., [$_{S[to]}$ NP[ACC] VP[*to*]]) is unstable; that is, it has a special property that its constituency only becomes manifest when it is immediately preceded by the head of the phrase of which it is a complement (the *want*-class verbs or the complementizer *for*). When S[*to*] is separated from the head, its property of being a single constituent is lost and it functions only as a sequence of NP VP[*to*] that does not form a constituent (36a-e). In this respect, the contrast between S[*to*] and S[PRP] (i.e., [$_{S[PRP]}$ NP[ACC] VP[PRP]]) is striking. We claim that S[PRP] is in fact [$_{NP[3SGN]}$ S[PRP]], that is, a third-person-singular-neuter NP node directly dominating the S[PRP] node (36f, g).

(36) a. They prefer [$_{S[to]}$ Mary to be reassigned].
 cf. They favor [$_{S[PRP]}$ Mary being reassigned].
 b. They prefer very much *(for) [$_{S[to]}$ Mary to be reassigned].
 cf. They favor very strongly [$_{S[PRP]}$ Mary being reassigned].
 c. We prefer, but they don't prefer, *(for) [$_{S[to]}$ Mary to be reassigned]
 cf. We favor, but they don't favor, [$_{S[PRP]}$ Mary being reassigned].
 d. *(For) [$_{S[to]}$ Mary to be reassigned] is preferred.
 cf. [$_{S[PRP]}$ Mary being reassigned] is favored.

e. What they prefer is *(for) [$_{S[to]}$ Mary to be reassigned]
  cf. What they favor is [$_{S[PRP]}$ Mary being reassigned].
  f. the picture/scene/sight of [$_{NP}$ [$_{S[PRP]}$ him singing]]
  g. The scene of [$_{NP}$ [$_{S[PRP]}$ [$_{S[PRP]}$ him attacking his wife] and [$_{S[PRP]}$ her stabbing him with a knife]]] is reenacted. (from the web)

4.3 Event Hierarchy and Control

4.3.1 Event Hierarchy

So far, we have introduced four kinds of events in RS, namely, event (EV), state (STATE) in 3.1.3 (9), volitional action (VA) in 3.3.1 (3), and situation (SITU) in 3.3.1 (4). There are phenomena that are sensitive to what kind of event is expressed by an S or VP: a state, an event, an action, or a volitional action. For example, the Passive Lexical Rule (3.1 (3)) is applicable to verbs that have both agent and patient in their RS (1a). Such an event is an action. But it does not have to be a volitional action (1b, c).

(1) *realize* (= 'become aware of')
  a. It was realized that it was raining.
  b. *John realized intentionally/deliberately that it was raining.
  c. *Realize it's raining! (Culicover and Jackendoff 2005: 428)

Passive and pseudo-cleft *what X did was* select actions, which may or may not be volitional. Another example of (nonvolitional) action is a sentence with an inanimate subject/agent, such as *The wind blew down the sign* (cf. *The sign was blown down by the wind*, *What the wind did was blow down the sign*) (Jerry Sadock (p.c.)). On the other hand, VP anaphora *do so* and the imperative select volitional actions (Culicover and Jackendoff 2005: 284, 427). Imperative (1c) and *do so* (2a) are bad when *realize* means nonvolitional 'become aware of.' However, they are good when it means 'achieve' (2c, d, e), which is a volitional action. VP anaphora *that happened* (*to/with*) and pseudo-cleft *what happened to X was* select events, covering both actions and nonactions (Culicover and Jackendoff 2005: 284) (3). VP ellipsis selects situations, covering both states and events (Culicover and Jackendoff 2005: 284) (4).

(2) a. ??John realized that it was raining and Mary did so too.
  b. ??What John did was realize that it was raining.
    cf. What the wind did was blow down the sign.

c. John realized his dream and Mary did so too. (*realize* = 'achieve')
d. What John did was realize his dream.
e. Realize your dream!

As for (2b) with ??, it looks as if when X in the pseudo-cleft *What X did was* ... is human, X is interpreted by default as a volitional agent, which is inconsistent with the nonvolitional action VP in the focus position: *realize that it was raining*.

(3) a. Robin read the newspaper today, but that didn't happen yesterday. (Culicover and Jackendoff 2005: 284)
 b. John slipped and fell but that didn't happen to/with Mary.
 c. What happened to John was that he slipped and fell.

(4) a. John likes the food and Mary does too. (state)
 b. John slipped and fell and Mary did too. (event)
 c. John read the newspaper and Mary did too. (volitional action)

We propose the Event Hierarchy (5) based on these facts. We will continue using the term *event* (EV) as a cover term when there is no need to distinguish the kind of event type under discussion.

(5) Event Hierarchy

```
        situation (SITU)
        /            \
    state          event (EV)
                   /        \
              nonaction    action (AC)
                           /         \
                  nonvolitional    volitional
                     action        action (VA)
```

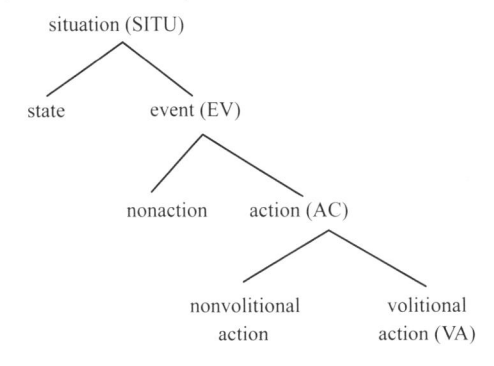

In the above hierarchy, the term *situation* (SITU) covers both *state* and *event* (EV). *Event* covers both *action* (AC) and *nonaction*. *Action* is characterized as an event one of whose participant roles is agent (AG), whereas nonaction is an event that lacks agent in its participant roles. The typical cases of *nonaction* are change of state and change of location. Action consists of *volitional action* (VA) and *nonvolitional action*.

4.3.2 The control construction

Verbs such as *try* and *persuade* syntactically take a VP[*to*] complement that is interpreted as a proposition. In (6a) and (6b), the semantic subject of the VP[*to*] is understood as *John*, which is evident from the reflexive pronoun *himself*. This phenomenon was originally explained in terms of a deletion rule called Equi-NP deletion in (7) that deletes the subject of the complement clause that is coreferent with a matrix NP.

(6) a. John tried to behave himself.
   b. Mary persuaded John to behave himself.

(7) Equi-NP deletion
   a. John tried [he to behave himself]. → John tried [to behave himself].
   b. Mary persuaded John [he to behave himself]. → Mary persuaded John [to behave himself].

In (7a), the pronoun subject of the complement clause that is coreferent with the matrix subject is deleted (McCawley 1998: 128). In fact, what is deleted must be a "bound individual variable" (McCawley 1993: 190, McCawley 1998: 155 note 11) if we look at such examples as *Every contestant expects to win* (McCawley 1998: 128) or *Several candidates expect to win the election* (McCawley 1998: 128). See 5.3 (3). (7a) is called subject-controlled Equi-NP deletion. In (7b), the pronoun subject of the complement clause that is coreferent with the matrix object is deleted. This is called object-controlled Equi-NP deletion. The other way to account for (6) is to assume a phonologically null pronominal NP called PRO as the SYNTACTIC subject of the complement clause. In (8a), PRO is coreferent with the matrix subject. In (8b), it is coreferent with the matrix object.

(8) complement clause with the PRO subject
   a. John tried [$_{S[to]}$ PRO to behave himself].
   b. Mary persuaded John [$_{S[to]}$ PRO to behave himself].

Although we do not adopt these analyses, we call the sentence patterns in (6) the control construction and, for descriptive purposes, use the terms subject control and object control for (6a) and (6b), respectively. We will call those verbs that appear in the control construction control verbs. The AMG analysis of the control construction (Sadock 2012: 47) is similar to the analyses proposed in LFG, GPSG, HPSG, and Culicover and Jackendoff (2005) in that control verbs take a VP complement in syntax and not a clausal complement.

The Event Hierarchy is related to the control construction in such a way that each control verb selects a specific event type for its VP[*to*] complement. Some control verbs, such as *tell* and *order*, select a volitional action (VA) for their VP[*to*] complement (9b), and others, such as *want* or *wish*, select a situation (SITU) (10a) (Culicover and Jackendoff 2005: 428).

(9) a. *John told Mary to realize that it was raining.
b. John told Mary to confirm that it was raining.

(10) a. I want to be tall/become a doctor/sing.
b. *Be tall!

Although the meaning of each control verb determines which event type it selects in the RS field of its lexical entry—VA complement or SITU complement— the default choice is a VA complement. This is seen in Unique Control of Actional Complement Hypothesis (Culicover and Jackendoff 2005: 427), which says in part "Infinitival and gerundive complements that are selected by their head to be of the semantic type Voluntary Action have unique control." Also, in HPSG's control theory (Sag and Pollard 1991, Pollard and Sag 1994: 286–287), control verbs are divided into three semantic classes: commitment (including intention and promising, e.g., *promise, intend, try*), influence (including ordering and causation, e.g., *persuade, appeal, cause*), and orientation (including desire and expectation, e.g., *want, hate, expect*). Of these three classes, verbs of commitment and influence take a VA complement and only verbs of orientation take a SITU complement.

4.4 Unique Control

4.4.1 Unique control verbs of *order* and *promise*

The verb *order* is an object-control verb, just like *persuade* in 4.3 (6b), in that the semantic subject of its VP[*to*] complement is coreferent with the verb's object NP. (The controller of an object-control verb is its object NP.) On the other hand, the verb *promise* is a subject-control verb, just like *try* in 4.3 (6a), in that the semantic subject of its VP[*to*] complement is coreferent with the verb's subject NP. (The controller of a subject-control verb is its subject NP.)

However, as stressed by Jackendoff and Culicover (2003: 529) and Culicover and Jackendoff (2005: 434), what is really at issue here is not the syntactic position or grammatical function of the controller but its participant role, specifically, the thematic-tier specification of the controller's role. In other words, controller choice is sensitive to thematic tier specification of roles. *Order* chooses as its controller the NP that carries a role whose thematic specification is goal (GO), whereas *promise* chooses as its controller the NP that carries a role whose thematic specification is source (SO). These NPs are underlined in (1) and (2). Recall that we have been using two-tiered roles (1.4), according to which, each role is a combination of two specifications: action tier specification (AG or PT) and thematic tier specification (SO, GO, TH, or LO). For example, as shown in (4), the verb *order* takes an [AG, SO] role for its subject NP and a [PT, GO] role for its object NP. In (1c), the verb *get* takes an [AG, GO] role for its subject NP. In (2c), the verb *give* takes an [AG, SO] role for its subject NP (1.4 (5)).

(1) *order* (cf. Culicover and Jackendoff 2005: 434)
 a. Mary ordered <u>John</u> to behave himself/*herself.
 b. the order from/by Mary to <u>John</u> to behave himself/*herself
 c. A: <u>John</u> got an order from Mary./Mary gave an order to <u>John</u>.
  B: What was it?
  A: It was to behave himself/*herself.
 d. a [$_A$ <u>state-wide</u>] order from the governor to evacuate

(2) *promise* (cf. Culicover and Jackendoff 2005: 434)
 a. <u>Mary</u> promised John to behave *himself/herself.
 b. the promise from/by <u>Mary</u> to John to behave *himself/herself
 c. A: John got a promise from <u>Mary</u>./<u>Mary</u> gave a promise to John.
  B: What was it?
  A: It was to behave *himself/herself.
 d. an [$_A$ <u>American</u>] promise to the EU to protect the euro

As shown in (1d), even an adjective is interpreted as the controller of the noun *order* if it allows goal interpretation. Recall that some adjectives correspond to an ARG in F/A (1.3 (12) and (13)). The same is true of the noun *promise*. In (2d), the adjective allows source interpretation and is interpreted as the controller (McCawley 1998: 538, Postal 1969).

4.4 UNIQUE CONTROL   187

The verbs *order* and *promise* do not allow their controllee (i.e., the semantic subject of the VP[*to*] complement that is coreferent with the controller NP) to have generic (gen) interpretation (PRO$_{arb}$ in GB terms) in (3a) nor a long-distance (remote) antecedent (super-equi) in (3b) nor a discourse antecedent (including the speaker and addressee) in (3c). These verbs are called unique control (a.k.a. obligatory control) verbs in the sense that their controller is uniquely determined in their lexical entries. In the following examples, the index in front of a nonfinite verb indicates how its subject is interpreted.

(3) a. *Mary$_i$ ordered/promised John$_j$ to $_{gen}$behave oneself.
    b. *They$_k$ said that Mary$_i$ ordered/promised John$_j$ to $_k$behave themselves.
    c. *Mary$_i$ ordered/promised John$_j$ to behave myself/yourself/ourselves.
    d. John$_i$ promised his son$_j$ to $_{i+j}$go to the movies together. (Landau 2000: 31)
    e. John$_i$ persuaded Mary$_j$ to $_{i+j}$kiss in the library. (Landau 2000: 31)
    f. John promised <u>Mary</u> to be allowed to get herself a new dog. (Pollard and Sag 1994: 316)

However, as shown in (3d, e), the controllee in some unique control constructions has split antecedents when the VP[*to*] is a collective predicate that requires a collective subject. Also, under certain conditions, controllers shift, as in (3f).

The controller of a unique control verb is determined by its lexical semantics. When a unique control verb takes an NP complement (as the object or the object of its PP complement) in addition to its subject NP (i.e., when the verb is Fpaa in F/A), a child determines which argument is the controller only by learning the lexical meaning of the unique control verb through observing what it represents in real life situations. Therefore, the semantic information in the lexical entry for a unique control verb must contain the specification of its controller. In AMG, this is done by stating the coreference requirement between the controller and controllee in the RS field of the lexical entry for a unique control verb, where participant roles are represented (Sadock 2012: 89). This accords with the observation in (1) and (2) that controller choice is sensitive to thematic-tier specifications of participant roles. Here are lexical entries for the unique control verbs *order* and *promise*.

(4) lexical entry for the unique control verb *order*
    syntax: V in [__, NP, VP[*to*]]
    F/A: Fpaa
    RS: [$_{TYPE}$ "order"] in [$_{VA}$ __ [AG, SO] [PT, GO] [$_{TH}$ [$_{VA}$ AG ...]]]

(5) lexical entry for the unique control verb *promise*
syntax: V in [__, NP, VP[*to*]]
F/A: Fpaa
RS: [$_{TYPE}$ "promise"] in [$_{VA\_}$ [AG, SO] [PT, GO] [$_{TH}$ [$_{VA}$ AG ...]]]

The dotted lines in (4) and (5) indicate the coreference requirement between the controller role and the controllee role. The controllee in both cases is the agent (AG) of the volitional action (VA) that corresponds to the PROP in F/A and the VP[*to*] in syntax. In the case of split antecedents in (3d, e), the coreference requirement in the RS of the unique control verb is still valid. What happens is that another coreference relation is added to the lexically specified coreference relation. This additional coreference relation is due to the collective predicate of the VP[*to*] complement (*to go to the movies together* in (3d) and *to kiss in the library* in (3e)) that requires a collective agent.

4.4.2 Notes on determining the controller

We claimed in the previous section that the controller of a unique control verb is determined by its lexical semantics. In terms of grammatical theorizing, how to predict the controller of a unique control verb has been a hotly debated issue. HPSG (Sag and Pollard 1991, Pollard and Sag 1994) divides the set of unique control verbs into three semantic classes: commitment (including intention and promising), influence (including ordering and causation), and orientation (including desire and expectation), and declares as part of its Control Theory (Pollard and Sag 1994: 302 (70)) that verbs of commitment and orientation are subject-control and those of influence are object-control. For example, *order* is of influence class and hence object-control, whereas *promise* is of commitment class and hence subject-control. On the other hand, Jackendoff and Culicover (2003) and Culicover and Jackendoff (2005) claim that the controller is determined by the basic control predicate embedded in the meaning (i.e., Jackendoff's Conceptual Structure (CS)) of a unique control verb. For example, they claimed that both *order* and *promise* contain in their CS the basic control predicate X$^\alpha$ OBLIGATED [α ACT] TO Y (Jackendoff and Culicover 2003: 537, Culicover and Jackendoff 2005: 446); that is, the person who is under obligation to do something is the controller. In the case of *order*, the object (goal) NP is the person who is under obligation, and therefore, the controller. In the case of *promise*, the subject (source) NP is the person who is under obligation, and therefore, the controller.

When we consider how a child learns which argument is the controller of a unique control verb, it is unlikely that a child first determines which semantic class the unique control verb in question belongs to, commitment, influence, or orientation, and then decides which argument is the controller based on the classification of the verb. In other words, it is unlikely that a child already has the three-way classification of unique control verbs at the start of its language acquisition and this classification is used in its acquisition process. It is also unlikely that a child already has the complete set of basic control predicates at the start of its language acquisition and the child first conducts the lexical decomposition of a unique control verb and then finds which basic control predicate is embedded in its Conceptual Structure, thereby deciding the controller argument. The point is that no matter how linguists may theorize the mechanism of predicting the controller, the undeniable fact still remains that a child must learn the lexical meaning of a unique control verb before it can determine its controller, and that learning the meaning of each lexical item is an integral part of language acquisition. As hinted in Jackendoff and Culicover 2003: 530 note 9 and Culicover and Jackendoff 2005: 435 note 10, "interpreting [$_S$ NP V NP VP[*to*]] as object control," which is predicted by the Minimal Distance Principle (Rosenbaum's (1967: 6) Erasure Principle) and also by Sadock's (2012: 48) reformulation of it in terms of F/A structure, is a default case and might be used in language acquisition process. That is, unless there is conflicting data available, the controller in the syntactic structure [$_S$ NP V NP VP[*to*]] is assumed by default to be the object NP (cf. Guasti 2002: 367, 369).

Radford (1981: 381) once observed about unique control verbs:

Pending the development of such a theory [*that is, Control Theory*], it would seem to be necessary simply to specify in the lexical entry for verbs like *persuade* or *promise* whether they are subject-control or nonsubject-control verbs. This is unsatisfactory as a solution to the control problem, however, for a number of reasons. Firstly, arbitrary lists of properties associated with predicates have no predictive or explanatory value: ask the question "How do you know this is a verb of subject control?," and you get the non-answer "Because it's listed as a verb of subject-control in the lexicon." Secondly, treating *control* (of PRO) as a *lexically governed* phenomenon implies that control properties are entirely arbitrary, and hence will vary in random fashion from dialect to dialect, and language to language: this would lead us to expect that the counterpart of *John persuade Bill to leave* in some dialect or language would have subject control rather than nonsubject control. But as far as we know, this is not the case. And we would hope that an adequate *Theory of Control* should explain why this is not the case.

As for Radford's question in the first part of the quotation, our answer is that we know this verb is subject control because we know the meaning of the verb (i.e., what kind of (speech) act it represents) and that knowledge determines the controller. As for the second part of the quotation, our claim is that control properties cannot be arbitrary, nor will they vary in random fashion from language to language. *Persuade* in English, *settoku suru* in Japanese, *überreden* in German, *persuader* in French, and *–qquaa* in Greenlandic all share the property of being an object control verb (controlled by the [PT, GO] role), because (i) they share the same meaning, roughly, 'cause someone to do something by reasoning' (i.e., they refer to the same kind of act), (ii) these languages share the same lexicalization pattern that when a verb takes an agent (AG) and a patient (PT), AG is realized as the syntactic subject (by occupying a more prominent syntactic position or by having a more prominent case marking, such as nominative or ergative) and PT is realized as the syntactic object (by occupying a less prominent syntactic position or by having a less prominent case marking, such as accusative or absolutive), because AG outranks PT (1.4 (6)), and (iii) the controllee of a volitional action complement is always its agent.

4.5 On the Controlled Argument RHO

The semantic subject of the VP complement of a unique control verb is not represented in syntax but is represented semantically in F/A and RS (Sadock 2012: 47), that is, "a semantic referential argument with no syntactic correspondent" (Sadock 2012: 71). Following Sadock (2012: 47), we call this defective lexical item RHO.

(1) lexical entry for RHO (cf. Sadock 2012: 47 (59))
    syntax: nil
    F/A: ARG[IND[j, AGR(j)]] (or informally [$_{ARG}$ RHO])
    RS: ROLE
    mphon: nil

RHO is in effect a zero pronoun that is not represented in syntax. It bears a certain participant role in RS and functions in F/A as an ARG carrying a certain INDEX value (1.3 (6)). In the following, we will sometimes treat RHO informally as a lexical item in F/A that occupies an ARG, as in (3), but this is just for ease of exposition. As shown in (1), the real substance of RHO in the F/A module is the value of its INDEX feature.

The distribution of RHO is restricted in English to the semantic subject of a nonfinite VP, that is, the subject ARG of the PROP headed by a functor that corresponds to a nonfinite verb (V[−FIN]) in syntax. First, RHO cannot appear as the object NP of a transitive verb or the complement NP of a preposition because it is not an NP and, in fact, it does not exist in syntax to begin with, and hence it cannot satisfy the syntactic subcategorization property of a transitive verb or preposition. Second, RHO cannot be the syntactic subject NP, that is, the NP in [$_S$ NP, VP], again for the same reason. In particular, a finite VP in English always requires its syntactic subject because of the PS rule [$_{S[FIN]}$ NP[NOM, AGR], VP[FIN, AGR]] (1.2 (11a)) for subject-verb agreement. However, nonfinite VPs (VP[*to*], VP[PRP], VP[PSP], and VP[PAS]) in English can occur without its syntactic subject as subject, object, complement, or adjunct of a clause.

(2) a. nonfinite VP as subject
   [$_{NP[3SG]}$ [$_{VP[PRP]}$ Watching TV]] is boring.
  b. nonfinite VP as object
   John believes [$_{NP[3SG]}$ [$_{VP[PRP]}$ watching TV]] to be boring.
   John knows little about [$_{NP[3SG]}$ [$_{VP[PRP]}$ watching TV]].
   How about [$_{NP[3SG]}$ [$_{VP[PRP]}$ watching TV]]?
  c. nonfinite VP as complement
   John likes [$_{VP[to]}$ to [$_{VP[BSE]}$ watch TV]].
  d. nonfinite VP as adjunct
   [$_{VP[PRP]}$ Watching TV], John drank wine.
   John stayed there [$_{VP[to]}$ to watch TV].
  e. nonfinite VP as fragment
   A: What did Mom tell you?
   B: To finish homework before watching TV.

In the examples in (2), the nonfinite VPs appear without their syntactic subject. In such cases, an innocuously mismatched correspondence (3a) is allowed between a nonfinite VP in syntax and its correspondent PROP in F/A, because there is nothing in syntax that corresponds to the RHO in F/A.

(3) a. intermodular correspondences of nonfinite VP without a syntactic subject

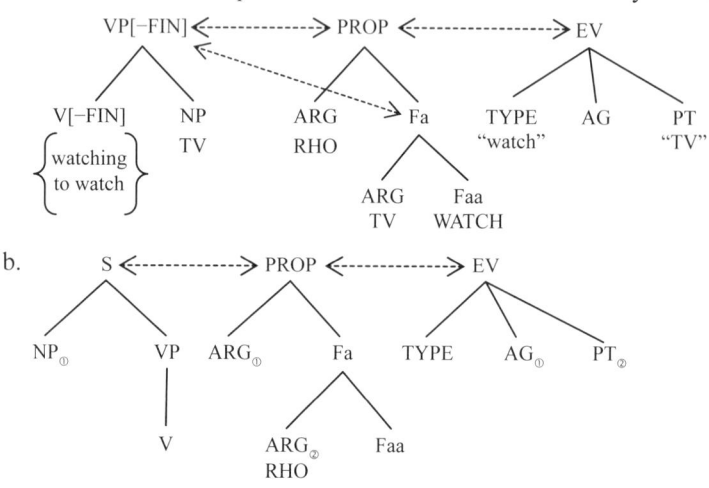

```
      VP[-FIN] <------------> PROP <-----------------> EV
         ⇐
       /     \              /     \              /     \
   V[-FIN]   NP          ARG ---> Fa          TYPE   AG    PT
   ⎧watching⎫ TV         RHO     /  \         "watch"      "TV"
   ⎨to watch⎬                  ARG   Faa
   ⎩        ⎭                  TV    WATCH
```

b.
```
         S <------------> PROP <-------------> EV
       /    \            /    \               /    \
     NP①    VP         ARG①    Fa           TYPE  AG①   PT②
             |                /  \
             V              ARG②  Faa
                            RHO
```

In (3a), the VP[-FIN] in syntax corresponds to the Fa in F/A by the default correspondence (1.4 (7)), and at the same time, it corresponds to the PROP that directly dominates the Fa, because the subject ARG (i.e., RHO) is not represented in syntax.

What needs to be prevented in English and other similar languages including French and German is the situation in (3b), where the verb is intransitive in syntax but its semantics is transitive both in F/A and in RS, and RHO appears as the object/lower ARG in F/A that corresponds to PT in RS. Some other similar situations must also be excluded including the one where the verb is transitive in syntax but its semantics is ditransitive both in F/A and in RS, and RHO appears as one of the lower ARGs in F/A. It is worth pointing out that this is what happens with a "zero pronoun" in such languages as Japanese and Malayalam that does not obey linear order restrictions (Mohanan 1983: 664–665, Bresnan 1995: 248, Dalrymple 2001: 171–172, 288–289). Note that linear order (precedence) restrictions can only be stated in syntax, because F/A and RS are order-free structures. Therefore, the lack of linear order restrictions of these zero pronouns indicates that they are not present in syntax. For example, (4) is a Japanese sentence consisting of a single verb in the past tense *age-ta* ('give-PAST'), and is interpreted as 'someone gave something to someone,' in which the actual referent of each zero pronoun (i.e., RHO in (1)) is determined by the context in which it is uttered.

4.5 ON THE CONTROLLED ARGUMENT RHO

(4) syntax: [$_{S[PAST]}$ [$_{VP[PAST]}$ [$_{V[PAST]}$ age-ta]]]
F/A: PAST(RHO(RHO(RHO [$_{Faaa}$ GIVE])))
RS: [$_{EV}$ [$_{TYPE}$ "give"] [AG, SO] [PT, GO] TH]

Therefore, we need something special for such languages as English (*I promise you* [*to be punctual*]), German (*Ich verspreche dir,* [*pünktlich zu sein*]), and French (*Je te promets* [*d'être ponctuel*]) that only allow RHO to appear as the semantic subject of a nonfinite VP. To restrict the distribution of RHO in these languages, we propose the following lexical rule, which is somewhat similar to LFG's Rule of Functional Anaphora (Bresnan 1982: 326).

(5) RHO Introduction Lexical Rule
    input   output
    F/A: Fφ   → Fφ in [$_{PROP}$ ARG[IND[j, AGR(j)]],
    morph: V[1, –FIN] or A[1]   [$_{Fa}$ … __ …]], where the ARG is the
                                    subject ARG of the PROP projected by Fφ

The input to this lexical rule is lexical entries for a functor whose morphology is a nonfinite verb or an adjective. Its output is lexical entries with the same morphology but with the F/A in which the subject ARG is RHO. Note that when the lexical entries for passive verbs (V[1, PSP] in morphology) are input to (5), the F/A of their output is such that RHO occupies the subject ARG, which corresponds to PT in RS. Therefore, a passive VP, such as *to be watched*, is interpreted properly. Here is a pair of active and passive examples.

(6) input to (5)   output
    lexical entry for *watching*
    syntax: V[PRP] in [__, NP]   → V[PRP] in [__, NP]
    F/A: Faa   → Faa in [$_{PROP}$ ARG[IND[j, AGR(j)]],
                                      [$_{Fa}$ ARG, __]]
    RS: [$_{TYPE}$ "watch"] in [$_{EV}$ __ AG PT] → [$_{TYPE}$ "watch"] in [$_{EV}$ __ AG PT]
    morph: V[1, PRP]   → V[1, PRP]
    mphon: [$_{V[1, PRP]}$ /wɑtʃɪŋ/]   → mphon: [$_{V[1, PRP]}$ /wɑtʃɪŋ/]

    lexical entry for passive participle *watched*
    syntax: V[PAS] in [__]   → V[PAS] in [__]
    F/A: Fa   → Fa in [$_{PROP}$ ARG[IND
                                      [j, AGR(j)]], __]

RS: [$_{\text{TYPE}}$ "watch"] in [$_{\text{EV}}$ __ <AG> PT]   → [$_{\text{TYPE}}$ "watch"] in [$_{\text{EV}}$ __ <AG> PT]
morph: V[1, PSP]   → V[1, PSP]
mphon: [$_{\text{V[1, PSP]}}$ /wɑʧt/]   → mphon: [$_{\text{V[1, PSP]}}$ /wɑʧt/]

The output lexical items in (6) cannot take a subject NP in syntax, because if they did, the subject NP would contribute its own F/A value with its IND feature to the subject ARG, which is impossible, because the subject ARG is already filled with the RHO (i.e., already has its own IND feature). However, such cases as (7) below, where the output lexical entries take the dummy *it* (2.4 (9)) as their subject NP, are not excluded yet.

(7) syntax: [$_{\text{S[PRP]}}$ [$_{\text{NP[}it\text{]}}$ it] [$_{\text{VP[PRP]}}$ [$_{\text{V[PRP]}}$ watching] TV]]
F/A: [$_{\text{PROP}}$ ARG[IND[j, AGR(j)]], [$_{\text{Fa}}$ WATCH(TV)]]
RS: [$_{\text{EV}}$ [$_{\text{TYPE}}$ "watch"] AG [$_{\text{PT}}$ "TV"]]

Both the S[PRP] *it watching TV* in (7) and the VP[PRP] *watching TV* express the same meaning; that is, they have the same F/A and RS. In this sense, the two forms are competing with each other. However, the former is syntactically and phonologically more complex than the latter, and therefore, the latter is chosen as a grammatical form, due to the economy of language use. (See the similar arguments based on the economy of language use in 2.2 (3), 2.3 (8)).

Our view about the distribution of RHO that has been discussed so far is that (i) for those languages such as Japanese and Malayalam that have order-free zero pronouns, their grammars contain the lexical entry for RHO (1) and lack the RHO Introduction Lexical Rule (5), and (ii) for those languages such as English, French, and German that allow RHO to appear only as the semantic subject of a nonfinite VP, their grammars contain the RHO Introduction Lexical Rule (5) instead of the lexical entry for RHO (1).

RHO is responsible not only for unique control (8a) but also for free control (8b).

(8) a. Amy$_i$ thinks Tom$_j$ enjoys [$_{\text{VP[PRP] *i/j/*i+j/*gen}}$ dancing with Dan].
  b. Amy$_i$ thinks that [$_{\text{VP[PRP] i/j/i+j/gen}}$ dancing with Dan] intrigues Tom$_j$. (Culicover and Jackendoff 2005: 422)
  c. Amy$_i$ thinks that it intrigues Tom$_j$ that she$_i$/he$_j$/one$_{\text{gen}}$ dances with Dan.
  d. Amy$_i$ thinks that it intrigues Tom$_j$ that they$_{i+j}$ dance with Dan.

Note that the range of interpretation possibilities of free control RHO in (8b) is the same as the range of interpretation possibilities of overt pronouns in (8c, d).

This is the primary reason why the F/A and RS of RHO are the same as those of an overt pronoun, namely, an IND feature in F/A and a ROLE in RS.

We can simplify both the lexical entry of each unique control verb (4.4 (4) and (5)) and the specification of free control (8b) by resorting to an inheritance hierarchy (1.1.2 (7), (8)).

(9) inheritance hierarchy of controlled VP

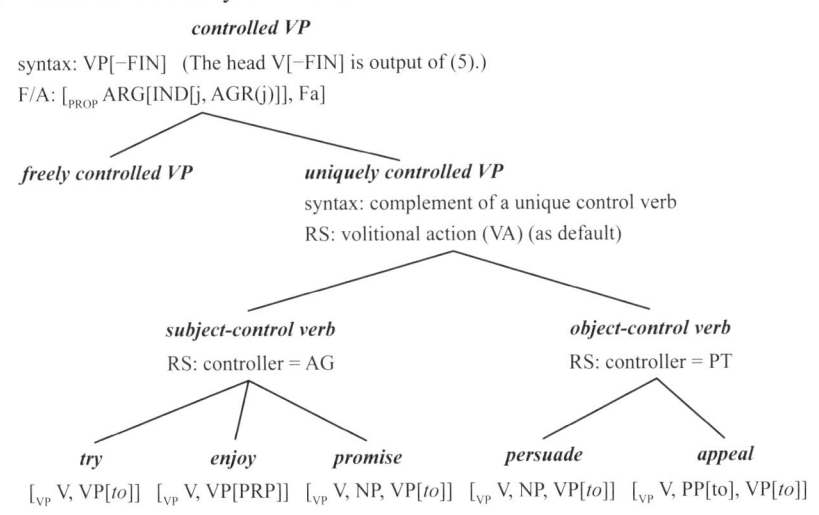

controlled VP
syntax: VP[−FIN] (The head V[−FIN] is output of (5).)
F/A: [$_{PROP}$ ARG[IND[j, AGR(j)]], Fa]

freely controlled VP   *uniquely controlled VP*
                             syntax: complement of a unique control verb
                             RS: volitional action (VA) (as default)

subject-control verb   *object-control verb*
RS: controller = AG   RS: controller = PT

try   *enjoy*   *promise*   *persuade*   *appeal*
[$_{VP}$ V, VP[*to*]] [$_{VP}$ V, VP[PRP]] [$_{VP}$ V, NP, VP[*to*]] [$_{VP}$ V, NP, VP[*to*]] [$_{VP}$ V, PP[to], VP[*to*]]

4.6 Passivization of Unique Control Verbs

4.6.1 Passivization of object-control verbs

When the Passive Lexical Rules (3.1 (3) for object NPs and 3.4 (2) for prepositional objects) apply to the lexical entry of an object-control verb (*order* in (1a) with its lexical entry (2) and *count on* in (1c) with its lexical entry in (4)), the output is a subject-control verb ((1b) and (1d)), because in the passive lexical entries (3) and (5), the controller patient role in their RS field corresponds to the subject NP in syntax.

(1) a. Mary ordered John to behave himself.
    b. John was ordered (by Mary) to behave himself.
    c. Mary counts on John to behave himself.
    d. John is counted on (by Mary) to behave himself.

(2) lexical entry for the object-control verb *order* (=4.4.1 (4))
syntax: V in [__, NP, VP[*to*]]
F/A: Fpaa
RS: [$_{TYPE}$ "order"] in [$_{VA\_}$ [AG, SO] [PT, GO] [$_{TH}$ [$_{VA}$ AG ...]]]

(3) passive output: lexical entry for the passive *ordered*
syntax: V[PAS] in [__, VP[*to*]]
F/A: Fpa
RS: [$_{TYPE}$ "order"] in [$_{VA\_}$ <[AG, SO]> [PT, GO] [$_{TH}$ [$_{VA}$ AG ...]]]

(4) lexical entry for the object-control verb *count on*
syntax: V in [__, [$_{PP[on]}$ P, NP], VP[*to*]]
F/A: Fpaa
RS: [$_{TYPE}$ "count-on"] in [$_{VA\_}$ [AG, SO] [PT, GO] [$_{TH}$ [$_{SITU}$ ROLE ...]]]

(5) passive output: lexical entry for the passive *counted on*
syntax: V[PAS] in [__, [$_{PP[on]}$ P], VP[*to*]]
F/A: Fpa
RS: [$_{TYPE}$ "count-on"] in [$_{VA\_}$ <[AG, SO]> [PT, GO] [$_{TH}$ [$_{SITU}$ ROLE ...]]]

In the RS field of (4) and (5), ROLE refers to the highest associable role (i.e., the associable role that outranks all the other roles listed on the RS) of the head verb of the complement VP[*to*].

4.6.2 Passivization of subject control verbs

When the Passive Lexical Rule applies to the lexical entry of a subject-control verb, such as *promise* in (6a), whose lexical entry is given in (7), sentences (6b, b') formed with the output lexical entry (8) are ungrammatical. This is known as Visser's Generalization (Bresnan 1982: 354, Pollard and Sag 1994: 304, Sadock 2012: 93). (6c) shows that the ditransitive use of *promise* is passivizable. (6d) shows that the control relation can be maintained in nominalization between the VP[*to*] and the object NP of the PP[*by*], which is in striking contrast with the ungrammatical agentive passive (6b').

(6) (cf. Culicover and Jackendoff 2005: 435 (47))
   a. Mary promised John to behave herself/*himself.
   b. *John was promised to behave herself/himself.
   b'. *John was promised by Mary to behave herself/himself.
   c. John was promised a new bike (by Mary).
   d. a promise to John by/from Mary to behave herself/*himself

(7) lexical entry for the subject-control verb *promise* (Sadock 2012: 91 (36a)) (=4.4.1 (5))
   syntax: V in [__, NP, VP[*to*]]
   F/A: Fpaa
   RS: [$_{TYPE}$ "promise"] in [$_{VA\_}$ [AG, SO] [PT, GO] [$_{TH}$ [$_{VA}$ AG ...]]]

(8) passive output (Sadock 2012: 93 (42)): lexical entry for the passive *promised*
   syntax: V[PAS] in [__, VP[*to*]]
   F/A: Fpa
   RS: [$_{TYPE}$ "promise"] in [$_{VA\_}$ <[AG, SO]> [PT, GO] [$_{TH}$ [$_{VA}$ AG ...]]]

In order to account for the ungrammaticality of (6b, b'), we propose a general condition on the controller of unique control verbs (cf. Bresnan 1982: 322, Dalrymple 2002: 345).

(9) condition on the controller of unique control verbs
   The controller role of a unique control verb must correspond to one of its ARGs in F/A.

In the RS field of the lexical entry for every unique control verb, by definition, the controller role is lexically specified as a coreference relation between it and the controllee role, as in (7). The lexically specified controller in the RS of (8), namely, <[AG, SO]>, being an unassociable role, does not correspond to any ARG in F/A. Therefore, (9) is violated in (8), which explains the ungrammaticality of (6b). In 3.3 (5), the passive *by*-phrase was analyzed as corresponding to an MFa (i.e., a modifier of Fa) and not an ARG in F/A. Therefore, (9) is violated in (6b').

(9) is formulated so as to only apply to (unique control) verbs. Hence, it does not apply to the nominalization (6d). What is special about control relations in NPs is that the controller is not obligatory (10b), though the interpretation always holds that the controllee RHO refers to the source of the promise in question (i.e., the person who makes the promise). The controllee RHO can be understood as generic (10c), as a discourse topic (10d), as a discourse participant (the speaker or addressee) (10e), or as having split antecedents (10f) (cf. 4.4 (3d)).

(10) a. a promise to John by/from Mary to behave herself/*himself (=(6d))
 b. a promise to John to buy a new bike
 c. A: What is the most important promise as a member of society?
   B: The promise to behave oneself in public.
 d. A: John gave me something.
   B: What was it?
   A: A promise to behave himself. (discourse topic = John)
 e. A: John wanted something.
   B: What was it?
   A: A promise to behave myself/yourself.
 f. A: John$_j$ gave Mary$_m$ something.
   B: What was it?
   A: A promise to $_{j+m}$go out together.
 g. lexical entry for the noun *promise* with VP[*to*]
   syntax: N in [$_{N'}$ ___, (PP[*to*]), (P[{*by* | *from*}]), VP[*to*]]
   F/A: ARG$_{p(a)(a)}$
   RS: [$_{VA}$ [$_{TYPE}$ "promise"]
   {[AG, SO] | <[AG, SO]>} {[PT, GO] | <[PT, GO]>} [$_{TH}$ [$_{VA}$ AG ...]]]

 morph: N[0]

The lexical entry for the noun *promise* when used with a VP[*to*] is given in (10 g), in which the PP[*to*] with a [PT, GO] role and the PP[{*by* | *from*}] with a [AG, SO] role are syntactically optional, and these roles can be unassociable. When the [AG, SO] role is associable, it must correspond to the PP[{*by* | *from*}] in syntax, and the noun exhibits subject-control-like properties, as in (10a). Note that the PP[{*by* | *from*}] is treated as a complement of the noun. By contrast, when the [AG, SO] role is unassociable, and hence does not correspond to anything in syntax, the noun exhibits free-control-like properties, as in (10c-f).

4.6.3 Impersonal passive with VP[*to*]

The following (11a) is what Jackendoff and Culicover called impersonal passive. They pointed out that there is no corresponding active for (11a). In fact, the apparent corresponding active (11b) is pretty bad.

(11) a. It is ordered by the authorities not to $_{gen}$shoot oneself.
(Jackendoff and Culicover 2003: 530, Culicover and Jackendoff 2005: 435)
b. ??The authorities order not to shoot oneself. (ibid.)

Besides being an object control verb, *order* is a passivizable transitive verb, as in *Silence was ordered*. The lexical entry for the transitive *order* and that for its passive counterpart are given below.

(12) Input: lexical entry for the   output: lexical entry for the passive
     transitive *order*   *ordered*
     syntax: V in [__, NP]   →   V[PAS] in [__]
     F/A: Faa   →   Fa
     RS: [$_{TYPE}$ "order"] in [$_{VA}$ __   →   [$_{TYPE}$ "order"] in [$_{VA}$ __ <[AG, SO]>
     [AG, SO] [PT, TH]]   [PT, TH]]

The [PT, TH] role in the RS field of the passive lexical entry (corresponding to the sole ARG in F/A) denotes the content of the order in question, as in *Silence/Curfew was ordered*, which means that the role is semantically compatible with a proposition. Hence, the Extraposition Lexical Rule (2.7 (5)) is applicable to the passive lexical entry in (12), and its output is as follows. Note that in (13), a VP[*to*] is used instead of a CP[*that*] in the Extraposition Lexical Rule.

(13) lexical entry for the extraposed passive *ordered* (output of the Extraposition Lexical Rule)
     syntax: V[PAS] in [[$_{VP[PAS]}$ __], VP[*to*]]
     F/A: Fp
     RS: [$_{TYPE}$ "order"] in [$_{VA}$ __ <[AG, SO]> [$_{[PT, TH]}$ VA]]

The impersonal passive sentence (11a) is licensed by the lexical entry (13). Because this is not a unique control structure (i.e., no coreference requirement in the RS field), the RHO in the F/A of (11a) can be interpreted in various ways, although the interpretation still holds in (11a) that the controller is a supposed goal role of the ordering event (i.e., a person to whom the order is issued). But such a goal role does not exist in the RS of (13). Therefore, this interpretation is not due to the RS of (13) but to our pragmatic knowledge of what the act of issuing an order is, that is, that an order is issued to someone, who then is required to carry it out. Other impersonal passives with a VP[*to*] can be explained in the same way. Here are examples of impersonal passive *try*.

(14) *try* in the passive (from the web)
   a. (?) Around 1800, it was tried to create a third West Indian Company, without any success.
   b. (?) Under the Articles of Confederation, it was tried to have states make their own currency.
   c. Es wird versucht, das Auto zu reparieren. (Dalrymple 2001: 345 note 5)
   d. lexical entry for the extraposed passive *tried*
      syntax: V[PAS] in [[$_{VP[PAS]}$ ___], VP[*to*]]
      F/A: Fp
      RS: [$_{TYPE}$ "try"] in [$_{VA}$ ___ <[AG, SO]> [$_{PT, TH}$ VA]]

The source of this impersonal passive is the same as that of (11a), namely, (14d): the lexical entry for the transitive *try* (Faa in F/A) first undergoes the Passive Lexical Rule and its output in turn undergoes the Extraposition Lexical Rule. Here are impersonal passives with *promise*.

(15) *promise* in the impersonal passive
   a. (?) I didn't even get my full commission but it was promised to me to be reimbursed in my salary check on the 22nd of June. (from the web)
   b. (?) It was promised to Susan to be allowed to take care of herself. (Culicover and Jackendoff 2005: 436)
   b'. It was never promised to Mary to be allowed to leave. (Bresnan 1982: 355)
   c. lexical entry for the extraposed passive *promised*
      syntax: V[PAS] in [[$_{VP[PAS]}$ ___, PP[*to*]], VP[*to*]]
      F/A: Fap
      RS: [$_{TYPE}$ "promise"] in [$_{VA}$ ___ <[AG, SO]> [$_{PT, TH}$ VA], GO]

The lexical entry (15c) is arrived at in such a way that the lexical entry for the transitive *promise* with the subcategorization frame [V, NP, PP[*to*]] first undergoes the Passive Lexical Rule and then the Extraposition Lexical Rule.

In (15a–b'), the goal argument (*me* in (15a), *Susan* in (15b), and *Mary* in (15b')) is interpreted as the controller of the VP[*to*]. Note that in (15c), GO in the RS field corresponds to ARG in F/A. Therefore, this ARG is the only candidate for the controller of the extraposed VP[*to*], if we try to find one within the sentence.

4.7 Causative Coercion

4.7.1 Need for causative coercion

Such verbs as *plan* take a complement that denotes a volitional action (VA) in the form of VP[*to*], CP[*for*], or CP[*that*], as is shown in the lexical entry below (Culicover and Jackendoff 2005: 429–430).

(1) lexical entry for *plan*
 syntax: V in [__, {VP[*to*] | CP[*for*] | CP[*that*]}]
 F/A: Fpa
 RS: [$_{TYPE}$ "plan"] in [$_{VA}$ __ AG [$_{PT}$ [$_{VA}$ AG ...]]]

But these verbs sometimes allow a CP complement that denotes a situation (SITU) as long as it can be interpreted as being brought about by the agent's volitional action (2b, c) (Jackendoff and Culicover 2003: 542, Culicover and Jackendoff 2005: 452).

(2) a. John plans to read the book/#realize the truth/#understand physics/#be much taller.
 b. John plans for Mary to realize the truth/understand physics/?be much taller.
 c. Hilary plans for there to be more light in here. (Jackendoff and Culicover 2003: 542)

In order to bridge the gap between the appearance of a situation CP complement, as in (2b, c), in which the coreference requirement in the RS field of (1) is not met, and the lexical requirements of *plan* in (1) that the verb take a volitional action complement and that the two agents be coreferent, Jackendoff and Culicover proposed causative coercion (*bring about* coercion in their terms). They claimed that the coerced material 'bring it about that' is inserted into their Conceptual Structure (CS). It is a two-place "cause$_2$" that takes two roles: a causer as its agent and a caused situation as its patient. "Coerced material" is "a conventionalized but freely available piece of semantic structure," according to Jackendoff and Culicover 2003: 543 note 24. In AMG terms, the coerced aspect of meaning is a defective lexical item that has an RS representation and lacks its syntax, F/A, and phonology, and it is freely available to ensure the RS well-formedness of a sentence. The lexical entry for causative coercion is given in (3), in which the RS field says that "$cause_2$" heads a volitional action (VA) and takes an agent ([AG, SO]) role and a patient ([PT, TH]) role, the latter directly dominating a situation (SITU).

(3) lexical entry for causative coercion (=3.3 (3))
   syntax: nil
   F/A: nil
   RS: [$_{TYPE}$ "$cause_2$"] in [$_{VA}$ ___ [AG, SO] [$_{[PT, TH]}$ SITU]]
   mphon: nil

If we apply this causative coercion lexical item to (2b) *John plans for Mary to understand physics*, its syntax and F/A stay the same but its RS is altered to (4). Compare this RS with the RS without causative coercion (5).

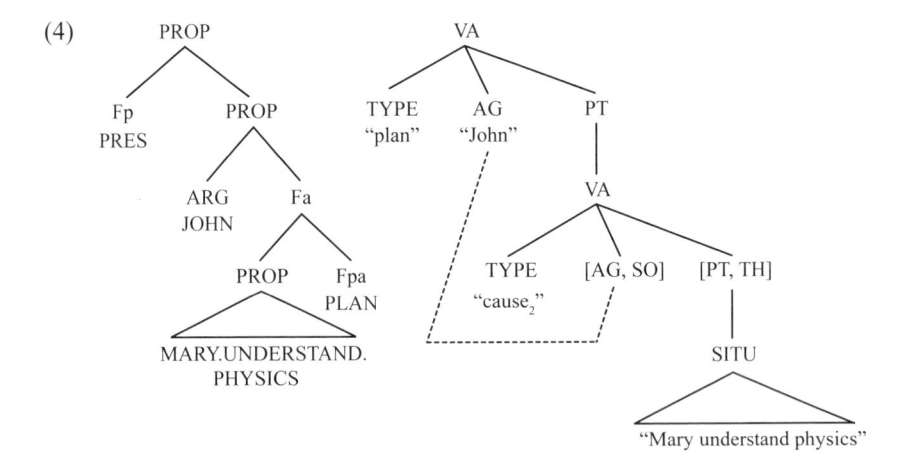

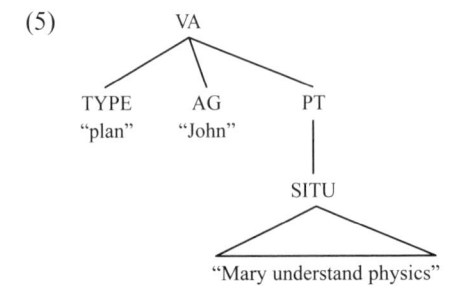

(4) [tree diagram]

(5) [tree diagram]

The RS without causative coercion in (5) violates two lexical requirements in the lexical entry for *plan* (1): that *plan* take a volitional action (VA) complement and that the AG of the verb corefer with the AG of the VA complement. Hence, (5) is an ill-formed RS. The speaker/addressee's intention to seek a well-formed RS and thus assign meaning to the sentence in question triggers causative coercion, producing a well-formed RS in (4), which meets the RS requirements of the verb *plan*. On the other hand, (2a) #*John plans to realize the truth/understand physics* cannot be improved by causative coercion, because the relevant predicates, *realize the truth* and *understand physics*, are not self-controllable (cf. Kuno 1970: 352), and hence it is impossible for *John* to bring about the respective situation on his own.

4.7.2 More examples of causative coercion

Promise is another verb that takes a volitional action complement. Therefore, when it occurs with a CP[*that*] complement that denotes a state, as in *John promised Mary that the children will be in bed by 8* (Farkas 1988: 36), the sentence is understood with causative coercion in such a way that *John promised Mary that he will bring it about that the children will be in bed by 8*. Searle (1969: 57) observed that "I cannot promise that someone else will do something (although I can promise to see that he will do it)" and gave an example *I promise that (I will see to it that) Henry will be here next Wednesday* (Searle 1979: 23). Sadock (1974: 33) gave a similar example *% I requested of Sam that Mary take out the garbage* and observed that some speakers find it almost grammatical, but only in the interpretation that 'I requested of Sam that he make/let Mary take out the garbage.' Another example of causative coercion is imperative sentences with a stative VP, such as *Be careful!* and *Be quiet!* (Farkas 1988: 39, Sag and Pollard 1991: 83). These imperatives are understood with causative coercion ('Make yourself careful/quiet!'). Still another example of causative coercion is the adverb *intentionally* used in sentences with nonagentive subject, such as *John fell off the ladder intentionally* (Farkas 1988: 39) or *John was intentionally seen by the best specialist* (Farkas 1988: 40). These sentences are interpreted with causative coercion ('John intentionally brought it about that he fell off the ladder' or 'John intentionally brought it about that he was seen by the best specialist'). Recall that causative coercion with its lexical entry (3) was already used to account for the passive *by*-phrase (3.3 (3)), passive imperatives (3.9 (4)), and raising imperatives (4.1 (37)).

Causative coercion is also triggered when the unique control verb *try*, which selects a volitional action (VA) VP[*to*] as its complement (6), takes a VP[*to*] complement that does not denote a VA, as in (7a).

(6) lexical entry for *try* (Sadock 2012: 89 (32))
syntax: V in [__, VP[*to*]]
F/A: Fpa
RS: [$_{TYPE}$ "try"] in [$_{VA}$ __ AG [$_{PT}$ [$_{VA}$ AG ...]]]

In (7a), the verb *try* takes a VP[*to*] complement that denotes a self-controllable state. The sentence is interpreted as 'John tried to make himself quiet/John tried to bring it about that he would be quiet.' The F/A structure in (7b) is well formed. Note that the verb *try* is a unique control verb and as such it needs an ARG controller of the RHO (4.6 (9)), which is the subject ARG of TRY, because it is an Fpa functor and takes only one ARG, on the one hand, and, on the other, the controller role AG specified in the RS field of (6) corresponds to this subject ARG.

(7) a. John tried to be quiet.
 b. the F/A, the ill-formed RS without causative coercion, and the well-formed RS with it

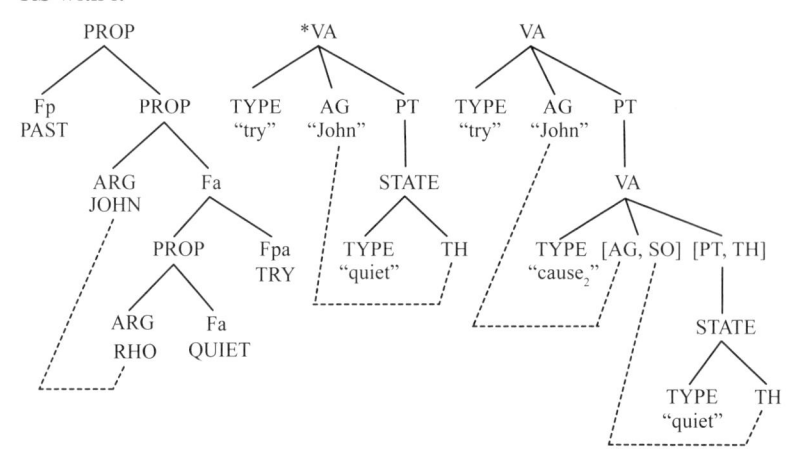

However, the corresponding RS without causative coercion is ill formed in two respects: first, the lexical requirement in (6) that *try* take a volitional action (VA) complement in RS is violated and second, the coreference requirement in (6) between the controller agent and the controllee agent is violated. Therefore, the speaker/addressee's intention to seek a well-formed RS and thereby assign meaning to the sentence in question triggers causative coercion, which is a freely available defective lexical item (3), resulting in the well-formed RS in (7b). Note that in the coerced RS, the two violations are resolved. The matrix verb *try* takes a VA complement and the agent of *try* and the agent of "cause$_2$" corefer. Note further that the coreference relation between JOHN and RHO in F/A is divided into two in RS: between the agent of *try* and the agent of coerced "cause$_2$," which is due to the coreference requirement of *try*, and between the agent of coerced "cause$_2$," and the theme of *quiet*.

(8a, a', a") are examples of controlled passive VP[*to*], and (8b, b', b") are examples of controlled *seem/appear*. Both types need causative coercion.

(8) a. John tried to be respected. (interpreted as 'John tried to get himself respected') (Sadock 2012: 236 note 8, Pollard and Sag 1994: 310)
   a'. I tried to be arrested. (Fodor 1974: 95)
   a". Throughout time women have tried to be treated as equals to males. (from the web)
   b. %Dick tried to seem to be a friendly person. (Sadock 2012: 51 (66))
   b'. I tried to appear to be asleep. (Fodor 1974: 99)
   b". During the 1988 New Hampshire primary, George H.W. Bush tried to appear to be an everyday guy by driving an 18-wheeler around a truck stop parking lot. (from the web)

The F/A and the two RS structures (with and without causative coercion) of (8a) are given in (9).

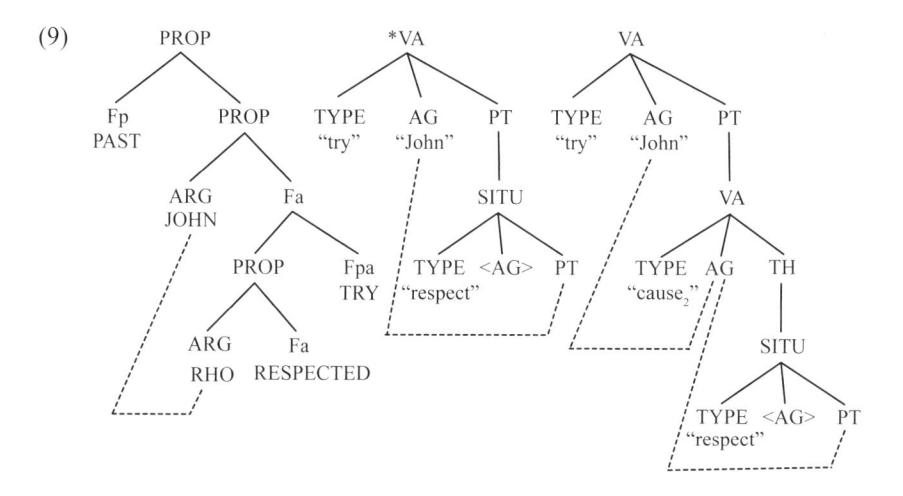

(9)
```
        PROP                    *VA                      VA
       /    \                  /    \                   /    \
     Fp     PROP            TYPE  AG   PT          TYPE   AG    PT
    PAST   /    \           "try" "John"           "try"  "John"
          ARG    Fa                  |                          |
         JOHN   /  \                SITU                        VA
               PROP  Fpa      TYPE <AG>  PT              TYPE   AG    TH
              /    \  TRY     "respect"                 "cause$_2$"
             ARG    Fa                                                |
             RHO  RESPECTED                                          SITU
                                                               TYPE <AG>  PT
                                                               "respect"
```

What is happening in (9) is the same as what happened in (7b). The subject ARG in F/A of the passive nonfinite VP, where RHO appears, corresponds to the patient role in RS. (This is due to the lexical entry for the passive participle *respected.*) Although the F/A structure in (9) is well formed, its corresponding RS prior to causative coercion is not. It violates two lexical requirements of *try* in (6): that it take a volitional action complement and that the two agents be coreferent. We assume in the RSs of (9) that the event type of the passivized *respect* is not a volitional action but a situation. The speaker/addressee's intention to seek a well-formed RS and assign meaning to the sentence in question triggers causative coercion, which is a freely available defective lexical item (3), leading to a well-formed RS. Here again, the coreference relation between JOHN and RHO in F/A is divided into two in RS: the coreference relation between the agent of *try* and the agent of the coerced "cause$_2$," and that between the agent of the coerced "cause$_2$," and the patient of *respect*.

The F/A structure and the two RS structures (with and without causative coercion) of (8b) are given in (10). Again, the F/A is well formed but the RS without causative coercion is not, and causative coercion is triggered, resulting in a well-formed RS. In the F/A structure, RHO is not an ARG of the complement PROP of *try*, because there is an intervening [$_{Fp}$ SEEM]. However, this is what happens in such control structures as *They claimed to have tried to escape* (Sadock 2012: 49), in which there is an intervening [$_{Fp}$ PAST] between CLAIM and the RHO subject of *tried*.

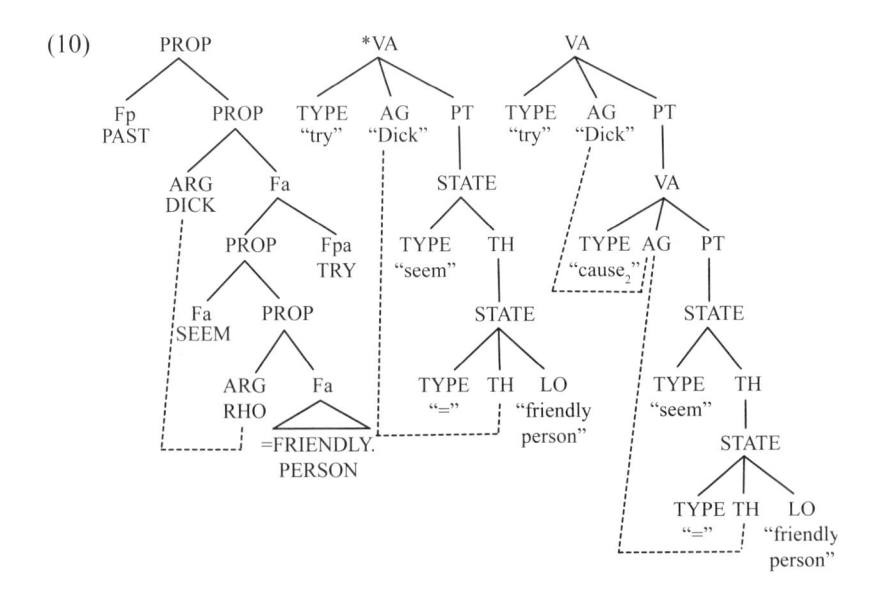

(10)

Pollard and Sag (1994: 311) observed that causative coercion is required in *We persuaded Sandy to be tall*, whereas it is not required in *Sandy wanted to be tall*. This is because *be tall* denotes a (non-self-controllable) state but *persuade* takes a volitional action complement, and hence causative coercion is required. On the other hand, *want* takes a situation complement and situations include states, according to the Event Hierarchy (4.3 (5)). Therefore, there is no need for causative coercion.

In (11a) below, *try* must take a volitional action complement, but *seem* does not denote one, thus triggering causative coercion. With causative coercion, the coreference between the agent of *try* and the agent of "cause$_2$" is established in the coerced RS, but (11a) is still ungrammatical, because *try* is a subject control verb and as such it must take as its complement a controlled VP, a VP[–FIN] that corresponds to a [$_{PROP}$ [$_{ARG}$ RHO], Fa] in F/A (4.5 (9)). However, the VP[*to*] in (11a) is semantically saturated and has no room for RHO. In other words, it is not a controlled VP, and hence lacks a controllee ARG in its F/A. In addition, the coreference requirement in the RS field of *try* in (6) is not met in the corresponding RS. Therefore, the F/A and the pre- and post-coerced RSs of (11a) are all ill formed, which explains the ungrammaticality of (11a).

(11) a. *John tried to seem that the earth is/was flat. (Sadock 2012: 87 (28))
 b. ?John tried to seem that he was sorry. (cf. (8b))
 c. Biden is the cookie cutter politician who tries to seem that he understands the working public but in fact he's never been one. (from the web)

When the CP[*that*] in (11a) has a pronoun subject that is coreferent with the matrix subject, as in (11b), the acceptability improves. (11c) is such an example. This is because the coerced RS of (11b, c) is well formed in that the agent of the matrix verb *try* and the agent of the coerced "cause$_2$" are coreferent and the latter agent and the subject of the state CP[*that*] are coreferent, too. The only problem is that the VP[*to*] complement of *try* is not a controlled VP that corresponds to [$_{PROP}$ [$_{ARG}$ RHO], Fa] in F/A. In other words, (11a) has a well-formed syntax but both its F/A and RS are ill formed, whereas (11b, c) have well-formed syntax and RS but their F/A is still ill formed. This explains the improved acceptability of (11b, c).

4.8 Controller Shift

4.8.1 Controller shift and its triggering factors

An NP that is not the lexically specified controller is sometimes interpreted as such. This phenomenon is called controller shift. Sadock (2012: 92), following Farkas (1988), claimed that our knowledge of the world is implicated in this phenomenon.

(1) a. The quarterback$_i$ promised the coach$_j$ to $_{i/*j}$be healthy by game time. (Sadock 2012: 92)

a'. ["promise" [$_{AG}$ "quarterback$_i$"] [$_{PT}$ "coach"] [$_{VA}$ "cause$_2$" AG$_i$ [$_{SITU}$ "healthy" TH$_i$]]]

b. The doctor$_i$ promised the quarterback$_j$ to $_{i/j}$be healthy by game time. (Sadock 2012: 92)

b'. ["promise" [$_{AG}$ "doctor$_i$"] [$_{PT}$ "quarterback$_j$"] [$_{VA}$ "cause$_2$" AG$_i$ [$_{SITU}$ "healthy" TH$_{i/j}$]]]

c. Fred$_i$ promised Nancy$_j$ to $_{*i/j}$be allowed to vote for herself$_j$. (Sadock 2012: 92)

c'. ["promise" [$_{AG}$ "Fred$_i$"] [$_{PT}$ "Nancy$_j$"] [$_{VA}$ "cause$_2$" AG$_i$ [$_{SITU}$ "allow" <AG> PT$_j$ [$_{VA}$ "vote" AG$_j$]]]]

d. lexical entry for the verb *promise* (=4.4.1 (5))
syntax: V in [__, NP, VP[*to*]]
F/A: Fpaa
RS: [$_{TYPE}$ "promise"] in [$_{VA}$ __ [AG, SO] [PT, GO] [$_{TH}$ [$_{VA}$ AG ...]]]

Although the verb *promise*, whose lexical entry is repeated in (1d), requires a volitional action complement VP[*to*], *to be healthy* in (1a, b) is a state and does not denote a volitional action. Furthermore, the coreference requirement between the two agents in the RS field of (1d) is not met. Therefore, causative coercion, which is a freely available defective lexical item, is triggered by the speaker/addressee's intention to seek a well-formed RS and thereby assign meaning to the sentence in question. The two-place "cause$_2$" (4.7.1 (3)) gets inserted in the RS of (1a), resulting in the coerced RS (1a'), whose interpretation is 'The quarterback$_i$ promised the coach$_j$ that he$_i$ would bring it about that he$_i$ would be healthy by game time.' In the coerced RS (1a'), the agent of *promise* and the agent of the coerced "cause$_2$" corefer due to the coreference requirement of *promise*, whereas the theme of *healthy* corefers with its immediately outranking role, namely, the agent of "cause$_2$." These two coreference relations are induced by the coreference relation in F/A between QUARTERBACK and RHO, which is what happened in 4.7.2 (7) and (9). This is a default case in that the original controller (i.e., the subject NP) is respected without controller shift.

On the other hand, (1b) is ambiguous and either the subject NP or the object NP is interpretable as the controller. When the subject *the doctor* is interpreted as the controller (default case), the same causative coercion and the same coreference between the theme of *healthy* and the agent of "cause$_2$," as in (1a') are responsible for this interpretation. However, this interpretation does not agree with our knowledge of the world that a doctor brings about improved conditions to his or her patients. Therefore, we prefer the other controller-shifted interpretation that accords with that knowledge (namely, 'the doctor$_i$ promised the quarterback$_j$ that he$_i$ would bring it about that he$_j$ would be healthy by game time'). In this interpretation, the controller is the object NP and the person who will be healthy is the doctor's patient, the quarterback. Note that the theme of *healthy* corefers with its second most immediately outranking role, the [PT, GO] role of *promise*. In this case, too, causative coercion is triggered for the same two reasons as above, resulting in the coerced RS (1b'), where the two lexical requirements of *promise* (1d) (that it take a volitional action complement and that the two agents be coreferent) are still met.

We claim about (1a, b) that unless there is pragmatic pressure toward the controller-shifted interpretation that agrees with our knowledge of the world, the default interpretation (1a') obtains, in which the role that corresponds to the RHO in F/A (i.e., the theme role of *healthy* in (1a)) corefers with its most immediately outranking role, the agent of "cause$_2$," which in turn corefers with the agent of *promise*, due to its lexical coreference requirement. Thus controller shift does not occur. However, when such pragmatic pressure does exist, the default interpretation is overridden by the other interpretation in which the role that corresponds to the RHO in F/A (i.e., the theme role of *healthy* in (1a, b)) corefers with its second most outranking role, the [PT, GO] role of *promise*. This results in controller shift and the interpretation obtains that accords with our pragmatic knowledge, as in the second interpretation of (1b'). The important point is that when the unique control verb *promise* in the matrix clause is used as a transitive (i.e., taking an object NP), causative coercion opens up two possibilities of controller choice. The controller of the complement VP[*to*] can be either the subject NP (the lexically specified controller) or the object NP (a case of controller shift). In either interpretation, the lexical requirements in the RS field of the lexical entry for *promise* are satisfied, thanks to causative coercion.

Our reasoning so far about (1a, b) is (i) that the controller-controllee coreference requirement is stated in the RS field of a unique control verb, (ii) that causative coercion is triggered to overcome the violation of two lexical requirements: that the matrix verb take a volitional action (VA) complement, which is violated in (1a, b), and that the agent of the matrix verb and the agent of the VA complement be coreferent, which is also violated in (1a, b), (iii) that these violations are resolved in the coerced RS. The net result is that causative coercion opens up two possibilities of controller choice: the controllee referring to the agent of "cause$_2$" (default case) or to the patient role of the matrix verb.

As for (1c), because the VP[*to*] complement contains the reflexive *herself*, the interpretation in which *Fred* is the controller of the VP[*to*] is impossible. More importantly, *be allowed* VP[*to*] denotes not a volitional action (VA) but a state (Pollard and Sag 1994: 309), which is shown in (2). Therefore, the two lexical requirements in the RS field of *promise* are violated as before. To overcome these difficulties, causative coercion is triggered in (1c).

(2) a. *What Nancy did was to be allowed to vote.
 b. ??Nancy was intentionally allowed to vote.
 c. Nancy happened to be allowed to vote.
 d. Nancy has been allowed to vote since she was 18 years old.

In (1c'), the coerced RS of (1c), the coreference relation between the agent of *promise* and the agent of "cause$_2$" holds, again, due to the lexical requirement of *promise*, and the coreference relation between the patient of *allow*, which takes a VA complement, and the agent of *vote* holds due to the lexical requirement of the unique control verb *allow*. As was the case with the theme of *be healthy* in (1b'), causative coercion opens up two options of what the patient of *allow* corefers with in (1c'): it corefers either with the agent of "cause$_2$" (default interpretation) or with the [PT, GO] role of *promise* (controller-shifted interpretation). Because the VP[*to*] contains *herself*, the default interpretation is impossible. (However, the default interpretation is available in appropriate contexts. See (3).) Therefore, the only available interpretation of (1c) is the latter (nondefault) interpretation ("Fred promised Nancy that he would bring it about that she would be allowed to vote for herself"), in which the patient of *allow* corefers with the [PT, GO] role of *promise*, as indicated in (1c, c'), resulting in controller shift. Again, under this interpretation, the lexical requirements of *promise* are satisfied that it take a volitional action complement and that the agent of *promise* and the agent of its VA complement corefer.

There is pragmatic pressure in (1c) toward choosing this controller-shifted interpretation. (In 4.9 (4), another pragmatic factor will be discussed.) Our knowledge about the notion of promise is that when X promises Y to do something, Y (=the [PT, GO] role of *promise*) is the beneficiary of the promised action (Jackendoff and Culicover 2003: 547). Also our knowledge about the notion of permission is that when X is allowed to do something, X (=the [PT, GO] role of *allow*) is the beneficiary of the permitted action. If we assume that there is at most one beneficiary participant in a single event in default cases, the interpretation of an event that involves both making a promise and being granted permission should be the one in which the beneficiaries of the two coincide. In (1c) with the controller-shifted interpretation, *Nancy* is the beneficiary of both promising and allowing. This uniqueness of the beneficiary participant in an event holds in (1a) and (1b), too. In (1a) with (1a') interpretation, the beneficiary of promising is its goal, *the coach*, and the beneficiary of predicting that *the quarterback* will be healthy by game time is also *the coach* (because, for example, his team will be able to win if the quarterback gets well in time and can take part in the game). In (1b) with (1b') interpretation, the beneficiary of promising is its goal, *the quarterback*, and the beneficiary of predicting that *the quarterback* will be healthy by game time is also *the quarterback* himself (because, for example, he wants to take part in the game).

However, the uniqueness of the beneficiary participant in an event holds as default and is not absolute. The examples in (3) show that the presence of *be allowed* VP[*to*] does not always result in controller shift. In fact, the default subject-control interpretation of the verb *promise* is still available with the complement *be allowed* VP[*to*].

(3) a. ?Jim promised Mary to be allowed to defend himself. (Pollard and Sag 1994: 312)
   b. John promised Mary to be allowed to marry her by their families.
   c. Aung San Suu Kyi had always wanted to run in a general election since she was placed under house arrest more than twenty years ago. But unfortunately, it became increasingly clear that she couldn't promise her supporters to be allowed to run in the next general election.

4.8.2 Passivization of *promise*: revisited

We discussed Visser's Generalization in 4.6.2 (6b, b') and (9), which says that a subject-controlled transitive verb with a VP[*to*] complement, for example, *promise*, cannot be passivized. However, when *promise* is interpreted as object control (due to controller shift resulting from causative coercion), passivization becomes possible, as in (4b).

(4) a. John promised <u>Mary</u> to be allowed to vote for herself.
 b. <u>Mary</u> was promised to be allowed to vote for herself.

This is apparently because once the control (coreference) relation between the [PT, GO] role of *promise* and a role in its VP[*to*] complement is established, it is maintained under passivization, in exactly the same way as the case of passivization of object control verb *order* (4.6 (3)). But we need to be careful here. There are two ways of accounting for the passivization in (4b): (i) the coerced *promise* (with its coerced RS) is input to the Passive Lexical Rule, or (ii) a passive sentence (based on a passive verb lexical entry that is the output of the Passive Lexical Rule) undergoes causative coercion, which leads to controller shift. We have so far taken the view that causative coercion is triggered by the speaker/addressee's intention to seek a well-formed RS and thereby assign meaning to the sentence in question, in which, for example, a control verb that requires a volitional action VP complement happens to take a state-denoting VP. Taking this into account, the coerced *promise* cannot be the input to the Passive Lexical Rule. There is no such thing as "the lexical entry for coerced *promise*," to begin with. The coerced material 4.7 (3) is inserted in the ill-formed RS of a sentence. Therefore, it exists in the RS of such a sentence, and not in the RS field of a lexical entry. This shows that we need to take option (ii). This entails that the lexical entry for passive *promised* (5) below is present in the lexicon, although its direct realization without causative coercion always results in violation of the condition on the controller of unique control verbs (4.6.2 (9)).

The passive participle of *promise* (5) takes a volitional action complement. But the VP[*to*] in (4b), *be allowed* VP[*to*], is not a volitional action but a state, as we saw in (2) above. In addition, the RS field of (5) requires that the unassociable AG and the AG of the VA complement be coreferent, which is not met in (4b), either. The speaker/addressee's intention to seek a well-formed RS of (4b) and thus overcome these discrepancies and assign meaning to (4b) triggers causative coercion (4.7 (3)), which is a freely available defective lexical item, as expected, resulting in the well-formed coerced RS of (4b), namely, (6).

(5) lexical entry for passive *promised* (=4.6.2 (8))
 syntax: V[PAS] in [__, VP[*to*]]
 F/A: Fpa
 RS: [$_{TYPE}$ "promise"] in [$_{VA}$ __ <[AG, SO]> [PT, GO] [$_{TH}$ [$_{VA}$ AG ...]]]

(6) coerced RS of (4b)
 ["promise" <[AG, SO]$_i$> [$_{[PT, GO]}$ "Mary$_j$"] [$_{VA}$ "cause$_2$" AG$_i$ [$_{SITU}$ "allow" <AG> PT$_{*i/j}$ [$_{VA}$ "vote" AG$_j$]]]]

As before, the patient of *allow* has two options: (i) coreferring with the agent of "cause$_2$," or (ii) coreferring with the [PT, GO] role of *promise*. If we take option (i), the condition on the controller of a unique control verb (4.6.2 (9)) is violated, because the controller is the unassociable agent and does not correspond to any ARG (violation of 4.6.2 (9)). If we take option (ii), the controller is the patient of *promise*, as indicated in (6), and the condition on the controller is met. Furthermore, the beneficiary participant of promising and that of allowing coincide in this interpretation, namely, *Mary*. That is, the uniqueness of the beneficiary role is also respected.

4.8.3 Other pragmatic and semantic factors

The controller shift we considered in 4.8.1 (1b, c) became available as a result of causative coercion (4.7 (3)), which opened up two options: the interpretation with controller shift ((1b) with (1b') as its RS and (1c) with (1c') as its RS) and the interpretation without it ((1a) with (1a') as its RS and (3)).

As shown in (3) below, there is another pragmatic/discourse factor that facilities the controller shift interpretation of the unique control verb *promise*. In direct discourse context, the speaker can give a promise to his or her addressee in two ways: with *I* as the subject (1a) or with *you* as the subject (1b). Therefore, (2a) and (3a) can be understood as reporting the promises (2b) and (3b), respectively. Note that (3a) is semantically very close to 'The doctor guaranteed the quarterback to be healthy by game time.' Searle (1969:58–59) observed that because *I (hereby) promise* is one of the strongest illocutionary force indicating devices for commitment, people say "I promise" when making an emphatic assertion.

(1) a. (a quarterback to his coach) "I'll be healthy by game time. I promise."
   b. (a doctor to a quarterback who is one of his patients) "You'll be healthy by game time. I promise."

(2) a. The quarterback promised the coach to be healthy by game time. (Sadock 2012: 92)
   b. reporting the quarterback's promise to his coach
   "I'll be healthy by game time. I promise."

(3) a. The doctor promised the quarterback to be healthy by game time. (Sadock 2012: 92)
   b. reporting the doctor's promise to the quarterback
   "You'll be healthy by game time. I promise."

In the same way, (4a) and (5a) can be understood as reporting Fred's promises to Nancy (4b) and (5b), respectively.

(4) a. Fred promised Nancy to be allowed to vote for herself. (Sadock 2012: 92)
   b. reporting Fred's promise to Nancy
   "You'll be allowed to/You may/You can vote for yourself. I promise."

(5) a. Fred promised Nancy to be allowed to marry her by their families. (= 4.8.1 (3b))
   b. reporting Fred's promise to Nancy
   "I'll be allowed to marry you by our families. I promise."

We have seen so far four factors that are involved in the controller-shifted interpretation of *promise*: (i) our knowledge of the world (for example, relationships between a quarterback and his coach and those between a quarterback and his doctor), (ii) causative coercion, (iii) the uniqueness of the beneficiary participant (for example, in an event involving both making a promise and granting permission), and (iv) the reporting of a promise expressed in the form of *You will* VP.

Some verbs, such as *ask*, *beg*, and *plead*, have two closely related meanings of *request for an action* and *request for permission for an action*. This polysemy of unique control verbs is a fifth factor that facilitates controller shift. Note that causative coercion is not triggered (6c, d, e, f), because *to leave* and *to go* are volitional actions and hence meet the verbs' lexical requirement that they take a volitional action VP[*to*].

(6) a. The coach begged <u>the quarterback</u> to be healthy by game time. (Sadock 2012: 92 (40))
cf. (the coach begging the quarterback) "You must be healthy by game time. I beg you."
b. <u>The quarterback</u> begged the doctor to be healthy by game time. (ibid.)
cf. (the quarterback begging the doctor) "I must be healthy by game time. I beg you."
c. John asked/begged <u>Susan</u> to leave the room. (Jackendoff and Culicover 2003: 546) (request for action)
cf. (*John*, the boss, to *Susan*, his secretary) "Please leave the room!"
d. <u>The student</u> asked/begged (the teacher) to leave the room. (ibid.) (request for permission for action)
cf. (the student to the teacher) "May I leave the room?"
e. <u>John</u> pleaded with <u>Mary</u> to go to the football game. (ambiguous) (Jackendoff and Culicover 2003: 547 note 26, Culicover and Jackendoff 2005: 458 note 27)
(request for action when *Mary* is the controller)
(request for permission for action when *John* is the controller)
f. <u>The student</u> pleaded (with the teacher) to leave the room. (request for permission for action)

What is special about *ask*, *beg*, and *plead* is that they have two closely related but distinct meanings: (i) request for an action and (ii) request for *permission* for an action. When they are used with meaning (i), they are object control verbs, as in (6c, e) that mean 'to request someone to do something.' On the other hand, when they are used with meaning (ii), they are subject control verbs, as in (6d, e, f) that mean 'to request for permission to do something' and the object NP becomes optional. Here are the lexical entries for *plead* with meanings (i) and (ii).

(7) lexical entry for *plead*₁ (with request-for-action meaning; object control)
syntax: V in [__, PP[*with*], VP[*to*]]
F/A: Fpaa
RS: [_TYPE_ "plead₁"] in [_VA_ __ [AG, SO] [PT, GO] [_TH_ [_VA_ AG ...]]]

(8) lexical entry for *plead₂* (with request-for-permission-for-action meaning; subject control)
syntax: V in [__, (PP[*with*]), VP[*to*]]
F/A: Fp(a)a
RS: [_TYPE "plead₁"] in [_VA __
[AG, SO] {[PT, GO] | <[PT, GO]>} [_TH [_VA [_TYPE "allow"] [AG, SO] [PT, GO] [_TH [_VA AG...]]]]]

(8) is the lexical entry for *plead₂* with request-for-permission-for-action meaning. In this RS field, *plead₁* in (7) takes "allow" as its [_TH VA] role. When the PP[*with*] does not appear in syntax in (8), the F/A is Fpa and the [PT, GO] of the matrix VA in RS is an unassociable role <[PT, GO]>. The coreference requirement between the matrix [PT, GO] role and the [AG, SO] role of "allow" is due to "plead₁" in (7), and the coreference requirement between the [PT, GO] role of "allow" and the lowest AG is due to the lexical property of "allow." The third coreference requirement between the matrix [AG, SO] role and the [PT, GO] role of "allow" is due to the meaning of this use of *plead₂* (i.e., asking for permission) that the [AG, SO] role of pleading is the recipient of the permission in question (i.e., the [PT, GO] role of "allow").

Jackendoff and Culicover (2003: 545) and Culicover and Jackendoff (2005: 455) used a new type of coercion, "the *allow/enable* coercion," to account for this case. Our claim here is that the controller shift with these verbs is simply due to their polysemy between 'requesting someone to do something' and 'requesting permission to do something from someone.'

Going back to the first factor (our knowledge of the world), here are examples in which this factor is dominant in determining the controller.

(9) a. John gave Susan $500 to take care of him/*himself. (Culicover and Jackendoff 2005: 438)
cf. "I gave you $500 to take care of me."
b. John got $500 from Susan to take care of her/*herself. (ibid.)
cf. "I got $500 from you to take care of you."
c. John contracted with Susan to take care of him/*her.
(Culicover and Jackendoff 2005: 437; under the reading that Susan got paid)
c'. John contracted with Susan to take care of *him/her.
(under the reading that John got paid)

d. John contracted with the housemaid to take care of him.
e. The housemaid contracted with John to take care of him.

In (9a, b), the recipient of the money is understood as the controller. In arriving at this interpretation, we need the real world knowledge (namely, the frame/script/schema of making a contract) that by getting paid, a person takes on a task (i.e., expressed by the VP[*to*]). This knowledge is also involved in controller determination with such verbs as *contract with, bargain with, arrange with*, and *make a deal with* when they take a VP[*to*] complement (Culicover and Jackendoff 2005: 437). In (9c), if *Susan* gets paid, she takes on the task and she is the person who does the task. That is, *Susan* is the controller and the controlled VP[*to*] is *to take care of him* (cf. 9d). On the other hand, in (9c'), if *John* gets paid, he takes on the task, and he is the person who does the task. The controller is *John* and the controlled VP[*to*] is *to take care of her* (cf. 9e).

4.9 Partial Control

Landau (2000: 28ff.) and Culicover and Jackendoff (2005: 459) discussed cases of what they called partial control such as (1a) below, cases of control relation in which unique control verbs, such as *want, hope, look forward to, intend, plan, agree*, and unique control adjectives, such as *eager, afraid* allow a noncollective controller subject when their VP[*to*] complement semantically requires a collective subject, such as *to meet at six* or *to gather during the strike*. On the other hand, verbs such as *manage, dare* (intransitive), and adjectives *rude, unwise* do not allow partial control (1b).

(1) Culicover and Jackendoff 2005: 460
 a. John wanted to meet at six/gather during the strike.
 b. *John managed to meet at six/gather during the strike.

The reason why (1b) is unacceptable is that (1b) has unacceptable entailments '#John met at six' and '#John gathered during the strike.' (The sign # is intended to show that the sentences are syntactically well formed but semantically anomalous.) Note that the matrix verb in (1b) *manage* is an implicative verb, whose defining property is that "an asserted main sentence with one of these verbs as predicate commits the speaker to an implied proposition which consists of the complement sentence" (Karttunen 1971: 340). Observe two more examples. The matrix verb in (2a) *dare* (subject-control) is another implicative verb and the adjective *unwise* in (2b) shares the same semantic property.

(2) a. *John dared to meet at six. (entailment '#John met at six')
    b. *John was unwise to meet at six. (entailment '#John met at six')

As long as a semantically ill-formed entailment does not arise, a joint/collective action VP allows a noncollective controller. This phenomenon is observed not only in subject-control structures (1a) but also in object-control structures.

(3) John dared/challenged Mary to meet at midnight.

Here are the F/A and RS of (1a), a partial control example with the subject-control verb *want*.

(4) the F/A and RS of *John wanted to meet (at six)* (=(1a))

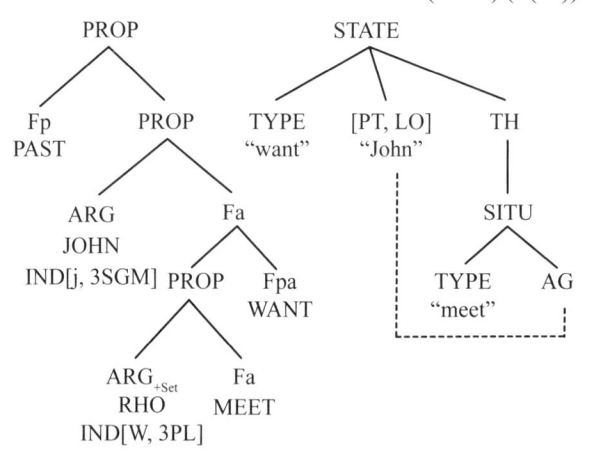

```
         PROP                    STATE
        /    \                  /  |  \
      Fp    PROP             TYPE [PT, LO]  TH
     PAST   /  \            "want"  "John"   |
           ARG   Fa                          SITU
          JOHN  /  \                         /  \
        IND[j, 3SGM] PROP  Fpa            TYPE   AG
                    /  \   WANT          "meet"
                ARG₊Set  Fa
                RHO    MEET
              IND[W, 3PL]
```

In the above F/A, JOHN carries the referential index j as part of its INDEX value, whereas RHO carries the INDEX value whose referential index is not an individual constant but a set of individuals W. (See 5.4 for details.) The partial control interpretation in (4) is nothing but the set-membership relation j∈ W in F/A, where W is the referential set of cardinality more than one that is required by the collective predicate MEET.

However, partial control interpretation is available even when the matrix subject NP is in the plural, as in (5a), if we can give an appropriate context, such as (5b).

(5) a. John$_i$ and Mary$_j$ wanted to $_w$ meet at six. ($\{i, j\}$ = W (default) or $\{i, j\} \subset W$)
 b. It was announced in the morning that [all the students]$_w$ must meet in the department lounge at some time this evening. John$_i$ and Mary$_j$ wanted to $_w$ meet at six. Surprisingly, [the other students]$_y$ did too.

In general, partial control is about set-inclusion relations, rather than set-membership relations, in that the referential index of the controller, a set, is included in W, the referential index of RHO: $\{j\} \subseteq W$ in (4) and $\{i, j\} \subseteq W$ and $Y \subseteq W$ in (5b). In the context of (5b), W = {all the students in the department} = $\{i, j\} \cup Y$. Note that partial control interpretation is maintained under VP ellipsis, as in the last sentence in (5b).

The coreference requirement stated in the RS field of the lexical entry of a unique control verb has been understood so far as the sharing of the INDEX value, that is, the identity of the two INDEX values. However, in view of partial control interpretation of unique control verbs, we need to relax the coreference requirement as follows.

(6) coreference requirements between the controller and the controllee RHO
 i. The referential index of the INDEX feature (1.3 (6)) is a set.
 ii. The referential index (as a set) of the controller's INDEX value must be included in the referential index (as a set) of the controllee's INDEX value.

Note that we take an individual referential index i as the single-membered set $\{i\}$. The default interpretation of unique control is the identity of the two sets in (6ii), such as $\{i\} = \{j\}$, a special case of set inclusion.

The referential index inclusion requirement in (6ii) between the controller and the controllee RHO is strikingly similar to the Greenlandic plural reflexives, whose antecedent can be a subset of the set referred to by the reflexive expression (Jerry Sadock (p.c.)).

(7) Hansip   illortik   ilisarinngilaa. (Sadock 2003: 41)
    Hansi-p   illu = (r)tik   ilisarinngit-laa
    Hansi-ERG/s house = ABS/3Rp/s not.recognize-IND/3 s/3 s
    "Hans$_j$ did not recognize their$_w$ (Hans's and somebody else's) house.'

Here, the antecedent *Hans* (with its referential index j) is a subset of the set referred to by the plural reflexive expression (with its referential index W), namely, $\{j\} \subseteq W$.

Jackendoff and Culicover (2003: 550) and Culicover and Jackendoff (2005: 463) proposed a new type of coercion GROUP INCLUDING α, where α is the controller, to explain partial control. In our view, however, what is needed to account for partial control is not a new type of coercion but a relaxed version of coreference requirement, such as (6).

Landau (2000: 6, 55, 91) classified unique control verbs into seven semantic classes and observed that partial control is possible with the verbs of four semantic classes: factive, propositional, desiderative, and interrogative. In the table below, PC and EC stand for partial control and exhaustive control, respectively.

(8) Landou's (2000) classification of control verbs

	semantic type	verbs
EC	implicative	manage, dare, make sure, bother, remember, get, avoid, forget, fail, force, compel
	aspectual	begin, start, continue, stop, finish
	modal	need, able, have, may, should, must
PC	factive	hate, regret, like, dislike, loath; glad, sad, shocked, sorry
	propositional	claim, assert, affirm, declare, deny
	desiderative	want, prefer, hope, arrange, refuse, agree, plan, decide, intend, demand, promise; afraid, eager, ready
	interrogative	wonder, ask, find out, inquire, guess, understand, know; unclear

Of the exhaustive control (EC) verbs, aspectual and modal verbs are our Fp's and are dealt with as subject raising predicates. That leaves implicative verbs as the only EC verbs. As noted above, these verbs do not and cannot allow partial control (PC) interpretation, because they would produce anomalous entailments. Therefore, in our terms, every unique control verb allows partial control unless it produces an anomalous entailment.

Chapter 5
Quantification

> In this chapter, we mainly focus on F/A structures and discuss such issues as the internal structure of a proposition, conditions on quantifiers and bound variables, quantifier scope ambiguities, and quantifier float.

5.1 Internal Structure of Proposition

We would like to justify the F/A structure of a proposition (PROP) with one or more quantifier phrases (QPs) in which the QPs are outside the matrix proposition. The F/A structures in 1.3 (17b) and (20), 2.3 (10), and 2.4 (12) and (15) are such examples. Before we present various pieces of evidence, a brief review of QPs, which were discussed in 1.3, might be in order. The F/A module is the place where quantifiers and their scopes are represented. The well-formedness conditions on QPs were given in 1.3 (15) and repeated here as (1), where a QP that quantifies a variable x is denoted by QP_x with the subscript x.

(1) the well-formedness conditions on QPs
   a. [$_{PROP}$ QP_x, PROP], where the matrix PROP must contain x.
   b. [$_{QPx}$ Q, PROP], where the domain expression PROP must contain x.

c. All the instances of the variable x must be either dominated or c-commanded by a single QP_x.

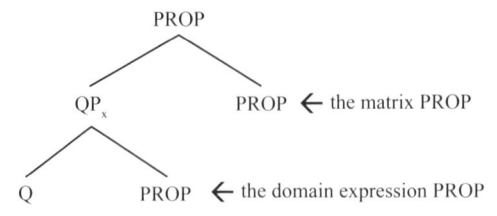

```
         PROP
        /    \
      QP_x   PROP  ← the matrix PROP
     /   \
    Q    PROP  ← the domain expression PROP
```

Note that (1) entails that the set {x, y, ...} of all the distinct variables contained in the topmost PROP and the set {QP_x, QP_y, ...} of all the distinct QPs contained in that PROP correspond one to one. That is, the correspondence from a variable x to the quantifier phrase QP_x that quantifies x defines a bijective mapping (namely, one-to-one and onto) from the former set to the latter set.

(2a) (repeated from 1.3 (17a)) is an example that has a quantified NP (QNP) *every baby* as its subject. The syntax of (2a) is (2c) and its F/A structure that satisfies the conditions (1) is (2b). The lexical entry for *every* is given in (3) (repeated from 1.3 (18)).

(2) a. Every baby sleeps.

b.
```
                    PROP
                  /      \
                QP_x      PROP
               /   \      /    \
              Q   PROP   Fp    PROP
            EVERY  / \  PRES   /   \
                ARG  Fa      ARG   Fa
                 x            x   SLEEP
                ARG  Faa
                BABY  =
```

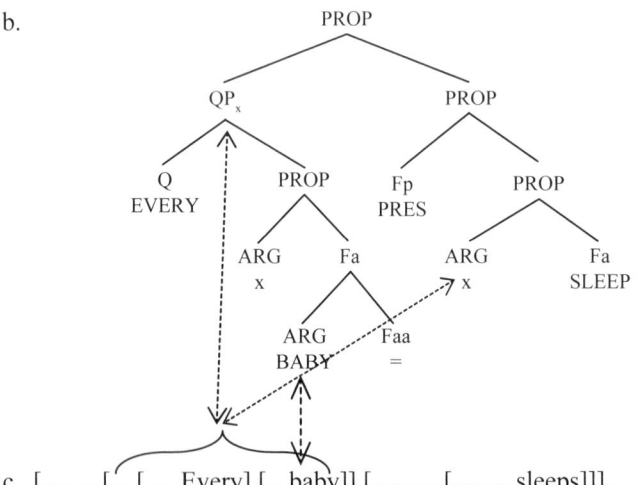

c. [$_{S[PRES]}$ [$_{NP}$ [$_{DET}$ Every] [$_{N'}$ baby]] [$_{VP[PRES]}$ [$_{V[PRES]}$ sleeps]]].

(3) lexical entry for *every*
 syntax: DET in [$_{NP}$ __, N'[3]]
 F/A: [$_Q$ EVERY]
 RS: nil

In (2b, c) above, the QNP *every baby* in syntax corresponds to the quantifier phrase QP$_x$ and one of the variables [$_{ARG}$ x] in the matrix PROP. (In (2b), there happens to be only one variable in the matrix PROP.) This is because a QP in F/A is required to be outside the matrix PROP by (1a), whereas a QNP in syntax is required to occupy an ordinary syntactic argument position, since it is an NP. Also, the N' of the QNP corresponds to the second ARG of the type-identity Faa functor = in the domain expression PROP. Recall that "*a* = *b*" means that '*a* is equal to *b* in type' or '*a* is an instance of type *b*' (cf. 1.3 (8) and (22)). See 1.3 (20) for an example of a PROP with two QPs. So much for a quick review from 1.3, and let us go back to the main point of this section.

The propositional structure in which QPs are outside the matrix proposition is justified by anaphora interpretation of the demonstrative *that*. In (4a), the demonstrative *that* refers to the propositional function 'x admires most philosophers.' Therefore, the second part of (4a) means 'Even Hockett admires most philosophers.' If we assume that the antecedent of *that* must be a semantic constituent in F/A, then (4a) must have the F/A structure in which the QP *most linguists* must be outside the propositional function, as in (4b).

(4) a. Most linguists admire most philosophers; that's true even of Hockett. (McCawley 1993: 200)
 b. [$_{QPx}$ MOST x = LINGUIST] [$_{PROP}$ x ADMIRE MOST PHILOSOPHERS]

In (5a), the demonstrative *that* refers to the propositional function 'Most linguists admire y.' Therefore, the second part means 'Most linguists admire even Sartre.' This shows that the QP *most philosophers* is outside the propositional function, as in (5b).

(5) a. Most linguists admire most philosophers; that's true even of Sartre. (McCawley 1993: 200)
 b. [$_{QPy}$ MOST y = PHILOSOPHER] [$_{PROP}$ MOST LINGUISTS ADMIRE y]

In (6), the version with *Halliday* is normal because both demonstratives refer to the same propositional function 'x admires most philosophers.' However, the version with *Sartre* is bad because the first demonstrative purports to refer to 'x admires most philosophers' whereas the second purports to refer to 'most linguists admire y.' This shows that the two propositional functions 'x admires most philosophers' and 'most linguists admire y' are distinct and cannot be separately referred to by the same demonstrative.

(6) Most linguists admire most philosophers; that's true even of Hockett, though that isn't true of {Halliday | *Sartre}. (McCawley 1993: 201)

In (7a, b), the demonstrative refers to the propositional function 'x admires y.' This shows that the two quantifier phrases are outside the propositional function ((7c) or (7d)).

(7) a. Most linguists admire most philosophers; that's true even of Sapir and Wittgenstein.
  b. Most linguists admire most philosophers; but that's not true of this pair of linguist and philosopher.
  c. [$_{QPx}$ MOST x = LINGUIST] [[$_{QPy}$ MOST y = PHILOSOPHER] [$_{PROP}$ x ADMIRE y]]
  d. [$_{QPy}$ MOST y = PHILOSOPHER] [[$_{QPx}$ MOST x = LINGUIST] [$_{PROP}$ x ADMIRE y]]

All sorts of propositional operators (Fp) are by definition outside the matrix proposition. The operator Fp is defined as [$_{PROP}$ Fp, PROP] (1.3 (2d)). For example, the tenses (PRES and PAST) have been treated as Fp. In (8a), the demonstrative refers to the proposition without a tense 'we eat out every weekend,' whose F/A is [$_{QPx}$ EVERY x = WEEKEND] [$_{PROP}$ WE EAT OUT ON x]. So the approximate F/A structure of the first clause in (8a) is (8b).

(8) a. We ate out every weekend but that's not true anymore.
  b. [$_{Fp}$ PAST] [[$_{QPx}$ EVERY x = WEEKEND] [$_{PROP}$ WE EAT OUT ON x]]

The F/A structures of modal auxiliaries are composite Fp, namely, Fp∘Fp, where the first Fp is a tense (2.1 (9), 2.2 (6), 4.1.1 (6)). For example, the epistemic *may*, which expresses the speaker's surmise at the moment of utterance, has an

F/A structure of $[_{Fp}$ PRES]∘$[_{Fp}$ MAY], which is to be interpreted as $[_{Fp}$ PRES]∘ $[_{Fp}$ MAY](PROP) = $[_{Fp}$ PRES]($[_{Fp}$ MAY](PROP)). In (9a), the noun *examples* refers to 'examples of energy being changed from one form to another,' where the complement of the noun is 'energy being changed from one form to another.' This corresponds to the innermost proposition in (9b). Also, *such process* refers to 'the process of kinetic energy being converted to potential energy,' where the complement of the noun is 'kinetic energy being converted to potential energy.' This corresponds to the innermost PROP in (9c).

(9) a. Energy may be changed from one form to another in innumerable ways. How many examples can you think of? Besides seeing that potential energy may be converted to kinetic energy, it is especially important to recognize that kinetic energy may be converted to potential energy, as in charging a battery or pumping water into a high-elevation reservoir. We shall see shortly that photosynthesis is another such process.
(from a university textbook)
   b. the F/A of *Energy may be changed from one form to another*
      $[_{Fp}$ PRES]($[_{Fp}$ MAY]($[_{PROP}$ ENERGY CHANGED FROM ONE FORM TO ANOTHER]))
   c. the F/A of *kinetic energy may be converted to potential energy*
      $[_{Fp}$ PRES]($[_{Fp}$ MAY]($[_{PROP}$ KINETIC ENERGY CONVERTED TO POTENTIAL ENERGY]))
   d. Mary said that John might be wrong. (cf. Mary said: "John may be wrong.")
   e. John might be wrong, but I doubt it. (cf. McCawley 1998: 57)

In (9d), *might* corresponds to $[_{Fp}$ PAST]∘$[_{Fp}$ MAY], whereas in (9e), *might* corresponds to $[_{Fp}$ PRES]∘$[_{Fp}$ MIGHT], which expresses the speaker's surmising a proposition at the moment of utterance. In (9e), whose first conjunct corresponds to $[_{Fp}$ PRES]∘$[_{Fp}$ MIGHT] (PRES(JOHN WRONG)), the pronoun *it* refers to the inner proposition PRES(JOHN WRONG). Note that the *be* verb in (9d, e) is an empty verb (2.1 (13e)) and that the PRES in PRES(JOHN WRONG) is a coerced tense "nonfinite PRES" (4.2.2 (5)).

The negation operator NOT is another example of Fp. In (10a), the relative pronoun *as* refers to the internal proposition CATS = ANIMALS in (10b). (10c) is a similar example.

(10) a. Suppose one day it was discovered that cats were not animals, as everyone has always thought, but highly sophisticated self-replicating robots. (Cruse 2004: 53)
b. [$_{Fp}$ IRREALIS] [[$_{Fp}$ NOT] [$_{PROP}$ CATS = ANIMALS]]
c. There are not, as Wittgenstein and many others have claimed, an infinite or indefinite number of language games or uses of language. (Searle 1979: 29)

The relative pronoun *as* in (10c) refers to the proposition 'There are an infinite or indefinite number of language games or uses of language.'

5.2 NP with Multiple Quantifiers

There are two quantifiers (*every* and *the*) in the object NP of (1) below. (Here, the definite article *the* is treated as a kind of existential quantifier. See 1.3 (24).) (1) seems to correspond to two F/A structures (2) and (3), both of which satisfy the well-formedness conditions in 5.1 (1).

(1) Mary knows every admirer of the professor. (cf. McCawley 1993: 34)

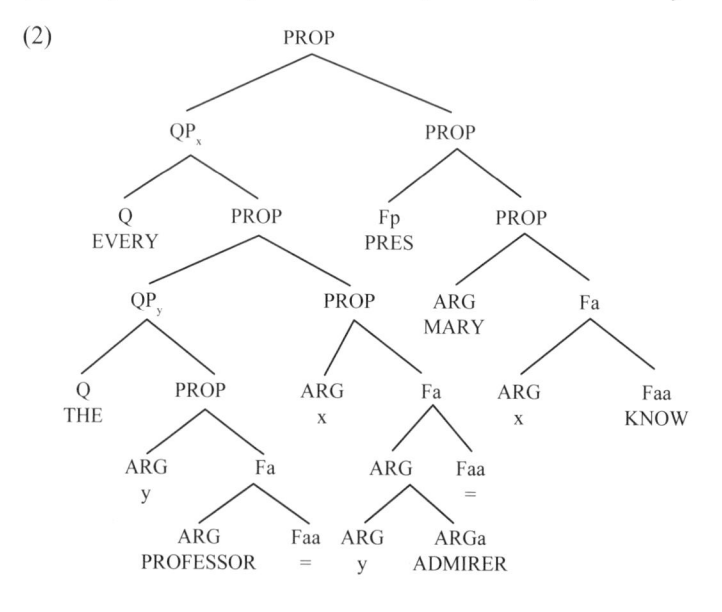

(2)
```
                    PROP
                   /    \
                QP_x     PROP
               /    \    /    \
              Q    PROP  Fp    PROP
           EVERY         PRES  /    \
                  QP_y        PROP   ARG        Fa
                 /    \      /    \  MARY      /  \
                Q    PROP  ARG   Fa  ARG      Faa
              THE          x    / \   x      KNOW
                /    \        ARG  Faa
              ARG    Fa       y    =
               y    /  \          /  \
                  ARG   Faa     ARG   ARGa
               PROFESSOR =       y   ADMIRER
```

5.2 NP WITH MULTIPLE QUANTIFIERS 227

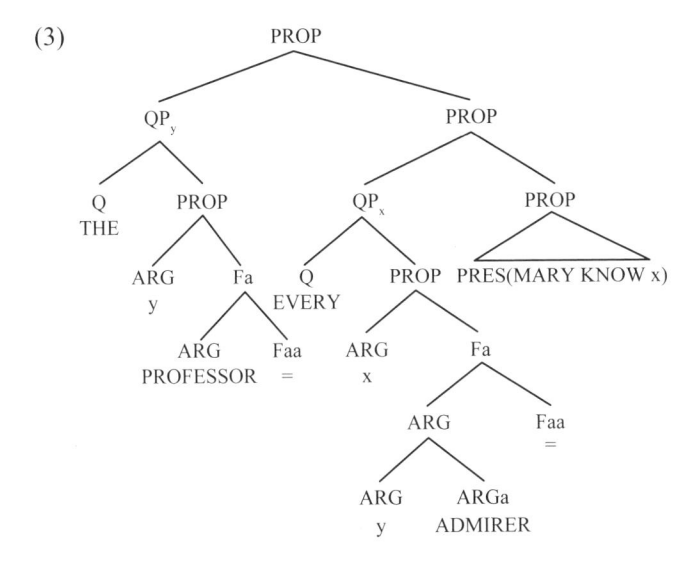

(3)
```
                    PROP
                   /    \
                QP_y    PROP
               /   \    /   \
              Q   PROP QP_x  PROP
             THE  / \  / \   /  \
             ARG Fa  Q  PROP PRES(MARY KNOW x)
              y     EVERY /  \
                  ARG   Faa  ARG   Fa
                PROFESSOR =   x   /  \
                                ARG   Faa
                                / \    =
                              ARG  ARGa
                               y  ADMIRER
```

In (2) and (3), the noun *admirer* is treated as ARGa, which means that this takes an ARG and returns an ARG: [$_{ARG}$ ARGa, ARG]. See 1.3 (10c) and (11c). So, the lexical entry for *admirer* includes syntax: N in [$_{N'}$ __, PP[*of*]] and F/A: ARGa[IND[3SG]]. In (2), the QNP *every admirer of the professor* corresponds to a single QP (QP$_x$), which dominates another QP (QP$_y$). Because QP$_x$ does not asymmetrically c-command QP$_y$ or vice versa in (2), there is no scope relationship between the two. (See 1.3 (20) for an example in which a QP asymmetrically c-commands another QP, thereby the former having the latter within its scope. See 1.3 (25) for the definition of c-command in F/A.) In (3), the QNP corresponds to two separate QPs (QP$_x$ and QP$_y$) in F/A, and QP$_y$ asymmetrically c-commands QP$_x$, which indicates that the former has wide scope and has the latter within its scope. Although this F/A structure may be easier to understand than the F/A in (2), the problem is that because the two QPs are separate, we would expect that there could be an Fp functor or an Mp modifier appearing between them, creating such scope relations as QP$_y$ > {Fp | Mp} > QP$_x$, where > indicates asymmetric c-command. But this possibility does not arise. Therefore, we adopt (2) as the F/A structure of (1) (cf. McCawley 1993: 34). We will need such F/A structures as (3) later when we deal with floated quantifiers in 5.6. F/A structures similar to (3) are also needed to deal with such inverse linking examples as *Somebody from every city despises it* (May 1985: 68), in which the pronoun *it* is a bound variable pronoun, namely, a pronoun interpreted as a bound variable, in this case, bound by the QNP *every city*. (4) is the F/A structure of this sentence.

(4) the F/A structure of *Somebody from every city_y despises it_y* (May 1985: 68)

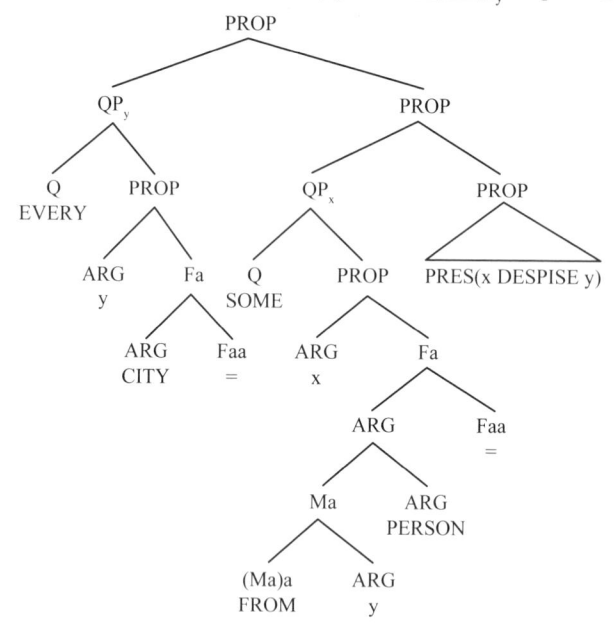

```
                            PROP
                    ╱               ╲
                QP_y                  PROP
              ╱     ╲            ╱         ╲
            Q       PROP       QP_x         PROP
          EVERY    ╱    ╲     ╱    ╲       ╱     ╲
                ARG    Fa    Q    PROP   PRES(x DESPISE y)
                 y          SOME  ╱   ╲
                ╱  ╲             ╱     ╲
              ARG  Faa         ARG     Fa
              CITY  =           x     ╱   ╲
                                    ARG    Faa
                                   ╱   ╲    =
                                 Ma    ARG
                                ╱  ╲  PERSON
                             (Ma)a  ARG
                             FROM    y
```

This F/A structure means 'For every city, there is somebody from it who despises it,' which is a rough paraphrase of *Somebody from every city despises it*. Note that in (4), the QP_y c-commands the variable [_ARG y] in the matrix PROP PRES([_PROP x DESPISE y]). Here is a more complex inverse linking example. In *Every daughter of every professor in some small college town wishes she could leave it* (Higginbotham 1980: 690), *she* and *it* are bound variable pronouns, the former being bound by the QNP *every daughter* and the latter by the QNP *some small college town*. Note that in the F/A of this example (5), QP_x and QP_z c-command the variables x and z in the matrix PROP, respectively. The F/A means 'There is some small college town such that for every professor in the town, every daughter of him wishes she could leave it.'

(5) the F/A of <u>Every daughter</u>$_z$ *of every professor in* <u>some small college town</u>$_x$ *wishes* <u>she</u>$_z$ *could leave* <u>it</u>$_x$ (Higginbotham 1980: 690)

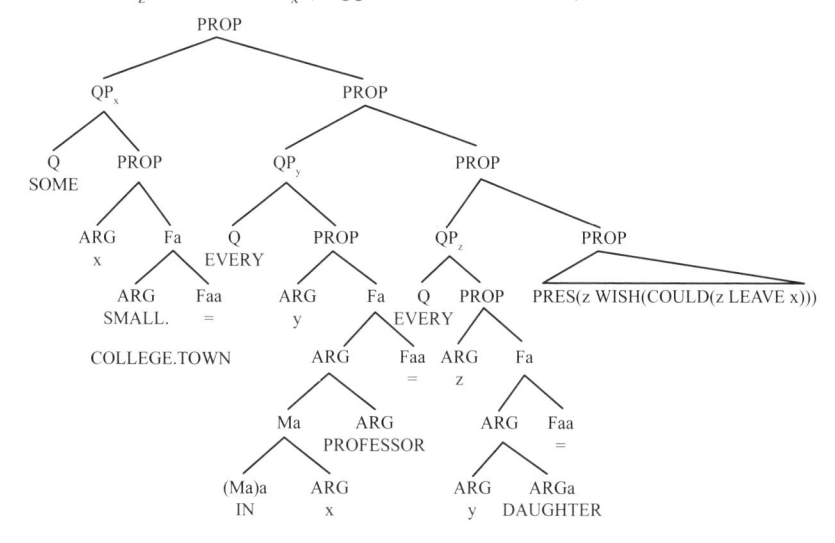

```
                              PROP
                            /      \
                         QP_x        PROP
                        /   \       /    \
                       Q    PROP   QP_y   PROP
                      SOME  /  \   / \    /   \
                          ARG  Fa  Q  PROP QP_z  PROP
                           x   /\ EVERY /\  /\   /     \
                             ARG Faa  ARG Fa Q PROP  PRES(z WISH(COULD(z LEAVE x)))
                           SMALL. =    y    EVERY
                         COLLEGE.TOWN     ARG    Faa ARG  Fa
                                          /\     =   /\
                                         Ma ARG    ARG Faa
                                         PROFESSOR  /\  =
                                        /\       ARG ARGa
                                     (Ma)a ARG    y  DAUGHTER
                                      IN    x
```

5.3 Quantifiers and Bound Variables

(1a) below has the interpretation [[$_{QPx}$ EVERY x = AMERICAN] [x ADMIRE x]], whereas (1b) is interpreted as [[$_{QPx}$ EVERY x = AMERICAN] [[$_{QPy}$ EVERY y = AMERICAN] [x ADMIRE y]]]. The latter entails the former. The syntax of (1a) is given in (1c), which also shows how subject-verb agreement is achieved. The F/A of (1a) is given in (1d).

(1) a. Every American admires himself. (McCawley 1993: 187)
 b. Every American admires every American. (McCawley 1993: 187)
 c. [$_{S[PRES]}$ [$_{NP[NOM, 3SG]}$ Every American] [$_{VP[PRES, 3SG]}$ [$_{V[PRES, 3SG]}$ admires] [$_{NP[ACC, 3SGM]}$ himself]]].

d. the F/A structure (under the assumption that QP > TENSE)

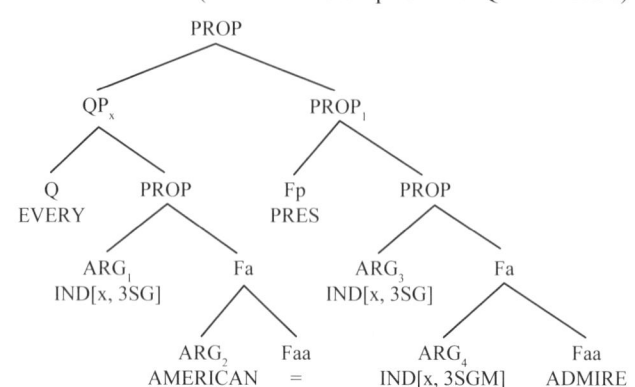

```
                            PROP
                   _____/    _____
                  QPₓ                    PROP₁
              ___/   \___           ___/     \___
             Q         PROP        Fp           PROP
           EVERY      /    \      PRES         /    \
                   ARG₁    Fa                ARG₃    Fa
                 IND[x,3SG]              IND[x,3SG]
                   /    \                    /     \
                ARG₂    Faa              ARG₄      Faa
              AMERICAN   =              IND[x,3SGM]  ADMIRE
              IND[3SG]
```

As we have assumed so far, the AGREEMENT (AGR) feature appears in both syntactic and F/A structures, due to Feature Osmosis (1.3, Sadock 2012: 154). First, let us see how the subject-verb agreement is achieved in the syntax of (1a), namely, (1c). The lexical entry for *every* in 5.1 (3) specifies its syntax as DET in [$_{NP}$ __, N'[3]]. The number (NUM) value comes from the N' *American*. Therefore, the N' carries AGR value 3SG. Because the AGR feature is a head feature (1.2 (4)), this AGR value 3SG on the N' *American* is shared with its mother NP by the Head Feature Convention (HFC) (1.2 (3)). This is why the subject NP node in (1c) above carries 3SG. The sister VP[PRES] gets the same AGR value by the agreement PS rule in 1.2 (11a), namely, [$_{S[FIN]}$ NP[AGR], VP[FIN, AGR]], and this AGR value is realized on the head of the VP, again by the HFC.

Let us now observe how the agreement between the subject *Every American* and the object *himself* in (1a) is achieved in the F/A structure (1d) above. Recall (i) that the INDEX (IND) feature consists of a referential index (ref) and the AGR feature, which in turn consists of three features: PERSON (PER), NUMBER (NUM), and GENDER (GEN) (1.3 (6)), (ii) that the variable x is technically IND[x, AGR(x)], where the IND's referential index is x, and (iii) that if two ARGs have the same referential index, they must have the same AGR value (1.3 (6)), because the AGR value is a function of the referential index, as in IND[j, AGR(j)]. The QP$_x$ and the matrix subject ARG₃ in (1d) share the same variable x, partly because this is required by 5.1 (1a) and partly because the QP$_x$ and the subject variable x correspond to the syntactic subject *every American*, as in 5.1 (2b).

The referential index on the object ARG_4 that corresponds to *himself* in syntax must also be x, because *himself* is a reflexive and needs a local binder, which is ARG_3. The AMERICAN at ARG_2 in (1d) has its AGR value 3SG, which comes from the lexical entry for *American*. ARG_1 gets this AGR value 3SG through the type-identity Faa functor = (1.3 (8b) and (21)) from ARG_2 AMERICAN. Therefore, the variable IND[x, 3SG] on ARG_1 must also be on ARG_3. The object ARG_4 of the matrix PROP has its AGR value 3SGM (IND[x, 3SGM]), because it corresponds to *himself* in syntax and the lexical entry for *himself* has 3SGM as its AGR value. This AGR value 3SGM on ARG_4 is consistent with the AGR value 3SG on ARG_1 and ARG_3.

This explanation predicts that *Every American admires themselves* is ungrammatical, because the IND value coming from *every American* is IND[x, 3SG] and the IND value coming from *themselves* is IND[x, 3PL] and the two AGR values are not consistent. However, this sentence is acceptable to most speakers. The reflexive *themselves* here, which is the reflexive form of the singular *they* (Huddleston and Pullum 2002: 493–494), functions as third person singular (3SG). We assume that the pronoun *they* (and its other inflected forms *them* and *themselves*) have two lexical entries, one for third person plural (as default) and the other for third person singular, just as *you* has two lexical entries for singular and plural. Both kinds of *they* lack their gender (GEN) value. For example, in *Every boy admires themselves*, the AGR value of *every boy* is 3SGM and that of *themselves* is 3SG and both values are consistent. Similarly, when a QNP is in the feminine singular, its bound variable pronouns can be either feminine singular, as in <u>Every woman</u> believes from the bottom of <u>her</u> heart that <u>she</u> will be rich and famous, or genderless singular *they*, as in <u>Every woman</u> believes from the bottom of <u>their</u> heart that <u>they</u> will be rich and famous.

When a quantified NP (QNP) is in the plural, its bound variable pronouns must also be in the plural (i.e., plural *they*), as in (2), because if the IND value coming from the bound variables were IND[x, 3SG], then it would not be consistent with the IND[x, 3PL] coming from the plural QNP.

(2) <u>All chemical reactions</u>, whether <u>they</u> occur in a test tube, in the environment, or inside living things, and whether <u>they</u> occur very slowly or very fast, involve rearrangements of atoms to form different kinds of matter. (from a university textbook)

Note that the QNP *all chemical reactions* in (2), although it is plural in number, is interpreted distributively (McCawley 1993: 37) in the same manner as

Every chemical reaction, whether *it* occurs in a test tube or inside living things, involves rearrangements of atoms.

When the controller of the control construction (discussed in 4.4 and 4.5) is a QNP, as in (3a) or it is a bound variable pronoun, as in *Every boy$_x$ knows that he$_x$ likes to stay up late*, the controllee RHO, the semantic subject of the VP[*to*], is interpreted as a bound variable (McCawley 1993: 190). Example (3a) below has the subject control verb *try* as the matrix verb. Its syntax, F/A, and RS are given in (3b, c).

(3) a. Every baby tries to walk.
 b. [$_{S[PRES]}$ [$_{NP}$ Every baby] [$_{VP[PRES]}$ [$_{V[PRES]}$ tries] [$_{VP[to]}$ [$_{V[to]}$ to] [$_{VP[BSE]}$ walk]]]]
 c. the F/A and RS of *Every baby tries to walk*

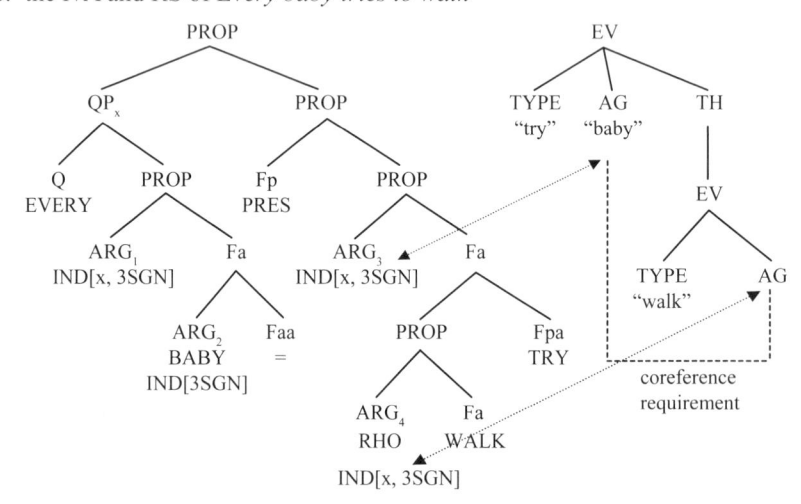

```
                    PROP                                    EV
                   /    \                                  /  \
                QP_x    PROP                        TYPE  AG   TH
               /  \    /    \                       "try" "baby"
              Q  PROP  Fp   PROP
            EVERY /  \ PRES  /  \                           EV
                ARG_1  Fa  ARG_3  Fa                       /  \
              IND[x,3SGN]    IND[x,3SGN]               TYPE   AG
                    /  \                               "walk"
                 ARG_2  Faa       PROP   Fpa
                 BABY   =        /   \   TRY
               IND[3SGN]       ARG_4  Fa                coreference
                              RHO   WALK                requirement
                            IND[x, 3SGN]
```

The coreference requirement stated in the RS field of the lexical entry of the verb *try* (4.7 (6)) forces the sharing of the same IND value in the F/A structure (3c) between the controller (the matrix subject ARG$_3$) and the controllee (the embedded subject ARG$_4$) (1.3 (6)). In (4a) below, which is a combination of (1a) and (3a), both the RHO and the reflexive pronoun receive bound variable interpretation, as is shown in (4b). Because of the coreference requirement of the lexical entry of the verb *try*, the IND value of the matrix subject ARG, IND[x, 3SG], is shared with the embedded subject RHO. The reflexive *himself* needs its local binder, which is RHO, and shares the same variable x. The IND value of the reflexive is IND[x, 3SGM], where masculine (M) comes from the lexical entry of *himself*. The IND[x, 3SGM] on *himself* and the IND[x, 3SG] coming from the LINGUIST are consistent, exactly as in (1).

(4) a. Every linguist tries to convince himself.
    b.

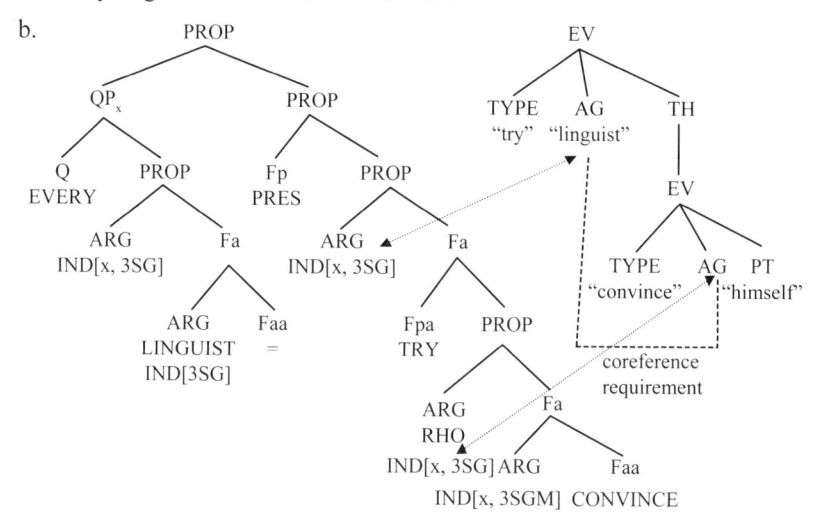

```
                    PROP                                      EV
                   /    \                                    /  \
                QP_x     PROP                          TYPE   AG    TH
               /   \    /    \                         "try" "linguist"
              Q    PROP  Fp   PROP                            |
           EVERY        PRES                                  EV
                 /  \        /   \                           /  \
              ARG   Fa    ARG    Fa                       TYPE  AG  PT
           IND[x,3SG]   IND[x,3SG]                      "convince" "himself"
                      /   \       /    \
                   ARG    Faa   Fpa   PROP              coreference
                LINGUIST   =    TRY                     requirement
                IND[3SG]              /   \
                                    ARG    Fa
                                    RHO
                              IND[x,3SG] ARG     Faa
                                    IND[x, 3SGM] CONVINCE
```

(5d) shows that the QNP *each of my teachers* cannot be coordinated with a nonquantified NP. The F/A structure of (5d) is given in (5e), in which [$_{ARG}$ JOHN] and [$_{ARG}$ x] are coordinated. If we assume that a constant ([$_{ARG}$ JOHN]) and a variable ([$_{ARG}$ x]) count as distinct categories in F/A, coordination of distinct F/A categories is the source of oddity in (5d).

(5) (McCawley 1993: 198)
    a. John had a fight with Bill.
    b. John had a fight with each of my teachers.
    c. John and Bill had a fight.
    d. ??John and each of my teachers had a fight.
    e. [$_{QPx}$ EACH x ∈ {MY TEACHERS}] ([$_{Fp}$ PAST] [$_{PROP}$ [$_{ARG}$ [$_{ARG}$ JOHN] AND [$_{ARG}$ x]] [$_{Fa}$ HAVE.A.FIGHT]])
    f. [Each of John's teachers] and [each of my teachers] had a fight.
    g. Each of my teachers and his TA had a fight.

Our assumption is justified by (5f), which sounds better than (5d). Note that there is a coordination of variables ($[_{ARG}$ x] and $[_{ARG}$ y]) in (5f). Furthermore, (5g) also sounds better than (5d). (5g) contains a coordination of a variable and its function ($[_{ARG}$ x] and $[_{ARG}$ x's TA]).

Jerry Sadock (p.c.) observed that *John and all of my uncles were born in Indiana* sounds perfect, although the constant NP *John* and the QNP *all of my uncles* are coordinated. It seems that a QNP with *all*, such as *all of my uncles* is interpreted as a definite NP, in that the QNP refers to the definite set of *all of my uncles*. With this collective interpretation (McCawley 1993: 37), the coordinated NP *John and all of my uncles* is simply a coordination of two definite NPs. In fact, we observe the following contrast. We cannot say [*Each of my uncles*]$_x$ *sang.* *He_x danced too.* (The second sentence is out, because the bound variable pronoun *he* is not c-commanded by its binder QNP.) However, we can say [*All of my uncles*]$_x$ *sang. They$_x$ danced too.* This shows that the QNP *all of my uncles* is interpreted in exactly the same way as a definite NP, such as *the group* in *The group sang. They danced too.*

5.4 Set Arguments and Set Variables

McCawley (1993: 214) pointed out that arguments need to represent not only individuals but also sets of individuals in order to deal with the following cases. In (1a), the predicate *an amiable couple* requires a two-membered set of people as its subject ARG. In (1b), the verb *conspire* is an Fpa functor in F/A that requires a set of people as its subject ARG. In (1c), the subject ARG of the Faa functor CARRY is interpreted as a set of boys. In these examples, the subject ARG is interpreted collectively, not distributively.

(1) a. The king and the queen are an amiable couple.
    b. Tom, Dick, and Harry conspired to assassinate The Postmaster General.
    c. The boys carried the piano up the stairs.

Here is another case where ARGs need to represent sets. (2a) below can be paraphrased as (2b), which shows that we need to treat the definite article as a kind of existential quantifier ($[_Q$ THE]) (1.3 (23)) that quantifies a set variable. To represent the F/A structure of (2a), we introduce set ARGs and set variables (as opposed to individual variables) and the Faa functor of set membership relation $\in$ (1.3 (22)). The F/A structure of (2a) is given in (2c) (cf. McCawley 1993: 214ff). For ease of exposition, we assume, following McCawley (1993: 217), that

5.4 SET ARGUMENTS AND SET VARIABLES   235

each ARG has the SET feature (±S), and add the subscript −S to an individual argument and +S to a set argument: ARG_{-S} and ARG_{+S}.

(2) a. Most of the boys danced.
   b. There is a specific set of boys such that most members of it danced.
   c. the F/A structure of *Most of the boys danced* (cf. 5.2 (1))

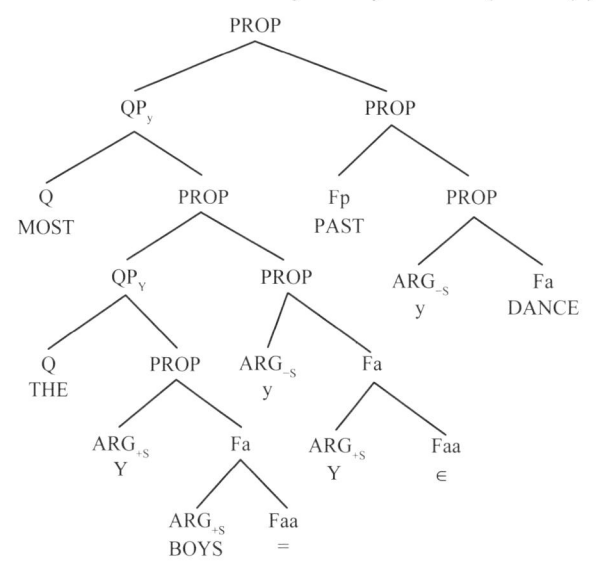

```
                            PROP
                    ┌────────┴────────┐
                  QP_y                PROP
              ┌────┴────┐         ┌────┴────┐
              Q        PROP       Fp       PROP
            MOST    ┌───┴───┐    PAST    ┌───┴───┐
                  QP_Y     PROP        ARG_{-S}   Fa
              ┌────┴────┐  ┌──┴──┐        y     DANCE
              Q        PROP ARG_{-S} Fa
            THE   ┌────┴────┐  y  ┌──┴──┐
                ARG_{+S}   Fa   ARG_{+S}  Faa
                  Y     ┌──┴──┐    Y      ∈
                      ARG_{+S} Faa
                      BOYS    =
```

Here is another example of set arguments and set variables, the F/A structure of (1c), in which the modifier PP[*up*] is ignored.

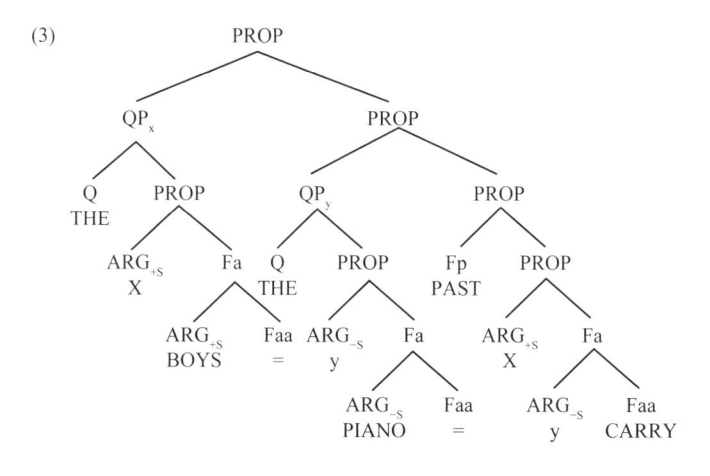

(3)
```
                         PROP
                ┌─────────┴─────────┐
              QP_x                 PROP
          ┌────┴────┐        ┌──────┴──────┐
          Q       PROP     QP_y            PROP
        THE    ┌───┴───┐ ┌───┴───┐     ┌────┴────┐
            ARG_{+S}  Fa Q     PROP    Fp       PROP
              X    ┌──┴──┐ THE ┌──┴──┐ PAST  ┌────┴────┐
                ARG_{+S} Faa ARG_{-S} Fa  ARG_{+S}   Fa
                BOYS   =     y   ┌──┴──┐    X    ┌───┴───┐
                              ARG_{-S} Faa   ARG_{-S}  Faa
                              PIANO   =        y      CARRY
```

In (4a) with its F/A (4b), the relative clause *who took the exam* is an individual modifier, which modifies the ARG_{-S} *students* and returns ARG_{-S}, namely, Ma in [$_{ARG-S}$ ARG_{-S}, Ma], whereas the numeral *three* is a set modifier, which modifies the ARG_{-S} *students who took the exam* and returns ARG_{+S}, namely, Ma in [$_{ARG+S}$ ARG_{-S}, Ma]. (4a) can be paraphrased as 'a three-membered set of students such that each member of the set took the exam.'

(4) a. [$_{N'}$ three [$_{N'}$ [$_{N'}$ students] who took the exam]] (McCawley 1993: 222)
    b. the F/A of (4a)

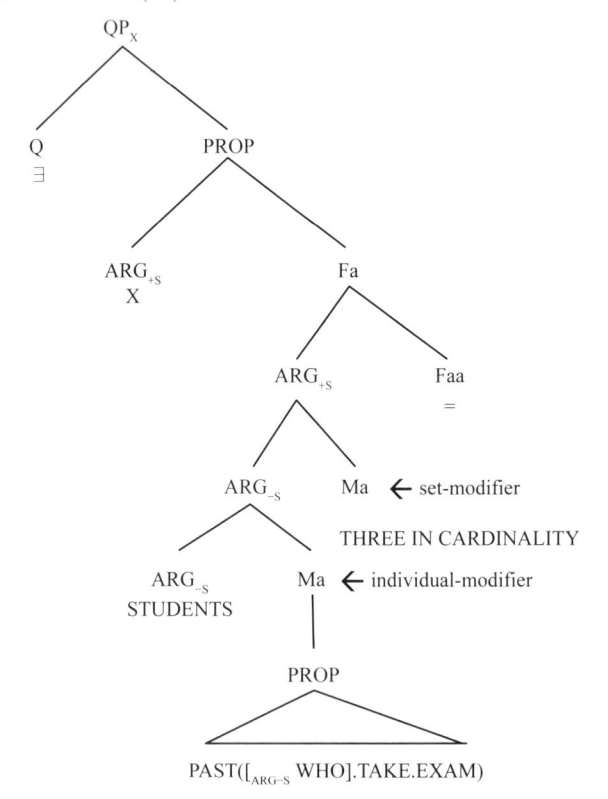

```
                QP_X
               /    \
              Q      PROP
              ∃     /    \
                 ARG_{+S}   Fa
                   X      /    \
                      ARG_{+S}   Faa
                       /    \      =
                   ARG_{-S}   Ma  ← set-modifier
                    /    \        THREE IN CARDINALITY
                ARG_{-S}  Ma  ← individual-modifier
                STUDENTS   |
                          PROP
                         /    \
                  PAST([_{ARG-S} WHO].TAKE.EXAM)
```

In (5a), the relative clause *who met at a conference on bilingual education* is a set modifier modifying *three linguists*.

(5) a. [$_{N'}$ [$_{N'}$ three [$_{N'}$ linguists]] who met at a conference on bilingual education] (McCawley 1993: 223)

b.

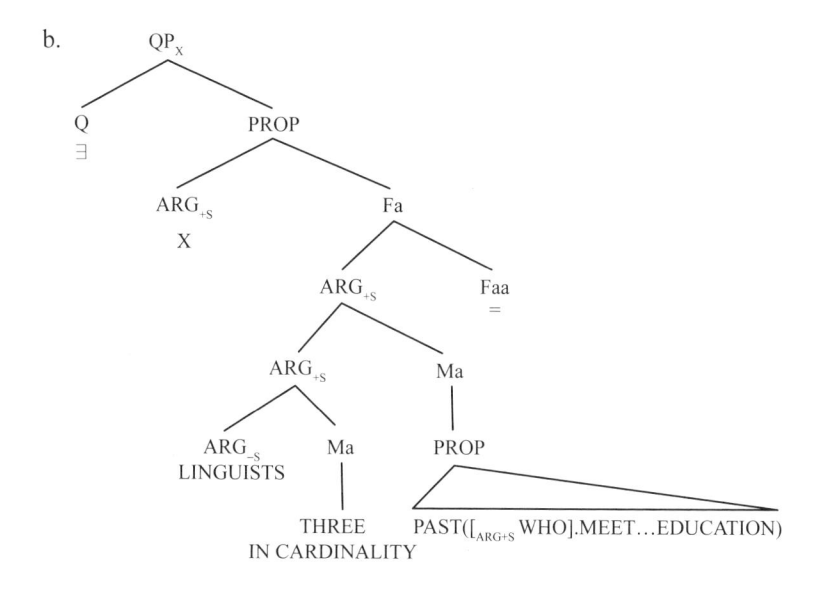

```
         QP_X
        /    \
       Q      PROP
       ∃     /    \
         ARG_{+S}   Fa
          X       /    \
             ARG_{+S}   Faa
            /    \       =
        ARG_{+S}  Ma
        /    \     |
     ARG_{-S}  Ma  PROP
    LINGUISTS  |   /────────────\
               THREE  PAST([_{ARG+S} WHO].MEET...EDUCATION)
             IN CARDINALITY
```

In (4a), the set modifier *three* is "higher" than the individual modifier *who took the exam* both in syntax and in F/A in the sense that an individual modifier is adjoined to the head N' first and then a set modifier is adjoined to the larger N', or in F/A terms, an individual modifier Ma is first adjoined to the head ARG and then a set modifier Ma is adjoined to the larger ARG. McCawley (1993: 222) pointed out that an individual modifier appears closer to the head noun in syntax than a set modifier. This is a natural consequence of the relevant F/A structures if we assume that there is no mismatch between syntax and F/A. So, the expected, default linear order is (6), where RRC stands for restrictive relative clause.

(6) [_{N'} set-modifying A < individual-modifying A < N' < individual-modifying RRC < set-modifying RRC]

Here are examples of the generalization (6).

(7) a. endangered hoofed animals   cf. ??hoofed endangered animals
  b. vanishing flightless birds   cf. ??flightless vanishing birds
  c. the ethnically diverse, hard-working community
     cf. ??the hard-working, ethnically diverse community
  d. the homogeneous religious community
     cf. ??the religious homogeneous community

In (7a), *endangered* is a set modifier and *hoofed* is an individual modifier. (7b) is a similar example, in which *vanishing* is a set modifier and *flightless* is an individual modifier. The first adjective *vanishing* in (7b) means 'becoming extinct.' In the N' with opposite adjective order *flightless vanishing birds*, the second adjective *vanishing* is forced to be interpreted as an individual modifier, because the first adjective *flightless* is an individual modifier. The only available interpretation of *vanishing* in this case seems to be 'physically disappearing.' When the head noun is a collective noun, namely, a count noun that denotes a group of individuals, the same generalization still holds; that is, a set-modifying adjective comes before an individual-modifying adjective. In (7c, d), *ethnically diverse* and *homogeneous* are set modifiers and *hard-working* and *religious* are individual modifiers. (7c) means 'the ethnically diverse community consisting of hard-working members' and (7d) means 'the homogeneous community consisting of religious members.'

Aggregation (McCawley 1993: 220) is an inference rule by which, when a propositional function $f(x)$ is an individual predicate (a predicate (Fa) that requires its subject ARG to represent an individual), $f(M)$ (i.e., $f(x)$ with a set M as the value of x) replaces the universally quantified proposition ($\forall x \in M$) $f(x)$. De-aggregation is the opposite inference rule by which $f(M)$ is expanded into its corresponding universally quantified proposition ($\forall x \in M$) $f(x)$ with distributive reading. These two rules are shown in (8).

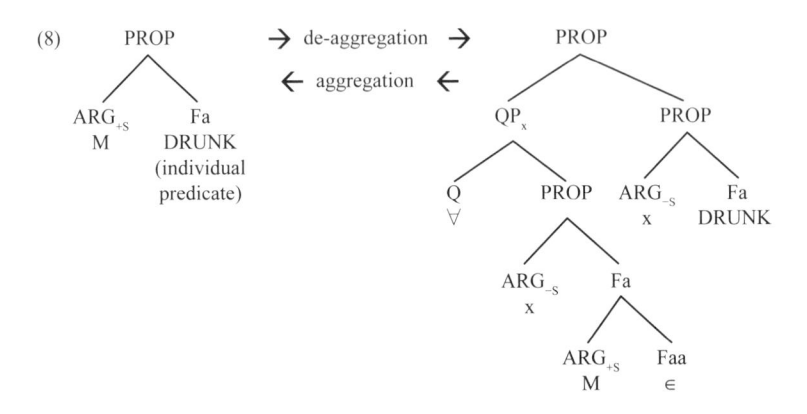

(8)   PROP   → de-aggregation →   PROP
      /   \   ← aggregation ←   /   \
   ARG$_{+S}$ Fa   QP$_x$ PROP
    M   DRUNK   / \   /   \
         (individual   Q   PROP ARG$_{-S}$ Fa
          predicate)   ∀   / \   x   DRUNK
                                             ARG$_{-S}$ Fa
                                              x   / \
                                               ARG$_{+S}$ Faa
                                                 M   ∈

When a set appears as the subject ARG of an individual predicate, the inference rule of de-aggregation applies. For example, in (8) above, because the Fa DRUNK is an individual predicate, DRUNK(M) for some set M is interpreted by de-aggregation as 'for each member x of the set M, DRUNK(x).' Sentences with a collective noun subject, such as *The group were drunk* or *The family are all early risers*, are interpreted in this way. Note that the NUM on the *be* verb is in the plural. Natural languages tend to prefer aggregated expressions (an individual predicate with a set argument subject) to de-aggregated expressions due to the economy of language use, because the former is structurally simpler than the latter.

Following McCawley's (1993: 220) analysis of numerals, we treat them as a combination of an existential quantifier and a set modifier Ma that specifies the cardinality of the set in question.

(9) a. Three linguists were drunk.
    b. F/A of *Three linguists were drunk* (in an aggregated expression)

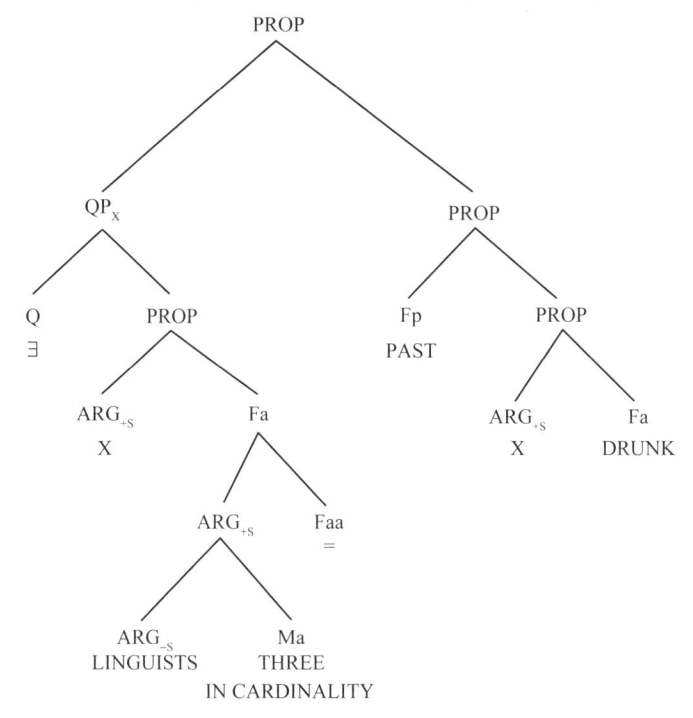

```
                          PROP
                         /    \
                       /        \
                    QP_x          PROP
                   /   \          /   \
                  Q    PROP      Fp    PROP
                  ∃   /    \    PAST   /   \
                   ARG_+S   Fa       ARG_+S  Fa
                    X      /  \        X    DRUNK
                        ARG_+S  Faa
                        /   \    =
                     ARG_-S   Ma
                   LINGUISTS THREE
                          IN CARDINALITY
```

Before we give the lexical entry for numerals, we need to consider where the existential quantifier in (9b) comes from. The reason for positing it in (9b) is that the NP *three linguists* is interpreted as existentially quantified, and in fact, it allows *there*-insertion (2.4 (8)): *There were three linguists drunk/at the party*. However, the singular and plural forms of a common noun and a mass noun allow *there*-insertion, too: *There was a linguist drunk*, *There were linguists drunk*, and *There was silence in the room*. In 2.4 (10), repeated here as (10) below, we proposed the modular correspondences of an existentially quantified NP (EQNP), an NP that is interpreted as existentially quantified, and assumed that the existential quantifier (∃) in (10) comes from existential quantifier uses of the indefinite article (1.3 (20)) and the definite article (1.3 (23)), or from the uses as an EQNP of a singular mass noun (*There is <u>time</u> left*) and a plural count noun (*There were <u>linguists</u> at the party*). Note that in the last two cases, there is no overt determiner (DET) that serves as an existential quantifier in F/A.

(10) modular correspondences for an EQNP
   syntax: [$_{NP}$ (DET), N']
   F/A: [$_{QPx}$ [$_Q$ ∃] [$_{PROP}$ [$_{ARG}$ x], [$_{Fa}$ ARG, [$_{Faa}$ =]]]]
   • The value of the ARG comes from the N'.

This entry for an EQNP simplifies the lexical entry for numerals given in (11), in which a numeral is a set modifier that specifies the cardinality of the set in question.

(11) lexical entry for *three*
   syntax: A in [$_{N'[PL]}$ __, N'[PL]]
   • The mother NP is an EQNP.
   RS: nil
   F/A: [$_{Ma}$ THREE IN CARDINALITY] in [$_{ARG+S}$ ARG, __]

5.5 Domain Expressions and Split Antecedents

In 5.1 (1b), which introduced the F/A structure [$_{QPx}$ Q, PROP], the PROP was called the domain expression for the quantifier Q. (1a) is an example in which the subject NP *a man who lived in Vienna* is a quantified NP (QNP) that corresponds to the QP$_x$ in its F/A (1b). The domain expression for the [$_Q$ A] is [$_{PROP}$ x = [$_{ARG}$ [$_{ARG}$ MAN] Ma]]].

(1) a. A man who lived in Vienna came in the front door.
    b. the F/A of (1a)

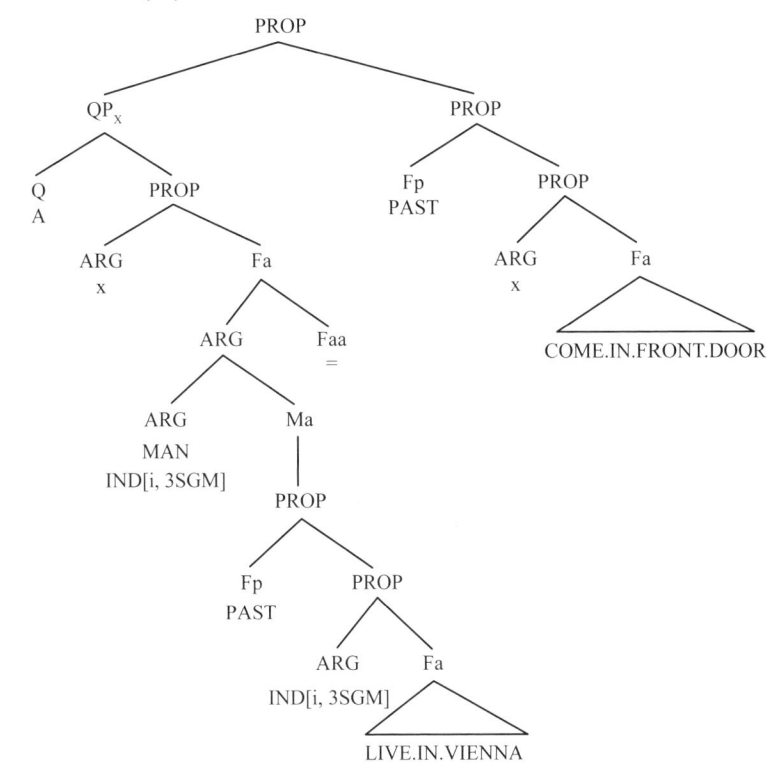

```
                            PROP
                   ┌─────────┴─────────┐
                  QPₓ                  PROP
             ┌─────┴─────┐         ┌────┴────┐
             Q          PROP       Fp       PROP
             A       ┌───┴───┐    PAST   ┌───┴───┐
                    ARG      Fa         ARG      Fa
                     x    ┌───┴───┐      x    COME.IN.FRONT.DOOR
                         ARG     Faa
                              =
                     ┌────┴────┐
                    ARG        Ma
                    MAN         │
                 IND[i, 3SGM]  PROP
                            ┌───┴───┐
                            Fp     PROP
                           PAST  ┌──┴──┐
                                ARG    Fa
                            IND[i, 3SGM]
                                    LIVE.IN.VIENNA
```

In (1b), the relative clause *who lived in Vienna* is an Ma (modifier of an ARG) and the relative pronoun *who* is treated as a pronoun, namely, an ARG with its IND value. The referential index (ref) of this IND is *i*, which is the same ref as that on the [₍ₐᵣ𝒸 MAN] (the head noun of the relative clause). This ref *i* is a type-identity (not token-identity) index, which is borne by an ARG that corresponds to an N' (not NP). (See 6.2.2 (1) for details.)

In (2a) below, there are two QNPs, *a man* and *a woman*, each being the subject of its own clause, and a restrictive relative clause at the end, whose relative pronoun takes the two QNPs as its antecedents (split antecedents). This is expected, because we treat relative pronouns as pronouns, which allow split antecedents, as in *A man_i came in the front door and a woman_j came in the side door. They_{i,j} had met in Vienna.*

(2) a. A man came in the front door and a woman came in the side door who had met in Vienna. (McCawley 1993: 240)
b. A man came in the front door and several/a few women came in the side door who had met in Vienna.

McCawley (1993: 242) explained (2a) by means of a polyadic quantifier, a quantifier that binds two or more variables (McCawley 1993: 240). His claim was that there is only one existential quantifier in (2a) that binds two variables. However, one of the two indefinite articles can be changed into some other existentially quantifying determiner, as in (2b). Therefore, we will assign an existential quantifier to each indefinite article, as in (3), which reduces the mismatch between its syntax and F/A.

(3) the F/A of (2a) PROP

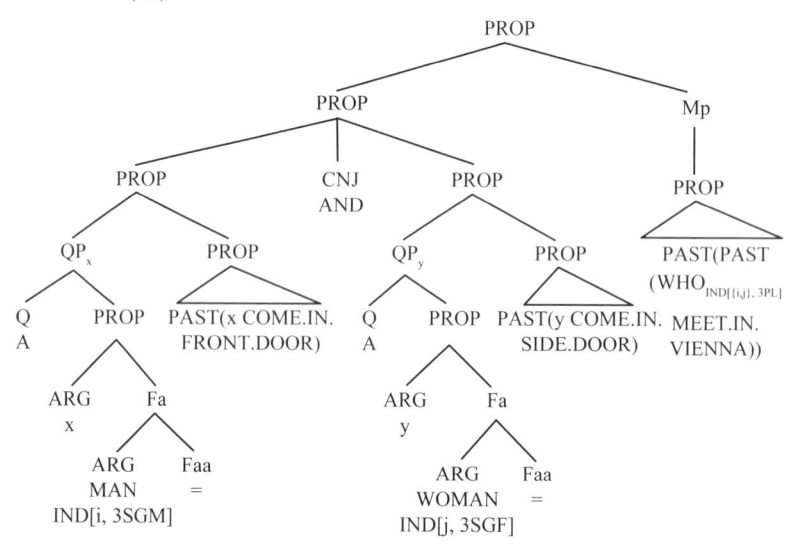

```
                                    PROP
                        ┌────────────┴────────────┐
                       PROP                       Mp
            ┌───────────┼───────────┐             │
          PROP         CNJ         PROP          PROP
         ┌──┴──┐       AND        ┌──┴──┐       ┌──┴──┐
        QP_x    PROP             QP_y   PROP   PAST(PAST
        ┌┴┐   ┌──┴──┐            ┌┴┐   ┌──┴──┐  (WHO_IND[{i,j}, 3PL]
        Q  A PROP  PAST(x COME.IN. Q  A PROP  PAST(y COME.IN.  MEET.IN.
             │     FRONT.DOOR)         │     SIDE.DOOR)        VIENNA))
           ┌─┴─┐                     ┌─┴─┐
          ARG  Fa                   ARG  Fa
           x  ┌┴┐                    y  ┌┴┐
             ARG Faa                   ARG Faa
             MAN  =                    WOMAN =
           IND[i, 3SGM]              IND[j, 3SGF]
```

One irregularity in (3) is that the F/A of the relative clause is not what it should be, namely, the Ma modifying the ARG in the domain expression for each Q, but is an Mp modifying the coordinated PROP. In other words, that part of the domain expression is displaced from each QP and adjoined to the coordinated PROP, exactly like the corresponding syntactic structure of (2a). This displacement is forced by the fact that the relative clause *who had met in Vienna*, having split antecedents, cannot modify *man* alone or *woman* alone, but must modify both at the same time. However, a benefit of accepting as an Mp the displacement of what should be an Ma is reducing the mismatch between syntax and F/A. Note that in (3), the relative pronoun is treated as a pronoun that is coreferent with its split antecedents and that the referential indices i on MAN and j on WOMAN are indices not of token identity but of type identity, exactly like (1b).

5.6 Quantifier-Float

In (1a), the quantified NP (QNP) *all the students* contains two quantifiers: *all* and *the*. The syntax, F/A, and RS of (1a) are given in (1b).

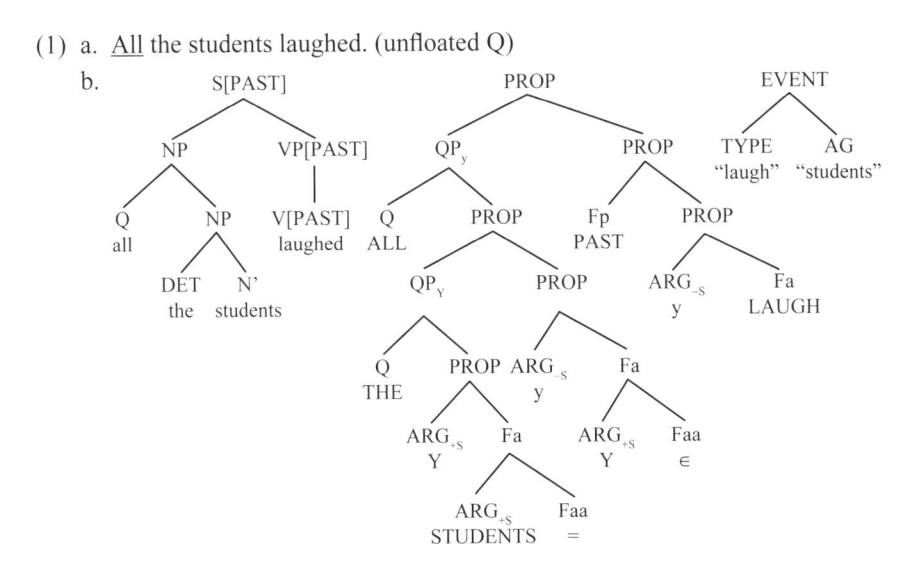

(1) a. All the students laughed. (unfloated Q)
  b.

```
         S[PAST]                    PROP                    EVENT
        /      \                   /    \                  /     \
      NP      VP[PAST]          QP_y     PROP         TYPE       AG
     /  \       |              /    \                "laugh"  "students"
    Q   NP   V[PAST]  Q       PROP   Fp      PROP
   all  / \  laughed ALL     /   \  PAST    /    \
      DET  N'              QP_y   PROP   ARG_-S   Fa
      the students        /   \          y     LAUGH
                         Q    PROP ARG_-S  Fa
                        THE    /\    y
                           ARG_+S  Fa   ARG_+S  Faa
                             Y          Y        ∈
                               ARG_+S    Faa
                              STUDENTS    =
```

In the F/A above, the lowercase y is an individual variable and the uppercase Y is a set variable (5.4). The F/A says that 'for all the members y of the specific set Y of students, y laughed.' On the other hand, the quantifier *all* in (2a) is floated and adjoined to the VP. The VP adjunction structure in (2a) is justified by VP coordination (2a') and pseudo-cleft (2a"). The syntax and F/A of (2a) are given in (2b). Note that the difference between the F/A structures in (1b) and (2b) is that the domain set quantifier QP_Y in (1b) that is contained in QP_y is taken out of it in

(2b) and is put at the immediately higher position that c-commands QP_y. This is the same difference that we saw between 5.2 (2) and (3).

(2) a. The students [$_{VP}$ all [$_{VP}$ laughed]]. (floated Q)
   a'. The neighbors either [all like punk rock] or [all want to annoy me]. (McCawley 1998: 99)
   a". What the children did was [all make obscene gestures]. (ibid.)
   b.
```
                S[PAST]                              PROP
              /        \                         /        \
           NP          VP[PAST]               QP_Y          PROP
          /  \         /    \               /    \        /    \
        DET   N'     ADV   VP[PAST]        Q    PROP    QP_y    PROP
        the students  all    |            THE   /  \    /  \    /    \
                           V[PAST]           ARG_+S Fa Q  PROP PAST(y LAUGH)
                           laughed            Y    /  \ ALL
                                                 ARG_+S Faa ARG_-S Fa
                                                 STUDENTS =      y
                                                              /    \
                                                           ARG_+S  Faa
                                                             Y      ∈
```

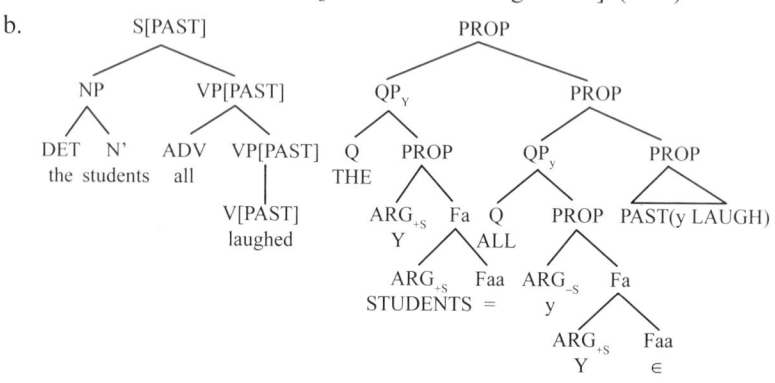

The F/A above says that 'there is a specific set Y of students such that for all y of the set Y, y laughed.' Note that the c-command relation between *the students* and *all* is maintained between syntax and F/A. A floated QP (QP_y in (2b)) must be c-commanded by the QP of the domain set (QP_Y in (2b)). This does not need to be stipulated independently, because if the floated QP_y and the domain QP_Y were reversed, the set variable Y in QP_y would not be bound, resulting in a violation of 5.1 (1c).

It has been known (e.g., in McCawley 1998: 161, 1999: 45) that, in transformational terms, Q-float is only possible from the surface subject position or that, in F/A terms, the QP that corresponds to a (VP-adjunct) floated quantifier in syntax must bind the subject variable. This is shown in (3). (The domain set and the floated Q are underlined.)

(3) (cf. McCawley 1993: 195; McCawley 1998: 161)
   a. The workers have all denounced the manager.
   b. *The manager has all denounced the workers.
   c. *The manager has all been denounced by the workers.
   d. *The workers, the manager has all denounced. (Jerry Sadock (p.c.))

Note that (3d), the topicalization of (3b), shares the same ill-formed F/A with (3b). (The difference between them is in Information Structure (IS).) What we need to require of a floated Q is that (i) it be a VP-adjunct in syntax and (ii) it (the QP_y in (2b)) quantify the subject ARG in F/A. (See the lexical entry for floated *all* in (9).)

Unfloated quantifiers exhibit scope ambiguity (McCawley 1993: 192–193, 1998: 631, 1999: 43–44). In (4a), the QNP *all the students* can be interpreted in two ways: one interpretation is that the QNP is outside the scope of *appeared* and the other is that it is inside the scope of *appeared*. If we abbreviate the QP_y in (1b) simply as ALL.THE.STUDENTS, the F/A structures of the two interpretations are given in (4b).

(4) a. <u>All the students</u> appeared to be cheating. (ambiguous with an unfloated Q) (McCawley 1993: 192, 1998: 631)

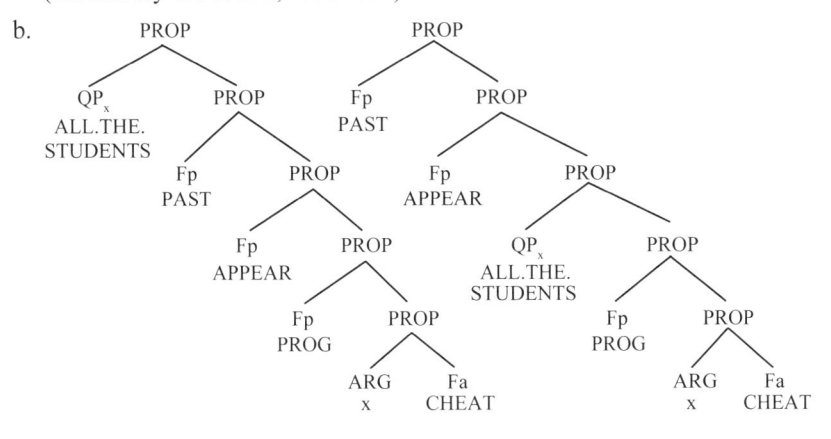

b.
```
         PROP                              PROP
        /    \                            /    \
    QP_x      PROP                    Fp        PROP
  ALL.THE.   /    \                  PAST      /    \
  STUDENTS  Fp     PROP                      Fp      PROP
           PAST   /    \                    APPEAR  /    \
                Fp      PROP                      QP_x    PROP
              APPEAR   /    \                   ALL.THE.  /    \
                      Fp     PROP              STUDENTS  Fp     PROP
                     PROG   /    \                      PROG   /    \
                          ARG    Fa                          ARG    Fa
                           x    CHEAT                         x    CHEAT
```

The F/A on the left means 'For all the members x of the specific set of students, it appeared that x was cheating' whereas the F/A on the right means 'It appeared that for all the members x of the specific set of students, x was cheating.' The ambiguity found in (4a) with the complex QNP (*all the students* with two quantifiers) is the same as that found in (5a) below, where a simple QNP (*a student* with one quantifier) is involved.

(5) a. <u>A student</u> appeared to be cheating.
  b. [$_{QPx}$ [$_Q$ A] x = STUDENT] [PAST(APPEAR(PROG(x CHEAT)))]
  c. [PAST(APPEAR([$_{QPx}$ [$_Q$ A] x = STUDENT](PROG(x CHEAT))))]

As for the floated versions of (4a), namely, (6a) and (7a), since a floated Q must be a VP adjunct, there are at least two positions available to the floated Q: adjoined to the VP headed by *appeared* (6a) and adjoined to the VP headed by *be* (7a). (6a) can be paraphrased as 'There is a specific set X of students such that for all x of X, it appeared that x was cheating,' which is the same interpretation as the F/A on the left in (4b). On the other hand, (7a) can be paraphrased as 'There was a specific set X of students such that it appeared that for all x of X, x was cheating,' which is roughly the same interpretation as the F/A on the right in (4b). The approximate F/A of each interpretation is given in (6b) and (7b). The lexical entries for *the* and the floated *all* are given in (8) and (9).

(6) a. The students <u>all</u> appeared to be cheating. (McCawley 1993: 192)
 b. [$_{QPX}$ [$_Q$ THE] X=STUDENTS] [$_{QPx}$ <u>ALL x∈X</u>] (PAST(APPEAR(PROG (x CHEAT))))

(7) a. The students appeared to <u>all</u> be cheating. (McCawley 1993: 192)
 b. [$_{QPX}$ [$_Q$ THE] X=STUDENTS] (PAST(APPEAR([$_{QPx}$ <u>ALL x∈X</u>](PROG (x CHEAT)))))

(8) lexical entry for *the* as a quantifier of a set variable
 syntax: DET
 F/A: [$_Q$ THE] in

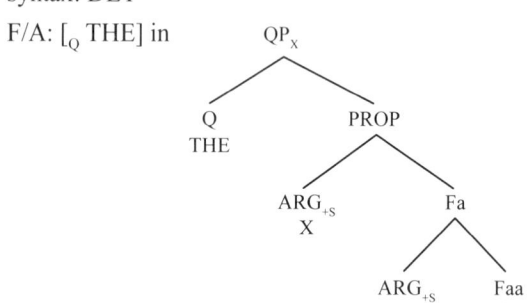

```
              QP_x
             /    \
            Q     PROP
           THE    /   \
               ARG_{+S}  Fa
                 X      /  \
                    ARG_{+S}  Faa
                              =
```

- The value of ARG$_{+S}$ comes from the sister N' of the DET.

(9) is the lexical entry for floated *all*. QP$_x$ must bind the subject [$_{ARG}$ x]. We will capture this relationship between QP$_x$ and the variable x by a dominance path condition (cf. 6.1.3 (2)).

(9) lexical entry for floated *all*
syntax: ADV in [$_{XP}$ __ XP], where XP corresponds to an Fa or PROP in F/A
F/A: [$_Q$ ALL] in

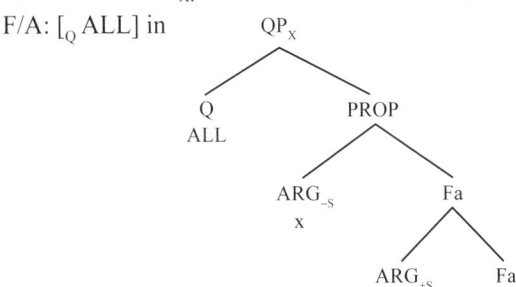

```
        QP_x
       /    \
      Q     PROP
     ALL   /    \
        ARG_-s   Fa
          x     /  \
              ARG_+s  Fa
                X     ∈
```

- Dominance path condition for QP$_x$
  {PROP}* [$_{ARG}$ x]

The dominance path condition for QP$_x$ above means that the variable [$_{ARG}$ x] can be reached from the mother PROP of QP$_x$ only by going down through any number of PROPs. This means that the variable is a subject ARG. Furthermore, the syntactic specification of *all* in (9) is not VP-adjunct but XP-adjunct, because we need to cover the following cases.

(10) *all* adjoined to a predicate phrase that is not a VP
   a. The students were [$_{AP}$ all [$_{AP}$ very quiet]].
   a'. Were the students [$_{AP}$ all [$_{AP}$ very quiet]]?
   b. The students were [$_{PP}$ all [$_{PP}$ in good shape]].
   b'. Were the students [$_{PP}$ all [$_{PP}$ in good shape]]?
   c. The students were [$_{NP}$ all [$_{NP}$ smart boys]].
   c'. Were the students [$_{NP}$ all [$_{NP}$ smart boys]]?
   d. the F/A of (10a)
      [$_{QPX}$ [$_Q$ THE] X=STUDENTS] (PAST ([$_{QPx}$ ALL x∈X] [$_{PROP}$ x [$_{Fa}$ VERY. QUIET]]))

In these examples, *all* is adjoined to an XP that corresponds to an Fa in F/A.

Just as the quantifier *all* and the following NP make up a single constituent, as in [$_{NP}$ *all* [$_{NP}$ *the students*]], a pronoun and the following *all* make up a single constituent, as in *I ate [them all]* or *Either [they all] or at least some of them knew the truth* (cf. "Quantifier-pronoun Flip" in McCawley 1998: 102). This means that (11) is syntactically ambiguous.

(11) They all appeared to be cheating. (syntactically ambiguous)

The quantifier *all* in (11) either makes up a constituent with the pronoun *they* or is adjoined to the VP. The former syntactic structure exhibits scope ambiguity just as (4a) with an unfloated *all* (12b, c), whereas in the latter, no scope ambiguity arises, which is shown in (13).

(12) a. [$_{NP}$ They all] appeared to be cheating. (ambiguous) (Jerry Sadock (p.c.))
   b. [$_{QPx}$ [$_Q$ ALL] x ∈ M](PAST(APPEAR(PROG(x CHEAT)))) (wide scope)
   c. PAST(APPEAR([$_{QPx}$ [$_Q$ ALL] x ∈ M](PROG(x CHEAT)))) (narrow scope)

(13) a. They [$_{VP}$ all appeared to be cheating]. (unambiguous)
   b. [$_{QPx}$ [$_Q$ ALL] x ∈ M](PAST(APPEAR(PROG(x CHEAT)))) (wide scope)

We can disambiguate the syntactic structure (11) by making a brief pause before *all* in (13a) or after *all* in (12a), or inserting a propositional modifier, such as *probably*: *They all probably appeared to be cheating* and *They probably all appeared to be cheating*. In the former (with the unfloated quantifier), the scope ambiguity remains, whereas in the latter (with the floated quantifier) it vanishes. The domain set for the (floated) quantifier *all* in (11) to (14) is the set of people referred to by the pronoun *they*, which is denoted in (14b, d) as M.

(14) a. They appeared to all be cheating. (unambiguous)
   b. PAST(APPEAR([$_{QPx}$ ALL x ∈ M](PROG(x CHEAT)))) (narrow scope)
   c. They appeared to be cheating.
   d. PAST(APPEAR(PROG(M CHEAT)))

The F/A of (14c) is (14d), which is an aggregated expression (5.4 (8)). The set M is technically the referential index of the IND value IND[M, 3PL] of the ARG that corresponds to the pronoun *they* (ARG[IND[M, 3PL]]) in (14c). (12c) and (14b) are, in a sense, de-aggregated expressions of (14d).

McCawley (1993: 194, 1998: 631, 1999: 46) observed that the auxiliary verbs that follow a floated quantifier are in its scope and those that precedes it are outside its scope (i.e., no mismatch between syntax and F/A), except when a floated quantifier immediately follows a tensed auxiliary verb (V[AUX, FIN]), as in (15a).

(15) a. The students must all have been cheating. (ambiguous) (McCawley 1993: 194)
 b. $QP_Y >$ PRES > MUST $> [_{QPy}$ ALL $y \in Y] >$ PAST > PROG (expected)
 c. $QP_Y > [_{QPy}$ ALL $y \in Y] >$ PRES > MUST $>$ PAST > PROG (unexpected)

The composite Fp PRES∘MUST, which expresses the speaker's strong belief at the moment of utterance, corresponds to the single node $[_{V[AUX, PRES]}$ *must*$]$ in syntax. No QP can intervene between PRES and MUST, because the latter two correspond to a single word (*must*) in syntax. (15a) can be interpreted either as the floated *all* (QP_y) being in the scope of *must*, as in (15b) or as *all* being outside its scope, as in (15c). The interpretation (15c) is the same as that of *The students all must have been cheating*. Note that in (15b, c), QP_Y corresponds to the quantified NP *the students* of the domain set in syntax (cf. (8)) and QP_y corresponds to the floated quantifier *all* (cf. (9)), and that A > B indicates that A asymmetrically c-commands B (in the case of scope relations, B is in the scope of A).

The same ambiguity as (15a) is observed with time/frequency adverbs that modify PROP (McCawley's (1998:197) ad-S). (16a) is ambiguous with respect to the scope relations between the finite auxiliary *can* and the immediately following adverb *always*. One interpretation is (16b), which is expected and involves no mismatch between syntax and F/A. The other interpretation is (16c), which shows a mismatch between syntax and F/A, and is synonymous with *You always can stay up late*.

(16) a. You can always stay up late. (ambiguous)
 b. What you are allowed to do is to always stay up late. (PRES > CAN > ALWAYS) (expected)
 c. What you are always allowed to do is to stay up late. (ALWAYS > PRES > CAN) (unexpected)

We would like to ascribe these mismatched cases, namely, (15a) with the interpretation (15c) and (16a) with the interpretation (16c), to the English V-2 constraint described by Sadock (2012: 122 (27)), according to which, English has a vestige of the Germanic V-2 constraint. This is divided into two cases.

(17) V-2 Constraint in English
  a. the V-2 template for main verbs (very weak)
     $[_{S[FIN]}$ XP ≼ V[FIN] …]
  b. the V-2 template for auxiliary verbs
     $[_{S[FIN, AUX]}$ XP ≼ V[FIN, AUX] …]
  c. The boy has now been missing for five days. (not ambiguous)

  c'. $[_{Mp}$ NOW] $[_{Fp}$ PRES] $[_{Fp}$ PAST] (THE.BOY MISSING.FOR.FIVE.DAYS)

The V-2 template for main verbs (17a) results from the two PS rules: $[_{S[FIN]}$ XP ≼ VP[FIN]] and the V-initial VP structure $[_{VP}$ V < XP]. The effect of this template is very weak, because all sorts of adverbs can intervene quite freely between XP (subject NP, clausal subject, or locative PP in the locative inversion construction) and the following finite main verb (V[FIN]). Hence (17a) can be violated without any loss of acceptability. By contrast, the V-2 template for auxiliary verbs (17b) is much stronger than (17a). First, in terms of adverb insertion, although two word orders are available: NP ≼ ADV ≼ V[FIN, AUX] (e.g., *John always has been at home*) that violates (17b) and NP ≼ V[FIN, AUX] ≼ ADV (e.g., *John has always been at home*) that respects it, the latter order is far more frequent than the former order (Carter and McCarthy 2006: 583, John Sinclair et al. 1990: 249, Huddleston and Pullum 2002: 782, Swan 2005: 20). Second, there are cases where (17b) is required: for example, when the emphatic *do* (e.g., **John indeed DOES speak Japanese* vs. *John DOES indeed speak Japanese*) or the negative *not* (e.g., **John not danced/did dance* vs. *John did not dance*) appears. The effect of (17b) is most clearly seen in such examples as (17c), in which the present perfect auxiliary *have/has* and the temporal adverb *now* appear side by side in this order. The corresponding F/A is (17c'), in which NOW modifies the whole proposition PRES(PAST(PROP)).

We take the V-2 template for auxiliary verbs (17b) to be an optional linear order rule in Sadock's (2012: 121–124) sense that it optionally places the relevant parts in the specified order, while keeping the syntactic constituency unchanged (cf. McCawley's (1982, 1998: 46–47, 94, 282, 284) discontinuous constituent structures). Our claim about (16a) with the interpretation (16c) and (15a) with the interpretation (15c) is that this word order is achieved by an optional application of the auxiliary V-2 template (17b) to the syntax of *You [always [can stay up late]]* or *The students [all [must have been cheating]]*. If the word order *You can always*

... or *The students must all* ... is achieved by (17b) on the basis of the syntax of *You [always [can stay up late]]* or *The students [all [must have been cheating]]*, the syntax of (16a) or (15a) must be kept intact. If the syntactic constituent structure of *John can always stay up late* (with the ALWAYS > PRES > CAN interpretation) were not *John [always [can stay up late]]*, which we claim to be the case, but *John [can [always [stay up late]]]*, we would expect that the VP[BSE] *[always [stay up late]]* could appear as the second conjunct with the same scope relations, as in (16c): ALWAYS > PRES > CAN.

(18) a. John <u>can</u> drink every night and <u>always</u> stay up late. (not ambiguous)
  b. The students <u>must</u> be sleeping or <u>all</u> be cheating. (not ambiguous)

However, the second conjunct in (18a) is not ambiguous. It can only be interpreted with the scope relation PRES > CAN > ALWAYS and lacks the interpretation ALWAYS > PRES > CAN. On the other hand, if the word order *You can always* ... is achieved by the template (17b) from *You always can* ..., as we claim is the case, the coordination in (18a) is impossible, because *always stay up late* does not form a syntactic constituent to begin with. (18b) shows the same point.

Chapter 6
Unbounded Dependency

> This chapter discusses how we can analyze from a multi-modular perspective the unbounded dependencies in *wh*-questions and relative clauses, various island phenomena, and strong and weak crossover phenomena. The syntax and semantics of quiz questions and non-bridge verbs are also discussed.

6.1 *Wh*-Questions

Wh-questions, such as (1a), have been explained in Mainstream Generative Grammar (MGG) by "*wh*-movement," which "moves" the *wh*-phrase *what* in (1b) in a successive cyclic way ("COMP-to-COMP") from the "D-structure" position to the specifier position of the immediately dominating CP, and then to the specifier position of the next immediately dominating CP, repeating the same local "Ā-movement" if necessary, and finally landing on the specifier position of the topmost CP. In some other versions of transformational grammar, for example, in McCawley (1998: 498, 655, 1999: 49), a *wh*-phrase "moves" from the "deep" structure position to the highest position "in one fell swoop" (according to McCawley's terminologies (1999: 49 note 15), "Newtonian *wh*-movement" as opposed to "Cartesian *wh*-movement" in (1b)) attracted by a coindexed C with the interrogative Q feature. To be precise, a *wh*-phrase at the surface structure *how many stories about Diana*, for example, corresponds to a *wh*-quantifier phrase (Q') *Wh: x cardinal number* and an existential quantifier phrase ∃: *M set of x-many stories about Diana*, the former c-commanding the latter, in McCawley's "deep" structure, and the latter first goes down to the corresponding variable by his "Q' Lowering" transformation and then goes up to the *wh*-quantifier phrase attracted by the topmost coindexed C with a Q feature, all according to his "Cyclic Principle" (McCawley 1998: 655).

(1) a. What did Susan tell you that Roger had ordered me to put in the vase? (McCawley 1998: 493)

b. [_CP ___ did Susan tell you [_CP___ that Roger had ordered me [_CP___ PRO to put [_NP what] in the vase]]]?

c. [_CP[WH[Q]] [_NP[WH[Q]] What] [_S[INV, PAST] did Susan tell you that Roger had ordered me to put NP[G] in the vase]]?

On the other hand, GPSG, HPSG, and Culicover and Jackendoff 2005 employed the slash category to capture the syntactic relations between the clause-initial *wh*-phrase and the gap at the bottom. In AMG, because there is no "movement" rule, a *wh*-question has a syntactic structure in which its *wh*-phrase NP[WH[Q]] is located at the clause-initial position and there is a corresponding gap NP[G] at its "extraction site," as in (1c), just as in other non-MGG approaches. However, we will capture the relationship between the clause-initial *wh*-phrase and the gap at the bottom by means of not the slash category but the dominance path conditions (6.1.3 (2)), which specify grammatical/licit paths of dominance relations from the top node CP[WP[Q]] (i.e., the mother node of the clause-initial *wh*-phrase) to the bottom gap XP[G]. This idea is borrowed from LFG's "functional uncertainty", but LFG formulated the conditions only in terms of f-structures. We will formulate our dominance path conditions in terms of syntactic and F/A structures.

One advantage of this AMG approach is that we can specify the grammatical instances of "*wh*-movement" positively without specifying the ungrammatical/illicit instances of "*wh*-movement" (i.e., island violations) negatively. Our approach to "*wh*-movement" by positively specifying its licit paths sounds plausible when we consider a possible scenario of language acquisition: children assume at their initial stage that they can't extract anything from anywhere and learn the "*wh*-movement" rule as "conservative generalizers" only from positive evidence (Culicover and Jackendoff 2005: 333). They learn syntactic environments where "*wh*-movement" is possible directly from positive evidence, and do not need to learn syntactic environments where "*wh*-movement" is impossible from negative evidence. Another advantage of our AMG approach is that because the *wh*-phrase is represented not only in syntax as XP[WH[Q]] but also in F/A as QP, we can formulate in F/A terms another set of dominance path conditions (6.1.4. (1)) similar to the ones formulated in syntactic terms. The two kinds of dominance path conditions will make slightly different predictions about grammatical/licit "*wh*-movement." If so, a picture would emerge quite naturally that in perfect cases of "*wh*-movement," both kinds of dominance path conditions would agree that they are grammatical, whereas, in completely impossible cases of "*wh*-movement," both kinds of dominance path conditions would agree that they are ungrammatical. There would be intermediate cases in which the "*wh*-movement" in question is allowed according to one kind of dominance path conditions but is not allowed according to the other kind. This opens up a possibility of explaining graded acceptability judgments in various *wh*-questions.

In the following sections, we assume that the F/A correspondent of a *wh*-phrase is a quantifier phrase (QP). This assumption is justified by at least the following three phenomena. First, a *wh*-phrase and an ordinary quantifier interact with each other and produce scope ambiguities, indicating that a *wh*-phrase functions semantically as a QP. For example, (2a) can be interpreted in two ways. In one interpretation, *what* has wide scope and *everyone* is within its scope, as in (2b). (2b') is an answer to (2a) with this interpretation. In the other interpretation, *everyone* has wide scope and *what* is within its scope, as in (2c). The *wh*-question (2a) with this interpretation can be answered by listing the pairs of eater and food, as in (2c'), or by giving a functional expression, as in (2c'').

(2) a. What did everyone eat? (ambiguous)
 b. $[_{QPy} [_Q \text{WH}] \text{ y} = \text{THING}] ([_{QPx} [_Q \text{EVERY}] \text{ x} = \text{PERSON}] (\text{PAST}(\text{x EAT y})))$
 b'. Everyone ate hamburgers.
 c. $[_{QPx} [_Q \text{EVERY}] \text{ x} = \text{PERSON}] ([_{QPy} [_Q \text{WH}] \text{ y} = \text{THING}] (\text{PAST}(\text{x EAT y})))$
 c'. John ate a hamburger, Mary fish, Jane a steak, and Tom sushi.
 c''. Everyone ate their favorite food.

Second, both regular quantifiers and *wh*-phrases allow pronouns in certain structural positions to be interpreted as bound variables.

(3) a. Everyone$_x$ loves his$_x$ mother.
 a'. Everyone$_x$ thinks that he$_x$ is a genius.
 b. Who$_x$ loves his$_x$ mother?
 b'. Who$_x$ thinks that he$_x$ is a genius?

Third, in (4a), the *wh*-phrase *which linguist* has wide scope and the QP *most philosophers* is in its scope. Since the latter QP is outside the matrix PROP in F/A, as in (4b), so is the former *wh*-phrase, c-commanding the latter.

(4) a. Which linguist admires most philosophers? (cf. 5.1 (4))
b. [$_{QPx}$ WH x = LINGUIST] [$_{QPy}$ MOST y = PHILOSOPHER] (PRES (x ADMIRE y))

6.1.1 Direct *wh*-questions

There are two ways in AMG of explaining the clause-initial *wh*-phrase XP[WH[Q]] in a *wh*-question CP[WH[Q]]: (i) the *wh*-phrase is *in situ* in syntax and a separate linear order rule places it where it should be, keeping the syntactic constituency intact (Sadock 2012: 122 (27) and 124 (33)) or (ii) the *wh*-phrase is admitted at the clause-initial position by the local PS rule [$_{CP[WH[Q]]}$ XP[WH[Q]] S[INV]] and at the same time a phonologically null gap XP[G] of the same syntactic category is introduced at its extraction site. The difficulty with (i) is when a *wh*-phrase is related to two or more extraction sites in a coordinate structure in the case of across-the-board (ATB) "*wh*-movement," such as 6.1.2 (1). To avoid this difficulty, we will take option (ii).

(1a) is an example of a direct *wh*-question. A direct *wh*-question is syntactically a local tree [$_{CP[WH[Q]]}$ XP[WH[Q]] S[INV]] (6.1.7 (1)), in which the clause CP with a WH[Q] feature dominates two daughters, a *wh*-phrase of the category XP (i.e., XP[WH[Q]]) and an inverted clause (S[INV]), the former preceding the latter. The syntactic category CP of *wh*-questions is justified by their external syntax: they can be a complement of certain verbs, just as CP[*that*] (e.g., *Everyone knows* {[$_{CP[WH[Q]]}$ *which medicine Mary took*] | [$_{CP[that]}$ *that Mary took that medicine*]}) and they can be a clausal subject, just like CP[*that*] (e.g., {[$_{CP[WH[Q]]}$ *Which medicine Mary took*] | [$_{CP[that]}$ *That Mary took that medicine*]} *is obvious to everyone*).

(1) a. Which medicine did Mary take? (cf. Sadock 2012:124 (33))
b. the syntax, F/A, and RS of (1a)

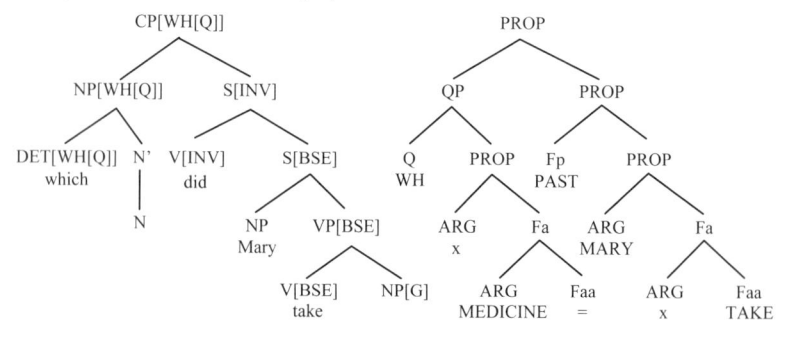

```
         CP[WH[Q]]                              PROP
         /        \                            /     \
   NP[WH[Q]]     S[INV]                      QP       PROP
    /    \      /    \                      /  \     /    \
DET[WH[Q]] N' V[INV] S[BSE]                Q  PROP  Fp    PROP
   |         |  |    /    \               WH  / \  PAST   /   \
 which       N did  NP   VP[BSE]             ARG Fa     ARG   Fa
                   Mary   /   \              x         MARY
                      V[BSE] NP[G]              ARG    Faa    ARG   Faa
                       take                    MEDICINE  =    x    TAKE
```

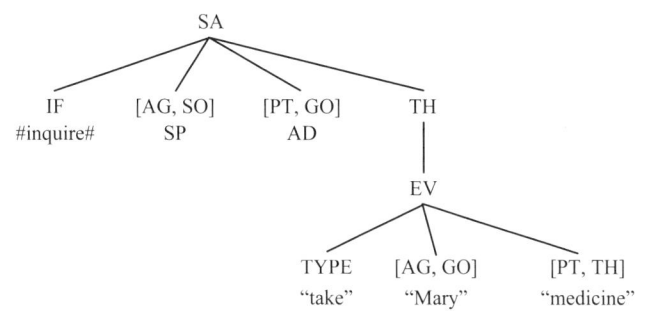

```
                    SA
         ┌──────┬────┴────┬──────┐
        IF    [AG, SO]  [PT, GO]  TH
      #inquire#   SP      AD      │
                                  EV
                         ┌────────┼────────┐
                       TYPE    [AG, GO]  [PT, TH]
                      "take"    "Mary"   "medicine"
```

c. the dominance path (from the top CP[WH[Q]] to the bottom NP[G]) of (1a)
CP[WH[Q]] S[INV] S[BSE] VP[BSE] NP[G]

d. What did John say that he ate?
syntax: [_CP[WH[Q]] [_NP[WH[Q]] What] [_S[INV, PAST] did [_S[BSE] John [_VP[BSE] say [_CP[*that*] that [_S[PAST] he [_VP[PAST] ate NP[G]]]]]]]]?
dominance path: CP[WH[Q]] S[INV, PAST] S[BSE] VP[BSE] CP[*that*] S[PAST] VP[PAST] NP[G]

Following Sadock (2012), we use the WH[Q] feature for *wh*-questions and the WH[R] feature for *wh*-relative clauses.

The internal syntax of CP[WH[Q]] in (1b) is an exocentric construction; that is, the CP lacks its own head C. However, the Head Feature Convention (HFC) (1.2 (3)) is not violated, because there is no head that the mother CP[WH[Q]] should share its head features with. In (1b), the clause-initial *wh*-phrase and the gap NP[G] in syntax correspond to the QP_x and the variable [$_{ARG}$ x] in F/A, respectively. This is guaranteed in the following manner. In the F/A structure, the quantifier [$_Q$ WH], which comes from the *wh*-word contained in the clause-initial XP[WH[Q]] (6.1.7 (6)-(9)), must instantiate a variable x in F/A and form a QP_x. The QP_x in turn must have a sister PROP that contains x. This is all due to the well-formedness conditions on quantifier phrases: [$_{QPx}$ Q, PROP] and [$_{PROP}$ QP_x, PROP] (1.3 (15), repeated as 5.1 (1)). Because of 1.3 (15a), repeated as 5.1 (1a), there must be a variable [$_{ARG}$ x] somewhere at the bottom of the F/A structure. This variable must correspond to the NP[G] in syntax, because any other syntactic node (lexical or phrasal) is filled with lexical items and hence has its own F/A value in the corresponding position in F/A. In the F/A structure of (1b), because of the interrogative determiner *which*, the variable x is interpreted as belonging to a definite set contextually evoked in the discourse (cf. "D-linked" in Pesetsky

1987: 108–109). See the lexical entry for the interrogative determiner *which* in 6.1.7 (9). The RS of (1b) shows that a direct *wh*-question in syntax corresponds to a speech act (SA) in RS with the illocutionary force (IF) #inquire#, in which the speaker (SP) asks the addressee (AD) a question (7.1 (6)). (The details of SA will be discussed in Chapter 7.) In the case of a direct *wh*-question, the CP[WH[Q]] in syntax corresponds to the SA with the #inquire# illocutionary force, which requires of the *wh*-question that its daughter be an inverted clause (S[INV]). By contrast, in the case of an indirect *wh*-question, the CP[WH[Q]] does not correspond to such an SA, and hence an inverted clause is not required. Furthermore, the [PT, TH] role of the verb *take* is borne by *medicine*, because the ARG that corresponds to the [PT, TH] role is the variable x, which represents MEDICINE in the domain expression for the quantifier [$_Q$ WH]. In other words, as far as the RS of a *wh*-question is concerned, the clause-initial *wh*-phrase is interpreted *in situ* as one of the roles in RS, as if there was no "movement." Recall that the c-command relations in syntax and F/A on the one hand and the outrank relations in RS are preserved under default correspondence (1.4 (7b)). In the case at hand, [$_{NP}$ Mary] c-commands NP[G] in syntax, [$_{ARG}$ MARY] c-commands [$_{ARG}$ x] in F/A, and [AG, GO] outranks [PT, TH] in RS.

(1c) shows that the relation between the top CP[WH[Q]] node and the bottom NP[G] node is captured by a dominance path, which represents the dominance relations of the nodes in the syntactic structure in (1b) from the top CP[WH[Q]] to the bottom NP[G]. Note that for every *wh*-question (CP[WH[Q]] in syntax), there is always a single dominance path from the top CP[WH[Q]] to the bottom gap XP[G]. (1d) is another example of dominance path. The issue of how to guarantee the presence of a gap XP[G] and the category identity between a *wh*-phrase and its gap will be discussed in 6.1.3 (1) and 6.1.7 (1).

When the matrix subject itself is a *wh*-phrase, as in (2a), inversion does not appear. If there were inversion in such a case, it would be ungrammatical (2b).

(2) a. Who sang with Mary?
    b. *Who did sing with Mary? (no stress on *did*)
       syntax: Who [$_{S[INV]}$ did [$_{S[BSE]}$ NP[G] [$_{VP[BSE]}$ sing with Mary]]]?
    c. Who did not sing with Mary?   cf. *Who not sang with Mary?
    d. Who DID sing with Mary?   (stress on *did*)

The ungrammatical status of (2b) with the syntactic structure indicated is explained in four ways. First, the most straightforward reason is the dominance path condition 6.1.3 (1c): the dominance path CP[WH[Q]] S[FIN] NP[G] is required of a matrix subject *wh*-question, and an S[FIN] (noninverted finite clause) is specified in the dominance path. So, lack of inversion in a matrix subject *wh*-question is forced by this dominance path condition. The second more pragmatic reason is that although (2a) and (2b) express the same information, (2b) is more costly than (2a) in terms of the number of words and the complexity of syntactic structures. Therefore, the simpler (2a) is chosen for the sake of the economy of language use. Note that (2b) is grammatical if its syntactic structure is [_{VP[AUX, PAST]} *did* [_{VP[BSE]} *sing with Mary*]] and *did* is stressed (2d), but this structure arises only when there is a need for such a structure. In a negative sentence, such as (2c), the negative *not* must be adjoined to a nonfinite VP ([_{VP[-FIN]} *not*, VP[-FIN]]) (2.2 (2)) and the auxiliary *did* is pressed into service to create such an environment ([_{VP[PAST]} *did* VP[BSE]]). Or when the polarity of the sentence (in this case, affirmativity) is emphasized in (2d), not the finite main verb (*Who SANG with Mary*) but the finite auxiliary verb (*Who DID sing with Mary*) is stressed, as in *John didn't sing with Mary. Tom didn't sing with her, either. Then, who DID sing with Mary?* Our view is that the VP[AUX, PAST] headed by *did* ([_{VP[AUX, PAST]} [_{V[AUX, PAST]} *did*], VP[BSE]]) is always available along with VP[PAST] (VP headed by a nonauxiliary V[PAST]) but the former, more complex structure is chosen only when there is a good reason for such a choice. When there is no such reason, the simpler, shorter form (VP[PAST]) is chosen again for the economy of language use. The third reason is the English V-2 constraint (5.6 (17), Sadock 2012: 122). *Wh*-questions must obey the V-2 constraint, namely, in this case, the first position must be a *wh*-phrase and the second position must be a finite verb. However, when the *wh*-phrase is the matrix subject, the V-2 word order is already achieved by the default [_{CP[WH[Q]]} NP[WH[Q]] [_{S[FIN]} NP[G] VP[FIN]]] without inversion. The fourth reason is more speculative and is related to Bresnan's Fixed Subject Condition (Bresnan 1972, McCawley 1998: 544). If we assimilate (3d) to such illicit cases as (3a, b, c), which violate the Fixed Subject Condition, we can claim that the four cases in (3) are illicit *wh*-phrase "extraction" from the left branch of the complement of the head (underlined below) that is not a main verb. In other words, a gap NP[G] can occur as the left branch of a binary-branching constituent, if the constituent is a complement of a main verb, as in (3d') and (3e).

(3) a. *Which applicant would you like [_{CP} <u>for</u> [_{S[to]} __ to get the job]]? (McCawley 1998: 528)
 b. *Who did you say [_{CP} <u>that</u> [_{S[PAST]} __ called me]]?
 c. *John is the one who I'm counting [_{PP[on]} <u>on</u> [_{S[PRS]} __ marrying her]]. (Kayne 1984: 29)

d. *Who [$_{S[INV]}$ did [$_{S[BSE]}$ ___ sing with Mary]]?
d'. Who do you [$_{VP[BSE]}$ want [$_{S[to]}$ NP[G] to sing with Mary]]? (1.3 (6), 4.2.2 (25))
e. [$_{VP}$ V [$_{XP}$ NP[G] < YP]]

(3a, b) are out because the gap occurs as the left branch of the complement of the complementizer. (3c) is out because the gap occurs as the left branch of the complement of the preposition. (3d) is out because the gap occurs as the left branch of the complement of the V[AUX], not a main verb.

When the matrix subject is a *wh*-phrase, this *wh*-phrase is outside the S it is the subject of and is directly dominated by CP[WH[Q]], and furthermore, there is an NP[G] at the subject position inside the S. This is forced by (i) the local tree for *wh*-question [$_{CP[WH[Q]]}$ XP[WH[Q]] S] and (ii) the dominance path condition for matrix subject CP[WH[Q]] S[FIN] NP[G] (6.1.3 (1c)). This is confirmed by the distribution of the idiom *the hell*.

(4) Nunberg et al. 1994: 515
   a. What the hell did you buy?
   b. I wonder who the hell bought what.
   c. *I wonder who bought what the hell.

The contrast between (4a) and (4c) shows that the idiom *the hell* occurs with a "moved" *wh*-phrase and does not occur with a *wh*-phrase *in situ*. In (4b), the idiom occurs with the subject *wh*-phrase, showing that it is "moved" and is outside the S it is the subject of. The same point is also confirmed by gapping, which applies to a coordinate structure of clauses in which, descriptively speaking, the conjuncts are identical except for two contrasting phrases, one constituent being outside the topmost VP constituent (subject NP or adverbial S-adjunct) and the other being a nonpredicate constituent contained in the topmost VP constituent, and "deletes" everything except those two nonidentical contrasting phrases from all conjuncts other than the first, as in (5a, b, c).

(5) a. [$_S$ [John] gave [$50] to the Cancer Foundation], [$_S$ [Mary] [$100]], and [$_S$ [Ted] [$75]]. (McCawley 1998: 62)
    b. [$_S$ [John] managed to find time to start writing [a novel]], and [$_S$ [Mary] [a movie script]]. (McCawley 1998: 63)

c. [$_S$ [On Tuesday], Lucy practices [the piano]], and [$_S$ [on Wednesday] [the clarinet]]. (McCawley 1998: 63)
d. (?)I wonder which student for three years has been learning Japanese and for two years Chinese.
d'. I wonder which student [$_S$ [for three years] [$_S$ NP[G] has been learning [Japanese]]] and [$_S$ [for two years] [Chinese]]?

(5d) is a barely acceptable gapping. This shows that the string *for three years has been learning Japanese* in the first conjunct is an S. Its constituent structure must be (5d'), in which *which student* must be outside the coordinated S and each conjunct S must have had the structure [$_S$ PP S] before the application of gapping (cf. (5c)). The third way to show the constituent structure of matrix subject *wh*-question (6a) concerns coordination.

(6) a. [$_{CP[WH[Q]]}$ NP[WH[Q]] [$_{S[FIN]}$ NP[G] VP[FIN]]]]
  b. I wonder who [$_{VP[PAST]}$ borrowed *Hamlet* in the morning] and [$_{VP[PAST]}$ returned it in the afternoon].
  c. I wonder who borrowed *Hamlet* in the morning and Mary said returned it in the afternoon.
  d. I wonder who [$_{S[PAST]}$ NP[G] borrowed *Hamlet* in the morning] and [$_{S[PAST]}$ Mary said NP[G] returned it in the afternoon].
  e. I wonder which book appeared last year and Smith reviewed for the *Post*. (cf. 6.1.11 (4c))

(6b) is an instance of VP-coordination. (6c) is an instance of S-coordination, because its second conjunct is an S[PAST], whose constituent structure must be (6d). This shows that the first conjunct must have the structure [$_{S[FIN]}$ NP[G] VP[FIN]], in which there must be a subject gap. (6e) is a similar example.

6.1.2 ATB "*wh*-movement"

When a *wh*-question contains a coordinate structure somewhere in its dominance path, "*wh*-movement" must take place from all the conjuncts; that is, a gap XP[G] must appear in all the conjuncts, as in (1) below. Otherwise, there will be a violation of the Coordinate Structure Constraint (CSC), which says in transformational terms that "a transformation can apply to a coordinate structure if and only if it has the same effect on all the conjuncts" (McCawley 1998: 270). For example, if a phrase is "extracted" from one of the conjuncts, it must be "extracted" from all the other conjuncts (across-the-board (ATB) rule application). In (1a), two S[BSE] nodes are coordinated and each S[BSE] conjunct contains an NP gap (NP[G]). In its F/A, two PROP nodes that contain the variable x are coordinated. In (1b), two VP[BSE] nodes are coordinated and each VP[BSE] conjunct contains an NP[G]. In its F/A, two Fa nodes that contain x are coordinated.

(1) a. Which theory did [Tom attack __] and [then Jane defend __]? (McCawley 1998: 268)
$[_{QPx} [_Q$ WH] x = THEORY] PAST $[_{PROP} [_{PROP}$ TOM ATTACK x] AND $[_{PROP}$ JANE DEFEND x]]
b. What did Susan tell you that Roger had ordered me to [take __ out of the box] and [put __ in the vase]? (McCawley 1998: 493)
$[_{QPx} [_Q$ WH] x = THING] PAST $[_{PROP}$ SUSAN TELL YOU $[_{PROP}$ PAST PAST $[_{PROP}$ ROGER ORDER ME $[_{PROP}$ RHO $[_{Fa} [_{Fa}$ TAKE.OUT.OF.BOX x] AND $[_{Fa}$ PUT.IN.VASE x]]]]]]

If "wh-movement" is only applied to some of the conjuncts, such sentences violate the CSC and are ungrammatical, for example, *Which theory did [Tom attack __] and [then Jane defend the standard theory]? or *Which theory did [Tom attack the standard theory] and [then Jane defend __]?). See 6.1.3 (14) for an account of obligatory ATB extractions by means of the dominance path conditions.

6.1.3 Unbounded dependency and islands

Wh-questions exhibit unbounded dependency; that is, however deeply the bottom gap XP[G] may be embedded, it can be associated with the clause-initial topmost wh-phrase XP[WH[Q]]. This is shown in (1).

(1) Borsley 1999: 188–189
a. Who $[_{S[INV]}$ did $[_{S[BSE]}$ Hobbs see __]]?
dominance path: CP[WH[Q]] S[INV] S[BSE] VP[BSE] NP[G]
b. Who $[_{S[INV]}$ do $[_{S[BSE]}$ you think $[_{S[PAST]}$ Hobbs saw __]]]?
dominance path: CP[WH[Q]] S[INV] S[BSE] VP[BSE] S[PAST] VP[PAST] NP[G]
c. Who $[_{S[INV]}$ do $[_{S[BSE]}$ you think $[_{S[PAST]}$ Hobbs said $[_{S[PAST]}$ he saw __]]]]?

dominance path: CP[WH[Q]] S[INV] S[BSE] VP[BSE] S[PAST]
VP[PAST] S[PAST] VP[PAST] NP[G]
d. Who [_{S[INV]} do [_{S[BSE]} you think [_{S[PAST]} Hobbs said [_{S[PAST]} he imagined [_{S[PAST]} he saw __]]]]]?
dominance path: CP[WH[Q]] S[INV] S[BSE] VP[BSE] S[PAST]
VP[PAST] S[PAST] VP[PAST] S[PAST] VP[PAST] NP[G]

The syntactic structure of every *wh*-question comes with its dominance path from the top CP[WH[Q]] to the bottom XP[G]. We can think of a *wh*-question dominance path as consisting of three parts: the top, the middle, and the bottom (cf. Gazdar et al. 1985: 138; Pollard and Sag 1994: 160). The top is always CP[WH[Q]] and the bottom is always XP[G]. Capturing the unbounded dependency in *wh*-questions boils down to how we can specify the infinite set of the middle parts of licit dominance paths. We do this by borrowing from LFG a similar idea called outside-in functional uncertainty (Kaplan and Zaenan 1995, Kaplan and Maxwell 1995, Bresnan 2001: 64, Ueno 1994: 435ff, and Dalrymple 2001: 139) and using the Kleene star operator * on the set of syntactic categories that allow "*wh*-movement" out of them. The dominance path conditions (2a, b, c) will eventually be encoded as part of the lexical entry for a clause-initial *wh*-phrase XP[WH[Q]] (6.1.7 (1)).

(2) the dominance path conditions for XP[WH[Q]]
  a. nonsubject gap:
     CP[WH[Q]] {S, VP, CP[{*that* | *for*}]}* VP {NP, N', PP}* XP[G]
  b. embedded subject gap:
     CP[WH[Q]] {S, VP, CP[{*that* | *for*}]}* VP S NP[G]
  c. matrix subject gap:
     CP[WH[Q]] S[FIN] NP[G]

For example, {S, VP, CP[{*that* | *for*}]}* in (2a, b) is to be interpreted as the set of dominance paths consisting of any number (including 0) of S, VP, CP[*for*], and CP[*that*] in any order. (Their correct order in each *wh*-question is determined independently in syntax by the relevant PS rules and lexical entries.) The dominance path condition (2b) says that a licit *wh*-question dominance path must be a member of the set that starts with its top CP[WH[Q]] and ends with VP S NP[G] and in between there can be any number (including 0) of S, VP, CP[*for*], and CP[*that*] in any order. {NP, N', PP}* in (2a) is interpreted in the same way. Note that the middle part {NP, N', PP}* in (2a) is very limited in *wh*-questions (3a-c), whereas this part is very robust in *wh*-relative clauses (3d).

(3) a. *Who did you hear stories about a picture of __ ? (Chomsky 1977: 105)
   b. ?Which actress did you read an article about a sensational picture of __ ?
   c. (?)Which framework did you receive request for an introductory article about __ ?
   d. Reports which the government prescribes the height of the lettering on the covers of __ are invariably boring. (Ross 1967/1986: 121)

The dominance path conditions (2a, b) account for many well-known islands. (4a) is an example in which the Complex NP Constraint (CNPC) is violated. The CNPC says in derivational terms that "derivational steps in which material is extracted from the S of a complex NP (an NP consisting of a noun and a relative clause or a complement clause) are excluded" (McCawley 1998: 523). That is, extraction out of a relative clause or a noun complement clause is impossible.

(4) a. Complex NP Constraint (CNPC)
   *What topics does Mary like to read books that are about?
   cf. What topics does Mary like to read books about?
   b. CP[WH[Q]] S[INV] S[BSE] VP[BSE] VP[*to*] VP[BSE] NP N' CP[*that*] S[FIN] VP[FIN] PP[*about*] NP[G]

The dominance path that accompanies (4a) is given in (4b). Every time the CNPC is violated in a *wh*-question, we find the offending sequence NP N' CP S as part of its dominance path. For example, if a *wh*-phrase is "extracted" out of a noun complement clause (e.g., [$_{NP}$ *the* [$_{N'}$ *fact* [$_{CP[that]}$ *that* [$_S$ ... XP[G] ...]]]]), its dominance path contains the sequence NP N' CP[*that*] S. Or if a *wh*-phrase is "extracted" out of a relative clause (e.g., [$_{NP}$ *the* [$_{N'}$ *man* [$_{CP[WH[R]]}$ *who* [$_S$ ... XP[G] ...]]]]), its dominance path contains the sequence NP N' CP[WH[R]] S. In either case, the dominance path contains the sequence NP N' CP S. The dominance path conditions (2a, b) exclude this sequence from the middle.

(5a) below is an example in which the *wh*-island is violated. A *wh*-island is a rather weak "constraint against extractions from any position in a Wh-complement" (McCawley 1998: 497). This is a weak constraint whose violation produces only a mild deviance, especially when the *wh*-word involved is a D-linked *which*. Every time *wh*-island is violated, we find an offending CP[WH[Q]] somewhere in the middle part of the dominance path, as in (5b). Again, the dominance path conditions (2a, b) exclude CP[WH[Q]] from the middle part.

(5) a. *Wh*-island
?Which books did you ask who had bought? (McCawley 1998: 497)
b. CP[WH[Q]] S[INV] S[BSE] VP[BSE] <u>CP[WH[Q]]</u> S[FIN] VP[FIN] VP[PSP] NP[G]

The reason why a *wh*-island violation produces only a mild deviance is that although *wh*-island violates the syntactic dominance path conditions (2), it does not violate the F/A dominance path condition. (See 6.1.4.)

(6a) below is an example in which the Subject Condition (SC) is violated. The SC says that extracting a constituent out of a subject is impossible. Every time the Subject Condition is violated, we find the offending sequence S NP in the middle part of the dominance path, as in (6ai, ii). Again, (2a, b) exclude this sequence from the middle part.

(6) a. Subject Condition (SC)
  i. *Who did [my talking to __] bother Hilary? (Pollard and Sag 1994: 188)
     CP[WH[Q]] S[INV, PAST] <u>S[BSE] NP</u> VP[PRP] PP[*to*] NP[G]
  ii. *Which Marx brother did she say [a biography of __] will appear this year?
     (Lasnik and Park 2003: 650)
     CP[WH[Q]] S[INV, PAST] S[BSE] VP[BSE] <u>S[PRES] NP</u> N' PP[*of*] NP[G]
  b. Sentential Subject Constraint (SSC)
   i. *Who does [that I voted for __] disturb you? (Culicover 2009: 347)
   ii. *Who would [for me to vote for __] be appalling? (ibid.)
   iii. *Tell me who [that I voted for __] disturbs you.
      CP[WH[Q]] <u>S[PRES] CP[*that*]</u> S[PAST] VP[PAST] PP[*for*] NP[G]
   iv. ??Tell me who [for me to vote for __] would be appalling to you.
   v. (?)Speaking of syntactic theories, I wonder which theory for me to try to understand would be a waste of time.
   vi. This is something which for you to try to understand would be futile.
      (Kuno and Takami 1993: 49)

A special case of the SC is the Sentential Subject Constraint (SSC), which says that extraction out of a sentential subject is impossible (6b). However, (6bi, ii) do not really show the effect of this constraint, because they have a clausal subject (indicated by brackets) in their embedded nonfinite clauses (*[$_{S[BSE]}$ CP

VP[BSE]]), which is excluded by 2.5 (2a, b), independently of "*wh*-movement" out of a clausal subject. Therefore, we need to look at indirect *wh*-questions, which lack interrogative inversion (6biii, iv). In this case, "*wh*-movement" out of a CP[*for*] subject is slightly better than that out of a CP[*that*] subject. Kuno and Takami pointed out a perfect example (6bvi) with a relative clause. (6bv) is a *wh*-question that violates the SSC and is similar to their relative clause example. The dominance paths of the examples in (6b) are admitted by the dominance path condition (2a), which we claim is a correct prediction in view of such examples as (6bv, vi). This means that we need to seek a different way of excluding (6biii). One relevant factor seems to be that when a *wh*-word is immediately followed by a CP[*that*] with a gap, as in *who* [*that I voted for* ___], it is interpretable as an interrogative pronoun modified by a *that*-relative clause, as in *Who that you know would make a good candidate?* (McCawley 1998: 436). In fact, (6biii) can be interpreted as "Tell me who disturbs you among those I voted for," in which the CP[*that*] is interpreted as a *that*-relative clause modifying the interrogative pronoun *who*. Note that because the domain necessary for choosing the relative clause interpretation (i.e., *who* [*that I voted for*]) in (6biii) is properly contained in the domain necessary for choosing the *wh*-question interpretation (i.e., *Tell me who* [[*that I voted for*] *disturbs you*]), it is plausible to think that the former interpretation preempts the latter interpretation, making the latter virtually unavailable, due to an extended interpretation of the Elsewhere Principle (1.1.2 (3)).

(7a) is an example of the *that*-trace effect, which shows the subject NP immediately following the complementizer *that* cannot be "extracted," which is a special case of the Fixed Subject Condition (6.1.1 (3)). The *that*-trace effect appears when the last part of the dominance path is CP[*that*] S[FIN] NP[G]. Again, none of the conditions in (2) allows this offending sequence. On the other hand, if there is no complementizer next to the subject extraction site, the sentence is grammatical, as in (7b), whose dominance path is correctly admitted by (2b).

(7) a. the *that*-trace effect
 *Who do you think that ___ admires Mary?
 CP[WH[Q]] S[INV, PRES] S[BSE] VP[BSE] <u>CP[*that*] S[PRES] NP[G]</u>
 b. Who do you think ___ admires Mary?
 CP[WH[Q]] S[INV, PRES] S[BSE] VP[BSE] S[PRES] NP[G]
 c. Who did you tell me ___ was your perfect man? (web)
 CP[WH[Q]] S[INV, PAST] S[BSE] VP[BSE] S[PAST] NP[G]

However, it has been well known since Bresnan (1977) that this effect is suspended or at least greatly reduced when an S-adjunct (i.e., a sentence-modifying PP or adverb phrase) appears between the C[*that*] and the following extraction site NP[G] (8a, b). (8a') shows that an S-final S-adjunct does not suspend the effect. (8b') shows an ad-VP does not suspend the effect.

(8) suspension of the "*that*-trace effect"
    a. ?Which doctor did you tell me that [$_{S[PAST]}$ [$_{PP}$ during an operation] [$_{S[PAST]}$ __ had had a heart attack]]? (Bresnan 1977: 194 note 6)
        CP[WH[Q]] S[INV, PAST] S[BSE] VP[BSE] CP[*that*] S[PAST] S[PAST] NP[G]
    a'. *Which doctor did you tell me that [$_{S[PAST]}$ [$_{S[PAST]}$ __ had had a heart attack] [$_{PP}$ during an operation]]?
        CP[WH[Q]] S[INV, PAST] S[BSE] VP[BSE] CP[*that*] S[PAST] S[PAST] NP[G]
    b. Who did you say that most recently __ called? (Culicover 2009: 368)
    b'. *Who did you say that most angrily called?
    c. Which doctor did you say that [$_{S[PAST]}$ [$_{ADVP}$ unfortunately] [$_{S[PAST]}$ [$_{PP}$ during an operation] [$_{S[PAST]}$ __ had had a heart attack]]]?

As a first attempt, we can tentatively add to (2b) a subsidiary dominance path condition with an ordering requirement (9), to deal with this adverb-effect.

(9) CP[WH[Q]] {S, VP, CP[*that*]}* VP CP[*that*] S S NP[G]
    C[*that*] ⩽ {PP | ADVP} ⩽ NP[G]

(9) specifically mentions the sequence S S, an S-adjunction structure, and the ordering requirement says that an S-adjunct must come between the complementizer C[*that*] and the subject gap NP[G]. We can combine (2b) and (9), arriving at (10). Note that the ordering requirement in (10) is effective only when the option of CP[*that*] S is taken. Recall that A ⩽ B means A immediately precedes B.

(10) dominance path condition for an embedded subject gap (revised version of (2b))
    CP[WH[Q]] {S, VP, CP[*that*]}* VP (CP[*that*] S) S NP[G]
    C[*that*] ⩽ {PP | ADVP} ⩽ NP[G]

The problem with (10) is that it only allows a single S-adjunction structure. However, there can be two or more S-adjuncts that suspend the adverb effect, as in (8c). To avoid this problem, we take the other option, namely, the option of replacing (2b) with a simpler dominance path condition (11a), which allows iterative S-adjunctions, and at the same time, registering the lexical entry (11b), which says that if the complementizer *that* and the subject gap are linearly adjacent, the CP[*that*] must be interpreted as a relative clause ([$_{Ma}$ PROP] in F/A).

(11) a. embedded subject gap: CP[WH[Q]] {S, VP, CP[{*that* | *for*}]}* S NP[G]
   b. lexical entry for *that*-relative clause with a subject gap (special case)
      syntax: CP[*that*], where C[*that*] ⩽ NP[G]
      F/A: [$_{Ma}$ PROP]

Every time we encounter the syntactic structures [$_{CP[that]}$ C[*that*] [$_{S[FIN]}$ NP[G] VP[FIN]]] or [$_{CP[that]}$ C[*that*] [$_{S[FIN]}$ [$_{S[FIN]}$ NP[G] VP[FIN]] S-adjunct]], the interpretation of the CP[*that*] as a relative clause overrides its interpretation as part of a *wh*-question dominance path, due to an extended interpretation of the Elsewhere Principle (1.1.2 (3)), because (11b) mentions only a single node CP[*that*] in syntax, and therefore, it is more local than a *wh*-question dominance path from CP[WH[Q]] to NP[G] through a CP[*that*]. On the other hand, when we encounter the syntactic structure [$_{CP[that]}$ C[*that*] [$_{S[FIN]}$ S-adjunct [$_{S[FIN]}$ NP[G] VP[FIN]]]], the lexical entry (11b) is irrelevant and this dominance path is admitted by (11a).

(12a, b) below are examples in which the Left Branch Constraint (LBC) is violated. The LBC says that "extraction of or from the X of an [X Y] constituent" is impossible (McCawley 1998: 526), which covers the cases where the left branch of an NP, namely, DET and NP[POS], cannot be extracted.

(12) Left Branch Constraint (LBC)
   a. *Which do you like [__ picture of Mary] best?
      CP[WH[Q]] S[INV, PRES] S[BSE] VP[BSE] NP DET[G]
   b. *Whose did you read [__ article on the accident]?
      CP[WH[Q]] S[INV, PAST] S[BSE] VP[BSE] NP NP[POS, G]
   c. *Leslie's, we liked __ book. (Gazdar et al. 1985: 148)
   d. *Kim's, I read a book of __. (ibid.)
   e. *Whose is this a picture of __? (Sadock 2012: 157)

As for (12a) with a determiner gap at the bottom, because the bottom of the dominance path conditions is XP[G] in (2a) and NP[G] in (2b, c), a determiner gap DET[G] is correctly excluded. As for (12b) with a possessive NP gap (NP[POS, G]), we interpret the bottom XP[G] in (2a) as nonpossessive, when XP is an NP. This interpretation of NP[G] as nonpossessive excludes the illicit bottom NP[POS]. We will treat the POS feature as a unary feature, and hence we will use NP[POS] to refer to a possessive NP and NP to refer to a nonpossessive NP. Note that a possessive NP (NP[POS]) resists extraction, whether it is pre-nominal (12c) or post-nominal (12d, e). By interpreting XP[G] in (2a) as nonpossessive, we can correctly exclude both cases.

A digression on the DP analysis. Lasnik and Uriagereka (2005: 6, 28–29 note 4) claimed about the LBC that *whose*, or for that matter, any possessive NP, cannot be moved because, according to the DP analysis, *who* or any other DP in the specifier position of a DP and the head of the DP (possessive clitic *'s*) do not form a syntactic constituent (13a).

(13) a. [$_{DP}$ [$_{DP}$ who] [$_{D'}$ [$_D$'s] NP]]
b. [$_{NP}$ DET [$_{N'}$ N' [$_{PP[of]}$ of NP's]]]
c. [$_{PP}$ of [$_{DP}$ NP [$_{D'}$ [$_D$'s] [$_{NP}$ ø]]]]
d. [$_{DP}$ [$_D$ which] [$_{NP}$ ø]]
e. [$_{DP}$ who [$_{D'}$ [$_D$'s] [$_{NP}$ ø]]]

However, this explanation does not extend to the ban on the preposing of a post-nominal possessive NP in the configuration (13b), which was illustrated in (12d, e). Rather, the DP analysis wrongly predicts that this preposing is possible, because the possessive NP used as the complement of the preposition *of* would have the structure (13c), where the D's complement NP is phonologically empty. So the whole DP, namely, *Kim's* in (12d) or *whose* in (12e) should be able to move, just as *which* in *Which do you like __?* or *whose* in *(Speaking of novels) whose do you like __?*, where *which* and *whose* are DPs with a phonologically null NP as their complement (13d, e).

As the last example of islands, we would like to reconsider the Coordinate Structure Constraint (CSC), which we discussed briefly in 6.1.2. Cases of CSC violation (i.e., cases of non-ATB extraction from a coordinate structure) can be looked at from the perspective of the dominance path conditions. When a coordinate structure appears in the middle of the dominance path, the path diverges at the mother node of the coordinate structure. We adopt the convention that the sequence of the mother node and each of its conjunct daughter nodes of a coordinate structure (shown by rectangles and circles in (14a)) counts as a single node for the purposes of the dominance path conditions. This convention is independently

270   6 UNBOUNDED DEPENDENCY

required for the adjacency requirement in inverted clauses (2.1 (3a, b)), nonrestrictive relative clauses (6.2.4 (4)), and bare relative clauses (6.2.5 (7)). This convention forces the dominance path to diverge at coordinate structures. (If the dominance path did not diverge at a coordinate structure in the middle part of the dominance path, it could not end there, because the single node consisting of the mother and its conjunct daughter node would still be in the middle part and the dominance path would be ill formed.)

(14) a. the dominance paths of 6.1.2 (1a) *Which theory did Tom attack and then Jane defend?*
first conjunct: CP[WH[Q]] S[INV] $\boxed{\text{S[BSE] S[BSE]}}$ VP[BSE] NP[G]
second conjunct: CP[WH[Q]] S[INV] $\boxed{\text{S[BSE] S[BSE]}}$ S[BSE] VP[BSE] NP[G]

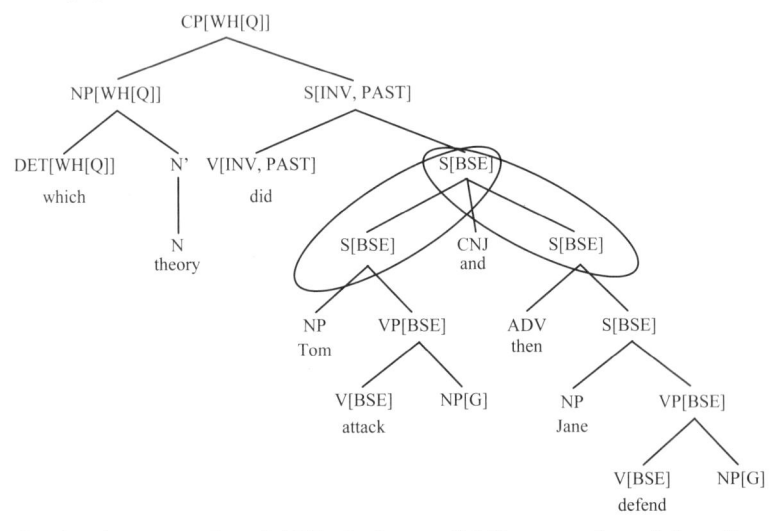

b. the dominance paths of *Which theory did Tom attack and then Jane defend the standard theory?*
first conjunct: CP[WH[Q]] S[INV] $\boxed{\text{S[BSE] S[BSE]}}$ VP[BSE] NP[G]
second conjunct: *CP[WH[Q]] S[INV] $\boxed{\text{S[BSE] S[BSE]}}$ S[BSE] VP[BSE] NP

When a coordinate structure appears in the middle of a dominance path, the dominance path conditions are applied to each branch on the basis of the convention proposed above. This forces the ATB "*wh*-movement." For example, in (14b), the dominance path of the second conjunct is ill formed because the path ends with NP, not NP[G].

The dominance path conditions (2) are a *positive* specification of infinite licit "*wh*-movement" paths. This is quite different from *negative* specifications of islands, which, in essence, list illicit paths of "*wh*-movement" (i.e., syntactic environments out of which "*wh*-movement" is impossible). What children learn from their primary data is not a list of islands per se but the positive specification of licit "*wh*-movement" paths (i.e., environments where "*wh*-movement" is *possible*) (cf. Culicover and Jackendoff 2005: 333). The islands that happen to have been discovered so far in the history of Generative Grammar since Ross 1967 are only a proper subset, a very small subset, in fact, of the complement set of licit dominance paths. That is, the following relations hold.

(15) {islands discovered so far} ⊂ {all dominance paths licit or illicit} − {dominance paths captured by the dominance path conditions}

In the above, the notation A−B refers to the complement of the set B with respect to the set A: A−B = {x∈A | x∉B}. In a sense, islands are side effects of illicit "*wh*-movement" dominance paths. Children do not need to learn those dominance paths that are excluded from the dominance path conditions (2).

The core part that characterizes unbounded dependency in the dominance path conditions (2) is {S, VP, CP[{*that* | *for*}]}*. Let us call this set U. Children need to learn U by finding what syntactic categories are the generators of U. For the sake of argument, let us assume that children learn that a syntactic category X is a generator of U if and only if they are exposed to *wh*-questions in which X appears at least twice in the middle part of the dominance path. If so, the set U can be learned from a very simple set of data. For example, a simple, short-distance *wh*-question such as (16a) contains in its dominance path two occurrences of S, namely, S[PAST] and S[BSE], and shows children that S is a generator of U. A *wh*-question such as (16b) contains in its dominance path two occurrences of VP, namely, VP[PRES] and VP[PSP], and tells children that VP is a generator of U. A *wh*-question such as (16c) is enough for children to learn that CP[*that*] is a generator of U. Such an example as (16d) is sufficient to learn that both S and VP are generators of U.

(16) a. What did you eat?

What [$_{S[PAST, INV]}$ did [$_{S[BSE]}$ you [$_{VP[BSE]}$ eat NP[G]]]]?

b. I don't know what you have eaten.
I don't know what [$_{S[PRES]}$ you [$_{VP[PRES]}$ have [$_{VP[PSP]}$ eaten NP[G]]]].
c. What did you say that Mary told you that John ate?
What [$_{S[PAST, INV]}$ did [$_{S[BSE]}$ you [$_{VP[BSE]}$ say [$_{CP[that]}$ that [$_{S[PAST]}$ Mary [$_{VP[PAST]}$ told you [$_{CP[that]}$ that [$_{S[PAST]}$ John [$_{VP[PAST]}$ ate NP[G]]]]]]]]]?
d. What did you say John ate?
What [$_{S[PAST, INV]}$ did [$_{S[BSE]}$ you [$_{VP[BSE]}$ say [$_{S[PAST]}$ John [$_{VP[PAST]}$ ate NP[G]]]]]]?

Furthermore, there seem to be clear implication relations between the generators of U: if CP[*that*] is a generator of U, so is S, and if S is a generator of U, so is VP.

In Mainstream Generative Grammar (MGG), it has been claimed for a long time that "*wh*-movement" is "successive cyclic" (COMP to COMP or from [SPEC, CP] to [SPEC, CP]), rather than "in one fell swoop" from the gap position to the clause-initial position crossing intermediate clauses. In AMG, along with other non-MGG theories including McCawley (1998: 498, 518 note 4; 1999: 48), "*wh*-movement" is "in one fell swoop" in the sense that, according to our current formulation of unbounded dependency, the dominance relations between the clause-initial *wh*-phrase XP[WH[Q]] and the bottom gap XP[G] are established all at once in the syntactic structure of a *wh*-question but simply checked by the dominance path conditions (2), or, according to Sadock's (2012: 123–124) view of "*wh*-movement," there is a modular mismatch between syntax, in which the *wh*-phrase is *in situ*, and the linear order component, in which there is a special linear order statement (namely, Sadock 2012: 122 (27)) that places the *wh*-phrase at the clause-initial position.

Evidence adduced in the MGG literature to support the successive cyclicity of "*wh*-movement" (Boeckx 2008: 12ff.) can be viewed from our perspective as the well-formedness conditions on the middle part ({S, CP[{*that* | *for*}], VP}*) of the dominance path conditions. The first evidence is iterative inversion. Some languages allow inversion (S[INV]) in embedded clauses when "*wh*-movement" is applied.

(17) a. French stylistic inversion (Boeckx 2008: 13)
Où crois-tu qu'est allé Jean?
"Where do you believe that Jean went?'
dominance path = CP[WH[Q]] S[INV] (VP) CP[que] S[INV] S[PSP] VP[PSP] ADVP[GAP]
b. Belfast English (Boeckx 2008: 13)
Who did John say did Mary claim had John feared would Bill attack?

dominance path = CP[WH[Q]] S[INV] S[BSE] VP[BSE] S[INV]
S[BSE] VP[BSE] S[INV] S[PSP] VP[PSP] S[INV] S[BSE] VP[BSE]
NP[GAP]
c. the dominance path condition for a nonsubject gap in Belfast English
CP[WH[Q]] {S[INV], S[–FIN], VP}* VP XP[G]

In these languages, the middle part of the dominance path conditions contains S[INV] instead of S[FIN] and/or CP[*that*]. The middle part for French is {CP[*que*], S[INV], S[–FIN], VP}* and the middle part for Belfast English is {S[INV], S[–FIN], VP}*. Similar data in Spanish and Basque can be dealt with in the same way. In these languages, S[INV] appears instead of S[FIN] and/or CP[*that*] in intermediate clauses when it is dominated by a CP[WH[Q]]. For example, the dominance path condition for a nonsubject gap in Belfast English looks like (17c).

The second evidence is concerned with agreement between the "moved" *wh*-phrase and the intermediate complementizers. In languages such as Irish, Kinande, and Chamorro, it has been observed that there is overt agreement between the *wh*-phrase and the intermediate complementizers, which has been interpreted as a morphological reflex of successive cyclicity of "*wh*-movement." For example, in Irish, the default complementizer is *goN* but when an embedded CP is dominated by a CP[WH[Q]] (i.e., in a *wh*-question) or dominated by a CP[WH[R]] (i.e., in a relative clause), its complementizer appears as *aL* (McCloskey 1979: 157). In these languages, the middle part of the dominance path condition (18b) contains CP[α], where α is an AGREEMENT (AGR) value that is equal to the AGR value on the *wh*-phrase NP[WH[Q], α] in (18a), in which the *wh*-phrase and its mother CP share not only the WH[Q] feature but also the same AGR value. This AGR value α is realized on the head C of CP[α] in (18c), due to the Head Feature Convention (HFC) (1.2 (3), (4)). Recall that AGR is a head feature (1.2 (4)).

(18) a. [$_{\text{CP[WH[Q], α]}}$ NP[WH[Q], α], S]
 b. dominance path condition: CP[WH[Q], α] {..., CP[α], ...}* ... NP[G]
 c. [$_{\text{CP[α]}}$ C[α], S] (by the HFC)

In the case of Irish, the relevant agreement feature α in (18) is, say, *wh* (covering both *wh*-questions and relative clauses), and we can say that the middle part of the dominance path conditions contains CP[*wh*], whose head C[*wh*] is realized as *aL*.

In this section, we proposed the dominance path conditions (2) (with slight modifications in (11)) to capture unbounded dependency between the *wh*-phrase and the gap in a *wh*-question, and considered how the various islands can be accounted for and how the alleged evidence for successive cyclicity of "*wh*-movement" can be interpreted in terms of these conditions.

Furthermore, what is interesting about these conditions is that they shed new light on parasitic gaps, and in particular, their licensing conditions. Because this issue is very complex and a full investigation would take us too far afield, we would like to briefly suggest our future research directions. Here are examples of parasitic gap (PG), which is labeled NP[PG] for descriptive purposes.

(19) Engdahl 1983: 5
   a. Which articles did John [$_{\text{VP[BSE]}}$ file NP[G] without reading NP[PG]]?
      dominance path: CP[WH[Q]] S[INV] S[BSE] $\boxed{\text{VP[BSE]}}$ VP[BSE] NP[G]
      parasitic dominance path: $\boxed{\text{VP[BSE]}}$ PP[*without*] VP[PRP] NP[PG]
   b. Which girl did you send a picture of NP[PG] to NP[G]?
      dominance path: CP[WH[Q]] S[INV] S[BSE] $\boxed{\text{VP[BSE]}}$ PP[*to*] NP[G]
      parasitic dominance path: $\boxed{\text{VP[BSE]}}$ NP N' PP[*of*] NP[PG]
   c. Which boy did Mary's talking to NP[PG] bother NP[G] most?
      dominance path: CP[WH[Q]] S[INV] $\boxed{\text{S[BSE]}}$ VP[BSE] VP[BSE] NP[G]
      parasitic dominance path: $\boxed{\text{S[BSE]}}$ NP VP[PRP] PP[*to*] NP[PG]

As is well known, parasitic gaps are allowed to appear in the constructions that exhibit unbounded dependency: "*wh*-movement," relative clauses, topicalization, and "*tough*-movement." In our current approach, these unbounded dependencies are all captured by the same dominance path conditions. Parasitic gaps are so called because they are parasitic on real gaps. In terms of the dominance path conditions, both real gaps and parasitic gaps have their own dominance paths. Real gaps must obey the dominance path conditions. The dominance path of a parasitic gap starts from the same top as the real gap and goes through the same middle part, and somewhere in the middle part branches into its own path. Therefore, parasitic gaps are dominated by one of the nodes of the middle part of the dominance path of a real gap. We would like to say that a parasitic gap is licensed by a parasitic dominance path condition that starts with one of the nodes of the middle part of the dominance path of a real gap. In each example in (19) above, the node enclosed by a rectangle is the one where the dominance path branches into two: the one leading to a real gap and the other leading to a parasitic gap.

Our future research must determine the parasitic dominance path conditions that licit parasitic gaps must meet.

6.1.4 F/A dominance path condition and role sharing

In the previous section, we proposed the dominance path conditions (6.1.3 (2) with slight modifications in (11)), which are stated in syntactic terms. Every *wh*-question has its dominance path in its syntactic structure from its top CP[WH[Q]] to its bottom gap XP[G]. At the same time, the *wh*-phrase of a *wh*-question is represented as a QP in its F/A structure, which contains another dominance path in F/A terms: from the top PROP to the bottom variable [$_{ARG}$ x]. The dominance relations along this path are captured by the F/A dominance path condition (1). This is needed anyway, because the syntactic dominance path conditions do not distinguish between extractions from a complement (e.g., an extraction from a complement VP) and those from an adjunct (e.g., an extraction from an adjunct VP). The relevant distinction can be made by the dominance path condition stated in F/A terms.

(1) F/A dominance path condition
    PROP {PROP, Fa, Faa, Fpa}* {ARG, POS}* [$_{ARG}$ x]

Note that the middle part {ARG, POS}* is very limited in *wh*-questions (6.1.3 (3)). Here are three examples: (2), (3), and (4).

(2) What did Susan tell you that Roger had ordered me to put in the vase? (=6.1 (1a))
    syntactic dominance path: CP[WH[Q]] S[INV] S[BSE] VP[BSE] CP[*that*] S[PAST] VP[PAST] VP[PSP] VP[*to*] VP[BSE] NP[G]
    F/A dominance path: PROP PROP PROP Fa Faa PROP PROP PROP Fa Faa PROP Fa [$_{ARG}$ x]

In (2) above, its syntactic dominance path is licensed by 6.1.3 (2a), and its F/A dominance path by (1) above. In (3a) below, the PP[*during*] is adjoined to the VP headed by *born* and its F/A category is MFa (a modifier of Fa). The syntactic dominance path is licensed by 6.1.3 (2a), but the F/A dominance path violates (1). This is why the acceptability of (3a) is slightly lower than (3b), in which MFa does not appear in its F/A dominance path and hence (1) is satisfied.

(3) a. (?)Which pope was Copernicus born during the reign of? (McCawley 1998: 499)
syntactic dominance path: CP[WH[Q]] S[INV] S[PAS] VP[PAS] PP[*during*] NP N' PP[*of*] NP[G]
F/A dominance path: PROP PROP PROP Fa <u>MFa</u> ARG [$_{ARG}$ x]
b. Which star was Copernicus interested in the movement of?
syntactic dominance path: CP[WH[Q]] S[INV] AS AP PP[*in*] NP N' PP[*of*] NP[G]
F/A dominance path: PROP PROP PROP Fa ARG [$_{ARG}$ x]

(4) a. (?) Which Greek authors does he have books by? (Ross 1986: 123)
Syntactic dominance path: CP[WH[Q]] S[INV] S[BSE] VP[BSE] NP N' PP[*by*] NP[G]
F/A dominance path: PROP PROP PROP Fa ARG <u>Ma</u> [$_{ARG}$ x]
b. Which Greek philosophers does he have pictures of?
Syntactic dominance path: CP[WH[Q]] S[INV] S[BSE] VP[BSE] NP N' PP[*of*] NP[G]
F/A dominance path: PROP PROP PROP Fa ARG [$_{ARG}$ x]

In (4a) above, the PP[*by*] is an N'-adjunct and its F/A category is Ma (a modifier of ARG). (4a) is slightly less acceptable than (4b), in which the PP[*of*] is a complement.

These two kinds of dominance path conditions make slightly different predictions. Let us look at two types of island: *wh*-island and the Complex NP Constraint that we discussed in the previous section. We pointed out that *wh*-island is a weak constraint. Here is the example we looked at, 6.1.3 (5), repeated here as (5).

(5) ?Which books did you ask who had bought?
syntactic dominance path: CP[WH[Q]] S[INV] S[BSE] VP[BSE] <u>CP[WH[Q]]</u> S[FIN] VP[FIN] VP[PSP] NP[G]
F/A dominance path: PROP PROP PROP Fa PROP PROP PROP PROP Fa [$_{ARG}$ x]

The F/A dominance path in (5) satisfies (1), but the syntactic dominance path does not satisfy 6.1.3 (2a). (The offending part is underlined in (5)). We claim that an impeccable *wh*-question satisfies both the syntactic and F/A dominance path conditions, and that an unacceptable *wh*-question violates both kinds of dominance path conditions. In the case of *wh*-island violation, only the syntactic dominance path condition is violated and the F/A dominance path condition is satisfied. This is why the effect of a *wh*-island violation is weak.

As for the Complex Noun Phrase Constraint (CNPC), which we discussed in 6.1.3 (4), there are two types of complex NP, an N with a complement CP[*that*] and an N' with a relative clause. In either case, the syntactic dominance path contains the offending sequence NP N' CP S. As for the F/A dominance path condition, an extraction out of a relative clause would contain an offending middle sequence ARG Ma PROP, whereas an extraction out of a noun complement clause would contain an offending middle sequence ARG PROP.

(6) a. complex NP (the case of relative clauses) (RRC = restrictive relative clause)

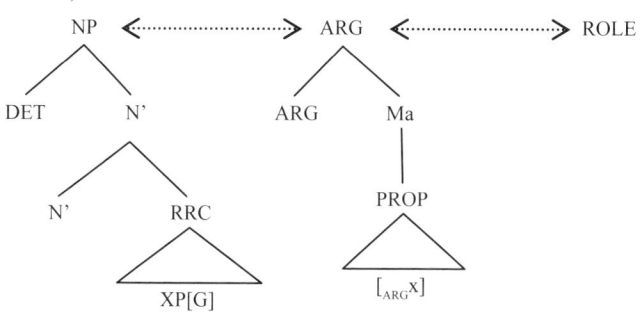

b. complex NP (the case of noun complement clauses)

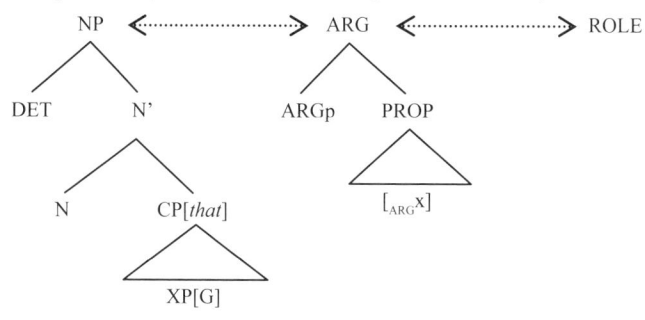

Therefore, a "*wh*-movement" out of a complex NP, whether it is a relative clause case or a noun complement case, violates both the syntactic dominance path conditions (6.1.3 (2a, b)) and the F/A dominance path condition (1), hence resulting in complete unacceptability.

However, there are notable cases of innocuous CNPC violation that involve the light verb (LV) construction, what Ross (1967/1986: 88) called modal construction following Modal Transformation proposed by Harris (1957). This is illustrated in (7).

(7) McCawley 1998: 525
   a. What company does Mike <u>hold the absurd belief that</u> he can get a job with?
      cf. What company does Mike absurdly believe that he can get a job with?
   b. the senator that Jack Anderson <u>made the claim that</u> the Mafia wanted to rub out
      cf. the senator that Jack Anderson claimed that the Mafia wanted to rub out
   c. The CIA, I <u>give</u> you <u>my assurance that</u> I would never accept a penny from.
      cf. The CIA, I assure you that I would never accept a penny from.

Other examples of the LV construction that take a CP[*that*] complement are *have a dream* CP[*that*] (Sadock 2012: 142), *have hopes/a feeling* CP[*that*], *make a proposal* CP[*that*] (Ross 1967/1986: 85). Following McCawley (1998: 526) and Sadock (2012: 145), we claim that the LV construction with a CP[*that*] complement constitutes a complex NP in syntax but not in F/A. More specifically, in the LV construction, the syntactic complex consisting of LV + determiner + head N + complement CP[*that*] corresponds to the F/A complex of functor + PROP. This means that there is a violation of the syntactic dominance path conditions but no violation of the F/A dominance path in such LV examples.

We implement this idea by means of role sharing in RS (Ueno 1994: 460–461), which triggers mono-clausalization in RS and, as a result, in F/A too. When the head verb in a transitive VP is an LV (*have, take, make, give, put* etc.) and the head noun of its object NP has its own set of participant roles, the LV construction requires that the highest role AG of the LV and that of the head noun be shared (i.e., unified or identified), leading to such single-layered event structures as (8) and (9).

(8) *have* (LV)   *try at*   →   *have a try at*
   [$_{EV}$ "have" AG PT]   [$_{EV}$ "try" AG PT]   [$_{EV}$ "have" AG [$_{PT}$ [$_{EV}$ "try" AG PT]]]

   the resultant RS after role sharing   [$_{EV}$ "have a try at" AG PT]

(9) *make* (LV)   *claim* CP[*that*] →   *make the claim* CP[*that*]
   [$_{EV}$ "make" AG PT]   [$_{EV}$ "claim" AG [$_{PT}$ EV]]   [$_{EV}$ "make" AG [$_{PT}$ [$_{EV}$ "claim" AG [$_{PT}$ EV]]]]

   the resultant RS after role sharing   [$_{EV}$ "make the claim" AG [$_{PT}$ EV]]

More generally, the LV construction requires that the common roles be shared between the LV and the head noun (cf. Complex Predicate Rule in Jackendoff 1974: 490, 493).

(10) *give* (LV)   *assurance* CP[*that*]
   [$_{EV}$ "give" [AG, SO] [PT, GO], TH]   [$_{EV}$ "assurance" [AG, SO] GO [$_{TH}$ EV]]

   →   *give one's assurance* CP[*that*]
     [$_{EV}$ "give" [AG, SO] [PT, GO], [$_{TH}$ [$_{EV}$ "assurance" [AG, SO] GO [$_{TH}$ EV]]]]

the resultant RS after role sharing [$_{EV}$ "give one's assurance" [AG, SO] [PT, GO] [$_{TH}$ EV]]

Strictly speaking, in (10), the [AG, SO] of the noun *assurance* is bound by the possessive determiner *one's*, which in turn is bound by the [AG, SO] of the LV *give*.

The sharing of two roles in the RS field of the LV construction is much stronger than the coreference requirement stated in the RS field (4.4 (4), (5)) of the lexical entry for a unique control verb. The former says that there is only one role that is shared by the LV and the head noun, thus resulting in a single-layered event structure, whereas the latter says that there are two distinct roles in RS that only covary in their INDEX feature values. Another way of looking at role sharing is that the event structure of the head noun overrides that of the LV and becomes the event structure of the whole LV construction. In other words, the LV provides a "syntactic skeleton onto which the syntactically deficient nominal can be grafted" in such a way as to "combine the readings" of the LV and the nominal "by superimposing parallel" roles (cf. Jackendoff 1974: 490, Culicover and Jackendoff 2005: 222–223). We are assuming here that each LV has its own set of participant roles and not that they lack participant roles. This is because there is a clear tendency that a particular noun co-occurs with a particular LV, more specifically, that a noun selects an LV that has a similar set of participant roles. For example, in (10), the noun *assurance* with [AG, SO], GO, and TH roles selects the LV *give* with [AG, SO], [PT, GO], and TH roles. The noun *blame* in *John's blame for the situation on Mary* takes [AG, SO] (blamer), GO (blamee), and TH (reason) roles and selects the LV *put*, which also takes [AG, SO], GO, and TH roles. In the LV construction *put* [$_{NP}$ *the blame for* NP] [$_{PP[on]}$ *on* NP], [AG, SO] and GO are shared between the LV *put* and the noun *blame*.

Recall that role sharing was needed to account for the passive *by*-phrase (3.3 (4)–(6)). Role sharing is also needed for the cognate object construction, such as *die a miserable death, live a happy life, smile a forced smile, laugh a hearty laugh*. For example, the patient role of the verb *die* (*John died*) and that of the noun *death* (*John's death*) are shared in the expression *die a miserable death*. Therefore, it expresses a single event with a single patient role.

We claim that the VP of the LV construction (as well as the cognate object construction), which results from role sharing, is registered in the lexicon (e.g., (11) and (12)), because children need to learn each LV construction one by one, including such properties as which noun goes with which LV and which determiner is used in the construction.

(11) lexical entry for the LV construction *make the claim* CP[*that*] (cf. (9))
syntax: [$_{VP}$ [$_V$ make] [$_{NP}$ the claim CP[*that*]]]
F/A: Fpa
RS: [$_{EV}$ [$_{TYPE}$ "make the claim"] AG [$_{PT}$ EV]] (after role sharing)

(12) lexical entry for the LV construction *give one's assurance* CP[*that*] (cf. (10))
syntax: [$_{VP}$ [$_V$ give] NP [$_{NP}$ [$_{DET}$ one's] assurance CP[*that*]]]
F/A: Fpaa
RS: [$_{EV\ TYPE}$ "give one's assurance"] [AG, SO] [PT, GO] [$_{TH}$ EV]] (after role sharing)

6.1.5 WH[Q] and preposition stranding

The WH[Q] feature is for interrogative *wh*-words and phrases and *wh*-questions, whereas the WH[R] feature is for relative *wh*-words and phrases and *wh*-relative clauses. Their distribution in syntax is different, which is shown in (1). Here, we ignore the interpretation of (1b) as an echo question or quiz question.

(1) Pollard and Sag 1994:159
 a. This is the farmer [$_{NP[WH[R]]}$ pictures of whom] appeared in *Newsweek*.
 b. *[$_{NP[WH[Q]]}$ Pictures of whom] appeared in *Newsweek*?

The WH[Q] feature is introduced into syntax by the lexical entry of an interrogative *wh*-word whose syntactic category is X[WH[Q]] (6.1.7 (6)–(9)). Metaphorically speaking, "*wh*-movement" must "move" the *wh*-phrase XP[WH[Q]] that is the highest node with a WH[Q] feature at D-structure (for example, *did you*

6.1 *WH*-QUESTIONS   281

like [~NP[WH[Q]]~ [~NP[WH[Q], POS]~ [~DET[WH[Q]]~ *which*] *student's*] *term paper*] *most?* being turned into (2i)), because all the categories except the top node CP[WH[Q]] in the dominance path conditions (6.1.3 (2)) lack WH[Q] (cf. (2a, b)). In (2) below, we restrict our attention to NP[WH[Q]] and PP[WH[Q]] for ease of description and observe how the WH[Q] feature percolates.

(2) a. [~NP[WH[Q]]~ [~DET[WH[Q]]~ Which] party] did John go to?
    dominance path: CP[WH[Q]] S[INV] S[BSE] VP[BSE] PP[*to*] NP[G]
  b. [~PP[*to*, WH[Q]]~ To [~NP[WH[Q]]~ [~DET[WH[Q]]~ which] party]] did John go?
    dominance path: CP[WH[Q]] S[INV] S[BSE] VP[BSE] PP[*to*, G]
  c. [Whose party] did John go to?
  d. [To whose party] did John go?
  e. [During which pope's reign] was Copernicus born? (McCawley 1998: 499)
  f. *[A picture of which cousin] did you put in the family album?
  g. [About what] does Mary read books?
  h. *[Books about what] does Mary read?
  i. [Which student's term paper] did you like most?
  j. [Which biographies of which poets] did the *Times* refuse to publish reviews of? (McCawley 1998: 518 note 5)

To account for the percolation of the WH[Q] feature in (1) and (2), we need to admit the local trees in (3) below, which license its percolation. These local trees are applied to the *wh*-phrase XP[WH[Q]] in a *wh*-question [~CP[WH[Q]]~ XP[WH[Q]] S[FIN]].

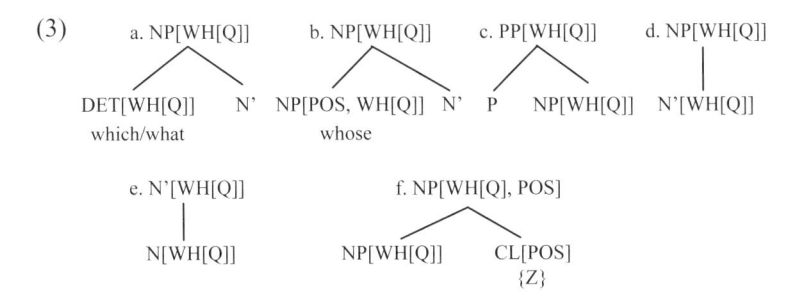

(3) a. NP[WH[Q]]   b. NP[WH[Q]]   c. PP[WH[Q]]   d. NP[WH[Q]]

    DET[WH[Q]]   N'   NP[POS, WH[Q]]   N'   P   NP[WH[Q]]   N'[WH[Q]]
    which/what   whose

       e. N'[WH[Q]]   f. NP[WH[Q], POS]

        N[WH[Q]]   NP[WH[Q]]   CL[POS]
                                             {Z}

In (3f), the possessive *'s* is treated as the clitic (CL) with the POS feature. What is significant about this list is that it does not include the local trees [~N'[WH[Q]]~ {N' | N}, PP[WH[Q]]]. (Recall the notation {A | B} indicates alternatives. Therefore, [~N'[WH[Q]]~ {N' | N}, PP[WH[Q]]] refers to [~N'[WH[Q]]~ N', PP[WH[Q]]] (N' with an adjunct PP) and [$_{N'[WH[Q]]}$ N, PP[WH[Q]]] (N with its complement PP).) That is, the WH[Q] feature cannot percolate up from a complement or adjunct PP to the head N'. This explains the ungrammatical cases in (1) and (2). As for (2 j), although the *wh*-phrase contains two *wh*-words, what makes it a *wh*-phrase in view of (3) is the first *which*, whose WH[Q] percolates up to its mother NP[WH[Q]] and the whole NP[WH[Q]] is "moved." The inner *wh*-phrase *which poets* "merely goes along for the ride" (McCawley 1998: 518 note 5).

In languages such as French and German, in which preposition stranding (P-stranding) is not allowed, the pied-piping of prepositions with their complement NP[WH[Q]] is obligatory. Therefore, the dominance path (4a) is not allowed and (4b) is forced.

(4) a. *[$_{CP[WH[Q]]}$ NP[WH[Q]] [$_{S[INV]}$ ... [$_{PP}$ P NP[G]]]]
    *dominance path: CP[WH[Q]] S[INV] ... PP NP[G]
  b. [$_{CP[WH[Q]]}$ PP[WH[Q]] [$_{S[INV]}$ .... PP[G]]]
    dominance path: CP[WH[Q]] S[INV] ... PP[G]

(5) and (6) show that P-stranding is impossible in French and German, respectively.

(5) Culicover 2009: 331
  a. Tu   parles   à Jean.
     you   speak   to
  b. A qui parles-tu __ ?
  c. *Qui parles-tu à __ ?

(6) Culicover 2009: 331
  a. Er hat das Buch   auf den Tisch   gestellt.
     He has the book   on   the table   put
  b. Auf welchen Tisch hat er das Buch __ gestellt?
  c. *Welchen Tisch hat er das Buch auf __ gestellt?

We can derive nonoccurrence of P-stranding in French and German from the condition (7).

(7) In non-P-stranding languages, the middle part of the dominance path conditions does not contain PP.

(7) entails that in these languages, no dominance path is possible that ends in the sequence PP NP[G]. We can state (7) as a parameter: P-stranding languages (e.g., English) contain PP in the middle part of the dominance path conditions, whereas non-P-stranding languages (e.g., French and German) do not. Therefore, in terms of the complexity of the middle part of the dominance path conditions, non-P-stranding languages are simpler than P-stranding languages in the sense that the former lack PP in the middle part of their dominance path conditions whereas the latter contain PP in it. In other words, non-P-stranding languages are unmarked and P-stranding languages are marked. In fact, P-stranding languages are extremely limited in their distribution (Merchant 2001: 92). Children need to learn the P-stranding property (i.e., the fact that the middle parts of the dominance path conditions contain PP) from positive evidence.

Here are the syntax and F/A of (2e) with the pied-piping of the N' *pope's reign* and the preposition *during*. Note that because of the lexical entry for *which* in 6.1.7 (9), the internal structure of QP$_x$ is [$_{QPx}$ [$_Q$ WH] [$_{PROP}$ x = POPE]]. This means that everything other than *which pope* in the *wh*-phrase *during which pope's reign* is forced to be in the matrix proposition. (As for the syntactic structure of NP[POS], see (3f).)

(8) a. During which pope's reign was Copernicus born? (=(2e))
 b. [$_{CP[WH[Q]]}$ [$_{PP[during,\ WH[Q]]}$ During which pope's reign] [$_{S[INV,\ PAST]}$ was [$_{S[PST]}$ Copernicus born PP[G]]]]?
 c. the internal syntax of the *wh*-phrase

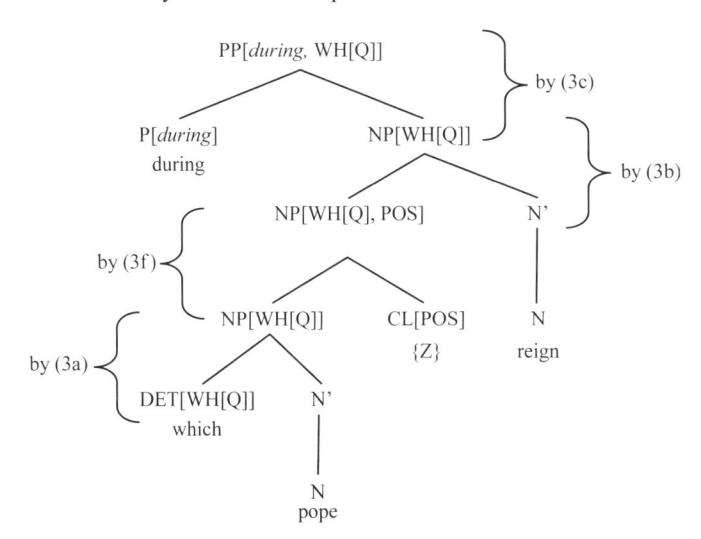

```
                    PP[during, WH[Q]]
                    ╱            ╲                  ⎫
              P[during]        NP[WH[Q]]            ⎬ by (3c)
               during          ╱      ╲             ⎭
                          NP[WH[Q], POS]    N'      ⎫
                          ╱        ╲         │      ⎬ by (3b)
              by (3f)  NP[WH[Q]]  CL[POS]    N      ⎭
                       ╱    ╲       {Z}    reign
              by (3a) DET[WH[Q]]  N'
                       which      │
                                  N
                                 pope
```

d. F/A

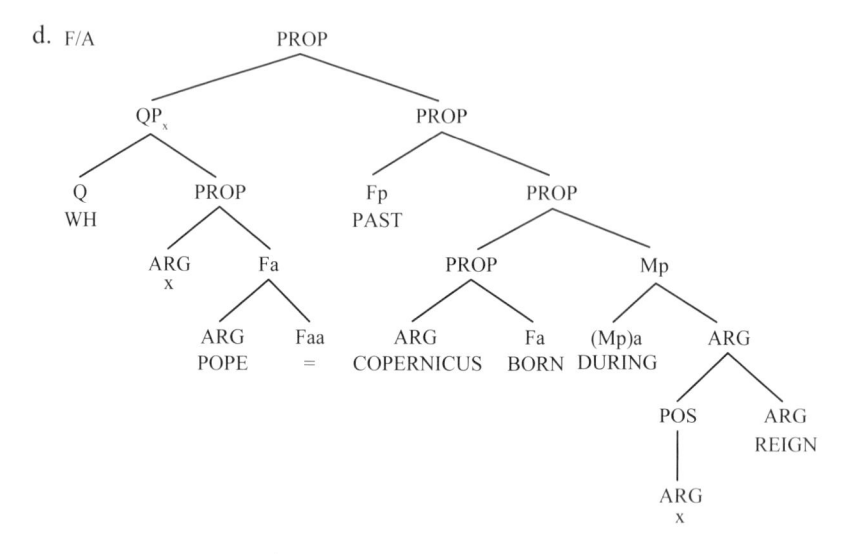

```
                        PROP
              ┌──────────┴──────────┐
             QPₓ                   PROP
           ┌──┴──┐              ┌───┴───┐
           Q    PROP            Fp     PROP
           WH   ┌┴┐            PAST   ┌──┴──┐
              ARG Fa                 PROP   Mp
               x ┌┴┐              ┌───┴┐   ┌┴──┐
                ARG Faa          ARG  Fa (Mp)a ARG
                POPE  =      COPERNICUS BORN DURING
                                              ┌──┴──┐
                                             POS   ARG
                                              │    REIGN
                                             ARG
                                              x
```

Note that the PP[*during*] can be either an Mp as above or an MFa as in 6.1.4 (3a).

6.1.6 Multiple *wh*-questions

The local tree that licenses a *wh*-phrase at the clause-initial position ([$_{CP[WH[Q]]}$ XP[WH[Q]] S]]) is not recursive in English and hence allows only one *wh*-phrase. (To introduce multiple *wh*-phrases to the clause-initial position, we would need, for example, another local tree that adjoins a *wh*-phrase to a CP[WH[Q]]: [$_{CP[WH[Q]]}$ XP[WH[Q]] CP[WH[Q]]].) Therefore, if there are multiple *wh*-phrases in a clause, one must be at the clause-initial position as required by the first local tree, but the other *wh*-phrases are forced to stay *in situ*, which is shown in (1).

(1) McCawley 1998: 499
   a. Who gave what to whom?
   b. What did who give to whom?
   c. To whom did who give what?
   d. *Who what to whom gave?
   e. *What to whom did who give?

The multiple *wh*-question (2a) is ambiguous and can be answered in two ways (2b, c).

(2) a. Who asked which students had bought which books? (McCawley 1998: 494)
    b. Tom did. (McCawley 1998: 494)

c. Tom asked which students had bought *War and Peace*, and Rita asked which students had bought *Fanny Hill*. (McCawley 1998: 494)
d. [[$_{QPx}$ who][x asked [[$_{QPy}$ which students] [[$_{QPz}$ which books] [y bought z]]]]] presupposition: Someone asked which students had bought which books. question: Who is that "someone"?
e. [[$_{QPx}$ who] [[$_{QPz}$ which books] [x asked [[$_{QPy}$ which students] [y bought z]]]]] presupposition: Someone asked which students had bought some books. question: Who is that "someone" and what are those "some books"?

The answer (2b) is possible when (2a) is interpreted as a simple *wh*-question with an embedded multiple *wh*-question. The approximate F/A structure of this interpretation is (2d). By contrast, (2c) is a possible answer when (2a) is interpreted as a multiple *wh*-question with an embedded simple *wh*-question. The approximate F/A structure of this interpretation is (2e). Note that the *wh*-phrase that is *in situ* (*which books* in (2a)) is allowed to take either the matrix scope (2e) or the embedded scope (2d), because its scope is not determined by the syntactic structure, whereas the other two clause-initial *wh*-phrases, *who* and *which students*, are already assigned their respective scope by being directly dominated by their respective CP[WH[Q]]. Note also that in (2d), *which students* has wide scope and has *which books* within its scope, whereas in (2e), *who* has wide scope and has *which books* within its scope. This is due to the default correspondence (1.4 (7b)), in which the c-command relations of the two *wh*-phrases between syntax and F/A are preserved.

McCawley (1998: 499–501) claimed that there is a strong tendency about multiple *wh*-questions that the clause-initial *wh*-phrase, which has wide scope and has the *in situ wh*-phrase within its scope, represents the key for sorting relevant pieces of information in the answer (an observation due originally to Kuno (1982)). For example, (3a) can best be answered by (4a) and (3b) by (4b).

(3) McCawley 1998: 499
  a. Which students did they give A's to in which subjects?
  b. In which subjects did they give A's to which students?
  c. shared presupposition: They gave A's to some students in some subjects.

(4) McCawley 1998: 499
  a. They gave A's to Peter Hanson in geometry, biology, and English, to Mary Murphy in history and music, ...

b. In Geometry, they gave A's to Peter Hanson, Martha Mooney, and Dave Isenberg, in history to Mary Murphy and Alice Jamison, ...

In (2e), one of the F/A structures of (2a), the quantifier phrase [$_{QPz}$ [$_Q$ WH] [$_{PROP}$ z = BOOKS]] (i.e., *which books*) has matrix scope, with its scope over the embedded proposition [[$_{QPy}$ which students] [y bought z]]. However, because the *wh*-phrase *which books* is *in situ* in the syntax of (2a), there is no violation of *wh*-island in syntax, thus accounting for the absence of the *wh*-island effect of reduced acceptability. In (5 A), the second *wh*-phrase *which book* is contained in a complex NP. However, because it is *in situ* in syntax, there is no violation of the Complex NP Constraint (CNPC) in syntax. In its F/A, the corresponding dominance path contains the offending sequence ARG Ma PROP in its middle part (cf. 6.1.4 (1) and (6a)).

(5) A: Which person knows the man who wrote <u>which book</u>? (Dayal 2006: 308)
cf. Which person knows the author of which book?
B: Bill knows the man who wrote *Aspects*.

(6) the approximate F/A of (5 A)
[$_{QPx}$ which person] [$_{QPy}$ which book] [$_{PROP}$ PRES [$_{PROP}$ x KNOW [$_{ARG}$ MAN$_j$ [$_{Ma}$ PAST [$_{PROP}$ IND[j, 3SG] WRITE y]]]]]

The acceptability of (2e) and (5 A) shows that the F/A dominance path condition (6.1.4 (1)) applies only to a clause-initial ("moved") *wh*-phrase, just like the syntactic dominance path conditions (6.1.3 (1)), and that *in-situ wh*-phrases are exempt from both conditions. To capture this observation, we will encode the syntactic and F/A dominance path conditions in the lexical entry of a clause-initial *wh*-phrase (6.1.7 (1)). (2e) and (5 A) show that a *wh*-phrase within an island can be asked without any loss of acceptability as long as it stays *in situ* within the island. This is also true of quiz questions (6.1.9) and echo questions.

6.1.7 Lexical entries

In this section, we will give the lexical entries for a clause-initial *wh*-phrase and individual *wh*-words. When the *wh*-words *who* and *what* are used as *wh*-phrases (as in *Who did you meet?* or *What did you do?*), their lexical entries are a composition of (1) and their respective lexical entry.

(1) lexical entry for clause-initial *wh*-phrase XP[WH[Q], α]
syntax: XP[WH[Q], α] in [_CP[WH[Q]] __ S[{FIN|INV|*to*}]], where α is a PFORM value if X = P
- the syntactic dominance path conditions
  a. nonsubject gap: CP[WH[Q]] {S, VP, CP[{*that*|*for*}]}* VP {NP, N', PP}* XP[G, α] (6.1.3 (2a))
  b. subject gap: CP[WH[Q]] {S, VP, CP[{*that*|*for*}]}* S[FIN] NP[G] (6.1.3 (2b, c) and (11a) with (11b))
- the F/A dominance path condition (6.1.4. (1))
  PROP {PROP, Fa, Faa, Fpa}* {ARG, POS}* [_ARG x]

There are four remarks about (1). First, (1) does not apply to an *in situ wh*-phrase, which is specified in the entry. Second, the three dominance paths 6.1.3 (2b, c) and (11a) are combined and reformulated as a single condition for a subject gap, which covers both a matrix subject and an embedded subject. Recall that the Kleene star operator * includes the null string (6.1.3 (2)). Third, for the dominance path condition for a subject gap (1b) above to function as desired, the lexical entry for *that*-relative clause with a subject gap (6.1.3 (11b)) must be assumed. Fourth, the choice between FIN and INV is determined by whether the *wh*-question is direct or indirect (6.1.1 (1)). When X in (1) is P, the lexical entry is as follows.

(2) lexical entry for clause-initial *wh*-phrase PP[WH[Q], α]
syntax: PP[WH[Q], α] in [_CP[WH[Q]] __ S[{FIN|INV|*to*}]], where α is a PFORM value
- the syntactic dominance path condition
  nonsubject gap: CP[WH[Q]] {S, VP, CP[{*that*|*for*}]}* VP {NP, N', PP}* PP[G, α]
- the F/A dominance path condition
  PROP {PROP, Fa, Faa, Fpa}* {ARG, POS}* [_ARG x]

This entails that when the clause-initial XP is a PP[WH[Q], *on*], the bottom gap must be PP[G, *on*] with the same PFORM value. Thus, the connectivity of syntactic category and that of PFORM value between PP[WH[Q], α] and PP[G, α] are guaranteed. These connectivities are especially necessary for complement PPs. When a complement PP[WH[Q]] appears at the clause-initial position, its bottom gap must be a PP with the same PFORM value, because it is a complement of a certain verb, adjective, or noun, whose lexical entry specifies which PFORM value it takes. For example, if the bottom PP[G] is a complement of the verb *depend*, it must be PP[G, *on*] with *on* as its PFORM value, and the clause-initial PP[WH[Q]] must have the same PFORM value by (2). When X in (1) is N, the lexical entry is as follows.

(3) lexical entry for clause-initial *wh*-phrase NP[WH[Q]]
   syntax: NP[WH[Q]] in [$_{\text{CP[WH[Q]]}}$ __ S[{FIN|INV}]]
   - the syntactic dominance path conditions
     a. nonsubject gap: CP[WH[Q]] {S, VP, CP[{*that*|*for*}]}* VP {NP, N', PP}* NP[G]
     b. subject gap: CP[WH[Q]] {S, VP, CP[{*that*|*for*}]}* S[FIN] NP[G]
   - the F/A dominance path condition
     PROP {PROP, Fa, Faa, Fpa}* {ARG, POS}* [$_{\text{ARG}}$ x]

When the bottom gap NP[G] is the subject of a finite clause, it needs its own agreement (AGR) value for subject-verb agreement. Here we need to consider two cases: (i) *Which boy do you think* NP[G] *likes Mary?*, in which the *wh*-phrase *which boy* corresponds to a QP$_x$ in F/A, and (ii) *Which boy's parents do you think* NP[G] *like Mary?*, in which only a part of the *wh*-phrase *which boy's parents* corresponds to a QP$_x$ in F/A. First, let us consider case (i), whose approximate syntax and F/A are given in (4) below. Recall that the subject-verb agreement is achieved by the PS rule [$_{\text{S[FIN]}}$ NP[AGR], VP[FIN, AGR]] (1.2 (11a)), in which the same AGR value is shared between the subject NP and the VP of a finite clause, and that because AGR is a head feature, the head of the finite VP also shares the same AGR value (1.2 (11b)), thanks to the Head Feature Convention. In the syntactic structure of (4), the verb *likes* agrees with the NP[G], due to the regular syntactic agreement. The NP[G] corresponds to the variable directly dominated by ARG$_3$. The variable x has the AGR value 3SGM. (Recall that the variable x is technically the IND feature with x as its referential index: IND[x, AGR]. This IND value is borne by ARG$_1$ in the F/A structure of (4). The AGR value 3SGM of this IND comes from [$_{\text{ARG2}}$ BOY] through the type-identity Faa =.) The same AGR value is shared by the NP[G] in syntax, due to Feature Osmosis (1.3, Sadock 2012: 154).

(4) approximate syntax and F/A of (i) *Which boy do you think* NP[G] *likes Mary?*

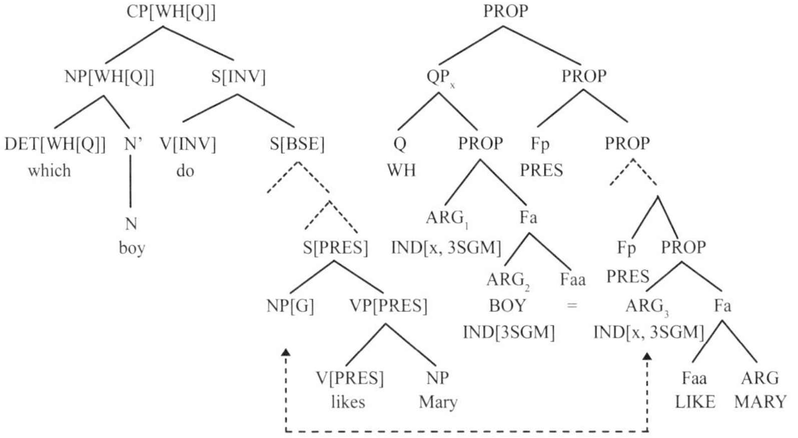

Second, let us consider case (ii), whose approximate syntax and F/A are given in (5) below. In the syntactic structure of (5), the finite verb *like* agrees with the NP[G], which in turn corresponds to the ARG_1. The AGR value of ARG_1 is determined by its head ARG_2, whose AGR value is 3PL.

(5) the approximate syntax and F/A of (ii) *Which boy's parents do you think* NP[G] *like Mary*?

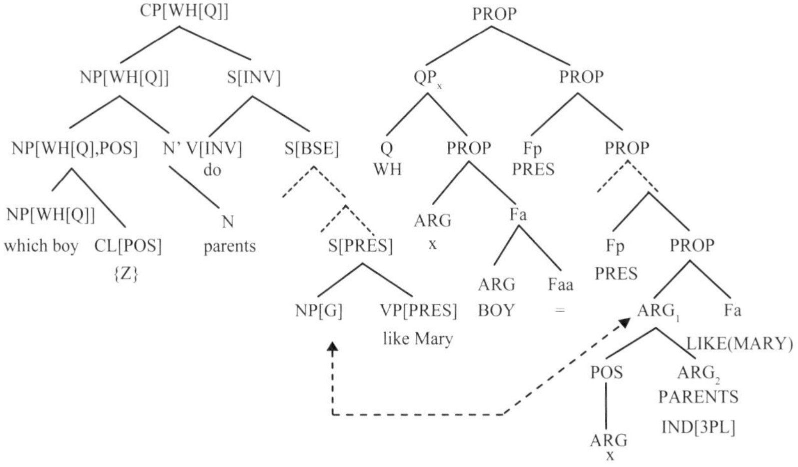

290   6 UNBOUNDED DEPENDENCY

Here are the lexical entries of interrogative pronouns *who* and *what*.

(6) lexical entry for interrogative pronoun *who*
    syntax: N[WH[Q]]
    F/A: [$_{QPx}$ [$_Q$ WH], [$_{PROP}$ x = PERSON]]

(7) lexical entry for interrogative pronoun *what*
    syntax: N[WH[Q]]
    F/A: [$_{QPx}$ [$_Q$ WH], [$_{PROP}$ x = THING]]

In (6) and (7), we take it that the syntactic category of the interrogative pronouns *who* and *what* is not NP[WH[Q]] but N[WH[Q]], because it can be followed by *of* NP[POS] (*What did he find of yours?* (McCawley 1998: 439)) and it can be modified by a restrictive relative clause, as in *What did you buy that you could have lived without?* (from the web) or *Who that you know would make a good candidate?* (McCawley 1998: 436). As will be shown in 6.2.3 (1b), a restrictive relative clause (RRC) is adjoined to an N', as in [$_{N'}$ N' RRC]. (8) and (9) are the lexical entries of interrogative determiners *what* and *which*.

(8) lexical entry for interrogative determiner *what*
    syntax: DET[WH[Q]]
    F/A: [$_{QPx}$ [$_Q$ WH], [$_{PROP}$ x = [$_{ARG}$ ...]]]
    • The value of [$_{ARG}$ ...] comes from the determiner's sister N'.

(9) lexical entry for interrogative determiner *which*
    syntax: DET[WH[Q]]
    F/A: [$_{QPx}$ [$_Q$ WH], [$_{PROP}$ x = [$_{ARG}$ ...]]]
    • The value of [$_{ARG}$ ...] comes from the determiner's sister N'.
    • The variable x is interpreted as a member of a contextually salient set evoked in the discourse.

As for the lexical entry for the interrogative possessive pronoun *whose*, we can derive it from that of *who* (6) by combining it with the lexical entries for the possessive clitic and NP[POS].

(10) lexical entry for interrogative pronoun *whose*
     syntax: NP[POS, WH[Q]]
     F/A: [$_{QPx}$ [$_Q$ WH], [$_{PROP}$ x = PERSON]] [$_{PROP}$ ... [$_{POS}$ [$_{ARG}$ x]] ...]

6.1.8 Crossover phenomena and presuppositions

Wh-questions are said to have existential presuppositions that are standardly assumed to contain an existentially interpreted indefinite pronoun, as in (1b) (Levinson 1983: 184). This indefinite pronoun can be referred to in a later discourse (1a). The pronoun *he* in the second conjunct in (1a) refers to *someone* in the presupposition (1b). (2) illustrates the same point.

(1) a. Who took the pictures and what camera did he use? (Comorovski 1996: 24)
    b. presupposition of the first part: Someone took the pictures.

(2) a. Who did you talk to and when did you talk to them? (Comorovski 1996: 24)
       presupposition of the first part: You talked to someone.
    b. What did they do and why did they do it? (from the web)
       presupposition of the first part: They did something.

For *wh*-questions to be well formed (i.e., to ask questions felicitously using a *wh*-phrase), let us assume that their existential presuppositions must be well formed and intelligible, in the first place. If this assumption is correct, we can explain why the strong crossover (SCO) and weak crossover (WCO) cases of *wh*-questions are unacceptable. Their existential presuppositions are all unintelligible, which is shown in (6b), (7), and (8b) below.

It has been claimed since Reinhart (1983: 122) that bound variable pronouns must be c-commanded by their quantified NP (QNP) in syntax. This condition is illustrated in (3), in which QNPs and their bound variable pronouns are underlined.

(3) QNP and its bound variable pronouns (Lasnik 1989: 103)
    a. Everyone/No one$_x$ seriously believes that he$_x$ is unattractive.
    b. *He$_x$ seriously believes that everyone/no one$_x$ is unattractive.
    c. Everyone/No one$_x$ sat down after he$_x$ walked in.
    d. Every businessman$_x$ was impoverished by the woman who loved him$_x$.
    e. *The woman who loved him$_x$ impoverished every businessman$_x$.

We cannot directly resort to this syntactic condition to account for the crossover phenomena for two reasons. First, we want to apply this kind of condition to presuppositions, which are, strictly speaking, not syntactic entities but semantic entities. Therefore, we need to formulate a relevant condition in semantic (i.e., F/A and or RS) terms. Second, Reinhart's condition has an important class of exceptions; that is, when a QNP is in the possessive and is part of the subject or object and at the same time, the bound variable pronouns are c-commanded by the subject or object NP that contains the possessive QNP in question. This type of exception is illustrated in (4).

(4) a. Every boy's father thinks he's a genius. (Higginbotham 1980: 691)
RS: [$_{EV}$ "think" [$_{AG}$ [$_{POS}$ "every boy"] "father"] [$_{PT}$ [$_{EV}$ "=" [$_{TH}$ "he"] [$_{LO}$ "genius"]]]]
a'. Every boy's father's friends think he's a genius.
RS: [$_{EV}$ "think" [$_{AG}$ [$_{POS}$ [$_{POS}$ "every boy"] "father"] "friends"] [$_{PT}$ [$_{EV}$ "=" [$_{TH}$ "he"] [$_{LO}$ "genius"]]]]
b. The headmaster asked every boy's mother to encourage him. (McCawley 1998: 657)
b'. The headmaster asked every boy's mother's friends to encourage him.
c. Everyone$_x$'s/No one$_x$'s mother thinks he$_x$ is unfriendly. (Lasnik 1989: 103)
d. Everyone$_x$'s pictures impressed him$_x$. (Lasnik 1989: 103)
cf. *Pictures of everyone$_x$ impressed him$_x$.

In the RS of (4a, a'), we used POS to indicate the role of a possessive NP. Note that in (4a, a', b, b'), the underlined pronoun is interpreted as a bound variable but is not c-commanded by the underlined QNP. Although this class of exceptions may eventually be reduced to a special function of the possessive NP, which tends to be the locus of the speaker's empathy, according to Kuno (1987: 205), or the reference point, according to Taylor (1996: 17), for the sake of our current discussion, we propose the notion of extended outrank relation (5b) and the RS condition (5a) that is based on it.

(5) a. the RS condition on quantified expressions
A quantified expression (QNP or *wh*-phrase) must outrank all the bound variable pronouns.
b. the definition of extended outrank relation
(i) A possessive NP outranks its mother NP.
(ii) The relation outrank is transitive, namely, if A outranks B and B outranks C, then A outranks C.
(iii) Otherwise, outrank relations are determined by 1.4 (6b), repeated in 3.1 (2iib).

(5bi) must be interpreted as "The role in RS that corresponds to a possessive NP outranks the role of its mother NP." For example, in (4a), *every boy* outranks its mother NP by (5bi), which in turn outranks the bound variable pronoun *he* by (5biii). Therefore, *every boy* outranks *he* by (5bii). In (4a'), *every boy* outranks its mother NP, which in turn outranks its mother subject NP. The latter outranks the bound variable *he*. Therefore, *every boy* outranks *he*. In other words, (4a) and (4a') meet the condition (5a). Similarly, (4b, b', c, d) meet (5a).

(6a) is an example of strong crossover (SCO).

(6) a. (SCO) *Who$_x$ does she$_x$ think John admires __?
 b. presupposition of (6a): *She$_x$ thinks John admires someone$_x$.
 c. Who$_x$ __ thinks John admires her$_x$?
 d. presupposition of (6c): Someone$_x$ thinks John admires her$_x$.
 e. [$_{PROP}$ [$_{QPx}$ WH x = PERSON] PRES([$_{PROP}$ x THINK [$_{PROP}$ PRES(JOHN ADMIRE x)]])]
 f. RS of (6a, b) [$_{EV}$ "think" [$_{AG}$ "she"] [$_{PT}$ [$_{EV}$ "admire" [$_{AG}$ "John"] [$_{PT}$ "who/someone"]]
 g. RS of (6c, d) [$_{EV}$ "think" [$_{AG}$ "who/someone"] [$_{PT}$ [$_{EV}$ "admire" [$_{AG}$ "John"] [$_{PT}$ "her"]]

Both the unacceptable SCO example (6a) and the acceptable (6c) share the same F/A structure (6e), but their presuppositions (6b) and (6d) are different. Because the quantified expression outranks its bound variable pronoun in (6 g), which is the RS of (6c, d), the *wh*-question (6c) and its presupposition (6d) meet the condition (5a). On the other hand, because the quantified expression does not outrank its bound variable pronoun in (6f), which is the RS of (6a, b), the *wh*-question (6a) and its presupposition (6b) violate the condition (5a). The unacceptability of (7) below can be explained in the same way. Note that the *wh*-phrase *who* in (7) is not "moved" but still exhibits the same effect as a regular SCO example, such as (6a).

(7) *She$_x$ thinks John admires who$_x$? (intended as a quiz question (6.1.9))
 presupposition: *She$_x$ thinks John admires someone$_x$.

In view of (6a) and (7), we conclude that whether there is an overt "*wh*-movement" in a *wh*-question or not, an example of SCO and its presupposition both violate the RS condition (5a). Recall our assumption about *wh*-questions stated above: for *wh*-questions to be well formed (i.e., to ask questions felicitously using a *wh*-phrase), their presuppositions must be well formed and intelligible, in the first place. In our analysis of (6a) and (7), not only the presuppositions but also the *wh*-questions themselves violate the RS condition on quantified expressions (5a).

Weak crossover (WCO) is explained in the same way. (8a) is an example of WCO.

(8) a. (WCO) *Who$_x$ does his$_x$ boss dislike? (Lasnik and Stowell 1991: 689)
  b. presupposition of (8a): *His$_x$ boss dislikes someone$_x$.
  c. Whose$_x$ boss dislikes him$_x$?
  d. presupposition of (8c): Someone's$_x$ boss dislikes him$_x$.
  e. [$_{PROP}$ [$_{QPx}$ WH x = PERSON] [$_{PROP}$ [$_{ARG}$ [$_{POS}$ [$_{ARG}$ x]] BOSS] DISLIKE x]]
  f. *His$_x$ boss dislikes who$_x$? (intended as a quiz question)

(8a) and (8c) share the same F/A structure (8e). However, (8a) and its presupposition (8b) violate (5a) whereas (8c) and its presupposition (8d) meet (5a).

The assumption that presuppositions of *wh*-questions must be well formed in order to ask them felicitously seems to be reasonable, if we consider the nature of *wh*-questions. A *wh*-question is a question with which the speaker requests the addressee to provide him or her with the information that completes the propositional function associated with the *wh*-question and turns it into a true proposition (Searle 1969: 66). That is, a *wh*-question seeks the value x that makes its associated propositional function P(x) a true proposition. Note that the propositional function associated with a *wh*-question is a proposition P(x) with a variable such that the F/A structure of the *wh*-question in question is [$_{QPx}$ [$_Q$ WH] x = …] P(x) and that of its presupposition is [$_{QPx}$ [$_Q$ ∃] x = …] P(x). By virtue of questioning a particular part of a sentence with a *wh*-word, the speaker takes the rest of the sentence (i.e., the propositional function) for granted (Kiparsky and Kiparsky 1971: 351). People cannot ask a *wh*-question properly with an ill-formed propositional function, namely, in our terms, a propositional function that violates (5a).

The question (9a) below with a *wh*-phrase and a QNP can be answered in various ways (cf. 6.1 (2)). The presupposition of (9a) is (9b), which is ambiguous. If we interpret it as (9c), in which *every man* is within the scope of *some woman*, the most plausible answer is 'every man likes the same woman.' If we interpret the presupposition as (9d), in which *some woman* is within the scope of *every man*, we can provide an answer by giving a list of which man likes which woman or by giving a propositional function, for example, 'x likes x's mother.'

(9) a. Which woman does every man like? (Dayal 2006: 301)
   b. presupposition: Every man likes some woman. (ambiguous)
      request for information: Who is that "some woman"?
   c. presupposition interpretation: [$_{QPy}$ some woman] [$_{QPx}$ every man] [PRES (x LIKE y)]
      Every man likes Mary.
   d. presupposition interpretation: [$_{QPx}$ every man] [$_{QPy}$ some woman] [PRES (x LIKE y)]
      Tom likes Mary, Dick likes Jane, and Harry likes Kim. (list answer)
      Every man likes his mother. (functional answer)

This account of SCO and WCO based on extended outrank relation (5b) extends to cases of unacceptable "*wh*-movement" that were explained in MGG by reconstruction.

(10) Hornstein 1984: 89
   a. *Which picture of John$_j$ does he$_i$ like?
      presupposition: *He$_i$ likes a certain picture of John$_j$.
   b. Which picture of himself$_i$ does John$_i$ like?
      presupposition: John$_i$ likes a certain picture of himself$_i$.
   c. *Which picture of John's$_j$ mother does he$_i$ like?
      presupposition: *He$_i$ likes a certain picture of John's$_j$ mother.
   d. Which picture of his$_x$ mother does everyone$_x$ like?
      presupposition: Everyone$_x$ likes a certain picture of his$_x$ mother.

The *wh*-questions and their presuppositions in (10a) and (10c) violate another RS condition that if X and Y are coreferential and X outranks Y, then Y must be a pronoun (McCawley 1998: 362). In the *wh*-question and its presupposition in (10d), *everyone* outranks its bound variable pronoun *his*, thus satisfying (5a).

Another advantage of our approach based on extended outrank relation defined on RS is that we can deal with another class of exceptions to Reinhart's c-command condition. It has been observed that a QNP allows pronouns to be interpreted as bound by it if it c-commands them at the level of McCawley's cyclic outputs, namely, "the structures at the end of the application of the cyclic transformations to each domain" (McCawley 1998: 360).

(11) a. What every candidate regretted was that he got so few votes. (McCawley 1998: 658)
cyclic output: Every candidate regretted that he got so few votes.
b. What I asked every candidate was whether he would vote to cut taxes. (ibid.)
cyclic output: I asked every candidate whether he would vote to cut taxes.

Here again, a possessive QNP behaves the same way as in (4).

(12) a. What every candidate's supporters regretted was that he got so few votes.
cyclic output: Every candidate's supporters regretted that he got so few votes.
b. What I asked every candidate's supporters was whether he would vote to cut taxes.
cyclic output: I asked every candidate's supporters whether he would vote to cut taxes.

If we assume that the pseudo-cleft construction and its noncleft version share the same RS, the outrank relations in these two are the same. (This assumption seems to be reasonable, because the pseudo-cleft construction and its noncleft version share the same (cognitive) meaning. The difference between the two lies in their Information Structure) If so, in the pseudo-clefts (11) and (12), *every candidate* outranks the bound variable *he*, thus satisfying (5a).

6.1.9 Quiz questions

Quizmaster/pedagogical questions (henceforth, quiz questions) are *wh*-questions in which the *wh*-phrase is not "moved" to the clause-initial position but stays *in situ*, as in (1). A quiz question is often used when the questioner (a quizmaster or a teacher) who already knows the answer requests the addressee (a panelist or a student) to provide the information corresponding to its *wh*-phrase, as in, a fill-in-the-blank question.

(1) a. For $100,000, Martha Washington was married to which famous American. (Culicover 2009: 335)
b. For $100,000, English is spoken in how many of the world's nations. (ibid.)

c. For $100,000, John said Martha Washington was married to who. (ibid.)
d. Everyone didn't eat what at the party.

Interestingly, a quiz question exhibits crossover phenomena (6.1.8 (7), (8f)). Furthermore, its *wh*-phrase always has the widest scope and hence cannot be embedded (Culicover and Jackendoff 2005: 325, Culicover 2009: 335). In (1c), the question is not about who Martha Washington was married to but about who John said Martha Washington was married to. In (1d), the interrogative pronoun *what* has the widest scope: [$_{QPy}$ WHAT] > [$_{QPx}$ EVERYONE] > [$_{Fp}$ PAST] > [$_{Fp}$ NOT] > [$_{PROP}$ x EAT y].

The dominance path conditions in 6.1.7 (1) are constraints on the dominance relations between the top CP[WH[Q]] that immediately dominates a "moved" *wh*-phrase and the bottom gap XP[G] in syntax. Because there is no clause-initial *wh*-phrase in quiz questions, there is no corresponding gap XP[G] at the bottom, either, that should be checked by the dominance path conditions. Because of this, we expect that the *wh*-phrase in a quiz question can stay *in situ* in an island. (Recall that we observed the same phenomenon in the case of multiple *wh*-questions in 6.1.6 (2a, e) and (5 A).) This expectation is borne out in (2) (cf. Culicover and Jackendoff 2005: 314, 337 note 24).

(2) a. For $100,000, Andy Griffith starred in CBS's *Andy Griffith Show* and played what role. (CSC)
  b. For $100,000, Andy Griffith played the role of a prominent defense attorney in Atlanta whose favorite food was what. (CNPC)
  c. For $100,000, the report that Andy Griffith passed away at what age shocked the entire nation last week. (Subject Condition)

The syntax of a quiz question is a syntactic structure in which the highest node is not CP[WH[Q]] but S[FIN]. If it were CP[WH[Q]], the local tree [$_{CP[WH[Q]]}$ XP[WH[Q]] S] would force "*wh*-movement" and the dominance path conditions would force an XP[G] to appear at the bottom, which is all due to 6.1.7 (1). Therefore, the top node of a quiz question cannot be CP[WH[Q]]. We simply take it as S[FIN].

The semantics of a quiz question consists of two parts: assertion of an existentially quantified proposition and request for the piece of information that identifies the existentially quantified variable. Putting it more precisely, a quiz question asserts the existentially quantified proposition in which the *wh*-word is replaced by its corresponding existential quantifier (e.g., *who* by *someone* or *what* by *something*) and at the same time, it requests the addressee to supply the information about the identity of the existentially quantified variable in the assertion. In other words, a quiz question serves double functions: (i) to assert an existentially quantified proposition and (ii) to request the addressee to provide the value for the existentially quantified variable so that the questioner can check its correctness.

Note that in an ordinary *wh*-question, the proposition obtained by replacing the *wh*-phrase by a corresponding existentially quantified expression is a presupposition and not an assertion. For example, in the *wh*-question *What did John eat last night?*, the corresponding existentially quantified proposition *John ate something last night* is a presupposition. This presupposition can be canceled by answering *John didn't eat anything.* (See Levinson 1983: 186ff. on the defeasibility of presupposition.) On the other hand, in the quiz question *John ate what last night?*, the corresponding existentially quantified proposition *John ate something last night* is an assertion, because the questioner claims it to be true (in fact, the questioner knows what John ate) and the addressee is required to give the identity of the existentially quantified variable, on the basis of the questioner's claim of the truthfulness of the existentially quantified proposition. Therefore, answering (1a) by saying "She wasn't married to any famous American" would be a contradiction and in fact does not qualify as an answer to the quiz question. This shows that the corresponding existentially quantified proposition of a quiz question is not a presupposition but an assertion. From the discussion so far, we claim that the meaning of (1a) and that of (1b) are (3) and (4), respectively.

(3) the meaning of (1a)
assertion: Martha Washington was married to [$_{NP}$ a certain famous American].
request for information: Who is the famous American?

(4) the meaning of (1b)
assertion: English is spoken in [$_{NP}$ a certain number of the world's nations].
request for information: What is the number?

If our understanding of quiz questions is on the right track, the F/A of a quiz question is a coordination of an existentially quantified PROP and a *wh*-quantified

PROP in which the matrix PROPs in both conjuncts are the same, whereas its RS is a coordination of two speech acts: assertion and request. (As for speech acts, see Chapter 7.)

(5) lexical entry for quiz question (as a construction)
syntax: [$_{S[FIN]}$ ... XP[WH[Q]] ...]
F/A: [$_{PROP}$ [$_{QPx}$ [$_Q$ ∃] x = ...] PROP] AND [$_{PROP}$ [$_{QPx}$ [$_Q$ WH] x = ...] PROP]
RS: [$_{SA}$ [$_{IF}$ #assert#] P(x)] and [$_{SA}$ [$_{IF}$ #request#] Identify the value of x]

The syntax of (5) says that a quiz question is a finite (declarative) sentence (S[FIN]) in which a *wh*-phrase is *in situ*. The F/A says that the QPs that correspond to the *wh*-phrase have the widest scope in each conjunct PROP.

6.1.10 Nonbridge verbs

Nonbridge verbs are verbs that do not permit or at least are resistant to "*wh*-movement" from their complement clauses. There are two types of nonbridge verbs: factive verbs (1) and manner-of-speaking verbs (2).

(1) "*wh*-movement" out of a complement clause of a factive verb
 a. ??What does Ginny regret that Don bought __? (Culicover and Jackendoff 2005: 336)
 b. *How do you regret that you behaved __? (Erteschik-Shir 1997: 231)
 c. Which politician do you regret that you spoke to __? (Erteschik-Shir 1997: 231)

(2) "*wh*-movement" out of a complement clause of a manner-of-speaking verb
 a. *What did John quip that Mary wore __? (Chomsky 1977: 85)
 b. *What did she simper that home economics was? (Erteschik-Shir 2006: 289)
 c. ??Who/??Which girl did you mumble that you'd seen __? (Erteschik-Shir 1997: 231)
 d. *Who/*Which girl did you lisp that you'd seen __? (Erteschik-Shir 1997: 231)

As for factive verbs in (1), they are a type of verbs that presuppose the truth of their complement clause; to be more precise, those verbs that take a CP[*that*] complement that denotes information whose truth the speaker takes for granted. *Regret* in (1) is such a verb. In the affirmative (3a), the negative (3b), and the interrogative (3c), the truth of 'Don bought a Porsche' is taken for granted by the speaker. (3a, b) assert Ginny's psychological attitude toward this proposition: 'regret it' in (3a) and 'not regret it' in (3b). In (3c), the focus of question is Ginny's psychological attitude toward the proposition: whether she regrets it.

(3) a. Ginny regrets that Don bought a Porsche. (Culicover and Jackendoff 2005: 335)
    cf. Don bought a Porsche. Ginny regrets it.
  b. Ginny doesn't regret that Don bought a Porsche. (ibid.)
    cf. Don bought a Porsche. Ginny doesn't regret it.
  c. Does Ginny regret that Don bought a Porsche?
    cf. Don bought a Porsche. Does Ginny regret it?

We discussed briefly in 1.5 the Information Structure (IS) module and a distinction between foreground information (FI) and background information (BI). Foreground information (FI) is information that the speaker intends to convey to the addressee (including assertion, focus, and new information). By contrast, background information (BI) is information that the speaker takes for granted and does not intend to convey to the addressee (including presupposition, topic, and old/given information). In general, information contained in an utterance (i.e., a sentence or a sentence fragment uttered in an actual context) is either FI or BI and no piece of information in it is both FI and BI at the same time.

Because the speaker already knows background information (BI), it is pragmatically odd to ask a part of it with a *wh*-phrase. Note that the CP[*that*] complement of a factive verb, such as *regret* in (1), corresponds to BI in IS. In (1a, b), the speaker, by choosing the verb *regret*, indicates that the content of the CP[*that*] is already taken for granted. Therefore, asking a part of it with a *wh*-phrase is pragmatically odd. This explains the reduced acceptability of "*wh*-movement" out of a complement clause of a factive verb in (1a, b). It is pragmatically anomalous not only to ask a part of BI with a *wh*-phrase but also to interpret such a part as the focus of negation and question. This is shown in (4) and (5).

(4) a. A: Ginny doesn't think that Don bought <u>a Porsche</u>.
      (intended focus of negation underlined)
      B: Right! She thinks that he bought a Toyota.

b. A: Ginny doesn't regret that Don bought <u>a Porsche</u>.
   B: Right! ??She regrets that he bought a Toyota.

(5) a. A: Does Ginny think that Don bought <u>a Porsche</u>?
      B. No, she thinks that he bought a Toyota.
   b. A: Does Ginny regret that Don bought <u>a Porsche</u>?
      B: ??No, she regrets that he bought a Toyota.

Interestingly enough, (1c) with the D-linked *which politician* is acceptable. We would like to claim, though tentatively, that the BI of (1c) is 'You spoke to a politician' and that the speaker requests the addressee to choose that politician from a set of politicians that is evoked in the discourse context by the *wh*-word *which* (6.1.7 (9)). It looks as if the set evoked by *which* serves as the topic of the sentence (6b).

(6) a. Which politician do you regret that you spoke to __? (=(1c))
   b. Of all the politicians we're talking about, which politician do you regret that you spoke to __?

Here is a lexical entry for the factive verb *regret*. The EV that corresponds to the CP[*that*] complement is specified as background information (BI) in Information Structure (IS).

(7) lexical entry for factive verb *regret*
   syntax: V in [__, CP[*that*]]
   F/A: F_{pa}
   RS: [$_{TYPE}$ "regret"] in [__ [AG, LO] [$_{[PT, TH]}$ EV]]
   IS: BI

Note that the specification of the embedded event as BI in the IS field of the lexical entry is default and can be overridden by an appropriate discourse context. In general, presuppositions are defeasible in certain contexts (Levinson 1983: 186ff.). In fact, Culicover and Jackendoff (2005: 336) pointed out that it is possible to set up a discourse context in which the BI status of the CP[*that*] is altered to FI, thereby producing an acceptable "*wh*-movement" out of it. In (8a, b) below, *regret* of the second sentence is backgrounded by *regret* of the first sentence, which in turn allows the content of the CP[*that*] complement in the second sentence to be foregrounded, permitting a "*wh*-movement."

(8) a. **I know** Ginny regretted that **Harry** bought a **tuba**, but what did she regret that **Don** bought __? (Culicover and Jackendoff 2005: 336)
  b. **I know** Ginny didn't regret that Don bought a **tuba**, but what **did** she regret that he bought __? (ibid.)

As for the manner-of-speaking verbs in (2), we follow Erteschik-Shir (1997: 232) and claim that in an utterance with such a verb, the verb itself necessarily represents foreground information (FI), which forces its CP[*that*] complement to represent background information (BI). For example, in the interrogative (9b), the focus of question is on *mumble* and not on the content of the clausal complement. In the negative (9c), too, the focus of negation is on *mumble* and not on the content of the clausal complement.

(9) a. John mumbled that he had seen the culprit.
    cf. John said mumblingly that he had seen the culprit.
  b. Did John mumble that he had seen the culprit?
    cf. Did John say mumblingly that he had seen the culprit?
  c. John didn't mumble that he had seen the culprit.
    cf. John didn't say mumblingly that he had seen the culprit.

To be exact, the focus of assertion in (9a), question in (9b), and negation in (9c) is on the manner ('mumblingly') of the act of saying. Levinson (1983: 184, note 13) pointed out that "manner adverbs trigger presuppositions." For example, *John ran/didn't run slowly* presupposes "John ran." By the same token, we claim that (9a, b, c) presuppose 'John said that he had seen the culprit' and that the manner of speaking ('mumblingly') is the focus of assertion in (9a), the focus of question in (9b), and the focus of negation in (9c). (10) is the lexical entry for the manner-of-speaking verb *mumble* (cf. Zwicky 1971).

(10) lexical entry for manner-of-speaking verb *mumble*
    syntax: V in [__, CP[*that*]]

F/A: F_{pa}
RS: [$_{TYPE}$ "say"] in [__ [AG, SO] [$_{TH}$ EV] [$_{MANNER}$ "mumbling"]]
$\underbrace{\qquad\qquad\qquad}\underbrace{\qquad\qquad\qquad\qquad\qquad}$
IS: BI   FI

Note that the specification in (10) of BI and FI is default, and that the information status can be changed by giving an appropriate discourse context. In (11a, b) below, the same manner-of-speaking verb is used in the first and second sentences. Therefore, the manner of speaking in the second sentence is no longer FI, which allows the complement clause to be new FI. This explains the improved acceptability of the *wh*-question in (11a, b).

(11) a. I know you mumbled about a woman you saw yesterday.
   ?Tell me who you mumbled that you saw? (cf. (2c))
   b. I know John simpered about a woman he's been seeing recently.
   ?But I don't know who he simpered that he's been seeing? (cf. (2b))

This semantic/pragmatic account of unacceptable "*wh*-movement" in (1) and (2) seems to be at least compatible with the fact that both factive verbs and manner-of-speaking verbs allow an in-situ *wh*-phrase in their complement clause when they are used in quiz questions.

(12) a. Ginny regrets that Don bought what. (cf. (1a))
   b. John regrets that he behaved how. (cf. (1b))
   c. John quipped that Mary wore what. (cf. (2a))
   d. Mary simpered that home economics was what. (cf. (2b))

When there is an in-situ *wh*-phrase in a declarative sentence, the lexical entry for quiz question (6.1.9 (5)) is triggered, overriding the default specification of BI and FI in (7) and (10), and the whole propositional function is asserted. For example, in (12a), the speaker asserts 'Ginny regrets that Don bought something' and asks the identity of that 'something.' As a quiz question, the *wh*-phrase is interpreted as having the widest scope in F/A.

6.1.11 The Coordinate Structure Constraint revisited
We discussed in 6.1.3 (14) how to account for the Coordinate Structure Constraint (CSC) in *wh*-questions and adopted the convention that the sequence of the

mother node and each of its daughter nodes of a coordinate structure constitutes a single node for the purposes of the dominance path conditions.

The *wh*-relative phrase and its corresponding gap in a relative clause also exhibit unbounded dependency, which can be captured by the dominance path conditions (6.2.3 (1), (4)). As will be discussed in 6.2.2, relative pronouns in *wh*-relative clauses are pronouns, not quantifiers, and as such, there is no QP, or for that matter, no variable, in the F/A structure of a relative clause. In this section, we would like to reconsider what happens to the dominance paths of a *wh*-question and a *wh*-relative clause when a coordinate structure occurs in its middle part.

When a coordinate structure appears in the middle part of a dominance path, we interpret the dominance path conditions according to the above convention. This interpretation forces the dominance path to diverge into a separate dominance path for each conjunct, thus resulting in an across-the-board (ATB) application of "*wh*-movement" in *wh*-questions and *wh*-relative clauses. When a dominance path diverges at a coordinate structure in its middle part, each branch must meet the dominance path conditions. Here is an example.

(1) a. Which student do you think Mary likes __ and John said he hates __?
  b. Which student [$_{S[PRES, INV]}$ do [$_{S[BSE]}$ you [$_{VP[BSE]}$ think [$_{\underline{S[FIN]}}$ [$_{\boxed{S[PRES]}}$ Mary [$_{VP[PRES]}$ likes NP[G]]] and
    [$_{\boxed{S[PAST]}}$ John [$_{VP[PAST]}$ said [$_{S[PRES]}$ he [$_{VP[PRES]}$ hates NP[G]]]]]]]]?
  c. the dominance path of the first gap
    CP[WH[Q]] S[PRES, INV] S[BSE] VP[BSE] $\boxed{\text{S[PRES]}}$ VP[PRES] NP[G]
  d. the dominance path of the second gap
    CP[WH[Q]] S[PRES, INV] S[BSE] VP[BSE] $\boxed{\text{S[PAST]}}$ VP[PAST] S[PRES] VP[PRES] NP[G]

In (1a), the complement clause of the verb *think* is a coordinate structure in the form of [$_{S[FIN]}$ S[PRES] *and* S[PAST]]. The mother node of the coordination S[FIN] is underlined in (1b) and its daughter conjunct nodes are enclosed in a rectangle in (1b, c, d). Following the convention, we take the sequence of the S[FIN] and its daughter node S[PRES] or S[PAST] as constituting a single node, and furthermore we take its category label as the same as that of the daughter node. This means in effect that we are treating the sequence of the mother and each of its conjunct daughters as if there were no coordinate structure. This is illustrated in (1c, d). We restate the convention in question as follows. This will be part of the dominance path conditions.

(2) Coordinate Structure Convention in dominance paths
When a coordinate structure occurs in the middle part of a dominance path, the mother node and each of its daughter conjunct nodes constitute a single node with the daughter's category label for the purposes of the dominance path conditions.

The convention (2) defines what happens when a coordinate structure occurs in the middle part of a dominance path. It guarantees that each conjunct node is still in the middle part of the dominance path, which implies that a conjunct itself cannot be a gap. Therefore, the following ungrammatical cases that violate the Conjunct Constraint (Ross 1986: 98, Pollard and Sag 1994: 201) (i.e., "In a coordinate structure, no conjunct may be moved") are correctly excluded by (2).

(3) Gazdar et al. 1985: 178
 a. *I wonder who you saw __ and __.
 a'. *I wonder who you saw [_NP_ NP[G] and NP[G]].
   the two dominance paths: CP[WH[Q]] S[PAST] VP[PAST] NP[G]
 b. *I wonder who you saw __ and a picture of __.
 b'. *I wonder who you saw [_NP_ NP[G] and a picture of NP[G]].
   the first dominance path: CP[WH[Q]] S[PAST] VP[PAST] NP[G]
 c. *I wonder who you saw a picture of __ and __.

On a related note, we need to make a remark on the CASE feature, whose value is NOM and ACC, of a *wh*-phrase and its corresponding gap. In (1a), *which student* is in the accusative, because both gaps are in the accusative. However, in (4a, b) below, the first gap is in the accusative but the second gap is in the nominative. In (4c), the first gap is in the nominative but the second gap is in the accusative.

(4) a. I know a man who Mary likes __ and hopes __ will win. (Gazdar et al. 1985: 178)
 b. I wonder which student Mary likes __ and hopes __ will pass the exam.

c. the book which __ appeared last year and Smith reviewed __ for the *Post* (McCawley 1998: 444)

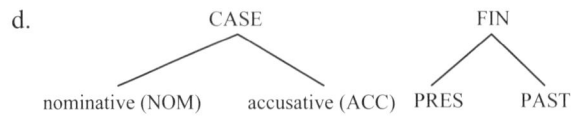

d.
```
          CASE                    FIN
         /    \                  /   \
nominative (NOM)  accusative (ACC)  PRES   PAST
```

To account for the grammaticality of (4a, b, c), in which the gaps have different CASE values, we need to take the CASE feature not as a binary feature <CASE, NOM> and <CASE, ACC> but as organized as (4d), in which CASE covers both NOM and ACC (i.e., CASE is the "common" case) and that both NP[ACC] and NP[NOM] are special instances of NP[CASE]. We understand the VFORM value FIN in exactly the same way (4d). Both V[PAST] and V[PRES] are special instances of V[FIN]. In (4a, b, c), the *wh*-phrase is NP[CASE], which is compatible with the two gaps NP[G, ACC] and NP[G, NOM]. Also, in (1a), the coordinate structure is [$_{S[FIN]}$ S[PRES] *and* S[PAST]], where the category of each conjunct (i.e., S[PRES] and S[PAST]) is compatible with that of their mother node, namely, S[FIN].

In the remainder of this section, we would like to consider well-known counterexamples to the Coordinate Structure Constraint (CSC). (5), (6), and (7) are counterexamples we would like to discuss.

(5) "extraction" from the second conjunct
   a. What did Harry go to the store and buy __? (Lakoff 1986 (1))
   a'. Who did he pick up the phone and call __? (Lakoff 1986 (20))
   b. Here's the whisky which I went to the store and bought __. (Ross 1986: 103)
   c. the screw which I've got to try and find __ (Ross 1986: 105)
   d. Which granny does Aunt Hattie want me to be nice and kiss __? (Ross 1986: 105)

Two VPs are coordinated in (5): *go somewhere and do something* in (5a, a', b), *try and do something* in (5c), and *be nice and do something* in (5d). The first conjunct VP expresses "an auxiliary action that was taken in preparation for the primary action described by the second conjunct" (Na and Huck 1992: 256). In this sense, these sequences of two VPs evoke a "scenario" of "a natural course of events"

(Lakoff 1986) that consists of two scenes. In (5a), for example, the first conjunct *go to the store* is an "auxiliary scene" and the second conjunct *buy* (*something*) is a "main scene." The two scenes evoke a scenario of a natural/expected course of events and the "extraction" takes place from the conjunct VP that represents a main scene.

Here is a different set of counterexamples.

(6) "extraction" from the first conjunct
   a. How much can you drink __ and not end up with a hangover the next morning? (Goldsmith 1985)
   b. How many lakes can we destroy __ and not arouse public antipathy? (Goldsmith 1985)
   c. That's the stuff that the guys in the Caucasus drink __ and live to be a hundred. (Lakoff 1986 (20a))
   d. That's the kind of firecracker that I set __ off and scared the neighbors. (Lakoff 1986 (20b))

In (6a, b), the two coordinated VPs express "a course of events that is counter to a natural course of events" (Lakoff 1986). However, the respective VP coordination still evokes a scenario of conventional expectations: 'if you drink a lot, you will end up with a hangover the next morning' in (6a) and 'if we destroy many lakes, we will arouse public antipathy' in (6b). In these examples, the first conjunct is a main scene and the second conjunct is an auxiliary scene in the sense that the second conjunct just "adds information that qualifies the first" (Na and Huck 1992: 257): 'you can drink x-much without ending up with a hangover the next morning' in (6a) and 'we can destroy x-many lakes without arousing public antipathy' in (6b). In (6c, d), the coordinated VPs express "cause and effect" (Lakoff 1986), which is another example of a natural course of events. The first conjunct describes a volitional act and is a main scene and the second conjunct is an auxiliary scene that "is regarded as an aftermath of the first conjunct" (Na and Huck 1992: 257). The examples we have looked at so far, (5) and (6), contain a coordinate structure with the conjunction *and* consisting of two VPs with the same VFORM value (i.e., coordinated VP[BSE], VP[PRES], or VP[PAST]). The VP coordination evokes a scenario of a natural course of events and "extraction" takes place from the main scene conjunct VP.

Lakoff (1986) pointed out the interesting examples in (7) below, in which "extraction" takes place from some but not all of the conjuncts. Here again, the coordinate structures involved are a coordination by *and* of VPs with the same VFORM value. We would like to claim again that "extraction" takes place from the main scenes of an evoked scenario of a natural/expected course of events.

(7) multiple "extractions"
   a. What did he go to the store, buy __, load __ in his car, drive home, and unload __? (Lakoff 1986 (3))
      presupposition: There is something such that he went to the store, bought it, loaded it in his car, drove home, and unloaded it.
   b. How many courses can you take __ for credit, still remain sane, and get all A's in __? (Lakoff 1986 (4))
      presupposition: There is a certain number such that you can take that many courses for credit, still remain sane, and get all A's in them.
   c. What problem did he sit there for a while, start thinking about __, get bored, and give up on __? (Lakoff 1986 (18))
      presupposition: There is a certain problem such that he sat there for a while, started thinking about it, got bored, and gave up on it.
   d. Sam is not the sort of guy you can just sit there, listen to __, and not want to punch __ in the nose. (Lakoff 1986 (7))
   e. This is the kind of brandy that you can sip __ after dinner, watch tv for a while, sip some more of __, work a bit, finish __ off, go to bed, and still feel fine in the morning.
   (Lakoff 1986 (8), also cited in McCawley 1998: 310 note 23)

The VP coordinations in these examples describe a series of temporally consecutive events that constitutes a normal course of events, which we see in the presuppositions of (7a–c). The gapped conjuncts are main scenes, whereas the nongapped conjuncts, for example, *go to the store* and *drive home* in (7a), are auxiliary scenes in that they simply give "background" (Lakoff 1986) that depicts stages that connect the main scenes of the gapped conjuncts.

So far we have argued for the following points about the counterexamples to the CSC, (5), (6), and (7): (i) they contain VP coordination with the same VFORM value by the coordinate conjunction *and*, (ii) the conjuncts evoke a scenario of a natural/expected course of events, (iii) the evoked scenario consists of auxiliary scenes and main scenes, and (iv) "extraction" takes place from the conjuncts that depict main scenes. As for claim (i) above, we claim that these VP coordinations correspond to Fa coordinations in F/A (cf. 4.1 (38c)). As for claim (ii), Na and Huck (1992: 254) pointed out that S coordination does not allow such an interpretation, even if all the S-conjuncts share the same subject and tense.

(8) a. I went to the store and I bought some whisky. (Na and Huck 1992: 254 (20))
  b. *This is the whisky which I went to the store and I bought (Na and Huck 1992: 254 (22))
  c. *Which whisky did you go to the store and you buy?

They observed that (8a) does not necessarily imply that 'I bought the whisky at the same store mentioned in the first conjunct.' It seems that S coordination signals that the VPs contained in it are not so closely related as to evoke a scenario of a natural course of events. They also pointed out that when two conjoined VPs are preceded by *both*, this coordination describes separate unrelated events and does not evoke such a scenario of a normal/expected course of events.

(9) a. I both went to the store and bought some whisky. (Na and Huck 1992: 254 (21))
  b. *the whisky I both went to the store and bought
  c. *Which whisky did you both go to the store and buy?
  d. Which whisky do you want to both drink every night and invest in the distiller of?

It seems that *both* forces each of the two VP conjuncts to be separate main scenes and hence such a VP coordination does not allow "extraction" from one of them. As shown in (9d), "extraction" is possible from the constituent structure *both* VP *and* VP if it is from both conjuncts.

We would like to maintain the Coordinate Structure Convention (2) as a general case. However, we need to relax it when the coordinate structure in question evokes a scene of a natural/expected course of events. In such a case, "extraction" is possible from main scene conjunct(s). Note that we have identified three factors for not evoking a scenario of a natural/expected course of events: (i) S coordination, (ii) VP coordination introduced by *both*, and (iii) VP coordination with different tenses. (iii) is illustrated in (10) below. A coordination of VPs with different tenses does not allow "extraction" from one of the conjuncts (10b, c) but allows

ATB "extraction" (10d). Note that (i) and (iii) are cases where PROP coordination is involved in F/A (cf. 4.1 (38)).

(10) a. I slept well last night and don't have a headache anymore. (Na and Huck 1992: 258 (34))
   b. *I wonder how well you slept __ last night and don't have a headache anymore.
   c. *I wonder what ache you slept well last night and don't have __ anymore.
   d. I wonder what ache you slept off __ and don't have __ anymore.

On the other hand, the factors that work toward evoking a scenario of a natural/expected course of events are: (i) Fa coordination in F/A (which corresponds to VP coordination with the same VFORM value) and (ii) coordination by *and* without *both*.

We do the necessary relaxing of the Coordinate Structure Convention (2) by proposing a special case of it. We assume that whether a VP coordination evokes a scenario of a natural/expected course of events or not is determined by reference to Information Structure (IS).

(11) Coordinate Structure Convention in dominance paths (special case of (2))
   When a VP coordinate structure that evokes a scenario of a natural/expected course of events occurs in the middle of a dominance path, the mother node and each of its main scene conjunct nodes constitute a single node with the daughter's category label for the purposes of the dominance path conditions.

(11) allows "extraction" from main scene conjunct VPs, because the daughter conjuncts that depict main scenes inherit the mother's dominance path by becoming unified with the mother node. On the other hand, conjunct VP nodes that depict auxiliary scenes are not unified with the mother node, thus not inheriting the dominance path from their mother, which means no gap in them. Because (11) only takes effect when the coordinate structure in question is a VP-coordination and evokes a scenario of a natural/expected course of events, thus a special case of (2), the application of (11) preempts that of (2), due to the Elsewhere Principle (1.1.2 (3)).

6.2 Relative Clauses

6.2.1 The WH[R] feature and its percolation

It is a well-known fact that interrogative pronouns (with the WH[Q] feature) and relative pronouns (with the WH[R] feature) are different in distribution. As a case in point, 6.1.5 (1) is repeated here. (We ignore the interpretation of (1b) as a *wh*-in-situ question, such as quiz question or echo question, in which no gap (NP[G]) is present.)

(1) Pollard and Sag 1994: 159
   a. This is the farmer [NP[WH[R]] pictures of whom] NP[G] appeared in *Newsweek*.
   b. *[NP[WH[Q]] Pictures of whom] NP[G] appeared in *Newsweek*?

Examples (2a, a') show that the syntactic feature WH[R] encoded in the relative pronouns *which* and *whose* can percolate up pretty high in each relative *wh*-phrase NP[WH[R]]. By contrast, (2b) shows that the dominance path for a relative clause can go down pretty deep into a series of NP, N', and PP to reach the bottom NP[G].

(2) a. The committee objected to all books [NP[WH[R]] the height of the covers of which] the government had prescribed NP[G]. (Gazdar et al. 1985: 156)
   [NP[WH[R]] the [N'[WH[R]] height [PP[WH[R]] of [NP[WH[R]] the [N'[WH[R]] covers [PP[WH[R]] of [NP[WH[R]] which]]]]]]]
   a'. Here's the minister [PP[WH[R]] in the middle of whose sermon] the dog barked. (Pollard and Sag 1994: 212)
   [PP[WH[R]] in [NP[WH[R]] the [N'[WH[R]] middle [PP[WH[R]] of [NP[WH[R]] [NP[WH[R], POS] whose] sermon]]]]]
   b. Reports [NP[WH[R]] which] the government prescribes [NP the height of the lettering on the covers of NP[G]] are invariably boring. (Ross 1986: 121)
   c. Here's the rabbi [NP[WH[R]] whose brother's son's friend's Bar Mitzvah] we attended NP[G]. (Pollard and Sag 1994: 212)
   d. an author [NP[WH[R]] most of whose works] NP[G] are completely forgotten (McCawley 1998: 435)

To license the percolation of the WH[R] feature in (1a) and (2), we need to admit the following set of local trees. The difference between WH[Q] (6.1.5 (3)) and WH[R] is (3b), in which WH[R] on a complement or adjunct PP can go up to its mother N'.

(3) a. NP[WH[R]]
          /\
      DET N'[WH[R]]

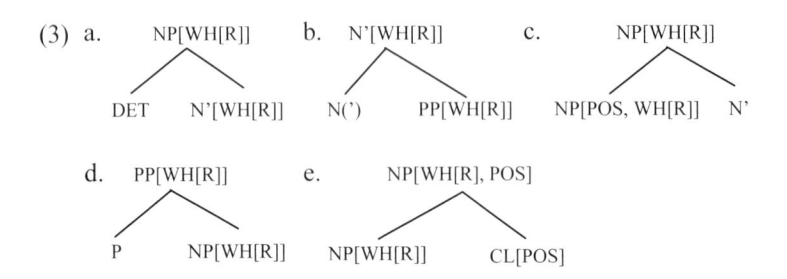

b. N'[WH[R]]
      /\
    N(') PP[WH[R]]

c. NP[WH[R]]
         /\
   NP[POS, WH[R]] N'

d. PP[WH[R]]
     /\
   P   NP[WH[R]]

e. NP[WH[R], POS]
       /\
  NP[WH[R]] CL[POS]

The local trees in (3) show that the WH[R] feature is shared between a daughter and its mother of any [−V] phrasal node (namely, N', NP, PP). The local trees (3c, e) admit the NP[WH[R]] in (2c) as follows.

(4) the syntax of [_{NP[WH[R]]} *whose brother's son's friend's Bar Mitzvah*] in (2c)

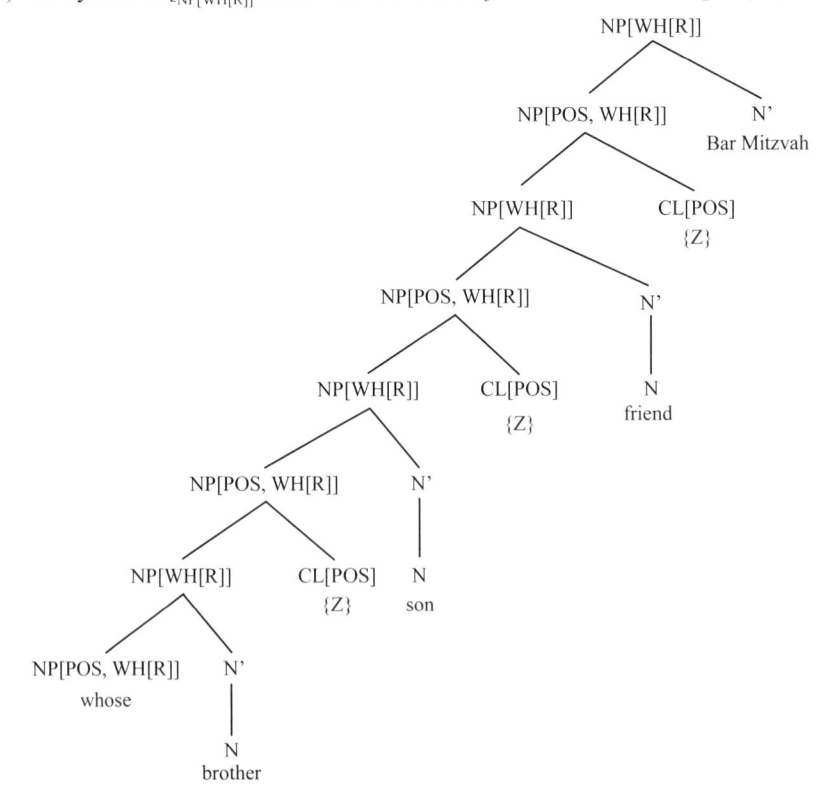

```
                                NP[WH[R]]
                                /        \
                    NP[POS, WH[R]]        N'
                    /          \          Bar Mitzvah
              NP[WH[R]]        CL[POS]
              /       \        {Z}
       NP[POS, WH[R]]  N'
        /      \       |
   NP[WH[R]]  CL[POS]  N
   /     \    {Z}     friend
NP[POS, WH[R]]  N'
 /     \        |
NP[WH[R]] CL[POS] N
 /    \   {Z}   son
NP[POS, WH[R]]  N'
  whose         |
                N
                brother
```

6.2.2 Relative pronouns

Following Sadock (2012: 131), we claim that (i) relative pronouns are definite pronouns (McCawley 1998: 430–431), (ii) relative pronouns have the syntactic feature WH[R], which restricts their distribution in syntax, and (iii) every relative pronoun must corefer with the N' to which the relative clause that contains it is adjoined (McCawley 1998: 430).

Claim (i) is best illustrated by the examples in (1), in which the relative pronoun, just like definite personal pronouns, has split antecedents. Note that a bound variable pronoun cannot have split antecedents (i.e., two quantified NPs as its antecedents) (1d), which suggests that a relative pronoun in (1a, b, c) is not a bound variable pronoun but an ordinary pronoun with the underlined N' (but not the quantified NP as a whole) as its antecedent.

(1) a. A <u>man</u>$_i$ entered the room and a <u>woman</u>$_j$ walked out <u>who</u>$_{\{i,j\}}$ had met in Vienna.
(McCawley 1998: 771, first noted by Ross and Perlmutter 1970)
cf. <u>A man</u>$_i$ entered the room and <u>a woman</u>$_j$ walked out. <u>They</u>$_{\{i,j\}}$ had met in Vienna.
b. A <u>man</u> came in the front door and a <u>woman</u> came in the side door <u>who</u> had met in Vienna. (McCawley 1993: 240)
c. ?Every <u>man</u>$_i$ wore a gaudy shirt and every <u>woman</u>$_j$ wore a matching blouse <u>who</u>$_{\{i,j\}}$ were partners in the dance marathon. (McCawley 1993: 244)
d. *<u>Everyone</u>$_x$ told <u>someone</u>$_y$ that <u>they</u>$_{\{x,y\}}$ had to leave. (Imanishi and Asano 1990:39)
cf. <u>Mary</u>$_i$ told <u>John</u>$_j$ that <u>they</u>$_{\{i,j\}}$ had to leave.

As for claim (iii), which is about coreference between the head N' and the relative pronoun, what is at issue here is not token identity but type identity in coreference relations. In general, a referential index on an NP with a definite determiner represents token identity (token-identity referential index), whereas a referential index on an N' represents type identity (type-identity referential index) (1.6 (5)). For example, in coordinated NPs, such as [[$_{NPi}$ *this* [$_{N'j}$ *picture of John*]] *and* [$_{NPk}$ *that* [$_{N'j}$ *one*]]], the indices i and k on the two NPs are token-identity referential indices and the index j on both N' nodes is a type-identity referential index. Note that two instances of the N' *picture of John* have the same type-identity referential index (i.e., coreferent in type) as long as the two instances of *John* refer to the same person (cf. McCawley 1998: 338). Third person pronouns, including relative pronouns, can carry a type-identity referential index, as in *While independent voters break strongly for Mr. Obama in Pennsylvania, a state that Mr. Romney has been trying to make more competitive, they are closely split in Florida and Ohio* (*New York Times*, August 1, 2012), in which the pronoun *they* refers to the preceding *independent voters* not as token identity (i.e., referring to one and the same set of independent voters) but as type identity (i.e., referring to another set of the same type). Coreference in type between an N' and the pro-N' form *one* obeys the usual constraint that a pronoun must not precede and c-command its antecedent. Observe the contrast between the following two (McCawley 1998: 358): *The young robin that the old one had pecked was bleeding* vs. *The young one that the old robin had pecked was bleeding. In the second example, the pro-N' *one* precedes and c-commands the N' *robin*, whether the *that*-relative clause is adjoined to the pro-N' *one* or to the larger N' *young one*. See the definition of c-command in syntax (1.2 (15) and (17)).

Here are the lexical entries for relative pronouns *who* (2) and *which* (3) (cf. Sadock 2012: 131).

(2) lexical entry for relative pronoun *who*
    syntax: NP[WH[R], IND[j, AGR]]
    • This must corefer with the N' to which the relative clause (CP[WH[R]]) that contains it is adjoined.
    F/A: ARG[IND[j, AGR]], where j∈ {[+HUMAN]}
    RS: ROLE

(3) lexical entry for relative pronoun *which*
    syntax: NP[WH[R], IND[j, 3 N]]
    • This must corefer with the N' to which the relative clause (CP[WH[R]]) that contains it is adjoined.
    F/A: ARG[IND[j, 3 N]], where j∈ {[–HUMAN]}
    RS: ROLE

The syntactic field of (2) and (3) specifies that it is an NP[WH[R]] with its INDEX (IND) value (1.3 (6)). Recall that we have been assuming that INDEX, is primarily a feature in F/A but syntax can access the same information as well due to Feature Osmosis (1.3). The coreference condition (i.e., claim (iii) above) is stated here. The F/A field specifies that the relative pronoun is an ARG with the same INDEX value. The RS specifies that the relative pronoun bears some role (agent, patient, etc.) in RS. The referential index j in (2) and (3) is a type-identity referential index. The domain of the referential index (i.e., the domain from which the referent of the referential index is chosen) is the set of humans in (2) and the set of nonhumans in (3).

The relative pronoun *who* is chosen when it purports to refer to a person or people ([+HUMAN]). For example, in reference transfer cases, such as *a blue shirt who was happy to have his picture taken* (from the web), which means 'a person in blue shirt who was happy to have his picture taken,' the relative pronoun *who* and the following VP *was happy to have his picture taken* determine that the referent of the head N' *blue shirt* is a person, that is, 'a person in a blue shirt' (shifted reading). On the other hand, the relative pronoun *which* is chosen when it purports to refer to a thing, a plant, or an animal ([−HUMAN]). For example, in *the former president which will be on display in Madame Tussaud's next month*, the relative pronoun *which* refers to 'the statue of the former president' (shifted reading). (See Jackendoff 1997: 54ff. and Jackendoff 2002: 389–90 for details on reference transfer.) To deal with these reference transfer cases, we assume in the lexicon a freely available defective lexical item (i.e., coerced material) {PERSON | THING} CONTEXTUALLY ASSOCIATED WITH with no phonology, morphology, or syntax. For example, the N' *blue shirt* in the above example has its coerced F/A structure [$_{ARG}$ PERSON CONTEXTUALLY ASSOCIATED WITH [$_{ARG}$ BLUE SHIRT]], in which the underlined part comes from the coerced material in question. (See 4.7 for another type of coercion.) The relative pronoun *who* also conveys "a greater degree of empathy or personal interest and involvement" (Huddleston and Pullum 2002: 1048) and is often used with animals, especially pets, as in *a dog who was licking my face* (Huddleston and Pullum 2002: 1048). Note furthermore that no specification of the AGR value is given in (2). This is because we need to cover cases such as *I, who am the owner of this company, have the right to decide who to hire*, and *You, who are the owner of this company, have the right to decide who to hire* (McCawley 1998: 479).

Here is an example of a relative clause: the syntax and F/A of the N' *pen with which John wrote the book*.

(4) the syntax and F/A of *pen with which John wrote the book*

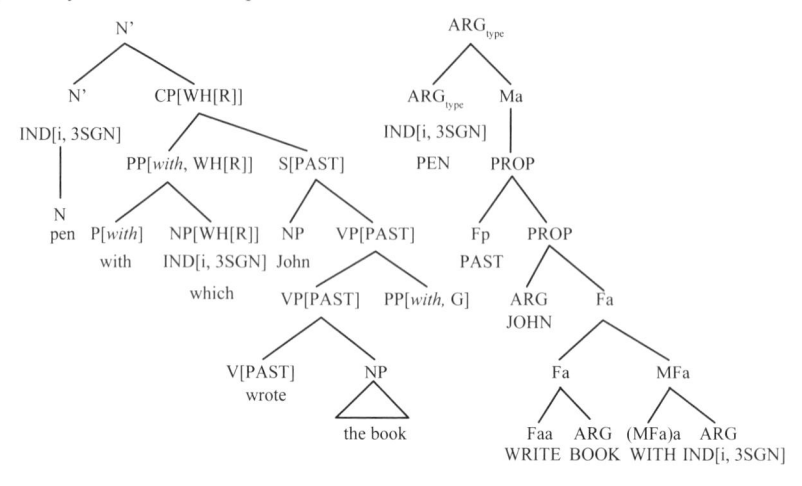

```
                N'                                    ARG_type
               / \                                    /      \
              N'      CP[WH[R]]                   ARG_type    Ma
         IND[i, 3SGN]  /    \                    IND[i, 3SGN]  |
              |    PP[with, WH[R]]  S[PAST]         PEN       PROP
              N     /        \       /    \                   /   \
             pen  P[with]  NP[WH[R]]  NP  VP[PAST]            Fp   PROP
                  with    IND[i,3SGN] John /    \            PAST  /   \
                            which      VP[PAST] PP[with, G]      ARG    Fa
                                        /    \                   JOHN  /  \
                                    V[PAST]   NP                     Fa    MFa
                                     wrote    △                     /  \   /  \
                                           the book              Faa  ARG (MFa)a ARG
                                                                WRITE BOOK WITH IND[i, 3SGN]
```

In the syntactic structure (4), CP[WH[R]] is a *wh*-relative clause, which consists of a relative *wh*-phrase (PP[*with*, WH[R]]) and a finite clause. The relative clause is adjoined to the head N'. The percolation of the WH[R] feature between the PP and its daughter NP is licensed by 6.2.1 (3d). In the F/A structure, the relative clause is a PROP directly dominated by an Ma, a modifier of argument. The relative pronoun is coreferent with the head N' in syntax and the head ARG in F/A. The referential index i is a type-identity referential index. Note that the relative pronoun is "moved" in syntax but stays *in situ* in F/A.

This analysis of relative clause can be extended to a QNP whose head N' is modified by a relative clause. In (5a), the relative pronoun *who* and the first *his* are definite pronouns that are coreferent with the head N' *man* and they carry the type-identity referential index j, as in (5b). The second *his* in (5a) is a variable pronoun bound by the QNP *every man who loves his children*. This situation is clearly represented in (5d), the F/A structure of (5a). Because pronouns in a relative clause that modifies a QNP (e.g., the first *his* in (5a)) are not variables, they allow split antecedents (5.5 (2), (3); cf. 6.2.2 (1d)). In (5c), *who* and *they* are coreferent and refer to the split antecedents *man* and *woman*.

(5) a. Every man who loves his children loves his wife.
    b. [$_{QNPx}$ Every [man$_j$ who$_j$ loves his$_j$ children]] loves his$_x$ wife.

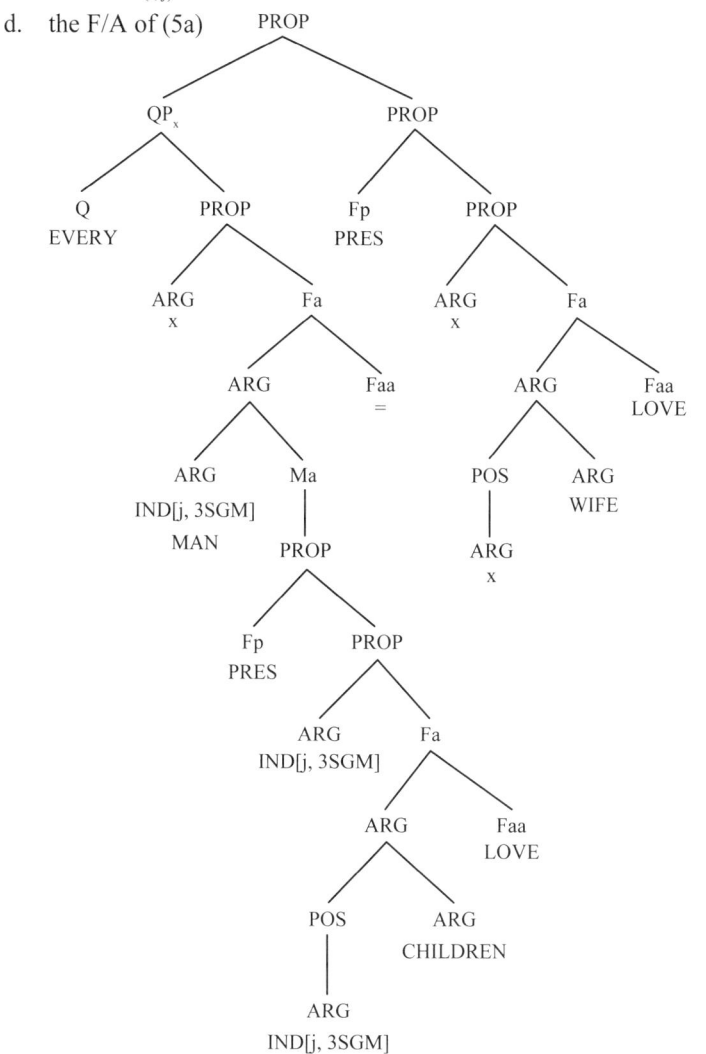

c. A <u>man</u>$_i$ came in the front door and a <u>woman</u>$_j$ came in the side door <u>who</u>$_{\{i,j\}}$ knew <u>they</u>$_{\{i,j\}}$ were late. (6.2.2 (1a))

d. the F/A of (5a)

```
                                    PROP
                    ┌─────────────────┴─────────────────┐
                   QP_x                                PROP
              ┌─────┴─────┐                      ┌──────┴──────┐
              Q          PROP                    Fp           PROP
           EVERY      ┌───┴───┐                 PRES      ┌────┴────┐
                     ARG      Fa                         ARG        Fa
                      x    ┌──┴──┐                        x      ┌───┴───┐
                         ARG    Faa                            ARG      Faa
                       ┌──┴──┐   =                          ┌───┴───┐   LOVE
                      ARG   Ma                             POS     ARG
                   IND[j, 3SGM] │                           │     WIFE
                      MAN     PROP                         ARG
                          ┌────┴────┐                       x
                          Fp       PROP
                         PRES   ┌───┴───┐
                               ARG      Fa
                           IND[j, 3SGM] ┌──┴──┐
                                       ARG   Faa
                                    ┌───┴───┐ LOVE
                                   POS     ARG
                                    │    CHILDREN
                                   ARG
                                IND[j, 3SGM]
```

6.2.3 Restrictive *wh*-relative clauses

The internal and external syntax of a restrictive *wh*-relative clause are (1a, b), where XP is NP or PP (cf. 6.1.7 (1)).

(1) the internal and external syntax of *wh*-relative clause
   a. the internal syntax of *wh*-relative clause
      [$_{\text{CP[WH[R]]}}$ XP[WH[R], α] S[FIN]], where α is a PFORM value if X = P.
      • the syntactic dominance path conditions on XP[WH[R], α]
         a. nonsubject gap: CP[WH[R]] {S, VP, CP[{*that* | *for*}]}* VP {NP, N', PP}* XP[G, α]
         b. subject gap: CP[WH[R]] {S, VP, CP[{*that* | *for*}]}* S[FIN] NP[G]
      • the F/A dominance path conditions on XP[WH[R], α]
         PROP {PROP, Fa, Faa, Fpa}* {ARG, POS}* ARG[IND[j, AGR]]
   b. the external syntax of *wh*-relative clause
      [$_{\text{N'}}$ N' CP[WH[R]]] (=1.2 (1c))

In (1a), the dominance path conditions on XP[WH[R], α] are the same as those on XP[WH[Q], α] (6.1.7 (1)) and capture unbounded dependency in a relative clause between the relative *wh*-phrase and the bottom gap. They require that there be a phonologically null XP[G] of the same category as the relative *wh*-phrase (XP[WH[R]]) within its sister S[FIN]. When the XP in (1a) is a PP, the same PFORM value is required for the PP[WH[R]] and the bottom PP[G]. (1a) also explains the ungrammaticality of **a shovel* [$_{\text{CP[WH[R]]}}$ *with which* [$_{\text{CP[that]}}$ *that* [$_{\text{S[FIN]}}$ *we will dig the hole*]]], because CP[WH[R]] must directly dominate S[FIN] and not CP[*that*]. The F/A of a relative pronoun is an ARG with its IND feature (6.2.2 (2), (3), (4)). In the F/A dominance path condition in (1a) above, the bottom ARG is the F/A of the relative pronoun and the top PROP corresponds to the top CP[WH[R]] in the syntactic dominance path conditions (cf. (3c)). Because the dominance path conditions are common to *wh*-questions and *wh*-relative clauses, the unbounded dependency in the former and that in the latter are sensitive to the same set of island constraints.

The external syntax of a restrictive *wh*-relative clause is (1b), where the relative clause (CP[WH[R]]) is adjoined to its head N' (Sadock 2012: 131, McCawley 1998: 381, McCawley 1993: 222, Gazdar et al. 1985: 155, Pollard and Sag 1994: 213, Huddleston and Pullum 2002: 1061), as in 6.2.2 (4). Because (1b) is recursive, stacked restrictive relative clauses (2) are possible (McCawley 1998: 382). See (8) and (9) for further details. (1a, b) will be incorporated into the lexical entry for relative *wh*-phrases in (4).

(2) a. [$_{\text{N'}}$ [$_{\text{N'}}$ N' CP[WH[R]]] CP[WH[R]]]
    b. the [[book [which I bought]] [which Ann had recommended]] (McCawley 1998: 428)

(3a) is an example of a relative clause used in a quantified NP. The syntactic structure of (3a) is given in (3b) and its F/A in (3c). See also 6.2.2 (5) for another example.

(3) a. Every person who knows Diane admires her. (McCawley 1998: 430)
  b. [_{S[PRES]} [_{NP} [_{DET} Every] [_{N'} [_{N'[IND[i, 3SG]]} person] [_{CP[WH[R]]} [_{NP[WH[R], IND[i, 3SG]]} who] [_{S[PRES]} NP[G] knows Diane]]]] [_{VP[PRES]} admires her]].
  c.

```
                        PROP    (tense ignored)
                       /    \
                     QP_x     PROP
                    /   \    /    \
                   Q    PROP ARG   Fa
                 EVERY  /  \  x   /  \
                      ARG  Fa    ARG    Faa
                       x   /\  IND[j, 3SGF] ADMIRE
                         ARG  Faa
                              =
                         /  \           N'
                       Ma   ARG        /  \
                        |   IND[i, 3SG] N'   CP[WH[R]]
                      PROP ◄--PERSON  person
                      /  \                 NP[WH[R]] --► S[PRES]
                    ARG ◄  Fa              who         /     \
                  IND[i, 3SG] /\  ---------------► NP[G]   VP[PRES]
                            ARG  Faa                        /  \
                         IND[j, 3SGF] KNOW              knows Diane
                            DIANE
```

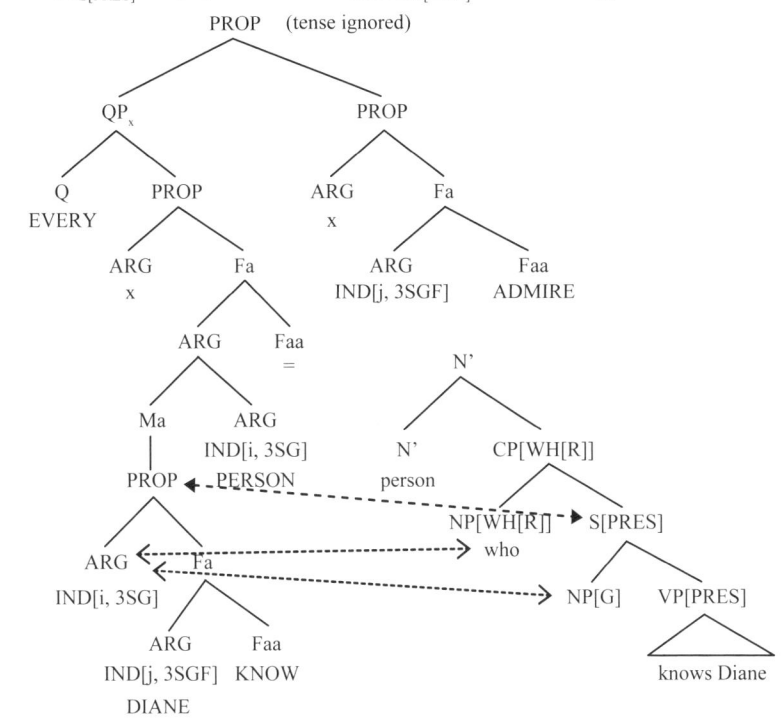

In this F/A structure, the relative clause is treated as a PROP directly dominated by an Ma (modifier of argument), as already illustrated in 6.2.2 (4), and within the PROP, one of the arguments (i.e., ARG[IND[i, 3SG]]) corresponds to a relative pronoun (NP[WH[R]]) in syntax, which is required by the lexical entry for relative pronoun *who* in 6.2.2 (2). At the same time, the ARG[IND [i, 3SG]] also corresponds to the NP[G] in syntax by the default correspondences between syntax and F/A (1.4 (7)). In other words, both the relative *wh*-phrase (*who*) and the NP[G] in syntax correspond to the F/A structure of the relative pronoun ARG[IND[i, 3SG]]. The ARG[IND[i, 3SG]] is coreferent with the head [$_{ARG}$ PERSON] and the two share the same IND value. The referential index i is a type-identity referential index, whereas j is a token-identity referential index.

There is a mismatch in (3c) between syntax and F/A in that although the relative pronoun *who* is directly dominated by the CP[WH[R]] and out of its sister S[PRES] in syntax, its F/A correspondent IND[i, 3SG] appears as one of the arguments inside the PROP that corresponds to the S[PRES]. This is because a relative *wh*-phrase XP[WH[R]] is forced by the internal syntax of relative clause (1a) to be outside the S to which it originally belongs, whereas a relative pronoun in F/A is treated as a regular pronoun and as such appears as an ARG (6.2.2 (2), (3)). (4a) is the lexical entry for the clause-initial relative *wh*-phrase (cf. (1) and 6.1.7 (1)). (4b) is the lexical entry for *wh*-relative clauses (1.2 (1c), 6.2.8 (4)).

(4) a. lexical entry for clause-initial relative *wh*-phrase (as a construction)
 syntax: XP[WH[R], α] in [$_{CP[WH[R]]}$ __ S[FIN]], where α is a PFORM value, if X = P.
 • the syntactic dominance path conditions
   a. nonsubject gap: CP[WH[R], α] {S, VP, CP[{*that* | *for*}]}* VP {NP, N', PP}* XP[G, α]
   b. subject gap: CP[WH[R]] {S, VP, CP[{*that* | *for*}]}* S[FIN] NP[G]
 • the F/A dominance path condition
   PROP {PROP, Fa, Faa, Fpa}* {ARG, POS}* ARG[IND[j, AGR]]
 b. lexical entry for *wh*-relative clause
  syntax: CP[WH[R]] in [$_N$, N' __]
  F/A: PROP in [$_{Ma}$ __]

In (3b), the subject relative pronoun *who* is outside the S of which it is the subject and c-commands the NP[G], because of the internal syntax [$_{CP[WH[R]]}$ XP[WH[R]] S[FIN]]. McCawley (1998: 444) pointed out that a time adverbial, such as PP[*for*], is a sentence-modifier (Mp in F/A) and as such occurs in front of the S it modifies but it does not usually occur between the subject and the verb (5a, b). However, when the subject is a relative pronoun, it can appear before the PP (5c). This is explained by our syntactic structure (5d), in which the relative pronoun is outside the S and directly dominated by the CP[WH[R]], and the time adverbial (PP[*for*]) is adjoined to the S whose subject is NP[G]. (5e) is an example in which the subject relative pronoun *which* is followed by a conditional PP[*if*].

(5) a. [For more than ten years] he has been harassing me.
   b. ??He [for more than ten years] has been harassing me.
   c. a person who [for more than ten years] has been harassing me
   d. a person [_CP[WH[R]] who [_S [for more than ten years] [_S NP[G] has been harassing me]]]
   e. "Or consider rhetorical questions like (36):
   (36) Was Mussolini going to be moderate?
   which [if the participants believe that whatever Mussolini was, he was not moderate], is likely to convey (37):
   (37) Mussolini was definitely not going to be moderate." (Levinson 1983: 110)

McCawley (1998: 444) also pointed out that the unacceptability of (6a) is due to a perceptual difficulty of interpreting this example as S-coordination rather than as VP-coordination. In order to make the S-coordination reading more salient, we insert a sentence adverbial in front of the second VP (6b), which indeed makes the reading (6c) more readily available.

(6) a. *the book which Smith reviewed for the *Post* and won a Pulitzer Prize (McCawley 1998: 444)
   b. the book which Smith reviewed for the *Post* and, according to the *Chicago Tribune*, won a Pulitzer Prize
   c. the book which [_S Smith reviewed NP[G] for the *Post*] and [_S according to the *Chicago Tribune* [_S NP[G] won a Pulitzer Prize]]

This amelioration effect by inserting a sentence adverbial is reminiscent of the amelioration of the *that*-trace effect by insertion of a sentence adverbial (6.1.3 (8)).

In (3c), the relative clause is treated as an Ma (a modifier of argument). Therefore, there is a clear structural asymmetry in F/A between the relative clause (the PROP dominated by an Ma) and the head noun (the ARG to which the Ma is adjoined). By contrast, McCawley (1993: 50) and Sadock (2012: 133) treated the semantics (F/A) of the head noun and the relative clause modifying it as the conjoined propositions. For example, the F/A of *every linguist who speaks Japanese* in their analysis would be [$_{QPx}$ [$_Q$ EVERY] [$_{RROP}$ [$_{RROP}$ x is linguist] AND [$_{RROP}$ x speaks Japanese]]. Some of the problems with this analysis are (i) that the relative pronoun is treated as a variable instead of a definite pronoun (cf. (3c), 6.2.2 (1)) and (ii) that the semantic asymmetry between the head noun and the relative clause is lost. As for (ii), there would be no distinction in their treatment of relative clause between (a) *every linguist who is Japanese* and (b) *every Japanese who is a linguist*. Although both (a) and (b) refer to every member of the intersection of the two sets {linguists} and {Japanese} (i.e., ∀x∈ {linguists}∩{Japanese}), (a) refers to every member of the intersection as the subset of {linguists} and (b) refers to every member of the intersection as the subset of {Japanese}. In each case, the head N' defines the domain set and the relative clause defines a subset within it: (a) {every linguist who is Japanese} ⊆ {linguists} vs. (b) {every Japanese who is a linguist} ⊆ {Japanese}. (This distinction is real in that "Every linguist who is Japanese can speak English" is a statement about linguists and not about the Japanese.) This asymmetry is captured by our treatment of relative clauses, according to which a relative clause is an Ma that modifies the head ARG.

(7a) below is an example of pied-piped PP[WH[R]]. See also 6.2.2 (4). The syntax and F/A of (7a) are given in (7b, d). The internal syntactic structure of PP[*from*, WH[R]] is given in (7c). See 6.2.1 (3) on how the WH[R] feature percolates. We assume that the verb *select* in this example takes two complements, NP and PP[*from*], namely, V in [__, NP, PP[*from*]] in syntax and Faaa in F/A.

(7) a. the poet from whose best-known work I selected that passage (McCawley 1998: 435)

   b. the [$_{N'[IND[i, 3SG]]}$ poet] [$_{CP[WH[R]]}$ [$_{PP[from, WH[R]]}$ from [$_{NP[WH[R]]}$ [$_{NP[WH[R], POS, IND[i, 3SG]]}$ whose] best-known work]] [$_{S[PAST]}$ I selected that passage PP[*from*, G]]]

   c. PP[*from*, WH[R]]
       /   \
   P[*from*]   NP[WH[R]]
   from   /   \
         NP[WH[R], POS]   N'
            whose   / \
                         A   N'
                    best-known |
                               N
                              work

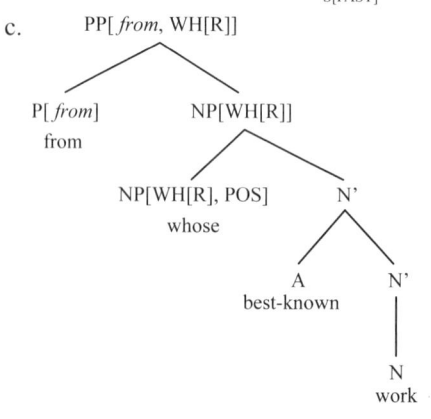

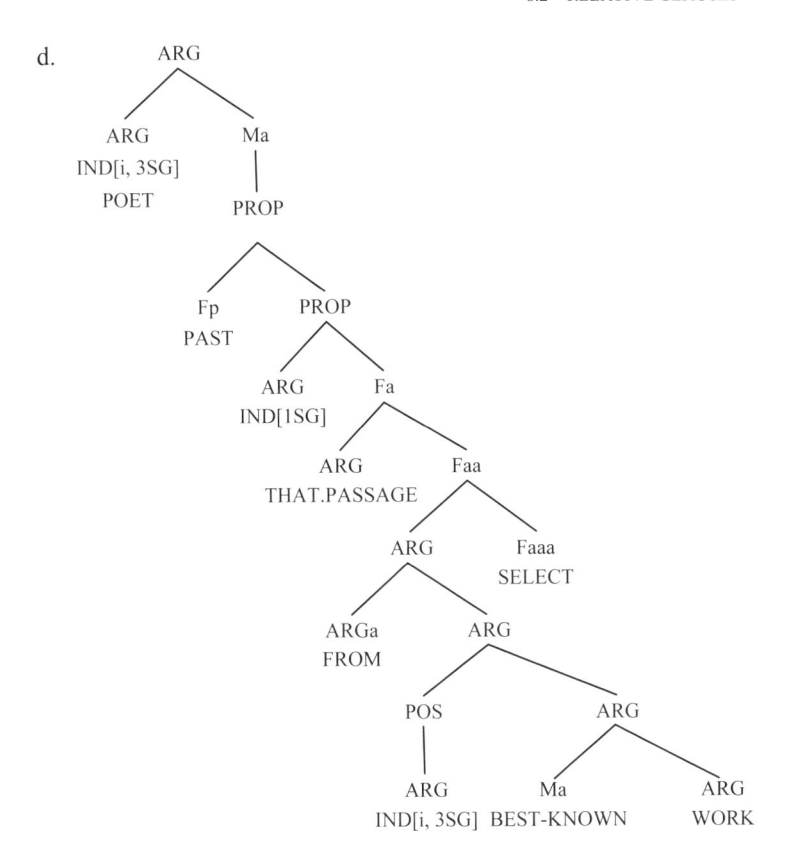

d.
```
            ARG
           /    \
        ARG      Ma
     IND[i, 3SG]  |
        POET     PROP
                /    \
              Fp     PROP
             PAST    /   \
                   ARG    Fa
                 IND[1SG] / \
                        ARG   Faa
                   THAT.PASSAGE / \
                              ARG  Faaa
                              / \  SELECT
                          ARGa  ARG
                          FROM
                               / \
                             POS   ARG
                              |    / \
                             ARG  Ma  ARG
                        IND[i, 3SG] BEST-KNOWN WORK
```

Note that although the whole PP[*from*] *from whose best-known work* is at the initial position of the relative clause in syntax because the PP[*from*] is marked as WH[R], the F/A correspondent of the PP[*from*] occurs *in situ* as one of the arguments of the Faaa within the PROP (cf. 6.1.5 (8)). Note also that the referential index i in (7d) is a type-identity referential index and appears in syntax on the head N' and on the relative pronoun (7b). The whole NP *the poet from whose best-known work I selected that passage* carries its own token-identity referential index.

Here is an additional remark about stacked relative clauses. As was pointed out in (2), the external syntax of relative clauses (1b), in which a relative clause is adjoined to the head N', allows stacked relative clauses, what Jespersen (1927: 87, 1933: 358) called double restriction. However, this does not mean that stacked relative clauses all modify the common innermost head N'. Because of the lexical entries for the relative pronouns 6.2.2 (2) and (3), according to which, the relative pronoun must corefer with the N' to which the relative clause that contains it is adjoined, each relative pronoun only corefers with the N' that is the sister of the relative clause that contains it. For example, in (8a), the relative pronoun contained in CP$_1$[WH[R]] corefers with its sister N' and the relative pronoun contained in CP$_2$[WH[R]] corefers with its sister N', namely, [$_{N'}$ N' CP$_1$[WH[R]]].

(8) a. [$_{N'}$ [$_{N'}$ N' CP$_1$[WH[R]]] CP$_2$[WH[R]]]
   b. the [[[$_{N'}$ book] [which I bought]] [which Ann had recommended]] (=(2b))

In (8b), the first *which* refers to the innermost N' *book* and the second *which* refers to the larger N' *book which I bought*. The approximate F/A of (8b) is (9) below.

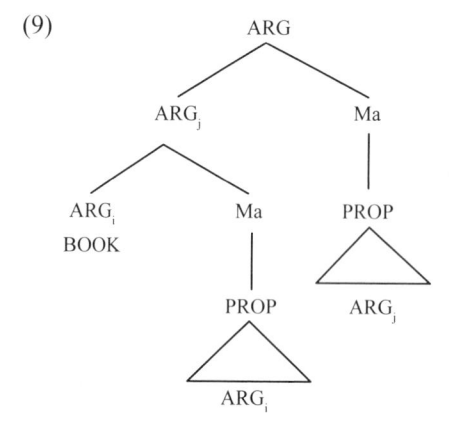

(9)
```
                    ARG
                   /    \
               ARG_j     Ma
              /    \      |
          ARG_i    Ma    PROP
          BOOK      |    /\
                  PROP  ARG_j
                   /\
                 ARG_i
```

The CP$_2$[WH[R]] *which Ann had recommended* is interpreted in such a way that it specifies a subset of the domain set {books which I bought}, just as the CP$_1$[WH[R]] *which I bought* is interpreted in such a way that it specifies a subset of the domain set {books}. (Recall the previous discussion on *every linguist who is Japanese*.)

6.2.4 Nonrestrictive relative clauses

A nonrestrictive relative clause, exemplified in (1), constitutes a speech act of its own separate from the sentence in which it appears (McCawley 1998: 448;

Sadock 2012: 137). In (1a), the matrix sentence is a declarative sentence, which carries out a speech act of assertion (making a statement), and the nonrestrictive relative clause is an interrogative sentence (tag question), which carries out a speech act of inquiry (asking a question) or confirmation.

(1) a. Marcia, who you wanted to meet, didn't you?, has just arrived. (McCawley 1998: 447)
 b. Has John, who was talking to Mary a minute ago, gone home? (McCawley 1998: 448)
 c. Put the turkey, which is in the refrigerator, in the oven. (McCawley 1998: 448)
 d. Symbolic logic, which who cares about anyway, is awfully tough. (Sadock 1974: 126).

In these sentences, the matrix sentence and the nonrestrictive relative clause accomplish different speech acts (SA) in RS, each with its own illocutionary force (IF). Although the antecedent NP and the nonrestrictive relative clause that follows must be adjacent (i.e., extraposition of nonrestrictive relative clause is impossible) (2), they do not form a syntactic constituent (McCawley 1998: 445) (3).

(2) a. Marcia, who you wanted to meet, has just arrived. (McCawley 1998: 447)
 b. *Marcia has just arrived, who you wanted to meet. (ibid.)

(3) a. Tom has <u>a violin which once belonged to Heifetz</u>, and Jane has <u>one</u> too. (McCawley 1998: 445)
 b. Tom has <u>a violin</u>, which once belonged to Heifetz, and Jane has <u>one</u> too. (ibid.)
 c. John <u>sold a violin</u>, which had once belonged to Nathan Milstein, <u>to Itzhak Perlman</u>, and Mary <u>did</u> too. (McCawley 1998: 450)

In (3a), the N' *violin* is modified by the restrictive relative clause *which once belonged to Heifetz* (i.e., [$_{NP}$ [$_{DET}$ *a*] [$_{N'}$ [$_{N'}$ *violin*] CP[WH[R]]]]), and the pronoun *one* in the second conjunct refers to the whole NP. However, when the NP *a violin* is followed by a nonrestrictive relative clause, as in (3b), the pronoun only refers to *a violin* and not *a violin, which once belonged to Heifetz*. The same thing happens with VP ellipsis. In (3c), the pro-VP form *did* in the second conjunct refers to the underlined part, namely, the matrix VP excluding the nonrestrictive relative clause, and not to *sold a violin, which had once belonged to Nathan Milstein, to Itzhak Perlman*.

Following McCawley (1998: 450–451) and Sadock (2012: 136–137), we propose the following lexical entry for nonrestrictive relative clause.

(4) lexical entry for nonrestrictive relative clause (as a construction)
syntax: CP[WH[R]] in {NP | N'} ⩽ __
- The relative pronoun must corefer with the immediately preceding NP or N'.

F/A: PROP
RS: EV in [$_{SA}$ [$_{IF}$ #...#] [$_{[AG, SO]}$ SP] [$_{[PT, GO]}$ AD] [$_{TH}$ __]], where [$_{IF}$ #...#] is the illocutionary force (IF) of the speech act (SA) accomplished by the nonrestrictive relative clause (CP[WH[R]]).

In the syntax of (4), a nonrestrictive relative clause is specified as CP[WH[R]], because nonrestrictive use of *that-* and bare relatives is not allowed. The nonrestrictive relative clause is placed immediately after an NP or N', with which the relative pronoun must be coreferent. It has no syntactic relation with its host S, namely, it is not part of its host S. In F/A, it constitutes a separate proposition, as opposed to [$_{Ma}$ PROP] in the case of restrictive relative clauses. In RS, it performs its own speech act. (See Chapter 7 for the details on speech acts.)

The lexical entry (4) accounts for some of the interesting peculiarities of nonrestrictive relative clauses. First, nothing can be "extracted" from a nonrestrictive relative clause, which is shown in (5). Because the PP[*from*] does not dominate the nonrestrictive relative clause, it does not dominate the gap NP[G] in the nonrestrictive relative clause, either. Therefore, there is no dominance path from the top CP[*that*] to the gap. Note that the CNPC is irrelevant here.

(5) *The knife that I've just heard from Mary, who carved the turkey with NP[G], has a serrated blade. (McCawley 1998: 451)
cf. I've just heard from Mary, who carved the turkey with the knife. The knife has a serrated blade.

Second, although restrictive relatives can be stacked freely (6.2.3 (2)), stacked nonrestrictive relatives are substantially low in acceptability (6a). This is because the adjacency requirement is violated between the head NP and the second nonrestrictive relative clause. In (6b), the second nonrestrictive relative clause follows the immediately preceding NP *the qualifying exam*, namely, the last NP of the first nonrestrictive relative clause, hence satisfying the adjacency requirement. In (6c), three nonrestrictive relative clauses are coordinated, and hence each of them counts as meeting the adjacency requirement.

(6) a. ??Sam Bronowski, who took the qualifying exam, who failed it, wants to retake it. (McCawley 1998: 447)
 b. Sam Bronowski, who took the qualifying exam, which almost everyone failed, did brilliantly on it. (McCawley 1998: 482 note 13)
 c. Sam Bronowski, who took the qualifying exam, who failed it, who took it again, and who failed it again, wants a third chance. (McCawley 1998: 482 note 13)

Third, only restrictive relative clauses can be combined with a quantified NP (QNP). Because the nonrestrictive relative clause in (7b, c) represents a proposition separate from the host proposition that contains the quantifier *everyone* or *every senator*, the nonrestrictive relative pronoun cannot be interpreted as a bound variable. Recall the well-formedness condition 1.3 (15d) (repeated as 5.1 (1c)) that all the instances of a variable x must be either dominated or c-commanded by a single QP_x. The second PROP in (7b') and (7c') violates this condition. The contrast between (8a, c) and (8b, d) can be explained in the same way.

(7) a. Everyone who attended the party had a good time. (McCawley 1998: 447)
 b. *$Everyone_x$, who_x attended the party, had a good time. (ibid.)
  cf. $Everyone_x$ attended the party. *He_x had a good time.
 b'. the F/A of (7b)
  $[_{PROP} [_{QPx}$ EVERY x = PERSON] PAST([x HAVE GOOD.TIME])]
  *$[_{PROP}$ PAST([x ATTEND PARTY])]
 c. *Susan interviewed $every\ senator_x$, who_x is crooked. (McCawley 1998: 451)
  cf. Susan interviewed $every\ senator_x$. *He_x is crooked.
 c'. the F/A of (7c)
  $[_{PROP} [_{QPx}$ EVERY x = SENATOR] PAST([SUSAN INTERVIEW x])]
  *$[_{PROP}$ PRES([x CROOKED])]

(8) a. $Everyone_x$ there had a wife who loved him_x. (Jackendoff 1977: 176)
 b. *$Everyone_x$ there had a wife, who loved him_x. (ibid.)
  cf. $Everyone_x$ there had a wife. *She loved him_x.

c. Most linguists$_x$ are grateful to the person who first introduced them$_x$ to linguistics. (McCawley 1998: 485 note34)
d. *Most linguists$_x$ admire Edward Sapir, whose works taught them$_x$ how fascinating language can be. (ibid.)

Fourth, when restrictive and nonrestrictive relative clauses modify the same NP, the restrictive relative clause precedes the nonrestrictive relative clause (9a), because the former is adjoined to the head N' (i.e., [$_{NP}$ DET [$_{N'}$ N' CP[WH[R]]]]), whereas the latter is placed immediately after the host NP. However, in (9c), the nonrestrictive relative precedes the restrictive relative, because the former adds a brief definition of the preceding N' *ophicleides*, and therefore, is placed immediately after it, namely, placed between the head N' and the restrictive relative clause CP[*that*], as in (9d).

(9) a. The contestant who won first prize, who is the judge's brother-in-law, sang dreadfully. (McCawley 1998: 447)
 b. *The contestant, who is the judge's brother-in-law, who won first prize sang dreadfully. (ibid.)
 c. Most ophicleides, which are a type of obsolete brass instrument, that are on display in museums are of German manufacture. (McCawley 1998: 453)
 d. [$_{NP}$ [$_{DET}$ Most] [$_{N'}$ [$_{N'}$ ophicleides], CP[WH[R]], CP[*that*]]] are of German manufacture.

Note that the coreference relation in (9c) between the head N' *ophicleides* and the relative pronoun *which* in the immediately following nonrestrictive relative clause is of type identity, whereas that in (9a) between the NP *the contestant who won first prize* and the relative pronoun *who* in the immediately following nonrestrictive relative clause is of token identity.

The nonrestrictive relative clause in (1d) *which who cares about anyway* contains two *wh*-words: *which* is a relative pronoun and *who* an interrogative pronoun. The internal syntax of the relevant part is as follows.

(10) Symbolic logic, [$_{CP[WH[R]]}$ which [$_{CP[WH[Q]]}$ who [$_{S[PRES]}$ NP[G] cares about NP[G] anyway]]], is awfully tough.
 dominance path for *which*: CP[WH[R]] <u>CP[WH[Q]] S[PRES]</u> VP[PRES] PP[*about*] NP[G]
 dominance path for *who*: <u>CP[WH[Q]] S[PRES]</u> NP[G]

The order between *which* and *who* in (10) is determined by at least three factors. First, this clause is primarily a nonrestrictive relative clause CP[WH[R]] and as such, the NP[WH[R]] *which* must come at the left edge of the clause and immediately follow its antecedent. Second, this order accords closely with the semantic scope relations between the two. *Who cares about* is used here to mean 'no one cares about symbolic logic' (what Sadock (1974: 125) called queclarative) by expressing doubt about the presupposition 'Someone cares about symbolic logic.' So the relevant part of (1d) can be paraphrased as '[$_{TOPIC}$ symbolic logic], [$_{COMMENT}$ who/no one cares about anyway].' Third, this order between *which* and *who* obeys the nested dependency constraint (Kaplan and Bresnan 1982: 259; Pesetsky 1987: 105 (24); Pollard and Sag 1994: 159 note 3, 169 note 9), which says in terms of the dominance path conditions that when there are two overlapping dominance paths involved in a sentence, the top and middle parts of one of the dominance paths must properly contain those of the other dominance path. This is shown in (10). The opposite order is completely unacceptable. (11a, b) with their parenthetical expressions are acceptable. However, the parenthetical in (11b) cannot be turned into a nonrestrictive relative clause, because the resultant (11b') violates the nested dependency constraint. This is shown in (12), where the *wh*-phrases and their corresponding NP[G] are coindexed.

(11) a. The professor—he cares about nothing anyway—is hard to please.
  a'. The professor, who cares about nothing anyway, is hard to please.
  b. The professor—what does he care about anyway—is hard to please.
  b'.*The professor, who what cares about anyway, is hard to please.

(12) crossed dependency in the nonrestrictive relative clause in (11b')
  who$_1$ [what$_2$ [NP[G]$_1$ cares about NP[G]$_2$ anyway]]
  dominance path for *who*: CP[WH[R]] CP[WH[Q]] S[PRES] NP[G]
  dominance path for *what*: CP[WH[Q]] S[PRES] VP[RPRES] PP[*about*] NP[G]

It is possible for the relative pronoun of a nonrestrictive relative clause to have split antecedents, although it is severely restricted due to the adjacency requirement in (4) between the host NP and the nonrestrictive relative clause. In (13a), the joint antecedents are in different conjuncts of the same coordinate structure.

(13) a. Sauter is living with his lawyer-wife Kathleen—the daughter of <u>Pat Brown</u> and sister of <u>Jerry Brown, who</u> are both former governors of California. (McCawley 1998: 469)
b. *A friend of <u>Pat Brown</u> has brought a lawsuit against a business associate of <u>Jerry Brown, who</u> are both former governors of California. (McCawley 1998: 485 note 33)

In general, when a coordinate structure is involved, an adjacency requirement between a constituent outside the coordinate structure and a constituent in each conjunct counts as being met, if we replace the whole coordinate structure with each conjunct and each conjunct meets the adjacency requirement. For example, in (6c), each nonrestrictive relative clause counts as meeting the adjacency requirement. We saw in 2.1 (3a) a different adjacency requirement between an inverted auxiliary verb and the subject NP of its complement clause. Again, it counts as being met, when the complement nonfinite clauses are coordinated, as in (14), where both *John* and *Mary* count as being adjacent to *did*.

(14) Did [John fix the car] and [Mary mow the lawn]? (=2.1 (2))

As for (13a), the adjacency requirement of the nonrestrictive relative clause counts as being met, because the two instances of N', *daughter of Pat Brown* and *sister of Jerry Brown*, are coordinated and the split antecedents of *who*, namely, *Pat Brown* and *Jerry Brown*, come at the end of each conjunct N'. We might be able to capture this situation about adjacency requirements in coordinate structures by resorting to an extended interpretation of the Coordinate Structure Convention in dominance paths (6.1.11 (2)) in such a way that the mother node and each of its daughter conjunct nodes count as constituting a single node, due to the convention, and therefore, each conjunct node inherits from its mother node the property of the adjacency requirement being met.

6.2.5 *That*-relatives and bare relatives
In addition to *wh*-relative clauses, there are *that*-relative clauses (1a, b), in which CP[*that*] is used as a relative clause, and a bare relative clause (1c), which lacks an overt subordinating marker.

(1) a. This is the girl that I met __ yesterday.
b. This is the girl that __ talked to me yesterday.

c. This is the girl I met __ yesterday.
d. *This is the girl __ talked to me yesterday.

As for (1d), in which the head N' *girl* is followed by a bare relative clause consisting of only a finite VP, we find a great deal of dialectal, idiolectal, and stylistic variation in (2).

(2) There's a woman wants to see you. (Quirk et al. 1972: 959) (colloquial)
There's a table stands in the corner. (Quirk et al. 1985: 1250) (colloquial)
It's Simon did it. (Quirk et al. 1985: 1250) (colloquial)
?It was my father did most of the talking. (Huddleston and Pullum 2002: 1055)
?There's something at the door wants to talk to you. (Huddleston and Pullum 2002: 1055)
!Anyone wants this can have it. (Huddleston and Pullum 2002: 1055)

The internal and external syntax of *that*-relative clause are given in (3).

(3) internal and external syntax of *that*-relative clause (cf. 6.2.3 (1))
a. internal syntax (same as the regular CP[*that*] local tree (1.2 (12d)))
[$_{CP[that]}$ C[*that*] S[FIN]]
b. external syntax
[$_{N'}$ N' CP[*that*]]
• The head N' must c-command a coreferent NP[G] in the CP[*that*].
c. [$_{N'}$ [$_{N'}$ N' CP[*that*]] CP[*that*]] (stacked *that*-relative clauses)

In (3a), we take *that* in *that*-relative clauses not as a relative pronoun but as the complementizer *that* (McCawley 1998: 429; Culicover and Jackendoff 2005: 322). This decision is based on the fact that *that* does not pied-pipe any other element, which is shown in *the conditions under which/*under that I'll sign the contract* and *the pope during whose/*during that's reign America was discovered* (McCawley 1998: 428–429). Furthermore, just as a pronoun allows the coordinated form *He and only he can do it*, so do the relative pronouns *who* and *which*, as in *designed by professionals who and only who can touch the code* (from the web) and *the presence of a corrupt system which and only which the believer will know is wrong* (from the web). On the other hand, *that* in *that*-relative clauses does not allow this coordinated form (4a) and neither do the other complementizers (4b, c, d). Note that the coordinated form *if and only if* is possible with the conditional *if*, which is a preposition and not a complementizer.

(4) a. The books that (*and only that) Mary bought were boring.
b. Mary said that (*and only that) she had bought the books.
c. Mary wanted very much for (*and only for) John to buy the books.
d. Mary wondered if (*and only if) she should buy the books.

(In fact, the syntactic status of relative *that* has been a very complex issue. See van der Auwera 1985.) The local tree (3b) is recursive and allows stacked relative clauses (3c), (5a). In fact, (3b) interacts freely with 6.2.3 (1b) [$_{N'}$ N' CP[WH[R]]], as in (5b, c).

(5) a. the [[book [that I bought]] [that Ann had recommended]] (McCawley 1998: 428)
b. the [[book [that I bought]] [which Ann had recommended]] (ibid.)
c. the [[book [which I bought]] [that Ann had recommended]] (ibid.)

Pollard and Sag (1994: 220) analyzed *that* in *that*-relative clauses with a matrix subject gap (6a) as a nominative relative pronoun. A problem with their analysis is that they may not be able to explain such a *that*-relative clause as (6b), in which two Ss are coordinated, the first S having an NP[G] in the subject position and the second S in the object position (6c).

(6) a. Here's the student that was telling you about cell structure. (Pollard and Sag 1994: 220)
b. the book that appeared last year and Smith reviewed for the *Post* (cf. McCawley 1998: 444)
c. the book [$_{CP[that]}$ that [NP[G] appeared last year] and [Smith reviewed NP[G] for the *Post*]]

The external syntax of bare relative clauses is given in (7) below.

(7) external syntax of bare relative clause S[FIN]
[$_{N'}$ N' S[FIN]]
• The head N' must c-command a coreferent NP[G].
[$_{N'}$ [$_{N'}$ N (XP)] ⩽ NP ...],
where the NP is the subject of the bare relative clause S[FIN] and the XP is a complement PP or a reduced relative clause (6.2.7).

The second rule in (7) requires that the innermost head N' and the subject NP of the following bare relative clause must be linearly adjacent (McCawley 1998: 433), which prevents a sentence adverb from appearing between the head N' and the subject of the bare relative (8a). Because the G feature in NP[G] is a unary feature, just as INV and AUX, NP (without the G feature) is interpreted as a nongapped NP. (See 2.1 for the details on unary features).

The first PS rule in (7) cannot be applied recursively because of the second rule in (7), which requires adjacency between the head N' and the subject NP of the relative S[FIN]. In fact, in (8b), the second bare relative *you talked about yesterday* can only be interpreted as modifying the immediately preceding N' *boy*. It cannot be interpreted as modifying the larger N' *book I borrowed from the boy*. By contrast, when two bare relatives are coordinated (8b'), each bare relative conjunct counts as meeting the adjacency requirement. Furthermore, when there are multiple relative clauses stacked in an NP, a bare relative clause must precede other CP relatives (*wh*-relatives and *that*-relatives) (McCawley 1998: 433), because of the adjacency requirement between the head N' and the subject NP of the bare relative clause (8c). This is shown in (8e, f). Interestingly enough, the adjacency requirement also forces the ordering of N' < bare relative clause < complement CP[*that*] (8 g).

(8) a. I discovered the criteria *(that) evidently I had not been meeting. (McCawley 1998: 433)
  b. I like the book I borrowed from the boy you talked about yesterday.
  b'. I like the book [I borrowed from the boy] and [you talked about yesterday].
  c. [$_{NP}$ (DET) < N' < S[FIN] < CP]
  d. The book (about Chicago) [that I bought] [that Ann had recommended] was boring. (cf. McCawley 1998: 433)
  e. The book (about Chicago) [I bought] [that Ann had recommended] was boring.
  f. *The book (about Chicago) [that I bought] [Ann had recommended] was boring.
  g. The rumor (about John) [we heard] [that he had his head blown off] was wrong. (from the web)

h. Furthermore, the representation of an individual's model of the world might include information about the people the individual knows that is structured in ways similar to the frames needed for linguistic description. (Fillmore 1976 "Frame semantics and the nature of language," p. 28)

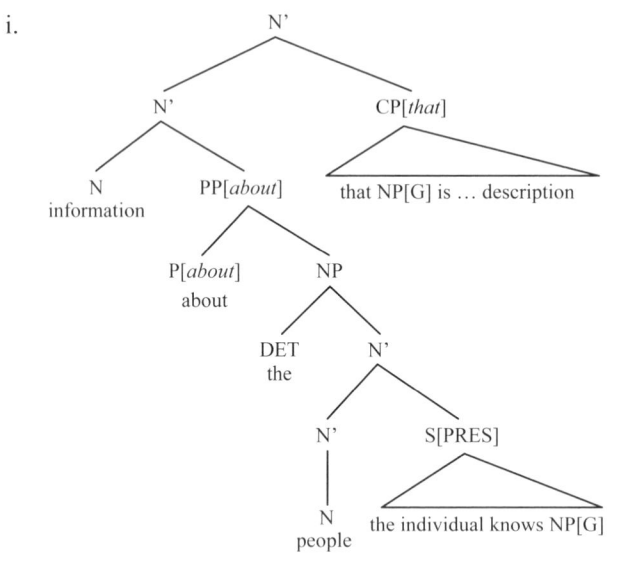

i.
```
                          N'
                  ┌────────┴────────┐
                 N'                CP[that]
             ┌────┴────┐       ╱          ╲
             N      PP[about]    that NP[G] is ... description
        information  ╱    ╲
                 P[about]  NP
                  about  ╱    ╲
                       DET    N'
                       the  ╱    ╲
                          N'     S[PRES]
                          │    ╱        ╲
                          N   the individual knows NP[G]
                        people
```

Note that adjacency of two relative clauses side by side in syntax does not guarantee a stacked relative clause structure in (3c) and 6.2.3 (8), in which the outer relative clause modifies the larger N' consisting of the head N' and the inner relative clause. In (8h) above, the inner bare relative *the individual knows* modifies the preceding N' *people* and the outer *that*-relative *that is structured in ways similar to the frames needed for linguistic description* modifies the N' *information about the people the individual knows*. The syntactic structure of (8h) is shown in (8i).

We would like to explore the possibility of extending the analysis by McCawley and Sadock that relative pronouns in *wh*-relative clauses are pronouns to the cases of *that*- and bare relative clauses, and we do this by proposing that the phonologically null NP (NP[G]) in such relative clauses is, in fact, a pronoun in F/A and RS that is coreferent with the head N', namely, it carries its own INDEX feature with referential index and AGR value in F/A, and carries a particular participant role in RS. (Note the condition in (3b) and (7) that the N' must c-command a *coreferent* NP[G].) Here are the syntactic and F/A structures of (1c) under this proposal.

(9) a. This is the [$_{N'}$ [$_{N'[IND[i, 3SGF]]}$ girl] [$_{S[PAST]}$ I met NP[G, IND[i, 3SGF]] yesterday]].

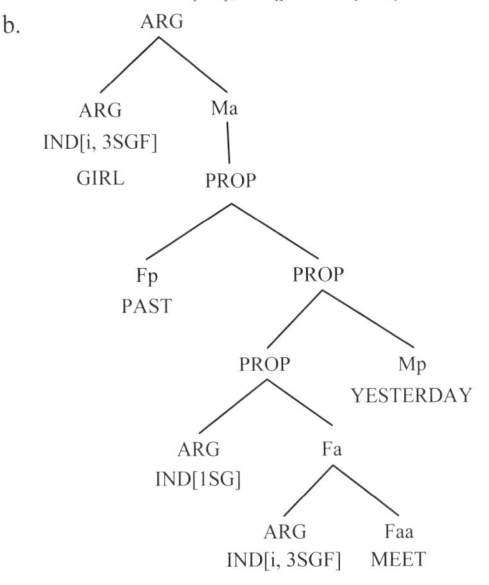

b.
```
                    ARG
                   /    \
              ARG        Ma
           IND[i, 3SGF]   |
              GIRL       PROP
                        /    \
                      Fp      PROP
                     PAST    /    \
                          PROP      Mp
                         /    \   YESTERDAY
                       ARG     Fa
                     IND[1SG]  /  \
                              ARG   Faa
                          IND[i, 3SGF]  MEET
```

In (9b), the ARG that corresponds to the NP[G, IND[i, 3SGF]] in syntax has the same IND value IND[i, 3SGF] and is coreferent with the head ARG that corresponds to the head N' *girl* in syntax. We need a separate lexical entry (10) for a pronominal NP[G] that appears in *that-* and bare relative clauses.

(10) lexical entry for pronominal NP[G] in *that-* and bare relative clauses
 syntax: NP[G, IND[i, 3]]
 F/A: ARG[IND[i, 3]]
 RS: ROLE
 mphon: nil

In (10), the pronominal NP[G] has its own INDEX value in the syntactic field that is the same as the IND value in its F/A structure, due to Feature Osmosis (1.3; Sadock 2012: 154). The distribution of pronominal NP[G] is restricted by the fact that it only occurs in a *that-* or bare relative clause, namely, any pronominal NP[G] must be c-commanded by a coreferent N' in syntax, which is required by (3b) and (7).

We now have two kinds of phonologically null NP[G]: an empty NP[G] (henceforth, NP[G]$_e$) for *wh*-relative clauses and *wh*-questions, which is null both in F/A and in RS, and a pronominal NP[G] (henceforth, NP[G]$_p$) for *that*- and bare relative clauses, which is a pronoun with its IND value in syntax and F/A and bears a role in RS (10). If we inserted an NP[G]$_p$ where an NP[G]$_e$ was required, or vice versa, we would end up with ill-formed F/A and RS.

The difference between the two kinds of NP[G] is real. First, observe the contrast between (11a) and (11b). Recall that (11a) is an example of the *that*-trace effect, which we discussed in 6.1.3 (7).

(11) a. *Who do you think [$_{CP[that]}$ that NP[G]$_e$ won the prize]?
b. I know the person [$_{CP[that]}$ that NP[G]$_p$ won the prize]

Second, this contrast is also observed in long-distance cases.

(12) a. Who do you think (*that) NP[G]$_e$ won the prize? (=(11a))
b. I know the person [$_{CP[WH[R]]}$ who I think (*that) NP[G]$_e$ won the prize].
c. The only person I think that NP[G]$_p$ will put a halt to such a love affair will be Dexter, himself. (from the web)
d. James is the only person I think that NP[G]$_p$ can settle my sister. (from the web)

Third, the pronominal nature of NP[G]$_p$ in *that*-relative clauses is evident in the following example of split antecedents.

(13) A <u>syntax book</u>$_i$ came out last month and a <u>semantics book</u>$_j$ is now in press [$_{CP[that]}$ that NP[G, IND[{i, j}], 3PLN]$_p$ were both written by a famous linguist].

Because *that* in *that*-relative clauses is a complementizer, as we have been claiming, it cannot bear a referential index or an agreement feature, such as number. The only candidate that can carry such information in the CP[*that*] in (13) is the pronominal NP[G]. Notice that the *be* verb in the CP[*that*] is in the plural. The floated quantifier *both* needs its licenser in the subject position and the NP[G]$_p$ or its corresponding ARG in F/A, to be exact, is serving as such (cf. 5.6. (12) and the preceding comments).

This NP[G]$_p$ is in fact pronominal, and not reflexive. The intended reading of (14a) is 'the man such that he is proud of himself.' When the antecedent of the NP[G]$_p$ is in a higher clause, as in (14b), the acceptability improves slightly, though the judgment is not so clear.

(14) a. *the man$_i$ [(that) he$_i$ is proud of __$_i$] (cf. (15c))
 b. ??the man$_i$ [(that) he$_i$ thinks Mary is proud of __$_i$]

Wh-questions exhibit the strong crossover (SCO) effect, which is illustrated in (15a) below and was discussed in 6.1.8. It is said that wh-relative clauses also exhibit the same SCO effect, as in (15b, b', b"), because both wh-question and wh-relative clause are said to involve the same "wh-movement." (However, recall that the SCO effect arises in quiz questions, in which the wh-phrase is not "moved." See 6.1.8 (7).) If our approach, according to which the relative pronoun in a wh-relative clause and the NP[G] in a that- and bare relative clause are pronouns, is on the right track, the oddity of (15b) seems to come from a juxtaposition of the two coreferential pronouns, who and he. In fact, (15b') can be improved, if we avoid the juxtaposition, either by removing the relative pronoun, as in (15c), or by inserting a new NP + V, as in (15d). Note that if we follow MGG's "wh-movement" analysis, (15c) is an instance of empty operator (Op) movement and therefore must be as bad as the pure SCO case (15a).

(15) a. *Who$_x$ does he$_x$ think Mary is fond of __? (SCO in wh-question)
 b. *the boy$_i$ [who$_i$ he$_i$ thinks Mary is fond of __] (SCO in relative clause)
  cf. the boy$_i$ such that he$_i$ thinks Mary is fond of him$_i$
 b'. *the man who$_i$ he$_i$ thinks __$_i$ won the game (Bhatt 2004:1)
  cf. the man$_i$ such that he$_i$ thinks he$_i$ won the game
 b". *the man who$_i$ he$_i$ thinks you saw __$_i$ (Bhatt 2004:1)
 c. ??the man$_i$ [(that) he$_i$ thinks __$_i$ won the game]
 d. ??the man$_i$ [who$_i$ you said he$_i$ thinks __$_i$ won the game]

Note that a wh-relative clause and a that- or bare relative clause have the same F/A structure in our approach.

There seems to be another factor involved in the SCO cases of wh-relative clauses (15b, b', b") and those of wh-questions (15a). When two expressions share the same F/A and RS structures (i.e., the same semantics) and obey the same dominance path conditions, the one with a shorter dominance path is preferred to the one with a longer dominance path. This is probably because of processing cost. A shorter dominance path is easier to process than a longer dominance path. For example, the dominance path in (15b', c) is much longer than the dominance path of *the man who thinks he won the game*.

As for the weak crossover (WCO) effect, Safir (1986) and Postal (1993), among others, claimed that it is present in restrictive relative clauses (16a, b), contrary to

Chomsky (1982: 93 note 11 (iii)), who assumed that WCO is not found in relative clauses at all. Again, if we avoid the juxtaposition of the coreferent *who* and *his* in (16a, b), the acceptability improves (16c, d). (16e, f) are examples of WCO taken from the web.

(16) a. *?A man$_i$ who$_i$ his$_i$ wife loves __ arrived early. (Safir 1986: 667)
   cf. John$_i$, who$_i$ his$_i$ wife loves __, arrived early. (Safir 1986: 667)
   b. *the kid$_i$ who$_i$ his$_i$ sister called __ a moron (Postal 1993: 540)
   c. ?A man$_i$ his$_i$ wife loves __$_i$ arrived early.
   d. ?the kid$_i$ his$_i$ sister called __$_i$ a moron
   e. Through the course of the movie, Crowe's Brennan transforms before our eyes from a non-violent man, into someone capable of committing murder. The question that remains unanswered by the end of the film is whether he'll be able to make his way back again—into the man$_i$ his$_i$ wife loves__$_i$, and who$_i$ his$_i$ son needs__$_i$. It is one of Crowe's best performances—at the heart of practically every scene of the movie. (from the web)
   f. A tribute to two women in this man's life who shaped him into the man$_i$ his$_i$ wife loves__$_i$ and chose to devote her life to__$_i$. (from the web)

So far, we have dealt with *that*- and bare relative clauses whose bottom gap is a pronominal NP[G]. However, these types of relative clause also seem to allow a phonologically null PP (PP[G]). This is shown in (17), where the underlined parts are a supposed PP[G].

(17) McCawley 1998: 427–428
   a. the place (that) I found the money __ (cf. in/at the place)
   b. the day (that) I went to the zoo __ (cf. on the day)
   c. the reason (that) I left early __ (cf. for the reason)
   d. the way (that) he tricked me __ (cf. in the way)

This type of relative clause also exhibits unbounded dependency, as in (18).

(18) a. This is the day I think that the Atlanta banks ran out of one-hundred-dollar bills __. (from the web)
   cf. I think that the Atlanta banks ran out of one-hundred-dollar bills on this day.

b. This is the place I believe that a great marketer is key ___ . (from the web)
cf. I believe that a great marketer is key in this place.
c. This is the way I believe that I will achieve my goal ___ . (from the web)
cf. I believe that I will achieve my goal in this way.
d. This is the reason it seems that the condenser has been damaged ___ . (from the web)
cf. It seems that the condenser has been damaged for this reason.

Note that the head nouns of the relative clauses in (17) and (18) belong to a semantically restricted class and the prepositions that accompany these head nouns are predictable from the head nouns themselves. On the basis of this fact, we propose (i) that there is no gap (PP[G]$_p$) in the syntax of the examples in (17) and (18) and (ii) that the relationship between the head ARG (*place*, *day*, *reason*, *way*, etc.) and the [$_{Mp}$ PROP] (relative clause) is determined semantically and pragmatically. Note that every event (expressed by the relative clause in question) can take a modifier of place (where did it happen?), time (when did it happen?), reason (why did it happen?), or manner (how did it happen?).

6.2.6 Infinitival *wh*-questions and relative clauses

In this section, we consider two constructions that are syntactically similar: infinitival *wh*-questions and infinitival relative clauses. Here are examples of infinitival *wh*-question, which is a nonfinite indirect question.

(1) a. I asked where to go ___ . (McCawley 1998: 492)
   I asked [$_{CP[WH[Q]]}$ [$_{ADVP[WH[Q]]}$ where] [$_{S[to]}$ [$_{VP[to]}$ to go ___]]].
b. *I asked where for John to go ___ . (ibid.)
c. *I asked where John to go ___ .
d. *I asked for where John to go ___ .
e. *I asked for John where to go ___ .

As shown in (1a), an infinitival *wh*-question (CP[WH[Q]]) consists of a *wh*-phrase (XP[WH[Q]]) and an S[*to*] that lacks an overt subject NP. The subject of an infinitival *wh*-question cannot appear overtly, which is shown in (1b-e). (1b) is out because its syntactic structure is [$_{CP[WH[Q]]}$ XP[WH[Q]] CP[*for*]], but English only allows the local tree [$_{CP[WH[Q]]}$ XP[WH[Q]] S] to introduce an interrogative *wh*-phrase. (1c) is out, because when a VP[*to*] has an overt subject and forms an S[*to*], namely, [_{S[to]} NP VP[*to*]], there are only two ways of admitting an S[*to*] with an overt subject in English (4.2.2 (36)): the S[*to*] must be either the complement of the complementizer *for* (1.2 (12e)) or the complement of a verb that belongs to the *want*-class, such as *like*, *hate*, and *prefer* (4.2.2 (25a)). The S[*to*] *John to go* in (1c) does not satisfy either of the two. (1d) is out, because the adjacency between the complementizer *for* and the subject NP is broken on the one hand, and *for* takes as its complement not S[*to*] but CP[WH[Q]] on the other. (1e) is out, because the *wh*-phrase *where*, being adjoined to the VP[*to*], violates the local tree [_{CP[WH[Q]]} XP[WH[Q]] S]. Here are some more examples of infinitival *wh*-question.

(2) a. I was wondering who to give the money to __. (Culicover 2009: 373)
   b. I was wondering on which table to put the book __. (Culicover 2009: 373)
   c. To be a savvy RV owner, you need to know what to expect __ and what to try to avoid __. (from the web)
   d. He insisted that he worked on an oil rig but his friends said he was in prison. It was very confusing and I didn't know what to believe that he was doing __ all those years. (from the web)
   e. I don't know what to do __ or who I should talk to __. (from the web)

In (2a, b), the infinitival *wh*-question is a complement of the verb *wonder*, which takes as its complement either CP[WH[Q]] or PP[*about*] (3.5 (8), (9)), but not VP[*to*]. This clearly shows that the syntactic category of an infinitival *wh*-question is CP[WH[Q]], and not VP[*to*] or its projection. (2c, d) are examples of "long-distance *wh*-movement" in an infinitival *wh*-question. In (2e), an infinitival *wh*-question is coordinated with a finite indirect *wh*-question. This shows again that the syntactic category of an infinitival *wh*-question is CP[WH[Q]]. Our conclusion is that the distribution of infinitival *wh*-questions coincides with that of (embedded) *wh*-questions (CP[WH[Q]]), and differs from that of VP[*to*].

Returning to (1a, c), we have two rules whose mother node is S[*to*].

(3) a. [_{S[to]} NP VP[*to*]] in [_{CP[for]} C[*for*] __] or [_{VP} V __], where V∈ {*want*, *like*, *hate*, ...}
   b. [_{S[to]} VP[*to*]]

Every time an S[*to*] appears, (3a) with an overt subject NP is chosen if it is a complement of the complementizer *for* or a complement of a verb of *want*-class, and (3b) is chosen otherwise. That is, the choice between the two depends on the external syntax of S[*to*]. (3a) is lexical information and requires a more specific environment than (3b). When that specific environment is present, (3a) preempts (3b), due to the Elsewhere Principle (1.1.2 (3)).

Adverbs that are adjoined to VP[*to*] or S[*to*] can intervene between the *wh*-phrase and the VP[*to*] of infinitival *wh*-question, as in (4).

(4) (examples from the web)
 a. I know what companies <u>never</u> to buy from.
 b. Instead, agents are to consider whether <u>always</u> to use addictive substances on every occasion.

Infinitival *wh*-questions have the following syntax and F/A, which will eventually be incorporated into the lexical entry of a clause-initial *wh*-phrase (XP[WH[Q]]). Just as is the case with the ordinary "*wh*-movement," a *wh*-phrase and its gap XP[G] in syntax correspond to a quantifier phrase QP_x and its variable [$_{ARG}$ x] in F/A, respectively.

(5) the syntax, F/A, and RS of infinitival *wh*-question
 syntax: [$_{CP[WH[Q]]}$ XP[WH[Q]] S[*to*]]
 F/A: [[$_{QPx}$ [$_Q$ WH] ...] [$_{PROP}$ [$_{ARG}$ RHO], Fa]]
 RS: EV in [$_{EV}$ [$_{TYPE}$ "should"] [$_{TH}$ __]]

As we pointed out already in connection with (1a, c) and (3), the S[*to*] in the syntax of (5) cannot have its own overt subject; that is, the S[*to*] must satisfy (3b), because an S[*to*] with an overt subject (3a) only appears when it is a complement of either the *want*-class verb or the complementizer *for*, and the S[*to*] in (5) does not meet this condition. Therefore, RHO is required as the F/A subject of the matrix PROP. In the RS of (5), "should" is a phonologically null deontic operator, whose lexical entry is (6).

(6) lexical entry for phonologically null deontic operator
 syntax: nil
 F/A: nil
 RS: [$_{TYPE}$ "should"] in [$_{EV}$ __ [$_{TH}$ EV]]

Note that the phonologically null deontic operator exists only in RS. This will predict that when an infinitival *wh*-question is negated with *not*, as in *I know what not to do*, the negated proposition QP_x [$_{PROP}$ NOT [[$_{ARG}$ RHO]

[$_{Fa}$ DO [$_{ARG}$ x]]]] in F/A must correspond to the internal EV in [$_{EV}$ [$_{TYPE}$ "should"] [$_{TH}$ EV]]; therefore, the interpretation is 'should not (do),' namely, *not* is interpreted as being within the scope of the deontic operator. The phonologically null deontic operator is also needed in the following examples. Certain verbs take a CP[*that*] complement that directly dominates an S[BSE], an S whose head is a verb in the base form (V[BSE]). S[BSE] is selected by these verbs not syntactically ("c-selection") but semantically and/or pragmatically, which is shown in (7b–d). Each S[BSE] in (7) is interpreted with the phonologically null deontic operator (6).

(7) a. The Case Filter requires that [$_{S[BSE]}$ an overt NP be Case-marked].
 b. A: What is the Case Filter?
    B: It is that [$_{S[BSE]}$ an overt NP be Case-marked].
 c. A: What was John's proposal?
    B: That [$_{S[BSE]}$ the system be updated].
 d. A: John proposed something. What was it?
    B: That [$_{S[BSE]}$ the system be updated].

In the F/A of (5), RHO is pressed into service to serve as the semantic subject of the proposition. The interpretation of RHO is free (4.5 (8b)), because (i) any matrix verb that takes an embedded interrogative (CP[WH[Q]]) as its complement can take an infinitival *wh*-question as well and (ii) these verbs lack a coreference requirement in the RS field of their lexical entry, as opposed to unique control verbs (cf. 4.4 (4), (5)), whose lexical entries specify coreference requirement in their RS field. In fact, the RHO of an infinitival *wh*-question can refer to the matrix subject (8a), to the object (8b), to both (8c), to some other person in the discourse (8d), or to an arbitrary person (what is called PRO$_{arb}$) (8e).

(8) a. A visitor asked a receptionist where to go.
 b. A receptionist asked a visitor where to go.
 c. John asked Mary where to go together.
 d. My kids didn't know which room they should go to, so I asked a receptionist where to go.
 e. The biggest question about early voting is not when and where to go but what ID to bring.

Because the semantic subject of the VP[*to*] in an infinitival *wh*-question is specified as RHO in (5), the interpretation of its *wh*-phrase as the semantic subject of the VP[*to*] is impossible (9b).

(9) a. I know who to vote for.
 b. *I know [_CP[WH[Q]]_ who [_S[to]_ [_VP[to]_ to vote for Obama]]]. cf. I know who should vote for Obama.

Here is an example of the syntactic and F/A structures of an infinitival *wh*-question. Note that in the F/A below, the QP_x corresponds to *which table* in syntax and that there is no pied piping of preposition in F/A.

(10) the syntax and F/A of *I was wondering on which table to put the book* (=(2b))

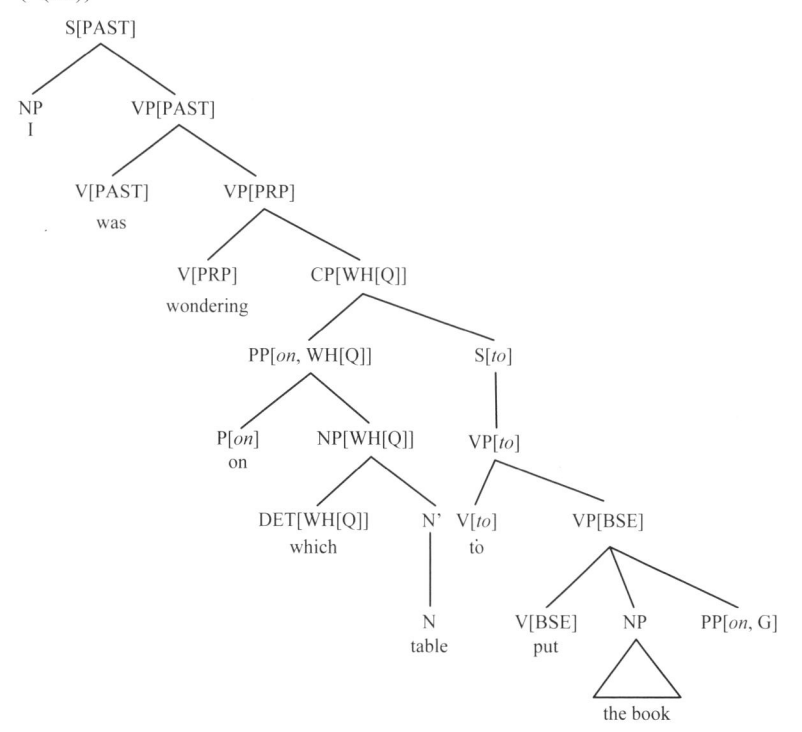

```
                    S[PAST]
                   /       \
                 NP         VP[PAST]
                 I         /        \
                      V[PAST]        VP[PRP]
                       was          /       \
                                V[PRP]       CP[WH[Q]]
                               wondering    /         \
                                      PP[on, WH[Q]]    S[to]
                                       /      \         |
                                    P[on]  NP[WH[Q]]   VP[to]
                                     on    /      \    /     \
                                       DET[WH[Q]]  N'  V[to]  VP[BSE]
                                        which     |    to    /       \
                                                  N      V[BSE]  NP   PP[on, G]
                                                table    put    /\
                                                              the book
```

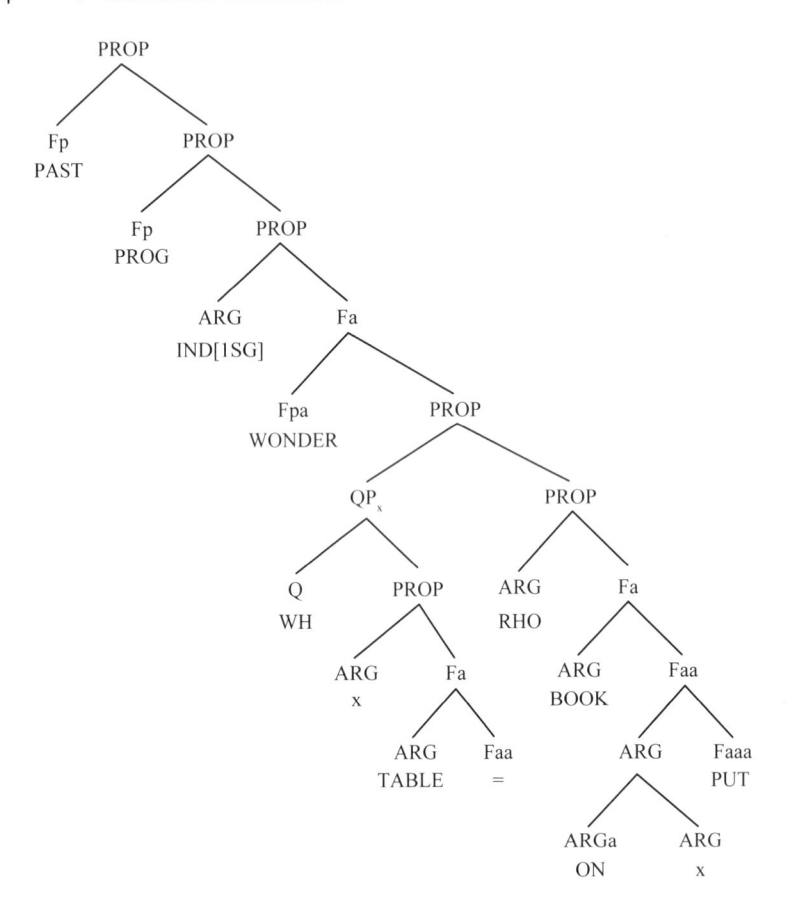

```
                    PROP
                   /    \
                 Fp     PROP
                 PAST   /   \
                      Fp    PROP
                      PROG  /   \
                          ARG    Fa
                          IND[1SG] / \
                                Fpa   PROP
                                WONDER /  \
                                     QPₓ   PROP
                                     / \   /   \
                                    Q  PROP ARG   Fa
                                    WH  / \  RHO  / \
                                      ARG Fa  ARG  Faa
                                       x  / \ BOOK / \
                                        ARG Faa  ARG  Faaa
                                        TABLE =   / \  PUT
                                                ARGa ARG
                                                ON    x
```

Infinitival relative clauses in (11) below are a nonfinite counterpart of finite restrictive relative clauses. Infinitival relatives allow an overt relative *wh*-phrase only in the form of PP[WH[R]] (McCawley 1998: 439) (11a, b). Infinitival relatives with an overt subject are in the form of CP[*for*] (McCawley 1998: 440) (11d). (11e, f) show that a PP *wh*-relative phrase (PP[WH[R]]) cannot appear before a CP[*for*] or between the subject NP and VP[*to*].

(11) McCawley 1998: 439–440
    a. a shovel with which to dig the hole
       a shovel [_CP[WH[R]] [_PP[WH[R], *with*] with which] [_S[*to*] [_VP[*to*] to dig the hole PP [G, *with*]]]]

b. *a shovel which [$_{VP[to]}$ to dig a hole with]
c. a shovel [$_{VP[to]}$ to dig a hole with]
d. a shovel [$_{CP[for]}$ for us to dig the hole with]
e. *a shovel [$_{CP[WH[R]]}$ with which [$_{CP[for]}$ for us to dig the hole]]
f. *a shovel [for us with which to dig the hole]

The syntactic structures of infinitival relative in (11a, c, d) are given in (12), (13), (14), respectively.

(12) syntax and F/A of (11a)
external syntax: CP[WH[R]] in [$_N$, N' __]
• The head N' must be coreferent with a relative pronoun contained in the PP[WH[R], α].
F/A: PROP in [$_{Ma}$ __]
internal syntax: [$_{CP[WH[R]]}$ PP[WH[R], α] S[to]], where α is a PFORM value
• The PP[WH[R], α] must c-command a PP[G, α].

Following the infinitival *wh*-question in (1a) and the PS rule (3b), we analyze the VP[*to*] in (11a) as an S[*to*] that exhaustively dominates the VP[*to*] (i.e., [$_{S[to]}$ VP[*to*]]). The local tree in the internal syntax of (12) correctly excludes the ungrammatical (11b), whose *wh*-relative phrase is NP, and (11e), in which the sister of the PP[WH[R]] is CP[*for*]. In (13) below, the internal syntax of the S[*to*] is (3b), because it is not a complement of the complementizer *for* or a complement of a verb of *want*-class.

(13) the syntax and F/A of (11c) (cf. 6.2.7 (1f))
external syntax: S[*to*] in [$_N$, N' __]
• The head N' must c-command a coreferent NP[G].
F/A: PROP in [$_{Ma}$ __]

(14) the syntax and F/A of (11d)
external syntax: CP[*for*] in [$_N$, N' __]
• The head N' must c-command a coreferent NP[G].
F/A: PROP in [$_{Ma}$ __]

The PP[WH[R]] in (12) allows embedding of a *wh*-relative pronoun (15a). Also, a "long distance" unbounded dependency between the top CP (CP[WH[R]] or CP[*for*]) or S[*to*] and the bottom XP[G] is possible (15b).

(15) a. the information <u>about whose source's identity</u> not to talk openly PP[G, *about*]
   b. the very thing for us to try to find out that he is doing NP[G] illegally

We can conflate (12), (13), and (14) into (16).

(16) the syntax and F/A of infinitival relative clauses
   external syntax: {CP[WH[R]] | CP[*for*] | S[*to*]} in [$_{N'}$ N' __]
   • The head N' must c-command a coreferent NP[G] in CP[*for*] or S[*to*].
   F/A: PROP in [$_{Ma}$ __]
   internal syntax: [$_{CP[WH[R]]}$ PP[WH[R], α] S[*to*]], where α is a PFORM value
   • The head N' must be coreferent with a relative pronoun contained in the PP[WH[R], α].
   • The PP[WH[R], α] must c-command a PP[G, α].

6.2.7 Reduced relative clauses

Reduced relative clauses (underlined in (1) below) are APs, PPs, NPs, and nonfinite VPs (VP[PRP], VP[PST], and VP[*to*]) that occur as postnominal modifiers.

(1) a. [$_{N'}$ N' < AP] two persons <u>both interested in music</u> (McCawley 1998: 393)
        any person <u>proud of himself</u> (McCawley 1998: 393)
        a lawyer <u>eager to make money</u> (McCawley 1998: 393)
   b. [$_{N'}$ N' < PP] the little house <u>on the prairie</u> (McCawley 1998: 391)
        a man <u>with a scar on his face</u> (McCawley 1998: 202)
        cf. a man who {has | *is with} a scar on his face
   c. [$_{N'}$ N' < NP] After 30 years, I met again my old patients <u>already adults</u>. (from the web)
        We are the only two people <u>still friends</u> from a large group of people. (from the web)
        I'm a deaf person <u>still a young girl</u> raised by a hearing family. (from the web)
        The runner <u>currently the record-holder in the 440 meter high hurdles</u> has announced his retirement. (McCawley 1998: 396)
   d. [$_{N'}$ N' < VP[PRP]] a vehicle <u>moving in this direction</u> (McCawley 1998: 391)

many persons <u>owning land in this city</u> (McCawley 1998: 396)
cf. many persons who own/*are owning land in this city
people <u>resembling their pets</u>
cf. people who resemble/*are resembling their pets

e. [$_{N'}$ N' < VP[PSP]] any money <u>taken from the victim by the defendant</u> (McCawley 1998: 393)

f. [$_{N'}$ N' < VP[*to*]] the most common example <u>to come to mind</u> (cf. 6.2.6 (11c), (13))
somebody <u>to fill your post</u>
a matter <u>to be judged by our readers</u>
the money <u>to be spent on books</u>

As for (1a, d, e, f), their status as reduced relative clause is not controversial. First, their syntactic category is AP or VP and they correspond to Fa in F/A. Second, their head is A or V, which has a role in the RS field of its lexical entry that must be carried by the subject ARG in F/A.

As for (1c), the reduced relative clauses of the type [$_{N'}$ N' < NP] are very rare, because they look very much like a mere juxtaposition of two NPs and are hence usually avoided. Therefore, this type of reduced relative clause takes an ad-S (S-modifying adverb), such as *still* or *already* before the NP (McCawley 1998: 396), so that it is readily interpreted as an Fa. Furthermore, as shown in (2), the floated quantifier *all* can be placed before the reduced relative clause. Because the syntactic category of the reduced relative clause is NP, there is no role in the lexical entry for its head N that can be carried by the subject ARG.

(2) a. I met a group of people <u>all</u> still [$_{NP}$ good friends].
  b. I met a group of people <u>all</u> [$_{NP}$ victims of the earthquake] themselves.

For these reasons, we analyze the NPs in (1c) and (2) as reduced relative clauses. In more concrete terms, the NPs correspond to the lower ARG of the type-identity Faa functor = (1.3 (22)), which carries the [$_{LO}$ *type*] role. The higher ARG of the functor is RHO and carries its [$_{TH}$ *token*] role.

As for (1b), the syntactic category of the reduced relative clause is PP. When the PP is used as a predicative PP, it corresponds to Fa in F/A and takes a subject ARG (i.e., RHO) in F/A. This is illustrated in (3a), in which the PP *on the table* is used to mean 'offered for discussion.' On the other hand, the same PP in (3b) is used as a locative modifier. This PP is also modified by an ad-S, as in (3c) and preceded by a floated quantifier, as in (3d).

(3) a. the proposals still <u>on the table</u>
    b. the newspaper <u>on the table</u>
    c. He glanced at yesterday's newspaper still <u>on the table</u>. (from the web)
    d. a huge pile of newspapers all <u>on the table</u>
    e. John was standing with his hand <u>in his pocket</u>.
    f. Mary closed her eyes with her glasses <u>on the table</u>.

For these reasons, we analyze these locative modifier PPs as reduced relative clauses. We claim that they correspond to the lower ARG of the existential Faa functor, whose lexical entry is given in (4). The locative PP carries the LO role of this functor. The subject RHO carries the TH role.

(4) lexical entry for the existential Faa functor (cf. 1.3 (22))
    syntax: nil
    F/A: $[_{Faa}$ EXIST]
    RS: $[_{TYPE}$ "exist"] in $[_{STATE}$ __ TH LO]
    mphon: nil

This lexical item is also necessary to account for such examples as (3e, f).
   The syntax and F/A of reduced relative clauses are given in (5). In the F/A field, the head ARG and the subject ARG of the PROP are coreferent (in type). We identify this ARG as RHO.

(5) the syntax and F/A of reduced relative clause
    syntax: XP in $[_{N'}$ N' <_], where X is not a finite verb.
    F/A:$[_{PROP}$ $[_{ARG[IND[i, AGR]]}$ RHO], Fa] in $[_{ARG}$ ARG[IND[i, AGR]], $[_{Ma}$ __]]

Since the syntax of reduced relative clause in (5) is recursive, reduced relative clauses can be stacked, just like *wh-* and *that-* relative clauses.

(6) a. the $[[_{N'}$ man] $[_{PP}$ with long hair]] $[_{PP}$ in the corner]
    b. the $[[_{N'}$ man] $[_{PP}$ with long hair]] $[_{VP[PRP]}$ standing in the corner]

c. the [[_N' lecture on nuclear physics] [_PP on Monday]] [_AP extremely rich in insights]

However, when there is a reduced relative clause and a CP relative clause (*wh-* and *that*-relative) side by side, the former must precede the latter. This is shown in (7b). There is a linear order rule that applies to post-nominal phrases and clauses (7e).

(7) a. the [[_N' man] [_PP with long hair]] [_CP[WH[R]] who was standing in the corner] (cf. (6b))
   b. *the [[_N' man] [_CP[WH[R]] who was standing in the corner]] [_PP with long hair]
   c. the report [from Tokyo] [that the Fukushima Daiichi nuclear power station continues to pose a major environmental threat]
   d. *the report [that the Fukushima Daiichi nuclear power station continues to pose a major environmental threat] [from Tokyo]
   e. the postnominal linear order rule under NP
      [_NP ... N < phrases < clauses]

The domain of application of the linear order rule (7e) is NP. The rule is sensitive to the distinction between phrases and clauses but not sensitive to the constituent structure or to the distinction between complements or adjuncts. For example, in (7c), the adjunct PP[*from*] precedes the complement CP[*that*]. (7e) is, in effect, a Heavy Constituent Shift within the domain of NP.

Reduced relative clauses do not involve gaps in syntax. (As stated in (5), the head ARG is required to be coreferent with the RHO subject of the reduced relative clause that modifies the head ARG.) Therefore, the dominance path conditions are not relevant to reduced relative clauses, which entails that they do not exhibit unbounded dependency.

6.2.8 Restrictive relative clause constructions in inheritance hierarchy

The four types of restrictive relative clause (*wh-*, *that-*, bare, and reduced relatives) have much in common, which can be extracted from the description of each type and stated separately once and for all. If we take this approach and extract commonalities from various types and subtypes, we will arrive at an inheritance hierarchy with the most general type at the top and the most specific subtypes at the bottom (1.1.2 (6), 1.6 (16), (17), 4.5 (10)) and thereby simplify the description of each subtype. The most basic property common to all types of restrictive relative clause is (1).

(1) restrictive relative clause (RRC)
   syntax: RRC in [$_{N'}$ N'__]
   - The RRC (except reduced relative clause) must obey the dominance path conditions (3).
   F/A: PROP in [$_{ARG}$ ARG [$_{Ma}$ __]]
   - The head ARG must c-command a coreferent ARG.

Here are the dominance path conditions on the three types of RRC (*wh-*, *that-*, and bare relatives). Note that no matrix subject gap is allowed in (2c), which makes such examples as [$_{NP}$ *the boy* NP[G] *came yesterday*] ungrammatical. For those speakers who accept this type of RRC (6.2.5 (2)), their relevant dominance path condition is (2c') instead of (2c). In (2a), the bottom XP[G] is either NP[G] or PP[G].

(2) dominance path conditions (cf. 6.1.7 (1))
   a. for *wh*-relatives
      nonsubject gap: CP[WH[R]] {S, VP, CP[{*that* | *for*}]}* VP {NP, N', PP}* XP[G]
      subject gap: CP[WH[R]] {S, VP, CP[{*that* | *for*}]}* S NP[G]
   b. for *that*-relatives
      nonsubject gap: CP[*that*] {S, VP, CP[{*that* | *for*}]}* VP {NP, N', PP}* NP[G]
      subject gap: CP[*that*] {S, VP, CP[{*that* | *for*}]}* S NP[G]
   c. for bare relatives
      nonsubject gap: S[FIN] {S, VP, CP[{*that* | *for*}]}* VP {NP, N', PP}* NP[G]
      subject gap: S[FIN] {S, VP, CP[{*that* | *for*}]}* S NP[G]
   c'. subject gap: S[FIN] {S, VP, CP[{*that* | *for*}]}* NP[G]
   d. F/A dominance path condition: PROP {PROP, Fa, Faa, Faaa}* {ARG, POS}* ARG[IND[j, AGR]] (=6.2.3 (1a))

Because the middle parts of the dominance path conditions contain repeated parts, (2a, b, c) can be simplified to (3).

(3) dominance path conditions
   a. CP[WH[R]] 𝓐 {𝓑 XP[G] | S NP[G]}
   b. {CP[*that*] | S[FIN]} 𝓐 {𝓑 | S} NP[G]
   where 𝓐={S, VP, CP[{*that* | *for*}]}* and 𝓑=VP {NP, N', PP}*

Recall that the notation {A | B | C} shows alternatives. These dominance path conditions are identical to those for *wh*-questions (6.1.3 (1)), which means that *wh*-questions and relative clauses obey the same set of islands.

(4) the inheritance hierarchy of restrictive relative clause (RRC)

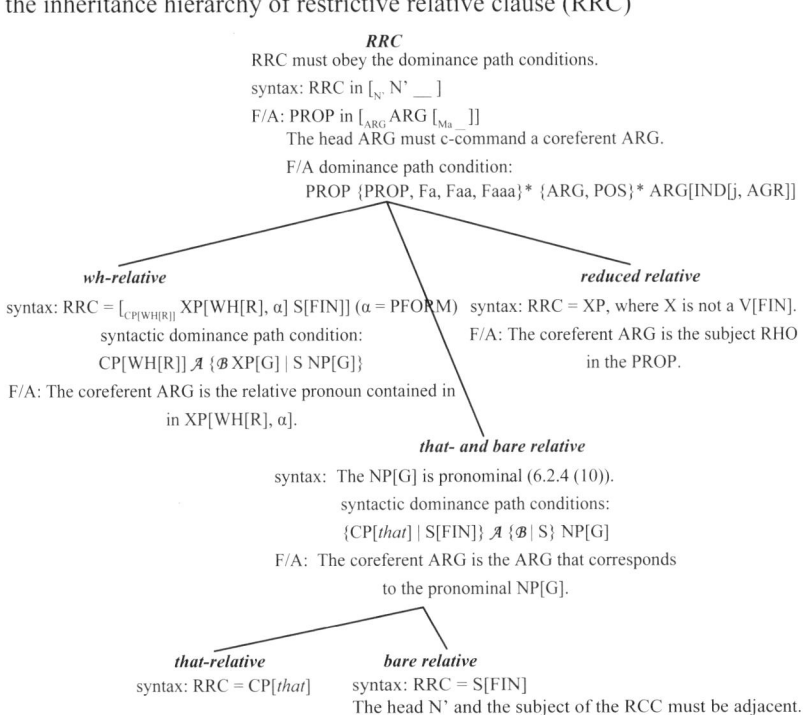

                  RRC
RRC must obey the dominance path conditions.
syntax: RRC in [$_{N'}$ N' __]
F/A: PROP in [$_{ARG}$ ARG [$_{Ma}$ __]]
   The head ARG must c-command a coreferent ARG.
F/A dominance path condition:
   PROP {PROP, Fa, Faa, Faaa}* {ARG, POS}* ARG[IND[j, AGR]]

wh-relative
syntax: RRC = [$_{CP[WH[R]]}$ XP[WH[R], α] S[FIN]] (α = PFORM)
syntactic dominance path condition:
   CP[WH[R]] 𝓐 {𝓑 XP[G] | S NP[G]}
F/A: The coreferent ARG is the relative pronoun contained in
   in XP[WH[R], α].

reduced relative
syntax: RRC = XP, where X is not a V[FIN].
F/A: The coreferent ARG is the subject RHO
   in the PROP.

that- and bare relative
syntax: The NP[G] is pronominal (6.2.4 (10)).
syntactic dominance path conditions:
   {CP[*that*] | S[FIN]} 𝓐 {𝓑 | S} NP[G]
F/A: The coreferent ARG is the ARG that corresponds
   to the pronominal NP[G].

that-relative
syntax: RRC = CP[*that*]

bare relative
syntax: RRC = S[FIN]
The head N' and the subject of the RCC must be adjacent.

𝓐={S, VP, CP[{*that* | *for*}]}* and 𝓑=VP {NP, N', PP}*

Chapter 7
Speech Acts

> This chapter discusses how we can capture the speech act aspects of utterance meaning. We extend the notion of Role Structure to speech acts and their illocutionary forces, and explain from a multi-modular perspective various phenomena that were dealt with under the Performative Hypothesis.

7.1 Speech Act Superstructure

The demonstrative *that* can refer to the proposition (PROP) in F/A or the speech act (SA) in RS of an utterance, depending on the context in which it is used. In the first exchange in (1) below, the demonstrative *that* refers to the proposition that A has just asserted. In the second exchange, *that* refers to the proposition expressed by the CP[*that*] *I took the money*. If A had said "I said that I took the money," B's utterance would have been ambiguous in that *that* could have referred to *I took the money* or *I said that I took the money*.

(1) A: The moon is owned by General Motors.
    B: That's false. (McCawley 1993: 290)

    A: I [$_{PV}$ confess] that I took the money. (PV = performative verb)
    B: That's not true. (Cruse 2011: 367)

On the other hand, the demonstrative *that* in (2) refers to the speech act (SA) of assertion that A has just performed.

(2) A: Your father is a retired pimp.
    B: That's pretty damn cheeky of you. (McCawley 1993: 290)

To capture the speech-act aspects of the meaning of an utterance, we propose to posit a speech act (SA) superstructure (a.k.a. performative clause) on top of an event structure (EV) in RS (cf. Sadock 2012: 137). As is shown in (3a), an SA superstructure consists of its illocutionary force (IF), the speaker (SP) with the [AG, SO] role, the addressee (AD) with the [PT, GO] role, and the theme (TH) role that dominates an event (EV), which corresponds to the PROP in F/A and the S in syntax of the utterance in question.

The correspondences in (3a) between the speech act of assertion in RS and the syntactic and F/A structures of a declarative clause are a default case, which can be overridden by various factors both linguistic and nonlinguistic. For example, the sentence *You will close the door* is ambiguous in its illocutionary force (Sadock 1974: 15): it can be either an assertion or an order. If this is produced/interpreted as an assertion, the correspondences between the modules are given in (4a). On the other hand, if this is produced/interpreted as an order, the correspondences are given in (4b).

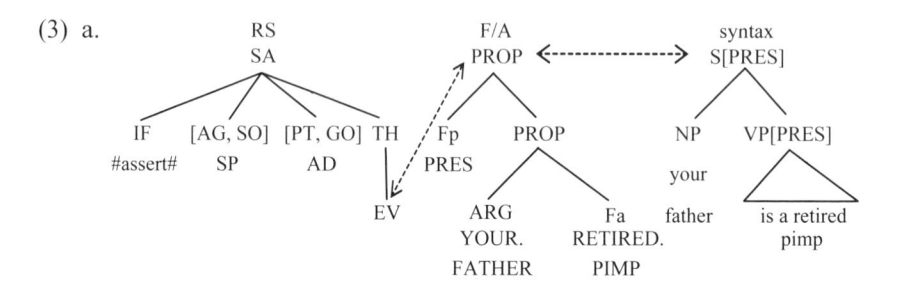

(3) a.

```
        RS                       F/A                    syntax
        SA                      PROP  <------------>   S[PRES]
       /  |  \                 /  \                     /   \
  IF [AG,SO] [PT,GO] TH       Fp   PROP              NP    VP[PRES]
  |     |      |              |   /    \             |
#assert# SP    AD            PRES ARG   Fa          your  father is a retired pimp
              EV                 YOUR. RETIRED.
                                 FATHER PIMP
```

b. lexical entry for SA superstructure
   syntax: nil
   F/A: nil
   RS: $[_{SA}$ IF $[_{[AG, SO]}$ SP$]$ $[_{[PT, GO]}$ AD$]$ $[_{TH}$ EV$]]$
   phonology: nil

(4) a. default case (direct speech act)
    declarative S   <--→   PROP   <--→   SA with the #assert#
    in syntax   in F/A   illocutionary force in RS
  b. nondefault case (indirect speech act)
    declarative S   <--→   PROP   <--→   SA with the #order#
    in syntax   in F/A   illocutionary force in RS

The speech act (SA) superstructure (3a) only exists in RS and does not correspond to anything in the other modules, which is guaranteed by the defective lexical entry (3b). This part of RS is an unassociable structure and is inaccessible to the other modules, just as unassociable roles and coerced materials. This means that there is no direct interaction between the SA superstructure in RS and the syntax and F/A of the sentence whose EV in RS is dominated by the SA superstructure in question, though there can be indirect interactions between them. In particular, an SA superstructure does not directly interact with QPs and Fp functors, such as NOT. The F/A structure of a sentence captures its propositional content (including truth conditions), whereas the SA superstructure in RS of an utterance captures the speech act/pragmatic aspects of its meaning.

An SA superstructure is not an obligatory part of RS, but optional in the sense that it is present only when its presence is required. For example, embedded clauses lack their SA superstructures. Again, this is a default case and can be overridden. We will discuss the cases in which a performative verb appears in an embedded clause in 7.3. We take an SA superstructure as freely available RS material. This is similar to freely available coerced materials, such as causative coercion. (See for example 4.7 (3). See also Pollard and Sag 1994: 308ff., Jackendoff 1997: 52, 2002: 389, and Culicover and Jackendoff 2005: 227ff.).

If a sentence is an explicit performative with an overt performative verb (*I order you to stay here*) and is uttered/interpreted as an expression of the illocutionary force named by the performative verb in question (*order*), the IF of the SA superstructure (#order#) and the TYPE of the EV ("order") coincide, as in $[_{SA} [_{IF} \#order\#]$ SP AD $[_{EV} [_{TYPE}$ "order"] AG PT $[_{TH}$ EV]]], though the SA superstructure may not be necessary. However, when an explicit performative sentence is uttered as an expression of an illocutionary force that is different from the illocutionary force of the performative verb in question, the SA superstructure is needed to represent the discrepancy. The examples of *I promise* in (5) are not used performatively to make a promise but are used to perform some other speech act.

(5) a. A: How do you get me to throw all these parties?
    B: I promise to come. (as an answer to the question; ellipsis of *I get you to do so by promising to come*) (Levinson 1983: 233)
  b. If you don't hand in your paper on time, I promise you I will give you a failing grade in the course. (as a warning or threat) (Searle 1969: 58)
  c. A: You stole that money, didn't you?
    B: No, I didn't. I promise you I didn't. (as an emphatic assertion) (Searle 1969: 58–59)
  d. I promise there won't be a next time/this won't happen again. (as an apology)
  e. I promise too many things to too many people. (statement of habitual practice) (Searle 1989: 537)
  f. Whenever I see you on Tuesday I always do the same thing: I promise to come and see you on Wednesday. (Searle 1989: 538)

Searle (1969: 58) remarked about (5b, c) that *I promise (you)* and *I hereby promise (you)* are among the strongest illocutionary force indicating devices for *commitment* provided by the English language. Therefore, speakers can use them either to emphasize the degree of their commitment to their intention to perform the speech act that is damaging to the addressee in (5b) or to emphasize the degree of their commitment to the truth of their statement in (5c). Constative sentences (nonperformative sentences, such as *The cat is on the mat* or *Birds eat*) may or may not have an SA superstructure. If a sentence uttered by a speaker is ambiguous in its illocutionary force (including cases of indirect speech act), there should be an SA superstructure to represent the speaker's intention or the addressee's interpretation.

Here are default correspondences between declaratives, interrogatives, and imperatives in syntax and their corresponding F/A and RS.

(6) a. default lexical entry for declaratives (as a construction)

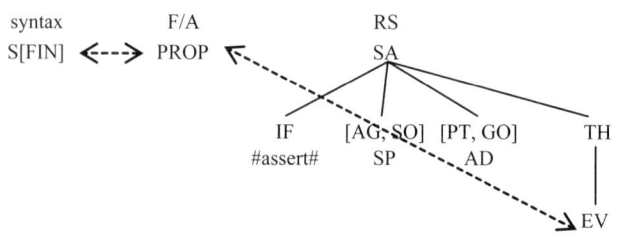

```
syntax         F/A              RS
S[FIN]  <-->  PROP              SA
                          ┌──────┼──────┐
                         IF   [AG, SO] [PT, GO]   TH
                       #assert#   SP      AD       │
                                                   ▼ EV
```

phonology: falling intonation

b. default lexical entry for yes/no interrogatives with inversion (as a construction)

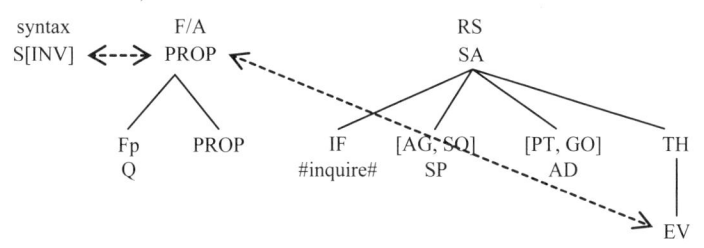

```
syntax          F/A              RS
S[INV]   <--->  PROP  <---       SA
  /\              /\             /|\
 Fp  PROP       IF   [AG,SQ]  [PT,GO]  TH
 Q             #inquire#  SP    AD      |
                                        EV
```

phonology: rising intonation

c. default lexical entry for imperatives (as a construction)

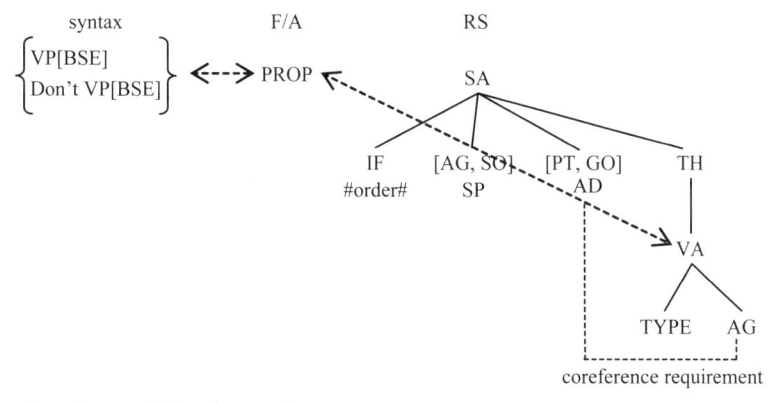

```
 syntax           F/A              RS
{ VP[BSE]    }
{ Don't VP[BSE] }  <--->  PROP  <---  SA
                                      /|\
                                    IF  [AG,SQ]  [PT,GO]  TH
                                  #order#  SP     AD       |
                                                           VA
                                                          /  \
                                                       TYPE   AG
                                  coreference requirement
```

phonology: falling intonation

These are all default correspondences. As for (6a), an utterance of a declarative sentence in syntax can correspond not only to an SA of assertion but also to an SA with some other illocutionary force if the sentence in question is an explicit performative with an IF other than #assert# (e.g., #promise# in *I promise to help you* uttered to make a promise). As for (6b), an utterance of an interrogative sentence (S[INV]) in syntax can correspond to a request (*Can you close the door?*), to an exclamative (*Boy, am I ticked off!*), to an assertion (*May I tell you that the square root of a quarter is a half?* (Levinson 1983: 266)), or to "queclarative" (*Does anyone study Aristotle anymore?* (Sadock 1974: 79)). As for (6c), an utterance of an imperative sentence in syntax can correspond to a wish (*Have a nice day!* or *Don't catch a cold!*), to an offer (*Have another drink!* (Levinson 1983: 275)), to a curse or swearing (*Shut up!* (Levinson 1983: 275)), or to a welcoming

(*Come in!* (Levinson 1983: 275)). In the RS of (6c), VA stands for volitional action (4.3 (5)). The coreference requirement between the addressee (AD) and the agent (AG) of the VA is not grammatically required but rather comes from the definition of the act of order, or more generally from the definition of "directive" (Searle 1979: 13), which is not part of grammatical knowledge but properly belongs to pragmatic knowledge. A speech act is an order if it counts as an attempt by the speaker to get the addressee to do something (Searle's essential condition for directives). See Searle 1969: 66 and 1979: 13.

In each utterance, the speaker (SP) and addressee (AD) are always available as part of its SA superstructure and can serve as the antecedent of the RHO subject of a nonfinite free-control VP or as that of a reflexive. In a sense, the SP and AD are "permanently available topics" (Erteschik-Shir 2007: 17–18).

(7) a. Undressing myself/yourself/ourselves in public may annoy Bill. (Culicover and Jackendoff 2005: 418)
  b. How about taking a swim together? (ibid.)
  c. Physicists like myself were never too happy with the parity principle. (Ross 1970: 230)
  d. As for myself, I won't be invited. (Ross 1970: 232)

In (7a), the agent role that corresponds to the F/A subject ARG (RHO) of *undressing oneself* refers to the SP, the AD, or both. In (7b), the agent role that corresponds to the F/A subject ARG (RHO) of *taking a swim together* refers to both the SP and AD. The reflexive *myself* in (7c, d) takes the SP in the SA superstructure as its antecedent.

We could go even further and posit a locutionary act (LA) superstructure (8b, d) on top of SA superstructure to represent a locutionary act (McCawley 1985; McCawley 1993: 584 note 3). As is shown in (8b, d), an LA consists of the TYPE #direct#, the SP with [AG, SO] role, the AD with [PT, GO] role, and the TH that dominates an SA, and represents the meaning that the SP directs this SA to the AD. Note that the SP and AD in an LA superstructure are the same as those in the SA superstructure that it dominates.

(8) a. Tom, you wash the dishes, and Lucy, you empty the garbage. (McCawley 1993: 295)
  a'. (pointing to different addressees) You wash the dishes, and you empty the garbage.

7.1 SPEECH ACT SUPERSTRUCTURE 359

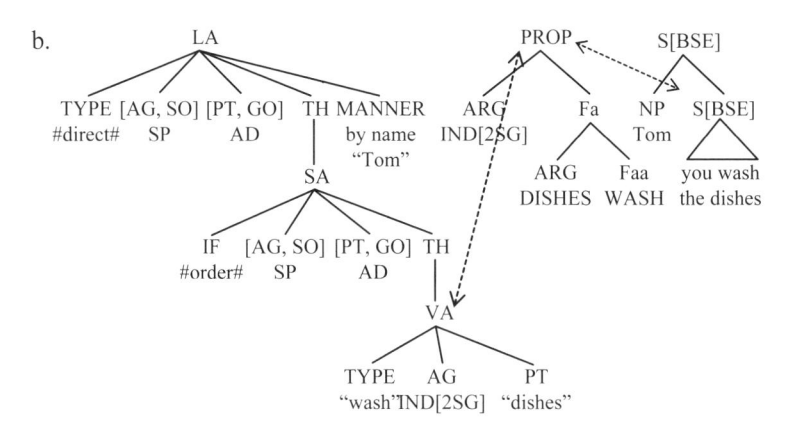

b.
```
                    LA                                PROP              S[BSE]
        ┌───────────┼──────────┐              ┌────────┼──────┐
   TYPE [AG, SO] [PT, GO]  TH  MANNER       ARG      Fa    NP   S[BSE]
   #direct#   SP      AD   │   by name    IND[2SG]        Tom
                           SA  "Tom"                    ┌──┼────┐
                 ┌─────────┼──────────┐              ARG  Faa  you wash
                 IF  [AG, SO] [PT, GO]  TH         DISHES WASH the dishes
              #order#   SP       AD    │
                                       VA
                                    ┌──┼──┐
                                  TYPE AG  PT
                               "wash"IND[2SG] "dishes"
```

c. I order you to shine these shoes, and I warn you that if you don't obey that order immediately, you'll be court-martialed. (McCawley 1993: 295)

d. lexical entry for LA superstructure
   syntax: nil
   F/A: nil
   RS: [_LA [_TYPE #direct#] [_[AG, SO] SP] [_[PT, GO] AD] [_TH SA] (MANNER)]
   phonology: nil

For example, an utterance of a sentence can express two locutionary acts, each with its own illocutionary force. This is illustrated in (8a), where the first LA is directed to Tom and the second LA to Lucy, and the IF of each conjunct SA is #order#. So, the whole modular representations of (8a) are those in which two Ss are coordinated in syntax, two PROPs are coordinated in F/A, and two LAs are coordinated in RS. Each LA dominates an SA whose illocutionary force is #order#. The correspondences between the syntax, F/A, and RS of the first conjunct S are given in (8b). According to McCawley (1985: 51, 1998: 752), LA is the level of RS where vocative expressions are represented. For example, the vocative expression *Tom* of the first conjunct in (8a) is represented as MANNER under the LA node in (8b). As another example of a vocative expression, the lexical entry for vocative *sir* is given in (9) below. There is no tense in the F/A of (8b), because the verb is in the base form (V[BSE]) when it is used in the imperative, as in *Everybody stand up*.

(9) lexical entry for vocative *sir*
    syntax: W in [_S rest < __] (a word in syntax that occupies the sentence-final position)

mphon: /sɚ/
F/A: nil

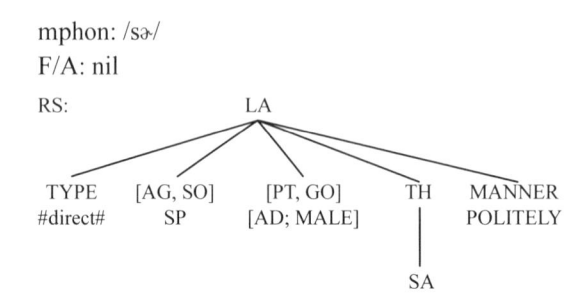

```
RS:                    LA
         ┌──────┬───────┬──────┬──────┐
       TYPE  [AG, SO]  [PT, GO]  TH  MANNER
      #direct#   SP    [AD; MALE]    POLITELY
                                │
                                SA
```

(8c) is an example of a sentence of two coordinated explicit performatives, whose utterance contains one LA that dominates two SAs, ordering and warning. In the syntax of (8c), two explicit performative Ss are coordinated. In F/A, two PROPs are coordinated. In RS, assuming that their SA superstructures are represented, the TH node of the LA dominates two coordinated SA nodes, each with its own IF: [$_{LA}$ [$_{TYPE}$ #direct#] SP AD [$_{SA}$ [$_{SA}$ [$_{IF}$ #order#] SP AD VA] [$_{SA}$ [$_{IF}$ #warn#] SP AD EV]]].

As has been often pointed out, there are two kinds of present tense: habitual present (h-PRES) and instantaneous present (i-PRES). Habitual present is used to report the usual state of affairs (McCawley 1993: 294), whereas instantaneous present is used to express what the speaker is doing (the speaker's verbal and nonverbal act) at the moment of speaking. Instantaneous present is used in demonstrations (10a, b) and play-by-play commentaries (10c).

(10) a. Magician: I display the inside of the box. I roll up my sleeves to show that they are empty. I reach into the box with my right hand... (McCawley 1993: 294)
b. I now beat the eggs till fluffy. (said in demonstration as a report of a concurrent action; Levinson 1983: 232)
c. Jones passes and Raul kicks the ball into the net.

In explicit performatives, such as (8c) or *I bet you sixpence it will rain tomorrow* (Austin 1975: 5), instantaneous present is used to express the speaker's verbal act at the moment of speaking (Austin 1975: 56, Searle 1989: 556). The distinction between habitual present (h-PRES) and instantaneous present (i-PRES) must be represented in F/A as part of propositional meaning, because this difference leads to another difference in what kind of time adverbial (Mp in F/A) the proposition can be modified by: for example, *now* or *every day*. Time adverbials are part of propositional content. Therefore, in (ii), when the utterance *I promise* VP[*to*] is used to give a promise, the tense F_p must be i-PRES.

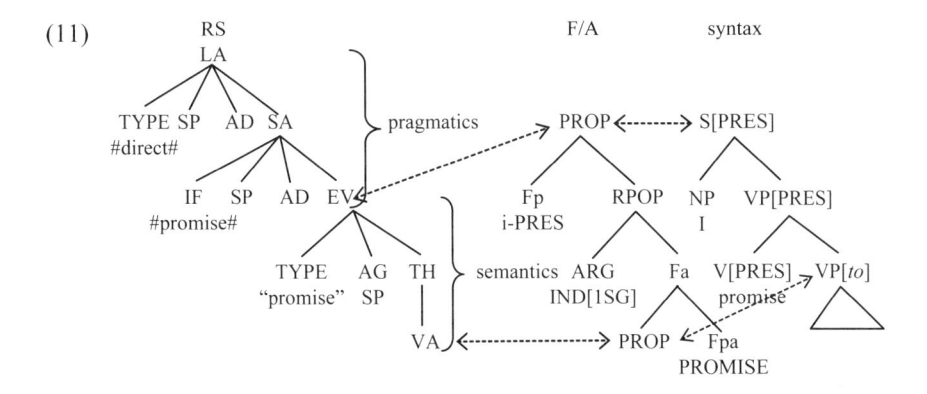

(11)

```
          RS                              F/A              syntax
          LA
        ╱     ╲
   TYPE SP   AD SA  ⎫                  PROP ◄------► S[PRES]
   #direct#   ╱  ╲  ⎬ pragmatics      ╱    ╲         ╱    ╲
             IF SP  AD EV ⎫          Fp    RPOP     NP   VP[PRES]
           #promise#   ╱  ╲⎬         i-PRES ╱ ╲      I     ╱    ╲
                   TYPE AG TH⎬ semantics ARG    Fa  V[PRES]→VP[to]
                  "promise" SP │         IND[1SG] ╱ ╲  promise
                              VA ◄--------► PROP  Fpa
                                                PROMISE
```

In the above representations, #promise# represents the IF (pragmatic notion) in RS of the performative verb *promise*, and "promise" represents the event type (cognitive semantic notion) in RS, which captures the RS aspects of the meaning of *promise*, and PROMISE represents the functor (propositional semantic notion) in F/A, which captures the F/A aspects of the meaning of *promise*. These representations allow a possibility that the utterance *I promise* CP[*that*] can be used to perform a speech act other than making a promise: for example, (5b) as a warning, (5c) as an assertion, and (5d) as an apology. In these cases, although the event type is "promise," the IF in the respective SA superstructure is #warn# in (5b), #assert# in (5c), and #apologize# in (5d).

7.2 Indirect Speech Acts

A speech act is said to be direct or literal if its default (literal) illocutionary force is realized, namely, (i) if the utterance in question is an explicit performative and has the illocutionary force named by the performative verb in the matrix clause (e.g., *I promise to be honest* is uttered to make a promise) or (ii) if the utterance in question follows one of the default correspondences between syntax and RS specified in 7.1 (6), that is, a declarative sentence uttered to make an assertion (6a), an interrogative sentence uttered to ask a question (6b), or an imperative sentence uttered to give an order (6c) (cf. Levinson 1983: 263–264). By contrast, a speech act is said to be indirect if its nondefault illocutionary force is realized, namely, cases where neither (i) nor (ii) above holds. For example, when the interrogative *Can you pass me the salt?* is uttered not to ask a question (default illocutionary force) but to make a request (nondefault illocutionary force), its illocutionary force is not the default #inquire# but the nondefault #request# (i.e., *Please pass me the salt*). Another example pointed out by Jerry Sadock (p.c.) is the imperative "Rise, Sir Antonio," which is uttered as the performative "I dub thee Sir Antonio." The intermodular correspondences of the former example are given in (1). The coreference requirement in the RS is not grammatical but rather comes from the definition of the act of making a request, which is an attempt by the speaker to get the addressee to do something (Searle 1969: 66). This belongs to pragmatic knowledge.

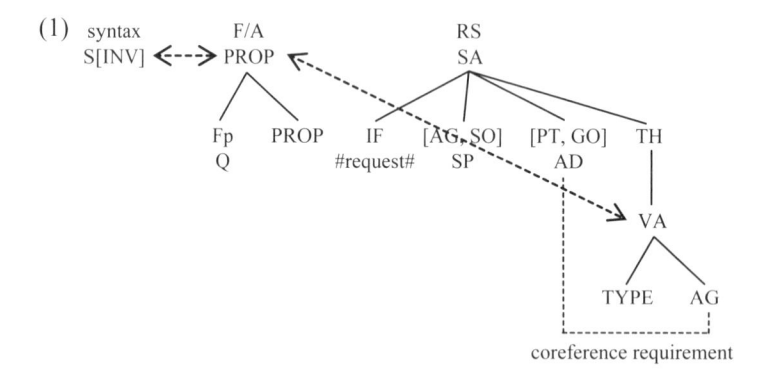

(1) syntax   F/A   RS
     S[INV] ⇔ PROP   SA
            Fp PROP   IF   [AG, SO] [PT, GO] TH
            Q   #request# SP   AD
                                          ⤳ VA
                                          TYPE AG
                            coreference requirement

Indirect speech acts form a continuum from the least indirect (i.e., the most direct) to the most indirect, depending on how much their interpretation as an indirect speech act (indirect interpretation) deviates from their interpretation as a direct speech act (literal interpretation).

(2) a. Can you pass me the salt? (as a request)
    b. Can you reach the salt? (as a request) (Searle 1979: 30)
    c. I wish you wouldn't do that. (as a request) (Searle 1969: 68)
    d. Sir, you are standing on my foot. (as a request) (Searle 1979: viii)
    e. Gosh, I'm cold. (as a request) (Jerry Sadock (p.c.))

As for (2a), its indirect interpretation is a speech act of making a request 'Please pass me the salt.' Although the speaker (SP) utters it as an indirect speech act with the #request# illocutionary force (IF), it can still be understood either literally as a question about the addressee (AD)'s physical ability or indirectly as a request to AD.

However, if this question is asked at dinner table where the salt is within easy reach of AD, AD can reject the literal interpretation and choose the indirect interpretation, because the answer to the question, if interpreted literally, is predictably "yes."

As for (2b), its intended indirect interpretation is not 'Please reach the salt' but 'Please pass me the salt.' AD can again reject the literal interpretation, which is irrelevant in this discourse context, and recover the intended indirect interpretation based by inference along the lines of the Gricean conversational maxims (Grice 1989: 22ff., Levinson 1983: 100ff.). In (2a) and (2b), a request is made by querying AD's ability (*Can you ...?*). As pointed out by Searle (1969: 66 and 1979: 45), AD's ability to do an act A (i.e., AD is able to do A) is a preparatory condition for SP's requesting AD to do A, and asking about the preparatory condition conventionally satisfies the essential condition for requesting AD to do A, that is, conventionally counts as an attempt by SP to get AD to do A. Note that *Can you ...?* is conventionalized as a requesting form, because *Are you able to ...?*, although it has the same meaning as *Can you ... ?*, is far more difficult to understand as a requesting form. Note also that (2b) is more indirect than (2a) in that the former questions AD's ability to reach the salt, which is a prerequisite for AD's ability to pass the salt, which in turn is a preparatory condition for SP's requesting AD to pass the salt.

As for (2c), AD interprets it literally as an expression of SP's wish and in addition interprets indirectly as a request. The literal interpretation is not rejected, as opposed to (2a, b). Rather, it acts as a conduit leading AD to the intended indirect interpretation. A request is made in (2c) by way of SP's stating his or her wish. Again, Searle (1969, 1979) pointed out that 'SP wants AD to do A' is a sincerity condition for requesting AD to do A, and stating the sincerity condition conventionally satisfies the essential condition for requesting AD to do A, that is, conventionally counts as an attempt by SP to get AD to do A.

As for (2d), AD interprets it literally as a statement of fact and in addition indirectly as a request through the Gricean conversational maxims. The literal interpretation is not rejected here, either.

As for (2e), AD interprets it literally as a statement of fact and in addition indirectly as a request ('Please close the window' or 'Please turn on the heater'). If this is said by a general to a private, it is interpreted as an order. (2e) can also be indirectly interpreted as a wish ('I want something to put on' or 'I want something hot to drink') or even as a proposal at the end of the day to a colleague that they stop in at a warm bar on their way home. All sorts of indirect interpretations are available depending on the discourse context in which it is uttered. The literal interpretation is not rejected here, either. The indirect interpretations of (2d, e) are quite different from their literal interpretations and hence must be recovered by means of AD's inference along the lines of the Gricean conversational maxims. In this respect, these indirect interpretations arise as conversational implicatures.

Searle (1969: 31) formulated illocutionary acts as F(p), where F is a variable that ranges over illocutionary indicating devices and p is a variable that ranges over propositions. He went on to claim (1969: 32) that there are two ways of negating this formula: "propositional negation" F(~p) and "illocutionary negation" ~F(p). He said that "I promise not to come" is a propositional negation and "I don't promise to come" is an illocutionary negation. In our AMG terms, the propositional negation "I promise not to come" is an utterance whose SA superstructure contains #promise# as its IF and dominates the EV whose event type is "promise," whose TH role corresponds to a negative proposition NOT(I.COME) in F/A (cf. 7.1 (11)). The problem with his formula is his notion of "illocutionary negation." Because illocutionary forces are "different types of function of language" (Austin 1975: 100), they are not amenable to the notion of negation. In AMG terms, negation is represented as an Fp functor NOT in F/A and corresponds to nothing in RS. Our view about Searle's example *I don't promise to come* of "illocutionary negation" is that an illocutionary force is not something that can be negated and that the illocutionary force of this utterance is not #promise# but #declare# (Searle's (1979:16) "declaration"). That is, the speaker of this utterance is merely declaring his or her lack of intention to promise. If our view is correct, the illocutionary force of "I don't promise to come" is not expressed in its overt form. This is another example of indirect speech act. The same is true of the utterance pair of *I order you to come* and *I don't order you to come*. The latter, when uttered by SP to AD, is an indirect speech act that declares SP's lack of intention to order.

7.3 Embedded Performative Verbs

The performative hypothesis was presented in Ross (1970) as a package of ideas that could each be theoretically independent issues. It consisted of the core part of the hypothesis, which McCawley (1985: 43) called the pristine performative hypothesis, and several other related but independent issues, such as what illocutionary forces a sentence may have, and what context performative verbs can occur in. Therefore, it is quite possible, as McCawley claimed, to accept the pristine performative hypothesis separately from the other issues.

The pristine performative hypothesis, according to McCawley (1985: 43), is "illocutionary forces are represented in underlying structure in terms of performative verbs occurring in positions in which performative verbs are allowed to occur anyway." We formulate this idea in AMG terms: (i) the illocutionary force of an utterance is represented as IF under the SA node in RS; (ii) claim (i) is neutral with regard to whether every sentence has an illocutionary force (i.e., has an SA superstructure); (iii) claim (i) is neutral with regard to how many illocutionary forces (i.e., how many SAs) a sentence can have; (iv) claim (i) is neutral with regard to where performative verbs may occur in syntax (in matrix or embedded clauses). This weakening of Ross' (1970) original performative hypothesis, according to which "Every sentence has a deep structure of the form [*I V you S*], where the V corresponds to the illocutionary force of the sentence; performative verbs occur in deep structure only in that position" (McCawley 1985: 43), is unavoidable to account for counterexamples to his original version.

Examples have been pointed out in which performative verbs, such as *inform*, appear in embedded clauses (1). We deal with these examples by simply admitting an occurrence of a performative verb (PV) in an embedded clause (claim (iv) above) and allowing the SA superstructure of the form [$_{SA}$ [$_{IF}$ #inform#] SP AD EV] to correspond locally to the PROP headed by INFORM in F/A. This is shown in (2).

(1) a. I regret that I must [$_{PV}$ inform] you that your goldfish has died. (Sadock 1974: 52)
  b. I regret to [$_{PV}$ inform] you of the death of your goldfish. (Sadock 1974: 53)
  c. I don't regret to [$_{PV}$ inform] you of the death of your goldfish.

(2) the intermodular correspondences of (1b)

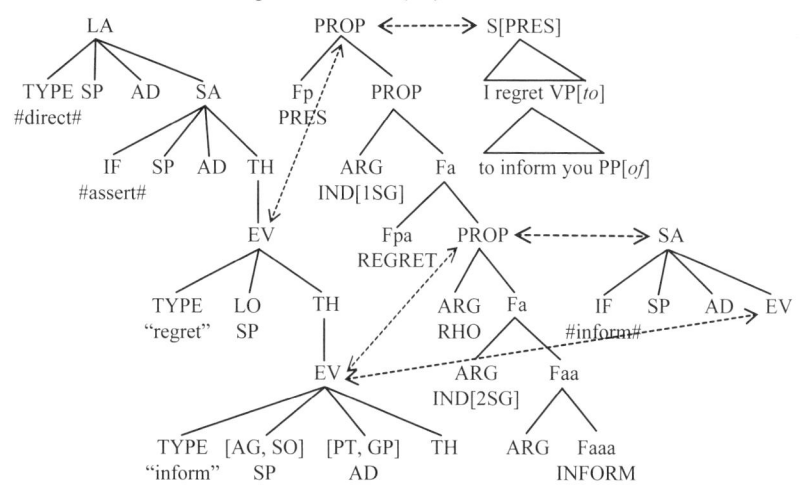

```
            LA                      PROP <--------> S[PRES]
           /|\                      /^\
    TYPE SP  AD  SA            Fp/  PROP    I regret VP[to]
    #direct#    /|\           PRES  /\
              IF  SP  AD  TH  /   ARG    Fa  to inform you PP[of]
            #assert#          /  IND[1SG]
                      EV              Fpa  PROP <---------> SA
                     /|\             REGRET/^              /|\
                 TYPE  LO  TH          ARG  Fa    IF   SP  AD -> EV
                "regret" SP            RHO       #inform#---
                         EV <---      ARG  Faa
                        /|\          IND[2SG]
                 TYPE [AG, SO] [PT, GP] TH   ARG   Faaa
                "inform"   SP      AD              INFORM
```

In (2), the topmost IF is #assert#, a default IF for a declarative sentence. The SA with the IF #inform# corresponds to the PROP headed by INFORM. Furthermore, the EV directly dominated by this SA corresponds to the EV with the event type "inform," which shows that the verb *inform* is used with the illocutionary force (IF) named by the verb itself.

The matrix verb *regret* in (1a, b) only expresses the speaker's attitude toward her speech act of informing (Sadock 1974: 62). As such, the matrix verb can also be expressed by sentence adverbs *regrettably, regretfully*, and *with great/deep regret*. Other expressions with similar properties are *I'm happy/pleased* VP[*to*] and *I'm sorry* VP[*to*] (Sadock 1974: 59). Jerry Sadock (p.c.) pointed out (1c) to me and observed that its illocutionary force is #inform#. That is, by uttering (1c), a negative sentence, the speaker still performs a speech act of informing but adds the information that he does not regret performing this speech act (cf. *Without regret, I inform you of the death of your goldfish*).

The matrix predicates *(don't) regret to/that* and the auxiliary *must* in (1) are, in a sense, orthogonal and transparent to the embedded illocutionary force. This orthogonality/transparency explains the occurrence of *hereby* in the matrix predicates in the following examples.

(3) (from the web)
   a. I hereby regret to [$_{PV}$ inform] you that our hospital will remain closed on Monday.
   b. We hereby regret to [$_{PV}$ inform] you that your employment contract with Five Forty Aviation Limited has been terminated effective 15th October 2012.
   c. We are hereby pleased to [$_{PV}$ inform] you that the following matters were reported and resolved.

In addition to embedded performative verbs in (1) and (3), examples in (4) with multiple performative verbs have been pointed out.

(4) (McCawley 1985: 45; a–c from Gazdar 1979 and Fraser 1974 and d from Sadock 1974: 57)
   a. I [$_{PV}$ announce] that I hereby [$_{PV}$ promise] to be timely.
   b. I [$_{PV}$ admit] that I [$_{PV}$ concede] the election.
   c. I [$_{PV}$ insist] I [$_{PV}$ dare] you to leave now.
   d. We regret to [$_{PV}$ inform] you that your insurance policy is hereby [$_{PV}$ cancelled].

In (4d), the performative adverb *hereby* shows that the embedded clause *your insurance policy is cancelled* is used performatively. Jerry Sadock (p.c.) pointed out to me that he can add another *hereby* to (4a, d), namely, *I hereby announce that I hereby promise to be timely* and *We hereby regret to inform you that your insurance policy is hereby cancelled*. If so, these sentences show that an utterance of a sentence can perform two different speech acts with one embedding the other. The intermodular correspondences of (4a) are given in (5).

(5) the intermodular correspondences of (4a)

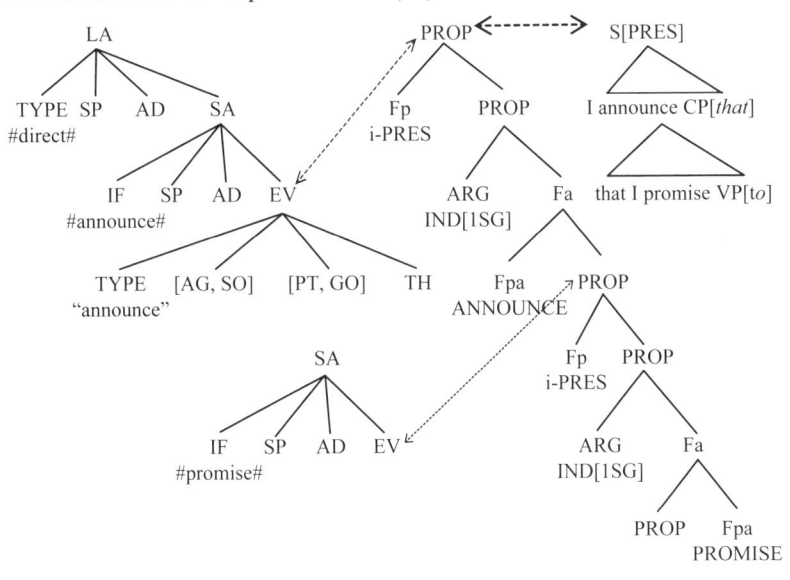

```
                LA                          PROP <------> S[PRES]
         /      |      \                   /                  /    \
     TYPE SP   AD     SA                  Fp     PROP       I announce CP[that]
    #direct#                            i-PRES    /    \
                 /   |   |   \                  ARG     Fa   that I promise VP[to]
              IF   SP  AD   EV                IND[1SG]
          #announce#                            /    \
              /      |        |     \         Fpa    PROP
          TYPE  [AG, SO]  [PT, GO]  TH     ANNOUNCE   /   \
        "announce"                                   Fp    PROP
                                                   i-PRES    /   \
                           SA                              ARG    Fa
                        /   |   |  \                     IND[1SG]
                      IF   SP  AD  EV                        /   \
                   #promise#                              PROP   Fpa
                                                                PROMISE
```

The RS of (5) shows that the speaker performs a speech act of announcing that contains another speech act of promising.

7.4 Antecedents in "Performative Clauses"

Examples such as (1a) below were counterexamples to Ross's (1970) performative analysis, because there was nothing that could trigger "reflexivization" of the first person singular pronoun according to his clause structure, where the "performative clause" headed by a performative verb (PV) was the highest clause. One way to account for this in our approach, following McCawley's (1985: 51) proposal, is to resort to a locutionary act (LA) superstructure in the form of [$_{LA}$ [$_{TYPE}$ #direct#] SP AD SA]

(7.1 (8b, d)). If we assume the existence of this structure, the antecedent of *myself* is available, namely, the speaker (SP) in the LA superstructure.

(1) a. As for myself, I [_PV_ declare] that these matters are beyond my ken.
   b. After arguing with him for two hours, I've finally gotten Jones to give in. The job will be pulled by Smith and himself tomorrow afternoon. (McCawley 1985: 52) the antecedent of *himself* = *Jones* (discourse topic)

As shown in (1b), a discourse topic can serve as the antecedent of an agreeing reflexive. We claim, following Erteschik-Shir (2007: 17–18), that the speaker (SP) and addressee (AD) are "permanently available topics" in any discourse because their existence is always taken for granted and they are always accessible. Therefore, a second way of accounting for (1a) is that SP and AD are permanently available discourse topics and hence can serve as the antecedent of an agreeing reflexive.

In (2a) below, the RHO subject of the verb *buy* refers to *John*, whose F/A correspondent is many PROPs higher than the reflexive. As shown in (2b), when the RHO subject refers to SP or AD, an overt antecedent is not required. Here, we claim again that the RHO can refer to SP and AD because they are permanently available discourse topics. In fact, the RHO in (2c, d) refers to an overt discourse topic.

(2) a. John thought it would be wise to buy himself a new hat. (McCawley 1993: 297)
   b. It would be wise to buy myself/yourself/*himself a new hat. (McCawley 1993: 298)
   c. John goes out without a hat for hours, no matter how hot it is. Doesn't he have a hat? It would be wise to buy himself a new hat. (discourse topic = *John*)
   d. Mary was happy and excited. To have involved herself in the group was a risky action. But it was proving that she could change her life. (discourse topic = *Mary*) (Bresnan 1982: 328)

7.5 Referring to "Performative Clauses"

In 7.1 (2), repeated here as (1), the demonstrative *that* refers to the speech act of assertion that A has just performed. However, it has been pointed out about implicit performatives that it is difficult to refer to the "performative clause" (SA superstructure in RS in our AMG terms) by the anaphoric device *do that* (2a), although it can refer to a situational antecedent (2b).

(1) McCawley (1993: 290)
   A: Your father is a retired pimp.
   B: <u>That</u>'s pretty damn cheeky of you.

(2) McCawley (1985: 54)
   a. *Jones is off on a bender, and his wife will <u>do that</u>, if you ask her.
      intended antecedent = 'tell you that Jones is off on a bender'
   b. (observing someone playing the piano) I could <u>do that</u>/*so for hours on end.

We can add to (2a) a PP that modifies the performative clause ('I tell you') and thereby increase its saliency so that it can be referred to more easily, but the result is still bad.

(3) *Since/In case you wanted to know, Jones is off on a bender, and his wife will <u>do that</u>, if you ask her.

Again, it is easy to refer to the speech act of telling/informing or any other speech act by the demonstrative *that* (4).

(4) a. (B has been looking for John.)
       A: Are you looking for John? He's waiting for you in the meeting room.
       B: Oh, <u>that</u>'s very kind of you. Thank you.
   b. A: I'll never tell any more lies.
       B: Can you really keep <u>that</u>?

In (4a), *that* refers to A's speech act of telling B that John is waiting for B in the meeting room. In (4b), *that* refers to A's speech act of promising that A will never tell any more lies.

We conclude that the anaphoric device *do that* requires that its antecedent be an action (an event one of whose participants is agent (4.3 (5) Event Hierarchy)), which covers two cases: an action VP in linguistic discourse context and a physical action in nonlinguistic/situational discourse context. The implicit SA superstructure [$_{SA}$ [$_{IF}$ #...#] SP AD [$_{TH}$ EV]] represents the speaker's intention to perform a certain type of speech act and as such it does not count as an action VP in linguistic discourse context or as a physical action in nonlinguistic/situational discourse context. Therefore, it does not qualify as an antecedent of the anaphoric device *do that*.

The anaphoric device *do so* is the same as *do that* in this respect. In (5a), *do so* refers to the overt performative in the first conjunct. In (5b), *do so* cannot refer to the implicit "performative clause" 'I promise you' in the first conjunct. McCawley (1993: 297) pointed out that *do so* requires an overt antecedent in syntax.

(5) McCawley (1993: 297); attributed to Davison 1973
   a. I [_PV_ promise] to never tell any more lies, and you should <u>do so</u> too.
   b. *I'll never tell any more lies, and you should <u>do so</u> too.

When the antecedent of *do so* is a VP headed by a performative verb (PV), it is possible to use *do so* as an explicit performative (6).

(6) a. I believe I have no choice but to [_PV_ resign] as a director, as chair of the Audit Committee, and from all other board committees, and I hereby <u>do so</u>, effective immediately. (from the web)
   b. A: I hereby [_PV_ announce] my candidacy for the position.
      B: <u>So do</u> I.

This shows that although the anaphoric device *do so* cannot refer to an implicit performative verb, it can refer to and inherit performativity from a VP headed by a performative verb.

7.6 "Performative Clause" Modifiers

7.6.1 Style disjuncts

Such adverbs as *frankly, truthfully, candidly, honestly, confidentially, briefly, bluntly*, which are said to be used by the speaker to comment on his or her choice of words or manner of speaking, are what Greenbaum (1969) called style disjuncts. They were said to modify performative verbs of abstract performative clauses in examples such as (1a), based on the alleged synonymity between (1a) and (1b). Therefore, they were called performative adverbs (Levinson 1983: 255). However, as pointed out by Lyons (1977: 783) and Levinson (1983: 255), what the adverb is doing in (1a) is warning the addressee, as a parenthetical comment, that a frank opinion is forthcoming, or to comment about the speaker's attitude toward the speech act of assertion that he is about to make. In (1c), what the adverb is doing is to assert that John was frank in the manner in which he performed the act of telling. (1b) is ambiguous between these two readings, according to Levinson (1983: 255).

(1) a. Frankly, Merlin is a genius. (Schreiber 1972: 321)
   b. I tell you frankly that Merlin is a genius. (Schreiber 1972: 321)
   c. John told Mary frankly that Merlin was a genius.

Lyons (1977: 783–784) also pointed out that the adverb in (1a) can be replaced by some other adverbs and adverbials, such as *actually*, *to tell you the truth*, or *speaking frankly* that serve roughly the same function, whereas the adverb in (1b) cannot be replaced by these expressions: **I tell you actually/to tell you the truth that Merlin is a genius*. The similar expressions with verbs of saying (*to tell you the truth, frankly speaking, to put it frankly*) clearly show that they are parenthetical comments about the way the speaker is performing or is about to perform his speech act.

McCawley (1985: 55) proposed that "style disjuncts are like nonrestrictive relative clauses: they correspond to an additional speech act that is separate from though subordinate to the primary speech act." If we follow his idea, (1a) consists of one locutionary act (LA) with two speech acts (SA).

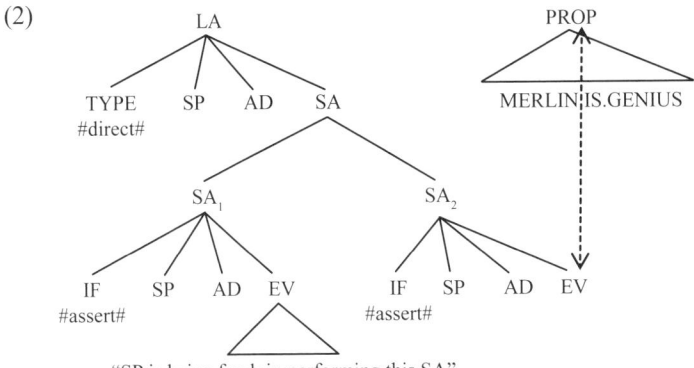

(2)

"SP is being frank in performing this SA"

The primary speech act (SA_2 in (2)) is of asserting the proposition that Merlin is a genius and the subordinate speech act (SA_1 in (2)) is of asserting to the addressee that 'I am being frank in performing this SA.' In (2), we tentatively assume that the IF of SA_1 is #assert#.

Mittwoch (1977) observed that performative adverbs occur in subordinate clauses (3a, b). Judging from our analysis in (2), this means that the subordinate clause (*I don't trust Bill* in (3a) and *I don't trust him* in (3b)) constitutes a separate speech act, which accords with our intuition.

(3) a. I voted for John because, <u>frankly</u>, I don't trust Bill. (Mittwoch 1977: 178)
   b. I voted for John though, <u>frankly</u>, I don't trust him. (ibid.)
   c. It is not the case that [I voted for John because I trusted him].
   d. *It is not the case that [I voted for John because, <u>frankly</u>, I trusted him].
   e. I don't beat my wife because I love her. (ambiguous)
   f. I don't beat my wife because, <u>frankly</u>, I love her. (unambiguous)

In (3c), the negative functor NOT can take the whole CP[*that*] within its scope. However, in (3d) with the performative adverb inserted, the PP[*because*] is felt to be outside the scope of NOT. This is because, according to (2), *I trusted him* is a separate speech act of assertion. Another piece of evidence is the contrast between (3e) and (3f). The former is ambiguous. In one interpretation, the PP[*because*] is outside the scope of *not* (i.e., The reason why I don't beat my wife is that I love her). In the other interpretation, it is inside the scope of *not* (i.e., I beat my wife for a reason other than that I love her). However, this ambiguity is gone in (3f), whose only interpretation is the former interpretation, because the second part of it (*I love her*) constitutes a separate speech act, due to the presence of *frankly*.

It has been observed that a style disjunct used with a declarative sentence and one used with an interrogative sentence are interpreted differently and that the latter exhibits ambiguity (Huddleston and Pullum 2002: 773).

(4) a. Frankly, you lied to me.
   b. Frankly, did you lie to me? (ambiguous) (cf. Schreiber 1972: 331, Huddleston and Pullum 2002: 773)
   c. the RS of (4a)

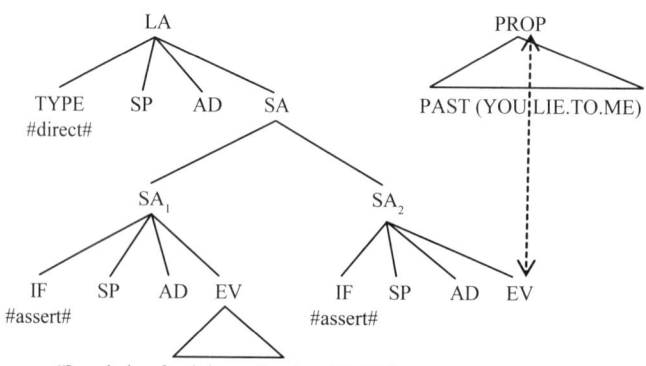

"I am being frank in performing this SA"

7.6 "PERFORMATIVE CLAUSE" MODIFIERS

d. the RS of the addressee-oriented interpretation of *frankly* in (4b)

```
              LA                                   PROP
          /   |   \                                 ↑
       TYPE  SP  AD  SA                         Fp     PROP
       #direct#      / \                         Q     /   \
                  SA₁   SA₂                        Fp    PROP
                 /|\    /|\                        PAST  /   \
               IF SP AD EV  IF SP AD EV            ↓   YOU.LIE.TO.ME
             #request#    #inquire#
```
"AD be frank in performing his SA"

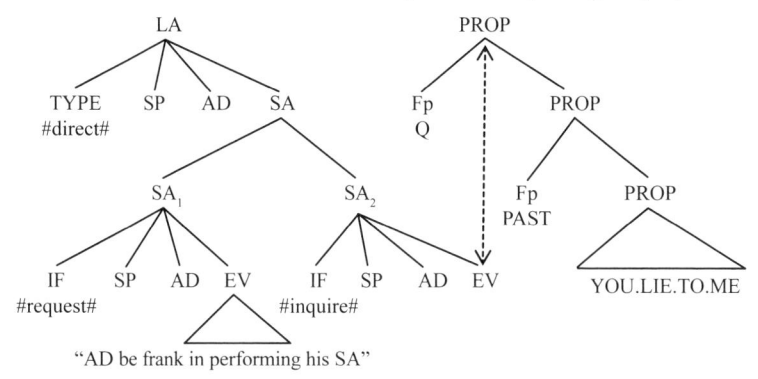

e. the RS of the speaker-oriented interpretation of *frankly* in (4b)

```
              LA                                   PROP
          /   |   \                                 ↑
       TYPE  SP  AD  SA                         Fp     PROP
       #direct#      / \                         Q     /   \
                  SA₁   SA₂                        Fp    PROP
                 /|\    /|\                        PAST  /   \
               IF SP AD EV  IF SP AD EV            ↓   YOU.LIE.TO.ME
             #assert#     #inquire#
```
"I am being frank in performing this SA"

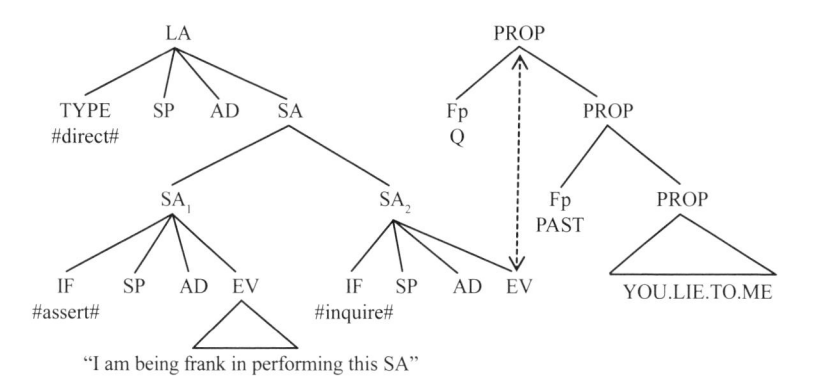

The speaker of (4a) is asserting that he is being frank about his speech act (SA) of assertion (cf. (2)). The RS of (4a) is given in (4c). On the other hand, the primary interpretation of (4b) is that the speaker is requesting the addressee to be frank about his answer (i.e., "Tell me frankly/I want you to be frank with me. Did you lie to me?"). The relevant part of its RS is given in (4d). Here again, we tentatively assume that the IF of this speech act is #request#. Schreiber (1972: 331 note 22; 332) pointed out about (4b) that it has another, secondary, interpretation that the speaker frankly asks a question (i.e., 'Let me ask you frankly. Did you lie to me?'). The RS of this interpretation is roughly a mixture of the first RS and the second RS and is given in (4e). Considering these three interpretations, the lexical entry for the style disjunct *frankly* is as follows.

(5) lexical entry for style disjunct *frankly*
syntax: ADV in [$_{S[FIN]}$ ___ {S[FIN] | S[INV]}]
F/A: nil
RS: [$_{SA}$ [$_{IF}$ #assert#] SP AD [$_{EV}$ "SP be frank about his SA"]] in
[$_{LA}$ [$_{SA}$ ___ [$_{SA}$ [$_{IF}$ #assert#] SP AD EV]]]
[$_{SA}$ [$_{IF}$ #request#] SP AD [$_{EV}$ "AD be frank about his SA"]] in
[$_{LA}$ [$_{SA}$ ___ [$_{SA}$ [$_{IF}$ #inquire#] SP AD EV]]]
[$_{SA}$ [$_{IF}$ #assert#] SP AD [$_{EV}$ "SP be frank about his SA"]] in
[$_{LA}$ [$_{SA}$ ___ [$_{SA}$ [$_{IF}$ #inquire#] SP AD EV]]]
mphon: /fræŋkli/

Sadock (1974: 15) observed that sentence adverbs, such as *fortunately*, occur freely only with declarative sentences. He also observed that when a sentence is ambiguous in its illocutionary force, the adverb *fortunately* co-occurs only with the assertive reading (6d). Huddleston and Pullum (2002: 771) commented on this class of adjuncts ("evaluative adjuncts") that "the residual proposition is presented as a fact, and the adjunct expresses the speaker's evaluation of it."

(6) a. Fortunately, Hilda hid the evidence. (Sadock 1974: 15)
    b. *Fortunately, did Hilda hide the evidence? (ibid.)
    c. *Fortunately, hide the evidence. (ibid.)
    d. Fortunately, you will close the door. (assertive reading only)

On the basis of these data, the lexical entry for sentence adverb *fortunately* would be as follows.

(7) lexical entry for sentence adverb *fortunately*
syntax: ADV in [$_{S[FIN]}$ ___ S[FIN]]
F/A: nil
RS: [$_{SA}$ [$_{IF}$ #assert#] SP AD [$_{EV}$ "I find this EV fortunate"]] in [$_{LA}$ [$_{SA}$ ___ [$_{SA}$ [$_{IF}$ #assert#] SP AD EV]]], where "this EV" refers to the event (EV) expressed by the primary SA of assertion.
mphon: /fɔɚtʃənətli/

In the RS of (7), the RS of the sentence adverb *fortunately* is the secondary SA of assertion and is a sister of the primary SA of assertion that corresponds to the matrix sentence.

7.6.2 Performative adverb *hereby*

The performative adverb *hereby* was said to modify explicit performatives (Sadock 1974: 37; Levinson 1983: 255). In (1) below, *hereby* modifies the matrix clause in (1a, b), and an embedded clause in (1c, d, e). In (1d, e), it modifies a nonfinite VP (VP[BSE]). In addition, when the first person present tense pro-VP form *do so* refers to a VP headed by a performative verb (PV), *do so* can be modified by *hereby* (7.5 (6)).

(1) a. I hereby [$_{PV}$ announce] my retirement. (Sadock 1974: 37)
    cf. *Bill hereby announces his retirement three times a year.
  b. I hereby [$_{PV}$ predict] that we will have seven lean years. (ibid.)
    cf. *We will hereby have seven lean years. (ibid.)
  c. I wish to [$_{PV}$ announce] that I hereby [$_{PV}$ tender] my resignation. (Sadock 1974: 52)
    cf. I hereby resign.
  d. I regret to hereby [$_{PV}$ inform] you of your dismissal. (from the web)
  e. I regret to hereby [$_{PV}$ sentence] you to a lifetime imprisonment in Azkaban prison. (from the web)

The verbs in the examples in (2) are performative verbs in the passive and still allow the performative adverb *hereby*. These examples belong to Searle's "declaration" illocutionary act (Searle 1979: 27).

(2) a. You are hereby [$_{PV}$ fired]. (Sadock 1974: 38)
  b. The meeting is hereby [$_{PV}$ adjourned]. (ibid.)
  c. War is hereby [$_{PV}$ declared]. (Searle 1979: 16)
  d. Your employment is hereby [$_{PV}$ terminated]. (Searle 1979: 17)
  e. Passengers are hereby [$_{PV}$ advised] that all flights to Phoenix have been cancelled. (Searle 1989: 537)

The examples in (3) do not contain an overt performative verb, but they are interpreted as a speech act of #declare# and therefore modified by the performative adverb.

(3) (from the web)
  a. A quick review of installation needs is hereby in order.
  b. A greater freedom of design is hereby present with respect to the pitches of the control section 36.
  c. Planned parenthood is hereby out of Knox County schools.

This adverb is "transparently an anaphoric device" (Sadock 1974: 61) and can be paraphrased as 'by saying this' or 'by means of these words,' in which *this* or *these words* refer to the speaker's locutionary act of uttering the sentence (cf. Lyons 1977: 781). Levinson's (1983: 254 note 17) paraphrase of this adverb is more elaborate: "I communicate this sentence to you in this situation and, by doing so, I [$_{PV}$ do]." Searle (1989: 552) claimed that *hereby* consists of the "self-referential part" *here* and the "executive part" *by* and paraphrased it as "by this here very utterance."

(4) lexical entry for performative adverb *hereby*
    syntax: ADV in [$_{VP}$ __ VP]
    F/A: nil
    RS: MEANS in LA

    TYPE   SP   AD   SA
    #direct#

                    IF   SP   AD   EV   MEANS
                    #PV#   "by performing this SA"

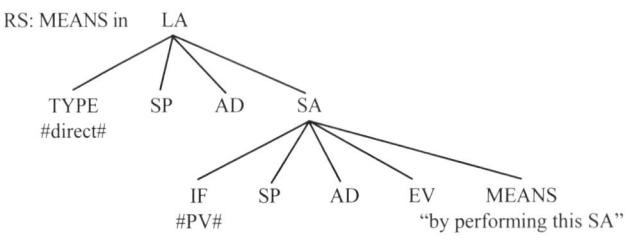

where #PV# is a performative verb if the utterance in question is an explicit performative, or it is #declare# otherwise.

In the lexical entry (4), "this SA" in RS refers to the speech act to which the performative adverb is adjoined (cf. "token-reflexivity" in Lyons 1977: 781 and Levinson 1983: 86, 254).

7.6.3 "Performative clause" modifying PPs

The adverbial clauses (syntactically PP adjuncts) in (1) are said to modify the implicit performative clauses. In fact, such a PP gives a reason for the speaker's performing the speech act in question. For example, the *in case* clause in (1a) gives a reason for informing the addressee of Bob and Frieda's marriage. The *since* clause in (1b) gives a reason for asking the question. The PP[*if*] in (1c, c')

7.6 "PERFORMATIVE CLAUSE" MODIFIERS

is interpreted not as a conditional but as a reason for asking a question or making a statement.

(1) a. In case you haven't heard, Bob and Frieda have decided to get married. (McCawley 1993: 299)
   b. Since you're so smart, what's the capital of South Dakota? (ibid.)
   b'. Feta is made from goat's milk, since you wanted to know. (Sadock 1974: 38)
   b". Close the door, since I'm busy. (Sadock 1974: 40)
   c. Who was the first German to visit Patagonia, if you know? (Sadock 1974: 39)
   c'. A ketch has two masts, if you didn't know that. (Sadock 1974: 39)

These adverbial PPs form a syntactic constituent with the matrix S: [$_S$ PP, S]. One piece of evidence comes from binding facts. As is well known, a pronoun may not precede and c-command its antecedent (McCawley 1998: 359) (assuming that (co)reference conditions apply to syntactic structures in addition to semantic representations F/A and RS). In (2d), the pronoun precedes and c-commands the antecedent, and hence the sentence is unacceptable, as expected. Another piece of evidence comes from coordination. In (2e), the first S and the second S are coordinated, the latter being adjoined by an S-adjunct PP.

(2) a. In case you haven't heard about them, Bob and Frieda have decided to get married.
   b. In case they haven't told you yet, Bob and Frieda have decided to get married.
   c. Bob and Frieda have decided to get married, in case you haven't heard about them.
   d. *They have decided to get married, in case you haven't heard about Bob and Frieda.
   e. [$_S$ Bob and Frieda will come tomorrow] and [$_S$ in case you haven't heard, they have decided to get married].

As for the F/A structure of (1a), there is no evidence that the adverbial clause (most plausibly Mp) and the matrix clause (PROP) form an F/A constituent: [$_{\text{PROP}}$ Mp, PROP]. If they did, it should be possible that some propositional operator (Fp), such as modal or negation, would take the whole constituent (i.e., [$_{\text{PROP}}$ Mp, PROP]) within its scope.

(3) a. *It seems that [in case you haven't heard, Bob and Frieda have decided to get married].
   b. *It seems that [Bob and Frieda have decided to get married in case you haven't heard].
   c. *It is not true that [in case you haven't heard, Bob and Frieda have decided to get married].
   d. *It is not true that [Bob and Frieda have decided to get married, in case you haven't heard].

Note that the only possible interpretation of the above examples is the one in which the *in case* clause is a parenthetical and modifies all the rest. That is, the *in case* clause is outside the scope of the Fp (SEEM or NOT). For example, it is possible to interpret (3c) in such a way that the *in case* clause modifies *It is not true that Bob and Frieda have decided to get married*. Therefore, we claim that the two parts (the *in case* clause and the rest *It is not true that Bob and Frieda have decided to get married*) are separate in F/A and do not form a constituent. This is shown in (4).

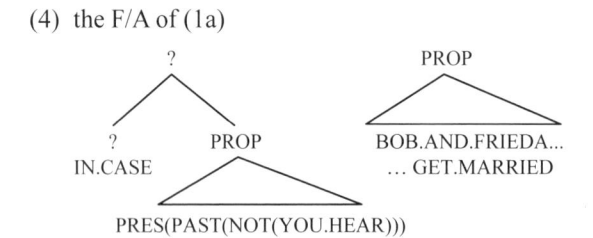

(4) the F/A of (1a)

```
              ?                              PROP
            /   \                          /      \
          ?      PROP              BOB.AND.FRIEDA...
       IN.CASE    |                ... GET.MARRIED
                 /\
        PRES(PAST(NOT(YOU.HEAR)))
```

As for the RS of (1a), we follow the structure for style disjuncts given in 7.6.1 (2) and claim that the adverbial clause constitutes a separate, subordinate speech act (SA) and is coordinated with the SA superstructure (primary speech act) of the matrix clause. We take these adverbial clauses as parentheticals that indicate that felicity conditions for performing a speech act of assertion or question are satisfied (Huddleston and Pullum 2002: 774). For example, (1a) consists of two

7.6 "PERFORMATIVE CLAUSE" MODIFIERS

speech acts: the matrix clause is the primary SA and the adverbial clause is the subordinate SA of asserting a reason for performing the primary SA of assertion. The intermodular correspondences are as follows.

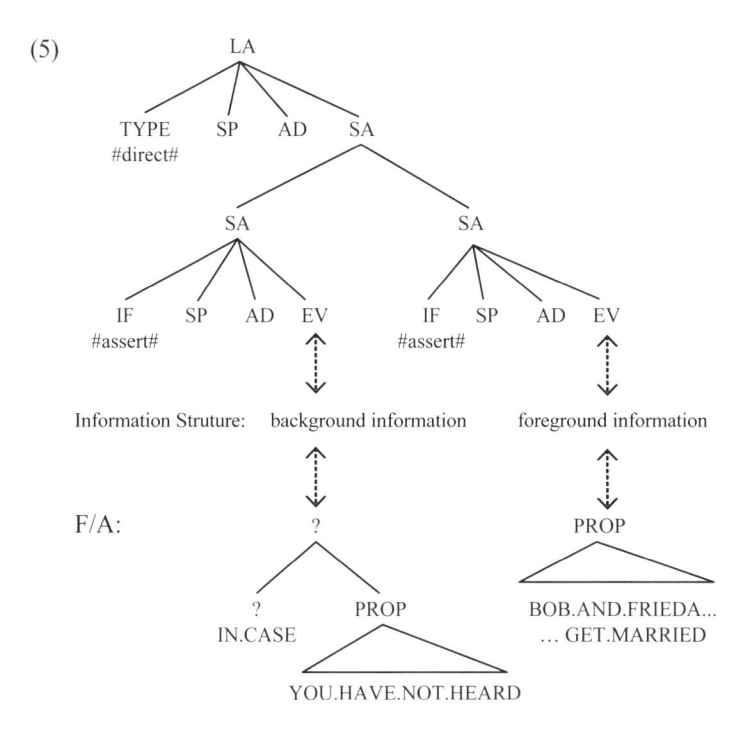

(5)

```
                              LA
                    ┌─────┬────┬─────┐
                  TYPE    SP   AD    SA
                 #direct#            ┌──────┴──────┐
                                    SA             SA
                              ┌──┬──┬──┐      ┌──┬──┬──┐
                              IF SP AD EV    IF SP AD EV
                            #assert#       #assert#
                                       ↕               ↕
      Information Structure:   background information   foreground information
                                       ↕               ↕
      F/A:                             ?               PROP
                                    ┌──┴──┐         ┌───┴───┐
                                    ?    PROP    BOB.AND.FRIEDA...
                                 IN.CASE  ┌─┴─┐   ... GET.MARRIED
                                      YOU.HAVE.NOT.HEARD
```

In (5), the adverbial clause (PP adjunct) represents background information (BI) and the matrix clause represents foreground information (FI).

It has been pointed out that modifiers of implicit performative clauses (6b) are subject to a more stringent restriction than those of overt performative clauses (6a, a') are subject to.

(6) a. Your breath smells. I tell you this <u>since I am your friend</u>. (Mittwoch 1977: 185)
   a'. I inform you that your breath smells, <u>since I am your friend</u>. (McCawley 1985: 54)
   b. *Your breath smells, <u>since I am your friend</u>. (Mittwoch 1977: 185)
   c. *Frankly, your breath smells, <u>since I am your friend</u>.
   d. <u>Since I am your friend</u>, frankly, your breath smells.

Following Mittwoch (1977: 188), we claim that the acceptability of a sentence with a performative-clause-modifying adverbial clause depends on whether and how clearly and easily we perceive the connection between the meaning of the adverbial clause and any of Searle's (1969: 66–67) preparatory and sincerity conditions of the speech act performed by uttering the main clause.

(7) preparatory and sincerity conditions of speech acts
(cf. Searle 1969: 66–67, Mittwoch 1977: 186)

types of speech act	assertion	question	order/command
preparatory conditions	➤ The speaker (SP) has evidence for the truth of the proposition (p). ➤ SP believes that the addressee (AD) does not know p.	➤ SP does not know whether p. ➤ SP expects that AD knows whether p.	➤ SP believes that AD is able to do the act (A). ➤ SP knows that he is in a position of authority over AD.
sincerity conditions	➤ SP believes p. ➤ SP believes that AD wants to know p.	➤ SP wants to know this information.	➤ SP wants AD to do A.

For example, we easily and clearly perceive a connection between the meaning of adverbial clause in (1a) and the second sincerity condition of assertion in (7). The adverbial clause in (1b) is clearly related to the second preparatory condition of question. The adverbial clause in (1b") is related to the sincerity condition of command. As for (6b), it is hard to perceive any connection between the meaning of the adverbial clause and any of the preparatory and sincerity conditions of assertion in (7), which explains its unacceptability. Adding a performative adverb (and thereby increasing the saliency of the implicit performative clause) does not help at all (6c). Interestingly, (6d) is more acceptable than (6c), because the PP[*since*] modifies the performative adverb *frankly* (giving a reason why the speaker is about to give a frank opinion) and does not directly modify the matrix clause. The fact that the performative adverb can be modified by a reason PP supports our analysis given in 7.6.1 (2), according to which an adverb of this type constitutes its own speech act. What is more interesting is that although (6b) is unacceptable, a slight change to it, as in *John's breath smells, since I am his friend* improves its acceptability a little, because we now perceive a slight connection between the meaning of the adverbial PP[*since*] and the first preparatory condition of assertion in (7).

Appendix

List of Definitions, Features, and Rules

Elsewhere Principle

When the conditions of application for one rule are a special case of those for another rule, the more general rule is inapplicable in those cases in which the conditions for the more specific rule are met, that is, specific rules preempt the application of general rules.

definition of directly dominate

For two nodes X and Y in a given tree, X directly dominates Y iff there is a branch in the tree that connects X and Y with X immediately above Y.

definition of dominate

For two nodes X and Y in a given tree, X dominates Y iff there is a series of nodes in the tree $X = X_1, \ldots, X_n = Y$, such that for each pair of X_i and X_{i+1}, X_i directly dominates X_{i+1}.

definition of x-command

For two nodes X and Y in a given tree, X x-commands Y iff (i) the first (lowest) non-adjoined node that dominates X and is a member of $\varphi(x)$, the set of bounding nodes for x, also dominates Y, and (ii) X does not dominate Y.

definition of non-adjoined node

The non-adjoined node in an adjunction structure is the node that dominates all the adjoined nodes.

definition of c-command in syntax

For two nodes X and Y in a given syntactic structure, X c-commands Y iff X x-commands Y, where $\varphi(x) = \{$all nodes in the syntactic structure$\}$.

definition of asymmetric c-command in syntax

For two nodes X and Y in a given syntactic structure, X asymmetrically c-commands Y iff X c-commands Y and Y does not c-command X.

definition of c-command in F/A

For two nodes X and Y in a given F/A structure, X c-commands Y iff X x-commands Y, where $\varphi(x) = \{$all nodes in an F/A structure$\}$.

definition of S-command in syntax

For two nodes X and Y in a given syntactic structure, X S-commands Y iff X x-commands Y, where $\varphi(x) = \{S\}$.

definition of S-mates in syntax

For two nodes X and Y in a given syntactic structure, X and Y are S-mates iff X and Y S-command each other.

Feature Osmosis

In the unmarked situations, there will be a correspondence of features between modules.

default correspondences

a. default categorial correspondences

syntax	F/A	RS
S	$\longleftrightarrow$ PROP $\longleftrightarrow$	EV
NP	$\longleftrightarrow$ ARG $\longleftrightarrow$	ROLE
VP	$\longleftrightarrow$ Fa	

b. default geometrical correspondences
  i. Dominance relations should be preserved between corresponding nodes in each module.
  ii. C-command relations in syntax and F/A should be preserved in RS as corresponding outrank relations.

Raising Principle

The subject ARG of the complement PROP of a raising predicate X_R (X = V or A) is allowed to correspond to a matrix NP position in syntax.

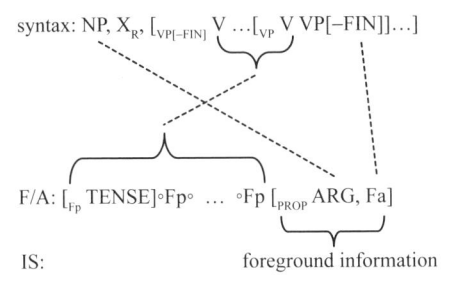

syntax: NP, X_R, $[_{VP[-FIN]}$ V ...$[_{VP}$ V VP[–FIN]]...]

F/A: $[_{Fp}$ TENSE]∘Fp° ... °Fp $[_{PROP}$ ARG, Fa]

IS: foreground information

Coordinate Structure Convention in dominance paths

When a coordinate structure occurs in the middle part of a dominance path, the mother node and each of its daughter conjunct nodes constitute a single node with the daughter's category label for the purposes of the dominance path conditions.

Coordinate Structure Convention in dominance paths (special case of the above)

When a VP coordinate structure that evokes a scenario of a natural/expected course of events occurs in the middle of a dominance path, the mother node and each of its main scene conjunct nodes constitute a single node with the daughter's category label for the purposes of the dominance path conditions.

Morphology Module

PS rules for morphology

derivation	$[_{X[0]}$ Y[0], AF]	inflection	$[_{X[1]}$ X[0], AF]
cliticization	$[_{Y[1]}$ X[1], CL]	compounding	$[_{Z[0]}$ X[m], Y[n]], where m, n = 0 or 1

definition of a well-formed morphological structure

a. A local morphological structure is well formed iff it is an instantiation of one of the local morphological rules (i.e., PS rules for morphology) permitted by the language in question and satisfies the morphological properties of the morphemes involved.

b. A morphological structure is well formed iff all the local morphological structures that it contains are well formed.

Syntax Module

PS rules for syntax

[$_S$ NP, VP] [$_{NP}$ {DET | NP[POS]}, N'] [$_{N'}$ {A | RRC}, N']
[$_{AP}$ {PP | ADVP}, AP] [$_{VP}$ {PP | ADVP}, VP] [$_S$ {PP | ADVP}, S]
[$_{S[FIN]}$ CP[*that*], VP[FIN]]

feature specifications

N = {<N, +>, <V, –>}, A = {<N, +>, <V, +>}, V = {<N, –>, <V, +>}, P= {<N, –>, <V, –>}

BAR values in syntax

category	N	V	A	P	ADV	C
<BAR, 0>	N	V	A	P	ADV	C
<BAR, 1>	N'	VP	AP	PP	ADVP	CP
<BAR, 2>	NP	S				

Head Feature Convention (HFC)

In each headed local tree, the mother and its head daughter must meet the conditions (i) and (ii), unless specified otherwise.

(i) The set of head features on the mother is identical to that on its head daughter, and
(ii) for each head feature in (i), its value on the mother must be identical to that on the daughter.

list of head features

BAR, form features (NFORM, PFORM, VFORM, and CFORM), part-of-speech features (<N, ±>, <V, ±>), AUX, INV, AGREEMENT (AGR), which subsumes PERSON (PER), NUMBER (NUM), and GENDER (GEN),

VFORM values

BSE (base form), PRP (present participial form), PSP (past participial form), PAS (passive participial form), *to*, FIN (finite, covering PRES (present tense) and PAST (past tense))

INV Feature Co-occurrence Restriction (FCR)

INV → {AUX, <VFORM, FIN>, <V, +>, <N, −>}

subject-verb agreement

[$_{S[FIN, AGR[3SGN]]}$ NP[AGR[α, β]], VP[FIN, AGR[α, β]]],
where α is a PER value and α ∈ {1, 2, 3}, and β is a NUM value and β ∈ {SG, PL}

subject-verb agreement (generalized)

a. definition of agreement controller
   The agreement controller of a finite (auxiliary) verb is the NP that the finite (auxiliary) verb agrees with.
b. generalized agreement
   The agreement controller of a finite (auxiliary) verb is the NP whose F/A correspondent is the subject ARG that is c-commanded by the TENSE that is realized on the finite (auxiliary) verb in question.

definition of a well-formed syntactic structure

a. A local syntactic structure is well formed iff it is either (ia) an instantiation of one of the PS rules for syntax admitted by the language in question or (ib) an instantiation of the syntactic field of one of the lexical entries of the language in question, and (ii) it meets all the relevant syntactic constraints on syntactic structures.
b. A syntactic structure is well formed iff all the local syntactic structures that it contains are well formed.

default linear order between sisters based on complexity

A less complex sister precedes a more complex sister by default.

a. pronoun < word < phrase < clause   b. NP < PP
c. syntactic correspondent of ARG < syntactic correspondent of Fa or PROP

English as head-initial language

In head-complement structures in English, where a lexical head (H[0]) takes one or more complements within its phrase (H[1]), the head must precede all the complements.

extended clause structures

head category	predicate phrase XP (<BAR, 1> except NP)	clause XS (<BAR, 2>) $[_{XS} NP, XP]$	
V	[$_{VP}$ likes music]	[$_{VS}$ Sally [$_{VP}$ likes music]]	VS (abbreviated as S)
N	[$_{NP}$ a carpenter]	[$_{NS}$ Sally [$_{NP}$ a carpenter]]	⎫
A	[$_{AP}$ very kind to you]	[$_{AS}$ Sally [$_{AP}$ very kind to you]]	⎬ small clause
P	[$_{PP}$ in the room]	[$_{PS}$ Sally [$_{PP}$ in the room]]	⎭

F/A Module

PS rules for F/A

a. [$_{F\varphi}$ Fxφ, x], where x is either a or p, and φ is a finite string of a's and p's, and Fe = PROP for the empty string e.
b. [$_\alpha$ Mα, α], where Mα is a modifier of an F/A category α.

definition of a well-formed F/A structure

a. A local F/A structure is well formed iff it is an instantiation of (a) or (b) of the PS rules for F/A, and its terminal nodes, if any, are instantiations of the F/A field of one of the lexical entries of the language in question.
b. An F/A structure is well formed iff all the local F/A structures that it contains are well formed.

feature structure of INDEX (IND)

$$\text{IND} \begin{pmatrix} \text{ref} & i \\ \text{AGR} & \begin{pmatrix} \text{PER} & \{1 \mid 2 \mid 3\} \\ \text{NUM} & \{SG \mid PL\} \\ \text{GEN} & \{M \mid F \mid N\} \end{pmatrix} \end{pmatrix}$$

well-formed conditions on QPs

a. [$_{PROP}$ QP$_x$, PROP], where the matrix PROP must contain x.
b. [$_{QP_x}$ Q, PROP], where the domain expression PROP must contain x.
c. All the instances of a variable x must be either dominated or c-commanded by a single QP$_x$.

condition on the controller of unique control verbs

The controller of a unique control verb must be an ARG in F/A of the unique control verb in question.

coreference requirements between the controller and the controllee RHO

The referential index (as a set) of the controller's INDEX value must be included in the referential index (as a set) of the controllee's INDEX value.

RS Module

PS rules for RS

a. $[_{EV}$ TYPE, ROLE$^n]$
b. $[_{ROLE}$ EV$]$

definition of a well-formed RS

a. A local RS is well formed iff it is an instantiation of (a) or (b) of the PS rules for RS, and is matched by the RS field of one of the lexical entries of the language in question.
b. An RS is well formed iff all the local RSs that it contains are well formed.

Role Hierarchy

(action tier) AG > PT > ø
(thematic tier) SO > GO > TH > LO

definition of outrank

i. Outrank is determined on the action tier. Otherwise, it is determined on the thematic tier.
ii. If A outranks B and B dominates C in RS, then A outranks C.
iii. If A outranks B and B outranks C, then A outranks C.

RS condition on quantified expressions

A quantified expression (QNP or *wh*-phrase) must outrank all the bound variable pronouns.

definition of extended outrank relations

(i) A possessive NP outranks its mother NP.
(ii) The relation outrank is transitive, namely, if A outranks B and B outranks C, then A outranks C.
(iii) Otherwise, outrank relations are determined by the above definition.

Event Hierarchy

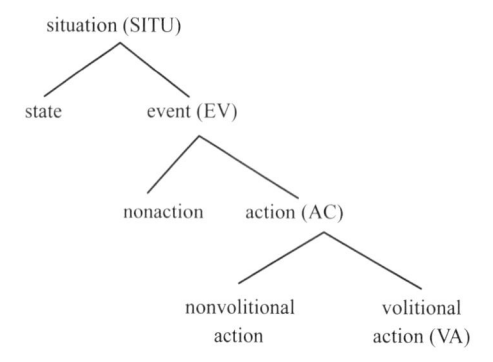

```
          situation (SITU)
           /            \
       state          event (EV)
                      /        \
                 nonaction    action (AC)
                              /         \
                      nonvolitional   volitional
                         action      action (VA)
```

Lexical Entries

lexical entry for the default transitive construction

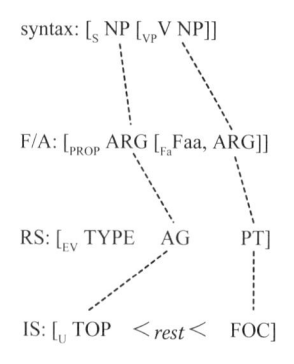

syntax: [$_S$ NP [$_{VP}$ V NP]]

F/A: [$_{PROP}$ ARG [$_{Fa}$Faa, ARG]]

RS: [$_{EV}$ TYPE   AG   PT]

IS: [$_U$ TOP $<$ *rest* $<$ FOC]

lexical entry for the negative inversion construction

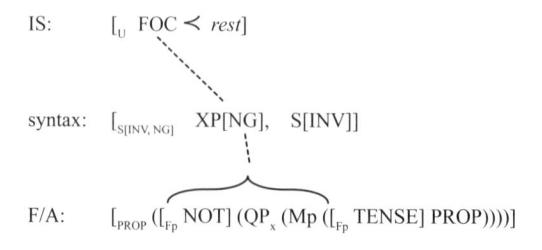

IS: [$_U$ FOC $\prec$ *rest*]

syntax: [$_{S[INV, NG]}$ XP[NG], S[INV]]

F/A: [$_{PROP}$ ([$_{Fp}$ NOT] (QP$_x$ (Mp ([$_{Fp}$ TENSE] PROP))))]

lexical entry for the *there* construction with verb-of-existence *be*

syntax: [$_{\text{V[AUX]}}$ be] in [$_{\text{VP}}$ __, EQNP, (PP)]
F/A: F$_{(a)a}$
RS: [$_{\text{TYPE}}$ "be"] in [__, TH, {LO | <LO>}]

IS: [$_{\text{U}}$ ... new ...]

lexical entry for the *there* construction with empty *be*

syntax: [$_{\text{VP}}$ [$_{\text{V[AUX]}}$ be], EQNP, XP], where XP is AP, PP, VP[−FIN].
F/A: [$_{\text{PROP}}$ ARG, Fa]
RS: [$_{\text{EV}}$ TYPE TH]

IS: [$_{\text{U}}$ ... new ...]

lexical entry for dummy *there*

syntax: NP[*there*, 3]
➢ NP[*there*] and an existentially quantified NP (EQNP) must be S-mates.
➢ NP[*there*] and its licensing verb must be S-mates.
F/A: nil
RS: nil
morph: Word
mphon: /ðɛɚ/

lexical entry for dummy *it*

syntax: NP[*it*, 3SGN]
F/A: nil
RS: nil
morph: Word
mphon: /ɪt/

lexical entry for the locative inversion construction

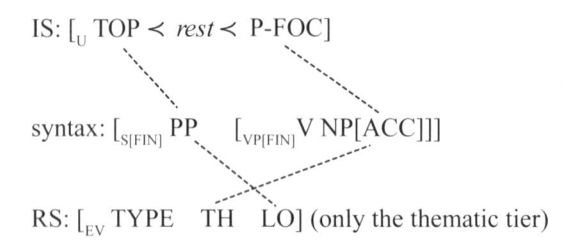

IS: [$_U$ TOP < rest < P-FOC]

syntax: [$_{S[FIN]}$ PP [$_{VP[FIN]}$ V NP[ACC]]]

RS: [$_{EV}$ TYPE   TH   LO] (only the thematic tier)

lexical entry for passive *by*-phrase

syntax: PP[*by*] in [$_{VP[PAS]}$ VP[PAS], __]
F/A: [$_{MFa}$ ARG]
RS: AG in [$_{VA}$[$_{TYPE}$ "cause$_2$"]__[$_{PT}$[$_{SITU}$<AG>]]] (due to causative coercion and role sharing)

bi-partite lexical entry for idiom *pull strings*

syntax: [$_{VP}$ [$_V$ pull] [$_{NP[3PL]}$ strings]]
F/A: [$_{Fa}$ [$_{Faa}$ EXPLOIT], [$_{ARG}$ PERSONAL.CONNECTIONS]]
RS: [$_{EV}$ [$_{TYPE}$ "exploit"] AG [$_{PT}$ "personal connections"]]

syntax: V in [__, NP]
F/A: Faa
RS: TYPE in [$_{EV}$ __ AG PT]
morph: V[0]

bi-partite lexical entry for sentence idiom *all hell break loose*

syntax: [$_{NP[3SGN]}$ all hell] in [$_S$ __, [$_{VP}$ break loose]]
F/A: [$_{ARG}$ PANDEMONIUM] in [$_{PROP}$ __, [$_{Fa}$ ARISE.SUDDENLY]]
RS: [$_{TH}$ "pandemonium"] in [$_{EV}$ [$_{TYPE}$ "arise suddenly"] __]

syntax: [$_{VP}$ break loose] in [$_S$ [$_{NP[3SGN]}$ all hell], __]
F/A: [$_{Fa}$ ARISE.SUDDENLY] in [$_{PROP}$ [$_{ARG}$ PANDEMONIUM], __]
RS: [$_{TYPE}$ "arise suddenly"] in [$_{EV}$ __ [$_{TH}$ "pandemonium"]]

lexical entry for the predicate inversion construction

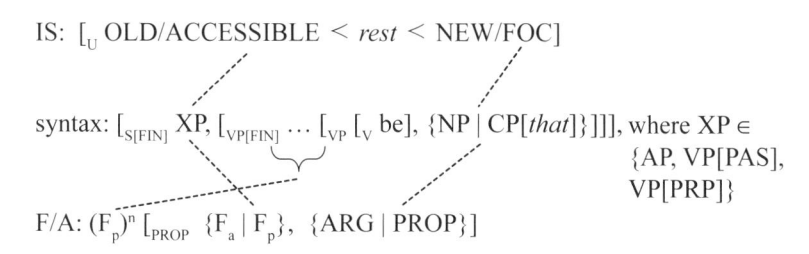

IS: [$_U$ OLD/ACCESSIBLE < rest < NEW/FOC]

syntax: [$_{S[FIN]}$ XP, [$_{VP[FIN]}$ ... [$_{VP}$ [$_V$ be], {NP | CP[*that*]}]]], where XP ∈ {AP, VP[PAS], VP[PRP]}

F/A: (F$_p$)^n [$_{PROP}$ {F$_a$ | F$_p$}, {ARG | PROP}]

lexical entry for RHO

syntax: nil
F/A: ARG[IND[j, AGR(j)]]
RS: ROLE
mphon: nil

lexical entry for causative coercion

syntax: nil
F/A: nil
RS: [$_{TYPE}$ "cause$_2$"] in [$_{VA}$ __ [AG, SO] [$_{[PT, TH]}$ SITU]]
mphon: nil

lexical entry for clause-initial *wh*-phrase XP[WH[Q], α]

syntax: XP[WH[Q], α] in [$_{CP[WH[Q]]}$ __ S[{FIN|INV}]]], where α is a PFORM value if X = P
- the syntactic dominance path conditions
  a. nonsubject gap: CP[WH[Q]] {S, VP, CP[{*that* | *for*}]}* VP {NP, N', PP}* XP[G, α]
  b. subject gap: CP[WH[Q]] {S, VP, CP[{*that* | *for*}]}* S[FIN] NP[G]
- the F/A dominance path condition
  PROP {PROP, Fa, Faa, Fpa}* {ARG, POS}* [$_{ARG}$ x]

lexical entry for quiz question (as a construction)

syntax: [$_{S[FIN]}$ ... XP[WH[Q]] ...]
F/A: [$_{PROP}$ [$_{QPx}$ [$_Q$ ∃] x = ...] PROP] AND [$_{PROP}$ [$_{QPx}$ [$_Q$ WH] x = ...] PROP]
RS: [$_{SA}$ [$_{IF}$ #assert#] P(x)] and [$_{SA}$ [$_{IF}$ #request#] Identify the value of x]

lexical entry for relative pronoun *who*

syntax: NP[WH[R], IND[j, AGR]]
  • This must corefer with the N' to which the relative clause (CP[WH[R]]) that contains it is adjoined.
F/A: ARG[IND[j, AGR]], where j∈ {[+HUMAN]}
RS: ROLE

lexical entry for relative pronoun *which*

syntax: NP[WH[R], IND[j, 3 N]]
  • This must corefer with the N' to which the relative clause (CP[WH[R]]) that contains it is adjoined.
F/A: ARG[IND[j, 3 N]], where j∈ {[−HUMAN]}
RS: ROLE

lexical entry for *wh*-relative clause (as a construction)

internal syntax: [$_{CP[WH[R]]}$ XP[WH[R], α] S[FIN]], where α is a PFORM value, if X = P.
  • the syntactic dominance path conditions on XP[WH[R], α]
    a. nonsubject gap: CP[WH[R], α] {S, VP, CP[{*that* | *for*}]}* VP {NP, N', PP}* XP[G, α]
    b. subject gap: CP[WH[R]] {S, VP, CP[{*that* | *for*}]}* S[FIN] NP[G]
  • the F/A dominance path condition
    PROP {PROP, Fa, Faa, Fpa}* {ARG, POS}* ARG[IND[j, AGR]]
external syntax: CP[WH[R]] in [$_{N'}$ N' __]
F/A: PROP in [$_{Ma}$ __]

lexical entry for nonrestrictive relative clause (as a construction)

syntax: CP[WH[R]] in NP ≼ __
  • The relative pronoun must corefer with the immediately preceding NP.
F/A: PROP
RS: EV in [$_{SA}$ [$_{IF}$ #...#] [$_{[AG, SO]}$ SP] [$_{[PT, GO]}$ AD] [$_{TH}$ __]], where [$_{IF}$ #...#] is the illocutionary force (IF) of the speech act (SA) accomplished by the nonrestrictive relative clause (CP[WH[R]]).

lexical entry for SA superstructure

syntax: nil
F/A: nil
RS: [$_{SA}$ IF [$_{[AG, SO]}$ SP] [$_{[PT, GO]}$ AD] [$_{TH}$ EV]]
phonology: nil

APPENDIX 393

default lexical entry for declaratives (as a construction)

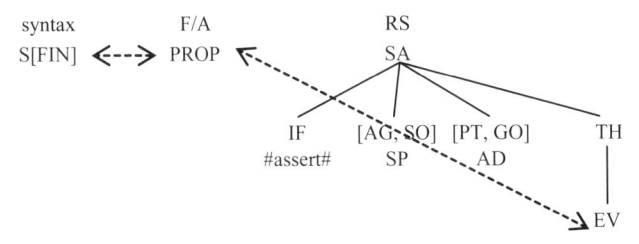

```
syntax          F/A              RS
S[FIN]  <-->   PROP              SA
                        ╱    ╱    ╲    ╲
                       IF  [AG, SO] [PT, GO]  TH
                    #assert#   SP      AD
                                          ↘ EV
```

phonology: falling intonation

default lexical entry for yes/no interrogatives with inversion (as a construction)

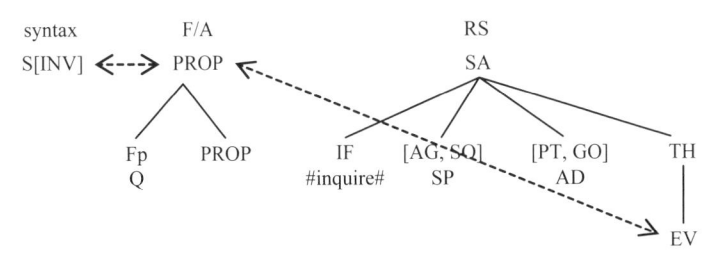

```
syntax          F/A              RS
S[INV]  <-->   PROP              SA
                ╱  ╲         ╱   ╱   ╲   ╲
               Fp  PROP     IF [AG, SO] [PT, GO] TH
               Q         #inquire#  SP     AD
                                                ↘ EV
```

phonology: rising intonation

default lexical entry for imperatives (as a construction)

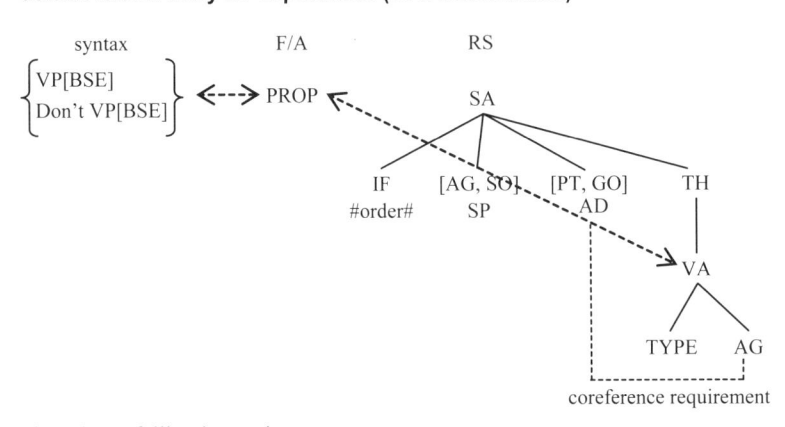

```
syntax              F/A              RS
{ VP[BSE]     }
{ Don't VP[BSE] } <-->  PROP          SA
                            ╱    ╱    ╲    ╲
                           IF [AG, SO] [PT, GO]  TH
                        #order#   SP      AD
                                              ↘ VA
                                              ╱  ╲
                                            TYPE  AG
                            coreference requirement
```

phonology: falling intonation

lexical entry for LA superstructure

syntax: nil
F/A: nil
RS: [$_{LA}$ [$_{TYPE}$ #direct#] [$_{[AG, SO]}$ SP] [$_{[PT, GO]}$ AD] [$_{TH}$ SA] (MANNER)]
phonology: nil

Lexical Rules

Inversion Lexical Rule

input
syntax: V[AUX, FIN] in
[$_{VP}$ __, VP[α]]

→

output
V[INV] in [$_{S[INV]}$ __, S[α]], where
[$_{S[INV]}$ V[INV] ⩽ NP...]

Extraposition Lexical Rule

input
syntax: V in [$_{VP}$ __, Σ]
F/A: Fφαχ

→
→

output
V in [[$_{VP}$ __, Σ], CP[*that*]]
Fφρχ

Passive Lexical Rule for transitive verbs

input (active)
syntax: V in [__, NP, ψ]
F/A: Fφα
RS: TYPE in [$_{EV}$ __ AG PT χ]
morph: V[0]

→
→
→
→

output (passive)
V[PAS] in [__, ψ]
Fφ
TYPE in [$_{EV}$ __ <AG> PT χ]
V[1, PSP]

Prepositional Passive Lexical Rule

input (active)
syntax: V in [__, [$_{PP}$ P, NP], ψ]
RS: TYPE in [$_{EV}$ __ AG PT χ]
morph: V[0]

→
→
→

output (passive)
V[PAS] in [__, [$_{PP}$ P], ψ]
TYPE in [$_{EV}$ __ <AG> PT χ]
V[1, PSP]

lexical rule for PP incorporation

input
syntax: V in [$_{VP}$ __, φ] →
RS: [$_{TYPE}$ χ] in [$_{EV}$ __ ψ] →

output
V in [$_{VP}$ __, φ, [$_{PP}$ P, NP]]
[$_{TYPE}$ χ-P] in [$_{EV}$ __ ψ, [PT, ROLE]],
where ROLE is a thematic-tier specification (either LO, GO, SO, or INSTR)

Middle Lexical Rule

input (transitive verb)
syntax: V in [__, NP] →
F/A: Faa →
RS: TYPE in [$_{VA}$ __ AG [PT, TH]] →
morph: V[0] →

output (middle)
V in [__, {ADVP | PP}]
Faa
TYPE in [$_{STATE}$ __ TH, MANNER]
V[0]

RHO Introduction Lexical Rule

input
F/A: Fφ
morph: V[1, –FIN] or A[1] →

output
Fφ in [$_{PROP}$ ARG[IND[j, ARG(j)]],
[$_{Fa}$ ... Fφ ...]], where the ARG is the subject ARG of Fφ

Inheritance Hierarchy

inheritance hierarchy of the lexical entries for the suffix {D}

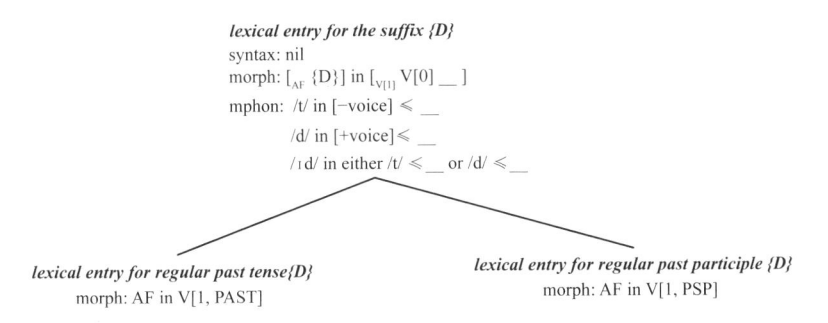

lexical entry for the suffix {D}
syntax: nil
morph: [$_{AF}$ {D}] in [$_{V[1]}$ V[0] __]
mphon: /t/ in [–voice] ≤ __
      /d/ in [+voice] ≤ __
      /ɪd/ in either /t/ ≤ __ or /d/ ≤ __

lexical entry for regular past tense {D}
morph: AF in V[1, PAST]

lexical entry for regular past participle {D}
morph: AF in V[1, PSP]

inheritance hierarchy of controlled VP

controlled VP
syntax: VP[−FIN]   (The head V[−FIN] is output of RHO Introduction Lexical Rule.)
F/A: [$_{PROP}$ ARG[IND[j, AGR(j)]], Fa]

freely controlled VP

uniquely controlled VP
syntax: complement of a unique control verb
RS: volitional action (VA) (as default)

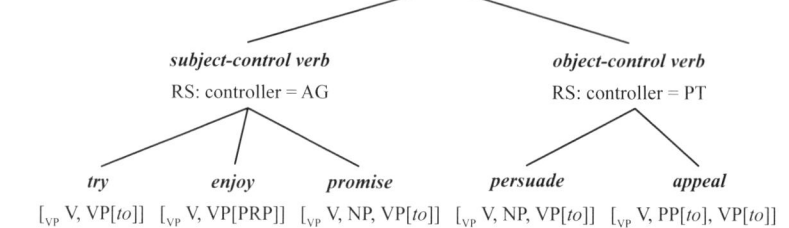

subject-control verb
RS: controller = AG

object-control verb
RS: controller = PT

try
[$_{VP}$ V, VP[*to*]]

enjoy
[$_{VP}$ V, VP[PRP]]

promise
[$_{VP}$ V, NP, VP[*to*]]

persuade
[$_{VP}$ V, NP, VP[*to*]]

appeal
[$_{VP}$ V, PP[*to*], VP[*to*]]

inheritance hierarchy of restrictive relative clause (RRC)

RRC
syntax: RRC in [$_{N'}$ N' __]
RRC obeys the dominance path conditions.
F/A: PROP in [$_{ARG}$ ARG [$_{Ma}$ __]]
The head ARG must c-command a coreferent ARG.

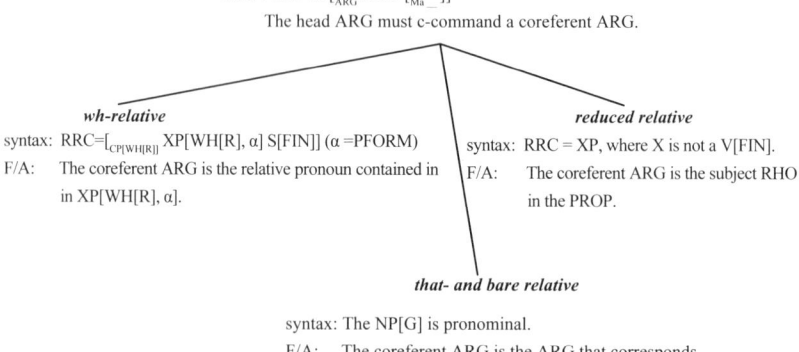

wh-relative
syntax: RRC=[$_{CP[WH[R]]}$ XP[WH[R], α] S[FIN]] (α =PFORM)
F/A: The coreferent ARG is the relative pronoun contained in
       in XP[WH[R], α].

reduced relative
syntax: RRC = XP, where X is not a V[FIN].
F/A: The coreferent ARG is the subject RHO
       in the PROP.

that- and bare relative
syntax: The NP[G] is pronominal.
F/A: The coreferent ARG is the ARG that corresponds
       to the pronominal NP[G].

that-relative
syntax: RRC = CP[*that*]

bare relative
syntax: RRC = S[FIN]
The head N' and the subject of the RCC must be adjacent.

References

Austin, John L. 1975. *How to Do Things with Words*. Second edition. Harvard University Press.
Birner, Betty J. and Gregory Ward. 1998. *Information Status and Noncanonical Word Order in English*. John Benjamins.
Boeckx, Cedric. 2008. *Understanding Minimalist Syntax*. Blackwell.
Bolinger, Dwight. 1975. On the passive in English. *LACUS Forum* 1:57–80.
Bolinger, Dwight. 1977. *Meaning and Form*. Longman.
Borsley, Robert. 1999. *Syntactic Theory: A Unified Approach*. Second edition. Arnold.
Bresnan, Joan. 1972. *Theory of Complementation in English Syntax*. Ph.D. thesis, MIT.
Bresnan, Joan. 1976. Nonarguments for raising. *Linguistic Inquiry* 7:485–501.
Bresnan, Joan. 1977. Variables in the theory of transformations. In Peter W. Culicover et al. eds., *Formal Syntax*, Academic Press, pp. 157–196.
Bresnan, Joan. 1982. The passive in lexical theory. In Joan Bresnan ed., *The Mental Representation of Grammatical Relations*, MIT Press, pp. 3–86.
Bresnan, Joan. 1982. Control and complementation. In Joan Bresnan ed., *The Mental Representation of Grammatical Relations*, MIT Press, pp. 282–390.
Bresnan, Joan. 1994. Locative inversion and the architecture of universal grammar. *Language* 70:72–131.
Bresnan, Joan. 1995. Linear order, syntactic rank, and empty categories: on weak crossover. In Mary Dalrymple et al. eds., *Formal Issues in Lexical Functional Grammar*, CSLI, pp. 241–274.
Bresnan, Joan. 2001. *Lexical-Functional Syntax*. Blackwell.
Carnie, Andrew. 2008. *Constituent Structure*. Oxford University Press.
Carter, Ronald and Michael McCarthy. 2006. *Cambridge Grammar of English*. Cambridge University Press.
Chomsky, Noam. 1977. On *wh*-movement. In Peter W. Culicover et al. eds., *Formal Syntax*, Academic Press, pp. 71–132.
Chomsky, Noam. 1981. *Lectures on Government and Binding*. Foris Publications.
Chomsky, Noam. 1982. *Some Concepts and Consequences of the Theory of Government and Binding*. MIT Press.
Chomsky, Noam. 1995. *The Minimalist Program*. MIT Press.
Comorovski, Ileana. 1996. *Interrogative Phrases and the Syntax and Semantics Interface*. Kluwer.
Cruse, Alan. 2004. *Meaning in Language*. Second edition. Oxford University Press.

Cruse, Alan. 2011. *Meaning in Language*. Third edition. Oxford University Press.
Culicover, Peter W. 1997. *Principles and Parameters*. Oxford University Press.
Culicover, Peter W. 2009. *Natural Language Syntax*. Oxford University Press.
Culicover, Peter W. and Ray Jackendoff. 2005. *Simpler Syntax*. Oxford University Press.
Dalrymple, Mary. 2001. *Lexical Functional Grammar*. Academic Press.
Davison, Alice. 1973. *Performatives, Felicity Conditions, and Adverbs*. PhD dissertation, University of Chicago.
Davison, Alice. 1980. Peculiar passives. *Language* 56:42–66.
Dayal, Veneeta. 2006. Multiple wh-questions. In M. Everaert and H. van Riemsdijk eds., *The Blackwell Companion to Syntax*, Volume III. Blackwell.
Dik, Simon C. 1997. *The Theory of Functional Grammar, Part 1: The Structure of the Clause*. Mouton de Druyter.
Dixon, Robert M.W. 2005. *A Semantic Approach to English Grammar*. Oxford University Press.
Dowty, David R. 1991. Thematic proto-roles and argument selection. *Language* 67:547–619.
Edelman, Gerald M. and Joseph A. Gally. 2001. Degeneracy and complexity in biological systems. *PNAS* 98, no.24:13763–13768.
Engdahl, Elisabet. 1983. Parasitic gaps. *Linguistics and Philosophy* 6:5–24.
Erteschik-Shir, Nomi. 1997. *The Dynamics of Focus Structure*. Cambridge University Press.
Erteschik-Shir, Nomi. 2006. Bridge phenomena. In Martin Everaert and Henk van Riemsdijk eds., *The Blackwell Companion to Syntax*, Volume I, pp. 284–294.
Erteschik-Shir, Nomi. 2007. *Information Structure*. Oxford University Press.
Farkas, Donka F. 1988. On obligatory control. *Linguistics and Philosophy* 11:27–58.
Firbas, Jan. 1992. *Functional Sentence Perspective in Written and Spoken Communication*. Cambridge University Press.
Fodor, Janet Dean. 1974. Like subject verbs and causal clauses in English. *Journal of Linguistics* 10:95–110.
Fraser, Bruce. 1974. An examination of performative analysis. *Papers in Linguistics* 7:1–40.
Gazdar, Gerald. 1979. *Pragmatics*. Academic Press.
Gazdar, Gerald, Geoffrey K. Pullum, and Ivan A. Sag. 1982. Auxiliaries and related phenomena in a restrictive theory of grammar. *Language* 58:591–638.
Gazdar, Gerald, Ewan Klein, Geoffrey Pullum, and Ivan Sag. 1985. *Generalized Phrase Structure Grammar*. Harvard University Press.
Goldsmith, John. 1985. A principled exception to the Coordinate Structure Constraint. CLS 21.
Greenbaum, Sidney. 1969. *Studies of English Adverbial Usage*. Longman.
Grice, Paul. 1989. *Studies in the Way of Words*. Harvard University Press.
Grimshaw, Jane. 1979. Complement selection and the lexicon. *Linguistic Inquiry* 10:279–326.
Grosu, Alexander and Sandra A. Thompson. 1977. The constraints on the distribution of NP clauses. *Language* 53:104–151.
Guasti, Maria Teresa. 2002. *Language Acquisition: The Growth of Grammar*. MIT Press.
Harris, Zellig S. 1957. Co-occurrence and transformation in linguistic structure. *Language* 33:283–340.

Higginbotham, James. 1980. Pronouns and bound variables. *Linguistic Inquiry* 11:679–708.
Hornsein, Nobert. 1984. *Logic as Grammar*. MIT Press.
Huddleston, Rodney and Geoffrey K. Pullum. 2002. *The Cambridge Grammar of the English Language*. Cambridge University Press.
Imanishi, Noriko and Ichiro Asano. 1990. *Shoo-oo to sakujo [Anaphora and Deletion]*. Taishukan.
Jackendoff, Ray. 1972. *Semantic Interpretation in Generative Grammar*. MIT Press.
Jackendoff, Ray. 1974. A deep structure projection rule. *Linguistic Inquiry* 5:481–505.
Jackendoff, Ray. 1977. *X-bar Syntax*. MIT Press.
Jackendoff, Ray. 1983. *Semantics and Cognition*. MIT Press.
Jackendoff, Ray. 1990. *Semantic Structures*. MIT Press.
Jackendoff, Ray. 1997. *The Architecture of the Language Faculty*. MIT Press.
Jackendoff, Ray. 2002. *Foundations of Language*. Oxford University Press.
Jackendoff, Ray. 2010. *Meaning and the Lexicon*. Oxford University Press.
Jackendoff, Ray and Peter W. Culicover. 2003. The semantic basis of control in English. *Language* 79:517–556.
Jacobson, Pauline. 1992. The lexical entailment theory of control and the *tough*-construction. In Ivan A. Sag and Anna Szabolcsi eds., *Lexical Matters*, CSLI. pp. 269–299.
Jespersen, Otto. 1927. *A Modern English Grammar on Historical Principles*. Vol. 3. George Allen and Unwin.
Jespersen, Otto. 1933. *Essentials of English Grammar*. George Allen and Unwin.
Kaplan, Ronald M. and Joan Bresnan. 1982. Lexical-Functional Grammar. In Bresnan ed., *The Mental Representation of Grammatical Relations*, MIT Press, pp. 173–281.
Kaplan, Ronald M. and Annie Zaenen. 1995. Long-distance dependencies, constituent structure, and functional uncertainty. In Mary Dalrymple et al. eds., *Formal Issues in Lexical Functional Grammar*, CSLI, pp. 137–165.
Kaplan, Ronald M. and John T. Maxwell III. 1995. An algorithm for functional uncertainty. In Mary Dalrymple et al. eds., *Formal Issues in Lexical Functional Grammar*, CSLI, pp. 177–197.
Karttunen, Lauri. 1971. Implicative verbs. *Language* 47:340–358.
Kayne, Richard, S. 1984. *Connectedness and Binary Branching*. Foris.
Kiparsky, Paul and Carol Kiparsky. 1971. Fact. In Danny D. Steinberg and Leon A. Jakobovits eds., *Semantics*, pp. 345–369.
Koster, Jan. 1978. Why subject sentences don't exist. In Samuel J. Keyser ed., *Recent Transformational Studies in European Languages*, MIT Press, pp. 53–64.
Koster, Jan. 1987. *Domains and Dynasties*. Foris.
Kuno, Susumu. 1970. Some properties of non-referential noun phrases. In R. Jakobson and S. Kawamoto eds., *Studies in General and Oriental Linguistics*. TEC Corporation, pp. 348–373.
Kuno, Susumu. 1972. Functional sentence perspective. *Linguistic Inquiry* 3:269–320.
Kuno, Susumu. 1982. The focus of the question and the focus of the answer. *CLS* 18:134–157.

Kuno, Susumu. 1983. *Shin-nihon-bunpoo-kenkyuu* [*A New Study of Japanese Grammar*]. Taishukan.
Kuno, Susumu. 1987. *Functional Syntax, Anaphora, Discourse and Empathy*. University of Chicago Press.
Kuno, Susumu and Takami Kenichi. 1993. *Grammar and Discourse Principles*. University of Chicago Press.
Lakoff, George. 1986. Frame semantic control of the coordinate structure constraint. *CLS* 22:152–167.
Lambrecht, Knud. 1994. *Information Structure and Sentence Form*. Cambridge University Press.
Landau, Idan. 2000. *Elements of Control*. Kluwer.
Lasnik, Howard. 1989. *Essays on Anaphora*. Kluwer.
Lasnik, Howard and Juan Uriagereka. 1988. *A Course in GB Syntax*. MIT Press.
Lasnik, Howard and Juan Uriagereka. 2005. *A Course in Minimalist Syntax*. Blackwell.
Lasnik, Howard and Mamoru Saito. 1992. *Move α*. MIT Press.
Lasnik, Howard and Myung-Kwan Park. 2003. The EPP and the Subject Condition under sluicing. *Linguistic Inquiry* 34:649–660.
Lasnik, Howard and Tim Stowell. 1991. Weakest crossover. *Linguistic Inquiry* 22:687–720.
Levin, Beth and Malka Rappaport Hovav. 1995. *Unaccusativity*. MIT Press.
Levinson, Stephen C. 1983. *Pragmatics*. Cambridge University Press.
Lyons, John. 1977. *Semantics*. In two volumes. Cambridge University Press.
Marantz, Alec. 1984. *On the Nature of Grammatical Relations*. MIT Press.
May, Robert Carlen. 1985. *Logical Form*. MIT Press.
McCawley, James D. 1973. *Grammar and Meaning*. Taishukan Publishing.
McCawley, James D. 1982. Parentheticals and discontinuous constituent structure. *Linguistic Inquiry* 13:91–106.
McCawley, James D. 1984. Anaphora and notions of command. *Papers from the 10th Annual Meeting*, Berkeley Linguistics Society, pp. 220–32.
McCawley, James D. 1985. What price the performative analysis? *University of Chicago Working Papers in Linguistics* 1:43–64.
McCawley, James D. 1993. *Everything that Linguists Have Always Wanted to Know about Logic* *but Were Ashamed to Ask*. Second edition. University of Chicago Press.
McCawley, James D. 1998. *The Syntactic Phenomena of English*. Second edition. University of Chicago Press.
McCawley, James D. 1999. Why surface syntactic structure reflects logical structure as much as it does, but only that much. *Language* 75:34–62.
McCloskey, James. 1979. *Transformational Syntax and Model Theoretic Semantics*. D. Reidel.
Merchant, Jason. 2001. *The Syntax of Silence*. Oxford University Press.
Mittwoch, Anita. 1977. How to refer to one's own words. *Journal of Linguistics* 13:177–189.
Mohanan, Karuvannur P. 1983. Functional and anaphoric control. *Linguistic Inquiry* 14:641–674.

Na, Younghee and Geoffrey J. Huck. 1992. On extracting from asymmetrical structures. In Diane Brentari et al. eds, *The Joy of Grammar*, John Benjamins, pp. 251–274.
Nunberg, Geoffrey, Ivan. A. Sag, and Thomas Wasow. 1994. Idioms. *Language* 70:491–538.
Pesetsky, David. 1987. Wh-in-situ: movement and unselective binding. In Eric J. Reuland and Alice G. ter Meulen eds., *The Representation of (In)definiteness*. MIT Press, pp. 98–129.
Pollard, Carl and Ivan A. Sag. 1987. *Information-Based Syntax and Semantics*. CSLI.
Pollard, Carl and Ivan A. Sag. 1994. *Head-Driven Phrase Structure Grammar*. CSLI.
Postal, Paul M. 1969. Anaphoric islands. *CLS* 5:205–239.
Postal, Paul M. 1971. *Cross-over Phenomena*. Holt, Rinehart and Winston.
Postal, Paul M. 1974. *On Raising*. MIT Press.
Postal, Paul M. 1977. About a "nonargument" for raising. *Linguistic Inquiry* 8:141–154.
Postal, Paul M. 1993. Remarks on weak crossover effects. *Linguistic Inquiry* 24:539–556.
Postal, Paul M. 2004. *Skeptical Linguistic Essays*. Oxford University Press.
Postal, Paul M and Geoffrey K. Pullum. 1988. Expletive noun phrases in subcategorized positions. *Linguistic Inquiry* 19:635–670.
Quirk, Randolph, Sidney Greenbaum, Geoffrey Leech, and Jan Svartvik. 1985. *A Comprehensive Grammar of the English Language*. Longman.
Radford, Andrew. 1981. *Transformational Syntax*. Cambridge University Press.
Reinhart, Tanya. 1983. *Anaphora and Semantic Interpretation*. University of Chicago Press.
Riemsdijk, Henk van and Edwin Williams. 1986. *Introduction to the Theory of Grammar*. MIT Press.
Rizzi, Luigi. 1990. *Relativized Minimality*. MIT Press.
Rochemont, Michael S. and Peter W. Culicover. 1990. *English Focus Constructions and the Theory of Grammar*. Cambridge University Press.
Rosenbaum, Peter S. 1967. *The Grammar of English Predicate Complement Constructions*. MIT Press.
Ross, John Robert. 1970. On declarative sentences. In Roderick Jacobs and Peter S. Rosenbaum eds., *Readings in English Transformational Grammar*, pp. 222–272.
Ross, John Robert. 1986. *Infinite Syntax!* (published version of his 1967 MIT dissertation *Constraints on variables in syntax*). Ablex Publishing.
Ross, John Robert and David M. Perlmutter. 1970. Relative clauses with split antecedents. *LI* 1:360.
Sadock, Jerrold M. 1974. *Toward a Linguistic Theory of Speech Acts*. Academic Press.
Sadock, Jerrold M. 1983. The necessary overlapping of grammatical components. *CLS* 18, *Parasession*, pp. 198–221.
Sadock, Jerrold M. 1984. The polyredundant lexicon. *CLS* 20, *Parasession*, pp. 250–269.
Sadock, Jerrold M. 1985. Autolexical syntax: a theory of noun incorporation and similar phenomena. *Natural Language and Linguistic Theory* 3:379–440.
Sadock, Jerrold M. 1991. *Autolexical Syntax*. University of Chicago Press.
Sadock, Jerrold M. 1996. The lexicon as bridge between phrase structure components. In J. Rooryck and L. Zaring eds., *Phrase Structure and the Lexicon*, Kluwer, pp. 173–185.

Sadock, Jerrold M. 2003. *A Grammar of Kalaallisut*. Lincom Europa.
Sadock, Jerrold M. 2012. *The Modular Architecture of Grammar*. Cambridge University Press.
Safir, Kenneth J. 1985. *Syntactic Chains*. Cambridge University Press.
Safir, Kenneth J. 1986. Relative clauses in a theory of binding and levels. *Linguistic Inquiry* 17:663–689.
Sag, Ivan A., Gerald Gazdar, Thomas Wasow, and Steven Weisler. 1985. Coordination and how to distinguish categories. *Natural Language and Linguistic Theory* 3:117–171.
Sag, Ivan A. and Carl Pollard. 1991. An integrated theory of complement control. *Language* 67:63–113.
Sag, Ivan A., Thomas Wasow, and Emily M. Bender. 2003. *Syntactic Theory*. CSLI.
Schreiber, Peter. 1972. Style disjuncts and the performative analysis. *Linguistic Inquiry* 3:321–348.
Searle, John R. 1969. *Speech Acts*. Cambridge University Press.
Searle, John R. 1979. *Expression and Meaning*. Cambridge University Press.
Searle, John R. 1989. How performatives work. *Linguistics and Philosophy* 12:535–558.
Sinclair, John et al. 1990. *Collins Cobuild English Grammar*. Harper Collins Publishers.
Stockwell, Robert P. 1977. Motivation for exbraciation in Old English. In Charles N. Li ed., *Mechanisms of Syntactic Change*, University of Texas Press, pp. 291–314.
Swan, Michael. 2005. *Practical English Usage*. Third edition. Oxford University Press.
Takami, Ken-ichi. 1992. *Preposition Stranding*. Mouton de Gruyter.
Takami, Ken-ichi. 1997. *Kinooteki-toogo-ron* [*Functional Syntax*]. Kurosio Publishers.
Takami, Ken-ichi. 2011. *Ukemi to Shieki* [*Passives and Causatives*]. Kaitaku-sha.
Takami, Ken-ichi and Susumu Kuno. 2002. *Nichi-eigo no Zidooshi-koobun* [*Functional Analysis of Intransitive Constructions in English and Japanese*]. Kenkyuu-sha.
Taylor, John R. 1996. *Possessives in English*. Oxford University Press.
Traugott, Elizabeth C. 1972. *A History of English Syntax*. Holt, Rinehart and Winston.
Ueno, Yoshio. 1994. *Grammtical Functions and Clause Structures in Japanese*. PhD dissertation, University of Chicago.
Ueno, Yoshio. 1997. Iwayuru ECM-kobun to sono shuhen [On the so-called ECM construction and related issues]. *Otsuma Women's University Bulletin* 29:43–61.
Ueno, Yoshio. 1998. Iwayuru ECM-kobun to sono shuhen (2) [On the so-called ECM construction and related issues (2)]. *Otsuma Women's University Bulletin* 30:63–78.
Van der Auwera, Johan. Relative *that*—a centennial dispute. *Journal of Linguistics* 21:149–179.
Zwicky, Arnold M. 1971. In a manner of speaking. *Linguistic Inquiry* 2:223–233.

Index

across-the-board (ATB) 175, 256, 262, 304
adjacency requirement 270, 326–330, 333
adjunction structure 17, 21, 41, 243, 267, 268
affix 3
aggregation 238
   de-aggregation 83, 238, 239
agreement 19, 25, 27, 55–58, 78–80, 82, 83, 90, 129, 230, 273
   agreement controller 57, 58, 79–81, 90, 91, 150
   generalized agreement 57, 79–81, 90
   subject-verb agreement 18, 19, 23, 56, 57, 191, 229, 230, 288
all hell break loose 155, 156, 167
argument 23
   individual argument 235
   set argument 234, 235, 239
assertion 42, 213, 297–300, 325, 354, 356, 357, 361, 368, 370, 372–374, 378–380
Automodular Grammar (AMG) v, vii, 1, 47

be (verb)
   empty 74, 75, 96, 147
   verb-of-existence 74, 75
blocking 14
branching
   binary 23, 49, 50, 76, 161, 168, 171, 173, 176, 178, 179, 259
   ternary 40, 49, 55, 76, 168, 169, 171, 173, 176

case assignment 123
c-command 21
   asymmetric c-command 227
clausal subject 81, 82, 84–86, 91, 108, 117, 118, 120, 147, 148, 158, 165, 167, 250, 256, 265, 266
cliticization 3, 4, 6
coercion 201
   causative coercion 105, 106, 108, 134, 136, 137, 158, 201–210, 212–214, 355
   coerced material 201, 212, 315, 355
comment 42, 329
Complex Noun Phrase Constraint (CNPC) 264, 276, 277, 286, 297, 326
complexity 39, 121, 259, 283
composite Fp functor 53
compounding 4, 6, 9
Conjunct Constraint 305
connectivity 287
constative sentence 356
construction 43
   cognate object construction 106, 280
   pseudo-cleft construction 156, 180–183, 243, 296
contracted forms of finite auxiliary verbs 64
control 184
   backward control 168
   condition on the controller of unique control verbs 197, 212
   control verb 185, 212
   controllee 187, 188, 190, 197, 198, 204, 207, 210, 219, 232

controller 29, 169, 185–190, 195, 197–201, 204, 208–210, 212, 213, 215–220, 232
controller shift 208–214, 216
controller-shifted interpretation 209–211, 214
free control 194, 195, 198, 358
object control 18, 184, 185, 188, 189, 190, 195, 199, 212, 215, 218
partial control 217–220
subject control 41, 156, 161, 184–186, 188–190, 195–198, 207, 211, 215, 216, 218, 232
unique control 185, 187–190, 194, 195, 197–199, 203, 204, 209, 210, 212–214, 217, 219, 220, 279, 342
conversion 8, 9, 131
Coordinate Structure Constraint (CSC) 160, 261, 269, 303, 306
Coordinate Structure Convention 305, 309, 310, 330
coordination 23, 50, 70, 71, 92, 104, 111, 159, 160, 172, 173, 176, 233, 234, 243, 251, 261, 298, 299, 304, 307–310, 321, 377
nonconstituent coordination 172
coreference 25, 137, 169, 188, 197, 205–207, 209, 210, 212, 313–315, 328
coreference requirement 135–137, 187, 188, 199, 201, 204, 205, 207–210, 216, 219, 220, 232, 233, 279, 342, 357, 358, 362

declaration 364, 375
default correspondence 1, 7, 37, 38, 75, 96, 98, 102, 126, 133, 161, 168, 192, 258, 285, 319, 356, 357, 361
default linear order 39, 69, 237
definition of
agreement controller 57
asymmetric c-command 22
c-command 21

c-command in F/A 33
directly dominate 21
dominate 21
extended outrank relation 292
non-adjoined node 21
outrank 37, 97
S-command 22
S-mates 22
well-formed F/A structure 24
well-formed RS 35
well-formed syntactic structure 22
x-command 21
degeneracy 45
derivation 3–5, 8, 20
derivational morphology 3
dominance path 257–259, 261–266, 268–271, 274–278, 281–283, 286, 287, 304, 305, 310, 311, 326, 328–330, 337
dominance path condition 246, 247, 254, 255, 258–260, 262–278, 281–283, 286–288, 297, 304, 305, 310, 318, 320, 329, 337, 349, 350, 351
parasitic dominance path condition 274
DP analysis 74, 269
dummy
do 51, 61, 69, 121, 147
it 55, 91, 93, 94, 119, 120, 123, 125, 141, 147, 148, 166, 194
there 78–80, 166

economy of language use 61, 69, 121, 194, 239, 259
Elsewhere Principle 11, 12, 14, 40, 51, 77, 110, 134, 166, 266, 268, 310, 341
empathy 292, 315
emphatic *do* 69, 250
empty NP[G] 336
English PS rules 15, 16, 41, 49
entailment 217, 218, 220
Event Hierarchy 33, 34, 102, 106, 182, 183, 185, 207, 369

Exceptional Case Marking (ECM) 161, 168, 181
existentially quantified NP 75, 77, 78, 149, 166, 172, 240
exocentric 17, 257
extraposition 91, 93, 94, 117, 148, 325

factive 148, 167
   factive verb 42, 167, 299–301, 303
feature
   binary feature 50, 306
   feature co-occurrence restriction (FCR) 48, 49, 68
   Feature Osmosis 25, 83, 230, 288, 315, 335
   head feature 16
   Head Feature Convention (HFC) 16, 23, 43, 48, 56, 80, 82, 160, 230, 257, 273, 288
   unary feature 50, 51, 269, 333
feeding 118, 120, 121
Fixed Subject Condition 69, 259, 266
focus (FOC) 42, 43, 67, 76, 86–88, 104, 134, 150, 153, 170, 177–181, 183, 300, 302
   focus-bearing element 104, 177
functional uncertainty 254, 263
Function-Argument (F/A) Structure 23

gapping 50, 174–176, 260, 261
graded acceptability 114, 156, 255

head 7, 14–19, 28, 29, 39–42, 48–50, 54, 56, 60
Heavy Constituent Shift (HCS) 42, 56, 76, 135, 170, 349
highest associable role 196

idiom chunk 129, 152, 154, 166, 167
idiomatically combining expression (ICE) 126, 130, 154, 167

illocutionary force (IF) 58, 136, 213, 258, 325, 326, 354, 355–357, 359, 361, 362, 364–366, 374
illocutionary negation 364
implicative verb 167, 217, 218, 220
INDEX (IND) 25, 26, 57, 80, 82, 83, 191, 218, 219, 230, 279, 314, 315, 334, 335
indirect interpretation 362–364
inflection 3, 4, 8
   inflectional morphology 3
   zero 5, 8
information
   background information (BI) 42, 167, 300–302, 379
   foreground information (FI) 42, 168, 300, 302, 379
   Information Structure (IS) 42, 43, 67, 75, 139, 150, 153, 170, 245, 296, 300, 301, 310
   new information 42, 76–78, 86, 153, 300
   old information 42, 153, 154, 300
inheritance hierarchy 12, 13, 49, 52, 140, 195, 349, 351
interface 1, 43
inverse linking 227, 228
inversion 16, 20, 47–49, 58, 59, 258, 259, 266, 272, 357
   inversion of finite main verb 49
   inversion PS rule 48
   locative inversion 42, 71, 72, 87, 133, 150, 152, 172, 250
   negative inversion 66
   predicate inversion construction 42, 43, 86, 150, 152, 153
   subject-auxiliary inversion 47, 85, 89
island 254, 262, 264, 269, 271, 274, 276, 286, 297, 318, 351

language acquisition 44, 45, 189, 254
Left Branch Constraint (LBC) 268

lexical entry 1, 12, 17, 19, 22, 24, 35, 43, 49, 98
bi-partite 126, 129, 154, 155
lexical entry for
all (floated quantifier) 247
all hell break loose (bi-partite) 155
aren't (first person singular inverted) 52
be (empty verb) 54
buy (transitive, ditransitive) 38
causative coercion 106, 202
declarative construction (default) 356
deontic operator (phonologically null) 341
direct yes/no question construction 58, 357
ditransitive construction (default) 44
do (dummy) 51
do (inverted dummy) 52
every 31
exclamative inversion 58
existential Faa functor 348
fortunately (sentence adverb) 374
frankly (style disjunct) 374
give (transitive with *to*, ditransitive) 36
have (perfect auxiliary) 145
hereby (performative adverb) 376
imperative construction (default) 135, 357
it (dummy) 77
LA superstructure 359
locative inversion construction 88, 133
mightn't (inverted, noninverted) 53
mumble (manner-of-speaking verb) 302
negative inversion construction 66
never 73
no (negative determiner) 72
nonfinite PRES 163
nonrestrictive relative clause construction 326
not (proposition-negating) 60
object raising verbs 162
order (transitive) 199
order (unique control verb, object-control verb) 187, 196

passive *by*-phrase 106
predicate inversion construction 154
present tense 143
promise (unique control verb, subject-control verb) 188, 197
propositional agentive phrase (in passive) 108
pull strings (bi-partite) 127
quiz question construction 299
rain (verb) 124
rain on 125
regret (factive verb) 301
regular past participle suffix 12
regular past tense suffix 12
RHO 190
SA superstructure 354
seem (subject raising) 146
set-membership Faa functor 33
sing (verb) 13
sir (vocative) 359
strike (subject raising) 157
surprising (adjective) 8
take advantage of (bi-partite) 131, 132
that-relative clause with subject gap 268
there construction with empty *be* 76
there construction with verb-of-existence *be* 75
there (dummy) 77
transitive construction (default) 44
try (unique control verb, subject-control verb) 204
type-identity Faa functor 32
what (interrogative determiner) 290
what (interrogative pronoun) 290
which (interrogative determiner) 290
which (relative pronoun) 314
who (interrogative pronoun) 290
who (relative pronoun) 314
whose (interrogative pronoun) 290
wh-phrase (clause-initial relative) 320
wh-phrase (clause-initial interrogative) 287

wh-relative clause 320
wonder (verb) 122
lexical item 19, 43, 44, 189
   defective lexical item 12, 106, 162, 190, 201, 204, 206, 208, 212, 315
lexical rule 1, 45, 49, 98, 101, 119, 120, *be* 55
   Extraposition 92, 118–121, 149, 199, 200
   Inversion 48–53, 64
   Middle 101, 102
   Passive 98, 109, 117–120, 126, 131, 133, 157, 158, 164, 165, 176, 182, 195, 196, 212
   PP Incorporation 114, 124, 125
   Prepositional Passive 108, 109, 111, 113, 119–121, 124–126
   RHO Introduction 193
light verb (LV) 106, 277
literal interpretation 362, 363
locutionary act (LA) 358, 359, 367, 371, 376
locutionary act (LA) superstructure 358, 359, 367, 368

Mainstream Generative Grammar (MGG) 49, 181, 253, 272
manner-of-speaking verbs 43, 299, 302
Minimal Distance Principle 189
mismatch 62, 63, 65, 142, 162, 242
   innocuous mismatch 26, 63, 142–145, 149, 150, 152, 154, 155, 159, 164, 167
modal (auxiliary) 20, 147, 220, 224
modifier
   individual modifier 236–238
   set modifier 236–240
morphology 3, 6–8, 15
   morphological word 3–5, 7–11, 15
morphophonology 10
   morphophonological rules for regular verbs 10

negation 53, 59, 67, 68, 72, 225, 300, 302, 364, 378
   propositional negation 59, 364
negative polarity item (NPI) 59
nested dependency constraint 329
nonbridge verbs 299

outrank relation 37
   extended outrank relation 292, 295

parasitic gap (PG) 70, 274
passive 95
   agentive 104–106, 108, 196
   agentless 95, 98, 103, 106,
   by-phrase 93, 104-107, 124, 134, 138, 139, 158, 197, 280
   impersonal 199, 200
   Kuno and Takami's functional constraints on passive sentences 138, 139
   prepositional passive 108–114, 116, 120, 121, 125, 138, 139
perfect auxiliary 26, 145, 250
performative
   explicit performative 355, 357, 360, 361, 370, 375, 376
   implicit performative clause 376, 379, 380
   performative adverb 367, 370–372, 375, 376, 380
   performative clause 43, 354, 367–370, 376, 379, 380
   performative hypothesis 364, 365
   performative verb 353, 355, 361, 364–367, 370, 375, 376
   pristine performative hypothesis 364
pied piping 129, 282, 283, 322, 331, 343
polyadic quantifier 242
PP incorporation 111, 112, 125
preparatory condition 363, 380
preposition stranding (P-stranding) 110, 111, 120, 121, 280, 282, 283

presupposition 42, 156, 285, 291, 293–295, 298, 300–302, 308, 329
  existential presuppositions 291
pronominal NP[G] 335, 336, 338, 351
propositional function 223, 224, 238, 294, 303
propositional operator 224, 378
proto-agent 115
proto-patient 115

quantifier phrase (QP) 29, 80, 149, 221–224, 253, 255, 257, 286, 341
  well-formedness conditions on 30, 221, 257
question
  concealed question 122
  direct *wh*-question 256, 258
  echo question 280, 286, 311
  indirect *wh*-question 258, 266, 340
  infinitival *wh*-question 338–343, 345
  multiple *wh*-question 284, 285, 297
  quiz question 280, 286, 293, 294, 296–299, 303, 337
  wh-question 17, 67, 89, 253–264, 266–268, 271–276, 280, 281
  yes/no (polar) question 58, 357

raising
  innocuous mismatches in object raising 164
  innocuous mismatches in subject raising 154
  object raising 41, 99, 140, 160
  Raising Principle 168
  subject raising 18, 26, 63, 80, 81, 89, 99, 141, 142, 144–150, 152–159, 163–167, 220
recursive 4, 67, 284, 318, 332, 333, 348
redundancy 44, 45, 49
reference point 292
reference transfer 315

referential index (ref) 25–27, 57, 80, 82, 136, 160, 218–220, 230, 231, 241, 248, 288, 313–316, 320, 323, 334, 336
  token-identity 241, 313, 320, 323
  type-identity 313–316, 320, 323
relative clause 156, 236, 241, 242, 264, 266, 268, 273, 274, 277, 304, 311, 313, 315, 316, 319–324, 334, 338, 351
  bare 270, 330–338
  infinitival 339, 344, 346
  nonrestrictive 89, 270, 324–330, 371
  reduced 15, 24, 41, 332, 346–351
  restrictive relative clause (RRC) 15, 24, 41, 55, 237, 241, 277, 290, 325–328, 337, 349, 350
  stacked 318, 323, 331–333, 348
  that- 266, 287, 314, 330–332, 335–338
  wh- 17, 257, 263, 280, 304, 316–318, 320, 334, 336, 337
relative pronoun 225, 226, 241, 243, 304, 311, 313–316, 318–324, 326–329, 331, 332, 334, 337, 345, 346, 351
RHO 168, 190–195, 198, 199, 204–207, 209, 218, 219, 232, 341–343, 347–349, 358, 368
Right Node Raising (RNR) 175, 176, 179, 180
Role Hierarchy 32, 37, 75, 91, 97
role sharing 105, 106, 108, 134, 158, 275, 278–280
Role Structure (RS) 34

SA superstructure 354–356, 358, 360, 361, 364, 365, 368, 369, 378
scene
  auxiliary scene 307, 308, 310
  main scene 307–310
self-controllable 203, 204, 207
Sentential Subject Constraint (SSC) 265
set-membership Faa 33, 218, 219, 234
shifted reading 315

sincerity condition 363, 380
singular *they* 231
slash category 254
small clause (SC) 41, 54, 55, 161
speech act (SA) 58, 136, 258, 299,
   324–326, 353–356, 358, 361, 362,
   364, 366–373, 375, 376, 378–380
  indirect speech act 355, 356, 361,
   362, 364
split antecedents 187, 188, 198, 240, 241,
   243, 313, 316, 329, 330, 336
stem 3–6, 8–10, 13, 15, 131
strong crossover (SCO) 291, 293, 337
style disjunct 370–373, 378
Subject Condition (SC) 265, 297
successive cyclic 253, 272–274

that-trace effect 89, 266, 267, 321, 336
  suspension of 267
tense (TENSE) 10, 23, 26, 51, 52, 57, 58,
   61, 90, 96, 142, 143, 160, 224
  habitual present (h-PRES) 360
  instantaneous present (i-PRES) 360
  nonfinite PRES 225
  past (PAST) 5, 7, 11, 12, 16, 17, 145
  past tense suffix 7, 12
  present (PRES) 7, 10, 11, 17, 27, 48, 55,
   64, 80, 81, 360
tier
  action 35–37, 88, 97, 114, 186
  thematic 35–37, 88, 97, 114, 133, 151,
   186, 187
  two-tiered (participant) roles 35, 88,
   97, 186
there-insertion 71, 240
token identity 241, 243, 313, 314, 328
topic (TOP) 42, 43, 67, 84–86, 88, 134,
   150, 198, 300, 301, 329, 358, 368
  default topic 42
  topicalization 85, 127, 245, 274

type identity 241, 243, 313, 314, 315, 328
  Faa functor 27, 31, 32, 55, 80, 223, 231,
   288, 347

unassociable 75, 102, 104, 106, 112–114,
   118, 125, 132, 133, 158, 197, 198,
   216, 355
  agent (<AG>) 97–99, 103, 106, 123–
   126, 212, 213
unbounded dependency 253, 262, 263,
   271, 272, 274, 304, 318, 338, 345, 349

V-2 constraint 249, 259
  template for auxiliary verbs 250
variable
  bound variable 228, 231, 232, 234, 255,
   291–293, 295, 296, 313, 327
  individual variable 184, 234, 243
  set variable 234, 235, 243, 244, 246
verbal communication 44
Visser's Generalization 196, 211
vocative expression 359

weak crossover (WCO) 291, 294, 337
wh-island 264, 265, 276, 286
"*wh*-movement" 85, 175, 253–255,
   261–263, 266, 271–274, 277, 280,
   293, 295, 297, 299, 300, 302, 303,
   337, 340, 341
  ATB 175, 176, 256, 261, 270, 304
wh-phrase (XP[WH[Q]]) 17, 67, 74, 89,
   253–260, 262–264, 272–275, 280–288,
   291–294, 296–300, 303, 305, 306, 329,
   337, 339–341, 343
  relative (XP[WH[R]]) 311, 316,
   318–320, 344

zero pronoun 191, 192, 194

著者紹介

上野 義雄（うえの　よしお）

早稲田大学理工学術院英語教育センター教授（言語学）
2012年度特別研究期間制度の適用を受け，シカゴ大学言語学科にて客員研究員として文法理論の研究に従事。

早稲田大学学術叢書 35

An Automodular View of English Grammar

2014年6月30日　　初版第1刷発行

著　者	上野　義雄
発行者	島田　陽一
発行所	株式会社　早稲田大学出版部
	169-0051 東京都新宿区西早稲田1-1-7
	電話 03-3203-1551　　http://www.waseda-up.co.jp/
校正協力・DTP	Cactus Communications K. K.
装　丁	笠井　亞子
印刷・製本	株式会社　平文社

Ⓒ 2014, Yoshio Ueno. Printed in Japan　　ISBN978-4-657-14705-9
無断転載を禁じます。落丁・乱丁本はお取替えいたします。

刊行のことば

　早稲田大学は、2007年、創立125周年を迎えた。創立者である大隈重信が唱えた「人生125歳」の節目に当たるこの年をもって、早稲田大学は「早稲田第2世紀」、すなわち次の125年に向けて新たなスタートを切ったのである。それは、研究・教育いずれの面においても、日本の「早稲田」から世界の「WASEDA」への強い志向を持つものである。特に「研究の早稲田」を発信するために、出版活動の重要性に改めて注目することとなった。

　出版とは人間の叡智と情操の結実を世界に広め、また後世に残す事業である。大学は、研究活動とその教授を通して社会に寄与することを使命としてきた。したがって、大学の行う出版事業とは大学の存在意義の表出であるといっても過言ではない。そこで早稲田大学では、「早稲田大学モノグラフ」、「早稲田大学学術叢書」の2種類の学術研究書シリーズを刊行し、研究の成果を広く世に問うこととした。

　このうち、「早稲田大学学術叢書」は、研究成果の公開を目的としながらも、学術研究書としての質の高さを担保するために厳しい審査を行い、採択されたもののみを刊行するものである。

　近年の学問の進歩はその速度を速め、専門領域が狭く囲い込まれる傾向にある。専門性の深化に意義があることは言うまでもないが、一方で、時代を画するような研究成果が出現するのは、複数の学問領域の研究成果や手法が横断的にかつ有機的に手を組んだときであろう。こうした意味においても質の高い学術研究書を世に送り出すことは、総合大学である早稲田大学に課せられた大きな使命である。

　「早稲田大学学術叢書」が、わが国のみならず、世界においても学問の発展に大きく貢献するものとなることを願ってやまない。

2008年10月

早稲田大学

「研究の早稲田」 早稲田大学学術叢書シリーズ

濱川 栄 著 **中国古代の社会と黄河** ¥5,500	五十嵐 誠一 著 **民主化と市民社会の新地平** フィリピン政治のダイナミズム ¥8,600
真辺 将之 著 **東京専門学校の研究** 「学問の独立」の具体相と「早稲田憲法草案」 ¥5,400	内田 悦生 著　下田 一太 (コラム執筆) **石が語るアンコール遺跡** 岩石学からみた世界遺産 ¥6,100
中垣 啓 著 **命題的推論の理論** 論理的推論の一般理論に向けて ¥6,800	青木 雅浩 著 **モンゴル近現代史研究** **：1921〜1924年** 外モンゴルとソヴィエト，コミンテルン　¥8,200
堀 真清 著 **一亡命者の記録** 池明観のこと ¥4,600	飯山 知保 著 **金元時代の華北社会と科挙制度** もう一つの「士人層」 ¥8,900
藤井 千春 著 **ジョン・デューイの経験主義哲学における思考論** 知性的な思考の構造的解明　¥5,800	上野 和昭 著 **平曲譜本による近世京都アクセントの史的研究** ¥9,800
鳥越 皓之 編著 **霞ヶ浦の環境と水辺の暮らし** パートナーシップ的発展論の可能性 ¥6,500	YOSHINO, Ayako 著 **Pageant Fever** Local History and Consumerism in Edwardian England　¥6,500
山内 晴子 著 **朝河貫一論** その学問形成と実践 ¥8,900	河西 宏祐 著 **全契約社員の正社員化** 私鉄広電支部・混迷から再生へ (1993年〜2009年)　¥6,100
金 孝淑 著 **源氏物語の言葉と異国** ¥4,900	市川 熹 著 **対話のことばの科学** プロソディが支えるコミュニケーション ¥5,600
鈴木 勘一郎 著 **経営変革と組織ダイナミズム** 組織アライメントの研究 ¥5,500	伊藤 りさ 著 **人形浄瑠璃のドラマツルギー** 近松以降の浄瑠璃作者と平家物語 ¥7,400
佐藤 洋一 著 **帝政期のウラジオストク** 市街地形成の歴史的研究 ¥9,300	石濱 裕美子 著 **清朝とチベット仏教** 菩薩王となった乾隆帝 ¥7,000

黒崎 剛 著 **ヘーゲル・未完の弁証法** 「意識の経験の学」としての『精神現象学』の批判的研究　　　¥12,000	高橋 勝幸 著 **アジア冷戦に挑んだ平和運動** タイ共産党の統一戦線活動と大衆参加　　　¥7,900
片木 淳 著 **日独比較研究 市町村合併** 平成の大合併はなぜ進展したか？　　　¥6,500	小松 志朗 著 **人道的介入** 秩序と正義, 武力と外交　　　¥4,900
SUZUKI, Rieko 著 **Negotiating History** From Romanticism to Victorianism　　　¥5,900	渡邉 将智 著 **後漢政治制度の研究**　　　¥8,400
杵渕 博樹 著 **人類は原子力で滅亡した** ギュンター・グラスと『女ねずみ』　　　¥6,600	石井 裕晶 著 **制度変革の政治経済過程** 戦前期日本における営業税廃税運動の研究　　　¥8,500
奥野 武志 著 **兵式体操成立史の研究**　　　¥7,900	森 佳子 著 **オッフェンバックと大衆芸術** パリジャンが愛した夢幻オペレッタ　　　¥8,200
井黒 忍 著 **分水と支配** 金・モンゴル時代華北の水利と農業　　　¥8,400	北山 夕華 著 **英国のシティズンシップ教育** 社会的包摂の試み　　　¥5,400
岩佐 壯四郎 著 **島村抱月の文藝批評と美学理論**　　　¥10,000	UENO, Yoshio 著 **An Automodular View of English Grammar**　　　¥8,400
高橋 弘幸 著 **企業競争力と人材技能** 三井物産創業半世紀の経営分析　　　¥8,200	すべて A5 判・価格は税抜き